Lecture Notes in Computer Science 5938

Commenced Publication in 1973
Founding and Former Series Editors:
Gerhard Goos, Juris Hartmanis, and Jan van Leeuwen

T0189830

Wu Zhang   Zhangxin Chen
Craig C. Douglas   Weiqin Tong (Eds.)

High Performance Computing and Applications

Second International Conference, HPCA 2009
Shanghai, China, August 10-12, 2009
Revised Selected Papers

 Springer

Volume Editors

Wu Zhang
Weiqin Tong
Shanghai University, School of Computer Engineering and Science
Shanghai 200072, P.R. China
E-mail: wzhang@shu.edu.cn, wqtong@mail.shu.edu.cn

Zhangxin Chen
University of Calgary, Schulich School of Engineering
Calgary AB T2N 1N4, Canada
E-mail: zhachen@ucalgary.ca

Craig C. Douglas
University of Wyoming, Department of Mathematics
1000 University Avenue, Laramie, WY 82071-3036, USA
E-mail: cdougla6@uwyo.edu

Library of Congress Control Number: 2010920846

CR Subject Classification (1998): D.4.8, D.2, D.3, C.5.1, C.1.4, C.2.4, C.2.1

LNCS Sublibrary: SL 1 – Theoretical Computer Science and General Issues

ISSN   0302-9743
ISBN-10   3-642-11841-0 Springer Berlin Heidelberg New York
ISBN-13   978-3-642-11841-8 Springer Berlin Heidelberg New York

Typesetting: Camera-ready by author, data conversion by Scientific Publishing Services, Chennai, India
Printed on acid-free paper   SPIN: 12985470   06/3180   5 4 3 2 1 0

Preface

The Second International Conference on High-Performance Computing and Applications (HPCA 2009) was a follow-up event of the successful HPCA 2004. It was held in Shanghai, a beautiful, active, and modern city in China, August 10–12, 2009. It served as a forum to present current work by researchers and software developers from around the world as well as to highlight activities in the high-performance computing area. It aimed to bring together research scientists, application pioneers, and software developers to discuss problems and solutions and to identify new issues in this area. This conference emphasized the development and study of novel approaches for high-performance computing, the design and analysis of high-performance numerical algorithms, and their scientific, engineering, and industrial applications. It offered the conference participants a great opportunity to exchange the latest research results, heighten international collaboration, and discuss future research ideas in HPCA.

In addition to 24 invited presentations, the conference received over 300 contributed submissions from over ten countries and regions worldwide, about 70 of which were accepted for presentation at HPCA 2009. The conference proceedings contain some of the invited presentations and contributed submissions, and cover such research areas of interest as numerical algorithms and solutions, high-performance and grid computing, novel approaches to high-performance computing, massive data storage and processing, hardware acceleration, and their wide applications.

The conference was co-organized by the School of Computer Engineering and Science and High-Performance Computing Center, Shanghai University and co-sponsored by Shanghai Jiao Tong University, Xi'an Jiao Tong University, and the University of Calgary. The conference organizers would like to thank Springer for their willingness to publish the conference proceedings as a volume in the series of *Lecture Notes in Computer Sciences*.

December 2009

Wu Zhang
Zhangxin Chen
Craig C. Douglas
Weiqin Tong

Organization

General Chair

Sanli Li   Shanghai University, China

Conference Co-chairs

Craig Douglas   University of Wyoming/Yale University, USA
Wu Zhang   Shanghai University, China

International Scientific Committee

Guoliang Chen	University of Science and Technology of China, China
Yaosong Chen	Beijing University, China
Zhangxin Chen (Chair)	University of Calgary, Canada
Junzhi Cui	Institute of Computational Mathematics, China
Jack Dongarra	University of Tennessee, USA
Jim Douglas, Jr.	University of Wyoming/Purdue University, USA
Roland Glowinski	University of Houston, USA
Shigeo Kawata	Utsunomiya University, Japan
Vipin Kumar	University of Minnesota, USA
Kaitai Li	Xi'an Jiaotong University, China
Tatsien Li	Fudan University, China
Qun Lin	Institute of Computational Mathematics, China
Yanping Lin	University of Alberta, Canada
Abani Patra	University of Buffalo and NSF, USA
Xianhe Sun	Illinois Institute of Technology, USA
Mary F. Wheeler	University of Texas at Austin, USA
Jinchao Xu	Penn State University, USA

Program Committee

Wenbin Chen	Fudan University, China
Yiqiang Chen	Insitute of Computing Technology, Academia Sinica, Taiwan
Zhihui Du	Tsinghua University, China
Kai Jiang	Shanghai Supercomputing Center, China
Jianguo Huang	Shanghai Jiaotong University, China
Linpeng Huang	Shanghai Jiaotong University, China
Zhou Lei	Shanghai University, China
Heping Ma	Shanghai University, China

Huadong Ma	Beijing University of Post and Telecommunication, China
Jun Ni	University of Iowa, USA
Weiqin Tong (Chair)	Shanghai University, China
Daping Yan	East China Normal University, China
Chaotung Yang	Tunghai University,Taiwan
Jifeng Yao	Shanghai Supercomputing Center, China
Xin Yuan	Florida State University, USA
Guosun Zeng	Tongji University, China

Organizing Committee

Yi Jin	Shanghai University, China
Wai-kin Lam	The Hong Kong Institute of High-Performance Computing, Hong Kong
Weimin Xu (Chair)	Shanghai University, China

Table of Contents

Invited Papers

Half-Duplex Dynamic Data Driven Application System for Forest Fire
Spread Prediction 1
    Ana Cortés

Advantages of Multiscale Detection of Defective Pills during
Manufacturing 8
    Craig C. Douglas, Li Deng, Yalchin Efendiev, Gundolf Haase,
    Andreas Kucher, Robert Lodder, and Guan Qin

Compressible Lattice Boltzmann Method and Applications 17
    Weibing Feng, Bing He, Anping Song, Yang Wang,
    Miao Zhang, and Wu Zhang

Studies on the Performance of a Heuristic Algorithm for Static and
Transportation Facility Location Allocation Problem 27
    Wei Gu and Xin Wang

A Parallel Algebraic Multigrid Solver on Graphics Processing Units 38
    Gundolf Haase, Manfred Liebmann, Craig C. Douglas, and
    Gernot Plank

Recent Advances in Time-Domain Maxwell's Equations in
Metamaterials 48
    Yunqing Huang and Jichun Li

Research on FPGA Based Evolvable Hardware Chips for Solving
Super-High Dimensional Equations Group 58
    Kangshun Li, Zhaolu Guo, Zhangxin Chen, and Baoshan Ge

An Efficient Splitting Domain Decomposition Approach for
Parabolic-Type Time-Dependent Problems in Porous Media 69
    Dong Liang and Chuanbin Du

New Shock Detector for Shock-Boundary Layer Interaction 78
    Chaoqun Liu and Maria Oliveira

Performance of Local Gauss Integration in Finite Element and Finite
Volume Methods for the Navier-Stokes Equations 88
    He Zhong and Zhangxin Chen

Contributed Papers

Performance Combinative Evaluation of Typical Virtual Machine
Monitors.. 96
Jianhua Che, Qinming He, Kejiang Ye, and Dawei Huang

Lunar Crater Rims Detection from Chang's Orbiter Data Based on a
Grid Environment.. 102
Shengbo Chen, Xuqing Zhang, and Shengye Jin

Study on Parallel System Performance Modeling Based on TCPN 108
Bin Cheng, Xingang Wang, Ying Li, and Weiqin Tong

A 3D Geological Modeling and Numerical Simulations of Near-Fault
Endangered Field 114
Haiying Cheng, Huagang Shao, Hualin Wang, and Hongwei Wang

Fast ARFTIS Reconstruction Algorithms Using CUDA 119
Deqi Cui, Ningfang Liao, Wenmin Wu, Boneng Tan, and Yu Lin

Numerical Methods for Nonequilibrium Solute Transport with
First-Order Decay and Zero-Order Production 127
Yazhu Deng and Ming Cui

Parallel Computing of Catchment Basins in Large Digital Elevation
Model 133
Hiep-Thuan Do, Sébastien Limet, and Emmanuel Melin

A Hybrid Parallel Evolutionary Algorithm Based on Elite-Subspace
Strategy and Space Transformation Search 139
Xiaojian Dong, Song Yu, Zhijian Wu, and Zhangxing Chen

Surface Reconstruction Technology from Dense Scattered Points Based
on Grid.. 146
Jianzhou Feng, Lingfu Kong, and Xiaohuan Wang

Parallel Branch Prediction on GPU Platform 153
Liqiang He and Guangyong Zhang

Calculation of TNT Equivalence of Composite Propellant and
Visualized Software Development 161
Ning He, Cong Xiang, Bin Qin, and Qi Zhang

The High Performance Computing on the Crash-Safety Analysis 169
Lei Hou, Haiyan Ding, Hanling Li, and Lin Qiu

A Heuristic Rule of Partitioning Irregular Loop for Parallelizing
Compilers.. 177
Changjun Hu, Yali Liu, Jue Wang, and Jianjiang Li

Numerical Simulation of Dimension Effect to Deformation in the
Cataclastic Medium Goafs Using UDEC 183
  *Jianhua Hu, Dezheng Lao, Qingfa Chen, Keping Zhou, and
  Yingmen Huang*

A Parallel Implementation of the Hybrid Algorithm for Electromagnetic
Scattering by Arbitrary Shaped Cavities 191
  Jungao Hu, Hu Yue, Cui Yanbao, and Zhi Xiaoli

A Fair Concurrent Signature Scheme Based on Identity 198
  Xiaofang Huang and Licheng Wang

Numerical Simulation of Rotating-Cage Bio-reactor Based on Dynamic
Mesh Coupled Two-Phase Flow 206
  Jiang Fan, Huang Chunman, Liang Zhongwei, and Wang Yijun

Energy-Efficient Intrusion Detection System for Wireless Sensor
Network Based on MUSK Architecture 212
  *Surraya Khanum, Muhammad Usman, Khalid Hussain,
  Rehab Zafar, and Muhammad Sher*

A Novel Parallel Interval Exclusion Algorithm 218
  Yongmei Lei, Shaojun Chen, and Yu Yan

Parallel Numerical Solution of the Time-Harmonic Maxwell
Equations 224
  Dan Li

The Semi-convergence of Generalized SSOR Method for Singular
Augmented Systems 230
  Jianlei Li and Tingzhu Huang

A Scientific Workflow System Based on GOS 236
  Lei Li, Bin Gong, and Yan Ma

Performance Optimization of Small File I/O with Adaptive Migration
Strategy in Cluster File System 242
  Xiuqiao Li, Bin Dong, Limin Xiao, and Li Ruan

Efficiently Packing Circles into a Larger Containing Circle 250
  Jingfa Liu, Yali Wang, and Jinji Pan

Heterogeneous Database Integration of EPR System Based on
OGSA-DAI 257
  Xuhong Liu, Yunmei Shi, Yabin Xu, Yingai Tian, and Fuheng Liu

RTTM: A New Hierarchical Interconnection Network for Massively
Parallel Computing 264
  Youyao Liu, Cuijin Li, and Jungang Han

Benchmarking Parallel I/O Performance for a Large Scale Scientific
Application on the TeraGrid 272
   Frank Löffler, Jian Tao, Gabrielle Allen, and Erik Schnetter

Reliability and Parametric Sensitivity Analysis of Railway Vehicle
Bogie Frame Based on Monte-Carlo Numerical Simulation 280
   Yaohui Lu, Jing Zeng, Pingbo Wu, Fei Yang, and Qinghua Guan

SVG-Based Interactive Visualization of PSE-Bio 288
   Guoyong Mao and Jiang Xie

A Modification of Regularized Newton-Type Method for Nonlinear
Ill-Posed Problems 295
   Ze-hong Meng, Zhen-yu Zhao, and Guo-qiang He

An Improved Technique for Program Remodularization 305
   Saeed Parsa and Mohammad Hamzei

Task Merging for Better Scheduling 311
   Saeed Parsa, Neda Reza Soltani, and Saeed Shariati

The Closure Temperature Fields and Shape Optimization of Arch Dam
Based on Genetic Algorithms 317
   Hui Peng, Wei Yao, and Ping Huang

Parallel Computing for Option Pricing Based on the Backward
Stochastic Differential Equation 325
   Ying Peng, Bin Gong, Hui Liu, and Yanxin Zhang

Dynamic Turbulence Simulation of Ceramic Roller Kiln Based on
Particle Systems 331
   Wenbi Rao and Weixia Shi

Rate Allocation in Overlay Networks Based on Theory of Firm
Consumer 337
   Mohammad Hossein Rezvani and Morteza Analoui

Retraction: Synthesizing Neural Networks and Randomized Algorithms ... 344
   Yonghong Shao, Qingyue Kong, and Yingying Ma

A Dynamic Update Framework for OSGi Applications 350
   Fei Shen, Siqi Du, and Linpeng Huang

Multiscale Stochastic Finite Element Method on Random Boundary
Value Problems 356
   Lihua Shen and X. Frank Xu

The BRI Algorithm for Double-Sides QBD Process 362
   Dinghua Shi and Hongbo Zhang

The Multi-dimensional QoS Resources Optimization Based on the Grid
Banking Model   369
    Guo Tang, Hao Li, and Shaowen Yao

A Cellular Automata Calculation Model Based on Ternary Optical
Computers   377
    Liang Teng, Junjie Peng, Yi Jin, and Mei Li

Performance Evaluation of Authentication Certificate Based Seamless
Vertical Handoff in GPRS-WLAN   384
    Muhammad Usman, Surraya Khanum, Wajahat Noshairwan,
    Ehtsham Irshad, and Azeem Irshad

Design and Implementation of Parallelized Cholesky Factorization   390
    Bailing Wang, Ning Ge, Hongbo Peng, Qiong Wei,
    Guanglei Li, and Zhigang Gong

Network Coding for Creating Replica in Grid Environments   398
    Banghai Wang, Jiangshou Hong, Lingxiong Li, and Dongyang Long

A Binary Method of License Plate Character Based on Object Space
Distribution Feature   404
    Mei Wang, Guang-da Su, and Sheng-lan Ben

The Load Balancing Algorithm Based on the Parallel Implementation
of IPO and FMM   410
    Ting Wang, Yue Hu, Yanbao Cui, Weiqin Tong, and Xiaoli Zhi

Sparse Matrix and Solver Objects for Parallel Finite Element
Simulation of Multi-field Problems   418
    Wenqing Wang and Olaf Kolditz

Vector-Matrix Multiplication Based on a Ternary Optical Computer   426
    Xianchao Wang, Junjie Peng, Yi Jin, Mei Li, Zhangyi Shen, and
    Shan Ouyang

Ultra High Throughput Implementations for MD5 Hash Algorithm on
FPGA   433
    Yuliang Wang, Qiuxia Zhao, Liehui Jiang, and Yi Shao

Stability Analysis and Numerical Simulation for a Class of
Multi-variable Networked Control Systems   442
    Lisheng Wei, Ming Jiang, and Minrui Fei

The Oblique Water Entry Impact of a Torpedo and Its Ballistic
Trajectory Simulation   450
    Zhaoyu Wei, Xiuhua Shi, Yonghu Wang, and Yuanbo Xin

Intelligent Traffic Simulation Grid Based on the HLA and JADE   456
    Junwei Wu and Xiaojun Cao

The Research and Emulation on PIM-SM Protocol 465
    Libing Wu, Shengchao Ding, Chanle Wu, Dan Wu, and Bo Chen

A Method for Querying Conserved Subnetwork in a Large-Scale
Biomolecular Network 473
    *Jiang Xie, Weibing Feng, Shihua Zhang, Songbei Li, Guoyong Mao,
    Luwen Zhang, Tieqiao Wen, and Wu Zhang*

Conflict Analysis of Multi-source SST Distribution 479
    *Lingyu Xu, Pingen Zhang, Jun Xu, Shaochun Wu, Guijun Han, and
    Dongfeng Xu*

Scientific Application Based Performance on Magic Cube 485
    Ying Xu, D.D. Zhang, and Lei Xu

Computation of Bounds for Exact Quantities of Interest in Elasticity
Based on FEM and SFEM 491
    Zhaocheng Xuan, Yaohui Li, and Hongjie Wang

Development of a Scalable Solver for the Earth's Core Convection 497
    Chao Yang, Ligang Li, and Yunquan Zhang

A Virtualized HPC Cluster Computing Environment on Xen with
Web-Based User Interface 503
    *Chao-Tung Yang, Chien-Hsiang Tseng, Keng-Yi Chou, and
    Shyh-Chang Tsaur*

Performance-Based Parallel Loop Self-scheduling on Heterogeneous
Multicore PC Clusters 509
    Chao-Tung Yang, Jen-Hsiang Chang, and Chao-Chin Wu

Sharing University Resources Based on Grid Portlet 515
    Shuhua Yu, Jianlin Zhang, and Chunjuan Fu

A Hybrid Particle Swarm Optimization Algorithm Based on Space
Transformation Search and a Modified Velocity Model 522
    Song Yu, Zhijian Wu, Hui Wang, and Zhangxing Chen

Adaptive Control in Grid Computing Resource Scheduling 528
    Jia-bin Yuan, Jiao-min Luo, and Bo-jia Duan

Study on Synchronously Driving Control System of Linear Move
Irrigator 534
    Yanwei Yuan, Xiaochao Zhang, Wenhua Mao, and Huaping Zhao

A Fast Morphological Reconstruction Algorithm for MRI Brain Image
Simplification 542
    Bofeng Zhang, Hui Zhu, Anping Song, and Wu Zhang

On Chip Cache Quantitative Optimization Approach: Study in Chip
Multi-processor Design 550
  Chi Zhang and Xiang Wang

A Novel CT Image Dynamic Fuzzy Retrieval Method Using Curvelet
Transform 557
  Guangming Zhang, Zhiming Cui, and Shengrong Gong

An Implementation Method of Parallel Finite Element Computation
Based on Overlapping Domain Decomposition 563
  Jianfei Zhang, Lei Zhang, and Hongdao Jiang

Numerical Simulation of Unsteady Flow in Centrifugal Pump Impeller
at Off-Design Condition by Hybrid RANS/LES Approaches 571
  Wei Zhang, Yunchao Yu, and Hongxun Chen

A Two-Level Stabilized Nonconforming Finite Element Method for the
Stationary Navier-Stokes Equations 579
  Liping Zhu and Zhangxin Chen

Author Index 587

Half-Duplex Dynamic Data Driven Application System for Forest Fire Spread Prediction*

Ana Cortés

Departament d' Arquitectura de Computadors i Sistemes Operatius, E.T.S.E.,
Universitat Autonoma de Barcelona, 08193 - Bellaterra (Barcelona) Spain

Abstract. Every year forest fires provoke enormous looses from the ecological, economical and social point of view, by burning millions of hectares and killing several people. Nowadays, several forest fire simulators are used for helping in forest fire prevention and mitigation. Most of these simulators are based on Rothermel model. However, in most cases it is not possible to know the exact real-time values of model input parameters. This input data uncertainty causes predictions that are far from the real fire propagation. For this reason, we propose a fire propagation prediction system based on two stages: a calibration stage and a prediction stage. The calibration stage bases on the observed real fire evolution, so that the behavior of the fire is assimilated by the system at run-time matching the Dynamic Data Driven Application Systems (DDDAS) paradigm.

1 Introduction

Forest fires are one of the most important threats to forest areas in the whole world. In the lasts years thousands of hectares were lost by forest fire action. Forest areas losses damage the nature, attempting on ecological balance. Death of different species of animals and plants, profitable areas loss, air pollution, water contamination, are some of the consequences of forest fires. At the same time these problems cause different diseases, famine, animals and vegetables extinction, etc. These facts attempt our standard of living. Some forest fires occur by nature itself: long dry seasons, elevated temperatures, electric storms, could generate wildland fires. These type of fires can help in the ecological balance: young plants take place where there were old and perhaps unproductive trees. Nature keeps number of fires limited, but in the last years this number was increased by human factors. More than 90% of forest fires are provoked by human hand (accidents, carelessness and negligence). For example, 16000 hectares were burned in Gran Canaria in 2007 during 6 days of strong fires. In Tenerife 15000 hectares were burned at the same time. In addition, more than 60 deaths occurred during forest fires in Greece in July 2007. Whereas the number of wildfires had increased in the last years, human research in this area had increased too. Main study areas are prevention and fighting against fires. There are different

---

* This work has been supported by the MEC-Spain under contracts TIN 2007-64974.

W. Zhang et al. (Eds.): HPCA 2009, LNCS 5938, pp. 1–7, 2010.

kind of studies, strategies and tools to prevent forest fires as well as to mitigate the fire damage during a disaster. Nowadays, several forest fire simulators exist for helping and improving this work. Most of these simulators are based on Rothermel mathematical model [8]. This model describes fire behavior through mathematical equations. Simulators are used to predict fire behavior, improving the accuracy of actions and reducing fire effects. Several of these simulators use a large number of input parameters for describing the environment where fire occurs. It is very difficult to dispose of exact real-time values of these parameters. Several of them change with time: wind and fuel humidity change along the day (day-night cycle), weather changes due to elevated temperatures provoked by fire, fires generate very strong gust of winds, etc. Furthermore, lots of these parameters have their own behavior pattern and it can change very strongly within a wildland fire. This input data uncertainty causes predictions that are far from the real fire propagation. During a real hazard such as wildland fire both, the accuracy of the prediction propagation and the prediction response time are crucial key points. For this reason, we propose a fire propagation prediction system based on two stages: a calibration stage and a prediction stage. The calibration stage bases on the observed real fire evolution, so that the behavior of the fire is assimilated by the system at run-time matching the Dynamic Data Driven Application Systems (DDDAS) paradigm [3][4].

2   DDDAS in Forest Fire Spread Prediction

DDDAS is a paradigm whereby application/simulations and measurements become a symbiotic feedback control system. DDDAS entails the ability to dynamically incorporate additional data into an executing application, and in reverse, the ability of an application to dynamically steer the measurement process. An optimal framework for a reliable DDDAS for Wildland Fire Prediction must consider, among others, the following issues: real-time data assimilation strategies for being further injected into the running system; the ability to dynamically couple models from different disciplines; steering strategies for automatic adjusting either models or input data parameters and to have access to enough computational resources to be able to obtain the prediction results under strict real-time constraints. Some current work on this area could be found in [6][1]. Our current research consists on a first step towards a DDDAS for Wildland Fire Prediction where our main efforts are oriented to take advantage of the computing power provided by High Performance Computing (HPC) systems to, in the one hand, propose computational data driven steering strategies to overcome input data uncertainty and, on the other hand, reducing the execution time of the whole prediction process in order to be reliable during real-time crisis. Our proposal consists of performing a forest fire spread prediction based on a two stages prediction scheme: calibration stage and prediction stage. The DDDAS bases are included in the calibration stage by assimilating the actual propagation of forest fire and using such information for input parameter calibration. Taking advantage of the computer power provided by HPC systems, several strategies such as Evolutionary Algorithms or Statistical Analysis are used to explore a huge number of input parameters combinations (called scenarios).

2.1 Two Stages Forest Fire Spread Prediction

The classical forest fire spread prediction is based on estimating the input parameters from direct or indirect measurements and then applying some simulator to predict the forest fire spread. However, as it has been mentioned above, in most cases such input parameters are not reliable and, therefore, the predictions provided does not match the actual behavior. So our proposal introduces a first calibration stage to determine a set of input parameters that represents the actual behavior of the fire in a more accurate way. For this stage being operative, it is necessary to have information about the forest fire front at two consecutive time instants (t_0 and t_1). These two forest fire fronts describe the actual evolution of the fire in the interval t_0-t_1. However, it must be considered that the models require several input parameters and, on the other hand, these parameters have a wide range of possible values and some of them affect the results very significantly. So, it means that the actual search space is huge; in a normal case we can easily have about half million scenarios. Consequently, some search technique must be applied to determine the input parameters values accomplishing the real-time constraints of a real emergency. Therefore, different methodologies are proposed considering different situations (see figure 1).

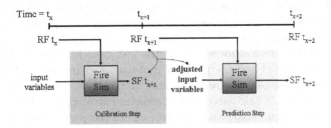

Fig. 1. Data Driven Prediction

Guided Genetic Algorithm. One methodology is based on applying a modified genetic algorithm. In a genetic algorithm a starting population (a set of initial scenarios) is selected randomly and then all the members of the population are evaluated considering a fitness or error function. In our case, the error function is the difference between the predicted fire front for each member and the real fire front. Then some genetic operators are applied (elitism, selection, crossover, mutation) and a new population is created. The process is iteratively repeated and the population is improved. The mutation operator is applied to few elements of the population selected randomly and the mutation itself is also random. This random operation is interesting because it allows skipping local minimums of the error function. However, the fact that the mutation is random provokes that some of the mutations generate worse elements than the original ones. So, a method has been developed to guide some of the mutations of certain elements. In this way, for these elements of the population the new values of the parameters are not selected randomly, but they are selected by analyzing the fire behavior. So, the system incorporates a data base that includes the results of many fires and when a real fire is propagating, the system analyses the real propagation in this case and looks for similar cases in the data base and then change the values of the selected parameters (mainly wind speed and wind direction) for those values found in the data base for similar cases. The main goal of guiding the mutation operation is to accelerate the convergence of the genetic algorithm, so that a reasonable scenario is reached in few iterations (actually, 5 iterations are enough). This is important due to the real time constraints of the emergency actuation. The best reached scenario is used as input scenario for the prediction stage and the prediction is only based on that best scenario provided by the calibration stage. For the prediction stage, the input fire front is the fire front at t_1 and it provides the prediction for the fire front at a later time t_2 [5].

Statistical analysis. Using the genetic algorithm the prediction provided by the system is based on a single scenario. It must be considered that in many cases there are parameters (such as wind speed) that change quickly and it is possible that the value of the parameter that represents the behavior of the fire from t_0 to t_1 could not be useful for predicting the behavior from t_1 to t_2. Therefore, a methodology based on a statistical analysis of multiple predictions provided by the whole population can adapt more easily to rapid changes in parameter values. So, after applying the guided genetic algorithm, the prediction provided by the system is not just the result of a single scenario, but all the scenarios in the final population are considered. Once the last generation is reached, all the scenarios are considered and the prediction of each scenario is evaluated. Then, all the predicted propagations are aggregated and applying a statistical analysis, the predicted fire line is calculated. This prediction strategy is called $SAPIFE^3$ [7]. This method adapts faster to situations where the parameters change more quickly.

Although both methods are based on evolutionary computation to avoid testing all the possible scenarios and guiding the process to accelerate the convergence, it must be considered that in any case many scenarios must be checked and, therefore, the proposed methods are computationally demanding. So, it is necessary to take advantage of the High Performance Computing (HPC) systems to accomplish the hard real time constraints of real emergencies.

3   Urgent Computing in Forest Fire Spread Prediction

As it has been mentioned above, real emergencies imply hard real time constraints, and therefore it is necessary to provide the prediction results as fast as possible by applying HPC solutions. However, in many cases the control centers does not own the HPC systems required to accomplish the real time requirements, and then the solutions provided do not have the necessary accuracy. Nowadays, there are many clusters and distributed systems that can be integrated in a global environment using some software layers (Grid systems). These systems offer a huge computing power and a transparent use, but usually they do not guarantee the exact time the system is available for the execution of the application. And this situation is critical for real emergency treatment. So, several projects are introducing the concept of Urgent Computing. In such systems there are many resources available and being used by the different users, but when a real emergency is detected; all the resources are derived to treat the emergency. In the case of forest fire, all the resources must be dedicated to estimate the predictions of the different scenarios and reach a feasible prediction that represents the behavior of the actual forest fire.

4   Real-Time Data Injection

Another key point when dealing with DDDAS for emergencies is the ability to inject real-time data at execution time in order to provide better forest fire spread prediction. For this reason, we have also developed and design strategies for real-time data gathering and injection, in order to establish a methodology from which DDDAS applications running in distributed environments can take benefit [2]. The proposal raises a great challenge, as there are many aspects to take into account. Our main goal is to provide an external-incoming-data assimilation schema in order to allow obtaining needed information in real time from not (necessarily) trusted platforms, which means to deal with certain key issues:

- To acquire new data from external sources as soon as it is available, to provide more efficicient application executions.
- To provide data sources with access to the execution platforms, which, security issues aside, also means to know which resources are being used by the application.
- To adapt current applications to be able for accepting new incoming data at execution time.
- To be as less intrusive with the execution environment as possible.

We have studied strategies to satisfy these points based on the use of interposition agents, which allow exploring and browsing external file systems in a non-intrusive way and without the need of having special privileges in the environment the users execute their applications, even when it is about a distributed-computing environment. Thereby, we can establish a methodology for solving the previously mentioned problems and allowing many HPC applications to fit in the DDDAS paradigm. Figure 2 shows the basic architecture for this scheme.

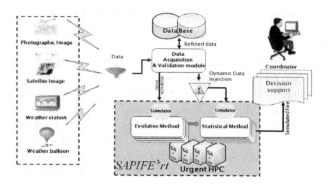

Fig. 2. Current *Forest Fire Spread Prediction System*

5   Conclusions

In this paper, we have described the main lines of our current research, which consists of a first step toward a DDDAS for Wildland Fire Prediction. Our main efforts are oriented to take advantage of the computing power provided by High Performance Computing (HPC) systems to, in the one hand, propose computational data driven steering strategies to overcome input data uncertainty and, on the other hand, reducing the execution time of the whole prediction process in order to be reliable during real-time crisis. Currently, we have deployed a basic prototype architecture of the proposed real-time prediction system that allows us to validate any prove the viability of any new feature that we introduce to the system.

References

1. Allen, G.: Building a Dynamic Data Driven Applications System for Hurricane Forecasting. In: Shi, Y., van Albada, G.D., Dongarra, J., Sloot, P.M.A. (eds.) ICCS 2007, Part I. LNCS, vol. 4487, pp. 1034–1041. Springer, Heidelberg (2007)
2. Cencerrado, A.: Real-time Data Flow Management for DDDAS-based Applications under Distributed Computing Environemnts, MSc Thesis. Universitat Autònoma de Barcelona (Spain) (July 2009)
3. Darema, F.: Dynamic Data Driven Applications Systems: A New Paradigm for Application Simulations and Measurements. In: Bubak, M., van Albada, G.D., Sloot, P.M.A., Dongarra, J. (eds.) ICCS 2004. LNCS, vol. 3038, pp. 662–669. Springer, Heidelberg (2004)
4. Dynamic Data Driven Application Systems homepage, http://www.dddas.org (Acceded, November 2007)
5. Denham, M., Cortés, A., Margalef, T., Luque, E.: Applying a Dynamic Data Driven Genetic Algorithm to Improve Forest Fire Spread Prediction. In: Bubak, M., van Albada, G.D., Dongarra, J., Sloot, P.M.A. (eds.) ICCS 2008, Part III. LNCS, vol. 5103, pp. 36–45. Springer, Heidelberg (2008)

6. Mandel, J., Beezley, J., Bennethm, L., Chakraborty, S., Coen, J., Douglas, C., Hatcher, J., Kim, M., Vodacek, A.: A Dynamic Data Driven Wildladnd Fire Model. In: Shi, Y., van Albada, G.D., Dongarra, J., Sloot, P.M.A. (eds.) ICCS 2007. LNCS, vol. 4487, pp. 1042–1049. Springer, Heidelberg (2007)
7. Rodríguez, R., Cortés, A., Margalef, T.: Injecting Dynamic Real-Time Data into a DDDAS for Forest Fire Behavior Prediction. In: Allen, G., Nabrzyski, J., Seidel, E., van Albada, G.D., Dongarra, J.J., Sloot, P.M.A. (eds.) ICCS 2009, Part II. LNCS, vol. 5545, pp. 489–400. Springer, Heidelberg (2009)
8. Rothermel, R.C.: A mathematical model for predicting fire spread in wildland fuels. USDA FS, Ogden TU, Res. Pap. INT-115 (1972)

Advantages of Multiscale Detection of Defective Pills during Manufacturing

Craig C. Douglas[1], Li Deng[2], Yalchin Efendiev[3], Gundolf Haase[4], Andreas Kucher[4], Robert Lodder[5], and Guan Qin[6]

[1] University of Wyoming Department of Mathematics, 1000 University Avenue, Dept. 3036, Laramie, WY 82071-3036, USA
cdougla6@uwyo.edu
[2] JSOL Corporation, Chuo-ku, Tokyo 104-0053, Japan
deng17jp@yahoo.co.jp
[3] Texas A&M University, Mathematics Department, College Station, TX, USA
efendiev@math.tamu.edu
[4] Karl-Franzens University of Graz, Mathematics and Computational Sciences Department, A-8010 Graz, Austria
gundolf.haase@uni-graz.at, andreas.kucher@gmail.com
[5] University of Kentucky Chemistry Department, Lexington, KY 40506, USA
lodder@uky.edu
[6] University of Wyoming Department of Chemical and Petroleum Engineering, 1000 University Avenue, Dept. 3295, Laramie, WY 82071-3295, USA
gqin@uwyo.edu

Abstract. We explore methods to automatically detect the quality in individual or batches of pharmaceutical products as they are manufactured. The goal is to detect 100% of the defects, not just statistically sample a small percentage of the products and draw conclusions that may not be 100% accurate. Removing all of the defective products, or halting production in extreme cases, will reduce costs and eliminate embarrassing and expensive recalls. We use the knowledge that experts have accumulated over many years, dynamic data derived from networks of smart sensors using both audio and chemical spectral signatures, multiple scales to look at individual products and larger quantities of products, and finally adaptive models and algorithms.

Keywords: manufacturing defect detection, dynamic data-driven application systems, DDDAS, integrated sensing and processing, high performance computing, and parallel algorithms.

1 Introduction

Diabetes is a problem worldwide. Of the more than 15 million Americans who have diabetes mellitus, about five million do not know it. Nearly 1 million new cases are diagnosed each year. The disease affects men and women of all ages and certain ethnic groups are more greatly affected than other groups [1]. With the more common type 2 diabetes, the body does not make or use insulin properly. Without enough

W. Zhang et al. (Eds.): HPCA 2009, LNCS 5938, pp. 8–16, 2010.

insulin, the glucose stays in the blood system. Having too much glucose in the blood system causes serious problems, e.g., damage to the eyes, kidneys, and nerves. Other side effects of diabetes include heart disease, stroke, and removal of limbs. Pregnant women can also have gestational diabetes [2].

The total annual economic cost of diabetes in 2007 in the U.S. was estimated to be 32% higher than just five years earlier. In 2007, medical expenditures totaled $116 billion ($27 billion for diabetes care, $58 billion for chronic diabetes-related complications, and $31 billion for excess general medical costs). Indirect costs resulting from increased absenteeism, reduced productivity, disease-related unemployment disability, and loss of productive capacity due to early mortality equaled the cost of chronic diabetes-related expenditures. One out of every five health care dollars is spent caring for someone with diagnosed diabetes, while one in ten health care dollars is attributed to diabetes [3].

While U.S. drug products are of generally high quality, there is an increasing trend toward manufacturing-related problems that lead to recalls, disruption of manufacturing operations, and loss of availability of essential drugs. The U.S. Food and Drug Administration (FDA) is combating these problems plus low manufacturing process efficiency (<30%) has also led to increased cost of drugs by emphasizing current good manufacturing practice (cGMP) as the means of controlling drug quality. An unfortunate side effect is that many companies are no longer innovating at the same rate as before. The FDA's response is that uses of new sensing technologies will be key to improving the regulation and quality of drug manufacturing using scientifically proven risk-based methods. Near infrared (NIR) is one of the process analytic technologies (PAT) that the FDA has chosen to improve manufacturing process quality [4].

In Section 2, we describe the smart sensors we are designing for use on manufacturing lines and how both offline high performance computing and integrated sensing and processing are involved.

In Section 3, we describe where multiscale techniques are useful and how to construct them.

In Section 4, we describe some identification results along with some simple timing information for the parallel computation needed to create libraries for our sensing devices.

In Section 5, we draw some conclusions.

2 Smart Sensors with Integrated Sensing and Processing

Smart sensors are a form of integrated sensing and processing (ISP). ISP optimizes systems that integrate sensing, signal processing, communication, and targeting. Traditional sensing systems lead to high dimensional and prohibitively expensive problems to solve. ISP based methods lead to reduced and low dimensional systems that can be solved through a combination of the on board computing on the sensors and by solving auxiliary problems on highly parallel computers in advance. We convert data directly to knowledge using programmable on demand ISP-based imaging spectrometers that produce detector signals that can be correlated directly to desired samples. Hence, we do not need to do a post collection chemometrics step. Parallel computers produce libraries that are downloaded to the ISPs and include environmentally

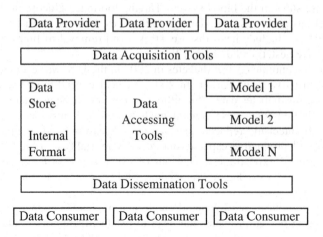

Fig. 1. A typical DDDAS

relevant information that is updated on a regular basis. While these libraries are expensive to create computationally, the use in the ISPs is both inexpensive and fast.

Dynamic data-driven application systems (DDDAS), [5], [6], and [7], place far different strains on high performance systems and centers than traditional applications due to dynamic and unpredictable changes in resources that are required during long term runs. An on demand environment is required that stresses traditional computing centers views on allocating resources. The number of processors, network resources, and location of computing and data can change unpredictably during the course of a long term DDDAS computation [8] and [9].

DDDAS assumes that application components, resource requirements, application mapping, interfaces and control of the measurement system can be modified during the course of the application simulation. Figure 1 provides a schematic of how typical DDDAS applications appear componentwise.

The longest running DDDAS we are aware of began its calculations in 1978 and still runs today even though all of the hardware and software have changed over time, but the application has never been turned off. The application monitors all oil and gas pipelines, storage tanks, wells, and tanker loading in Saudi Arabia.

The devices we are designing for this project are designed to reduce the over abundance of data that is prevalent in most pharmaceutical manufacturing environments today [10]. We envision using similar devices in related fields, e.g., handheld devices to ensure correct pill delivery wherever health caregivers are involved.

Providing a reprogrammable, networked embedded system that can automatically determine quality and control end products in a manufacturing line will impact not only the pharmaceutical industry, but any similar chemically-based production facility. A likely offshoot is a handheld acoustic device that medical providers can use to correctly identify all medications that will be given to patients. Taking the wrong medications is the fifth leading cause of death in the United States.

The identification of pills by using acoustic waves is a challenging problem in technical pharmacy. Manufacturing lines are extremely noisy and we typically only have 8-10 milliseconds to identify each defective or incorrect pill. Our goal is to catch 100% of the possible problem pills and get them out of the manufacturing line before they reach packaging.

In the U.S., a pilot line is created, tested, and eventually approved by the FDA. Once approved, it becomes a production line and cannot be modified in any significant way. Any significant modification to a production line makes it a pilot line again with all of the testing and approvals required again. Further, the FDA has to approve to conversion back to a pilot line, which it may not do.

Spherix is a small pharmaceutical company that created Tagatose [11], [12], and [13]. The manufacturing line belongs to a much larger company that is in Italy that does contract work for others. We are in a position to create a complete DDDAS and test it on a real pharmaceutical manufacturing line in Italy, where the rules for testing new pharmaceutical technology is quite different than in the U.S. In particular, we do not have to get FDA approval to make an adjustment to the manufacturing line in order to improve the quality control mechanisms.

The system we are creating corresponds to a true DDDAS since it involves combining pill manufacturing and environmental factors with integrated sensing and processing. A number of human factors also are included based on who is working on the manufacturing line during a work shift and the peculiarities of the individual workers. Incoming raw materials vary, too, and the system needs small, but significant adjustments on a regular basis, typically timed for work shifts. The updates require some substantial high performance computing to create downloadable libraries for the actual devices.

The DDDAS is built using a cumulative set of components:

- The production process is modeled using TagSim, a semi-empirical Simulink [14] program written in Matlab. TagSim predicts both the output yield and impurities for the tagatose production process.
- Remote access to the system uses a secure client-server approach on the Internet.
- Servers are connected to the processes through standard data acquisition hardware and the Matlab Communication Toolbox. The combination provides security, data validation, and session management.

The remote access provides a secondary side effect, namely a nice mechanism for training students in process control.

The choice of Matlab speeded up the development of the entire system. In part because Matlab is well known by students, but also that it was easy to design, test, and verify control strategies in real time over the Internet. Both interlocks and cutoffs were easy to implement, both of which guarantee safe and secure operation of the remote processing units.

One problem that came to light was that computation and networking speeds have to be carefully monitored. Using remote supercomputers to generate the libraries for the ISP devices must minimize data transfers in order to be useful. It is not yet practical to transfer the data to a remote supercomputer, do a fast calculation on it, and transmit the result for an individual pill back to the manufacturing line. It is essential to do the identification on the ISP directly.

The actual acoustic devices use a combination of integrated sensing and processing and acoustic resonance spectroscopy (ISP-ARS). This is a novel approach to acoustic spectroscopy that can be implemented using instruments as simple as a MP3 player like an Apple iPod Touch^{TM} or one that is extremely complex. The choice depends on the environment that the ISP-ARS will be used in. A wireless networked MP3 player is ideal since the library can be downloaded from a server at selected times or pushed by the server.

ISP-ARS is both fast and non-destructive. Unlike near-infrared or optical methods, acoustic methods are can penetrate deeply many common forms of opaque packaging. The penetration ability is a significant advantage in preparing clinical trial lots since drugs and placebos should be indistinguishable by the patients.

Pharmaceutical manufacturing lines for pills are extremely noisy environments. Simple acoustic devices are worthless unless a sound box is created to house the acoustic device while letting pills pass by. In addition, the pills move on manufacturing line at a considerable speed. At any physical region of the line, the pills are only available for defect identification for 5-10 milliseconds and must then be eliminated from the line. Further, our goal is to eliminate every single defective pill, not just some of them.

The ISP-ARS device must perform an optimization of a functional that is equivalent to solving a complicated nonlinear equation. We use automatic differentiation techniques to simplify the entire process to something that can be put into an embedded system. Numerical approximations are used to further simplify the computing tasks to something practical for the embedded system. All we care about is that the ISP computation is accurate and fast enough to catch each defective pill.

All pills sold in the world are supposed to be unique in shape, size, and coloring. All pills have a unique audio spectra footprint. We play specific noise patterns at pills and measure the resulting spectra. We look for specific spectra to identify specific types of pills. We have to identify which spectra to look for given environmental factors that may change over time as short as a work shift.

In ISP-ARS, an acoustic waveform is created that comprises just the distinguishing spectral details associated with an analyte of interest. Fourier transform acoustic resonance spectroscopy (FTARS) is used to develop ISP acoustic waveforms employed in differentiating different drugs.

As a PAT, a series of ISP-ARS sensors must scan every pill produced by a manufacturer, enabling the removal of only those pills that do not meet quality standards or controls. Measurements from a series of ISP-ARS sensors should control the manufacturing line dynamically and adjust the process conditions and ingredients in real time based on actual process measurements [15] and [16].

ISP-ARS reduces the time required for processing that normally occurs with full spectrum FTARS. An ISP acoustic waveform results from chemometric analysis of the FTARS spectrum. By weighting the frequency changes according to individual component scores, an acoustic waveform can be constructed that excites just the frequencies important to the analyte in question. The ISP output is a voltage that can be read immediately and corresponds to just the analyte in question.

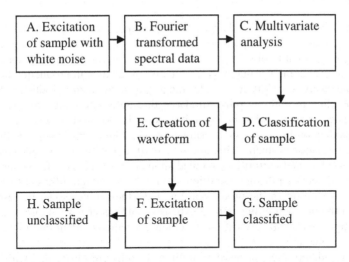

Fig. 2. A classification of the steps in FTARS and ISP-ARS

The ISP acoustic wave design starts with the chemometric analysis of the initial FTARS data. FTARS makes a prediction about what works as an ISP acoustic waveform for a given set of samples. The training process can be interpreted as a DDDAS that continuously monitors the performance of the ISP waveform that is continuously adjusted through retraining. In essence, a symbiotic relation between the computation and the sensing that results in highly quality manufacturing.

Consider Figure 2. The traditional FTARS cycle is steps A→B→C→D→A. In traditional FTARS, samples are scanned and classified according to their inter-cluster distances found via multivariate analysis (steps A-D). For each sample or groups scanned the process is repeated. The FTARS data is used as a predictor for ISP-ARS. The prediction (E) is used to construct an ISP acoustic waveform. The traditional FTARS cycle is no longer needed once the ISP waveform is constructed. Samples scanned with the ISP waveform are classified according to their voltages (F-G). If a sample cannot be classified (H), then FTARS is employed to construct chemometrically a new ISP acoustic waveform usingth a training set that it includes the new unknown. As samples change during time, the ISP waveform adapts to the new data.

FTARS can be used to differentiate liquids, powders, drugs, and predict dissolution rates in seemingly identical samples. FTARS is nondestructive and complete scans can be made in seconds, therefore it should be a prime candidate for use as a PAT. Following data collection, FTARS relies on intensive computer processing due to the amount of information gained in each scan. An ARS spectrum recorded over the interval of 20 Hz to 20 kHz with a sample rate of 44.1 kHz for one second generates a large amounts of data from the 44100 data points. Chemometric analysis of multiple FTARS data sets requires too much computation, which limits the production rate of tablets, which is unacceptable. ISP-ARS is fast enough to not limit production rates since it directly produces the analyte identity as an output, thus eliminating the computational time of FTARS.

3 Multiscale Advantages

We can assume that the ISP-ARS devices are in multiple locations in the production line and that there are local computing resources. The ISP-ARS devices are identifying defective or low quality pills on the manufacturing line as defective. Data can be transmitted to a local computer that maps the quality of the overall production line.

The map can easily be on different scales ranging from the entire production line to space corresponding to multiple pills. Similarly, disparate time scales are present in the process. The advantage of using a multiscale technique is that when problems arise on the production line, we can determine quickly and automatically whether we have a minor or major problem. This allows identifying both spatial and temporal scales of the problem and performing detailed simulations, if needed, for better accuracy. If enough defective pills are identified at once or in enough different locations, we may want to shut down the production line until the problems can be resolved. Shutting down the production line is both expensive and under normal circumstances not done. Doing so automatically with the problem area already identified will reduce the expenses considerably.

In packaging, identifying that possibly millions of pills are mislabeled will save a costly product recall. For a drug test, it will possibly save the entire set of human trials from having to be discarded and a new country targeted for the trials.

4 Identification and Computational Results

We identified several toll-manufactured drugs (aspirin, acetaminophen, D-tagatose, ibuprofen, vitamin C, and vitamin B) in a controlled lab environment using ISP acoustic waveforms composed of 10, 100, and 1000 frequencies. We found that just the top 10 frequencies properly classified each pill. Intra-cluster distances were calculated to be less than 3 multidimensional standard deviations (MSD) for each pill type. The average accuracy of prediction was 98.47, 97.45 and 95.41 percent for the 10, 100 and 1000 frequency component acoustic waveforms respectively []$i7-i8.

Computing the libraries for the ISP-ARS devices requires a large number of independent calculations. We used a cluster made up of Intel Core i7-920 running at 2.67GHz and 6GB DDR3 RAM. Each potential frequency was computed using 8 cores. We used 10,000 point datasets and 9-way parallelism (the ninth is the controlling process and uses minimal time).

Using the g++ compiler, run times per frequency calculation were approximately 160, 260, and 321 seconds for third through fifth degree arc lengths used to find the best frequencies.

We can deliver an infinite number of acoustic spectra, but that defeats the creation of a small, embedded DDDAS device that is useful in itself. Instead we choose a small number of spectra, which changes slightly over time based on environmental and personnel factors. However, we compute on as many processors as we can for a set period of wall clock time. For real production of pills, we need to recalibrate the libraries once per work shift. We can predict how long we need to compute based on timings like above and the number of processors we can access on a supercomputer. Alternately, we can predict how many processors we need based on how much time we are allowed.

5 Conclusions

We have described a multiscale prototype DDDAS to identify defective, inadequately low quality, or mislabeled pills. ISP-ARS can differentiate between different types of pills. The results are preliminary and much more research and development is necessary to produce systems that can be deployed on pharmaceutical manufacturing lines with government approvals.

Acknowledgments. This research was supported in part by NSF grants OISE-0405349, ACI-0305466, CNS-0719626, and ACI-0324876, DOE grant DE-FC26-08NT4, and Award No. KUS-C1-016-04, made by King Abdullah University of Science and Technology (KAUST).

References

1. http://www.fda.gov/diabetes/qna.htm
2. http://www.nlm.nih.gov/medlineplus/diabetes.html
3. http://www.diabetes.org/diabetes-statistics/cost-of-diabetes-in-us.jsp
4. http://www.fda.gov/ohrms/dockets/ac/02/briefing/3869B1_08_woodcock/sld001.htm
5. http://www.dddas.org
6. Baldridge, K., Biros, G., Chaturvedi, A., Douglas, C.C., Parashar, M., How, J., Saltz, J., Seidel, E., Sussman, A.: DDDAS Workshop Report, National Science Foundation (January 2006)
7. Douglas, C.C., Deshmukh, A., Ball, M., Ewing, R.E., Johnson, C.R., Kesselman, C., Lee, C., Powell, W., Sharpley, R.: Dynamical data driven application systems: Creating a dynamic and symbiotic coupling of application/simulations with measurements/ experiments, National Science Foundation, Arlington, VA (2000)
8. Darema, F. (ed.): 2007 Dynamic Data-Driven Application Workshop, in Computational Science – ICCS 2007: 7th International Conference, Beijing, P.R. China, May 28-31 (2007); Shi, Y., van Albada, G.D., Dongarra, J., Sloot, P.M.A. (eds.): ICCS 2007. LNCS, vol. 4487, pp. 955–1245. Springer, Heidelberg (2007)
9. Douglas, C.C. (ed.): 2009 Dynamic data-driven application systems - DDDAS 2008, in Computational Science – ICCS 2008: 8th International Conference, May 25-27 (2009); Allen, G., Nabrzyski, J., Seidel, E., van Albada, G.D., Dongarra, J.J., Sloot, P.M.A. (eds.): ICCS 2009, Part II. LNCS, vol. 5545, pp. 445–509. Springer, Heidelberg (2009)
10. Dai, B., Urbas, A., Douglas, C.C., Lodder, R.A.: Molecular factor computing for predictive spectroscopy. Pharm Res. 8, 1441–1444 (2007)
11. Beadle, J.R., Saunders, J.P., Wajda Jr., T.J.: Process for Manufacturing Tagatose. Biospherics Incorporated (US patent 5,002,612) (1991),
http://www.uspto.gov/patft/index.html
12. Beadle, J.R., Saunders, J.P., Wajda Jr., T.J.: Process for Manufacturing Tagatose. Biospherics Incorporated (US patent 5,078,796) (1992),
http://www.uspto.gov/patft/index.html
13. Lu, Y., Levin, G.V., Donner, T.W.: Tagatose, a new antidiabetic and obesity control drug. Diabetes Obes Metab. 10, 109–134 (2008)

14. The MathWorks, Simulink and the Communications Toolbox,
    http://www.mathworks.com
15. Woodcock, J.: US Food and Drug Administration,
    http://www.fda.gov/ohrms/dockets/ac/02/briefing/
    3869B1_08_woodcock/sld001.htm
16. Parashar, M., Matossian, V., Klie, H., Thomas, S.G., Wheeler, M., Kurc, T., Saltz, J.,
    Versteeg, R.: Towards Dynamic Data-Driven Management of the Ruby Gulch Waste Re-
    pository. In: Alexandrov, V.N., van Albada, G.D., Sloot, P.M.A., Dongarra, J. (eds.) ICCS
    2006, Part III. LNCS, vol. 3993, pp. 384–392. Springer, Heidelberg (2006)
17. Medendorp, J.P., Fackler, J.A., Douglas, C.C., Lodder, R.A.: Integrated sensing and proc-
    essing acoustic resonance spectrometry (ISP-ARS) for sample Classification. J. Pharm. In-
    nov. 2, 125–134 (2007)
18. Hannel, T., Link, D., Lodder, R.A.: ISP-ARS in discriminating Tagatose and other toll
    manufactured drugs. ISPE Journal of Pharmaceutical Innovation 3, 152–160 (2008)

Compressible Lattice Boltzmann Method and Applications

Weibing Feng[1,2], Bing He[1,2], Anping Song[1], Yang Wang[2],
Miao Zhang[3], and Wu Zhang[1,2,*]

[1] School of Computer Engineering and Science, Shanghai University,
Shanghai 200072, China
[2] High Performance Computing Center, Shanghai University,
Shanghai 200072, China
wzhang@shu.edu.cn
[3] Shanghai Aircraft Design and Research Institute, Commercial Aircraft
Corporation of China, Ltd., Shanghai 200232, China

Abstract. Lattice Boltzmann Method (LBM) is a novel numerical method for flows simulations. Compared with classic methods of Finite Difference Method, Finite Volume Method and Finite Element Method, LBM has numerous advantages, including inherent parallelization and simplicity of boundary condition treatment. The LBM usually has a constraint of incompressible fluid (Mach number less than 0.4). A variant of the LBM is studied and used to deal with compressible fluid with Mach number up to 0.9 in this paper. Special emphasis is placed on mesh generation of 3-D complete geometry in Cartesian coordinate system. Numerical experiments are fulfilled in 2-D and 3-D compressible flows. Performance evaluation of the algorithm demonstrates high parallel efficiency and prefect scalability. Numerical results indicate that the LBM is successful with the simulation of compressible fluid.

Keywords: Lattice Boltzmann Method, Compressible fluid, Mesh generation.

1 Introduction

There are two different ways to numerically simulate fluid flow, i.e., one based on macro-continuous model from top to button and one of micro-discrete model from button to top. From Euler equations and Navier-Stokes equations, classical numerical methods of finite different method, finite volume method and finite element discretize the equations, obtain the liner systems and solve the systems. While such from top to button approaches intuitive, there are still many deficiencies. For example, in such method, often focus on analysis from the continuous differential equations to the discrete algebraic equations of the truncation error, but ignored the discrete process of

---

*Corresponding author.

W. Zhang et al. (Eds.): HPCA 2009, LNCS 5938, pp. 17–26, 2010.

conservation of certain physical quantities. Furthermore, in dealing with complex flow systems, to solve this type of nonlinear differential equations is very difficult or impossible.

In recent years, much attention of the Lattice Boltzmann method [1,2] (hereinafter referred to as LBM) belong to micro-discrete model based on from button to top approach. In the LBM method, the fluid is an abstract for a large number of micro-particles, and these micro-particles in a discrete lattice migrate and collide in accordance with a simple movement rules. By the statistical particle can get the macro movement of fluid characteristics. This particle properties of LBM method also make the conventional numerical methods do not have many unique advantages, such as the physical image is clear, the boundaries treat easier and the computing is nature of parallel processing and so on. LBM method also provides the possibility and the reality of macro and micro. It is both a direct calculation of the viscous fluid, and also approximate Navier-Stokes equations under certain conditions. At the same time, LBM modeling is achieved with a simple mathematical modeling of complex systems, it also breaks the traditional concept of modeling for other complex systems and provides a new way. The evolution process of LBM method (in particular, LBGK model) is very simple and clear, its program more concise. Lattice Boltzmann method involved in the calculations are localized, with the natural parallelism, very suitable for large-scale parallel computer. Because of these advantages, LBM method is considered a promising method of calculation and raised a strong interest.

Currently, LBM has been in the multi-phase flow, porous media flow, particulate flow, reacting flow, magnetic fluid mechanics and bio-mechanics have achieved great success, their efficiency, accuracy and robustness have been widely confirmed. The traditional LBM methods can only handle low-speed incompressible fluid flow, can not be used for high-speed moving objects such as aircraft simulation, thereby limiting the application of the method. To calculate the high-speed compressible fluid flow, researchers have begun a new model of research, such as Alexander et al [7] approaches such as the use of controlled speed of sound; Yu and Zhao [8] introduce magnetism to reduce the speed of sound, thus alleviating the constraints of small Mach number impact, but these methods do not restore the energy equation, and apply to a limited extent. Palmer and Rector et al [9-10] made the thermal LBM model, but still do not reflect the high Mach number phenomenon; Qu et al [11] proposed to use a circle function instead of using the Maxwell distribution function; Li et al [12] proposed a pairs of distribution function method; Sun et al [13] made the locally adaptive LB model, the speed of his model can get a very wide speed unlimited size; Yan Guang-wu [14] proposed multi-level multi-speed compressible model. These methods are the methods of changing the model of LBM proceed to find a distribution function and lattice model of a suitable compressible problem, in order to solve compressible fluid flow problems. These models themselves are some shortcomings, such as some models require large amount of computing, and some itself is complex, and some lack of rigorous theoretical derivation, and some extended to three-dimensional problem more difficult, reducing the usefulness. Recently, Shan Xiao-wen et al [15] introduced Hermite functions and derived distribution function, and made theoretically the LBM method for solving compressible fluid flow problems, this method has a more rigorous mathematical derivation. This paper will use this method to study high-speed compressible fluid problems.

2 The Lattice Boltzmann Method

Qian [2-4] and Chen [5-6] et al used independently Bhatnagar-Gross-Krook (BGK) collision relaxation model, and proposed lattice BGK (Lattice BGK, LBGK) model, the complex collision operation transformed into a simple relaxation process:

$$f_i(\mathbf{x}+\mathbf{e}_i,t+1) = (1-\omega)f_i(\mathbf{x},t) + \omega f_i^{eq}(\mathbf{x},t) , \qquad (1)$$

where $f_i(\mathbf{x},t)$ is defined in the discrete velocity set $\mathbf{e}_i$, is particle density distribution function at time t in the space grid points $\mathbf{x}$, $f_i^{eq}(\mathbf{x},t)$ is the amount by the system's current macro-constructed local dynamic equilibrium distribution function, relaxation factor ω depends on the physical properties (such as fluid viscosity, thermal conductivity coefficient, mass diffusion coefficient). In LBGK model, The macro-system state is constructed by the micro-particle group, on the other hand, the micro-particle group movement is controlled by the local macro-state of dynamics system. This reflects the individual partial discipline and adaptability. The local dynamic equilibrium distribution function $f_i^{eq}(\mathbf{x},t)$ is like a "Wizard" lead dynamically the system towards the state in line with objective laws. This relaxation technique makes the computational efficiency is very high.

Currently, LBM is no longer a pure fluid computing method, it is the design and modeling of complex systems provides a new way and means. The simplest and most commonly used LB model is the LBGK model useing relaxation BGK collision model. The evolution equation of the LBGK model is:

$$f_i(\mathbf{x}+\mathbf{c}_i\Delta t, t+\Delta t) - f_i(\mathbf{x},t) = \Omega_i(f) = \omega(f_i^{(0)}(\mathbf{x},t) - f_i(\mathbf{x},t)) , \qquad (2)$$

where $f_i(\mathbf{x},t)$ is particle density distribution function at time t in the space grid points $\mathbf{x}$ along the direction $\mathbf{e}_i$, $f_i^{(0)}(\mathbf{x},t)$ is the corresponding local dynamic distribution function, $\mathbf{c} = \Delta\mathbf{x}/\Delta t$ is particle speed, the relaxation factor $\omega = 1/\tau$, τ said the relaxation time that particle distribution function reach the equilibrium state. The macro-density and macro-velocity of fluid determined by the following formula:

$$\begin{cases} \rho = \displaystyle\sum_{i=0}^{n} f_i = \sum_{i=0}^{n} f_i^{eq} , \\ \rho\mathbf{u} = \displaystyle\sum_{i=0}^{n} f_i\mathbf{c}_i = \sum_{i=0}^{n} f_i^{eq}\mathbf{c}_i , \end{cases} \qquad (3)$$

The pressure is calculated by

$$p = c_s^2 \rho . \tag{4}$$

The evolution of LBGK model is a relaxation process, through the micro-particle density distribution function f_i and the equilibrium state f_i^{eq} to speed up relaxedly, allowing the system to quickly evolve to meet the objective laws of the state. LBGK model is a class of high-efficient computing models, since it has been proposed, due to the high computational efficiency, the strong parallel, and the easy implement of program, as well as the advantages of the boundary handling simple, it is made the most significant LBM and used most widely model, was applied to many complex flow simulation. In LBGK model, The most common is Qian [2] made DdQq series model, where d is the space dimension, q represents the number of discrete speeds. The local dynamic equilibrium distribution functions of such models usually take the following format:

$$f_i^{eq} = \omega_i \rho \left\{ 1 + \frac{3(\mathbf{e}_i \cdot \mathbf{u})}{c^2} + \frac{9(\mathbf{e}_i \cdot \mathbf{u})^2}{2c^4} - \frac{3\mathbf{u}^2}{2c^2} \right\} . \tag{5}$$

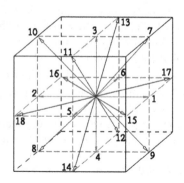

Fig. 1. Qian's D3Q19 model

3　The Complex Boundary Conditions Handling

In the compressible lattice Boltzmann method, the boundary conditions handling approach plays an important effect on the accuracy and stability of the Boltzmann model. Macroscopic hydrodynamic equations, such as the Navier-Stokes equations, by the fluid velocity, pressure and so on the actual situation, is more convenient and directly given boundary conditions. But the compressible lattice Boltzmann method, through the dynamic equations of a particle distribution function of micro-state to describe fluid movement, the distribution function is not known on the boundary, and therefore need to construct a definite pattern, from the microscopic point of view the distribution function is given boundary conditions, so a lot of the boundary conditions handling approach are designed to appease the macro-flow boundary conditions.

In the computing fluid problem, the no-slip boundary condition is a very important type of boundary condition. In the lattice Boltzmann method, the bounce back reflection is most common as the no-slip boundary condition. This method is relatively simple and handle easily, but this format is only a first-order accuracy, while the formula (2) is the second-order accuracy at the internal nodes, thereby reducing the overall accuracy of lattice Boltzmann method, and can only be used for no-slip boundary and not for movement boundary and Neumann boundary conditions and other complex boundary conditions.

In this paper, we use a non-equilibrium extrapolation method to handle boundary conditions. The non-equilibrium extrapolation boundary handling method draw the basic idea of extrapolation method in the design of numerical algorithm, it divide the distribution function f_i at the boundary nodes x_b into equilibrium and non-equilibrium two parts as follow:

$$f_i(\mathbf{x}_b,t) = f_i^{(0)}(\mathbf{x}_b,t) + f_i^{(1)}(\mathbf{x}_b,t), \tag{6}$$

the non-equilibrium part $f_i^{(1)}$ is the error of the equilibrium part $f_i^{(0)}$, satisfy $|f_i^{(1)}| \ll |f_i^{(0)}|$. So depending on the boundary conditions define a new equilibrium distribution to approximate equilibrium part, the non-equilibrium part obtained by the non-equilibrium extrapolation (a first-order format), the overall approximation accuracy of the attaining distribution function possess second order accuracy.

In this paper, this method is improved so that it applies more broadly, in particular the transition at the boundary corner points in the following ways will be more smooth, and the error smaller. Specific treatment methods are as follows. For velocity boundary condition, $\mathbf{u}(\mathbf{x}_b,t)$ is known, but the pressure $p(\mathbf{x}_b,t)$ is unknown, at this time the distribution function at boundary is determined by the following formula:

$$f_i(\mathbf{x}_b,t) = \overline{f}_i^{(0)}(\mathbf{x}_b,t) + (f_i(\mathbf{x}_f,t) - f_i^{(0)}(\mathbf{x}_f,t)), \tag{7}$$

Where $\mathbf{x}_f$ is the nearest fluid grid point with $\mathbf{x}_b$, $f_i^{(0)}(\mathbf{x}_b,t)$ is a approximationof $f_i^{(0)}(\mathbf{x}_b,t)$, it is computed by the following formula:

$$\overline{f}_i^{(0)}(\mathbf{x}_b,t) = \begin{cases} \dfrac{w_0-1}{c_s^2} p(\mathbf{x}_f,t) + s_0(\mathbf{u}(\mathbf{x}_b,t)) & i = 0, \\ \dfrac{w_i}{c_s^2} p(\mathbf{x}_f,t) + s_i(\mathbf{u}(\mathbf{x}_b,t)) & i \neq 0, \end{cases} \tag{8}$$

4 The Advantages of LBM Method

With the traditional finite element and finite volume methods, LBM method has the following advantages:

1) The natural parallel performance. LBM method only requires each node to independently calculate the collision and moving process, so the parallel performance of LBM method is very good, according to tests was almost linear speedup, see Fig.2.

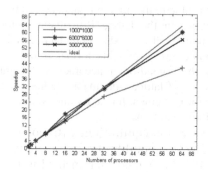

Fig. 2. The speedup of cave flow in different computing scales

2) Simple boundary conditions handling. Just at the boundary can be a simple reflection.

3) Simple mesh generation. In the usual entire aircraft CFD calculation, the mesh generation is generally the total workload of 60-70%, This is because the entire aircraft has very complex geometry, to obtain high-quality three dimensional structural or non-structural mesh, need to do a lot of meticulous work. However, The LBM method needs only the geometric shape of the entire aircraft to make a three dimensional surface mesh, and then can generate three dimensional Cartesian meshes. At the same time, we can see from their generation process, in the traditional method, the total number of body mesh and the number of the surface mesh are related, such as generating 10,000,000 body meshes, its surface meshes only 500,000-600,000(for example, the boundary layer is generated 10 layer). In the LBM method, the total number of body mesh and the number of the surface mesh are irrespective, in order to

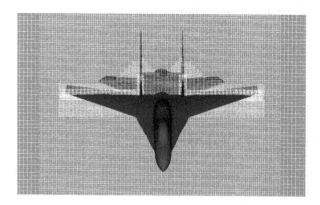

Fig. 3. Mesh profile diagram of an aircraft model

characterize the complex geometric structure of the entire aircraft, resulting in 10,000,000 body meshes, we can use 1,000,000 or more surface meshes, which can be more subtle describe the complex geometry of the entire aircraft, in order to obtain accurate results lay the foundation.

5 Numerical Experiments

5.1 One-Dimensional Shock Tube

Sod shock tube problem is a classic problem, it can be verified that the algorithm is reasonable.

Initial conditions: At $t = 0$,

$$p_l = 10, \quad \rho_l = 8, \quad v_l = 0, \quad x < 250,$$

$$p_r = 1, \quad \rho_r = 1, \quad v_r = 0, \quad x > 250,$$

For the ideal gas, gas constant $\gamma = 1140$, in Calculation, taking quality points to 500.

Fig.4 shows the calculation results, we can see that these new LBM method can be well simulated shock interruption to verify our algorithm.

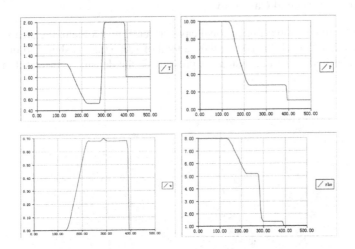

Fig. 4. The calculation results of Sod shock tube

5.2 Two-Dimensional NACA0012 Transonic Airfoil

Transonic flow region, including the flow Mach number is greater than 1, less than 1, equal to 1 situation, the flow phenomenon more complicated, more difficult to solve, the next figure shows the calculation results of new LBM methods.

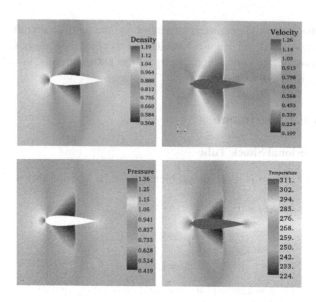

Fig. 5. The calculation results of NACA0012 transonic airfoil

5.3 Three-Dimensional Cave Flow

In this calculation of three-dimensional cave driven flow problem, the area size is the length width height each for 100 meshes, a total of 1,000,000 meshes. Lid-driven flow Mach number is 0.7, the dimensionless pressure 1, the density 1, the result as shown below.

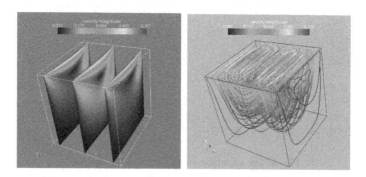

Fig. 6. The calculation results of three-dimensional cave flow

5.4 High-Speed Train

This Calculation takes into account three trains models (including the locomotive, the middle compartment, and tail each one). The space mesh is Cartesian orthogonal mesh, a total number of space mesh is about 40 million. Speed is 250 km/h.

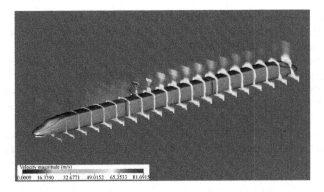

Fig. 7. The calculation results of high-speed train

6 Conclusion

Compressible LBM are studied and the applications to 2-D and 3-D flows are fulfilled. Large-scale 3-D transient Lattice Boltzmann code with the capabilities of handling multi-component flow, complex geometry and turbulence modeling will be studied in the future.

Acknowledgement

This work is partly supported by the CFD Sub-Project of the State Special Key Project of Large Commercial Aircraft and Shanghai Leading Academic Discipline Project under Grant No.J50103.

References

1. Qian, Y.H., d'Humieres, D., Lallemand, P.: Lattice BGK models for Navier-Stokes equation. Europhys. Lett. 17, 479 (1992)
2. Alexander, F.J., Chen, H., Doolen, G.D.: Lattice Boltzmann model for compressible fluids. Phys. Rev. A 46(4), 1967–1970 (1992)
3. Alexander, F., Chen, H., Chen, S., et al.: Lattice Boltzmann model for compressible fluids. Physical Review A 46(4), 1967–1970 (1992)
4. Yu, H., Zhao, K.: Lattice Boltzmann method for compressible flows with high Mach numbers. Physical Review E 61(4), 3867–3870 (2000)
5. Palmer, B., Rector, D.: Lattice Boltzmann algorithm for simulating thermal flow in compressible fluids. J. Comput. Phys. 161(1), 1–20 (2000)
6. He, X., Chen, S., Doolen, G.D.: A Novel Thermal Model for the Lattice Boltzmann Method in Incompressible Limit. Journal of Computational Physics 146(1), 282–300 (1998)
7. Qu, K., Shu, C., Chew, Y.: Alternative method to construct equilibrium distribution functions in lattice-Boltzmann method simulation of inviscid compressible flows at high Mach number. Physical Review E 75(3), 36706–1 (2007)

8. Li, Q., He, Y., Wang, Y., et al.: Coupled double-distribution-function lattice Boltzmann method for the compressible Navier-Stokes equations. Physical Review E - Statistical, Nonlinear, and Soft Matter Physics 76(5), 056705–056735 (2007)
9. Sun, C., Hsu, A.: Multi-level lattice Boltzmann model on square lattice for compressible flows. Computers and Fluids 33(10), 1363–1385 (2004)
10. Yan, G., Zhang, J., Liu, Y., et al.: A multi-energy-level lattice Boltzmann model for the compressible Navier-Stokes equations. International Journal for Numerical Methods in Fluids 55(1), 41–56 (2007)
11. Shan, X., Yuan, X.F., Chen, H.: Kinetic theory representation of hydrodynamics: A way beyond the Navier-Stokes equation. Journal of Fluid Mechanics 550, 413–441 (2006)

Studies on the Performance of a Heuristic Algorithm for Static and Transportation Facility Location Allocation Problem

Wei Gu and Xin Wang

Department of Geomatics Engineering, University of Calgary, Calgary, AB, Canada
{wgu,xcwang}@ucalgary.ca

Abstract. Static and transportation facility location allocation problem (STAFLA) is a new problem in facility location research. It tries to find out optimal locations of static and transportation facilities to serve an objective area with minimum costs. STFLS [2], a heuristic algorithm, has been proposed to solve STAFLA problem successfully and used into real applications. In this paper, an extended formalization of STAFLA problem is given first. Then the thorough analysis on the computing performance of the algorithm STFLS is discussed. Experiments have been conducted to demonstrate the efficiency and practicality of STFLS.

Keywords: Facility Location Problem, Static facility, Transportation facility, STFLS.

1 Introduction

Spatial analysis research is an important research field and has a variety of applications. Facility location allocation problem is one type of spatial analysis which solves problems of matching the supply and demand by using sets of objectives and constraints [1]. The objective is to determine a set of locations for the supply so as to minimize the total supply and assignment cost. For instance, decision makers may want to know how to allocate public service facilities such as hospitals and post offices for new residence area. The decision will be made based on the local populations and the capability of the limited resources. For another example, a local school board may provide accessible service to a population while minimizing the total distance travelled by the students. These examples are involved with single type of facilities such as hospitals, fire stations or schools.

In reality, we also face two types of facilities location problem when the number of the single type of facilities within a service area is inefficient [2]. For example, for emergency medical services, we can locate the hospital locations in such a way that it achieves full coverage of a service with the minimum total travelling distance. This usually ends up the hospital locations close to the dense community. However, for the residents in the sparse and remote area, since the number of hospitals is limited, in order to offer fast response time, the ambulance should be located to shorten the time

W. Zhang et al. (Eds.): HPCA 2009, LNCS 5938, pp. 27–37, 2010.

to access medical services. In this application, two types of facilities need to be located in a region, static facilities (e.g. hospitals) and transportation facilities (e.g. ambulances). The service is supplied to the customers by the cooperation of these two types of facilities. In addition, dependency relations usually exist between different types of facilities. Specifically, the locations of transportation facilities are dependent on the locations of static facilities and demand objects. For example, the locations of ambulances will be determined by both residence locations and hospital locations.

The solution of facility location allocation problem includes two steps: designing models to simulate real problems and developing algorithms to solve models. Many models and algorithms have been developed for solving single type of faculty location allocation problem during the past thirty years [1, 3]. Three basic facility location models, *P-median model* [4], *covering model* [5], and *center model* [6], have been proposed that form the foundation for other advanced models. Based on them, different constraints are added, such as capability, delay and probability to evolve into many specific models [7, 8, 9, 10, 11]. As for algorithms, two types of algorithms have been developed. The first approach is to apply mixed-integer programming (MIP) algorithms [12].While these algorithms work well on some instances of most location models, they are typically only useful on small problems. Considering that realistically scaled location models can easily have thousands even hundreds of thousands of constraints and variables, using these standard optimization algorithms to find optimal solutions will quite often consume unacceptable computational resources in terms of both computer memory and time and with no guarantee of success. The second is to apply heuristic algorithms. The simplest options are constructive heuristics that build solutions from scratch, usually in a greedy fashion [13]. A further step is to use a local search procedure, which uses an existing solution as input and tries to improve it [14, 15]. Recently, some metaheuristics have been developed for exploring a large portion of the search space in an organization fashion to obtain close-to-optimal solutions, such as variable neighbourhood search (VNS) [16], tabu search [17], and scatter search [18].

Static and transportation facility location allocation problem has been concerned recently. Gu et al. [2] first formalized the problem and proposed a new algorithm named STFLS (Static Transportation Facilities Location Searching Algorithm) to solve it. STFLS is a local search heuristic algorithm which uses clustering method to reduce the searching space. The problem has also been considered in some real applications. For example, a Geographic Information System (GIS) platform named GIS-FLResolution [19] was developed for helping geographers and civil researchers to solve static and transportation facility location allocation problem.

Although STFLS has been proved that it can solve static and transportation facility location allocation problem efficiently, there is no research to reveal the computing performance of STFLS thoroughly. This paper aims to evaluate the STFLS on different computing environments. Firstly, an extended formalization of static and transportation location allocation problem is given in section 2. Secondly, the analysis on the performance of the algorithm STFLS in terms of executing time is discussed in section 3. Experimental studies on are presented in Section 4. Section 5 concludes the paper with future research directions.

2 Static and Transportation Facility Location Allocation Problem

The formalization of static transportation facility location allocation problem proposed here extends the one in [2].

Static and Transportation Facility Location allocation (STFLA) problem is about how to allocate capacitated static and transportation facilities in a given region, which aims to minimize the average travelling distance from demand objects to static facilities and the maximal travelling distance by transportation facilities.

Let Loc be a set of locations $Loc = \{\, l_1 \ldots l_k \mid K \in N^+ \,\}$ in a region. In this paper, the discussion is based on the following definitions.

Definition 1 (Demand Object). A demand object d is defined as a tuple (l, w) which $l \in Loc$ represents the location of the demand object; w is a positive number representing the demand of the demand object. A set of demand objects is denoted by $D = \{ d_1 \ldots d_e \mid e \in N^+ \}$.

Definition 2 (Facility). A facility is an object that has a location in Loc. We classify the facilities into two categories in term of functionality: static and transportation.

Definition 3 (Static Facility). A static facility s is defined as a tuple (l, u) which $l \in Loc$ represents the location of the static facility; u is a positive number representing the capability of the static facility. S is a set of static facilities, denoted by $S = \{ s_1 \ldots s_n \mid n \in N^+ \}$. A facility is static iff its location depends on the locations and demands of demand objects.

Definition 4 (Transportation Facility). A facility is a transportation facility if its location depends on not only demand objects but also static facilities. It is used to connect static facilities with demand objects. Each transportation facility t has a location $l \in Loc$. T is a set of transportation facilities, denoted by $T = \{ t_1 \ldots t_m \mid m \in N^+ \}$.

Definition 5 (Assignment). Given a set of demand objects D and a set of static facilities S, a couple (s_i , d_j) is an assignment between S and D if

$$ s_i.u \geq d_j.w + \sum_{d_z \in D'} d_z.w, \text{ where } s_i \in S, \ d_j \in D \text{ and D' is a set of the demand}$$

objects that have already been assigned to the static facility s_i. If (s_i , d_j) is an assignment, we call s_i is an **available static facility** to d_j. The 0-1 variable x_{ij} indicates if a demand object d_j is assigned to a static facility s_i. $x_{ij} = 1$ if (s_i , d_j) is an assignment, otherwise $x_{ij} = 0$.

Definition 6 (Static Facility Reachability). Given s set of demand objects D and a set of static facilities S, the static facility reachability function of a demand object d_j is defined as:

$\quad$ SRF(d_j)= $dist(d_j, s_i)$, where s_i is d_j 's assigned static facility. The static reachability function defines the distance from the demand object to its assigned static facility.

$\quad$ Taking the demands into account, the weighted static facility reachability function of a demand object d_j is defined as: WSRF(d_j)= $dist(d_j, s_i) * d_j.w$.

Definition 7 (Transportation Facility Reachability). Given a set of demand objects D, a set of static facilities S and a set of transportation facilities T, the transportation reachability function (TRF) of the demand object d_j is defined as:

$$TRF(d_j) = dist(d_j, s_i \parallel t_k) + SRF(d_j, s_i)$$,where $dist(d_j, s_i \parallel t_k)$ is the distance from a location of a demand object d_j to its assigned static facility location s_i or the closest transportation facility location t_k , whichever is shorter; the function Max{TRF(d_j), $d_j \in D$ } is to get the maximal transportation travelling distance value among all the demand objects.

Definition 8 (Static and Transportation Facility Location Allocation Problem)
Given a set of demand objects D, the STFLA problem is to determine locations for a set of static facilities S and a set of transportation facilities T, which satisfies the following conditions:

$\quad$ (1) Minimize the value of the average weighted traveling distance function

$$\frac{\sum_{d_j \in D} WSRF(d_j)}{\sum_{d_j \in D} d_j.w}$$

$\quad$ (2) For $\forall$ $s_i \in$ S, $s_i.u \geq \sum_{d_j \in D} d_j.w * x_{ij}$

$\quad$ (3) for $\forall$ $d_j \in D, \sum_{s_i \in S} x_{ij} = 1$.

$\quad$ (4) Minimize Max{TRF(d_j), $d_j \in D$ }

In the definition, the condition (1) minimizes the average weighted travelling distance from every demand object to its assigned static facility. The condition (2) guarantees that every static facility has sufficient resources for its assigned demand objects. The condition (3) ensures that each demand object can only be assigned to one static facility. The condition (4) stipulates to minimize the maximum value of traveling distance for each transportation facilities.

3   STFLS: A Heuristic Algorithm for STFLA Problem

STFLS contains of two steps (shown in figure 1): static facility location searching and transportation facility location searching.

Static Facility Location Searching

In this step, we find local optimal locations for static facilities by using clustering. Clustering is the process of grouping a set of objects into classes so that objects within a cluster have high similarity to one another, but are dissimilar to objects in other clusters [20]. The clustering process is used to reduce the searching area. Static facility location searching involves three steps:

Step 1: initialization. Randomly pick up the locations for static facilities. Assign every demand object to a static facility by using urgency capability constraint assignment method [21]. After the assignment, each static facility together with its assigned demand objects is considered as a cluster.

Step 2: intra-cluster searching. The goal of the step is to find the local optimal location to minimize the average travelling distance from demand points to the static facility in each cluster. Because the objects in a cluster are closer to each other than the objects from other clusters, for every static facility in a cluster, we assume that its optimal location should be in that cluster. Through separating the whole area into different clusters, the searching space for every static facility is reduced from the whole area to its cluster. The local optimal location for each static facility from its cluster is found out.

Step 3: inter-cluster searching. The goal of the step is to compare the local optimal static facilities' location in every cluster and select one which can reduce the average distance most. The reason we only change one static facility to its new local optimal location is that all the local optimal locations for static facilities are determined under the same distribution of static facilities. Thus, once one static facility's location is changed, the other static facilities' local optimal locations could be changed.

Step 2 and step 3 are iterated until no change happened in step 3.

```
STFLS(D, S, T)
Input: a set of demand objects D, a set of static
facilities S with unknown locations, and a set of
transportation facilities T with unknown locations
Output: locations of S and T
   /* static facilities locations searching step */
   1 SearchStaticFacilityLocations (D,S)
   /* transportation facilities locations searching step*/
   2 SearchTransportationFacilitiesLocations(D,S,T,
     threshold)
```

Fig. 1. Pseudo code of STFLS

Transportation Facility Location Searching

Locations of transportation facilities depend on both locations of demand objects and static facilities. To reduce the computation time, we use a greedy method in this step. Transportation facility location searching includes 3 steps:

Step 1: initialization. Randomly choose the initial locations for all transportation.

Step 2: exchanging. The strategy is that it changes every transportation facility to the location whichever reduces the maximum transportation travelling distance most within each iteration.

Step 3: calculation. Calculate the transportation facility travelling distance of every demand point and determine every transportation facility's service area.

Step 2 and step 3 are iterated until no change is made in step 2 or the iteration times reach the predefined threshold.

The cost of STFLS is dominated by two operations: static facility location searching and transportation facility location searching. For static facility location searching, it can also be separated into two parts: urgency capability constraint assignment method and find local optimal locations. The executing time of urgency capability constraint assignment method is $O(|D|\cdot|S|)$, where |D| is the number of demand points and |S| is the number of static facilities. The executing time of finding local optimal static facility location is $O(|D|\cdot|S|)$. Thus, in each iteration, the executing time of static facility location searching is $O(|D|\cdot|S|)$. The executing time of transportation facility location searching in each iteration is $O(T\cdot|D|^2)$, where |T| is the number of transportation facilities. So, the total time complexity of the algorithm is $O(|D|\cdot|S|+|T|.|D|^2)$.

4 Experiments

We have conducted extensive experiments to evaluate the performance of STFLS. The algorithm was implemented in Java and experiments were performed on a Core 2 Quad 2.40GHz PC with 3GB memory, running on Windows XP platform.

4.1 Data Generation and Problem Setting

Seventy-six synthetic datasets for demand objects were created in a $300 \otimes 300$ area. All experiments run on three datasets, in which 80% of the points consist of 4, 6, 8 dense clusters, and the remaining 20% are uniformly distributed in the area. All values in the following experiments are the average of the results which are got from running the algorithm six times on three datasets with different distribution. Table 1 shows the range of values for different parameters. Without specifying, the underlined default values are used for experiments.

Table 1. Parameter Values for experiments on synthetic datasets

Parameter	Value
Number of demand objects	1000, 5000, <u>10000</u>, 20000, 40000, 60000, 80000, 100000
Number of static facilities	1, 3, <u>5</u>, 10, 15, 20
Capability of static facility	<u>40000</u>, 80000, 120000, 160000, 200000, 300000, 400000
Number of transportation facilities	1, 5, <u>10</u>, 20, 40, 60, 80, 100
Capability range of demand object	(1,30)

4.2 Experiments on STFLS

The evaluation on STFLS includes the following parts: the number of static facilities, the number of transportation facilities, the number of the demand points, the capability of static facilities and the distribution of demand points and static facilities' capabilities.

We first evaluate the performance on locating static facility in the method. The capability of each static facility is 200,000. When the number of static facilities increases from 1 to 20 and the maximal transportation travelling distance decreases from 308.1 to 143.3, the average travelling distance decreases from 112.0 to 19.8 as shown in figure 2 (a). In figure 2 (b), when the number of static facilities increases from 1 to 20, the execution time increases from 259 seconds to 4,635 seconds.

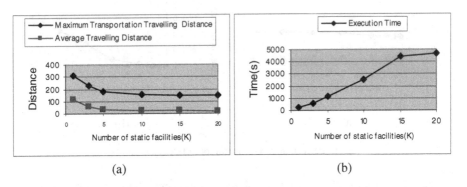

(a)   (b)

Fig. 2. Performance vs. the number of static facilities

Figure 3 investigates the effect of the number of transportation facilities on execution time and maximum transportation travelling distance. In Figure 3 (a), as the number of transportation resources increases, the maximal transportation travelling

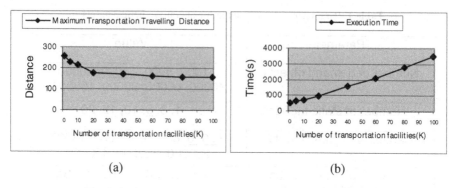

Fig. 3. Performance vs. the number of transportation facilities

distance shrinks from 259.2 for one facility to 155.3 for 100 facilities. Figure 3 (b) shows the execution time versus the number of transportation facilities. The execution time ranges from 495 seconds for 1 transportation facility to 3,475 seconds for 100 transportation facilities.

Figure 4 evaluates the effect of the number of demand points on execution time, average travelling distance and maximum transportation travelling distance. When the number of demand points increases from 1000 to 100,000, the maximum transportation travelling distance increases from 171 to 215 and the average travelling distance increases from 25 to 28 as shown in figure 4 (a). In figure 4 (b), when the number of demand points increases from 1000 to 100,000, the execution time increases from 8 seconds to 156,311 seconds.

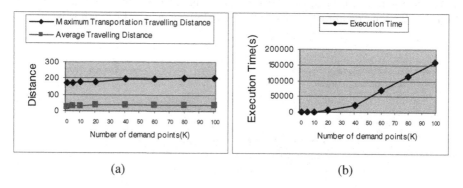

Fig. 4. Performance vs. the number of demand points

Figure 5 shows the effect of the distribution of demand points and static facilities' capabilities on execution time, average travelling distance and maximum transportation travelling distance. For the distribution of demand points, we have Uniform distribution and Clustered distribution. Uniform distribution (U) places points uniformly in the given region, while clustered distribution (C) generates datasets in the way described in Section 4.1. For the distribution of static facilities' capabilities, we have Average distribution and Particular distribution. Average distribution (A) gives the capability of all the static facilities with similar capability, while particular distribution (P) generates the capability of one static facility which are ten times less than other static facilities. For example, label "U&A" on the horizontal axis corresponds to uniformly distribute demand points and give the capability of all the static facilities with similar capability. We observe that when particular distribution generates capability, the execution time is reduced but maximal transportation travelling distance and average travelling distance increase. The reason is that the static facilities with small capability needs less time to allocate its location. Since the static facilities with small capability cannot serve all the demand points around it, some demand points should be assigned to other remote static facility, which leads to the increment of maximal transportation travelling distance and average travelling distance.

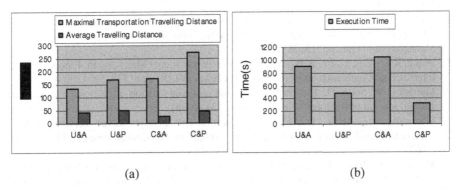

(a)   (b)

Fig. 5. Performance comparison for different distribution of demand points and static facilities' capability

5 Conclusion and Future Work

Static and transportation facility location allocation problem is a new problem in facility location research. It tries to find out optimal locations of static and transportation facilities to serve an objective area with minimum costs. The problem is challenging because two types of facilities are involved and cooperate with each other. STFLS as a local search heuristic algorithm has been proposed recently. In this paper, we give an extended formalization of static and transportation location allocation problem and evaluate the performance of STFLS on different datasets. According to the experimental results, the executing time of STFLS on large dataset is acceptable with a reasonable accuracy.

In the future, we will extend the problem to multiple types of facilities and develop an algorithm with flexible interface which can be used in a wide range of applications. In addition, we seek to introduce a pre-processing method and spatial data index in our algorithm to reduce the execution time and memory usage. Finally, we will extend the algorithm from using Euclidean distance to spatial network.

References

1. Owen, S.H., Daskin, M.S.: Strategic facility location: A review. European Journal of Operational Research 111(3), 423–447 (1998)
2. Gu, W., Wang, X., Geng, L.: STFLS: A Heuristic Method for Static and Transportation Facility Location Allocation in Large Spatial Datasets. In: Proceedings of the 22th Canadian Conference on Artificial Intelligence, pp. 211–214 (2009)
3. Longley, P., Batty, M.: Advanced Spatial Analysis: The CASA Book of GIS. ESRI (2003)
4. Church, R.L., ReVelle, C.S.: Theoretical and computational links between the p-median location set-covering and the maximal covering location problem. Geographical Analysis 8, 406–415 (1976)
5. Pacheco, J., Casado, S., Alegre, J.F.: Heuristic Solutions for Locating Health Resources. IEEE Intelligent Systems 23(1), 57–63 (2008)
6. Daskin, M.S.: Network and Discrete Location: Models Algorithms and Applications. Wiley, Chichester (1995)
7. Yiu, U.L.H., Mouratidis, M.L., Mamoulis, K.: N.: Capacity Constrained Assignment in Spatial Databases. In: Proceedings of ACM-SIGMOD international conference on Management of data, pp. 15–28 (2008)
8. Wong, R.C., Tao, Y., Fu, A.W., Xiao, X.: On efficient spatial Matching. In: Proceedings of International Conference on Very Large Data Bases (VLDB), pp. 579–590 (2007)
9. Marianov, V., Serra, D.: Probabilistic maximal covering location–allocation for congested system. Journal of Regional Science 38, 401–424 (1998)
10. Marianov, V., Serra, D.: Location–allocation of multiple-server service centers with constrained queues or waiting times. Annals of Operations Research 111, 35–50 (2002)
11. Marianov, V., Rios, M., Icaza, M.J.: Facility location for market capture when users rank facilities by shorter travel and waiting times. European Journal of Operational Research 191, 32–44 (2008)
12. Willoughby, K.A.: A mathematical programming analysis of public transit systems. Omega 30, 137–142 (2002)
13. Mahdian, M., Markakis, E., Saberi, A., Vazirani, V.V.: A greedy facility location algorithm analyzed using dual fitting. In: Goemans, M.X., Jansen, K., Rolim, J.D.P., Trevisan, L. (eds.) RANDOM 2001 and APPROX 2001. LNCS, vol. 2129, pp. 127–137. Springer, Heidelberg (2001)
14. Teitz, M.B., Bart, P.: Heuristic methods for estimating generalized vertex median of a weighted graph. Operations Research 16, 955–961 (1968)
15. Densham, P.J., Rushton, G.: Strategies for solving large location-allocation problems by heuristic methods. Environment and Planning A 24, 280–304 (1992)
16. Hansen, P., Mladenović, N.: Variable Neighborhood Search for the p-Median. Location Science 5, 207–226 (1997)
17. Rolland, E., Schilling, D.A., Current, J.R.: An Efficient Tabu Search Procedure for the p Median Problem. European Journal of Operational Research 96, 329–342 (1996)
18. García-López, F., Melián-Batista, B., Moreno-Pérez, J.A., Moreno-Vega, J.M.: Parallelization of the Scatter Search for the p-Median Problem. Parallel Computing 29(5), 575–589 (2003)

19. Gu, W., Wang, X., Geng, L.: GIS-FLSolution: A Spatial Analysis Platform for Static and Transportation Facility Location Allocation Problem. In: Proceedings of the 18th International Symposium on Methodologies for Intelligent Systems, pp. 453–462 (2009)
20. Han, J., Kamber, M., Tung, A.K.H.: Spatial Clustering Methods in Data Mining: A Survey. In: Miller, H., Han, J. (eds.) Geographic Data Mining and Knowledge Discovery. Taylor and Francis, Abington (2001)
21. Ghoseiri, K., Ghannadpour, S.F.: Solving Capacitated P-Median Problem using Genetic Algorithm. In: Proceedings of International Conference on Industrial Engineering and Engineering Management (IEEM), pp. 885–889 (2007)

A Parallel Algebraic Multigrid Solver on Graphics Processing Units[*]

Gundolf Haase[1], Manfred Liebmann[1,2], Craig C. Douglas[2], and Gernot Plank[3]

[1] Institute for Mathematics and Scientific Computing, University of Graz
[2] Department of Mathematics, University of Wyoming
[3] Computing Laboratory, Oxford University

Abstract. The paper presents a multi-GPU implementation of the pre-conditioned conjugate gradient algorithm with an algebraic multigrid preconditioner (PCG-AMG) for an elliptic model problem on a 3D unstructured grid. An efficient parallel sparse matrix-vector multiplication scheme underlying the PCG-AMG algorithm is presented for the many-core GPU architecture. A performance comparison of the parallel solver shows that a singe Nvidia Tesla C1060 GPU board delivers the performance of a sixteen node Infiniband cluster and a multi-GPU configuration with eight GPUs is about 100 times faster than a typical server CPU core.

1 Introduction

Key elements of numerical algorithms in scientific computing are now accessible on graphics processing units (GPUs) due to recent hardware and software advancements. Specifically, the support of IEEE 754 double precision floating point arithmetics and the introduction of the Nvidia CUDA technology. The hardware and software enhancements of Nvidia CUDA technology remove the limitations of the stream computing concepts of the previous generation of graphics processors and significantly simplify the design and implementation of complex numerical algorithms on many-core GPU architectures. The paper presents the design and implementation of a parallel preconditioned conjugate gradient algorithm with algebraic multigrid preconditioner (PCG-AMG) [6,3,14,9,8]. The PCG-AMG algorithm requires symmetric positive definite system matrices, that typically appear in finite element simulations of potential problems in electrodynamics or in fluid dynamics simulations. A performance comparison of the PCG-AMG solver on different hardware platforms shows a significant performance advantage for GPU based systems over traditional shared memory servers and cluster computers. A benchmark for an elliptic model problem derived from a 3D virtual heart simulation [13] shows that a single Nvidia Tesla

[*] This publication is based on work supported in part by NSF grants OISE-0405349, ACI-0305466, CNS-0719626, and ACI-0324876, by DOE project DE-FC26-08NT4, by FWF project SFB032, by BMWF project AustrianGrid 2, and Award No. KUS-C1-016-04, made by King Abdullah University of Science and Technology (KAUST).

W. Zhang et al. (Eds.): HPCA 2009, LNCS 5938, pp. 38–47, 2010.

C1060 board delivers the same performance as a sixteen node Infiniband cluster with 32 Opteron CPU cores. A GPU server with four Nvidia Geforce GTX 295 dual-GPU boards is about 100x times faster than a typical AMD Opteron CPU core. A detailed performance comparison of the PCG-AMG solver for the elliptic model problem on a variety of hardware is given in Table 1. Table 2 details the parallel performance for the setup of the algebraic multigrid (AMG) preconditioner. The key performance ingredient for the GPU implementation of the PCG-AMG algorithm is an efficient implementation of the sparse matrix-vector multiplication. An interleaved compressed row storage (ICRS) data format for sparse matrices is introduced in §3.2, that provides the basis for an efficient matrix-vector multiplication scheme for unstructured matrices. Previous work on multigrid algorithms on graphics processors can be found in [8,15].

2 Algebraic Multigrid

We solve a sparse system of linear equations $A\underline{u} = \underline{f}$ with an unknown solution vector $\underline{u}$ and a quadratic, positive definite system matrix A derived from a finite element discretization of a partial differential equation in a 3D domain. We solve this system of linear equations using multigrid and especially an algebraic version. We give a brief sketch of the methods (see [4,14,16] for more details).

2.1 Multigrid

The standard multigrid V-cycle is formulated as a recursive scheme in Algorithm 1. The algorithm requires as inputs the matrix hierarchy A_l ($A_0 := A$), the prolongation and restriction operator P_l and R_l, and the pre- and post-smoothers S_l and T_l are typically Jacobi or forward/backward Gauss-Seidel smoothers, for $0 \le l < L$. Furthermore a coarse grid solver is required denoted as A_L^{-1} and the right hand side on the finest level $f_0 := f$. The algorithm returns the solution at the finest level $u := u_0$. Implementation details for these algorithms can be found in [7,4,5].

Most steps of Alg. 1 require a sparse matrix-vector multiplication, which motivates us to investigate this operation in §3.2 in more detail.

2.2 Algebraic Multigrid

Algorithm 1 assumes that all coarser discretizations, all matrices A_l, and all intergrid transfer operators R_l and P_l are known. If only the finest matrix A_0 is given, then all of the missing information must be created [14,16] using a setup process. AMG contains the following setup steps on each level $l = 0, 1, \ldots, L-1$:

1. Coarsening the set of nodes ω_l, such that $\omega_{l+1} \subset \omega_l$.
2. Derive the restriction $R_l : \mathbb{R}^{\omega_l} \mapsto \mathbb{R}^{\omega_{l+1}}$ and the prolongation $P_l : \mathbb{R}^{\omega_{l+1}} \mapsto \mathbb{R}^{\omega_l}$ for nodes in ω_l and ω_{l+1} from their entries in matrix A_l.
3. Calculate the coarse matrix by the sparse triple product $A_{l+1} = R_l \cdot A_l \cdot P_l$.

The parallelization of multigrid and AMG on distributed memory systems follows [10,12].

Algorithm 1. Sequential Multigrid Algorithm: multigrid(l)

Require: $f_l, u_l, r_l, s_l, A_l, R_l, P_l, S_l, T_l, \quad 0 \le l < L$

$f_0 \leftarrow f$

if $l < L$ **then**

$\quad u_l \leftarrow 0$ {Initial guess}

$\quad u_l \leftarrow S_l(u_l, f_l)$ {Presmoothing}

$\quad r_l \leftarrow f_l - A_l u_l$ {Calculation of residual}

$\quad f_{l+1} \leftarrow R_l r_l$ {Restriction of residual}

$\quad$ multigrid(l+1)   {Multigrid recursion}

$\quad s_l \leftarrow P_l u_{l+1}$ {Prolongation of correction}

$\quad u_l \leftarrow u_l + s_l$ {Addition of correction}

$\quad u_l \leftarrow T_l(u_l, f_l)$ {Postsmoothing}

else

$\quad u_L \leftarrow A_L^{-1} f_L$ {Coarse grid solver}

end if

$u \leftarrow u_0$

---

3 Parallelization on Graphics Processing Units

3.1 An Introduction to GPU Computing

Although the idea of general purpose computing in graphics processing units has been considered for about a decade, it has been a curiosity rather than a mainstream tool. During this period of time GPU programming models all involved stream computing, which limits access to data in a sequential manner. While stream computing is natural for 3D graphics, where thousands of triangles are processed piece by piece by the graphics pipeline, it is unacceptable for implementing general purpose algorithms.

In 2007 NVIDIA made significant changes in the processing cores in their GPUs to allow random access of memory for all data structures on a GPU. With corresponding changes to their software environment CUDA (Compute Unified Device Architecture), general purpose GPUs came into existence (and are sometimes found in the literature as GP-GPUs). As a result, any such GPU can now be thought of as a shared memory machine with hundreds of processing cores or as a many core CPU.

The CUDA toolkit has both C/C++ compilers and runtime libraries so that standard C/C++ code can be compiled to run on a GPU. The GPU is treated as a coprocessor for the host computer that holds the GPU (which may be on one or more separate GPU boards). The CUDA programming model is built on the concept of running a program on the host while compute intense functions are handled by the GPUs. Recent high end GPUs contain several hundred thread processors and more than 1 GB of high speed memory. NVIDIA's TESLA products are pure compute boards that hold up to 4 GPUs that have up to 4 GB of onboard memory per GPU.

The CUDA toolkit allows for an incremental software design approach. Hence, a given C/C++ code can be extended step by step using computational kernels that run on the GPU (using it as a coprocessor). Often the performance of an algorithm is dominated only by a few computational bottlenecks, where most of the compute time is spent. Replacing the bottlenecks incrementally by GPU optimized implementations has the potential of speeding up the whole algorithm with minimal effort.

Well implemented GPU kernels are $10 - 100$ times faster than their CPU counterparts, which can be attributed to the hundreds of processing cores on the GPU and the very fast onboard memory that is typically an order of magnitude faster than typical server memory.

GPUs have one serious limitation: transferring data to or from the GPU takes time and possibly large amounts of time. GPU kernels only work with data in the onboard memory. Hence, data has to be transferred in and out of the GPU. GPU boards are currently connected via the PCIE bus on the host computer. The speed of the PCIE bus is comparable to the speed of typical memory chips in the host computer and gives about 5 GB/s of memory copy performance. GPU memory has memory copy performance of 120 GB/s, which is much faster than the host to GPU copy speed. It is extremely important to limit data transfers between the host and a GPU, much like limiting communication is essential to good parallel computing performance. All data structures required for the computational kernel must be kept in GPU memory as long as possible in order to use the full potential of the GPU.

3.2   Sparse Matrix-Vector Multiplication Kernel

The most challenging kernel within the PCG-AMG solver is the sparse matrix-vector multiplication $v := Au$. Different approaches to the sparse matrix-vector multiplication are discussed in [11,1,2]. Due to the coalescing restriction in accessing the GPU memory it is not efficient to use the standard compressed row storage (CRS) data format. Since there is no natural blocking within the data structure, memory access will not be coalesced and thus leads to very poor performance. The performance drop for non-coalesced memory access is up to one order of magnitude in memory bandwidth. Extensive performance tests with different data structures for sparse matrices singled out an interleaved compressed row storage (ICRS) format as the best format for typical finite element matrices. The computational complexity for the generation of the interleaved data structure is also low. See §3.3 for a detailed explanation.

Except for the modified data structure for the sparse matrix storage the standard CRS matrix-vector multiplication algorithm can be used with only minor modifications. The code listing below shows the actual implementation of the kernel using CUDA. Further optimizations of the code involve the random access to the vector u using the texture cache of the GPU, which is a small read only cache (typically 16KB) that is optimized for memory access with 1D and 2D locality. Originally designed for fast access to color information stored in 1D or 2D arrays the texture cache can also enhance the performance of the matrix-vector multiplication by up to a factor of about two.

```
#define L 256
struct linear_operator_params {          //ICRS data structure
    const int *cnt;                      //ICRS count vector
    const int *dsp;                      //ICRS displacement vector
    const int *col;                      //ICRS column indices
    const double *ele;                   //ICRS matrix entries
    const double *u;                     //Input vector
    double *v;                           //Output vector
    int n;                               //Matrix dimension
};

texture<int2> tex_u;                     //Define texture reference

//Function on device
__global__ void __device_linear_operator(struct linear_operator_params parms)
{
    unsigned int j = N * blockIdx.x + threadIdx.x;
    if(j < parms.n)
    {
        unsigned int blkStart = parms.dsp[j];
        unsigned int blkStop = blkStart + L * parms.cnt[j];

        double s = 0.0;
        for(unsigned int i = blkStart; i < blkStop; i += L)
        {                                              //Stride L for interleaved access
            unsigned int q = parms.col[i];             //Load column index
            double a = parms.ele[i];                   //Load matrix entry
            int2 c = tex1Dfetch(tex_u, q);             //Load entry from texture cache
            double b = __hiloint2double(c.y, c.x);     //Convert texture entries to double
            s += a * b;                                //Calculate the sparse scalar product
        }
        parms.v[j] = s;                                //Store the sparse scalar product
    }
}

//Function on host
extern "C" {
void _device_linear_operator(int *cnt, int *dsp, int *col, double *ele,
    int m, int n, double *u, double *v)
{
    cudaBindTexture(0, tex_u, (int2*)u, sizeof(double) * m); //Bind the texture

    struct linear_operator_params parms;
    parms.cnt = cnt;
    parms.dsp = dsp;
    parms.col = col;
    parms.ele = ele;
    parms.u = u;
    parms.v = v;
    parms.n = n;
    __device_linear_operator<<< (n + N - 1)/N, N >>>(parms); //GPU kernel launch

    cudaUnbindTexture(tex_u);                        //Unbind the texture
}
}
```

3.3 Interleaved Compressed Row Storage Data Format

The standard compressed row storage data format for a matrix $A \in \mathbb{R}^{n \times n}$ with $m = \#A$ non-zero elements is defined by the three vectors $\mathtt{cnt} \in \mathbb{N}^n$, $\mathtt{col} \in \mathbb{N}^m$, and $\mathtt{ele} \in \mathbb{R}^m$. The vector $\mathtt{cnt}$ represents the number of non-zero elements per row. The vector $\mathtt{col}$ stores the column indices of the non-zero matrix entries row wise in sequential order and finally $\mathtt{ele}$ stores the non-zero matrix elements corresponding to the column indices. The vector $\mathtt{dsp}$ complements the

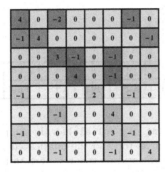

Fig. 1. A sample matrix with the rows colored in different hues

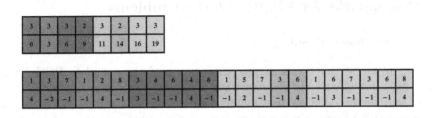

Fig. 2. CRS data structure (`cnt`, `dsp`, `col`, `ele`) for the sample matrix with the count and displacement vector on top and the column indices and matrix entries below

data structure with the offsets to the first element of a matrix row. Using the traditional vector of pointers to the first element of a matrix row violates the coalescence restriction and leads to bad performance. The adapted CRS format is depicted in Fig. 2 for the simple example matrix from Fig. 1. The interleaved compressed row storage (ICRS) data format leaves the vector `cnt` untouched, but rearranges the other three vectors. A block of L rows of column indices is grouped together by storing all the column indices of the first non-zero elements in a row in sequential order, then the second ones, and then third ones up to the maximum row length in the block. If not all rows in the block have the same number of column indices then the data structure contains holes. Although this reduces the storage efficiency of the data format for finite element matrices the number of non-zero elements per row is roughly the same. Even in the case of greater variations in the row lengths the data structure adapts since only blocks of L rows are grouped together. Typically L is chosen in the range of $16 - 256$ as a multiple of sixteen, which corresponds to the minimum coalescence requirement. The example matrix is stored in the ICRS data structure with eight rows interleaved which can be seen in Fig. 3.

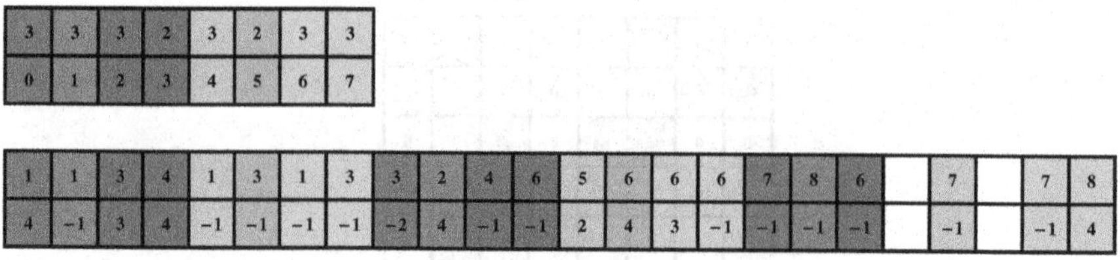

Fig. 3. ICRS data structure (`cnt`, `dsp`, `col`, `ele`) for the sample matrix in Fig. 1 with the count and displacement vector on top and the interleaved column indices and matrix entries below. The $L = 8$ interleaved matrix rows create holes in the data structure represented by the white boxes.

4   Benchmarks for Elliptic Model Problems

4.1   Performance Results

The key result of this paper is the performance of the complete PCG-AMG algorithm running on a GPU server when compared to traditional cluster computers and servers. The system matrix used in the tests originates from the unstructured 3D finite element discretization of an elliptical subproblem of the biharmonic equations describing a virtual heart simulation [13]. The resulting matrix has $n = 862,515$ rows and $m = 12,795,209$ non-zero entries. The benchmark times the setup of the AMG algorithm in Table 2 and 64 iterations of the PCG-AMG algorithm in Table 1 for details. We compare the performance of

Table 1. PCG-AMG Solver in seconds for the servers: *kepler* (AMD Opteron 248 Infiniband Cluster), *liebmann* (AMD Opteron 8347 Quad Socket Shared Memory Server), *mgser1* (Intel Xeon E5405 Dual Socket Server), *gtx* (AMD Phenom 9950 Server), *gpusrv1* (Intel Core i7 965 Server) and for the GPU configurations: *mgser1* (1x Nvidia Tesla C1060), *gtx* (4x Nvidia Geforce GTX 280), *gpusrv1* (4x Nvidia Geforce GTX 295)

#cores	kepler	liebmann	mgser1	gtx	gpusrv1	mgser1	gtx	gpusrv1
			CPU–cores				GPU–cores	
1	29.239	30.253	22.615	17.026	9.607	**1.217**	1.016	1.238
2	14.428	15.954	11.999	9.709	5.662		0.612	0.726
4	7.305	7.544	8.490	**6.562**	**3.885**		**0.367**	0.409
8	3.607	4.054	**8.226**		4.105			**0.284**
16	1.909	**3.493**						
32	**1.167**							
					Speedup			
wrt. one core	28.7	29.8	22.3	16.8	9.5	1.2	1.0	1.2
parallel	**25.0**	8.7	2.8	2.6	2.5		2.8	**4.4**

Table 2. Timings in seconds for the parallel algebraic multigrid (AMG) preconditioner setup for the same hardware as in Table 1

#cores	kepler	liebmann	mgser1	gtx	gpusrv1	mgser1	gtx	gpusrv1
			CPU–cores				GPU–cores	
1	6.302	5.812	3.836	3.583	2.106	**5.452**	4.714	2.888
2	3.280	3.182	2.209	2.069	1.217		2.765	1.745
4	1.601	1.640	1.239	**1.165**	0.684		**1.698**	**1.118**
8	0.787	0.877	**0.850**		0.581			1.159
16	0.501	**0.564**						
32	**0.426**							
Parallel speedup	**14.8**	10.3	4.5	3.1	3.6		**2.8**	2.6

the Infiniband cluster computer *kepler* with 16 dual-socket single core Opteron 2.2GHz nodes and the quad-socket shared memory server *liebmann* with quad-core Opteron 1.9GHz processors and the dual-socket quad-core Xeon 2.6GHz server *mgser1* and the single socket quad-core Phenom 2.6GHz server *gtx* and the single socket quad-core Intel Core i7 3.2GHz server *gpusrv1* with three GPU servers setups. The first GPU server *mgser1* has a single Tesla C1060 board with 4GB of memory and 240 processing cores. The second custom built GPU server *gtx* has four Nvidia GTX 280 boards with 1GB memory each and 960 processing cores. The third most powerful GPU server *gpusrv1* has four Nvidia GTX295 dual GPU boards with 1.8GB memory each and 1920 processing cores.

The performance of the GPU server *gpusrv1* with all eight GPUs active is about 100x that of a single Opteron core on the cluster computer or shared memory machine. Even compared to the fastest Intel Core i7 CPU with all four cores active the GPU server is more than 13x faster. A single Tesla board is essentially as fast as the whole Infiniband cluster with all 32 CPUs active and the fastest GPU server beats the Infiniband cluster by a factor of four. The setup phase of AMG requires too many data synchronizations between the GPU cores and therefore this part of the algorithm has not been accelerated by the GPU. At least the whole setup process runs on the GPU and we have all of the data available in the GPU memory afterwards. The saves time for starting the AMG solver on one hand and allows a cheap update of AMG-components on the GPU in case of a nonlinear problem.

5 Conclusions

We showed that even with algorithms on unstructured data the GPU outperforms the CPU and even a complex algorithm such as AMG can be completely implemented on the GPU. Considering the GPU as a processor with high inherent parallelism and combining it into clusters opens new opportunities for low budget parallel computing. Not all algorithm parts should be transferred to the GPU as the differences in in Tables 1 and 2 show. Over time, GPUs may evolve so that all parts can be productively transferred, however.

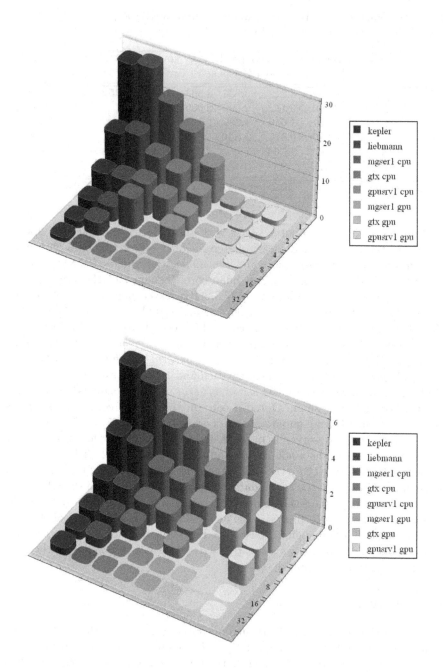

Fig. 4. Parallel solver and setup performance data for the *kepler* cluster and the servers *liebmann*, *mgser1*, *gtx*, and *gpusrv1*

References

1. Baskaran, M.M., Bordawekar, R.: Optimizing sparse matrix-vector multiplication on gpus. IBM Technical Report RC24704 (2008)
2. Bell, N., Garland, M.: Efficient sparse matrix-vector multiplication on cuda. NVIDIA Technical Report NVR-2008-004 (2008)
3. Bornemann, F.A., Deuflhard, P.: The cascadic multigrid method for elliptic problems. Numer. Math. 75, 135–152 (1996)
4. Briggs, W.L., Henson, V.E., McCormick, S.: A Multigrid Tutorial, 2nd edn. SIAM, Philadelphia (2000)
5. Douglas, C.C.: Madpack: A family of abstract multigrid or multilevel solvers. Comput. Appl. Math. 14, 3–20 (1995)
6. Douglas, C.C., Haase, G., Langer, U.: A Tutorial on Elliptic Pde Solvers and Their Parallelization. Society for Industrial and Applied Mathematics (2003)
7. Barrett, R., et al.: Templates for the Solution of Linear Systems: Building Blocks for Iterative Methods. SIAM, Philadelphia (1994)
8. Göddeke, D., Strzodka, R., Mohd-Yusof, J., McCormick, P., Wobker, H., Becker, C., Turek, S.: Using GPUs to improve multigrid solver performance on a cluster. International Journal of Computational Science and Engineering 4(1), 36–55 (2008)
9. Gropp, W., Lusk, E., Skjellum, A.: Using MPI: Portable Parallel Programming with the Message Passing Interface. The MIT Press, Cambridge (1999)
10. Haase, G., Kuhn, M., Reitzinger, S.: Parallel AMG on distributed memory computers. SIAM SISC 24(2), 410–427 (2002)
11. Im, E.-J., Yelick, K., Vuduc, R.: Sparsity: Optimization framework for sparse matrix kernels. Int. J. High Perform. Comput. Appl. 18(1), 135–158 (2004)
12. Liebmann, M.: Efficient PDE Solvers on Modern Hardware with Applications in Medical and Technical Sciences. PhD thesis, University of Graz, Department of Mathematics and Scientific Computing (July 2009)
13. Plank, G., Liebmann, M., Weber dos Santos, R., Vigmond, E.J., Haase, G.: Algebraic multigrid preconditioner for the cardiac bidomain model. IEEE Transactions on Biomedical Engineering 54(4), 585–596 (2007)
14. Ruge, J.W., Stüben, K.: Efficient solution of finite difference and finite element equations by algebraic multigrid (amg). In: Multigrid methods for integral and differential equations. The Institute of Mathematics and Its Applications Conference Series, pp. 169–212. Clarendon Press, Oxford (1985)
15. Thoman, P.: Multigrid Methods on GPUs, p. 62. VDM, Saarbrücken (2008)
16. Vassilevski, P.S.: Multilevel Block Factorization Preconditioners: Matrix-based Analysis and Algorithms for Solving Finite Element Equations, 1st edn. Springer, New York (2008)

Recent Advances in Time-Domain Maxwell's Equations in Metamaterials

Yunqing Huang[1,*] and Jichun Li[2,**]

[1] Hunan Key Laboratory for Computation and Simulation in Science and
Engineering, Xiangtan University, China
[2] Department of Mathematical Sciences, University of Nevada, Las Vegas, Nevada
89154-4020, USA

Abstract. In this paper, we present three second-order finite element
methods solving Maxwell's equations when metamaterials are involved.
The first method is based on integral-differential equations transformed
from the governing equations; the other two methods solve the original
governing differential equations. Numerical results are presented for the
last two methods.

1 Introduction

The double negative (DNG) metamaterials are artificially structured electromagnetic materials with both negative permittivity and permeability. The successful
construction of DNG metamaterials in 2000 triggered a new wave in the study and
design of DNG metamaterials and exploration of applications in diverse areas such
as sub-wavelength imaging and cloaking. Since 2000, engineers and physicists have
proposed some mathematical models and initiated some numerical simulations for
DNG metamaterials. Most methods are either based on the finite-difference time-
domain (FDTD) methods or finite element methods on frequency domain (mainly
using commercial packages such as HFSS and FEMLAB).

Though there exist many work (e.g., [5] and references cited therein) devoted
to Maxwell's equations, to our best knowledge, most are for the simple media
case. There are very few numerical analysis work when metamaterials are involved except our recent effort in time-domain finite element methods [4,3,1].
In this paper, we systematically present three second-order methods: one solved
as integral-differential equations; the other two solved directly from the original
differential equations either implicitly or explicitly.

2 The Governing Equations

The DNG metamaterials can be simulated using lossy Drude polarization and
magnetization models. The governing equations for modeling wave propagation
in metamaterials are [4]:

* Supported by the NSFC for Distinguished Young Scholars (10625106) and National
Basic Research Program of China under the grant 2005CB321701.
** Supported by National Science Foundation grant DMS-0810896.

W. Zhang et al. (Eds.): HPCA 2009, LNCS 5938, pp. 48–57, 2010.

$$\epsilon_0 \frac{\partial \boldsymbol{E}}{\partial t} = \nabla \times \boldsymbol{H} - \boldsymbol{J}, \quad \mu_0 \frac{\partial \boldsymbol{H}}{\partial t} = -\nabla \times \boldsymbol{E} - \boldsymbol{K}, \tag{1}$$

$$\frac{1}{\epsilon_0 \omega_{pe}^2} \frac{\partial \boldsymbol{J}}{\partial t} + \frac{\Gamma_e}{\epsilon_0 \omega_{pe}^2} \boldsymbol{J} = \boldsymbol{E}, \quad \frac{1}{\mu_0 \omega_{pm}^2} \frac{\partial \boldsymbol{K}}{\partial t} + \frac{\Gamma_m}{\mu_0 \omega_{pm}^2} \boldsymbol{K} = \boldsymbol{H}, \tag{2}$$

where ϵ_0 and μ_0 are the vacuum permittivity and permeability respectively, ω_{pe} and ω_{pm} are the electric and magnetic plasma frequencies respectively, Γ_e and Γ_m are the electric and magnetic damping frequencies respectively, $\boldsymbol{E}(\boldsymbol{x},t)$ and $\boldsymbol{H}(\boldsymbol{x},t)$ are the electric and magnetic fields respectively, and $\boldsymbol{J}(\boldsymbol{x},t)$ and $\boldsymbol{K}(\boldsymbol{x},t)$ are the induced electric and magnetic currents respectively.

For simplicity, we assume that the modeling domain be $\Omega \times (0,T)$, where Ω is a bounded Lipschitz polyhedral domain in $\mathcal{R}^3$ with connected boundary $\partial\Omega$. Furthermore, we assume that the boundary of Ω is perfect conducting so that

$$\mathbf{n} \times \boldsymbol{E} = 0 \quad \text{on} \quad \partial\Omega, \tag{3}$$

where $\mathbf{n}$ is the unit outward normal. Also we assume the initial conditions:

$$\boldsymbol{E}(\mathbf{x},0) = \boldsymbol{E}_0(\mathbf{x}), \quad \boldsymbol{H}(\mathbf{x},0) = \boldsymbol{H}_0(\mathbf{x}), \quad \boldsymbol{J}(\mathbf{x},0) = \boldsymbol{J}_0(\mathbf{x}), \quad \boldsymbol{K}(\mathbf{x},0) = \boldsymbol{K}_0(\mathbf{x}).$$

Lemma 1. *[1] There exists a unique solution for the system (1)-(2). Furthermore, the solution of (1)-(2) satisfies the following stability estimate*

$$\epsilon_0 \|\boldsymbol{E}(t)\|_0^2 + \mu_0 \|\boldsymbol{H}(t)\|_0^2 + \frac{1}{\mu_0 \omega_{pm}^2} \|\boldsymbol{K}(t)\|_0^2 + \frac{1}{\epsilon_0 \omega_{pe}^2} \|\boldsymbol{J}(t)\|_0^2$$

$$\leq \epsilon_0 \|\boldsymbol{E}(0)\|_0^2 + \mu_0 \|\boldsymbol{H}(0)\|_0^2 + \frac{1}{\mu_0 \omega_{pm}^2} \|\boldsymbol{K}(0)\|_0^2 + \frac{1}{\epsilon_0 \omega_{pe}^2} \|\boldsymbol{J}(0)\|_0^2. \tag{4}$$

3   Three Different Numerical Methods

To construct a finite element method, we partition Ω by a family of regular tetrahedral meshes T^h with maximum mesh size h. For simplicity, consider the lowest order Raviart-Thomas-Nédélec's spaces: for any $K \in T^h$,

$$\boldsymbol{U}_h = \{\boldsymbol{u}_h \in H(div; \Omega) \mid \boldsymbol{u}_h|_K = \boldsymbol{c}_K + d_K \boldsymbol{x}\},$$
$$\boldsymbol{V}_h = \{\boldsymbol{v}_h \in H(curl; \Omega) \mid \boldsymbol{v}_h|_K = \boldsymbol{a}_K + \boldsymbol{b}_K \times \boldsymbol{x}\}, \quad \boldsymbol{V}_h^0 = \boldsymbol{V}_h \cap \{\mathbf{n} \times \boldsymbol{v}_h = 0 \quad \text{on} \quad \partial\Omega\},$$

where $\boldsymbol{a}_K, \boldsymbol{b}_K, \boldsymbol{c}_K$ are constant vectors in R^3, and d_K is a real constant.

For any $\boldsymbol{v} \in H^\alpha(curl; \Omega), \frac{1}{2} < \alpha \leq 1$, it is known that we can define the Nédélec interpolant $\Pi_h \boldsymbol{v} \in \boldsymbol{V}_h$ on each tetrahedron K and have ([5]):

$$\|\boldsymbol{v} - \Pi_h \boldsymbol{v}\|_0 + \|\nabla \times (\boldsymbol{v} - \Pi_h \boldsymbol{v})\|_0 \leq Ch^\alpha \|\boldsymbol{v}\|_{\alpha,\text{curl}}. \tag{5}$$

Denoting by $P_h \boldsymbol{u} \in \boldsymbol{U}_h$ the standard $(L^2(\Omega))^3$-projection onto $\boldsymbol{U}_h$, we have

$$\|\boldsymbol{u} - P_h \boldsymbol{u}\|_0 \leq Ch^\alpha \|\boldsymbol{u}\|_\alpha \quad \forall \boldsymbol{u} \in H^\alpha(\Omega). \tag{6}$$

To define a fully discrete scheme, we divide the time interval $(0,T)$ into M uniform subintervals by points $t_k = k\tau$, where $\tau = \frac{T}{M}$. Moreover, we denote the k-th subinterval $I^k = [t_{k-1}, t_k]$, and define $\boldsymbol{u}^k = \boldsymbol{u}(\cdot, k\tau)$.

3.1   Treated as Integral-Differential Equations

Solving (2) with initial currents $\boldsymbol{J}_0(\boldsymbol{x})$ and $\boldsymbol{K}_0(\boldsymbol{x})$, we obtain

$$\boldsymbol{J}(\boldsymbol{x}, t; \boldsymbol{E}) = e^{-\Gamma_e t} \boldsymbol{J}_0(\boldsymbol{x}) + \epsilon_0 \omega_{pe}^2 \int_0^t e^{-\Gamma_e(t-s)} \boldsymbol{E}(\boldsymbol{x}, s) ds \equiv \boldsymbol{J}_0^N(\boldsymbol{x}) + \boldsymbol{J}_N(\boldsymbol{E}), \qquad (7)$$

$$\boldsymbol{K}(\boldsymbol{x}, t; \boldsymbol{H}) = e^{-\Gamma_m t} \boldsymbol{K}_0(\boldsymbol{x}) + \mu_0 \omega_{pm}^2 \int_0^t e^{-\Gamma_m(t-s)} \boldsymbol{H}(\boldsymbol{x}, s) ds \equiv \boldsymbol{K}_0^N(\boldsymbol{x}) + \boldsymbol{K}_N(\boldsymbol{H}).$$

Hence, the governing equations (1)-(2) become: find $(\boldsymbol{E}, \boldsymbol{H})$ such that

$$\epsilon_0 \frac{\partial \boldsymbol{E}}{\partial t} - \nabla \times \boldsymbol{H} + \boldsymbol{J}_N(\boldsymbol{E}) = -\boldsymbol{J}_0^N(\boldsymbol{x}) \quad \forall\, (\boldsymbol{x}, t) \in \Omega \times (0, T), \qquad (8)$$

$$\mu_0 \frac{\partial \boldsymbol{H}}{\partial t} + \nabla \times \boldsymbol{E} + \boldsymbol{K}_N(\boldsymbol{H}) = -\boldsymbol{K}_0^N(\boldsymbol{x}) \quad \forall\, (\boldsymbol{x}, t) \in \Omega \times (0, T). \qquad (9)$$

Now we can formulate a Crank-Nicolson mixed finite element scheme for (8)-(9) as follows: for $k = 1, 2, \cdots, M$, find $\boldsymbol{E}_h^k \in \mathbf{V}_h^0, \boldsymbol{H}_h^k \in \mathbf{U}_h$ such that

$$\epsilon_0 (\delta_\tau \boldsymbol{E}_h^k, \boldsymbol{\phi}_h) - (\overline{\boldsymbol{H}}_h^k, \nabla \times \boldsymbol{\phi}_h) + (\overline{\boldsymbol{J}}_h^k, \boldsymbol{\phi}_h) = -(\tilde{\boldsymbol{J}}_0^N, \boldsymbol{\phi}_h), \qquad (10)$$

$$\mu_0 (\delta_\tau \boldsymbol{H}_h^k, \boldsymbol{\psi}_h) + (\nabla \times \overline{\boldsymbol{E}}_h^k, \boldsymbol{\psi}_h) + (\overline{\boldsymbol{K}}_h^k, \boldsymbol{\psi}_h) = -(\tilde{\boldsymbol{K}}_0^N, \boldsymbol{\psi}_h) \qquad (11)$$

for any $\boldsymbol{\phi}_h \in \mathbf{V}_h, \boldsymbol{\psi}_h \in \mathbf{U}_h$ and $0 < t \leq T$, subject to the initial conditions

$$\boldsymbol{E}_h^0(\boldsymbol{x}) = \Pi_h \boldsymbol{E}_0(\boldsymbol{x}) \quad \text{and} \quad \boldsymbol{H}_h^0(\boldsymbol{x}) = P_h \boldsymbol{H}_0(\boldsymbol{x}). \qquad (12)$$

Here we denote $\tilde{\boldsymbol{u}} = \frac{1}{\tau} \int_{I^k} \boldsymbol{u}(t) dt$ for any $\boldsymbol{u}$. The $\overline{\boldsymbol{J}}_h^k$ is defined as

$$\overline{\boldsymbol{J}}_h^k = \frac{1}{2}(1 + e^{-\Gamma_e \tau}) \boldsymbol{J}_h^{k-1} + \epsilon_0 \omega_{pe}^2 \cdot \frac{\tau}{2} \cdot \frac{1}{2}(e^{-\Gamma_e \tau} \boldsymbol{E}_h^{k-1} + \boldsymbol{E}_h^k), \quad 1 \leq k \leq M, \quad (13)$$

$$\boldsymbol{J}_h^0 = 0, \quad \boldsymbol{J}_h^k = e^{-\Gamma_e \tau} \boldsymbol{J}_h^{k-1} + \epsilon_0 \omega_{pe}^2 \cdot \frac{\tau}{2}(e^{-\Gamma_e \tau} \boldsymbol{E}_h^{k-1} + \boldsymbol{E}_h^k), \quad 1 \leq k \leq M. \quad (14)$$

Similar formula will be used for $\overline{\boldsymbol{K}}_h^k$.

Lemma 2. *[1] For $S = H^1(\mathrm{curl}; \Omega)$ or $S = (H^\alpha(\Omega))^3$ with $\alpha \geq 0$, we have*

$$(i) \quad \|\delta_\tau \boldsymbol{u}^k\|_S^2 \leq \frac{1}{\tau} \int_{t_{k-1}}^{t_k} \|\boldsymbol{u}_t(t)\|_S^2 dt \quad \forall \boldsymbol{u} \in H^1(0, T; S),$$

$$(ii) \quad \|\overline{\boldsymbol{u}}^k - \frac{1}{\tau} \int_{t_{k-1}}^{t_k} \boldsymbol{u}(t) dt\|_S^2 \leq \frac{\tau^3}{4} \int_{t_{k-1}}^{t_k} \|\boldsymbol{u}_{tt}(t)\|_S^2 dt \quad \forall \boldsymbol{u} \in H^2(0, T; S).$$

Lemma 3. *Let $\boldsymbol{J}_N^k \equiv \boldsymbol{J}_N(\boldsymbol{E}(\cdot, t_k))$ and $\overline{\boldsymbol{J}}_h^k$ be defined by (7) and (13), respectively. Then for any $1 \leq k \leq M$, we have*

$$|\overline{\boldsymbol{J}}_h^k - \boldsymbol{J}_N^k|^2 \leq C[\tau \sum_{l=0}^k |\boldsymbol{E}_h^l - \boldsymbol{E}^l|^2 + \tau^4 \int_0^{t_k} (|\boldsymbol{E}(t)|^2 + |\frac{\partial \boldsymbol{E}}{\partial t}(t)|^2 + |\frac{\partial^2 \boldsymbol{E}}{\partial t^2}(t)|^2) dt].$$

Proof. Recall that $\boldsymbol{J}_N(\boldsymbol{E}) = \epsilon_0\omega_{pe}^2\int_0^t e^{-\Gamma_e(t-s)}\boldsymbol{E}(s)ds$. For clarity, we denote $\boldsymbol{J}^k = \boldsymbol{J}_N(\boldsymbol{E}(t_k))$. By definitions of $\boldsymbol{J}$ and $\boldsymbol{J}_h^k$, we have

$$|\boldsymbol{J}^k - \boldsymbol{J}_h^k| = |\frac{1}{2}(1+e^{-\Gamma_e\tau})(\boldsymbol{J}^{k-1} - \boldsymbol{J}_h^{k-1})$$

$$+\epsilon_0\omega_{pe}^2 \cdot \frac{\tau}{2}[\frac{1}{\tau}\int_{t_{k-1}}^{t_k} e^{-\Gamma_e(t_k-s)}\boldsymbol{E}(s)ds - \frac{1}{2}(e^{-\Gamma_e\tau}\boldsymbol{E}^{k-1} + \boldsymbol{E}^k)]$$

$$+\epsilon_0\omega_{pe}^2 \cdot \frac{\tau}{2} \cdot \frac{1}{2}[(\boldsymbol{E}^k - \boldsymbol{E}_h^k) + e^{-\Gamma_e\tau}(\boldsymbol{E}^{k-1} - \boldsymbol{E}_h^{k-1})]$$

$$\leq |\boldsymbol{J}^{k-1} - \boldsymbol{J}_h^{k-1}| + \epsilon_0\omega_{pe}^2 \cdot \frac{\tau}{2} \cdot \frac{\tau}{2}\int_{t_{k-1}}^{t_k} |\frac{\partial^2}{\partial s^2}(e^{-\Gamma_e(t_k-s)}\boldsymbol{E}(s))|ds$$

$$+\epsilon_0\omega_{pe}^2\frac{\tau}{4}(|\boldsymbol{E}^k - \boldsymbol{E}_h^k| + |\boldsymbol{E}^{k-1} - \boldsymbol{E}_h^{k-1}|), \tag{15}$$

where in the last step we used the inequality

$$|\frac{1}{2}(\boldsymbol{u}^k + \boldsymbol{u}^{k-1}) - \frac{1}{\tau}\int_{t_{k-1}}^{t_k} \boldsymbol{u}(t)dt| \leq \frac{\tau}{2}\int_{t_{k-1}}^{t_k} |\boldsymbol{u}_{tt}(t)|dt$$

for $\boldsymbol{u}(s) = e^{-\Gamma_e(t_k-s)}\boldsymbol{E}(s)$.

From [2, (Eq. (27))], for $k \geq 2$, we have

$$|\boldsymbol{J}^{k-1} - \boldsymbol{J}_h^{k-1}| \leq \epsilon_0\omega_{pe}^2[\tau\sum_{l=0}^{k-1} |\boldsymbol{E}_h^l - \boldsymbol{E}^l| + C\tau^2\int_0^{t_{k-1}}(|\boldsymbol{E}| + |\boldsymbol{E}_s| + |\boldsymbol{E}_{ss}|)ds]. \tag{16}$$

When $k = 1$, we have $\boldsymbol{J}^0 = \boldsymbol{J}_h^0 = 0$. Hence (16) holds true for $k = 1$.

Combining (15)-(16), we obtain (for any $k \geq 1$)

$$|\boldsymbol{J}_h^k - \boldsymbol{J}^k| \leq C[\tau\sum_{l=0}^{k} |\boldsymbol{E}_h^l - \boldsymbol{E}^l| + \tau^2\int_0^{t_k}(|\boldsymbol{E}| + |\boldsymbol{E}_t| + |\boldsymbol{E}_{tt}|)dt], \tag{17}$$

where we absorbed the dependence of $\epsilon_0, \omega_{pe}, \Gamma_e$ into the generic constant C.

Squaring both sides of (17) and using Cauchy-Schwarz inequality leads to

$$|\boldsymbol{J}_h^k - \boldsymbol{J}^k|^2 \leq C[\tau^2(\sum_{l=0}^{k} |\boldsymbol{E}_h^l - \boldsymbol{E}^l|)^2 + \tau^4(\int_0^{t_k}(|\boldsymbol{E}| + |\boldsymbol{E}_t| + |\boldsymbol{E}_{tt}|)dt)^2]$$

$$\leq C[\tau\sum_{l=0}^{k} |\boldsymbol{E}_h^l - \boldsymbol{E}^l|^2 + \tau^4\int_0^{t_k}(|\boldsymbol{E}|^2 + |\boldsymbol{E}_t|^2 + |\boldsymbol{E}_{tt}|^2)dt]$$

which concludes the proof.

Theorem 1. *Let $(\boldsymbol{E}^n, \boldsymbol{H}^n)$ and $(\boldsymbol{E}_h^n, \boldsymbol{H}_h^n)$ be the solutions of (1)-(2) and (10)-(11) at time $t = t_n$, respectively. Assume that for $\frac{1}{2} < \alpha \leq 1$,*

$$\boldsymbol{E}, \boldsymbol{E}_t \in L^\infty(0, T; H^\alpha(curl; \Omega)), \quad \boldsymbol{H}, \boldsymbol{H}_t \in L^\infty(0, T; H^\alpha(\Omega)),$$

$$\boldsymbol{E}_{tt}, \nabla \times \boldsymbol{E}_{tt}, \boldsymbol{H}_{tt}, \nabla \times \boldsymbol{H}_{tt} \in L^\infty(0, T; (L^2(\Omega))^3).$$

Then there is a constant $C = C(T, \epsilon_0, \mu_0, \omega_{pe}, \omega_{pm}, \Gamma_e, \Gamma_m, \boldsymbol{E}, \boldsymbol{H})$, independent of both the time step τ and the mesh size h, such that

$$\max_{1\leq n\leq M}(\|\boldsymbol{E}^n - \boldsymbol{E}_h^n\|_0 + \|\boldsymbol{H}^n - \boldsymbol{H}_h^n\|_0) \leq C(\tau^2 + h^\alpha).$$

Proof. Multiplying (8)-(9) by test functions ϕ and ψ, integrating the resultants in time over I^k, then choosing $\phi = \frac{1}{\tau}\phi_h, \psi = \frac{1}{\tau}\psi_h$ and subtracting (10) and (11), respectively, we obtain the error equations

$$\epsilon_0(\delta_\tau \xi_h^k, \phi_h) - (\overline{\eta}_h^k, \nabla \times \phi_h) = \epsilon_0(\delta_\tau(\Pi_h E^k - E^k), \phi_h)$$

$$-(P_h \overline{H}^k - \frac{1}{\tau}\int_{I^k} H(s)ds, \nabla \times \phi_h) + (\overline{J}_h^k - \frac{1}{\tau}\int_{I^k} J_N(s)ds, \phi_h), \qquad (18)$$

$$\mu_0(\delta_\tau \eta_h^k, \psi_h) + (\nabla \times \overline{\xi}_h^k, \psi_h) = \mu_0(\delta_\tau(P_h H^k - H^k), \psi_h)$$

$$+(\nabla \times (\Pi_h \overline{E}^k - \frac{1}{\tau}\int_{I^k} E(s)ds), \psi_h) + (\overline{K}_h^k - \frac{1}{\tau}\int_{I^k} K_N(s)ds, \psi_h), \quad (19)$$

where we introduced the notation $\xi_h^k = \Pi_h E^k - E_h^k$ and $\eta_h^k = P_h H^k - H_h^k$. Choosing $\phi_h = \tau(\xi_h^k + \xi_h^{k-1}) = 2\tau\overline{\xi}_h^k, \psi_h = \tau(\eta_h^k + \eta_h^{k-1}) = 2\tau\overline{\eta}_h^k$ in (18)-(19), and adding the resultants together, we have

$$\epsilon_0(||\xi_h^k||_0^2 - ||\xi_h^{k-1}||_0^2) + \mu_0(||\eta_h^k||_0^2 - ||\eta_h^{k-1}||_0^2)$$

$$= 2\tau\epsilon_0(\delta_\tau(\Pi_h E^k - E^k), \overline{\xi}_h^k) - 2\tau(P_h \overline{H}^k - \frac{1}{\tau}\int_{I^k} H(s)ds, \nabla \times \overline{\xi}_h^k)$$

$$+2\tau(\overline{J}_h^k - \frac{1}{\tau}\int_{I^k} J_N(s)ds, \overline{\xi}_h^k) + 2\tau\mu_0(\delta_\tau(P_h H^k - H^k), \overline{\eta}_h^k)$$

$$+2\tau(\nabla \times (\Pi_h \overline{E}^k - \frac{1}{\tau}\int_{I^k} E(s)ds), \overline{\eta}_h^k) + 2\tau(\overline{K}_h^k - \frac{1}{\tau}\int_{I^k} K_N(s)ds, \overline{\eta}_h^k)$$

$$= \sum_{i=1}^{6}(Err)_i. \qquad (20)$$

Using the inequality $|ab| \le \delta a^2 + \frac{1}{4\delta}b^2$ and Lemma 2, we have

$$(Err)_1 \le 2\delta_1\tau\epsilon_0||\overline{\xi}_h^k||_0^2 + \frac{\tau\epsilon_0}{2\delta_1}||\delta_\tau(\Pi_h E^k - E^k)||_0^2$$

$$\le \delta_1\tau\epsilon_0(||\xi_h^k||_0^2 + ||\xi_h^{k-1}||_0^2) + \frac{\epsilon_0}{2\delta_1}\int_{I^k}||\partial_t(\Pi_h E^k - E^k)||_0^2 dt. \qquad (21)$$

Similarly, by the projection property of P_h and integration by parts, we have

$$(Err)_2 = -2\tau(\nabla \times (\overline{H}^k - \frac{1}{\tau}\int_{I^k} H(s)ds), \overline{\xi}_h^k)$$

$$\le 2\delta_2\tau||\overline{\xi}_h^k||_0^2 + \frac{\tau}{2\delta_2}||\nabla \times (\overline{H}^k - \frac{1}{\tau}\int_{I^k} H(s)ds)||_0^2,$$

$$\le \delta_2\tau(||\xi_h^k||_0^2 + ||\xi_h^{k-1}||_0^2) + \frac{\tau^4}{8\delta_2}\int_{I^k}||\nabla \times H_{tt}(t)||_0^2 dt. \qquad (22)$$

Similarly, by Lemmas 2 and 3, we can obtain

$$(Err)_3 = 2\tau(\overline{J}_h^k - \overline{J}_N^k + \overline{J}_N^k - \frac{1}{\tau}\int_{I^k} J_N(s)ds, \overline{\xi}_h^k)$$

$$\le \delta_3\tau(||\xi_h^k||_0^2 + ||\xi_h^{k-1}||_0^2) + \frac{\tau}{\delta_3}(||\overline{J}_h^k - \overline{J}_N^k||_0^2 + ||\overline{J}_N^k - \frac{1}{\tau}\int_{I^k} J_N(s)ds)||_0^2)$$

$$\le \delta_3\tau(||\xi_h^k||_0^2 + ||\xi_h^{k-1}||_0^2) + \frac{C\tau^2}{\delta_3}\sum_{l=0}^{k}||E_h^l - E^l||_0^2$$

$$+\frac{C\tau^5}{\delta_3}\int_0^{t_k}(\|\boldsymbol{E}\|_0^2+\|\boldsymbol{E}_t\|_0^2+\|\boldsymbol{E}_{tt}\|_0^2)dt+\frac{\tau^4}{4\delta_3}\int_{I^k}\|\frac{\partial^2\boldsymbol{J}_N}{\partial t^2}\|_0^2ds$$

$$\leq\delta_3\tau(\|\xi_h^k\|_0^2+\|\xi_h^{k-1}\|_0^2)+\frac{C\tau^2}{\delta_3}\sum_{l=0}^k(\|\xi_h^l\|_0^2+\|\Pi_h\boldsymbol{E}^l-\boldsymbol{E}^l\|_0^2)$$

$$+\frac{C\tau^5}{\delta_3}\int_0^{t_k}(\|\boldsymbol{E}\|_0^2+\|\boldsymbol{E}_t\|_0^2+\|\boldsymbol{E}_{tt}\|_0^2)dt+\frac{\tau^4}{4\delta_3}\int_{I^k}\|\frac{\partial^2\boldsymbol{J}_N}{\partial t^2}\|_0^2ds. \qquad (23)$$

Similarly, we can easily obtain

$$(Err)_4\leq\delta_4\tau\mu_0(\|\eta_h^k\|_0^2+\|\eta_h^{k-1}\|_0^2)+\frac{\mu_0}{2\delta_4}\int_{I^k}\|\partial_t(P_h\boldsymbol{H}^k-\boldsymbol{H}^k)\|_0^2dt,$$

$$(Err)_6\leq\delta_6\tau(\|\eta_h^k\|_0^2+\|\eta_h^{k-1}\|_0^2)+\frac{C\tau^2}{\delta_6}\sum_{l=0}^k(\|\eta_h^l\|_0^2+\|P_h\boldsymbol{H}^l-\boldsymbol{H}^l\|_0^2)$$

$$+\frac{C\tau^5}{\delta_6}\int_0^{t_k}(\|\boldsymbol{H}\|_0^2+\|\boldsymbol{H}_t\|_0^2+\|\boldsymbol{H}_{tt}\|_0^2)dt+\frac{\tau^4}{4\delta_6}\int_{I^k}\|\frac{\partial^2\boldsymbol{K}_N}{\partial t^2}\|_0^2ds,$$

$$(Err)_5=2\tau(\nabla\times(\Pi_h\overline{\boldsymbol{E}}^k-\overline{\boldsymbol{E}}^k+\overline{\boldsymbol{E}}^k-\frac{1}{\tau}\int_{I^k}\boldsymbol{E}(s)ds),\overline{\eta}_h^k)$$

$$\leq2\delta_5\tau\|\overline{\eta}_h^k\|_0^2+\frac{\tau}{\delta_5}(\|\nabla\times(\overline{\boldsymbol{E}}^k-\frac{1}{\tau}\int_{I^k}\boldsymbol{E}(s)ds)\|_0^2+\|\Pi_h\overline{\boldsymbol{E}}^k-\overline{\boldsymbol{E}}^k\|_0^2)$$

$$\leq\delta_5\tau(\|\eta_h^k\|_0^2+\|\eta_h^{k-1}\|_0^2)+\frac{\tau^4}{4\delta_5}\int_{I^k}\|\frac{\partial^2(\nabla\times\boldsymbol{E})}{\partial t^2}\|_0^2dt+\frac{\tau}{\delta_5}\|\Pi_h\overline{\boldsymbol{E}}^k-\overline{\boldsymbol{E}}^k\|_0^2.$$

Finally, summing up both sides of (20) from $k=1$ up to any $n\leq M$, using the estimates of $(Err)_i$, the fact that $\xi_h^0=\eta_h^0=0$, and choosing δ_i small enough so that ξ_h^n and η_h^n can be controlled by the left hand side, we have

$$\epsilon_0\|\xi_h^n\|_0^2+\mu_0\|\eta_h^n\|_0^2$$

$$\leq C_1\tau\sum_{k=1}^{n-1}(\|\xi_h^k\|_0^2+\|\eta_h^k\|_0^2)+\frac{\epsilon_0}{2\delta_1}\sum_{k=1}^n\int_{I^k}\|\partial_t(\Pi_h\boldsymbol{E}^k-\boldsymbol{E}^k)\|_0^2dt$$

$$+\frac{\tau^4}{8\delta_2}\int_0^{t_n}\|\nabla\times\boldsymbol{H}_{tt}(t)\|_0^2dt+\frac{C\tau}{\delta_3}\sum_{l=1}^n\|\Pi_h\boldsymbol{E}^l-\boldsymbol{E}^l\|_0^2$$

$$+\frac{C\tau^4}{\delta_3}\int_0^{t_n}(\|\boldsymbol{E}\|_0^2+\|\boldsymbol{E}_t\|_0^2+\|\boldsymbol{E}_{tt}\|_0^2)dt+\frac{\tau^4}{4\delta_3}\int_0^{t_n}\|\frac{\partial^2\boldsymbol{J}_N}{\partial t^2}\|_0^2ds$$

$$+\frac{\mu_0}{2\delta_4}\sum_{k=1}^n\int_{I^k}\|\partial_t(P_h\boldsymbol{H}^k-\boldsymbol{H}^k)\|_0^2dt+\frac{\tau}{\delta_5}\|\Pi_h\overline{\boldsymbol{E}}^k-\overline{\boldsymbol{E}}^k\|_0^2$$

$$+\frac{\tau^4}{4\delta_5}\int_0^{t_n}\|\frac{\partial^2(\nabla\times\boldsymbol{E})}{\partial t^2}\|_0^2dt+\frac{C\tau}{\delta_6}\sum_{k=1}^n\|P_h\boldsymbol{H}^k-\boldsymbol{H}^k\|_0^2$$

$$+\frac{C\tau^4}{\delta_6}\int_0^{t_n}(\|\boldsymbol{H}\|_0^2+\|\boldsymbol{H}_t\|_0^2+\|\boldsymbol{H}_{tt}\|_0^2)dt+\frac{\tau^4}{4\delta_6}\int_0^{t_n}\|\frac{\partial^2\boldsymbol{K}_N}{\partial t^2}\|_0^2ds, \qquad (24)$$

where we used the fact $k\tau\leq T$ and absorbed T into the generic constant C.
Using interpolation estimates (5) and (6) to (24) and the inequality

$$\|\frac{\partial^2\boldsymbol{J}_N}{\partial t^2}\|_0^2\leq C(\int_0^T\|\boldsymbol{E}(s)\|_0^2ds+\|\boldsymbol{E}(t)\|_0^2+\|\boldsymbol{E}_t(t)\|_0^2), \qquad (25)$$

we obtain

$$\epsilon_0||\xi_h^n||_0^2 + \mu_0||\eta_h^n||_0^2 \leq C_1\tau \sum_{k=1}^{n-1}(||\xi_h^k||_0^2 + ||\eta_h^k||_0^2) + C \cdot (\tau^4 + h^{2\alpha}), \qquad (26)$$

which concludes the proof by the standard technique [1].

3.2   Treated as Differential Equations: Crank-Nicolson Method

Recently, we found that we can solve (1)-(2) directly and efficiently by constructing a Crank-Nicolson scheme[3]: for $k = 1, 2, \cdots, M$, find $\boldsymbol{E}_h^k \in \mathbf{V}_h^0, \boldsymbol{J}_h^k \in \mathbf{V}_h, \boldsymbol{H}_h^k, \boldsymbol{K}_h^k \in \mathbf{U}_h$ such that

$$\epsilon_0(\delta_\tau \boldsymbol{E}_h^k, \boldsymbol{\phi}_h) - (\overline{\boldsymbol{H}}_h^k, \nabla \times \boldsymbol{\phi}_h) + (\overline{\boldsymbol{J}}_h^k, \boldsymbol{\phi}_h) = 0, \qquad (27)$$

$$\mu_0(\delta_\tau \boldsymbol{H}_h^k, \boldsymbol{\psi}_h) + (\nabla \times \overline{\boldsymbol{E}}_h^k, \boldsymbol{\psi}_h) + (\overline{\boldsymbol{K}}_h^k, \boldsymbol{\psi}_h) = 0, \qquad (28)$$

$$\frac{1}{\epsilon_0\omega_{pe}^2}(\delta_\tau \boldsymbol{J}_h^k, \tilde{\boldsymbol{\phi}}_h) + \frac{\Gamma_e}{\epsilon_0\omega_{pe}^2}(\overline{\boldsymbol{J}}_h^k, \tilde{\boldsymbol{\phi}}_h) = (\overline{\boldsymbol{E}}_h^k, \tilde{\boldsymbol{\phi}}_h), \qquad (29)$$

$$\frac{1}{\mu_0\omega_{pm}^2}(\delta_\tau \boldsymbol{K}_h^k, \tilde{\boldsymbol{\psi}}_h) + \frac{\Gamma_m}{\mu_0\omega_{pm}^2}(\overline{\boldsymbol{K}}_h^k, \tilde{\boldsymbol{\psi}}_h) = (\overline{\boldsymbol{H}}_h^k, \tilde{\boldsymbol{\psi}}_h), \qquad (30)$$

are true for any $\boldsymbol{\phi}_h, \tilde{\boldsymbol{\phi}}_h \in \mathbf{V}_h$, and $\boldsymbol{\psi}_h, \tilde{\boldsymbol{\psi}}_h \in \mathbf{U}_h$. In practical implementation, at each time step we just need to first solve a smaller system

$$(\frac{2\epsilon_0}{\tau} + \frac{\epsilon_0\omega_{pe}^2\tau}{2 + \tau\Gamma_e})(\boldsymbol{E}_h^k, \boldsymbol{\phi}_h) - (\boldsymbol{H}_h^k, \nabla \times \boldsymbol{\phi}_h)$$
$$= (\frac{2\epsilon_0}{\tau} - \frac{\epsilon_0\omega_{pe}^2\tau}{2 + \tau\Gamma_e})(\boldsymbol{E}_h^{k-1}, \boldsymbol{\phi}_h) + (\boldsymbol{H}_h^{k-1}, \nabla \times \boldsymbol{\phi}_h) - \frac{4}{2 + \tau\Gamma_e}(\boldsymbol{J}_h^{k-1}, \boldsymbol{\phi}_h), \qquad (31)$$

$$(\frac{2\mu_0}{\tau} + \frac{\mu_0\omega_{pm}^2\tau}{2 + \tau\Gamma_m})(\boldsymbol{H}_h^k, \boldsymbol{\psi}_h) + (\nabla \times \boldsymbol{E}_h^k, \boldsymbol{\psi}_h)$$
$$= (\frac{2\mu_0}{\tau} - \frac{\mu_0\omega_{pm}^2\tau}{2 + \tau\Gamma_m})(\boldsymbol{H}_h^{k-1}, \boldsymbol{\psi}_h) - (\nabla \times \boldsymbol{E}_h^{k-1}, \boldsymbol{\psi}_h) - \frac{4}{2 + \tau\Gamma_m}(\boldsymbol{K}_h^{k-1}, \boldsymbol{\psi}_h). \qquad (32)$$

for $\boldsymbol{E}_h^k$ and $\boldsymbol{H}_h^k$, then update $\boldsymbol{J}_h^k$ and $\boldsymbol{K}_h^k$ as follows:

$$\boldsymbol{J}_h^k = \frac{\epsilon_0\omega_{pe}^2\tau}{2 + \tau\Gamma_e}(\boldsymbol{E}_h^k + \boldsymbol{E}_h^{k-1}) + \frac{2 - \tau\Gamma_e}{2 + \tau\Gamma_e}\boldsymbol{J}_h^{k-1}, \qquad (33)$$

$$\boldsymbol{K}_h^k = \frac{\mu_0\omega_{pm}^2\tau}{2 + \tau\Gamma_m}(\boldsymbol{H}_h^k + \boldsymbol{H}_h^{k-1}) + \frac{2 - \tau\Gamma_m}{2 + \tau\Gamma_m}\boldsymbol{K}_h^{k-1}. \qquad (34)$$

In [3], we proved the following optimal error estimate:

$$\max_{1 \leq n \leq M}(||\boldsymbol{E}^n - \boldsymbol{E}_h^n||_0 + ||\boldsymbol{H}^n - \boldsymbol{H}_h^n||_0 + ||\boldsymbol{J}^n - \boldsymbol{J}_h^n||_0 + ||\boldsymbol{K}^n - \boldsymbol{K}_h^n||_0) \leq C(\tau^2 + h^\alpha).$$

3.3   Treated as Differential Equations: Leap-Frog Method

Inspiring from the classic FDTD scheme, we can formulate a leap-frog scheme: Given initial approximations $E_h^0, K_h^0, H_h^{\frac{1}{2}}, J_h^{\frac{1}{2}}$, for $k = 1, 2, \cdots$, find $E_h^k \in V_h^0, J_h^{k+\frac{1}{2}} \in V_h, H_h^{k+\frac{1}{2}}, K_h^k \in U_h$ such that

$$\epsilon_0(\frac{E_h^k - E_h^{k-1}}{\tau}, \phi_h) - (H_h^{k-\frac{1}{2}}, \nabla \times \phi_h) + (J_h^{k-\frac{1}{2}}, \phi_h) = 0, \tag{35}$$

$$\mu_0(\frac{H_h^{k+\frac{1}{2}} - H_h^{k-\frac{1}{2}}}{\tau}, \psi_h) + (\nabla \times E_h^k, \psi_h) + (K_h^k, \psi_h) = 0, \tag{36}$$

$$\frac{1}{\epsilon_0 \omega_{pe}^2}(\frac{J_h^{k+\frac{1}{2}} - J_h^{k-\frac{1}{2}}}{\tau}, \tilde{\phi}_h) + \frac{\Gamma_e}{\epsilon_0 \omega_{pe}^2}(\frac{1}{2}(J_h^{k+\frac{1}{2}} + J_h^{k-\frac{1}{2}}), \tilde{\phi}_h) = (E_h^k, \tilde{\phi}_h), \tag{37}$$

$$\frac{1}{\mu_0 \omega_{pm}^2}(\frac{K_h^k - K_h^{k-1}}{\tau}, \tilde{\psi}_h) + \frac{\Gamma_m}{\mu_0 \omega_{pm}^2}(\frac{1}{2}(K_h^k + K_h^{k-1}), \tilde{\psi}_h) = (H_h^{k-\frac{1}{2}}, \tilde{\psi}_h), \tag{38}$$

for any $\phi_h \in V_h^0, \psi_h \in U_h, \tilde{\phi}_h \in V_h, \tilde{\psi}_h \in U_h$. Conditional stability and the following optimal error estimate were obtained in [1]:

$$\max_{1 \leq n}(\|E^n - E_h^n\|_0 + \|H^{n+\frac{1}{2}} - H_h^{n+\frac{1}{2}}\|_0 + \|J^{n+\frac{1}{2}} - J_h^{n+\frac{1}{2}}\|_0 + \|K^n - K_h^n\|_0)$$

$$\leq C(\tau^2 + h^\alpha) + C\Big(\|E^0 - E_h^0\|_0 + \|H^{\frac{1}{2}} - H_h^{\frac{1}{2}}\|_0 + \|J^{\frac{1}{2}} - J_h^{\frac{1}{2}}\|_0 + \|K^0 - K_h^0\|_0\Big).$$

4   Numerical Examples

Here we show some numerical results obtained by the Crank-Nicolson (CN) scheme (27)-(30) and Leap-Frog (LP) scheme (35)-(38). We implemented our algorithms using the lowest order rectangular edge element basis functions [1]. Our tests were carried out using MATLAB 7.2 running on Dell Latitude D630 laptop with 1GB memory and 2.00 GHz CPU. In order to test our algorithm with an analytical solution, we add source terms to the original governing equations, i.e., the LP scheme (35)-(38) becomes:

$$(E_h^k, \phi_h) = (E_h^{k-1}, \phi_h) + \frac{\tau}{\epsilon_0}[(H_h^{k-\frac{1}{2}}, \nabla \times \phi_h) - (J_h^{k-\frac{1}{2}}, \phi_h) + (f^{k-\frac{1}{2}}, \phi_h)], \tag{39}$$

$$(H_h^{k+\frac{1}{2}}, \psi_h) = (H_h^{k-\frac{1}{2}}, \psi_h) - \frac{\tau}{\mu_0}[(\nabla \times E_h^k, \psi_h) + (K_h^k, \psi_h) - (g^k, \psi_h)], \tag{40}$$

$$J_h^{k+\frac{1}{2}} = \frac{2\epsilon_0 \omega_{pe}^2 \tau}{2 + \tau\Gamma_e} E_h^k + \frac{2 - \tau\Gamma_e}{2 + \tau\Gamma_e} J_h^{k-\frac{1}{2}}, \tag{41}$$

$$K_h^k = \frac{2\mu_0 \omega_{pm}^2 \tau}{2 + \tau\Gamma_m} H_h^{k-\frac{1}{2}} + \frac{2 - \tau\Gamma_m}{2 + \tau\Gamma_m} K_h^{k-1}, \tag{42}$$

where $f^{k-\frac{1}{2}}$ and g^k are added source terms. While for CN scheme, we add $\overline{f}^k$ and $\overline{g}^k$ to the right hand side of (27) and (28), respectively.

To compare the performance between CN and LP schemes, we used the exact solution developed for the 2-D transverse electrical model in [1]. Through many

Table 1. L^2 errors obtained by the CN scheme with $\tau = 10^{-8}$

Time steps	$nt = 1$		$nt = 100$			DOF
Mesh sizes	E_x	H_z	E_x	H_z	Time (sec)	
10×10	5.689190e-3	4.307665e-13	5.695761e-3	3.193383e-10	8.18	280
20×20	1.446042e-3	1.376676e-13	1.452879e-3	1.126767e-9	32.09	1160
40×40	3.630540e-4	4.503064e-13	3.770630e-4	4.504495e-9	137.24	4720
80×80	9.090923e-5	1.802114e-12	2.011538e-4	1.802440e-8	780.07	19040
160×160	2.302692e-5	7.210232e-12	3.908776e-4	7.210453e-8	5716.29	76480

Table 2. L^2 errors obtained by the CN scheme with $\tau = 10^{-10}$

Time steps	$nt = 1$		$nt = 100$			DOF
Mesh sizes	E_x	H_z	E_x	H_z	Time (sec)	
10×10	5.689124e-3	4.440892e-15	5.689190e-3	4.352074e-13	8.28	280
20×20	1.445973e-3	8.881784e-16	1.446042e-3	1.545430e-13	32.23	1160
40×40	3.629851e-4	1.776356e-15	3.630541e-4	4.698463e-13	138.45	4720
80×80	9.084018e-5	1.776356e-15	9.090923e-5	1.819877e-12	748.18	19040
160×160	2.271640e-5	1.776356e-15	2.302692e-5	7.230660e-12	5650.04	76480

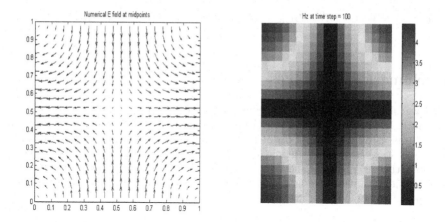

Fig. 1. Numerical solution on 20×20 mesh: (Left) electric field; (Right) magnetic field

tests, we found that even for CN scheme good results can only be achieved until $\tau = 10^{-8}$ or smaller. Our numerical results obtained with CN scheme using $\tau = 10^{-8}$ and $\tau = 10^{-10}$ are presented in Table 1 and Table 2, respectively. Also presented are the total number of degree of freedom (DOF) and computational time. Tables 1-2 show clearly $O(h^2)$ convergence for $\boldsymbol{E}$, which is superconvergent for rectangular meshes [1]. The accuracies for $\boldsymbol{H}$ are really excellent, but it shows $O(h^{-2})$ as mesh gets finer. We think this is due to the larger sampling errors coming with finer meshes since $\boldsymbol{H}$ are approximated by piecewise constants.

Comparing Tables 1-2 to Tables 2-3 of [1] (results obtained by LP scheme), we see that with the same mesh and time step CN scheme achieves similar accuracy for E as LP scheme and has much more accurate results for H than LP scheme. However, CN scheme takes much longer computational time than LP scheme.

5 Concluding Remarks

In this paper, we presented three second order methods for solving the metamaterial Maxwell's equations in time-domain. Considering the accuracy and computational cost, it seems that the LP scheme is the best choice of the three methods. More rigorous comparisons will be carried out in our future work. For practical applications, we have to work on high performance computers, since our laptop runs out of memory for 320×320 mesh.

References

1. Li, J.: Numerical convergence and physical fidelity analysis for Maxwell's equations in metamaterials. Comput. Methods Appl. Mech. Engrg. 198, 3161–3172 (2009)
2. Li, J., Chen, Y.: Analysis of a time-domain finite element method for 3-D Maxwell's equations in dispersive media. Comput. Methods Appl. Mech. Engrg. 195, 4220–4229 (2006)
3. Li, J., Chen, Y., Elander, V.: Mathematical and numerical study of wave propagation in negative-index materials. Comput. Methods Appl. Mech. Engrg. 197, 3976–3987 (2008)
4. Li, J., Wood, A.: Finite element analysis for wave propagation in double negative metamaterials. J. Sci. Comput. 32, 263–286 (2007)
5. Monk, P.: Finite Element Methods for Maxwell's Equations. Oxford University Press, Oxford (2003)

Research on FPGA Based Evolvable Hardware Chips for Solving Super-High Dimensional Equations Group

Kangshun Li[1], Zhaolu Guo[2], Zhangxin Chen[3], and Baoshan Ge[4]

[1] School of Information, South China Agricultural University, Guangzhou 510642,
School of Information Engineering, Jiangxi University of Science and Technology,
Ganzhou 341000, China
Department of Chemical and Petroleum Engineering, University of Calgary,
Calgary, Alberta, Canada
Institue of Automation, Chinese Academy of Sciences, Beijing 100190, China
[2] School of Information Engineering, Jiangxi University of Science and Technology,
Ganzhou 341000, China
[3] Department of Chemical and Petroleum Engineering, Schulich School of
Engineering, University of Calgary, Calgary, AB T2N 1N4, Canada
[4] Institue of Automation, Chinese Academy of Sciences, Beijing 100190, China

Abstract. Solving a super-high dimensional equations group is widely used in science and engineering, but the slow solution speed is the biggest problem researchers face. Research on FPGA based evolvable hardware chips for solving the super-high dimensional equations group (SHDESC) is proposed in this paper. These chips can be implemented on a million-gate scale FPGA chip. The core architecture of SHDESC is a systolic array which consists of thousands of special arithmetic units and can execute many super-high dimensional matrix operations parallelly in short time as well as really achieve the purpose of high speed solution in hardware/software codesign. The experiments show that these chips can achieve high precision results in a short period of time to solve a super-high dimensional equations group.

Keywords: Evolvable hardware super-high dimension equations group, FPGA hardware/software Codesign, systolic array.

1 Introduction

Solving a super-high dimensional equations group is widely used in science and engineering, for instance, in optimization structure of oil wells and mining, structural analysis of mineral resources, calculation of deformation of bridges and housing construction after the force, computation of the flow field around the aircraft in aerodynamics, and evaluation of the flow of the atmosphere in weather forecast. These problems are transformed into a super-high dimensional equations group to solve ultimately. The process of solving these problems is described

W. Zhang et al. (Eds.): HPCA 2009, LNCS 5938, pp. 58–68, 2010.

by a number of differential equations. In general, solving these differential equations is acquiring a super-high dimensiona equations group which has thousands or even millions of unknowns after discretizing differential equations, no matter whether the difference method or finite element method is used. Thus the advantages and disadvantages of a method to solve the super-high dimensional equations group are restricted to solving these problems largely. To find an efficient, fast algorithm to solve a super-high dimensional equations group, many scholars continue to carry out in-depth and long-term studies.

With the advances in modern microelectronic technology, The EDA technology has developed greatly in every aspect. One of this technology is evolvable hardware [1,2] which uses an intelligent, self-reproduction and self-healing method to design hardware. It refers to hardware that can change its architecture and behavior automatically and dynamically through interacting with its environment, which can be presented in the following formula [2]: Evolutionary Algorithm + Programmable Logical Devices = Evolvable Hardware.

Research on FPGA based evolvable hardware chips for solving a super-high dimensional equations group (SHDESC) is proposed in this paper. This method is researched on solving the super-high dimensional equations group with the evolvable hardware theory and hardware/software codesign technology, and implemented on a million-gate scale FPGA chip. The bottleneck of slow speed is mainly concentrated on the super-high dimensional matrix operations in the process of solving the super-high dimensional equations group using traditional algorithms. But the chips are implemented on a million-gate scale FPGA chip, and its core architecture is a systolic array which consists of thousands of special arithmetic units that execute matrix operations concurrently, break through the bottleneck of slow solution speed, make super-high dimensional matrix operations in a short period of time, and really achieve the purpose of hardware/software codesign to solve with high speed. On the one hand, this chip combines the advantages of evolvable hardware, which are intelligence, efficiency, and parallelism. On the other hand it makes full use of the advantages of modern VLSI, which are high integration, low cost, and easy to achieve the operation of parallel computing. Therefore, it improves the speed of solving the super-high dimensional equations group greatly and really achieve the purpose of hardware/software codesign to solve with high speed.

2   Design Process of FPGA

The designing process of FPGA (Field Programmable Processor Arrays) is the process of using EDA development software and program utilities to develop FPGA chips. The development process of FPGA includes design of function circuit, design entry, function simulation, synthesis optimization, simulation after synthesis optimization, system implement, circuits and wires distribution, time sequence simulation and verifying, circuit board level simulation and verify, and programming of Soc (System of chip) and verifying.

2.1   Design of Function Circuit

Before system designing, some preparations such as schematic verifying and the selection of FPGA chip have to be done. Then the complexity of the indexes in system, running speed of FPGA, resources provided by chips and cost should be analyzed according to the requests of projects. After that, reasonable design schedule and suitable types of devices have to be selected; and at last the design method from top to down is used in general in the world. In this method we partition the circuit system to some base units as a top layer, and partition every unit to next base unit of next layer and so on, until we can find and load the EDA components from the components library to construct the complete circuit of the project.

2.2   Design Entry

The goal of design entry is to demonstrate the circuit system according to the requests of software development, and design entry is a process for input program to EDA utilities, and for input the components loaded from circuit components library to the circuit system using software or other design utilities. These software or design utilities are the main design utilities of EDA of FPGA, such as hard description language (HDL), Handle-C language and utility of schematic diagram description.

2.3   Function Simulation

Function simulation is called pre-simulation. Namely, function simulation is to verify the logic function of circuit system designed by using HDL programs before compiling the HDL programs, and this function simulation doesn't include the verification of delay circuits. In the first place, we use wave editor and HDL to build wave file and verified vector (namely, combining input signals to a execution sequence), and then the results will be saved in a report file and output signal waves which show the signals' change of all the circuit notes.

2.4   Synthesis Optimization

Synthesis is to transfer the abstract circuit layers in up level to the circuit layers in down level by using program description. Synthesis optimization is to optimize the circuits to be complanation circuits according to the goals and requests of the logic connection circuits, which are provided to implement distributed wires software of FPGA. In recent design circuit layers, synthesis optimization is to compile design entry to the logic connected network table composed with the based logic units such as 'and' gate, 'or' gate, 'not' gate, 'RAM' and trigger which are not the truly gate circuits. The truly gate circuits in FPGA have been produced through the function of circuits and wires distribution of FPGA producer and according to the standard network table of the gate level structures after synthesis optimization.

2.5   Simulation after Synthesis Optimization

The goal of simulation after synthesis optimization is to verify the consistency between synthesis results and original designed circuits. In the simulation process, we reversely label standard delay files generated through synthesis optimization to the synthesized simulation models and then we can estimate the effects brought by gates delay. Therefore, the running results in simulation after synthesis optimization are not accurate sometimes and are differences from the running results of FPGA after the wires are distributed. Because the recent synthesis utilities are relatively sophisticated, this step can be omitted in general FPGA designing.

2.6   System Implement, Circuits and Wires Distribution

System implement is to configure logic network generated through synthesis optimization on concrete FPGA chips, and the wires distribution is a most important process in system implement. Circuits distribution is to reasonably configure the hardware primitives and bottom units in the logic network tables to be the inherent hardware structure in chips of FPGA, and either speed optimal or area optimal must be selected. Wires distribution is also requested to reasonably connect all circuit units in FPGA correctly according the topology structure of circuit distribution and inner structure of chips.

2.7   Time Sequence Simulation and Verifying

Time sequence simulation and verifying is called post-simulation. It is to reversely label the delay information in circuits distribution and wires distribution on the designed network table to verify whether the phenomenon of violating time sequence (dissatisfying constrained condition of time sequence or violating the inherent rules of the time sequence) exist in the design process or not. Time sequence simulation includes all the delay information of circuits, and it will report the accurate truly state of the FPGA chips.

2.8   Circuit Board Level Simulation and Verification

Circuit board level simulation and verify is mainly to apply to the high-speed circuit design, and analyse the integrality of the high-speed system signals and the character of the magnetic disturbance. In general, we use the third part's utilities to conduct the circuit board level simulation and verification.

2.9   Programming of Soc and Verifying

Programming of Soc and debugging is the last step in FPGA circuits design. Programming of Soc is to produce the usable data files (Bitstream Generation) derived from HDL program, and then download these data bitstram files into the chips of FPGA (we call these types of program as chips-level program). Chips-level programming must satisfy some constrained conditions such as voltage programming, time sequence programming and algorithm programming etc.

3   Solving Super-High-Dimension Equations Group Based on Evolvable Hardware

The essence of solving super-high-dimension equations group is to find groups of vector X which satisfy: $AX = b$, for a given matrix A, vector b. An elite-subspace evolutionary algorithm which has very high efficiency has been presented in [3]. Its idea will be used in solving super-high-dimension equations group in the SHDESC chip. In the design of SHDESC, real coding is adopted, and the individuals are represented by vector X'. The core question of design SHDESC are the storage of matrix A, the design of fitness function, selection and cross-replace operator.

3.1   The Storage of Matrix A

The storage of matrix A is considerable cost determined by the characteristics of super-high-dimension equations group. For example, a 20000-dimensional equations group, the storage of matrix A costs 4*20000*20000 bytes, nearly 2G bytes, if stored with traditional method. Apparently, it is not realistic, as well as not feasible. Actually, the matrix A is always sparse matrix in science and engineering and it exists a large number of zero elements. Thus, it's necessary to adopt triad (row, col, value) to store the matrix A compressingly and it is effective proved by experiments.

3.2   The Design of Fitness Function

In the EHW, The design of fitness function is essential, for it directly affects the convergence speed and accuracy of the solution. In this paper, the fitness function adopts 2-norm. For every individual X', the formula of fitness value calculation is:

$$Fitness(X') = \left\| AX' + b \right\|_2 \text{ ,where } \left\| X \right\|_2 \text{ is 2-norm of the vector } X \qquad (1)$$

This fitness function can reflect the sum-gap between individual X' and the aim solution. While the less the fitness value is, the closer between the individual X' and the target solution is, the individual X' is better.

3.3   The Design of Selection Operator

In the EHW, the selection operator is based on the idea of the elite-subspace selection and is depicted as follows:

Step 1: Using formula (1), calculate the fitness value of each individual in the population as follows:

$$P(t) = \{X'_1, X'_2, X'_3, ..., X'_{Popsize}\}$$

Step 2: Sort the individuals in population $P(t)$ according to the fitness value in ascending order. After sorting still recorded as follows:

$$P(t) = \{X_1', X_2', X_3', ..., X_{Popsize}'\}. \text{ Where } X_1' \text{ is the best individual,}$$

and $X_{Popsize}'$ is the worst individual.

Step 3: Select the best $Elite\_K(Elite\_K \leq Space\_M)$ individuals:

$$X_1'', X_2'', X_3'', ..., X_{Elite\_K}''$$

Step 4: Select $Space\_M - Elite\_K$ individuals from the remaining $PopSize - Elite\_K$ individuals in the population $P(t)$ randomly, and recorded as follows:

$$X_{Elite\_K+1}'', X_{Elite\_K+2}'', X_{Elite\_K+3}'', ..., X_{Space\_M}''$$

Step 5: End of selection operator.

In the selection operator above, there are $Space\_M$ individuals are selected, in which the best $Elite\_K$ individuals are selected in the step 3, which sufficiently exert the oriented effect of the better individuals to enhance the precision and convergent speed. While in the step 4, $Space\_M - Elite\_K$ individuals are selected from the remaining $PopSize - Elite\_K$ individuals in the population $P(t)$ randomly, which ensure the diversity of the population, avoid falling into local optima and leading to precocity.

3.4   The Design of Cross-Replace Operator

In the EHW, the cross-replace operator adopts the idea of Multi-Parent-Crossover operator which was proposed in [4].When using the Multi-Parent-Crossover operator to solve the question in this paper, the detail design is depicted as follows:

Step 1: $I = 1$;

Step 2: If $(I > Replace\_L)$ then goto Step 8;

Step 3: Generate $a_1, a_2, ..., a_{Space\_M}$ randomly, which satisfy :

$$\sum_{j=1}^{Space\_M} a_j = 1, -0.5 \leq a_j \leq 1.5.$$

Step 4: Generate a new individual $\overline{X}$:

$$\overline{X} = \sum_{j=1}^{Space\_M} a_j X_j''.$$

In the formula above, the $Space\_M$ individuals:

$$X_1'', X_2'', X_3'', ..., X_{Space\_M}'' \text{ are produced by the selection operator.}$$

Step 5: Assume X_{worst} is the worst individual.
If individual $\overline{X}$ is better than X_{worst} then $\overline{X}$ replaces X_{worst}.

Step 6: $I = I + 1$;

Step 7: Goto Step 2;

Step 8: End of cross-replace operator.

In the cross-replace operator above, $Replace\_L$ is the number of elimination individuals. it determines the pressure of elimination in the algorithm. Step 4 is Multi-Parent-Crossover operation.

3.5   The General Description of the Algorithm

All the steps of the algorithm to solve Super-High-Dimension Equations Group are depicted as follows:

Step 1: $t = 1$;

Step 2: Initialize the population $P(t)$, generate $Popsize$ individuals randomly:

$$X_1', X_2', ..., X_{Popsize}'.$$

Step 3: Execute the selection operator.

Step 4: Execute the cross-replace operator.

Step 5: Assume X_{worst} is the worst individual, X_{best} is the best individual in the population $P(t)$.

If $Fitnes(Xworst) == Fitnes(X_{best})$ then goto Step 8;else goto Step 6.

Step 6: $t = t + 1$;

Step 7: Goto Step 3;

Step 8: The end.

4   The Design and Implementation of SHDESC

4.1   Speed Bottleneck Analysis and Breakthrough

The algorithm to solve super-high-dimension equations group above is simulated with software. The analysis of the simulation results shows convergent speed of the algorithm is very fast when the dimension of the equations group is low, but the convergent speed of the algorithm is rapidly declining when the dimension of the equations group is more than 1000.Through the analysis, it is known that the Bottleneck of slow speed is mainly concentrated in the operations of calculating the fitness value of each individual using formula (1). For an equations group which has N dimensions, calculating the fitness value of a single individual should operate: $N * (N + 1)$ floating-point multiplications $+ N * (N + 1)$ floating-point additions. If N is more than 1000, the operations of floating-point are so large that is led to the Bottleneck of the speed of the whole algorithm.

Thus, the key to break through the Bottleneck is to accelerate the speed of calculating the fitness value of individuals using formula (1). The method of SHDESC is that the core architecture of SHDESC is a systolic array which consists of thousands of special arithmetic units, which execute matrix operations concurrently, break through the Bottleneck of slow solving speed, and make super-high-dimension matrix operations in a short period of time.

4.2   The Core Structure of Parallel Processing of SHDESC

From the algorithm design above, it is known that the structure of SHDESC has four parts: Initializing Population Module, Calculating Fitness Value Module, Selection Operator Module, and Cross-Replace Operator Module. The whole structure and data flow diagram is shown in Figure 1.Where the Control Module generates the entire control signal and synchronizes all the other Module as well as generates random number to the Initializing Population Module, Selection Operator Module and Cross-Replace Operator Module. The Storage Module, consists of memory bank and read/write controller, in which the matrix A, vector b, and all the individuals of population $P(t)$ are stored. The read/write controller generate read/write control signal to the memory bank for every address which any other module provider.

In the structure of SHDESC, the core Module is Calculating Fitness Value Module is a systolic array which consists of N special ALUs shown in Figure 2.

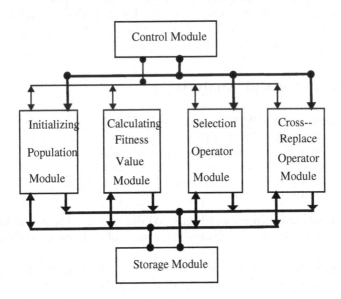

Fig. 1. The whole Structure and Data Flow Diagram of SHDESC

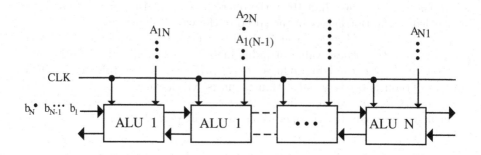

Fig. 2. The Systolic Array of Calculating Fitness Value

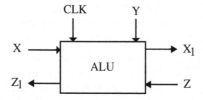

Fig. 3. The Structure of Special ALU

In the figure 2, CLK is clock signal, and $b_N b_{N-1}, ..., b_1$ are elements of vector b, which come into the systolic array one by one for every clock according to the order from 1 to N. The structure of each special ALU is shown in figure 3, which has four input terminals: CLK,X, Y, Z and two output terminals: Z_1, X_1. Where $Z_1 = XY + Z, X_1 = X$ and CLK is clock signal.

5　Experiments and Analysis

The whole design of SHDESC is depicted by VHDL and implemented on the XC2V1000 (100 million gates) FPGA. The following experiments have been done, and compared with the software implementation.

5.1　Experiment 1

Generate an equations group which has 100 dimensions. The algorithm is implemented by software and hardware. The results of experiment 1 are shown in table 1.

From the results of experiment 1, it is known: when solving the equations group of 100-dimensions, both the Solution Error is 0 when the algorithm is implemented by software to solve this question and when the algorithm is implemented by hardware. It is obvious that the precision is very high. And also

Table 1. The results of Experiment 1

Method	Running Time (Unit:s)	Solution Error
Software	21.56	0
Hardware	10.18	0

the speed of the algorithm implemented by hardware is about 1 times faster than implemented by software. As a result, the matrix operations executed by hardware concurrently could increase the speed of the algorithm.

5.2 Experiment 2

Generate an equations group which has 1000 dimensions. The algorithm is implemented by software and hardware. The results of experiment 2 are shown in table 2.

Table 2. The results of Experiment 2

Method	Running Time (Unit:s)	Solution Error
Software	218.38	2.4703179247e-27
Hardware	20.27	0

From the results of experiment 2, it is known: when solving the equations group of 1000-dimensions, the Solution Error is 2.4703179247e-27 when the algorithm is implemented by software to solve this question and the Solution Error is 0 when the algorithm is implemented by hardware. And also the speed of the algorithm implemented by hardware is obviously faster than implemented by software, which is faster more than about 10 times. As a result, when the dimension of equations group is high, the super-high-dimension matrix operations executed by hardware concurrently could increase the speed of the whole algorithm and could acquire high precision results much faster than software implement.

6   Conclusions

A research on FPGA based evolvable hardware chips for solving super-high-dimension equations group (SHDESC) was proposed in this paper. This method was researched on solving super-high-dimension equations group with evolvable hardware theory and Hardware/Software Codesign technology, and implemented on a million-gate scale FPGA chip. The Bottleneck of slow speed are mainly concentrated in the super-high-dimension matrix operations in the process of solving super-high-dimension equations group using traditional algorithm. But this chip is implemented on a million-gate scale FPGA chip, and its core architecture was a systolic array which consists of thousands of special arithmetic units, which execute matrix operations concurrently, break through the Bottleneck of slow solving speed, make super-high-dimension matrix operations in a short period of time, and really achieve the purpose of Hardware/Software Codesign to solve with high speed. On the one hand, this chip combines the advantages of evolvable hardware, which are intelligence, efficiency, and parallelism; On the other hand it makes full use of the advantages of modern VLSI, which are high integration, low cost and easy to achieve the operation of parallel computing. Therefore, it improves the speed of solving super-high-dimension equations group greatly, really achieve the purpose of Hardware/Software Codesign to solve with high speed and solve the problems which are slow speed of solving super-high-dimension equations group in science and engineering.

References

1. Pan, Z., Kang, L., Chen, Y.: Evolutionary Computation. Tsinghua University Press, Beijing (1998)
2. de Garis, H.: Evolvable Hardware: Genetic Programming of a Darwin Machine. In: Artificial Neural Nets and Genetic Algorithms, pp. 441–449. Springer, Heidelberg (1993)
3. Wu, Z.-j., Kang, L.-s., Zou, X.-f.: An Elite-subspace Evolutionary Algorithm for Solving Function Optimization Problems. Computer Applicafions 23(2), 13–15 (2003)
4. Tao, G., Kang, L., Li, Y.: A New Algorithm for Solving Inequality Constrained Function Optimization Problems. Wuhan University Journal of Natural Sciences 45(5B), 771–775 (1999)

An Efficient Splitting Domain Decomposition Approach for Parabolic-Type Time-Dependent Problems in Porous Media*

Dong Liang** and Chuanbin Du

Department of Mathematics and Statistics
York University
Toronto, Ontario, Canada M3J 1P3
dliang@mathstat.yorku.ca

Abstract. In this paper, we develop a new and efficient splitting domain decomposition method for solving parabolic-type time-dependent equations in porous media. The method combines the multi-block non-overlapping domain decomposition and the splitting technique. On interfaces of sub-domains, the local multilevel explicit scheme is proposed to solve the interface values of solution, and then the splitting implicit scheme is proposed to solve the solution in interiors of sub-domains. The developed method reduces computational complexities, large memory requirements and long computational durations. Numerical experiments are performed to illustrate the accuracy and efficiency of the method.

1 Introduction

Parabolic-type time-dependent partial differential equations in porous media are widely used in science and engineering, such as in groundwater modeling and in petroleum reservoir simulation, etc (see, for example, [1, 2, 3, 5]). The objective of simulating fluid flows in porous media in groundwater modeling and reservoir simulation is to quantify the transport of the pollutants, to predict, control, and re-mediate contaminations in subsurface contaminant transports and re-mediations, seawater intrusion and control, and many other applications. The mathematical model of contamination fluid flows in porous media is a coupled nonlinear system of time-dependent partial differential equations, in which one equation is a parabolic equation and the other is a convection-diffusion equation. Due to the computational complexities and the huge computational costs in realistic long term and large scale simulations, there are strong interests in developing efficient solution techniques for solving these problems in porous media. By combining domain decomposition methods, which reduce the sizes of problems by decomposing domain into smaller ones (see [6, 11, 15], etc), and the splitting technique, which reduces high-dimensional problems to a series of

---

* This work was partially supported by the Natural Sciences and Engineering Research Council of Canada (NSERC) and by Mathematics for Information Technology and Complex Systems (MITACS).
** Corresponding author.

W. Zhang et al. (Eds.): HPCA 2009, LNCS 5938, pp. 69–77, 2010.

one-dimensional problems at each time interval (see [7, 16, 4, 8, 10, 12], etc), we develop efficient splitting domain decomposition methods to solve multi-dimensional parabolic-type time-dependent problems in this study.

Since non-overlapping domain decomposition methods have low computation and communication cost for each time step, they are preferable for large problems on massively parallel machines ([6, 9, 13, 14], etc). For treating interface boundaries of sub-domains, an explicit-implicit algorithm was developed for non-overlapping sub-domain decompositions in [6], which relaxed the stability condition by using the larger spacing step size in the explicit scheme at the points of the interface boundaries of sub-domains. Further, paper [9] proposed an explicit-implicit domain decomposition method by using either a high-order explicit scheme or a multi-step explicit scheme on the interface which further relaxed the stability requirement. The methods in [6, 9] work efficiently for stripe-divided non-overlapping sub-domains along one spatial variable for parabolic equations. However, it has been an important and challenging task to develop efficient explicit-implicit domain decomposition methods over multiple block-divided non-overlapping sub-domains so that it is more suitable and powerful to simulate large scale time-dependent problems in porous media.

In this paper, we propose a new splitting domain decomposition approach over multiple block-divided sub-domains for parabolic-type time dependent partial differential equations in porous media by combining the non-overlapping domain decomposition technique and the splitting technique. The domain is divided into multi-block non-overlapping sub-domains and is further partitioned into fine meshes on sub-domains. On each sub-domain, the high-dimensional parabolic equation is solved by the splitting technique iteratively in each time interval. At each time step, we first solve the interface values of solution by a local multilevel explicit scheme on the interface boundaries of sub-domains and then solve the interior solutions in interiors of sub-domains by the splitting implicit scheme. The developed S-DDM overcomes the limitation of the stripe-divided sub-domains in previous work ([6, 9]) and is an efficient and simple explicit-implicit domain decomposition method over multi-block sub-domains. It keeps the excellent advantages of the non-overlapping domain decomposition method and the splitting technique. It reduces computational complexities, large memory requirements and long computational durations and is more suitable and powerful for parallel computing. The method has been extended to solve high-dimensional large scale problems of compressible fluid flows in porous media. Theoretical results of stability analysis and convergence analysis are reported. Numerical experiments are given to show the excellent performance of the method.

2   Mathematical Models

In simulating fluid flows in porous media, mathematical models are built by the mass conservations for the fluid and the contaminant, the Darcy's law for momentum, and the equations of state that provide fluid properties in porous media ([1, 2, 5, 3]).

The mass conservation for the fluid and the equations of state lead to the equation for pressure p

$$s_p \frac{\partial p}{\partial t} + \nabla \cdot \rho \mathbf{u} = Q, \qquad \mathbf{x} \in \Omega, t \in (0, T], \tag{1}$$

where ρ is the mass density of the fluid, $s_p(\mathbf{x}, p)$ is the storage coefficient, Q is the source and sink, and the velocity $\mathbf{u}$ is given by Darcy's law as

$$\mathbf{u} = -\frac{\mathbf{k}}{\mu} \cdot (\nabla p + \rho g \nabla Z), \tag{2}$$

where g is the gravity constant, Z is the elevation height of the fluid measured from some chosen datum level, $\mathbf{k}$ is the permeability, and μ is the dynamical viscosity of the fluid.

The conservation of mass for the contaminant in the fluid leads to the partial differential equation of contaminant concentration c:

$$\frac{\partial(\phi c)}{\partial t} + \nabla \cdot (\mathbf{u}c - \mathbf{D}\nabla c) = Qc^*, \qquad \mathbf{x} \in \Omega, t \in (0, T], \tag{3}$$

where ϕ is the porosity of a porous medium and $\mathbf{D}$ is the diffusion coefficient.

The system (1)-(3) is time-dependent. Providing proper boundary conditions for pressure p and concentration c, and initial conditions $p(\mathbf{x}, 0) = p_0(\mathbf{x})$, $\mathbf{x} \in \Omega$, $c(\mathbf{x}, 0) = c_0(\mathbf{x})$, $\mathbf{x} \in \Omega$ closes the system.

This time-dependent system is often used to model water-head in groundwater modeling, pressure in petroleum reservoir simulations, temperature in heat transfer, and other qualities in many applications (see, [1, 2, 5], etc). This system is characterized by the nonlinearity, the coupling among these equations, the compressibility of the fluid and the medium, the enormous size of field-scale application, and the required long time period of prediction. numerical simulations of these systems encounter serious difficulties and complexities. It is important to develop efficient domain decomposition methods for solving this parabolic-type time-dependent system of partial differential equations. In this paper, we will construct and analyze an efficient splitting domain decomposition method (S-DDM) for solving the parabolic equations by combining non-overlapping domain decomposition and the splitting technique.

3   The S-DDM Scheme

Consider the parabolic-type time-dependent model problems on two dimensions

$$\frac{\partial u}{\partial t} - \frac{\partial}{\partial x}\left(a\frac{\partial u}{\partial x}\right) - \frac{\partial}{\partial y}\left(b\frac{\partial u}{\partial y}\right) = f(x, y, t), \qquad (x, y) \in \Omega, t \in (0, T], \tag{4}$$

$$u(x, y, 0) = u_0(x, y), \qquad (x, y) \in \Omega, \tag{5}$$

$$u(0, y, t) = u(L_x, y, t) = 0, \qquad y \in [0, L_y], t \in (0, T], \tag{6}$$

$$u(x, 0, t) = u(x, L_y, t) = 0, \qquad x \in [0, L_x], t \in (0, T], \tag{7}$$

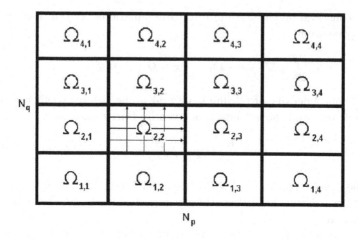

Fig. 1. The domain Ω and the sub-domains $\Omega_{p,q}$

where domain is $\Omega = (0, L_x) \times (0, L_y)$ with large numbers $L_x > 0$ and $L_y > 0$; $T > 0$ is the time period; and $a > 0$ and $b > 0$ are diffusion coefficients. We shall assume that $f(x, y, t)$ and $u_0(x, y)$ are smooth functions.

For constructing efficient domain decomposition methods, we divide large domain Ω into $d = N_p \times N_q$ multiple block-divided sub-domains $\Omega_{p,q}$ which are further partitioned into fine meshes by using small step sizes, see Figure 1. In general, the number d of sub-domains is related to the size of problem and the number of processors in the computer platform, and the sub-domains may be of different lengths.

For simplicity of description, let us consider $\Omega = (0, 1) \times (0, 1)$ and the number of sub-domains $d = 2 \times 2$ at this moment. Let us introduce an uniform block mesh Ω_h as the tensor direct product of $I_h \times J_h$ of one-dimensional mesh, where $I_h = \{0 = x_0, x_1, \cdots, x_p, \cdots, x_{I-1}, x_I = 1\}$ and $J_h = \{0 = y_0, y_1, \cdots, y_{J-1}, y_J = 1\}$. Then, we denote the spatial step sizes by $h_x = \frac{1}{I}$ and $h_y = \frac{1}{J}$ along x- and y-directions respectively. We denote the uniform spatial step as h for the case of $h = h_x = h_y$. $x = x_p$ and $y = y_q$ divide Ω into four sub-domains $\Omega_{l,m}$, $l = 1, 2; m = 1, 2$. Take the time step $\Delta t = T/N$, where N is a positive integer. For interfaces, we introduce the multilevel time step $\Delta \tau = \Delta t/K$ by dividing the time level $[t^n, t^{n+1}]$ into K sub-intervals, and the interface spatial step size is defined by $\hat{h} = mh$, where $K \geq 1$ and $m \geq 1$ are integer numbers. Let $\tau^k = k\Delta\tau$ and then k'th time level is $t^n + \tau^k$ in the time interval on interfaces.

We denote $u_{i,j}^n = u(x_i, y_j, t^n)$ as well as $u_{i,j}^{n,k} = u(x_i, y_j, t^n + \tau^k)$. Then, we denote $U_{i,j}^n$ (or $U_{i,j}^{n,k}$) to be the numerical value to $u_{i,j}^n$ (or $u_{i,j}^{n,k}$). In general, let N_p be the number of sub-domains along x-direction and N_q be the number of sub-domains along y-direction. Let I_p be the index set of interior points of the p'th part along x-direction and J_q be the index set of interior points of the q'th part along y-direction. Let IN_p be the index number of interface points and IN_q be the index number of interface points.

To construct the scheme, we introduce a splitting spatial differential operator and a decomposition of the right side term:

$$L_x u \equiv -\frac{\partial}{\partial x}\left(a\frac{\partial u}{\partial x}\right), \qquad L_y u \equiv -\frac{\partial}{\partial y}\left(b\frac{\partial u}{\partial y}\right), \tag{8}$$

$$f(x,y,t) = f_1(x,y,t) + f_2(x,y,t). \tag{9}$$

Then, we introduce some notations. For the interior points of sub-domains, we define the discrete operators L_{x,h_x} and L_{y,h_y} to be the discretization of the operators L_x and L_y by the central finite difference scheme on I_h and J_h respectively, i.e., for each $y_j \in J_h$ we have

$$(I + \Delta t L_{x,h_x})u_{i,j}^n \equiv -r_x u_{i-1,j}^n + (1+2r_x)u_{i,j}^n - r_x u_{i+1,j}^n \tag{10}$$

where $r_x = \frac{a\Delta t}{h_x^2}$. Similarly, for each $x_i \in I_h$, we have

$$(I + \Delta t L_{y,h_y})u_{i,j}^n \equiv -r_y u_{i,j-1}^n + (1+2r_y)u_{i,j}^n - r_y u_{i,j+1}^n \tag{11}$$

where $r_y = \frac{b\Delta t}{h_y^2}$.

Similarly, for the interface points, we can define the discrete operators $L_{x,\hat{h}_x}$ and $L_{y,\hat{h}_y}$ to be the discretization of the operators L_x and L_y with spatial step $\hat{h}_l = mh_l$, $l = x,y$, and $m \geq 1$ is positive integer. $\Delta\tau = \frac{1}{K}\Delta t$, $K \geq 1$ is the number of multilevel on interfaces. For each $y_j \in J_h$, at point (x_p, y_j), we have

$$(I - \Delta\tau L_{x,\hat{h}_x})u_{p,j}^{n,k-1} \equiv \bar{r}_x u_{p-m,j}^{n,k-1} + (1-2\bar{r}_x)u_{p,j}^{n,k-1} + \bar{r}_x u_{p+m,j}^{n,k-1} \tag{12}$$

where $\bar{r}_x = \frac{a\Delta\tau}{\hat{h}_x^2}$, and

$$(I - \Delta\tau L_{y,\hat{h}_y})u_{i,q}^{n,k-1} \equiv \bar{r}_y u_{i,q-m}^{n,k-1} + (1-2\bar{r}_y)u_{i,q}^{n,k-1} + \bar{r}_y u_{i,q+m}^{n,k-1} \tag{13}$$

where $\bar{r}_y = \frac{b\Delta\tau}{\hat{h}_y^2}$.

Therefore, based on the notations above, we can propose the splitting domain decomposition method (S-DDM) for parabolic equations. Let $U_{i,j}^n$ approximate $u_{i,j}^n$ for $n \geq 0$ and any (i,j). Set $U_{i,j}^0 = u^0(x_i, y_j)$ for any (i,j). Then, in each time interval $(t^n, t^{n+1}]$ for $n \geq 0$, we do as follows:

Firstly, along x - direction, $\forall j \in J_q$, $1 \leq q \leq N_q$, (a) the local multilevel explicit scheme is defined on interface points x_p for finding the interface values by setting

$$U_{p_l,j}^{n,0} = U_{p_l,j}^n, \ p_l = p, p \pm m, \cdots, p \pm Km; \ p \in IN_p, \tag{14}$$

and for $k = 1, 2, \cdots, K$, computing

$$U_{p_l,j}^{n,k} = (I - \Delta\tau L_{x,\hat{h}_x})U_{p_l,j}^{n,k-1} + \Delta\tau f_{1\ p_l,j}^{n+1},$$
$$p_l = p, p \pm m, \cdots, p \pm (K-k)m; \ p \in IN_p, \tag{15}$$

and set $U_{p,j}^{n+\frac{1}{2}} = U_{p,j}^{n,K}$; (b) after getting the interface values, the implicit x-directional splitting scheme within interior nodes of sub-domains is defined to find the interior point values, by solving tri-diagonal systems

$$(I + \Delta t L_{x,h_x}) U_{i,j}^{n+\frac{1}{2}} = U_{i,j}^n + \Delta t f_{1\,i,j}^{n+1}, \ \forall i \in I_p, p \in IN_p. \qquad (16)$$

Secondly, along y - direction, $\forall i \in I_p, 1 \leq p \leq N_p$, (a) the values at the interface points y_q is computed by the local multilevel explicit scheme by setting for $k = 1, 2, \cdots, K$ with

$$U_{i,q_l}^{n+1,0} = U_{i,q_l}^{n+\frac{1}{2}}, \ q_l = q, q \pm m, \cdots, q \pm Km; \ q \in IN_q, \qquad (17)$$

and for $k = 1, 2, \cdots, K$, computing

$$U_{i,q_l}^{n+\frac{1}{2},k} = (I - \Delta \tau L_{y,\hat{h}_y}) U_{i,q_l}^{n+\frac{1}{2},k-1} + \Delta t f_{2\,i,q_l}^{n+1},$$
$$q_l = q, q \pm m, \cdots, q \pm (K-k)m, \ q \in IN_q \qquad (18)$$

and let $U_{i,q}^{n+1} = U_{i,q}^{n+\frac{1}{2},K}$; (b) the interior point values of sub-domains are solved by the implicit y−directional splitting scheme:

$$(I + \Delta t L_{y,h_y}) U_{i,j}^{n+1} = U_{i,j}^{n+\frac{1}{2}} + \Delta t f_{2\,i,j}^{n+1}, \ \forall j \in J_q, 1 \leq q \leq N_q. \qquad (19)$$

Scheme (14)-(19) constructs the splitting domain decomposition method (S-DDM) on multiple block-divided sub-domains for parabolic equations.

4   Theoretical Analysis

In this section, we will discuss the stability of the splitting domain decomposition method (14)-(19). We have the following theorem of stability.

Theorem 1. *Suppose that* $f = f_1 + f_2$, *and* $f_1, f_2 \in C^0(\Omega \times (0, T])$, *and the stability condition* $1 - 2\bar{r}_l \geq 0, l = x, y$, *holds. Then the splitting domain decomposition scheme (14)-(19) satisfies that for* $n \geq 0$

$$\max_{i,j} |U_{i,j}^{n+1}| \leq \max_{i,j} |U_{i,j}^0| + \Delta t \sum_{s=0}^n \max_{i,j}(|f_{1\,i,j}^{s+1}| + |f_{2\,i,j}^{s+1}|), \qquad (20)$$

where $\bar{r}_x = \frac{a\Delta\tau}{\hat{h}_x^2}$ *and* $\bar{r}_y = \frac{b\Delta\tau}{\hat{h}_y^2}$.

Remark 1. In Theorem 4.1, we prove the stability for the S-DDM. As we know, the standard explicit scheme on interface boundaries of sub-domains will require the stability condition $r = \frac{\Delta t \max\{a,b\}}{h^2} \leq \frac{1}{2}$. Using multilevel time step size $\Delta\tau = \Delta t/K$ and interface spatial step size $\hat{h} = mh$, where $K > 1$ and $m > 1$, relaxes the stability condition of the S-DDM to $\bar{r} = \frac{r}{Km^2} \leq \frac{1}{2}$. It is clear that we can increase the values of K and m so that the condition is always true with respect to any h and Δt, therefore, the S-DDM is stable. Further, we have obtained the convergence analysis of our S-DDM scheme and its optimal error estimate. The theoretical proofs of the stability and error estimate can be extended to higher dimensional parabolic problems.

Remark 2. In the previous work on non-overlapping domain decomposition methods for parabolic problems ([6, 9]), the domain was divided into stripe-divided sub-domains. Our S-DDM overcomes the limitation of stripe sub-domains of the previous methods and works efficient for multiple block-divided sub-domains for large scale parabolic problems. Numerical experiments will further show the efficiency of the S-DDM in Section 5.

5   Numerical Experiments

In numerical experiments, we will focus on the efficiency and accuracy of the S-DDM method, the effects of multilevel numbers K and m of the local multilevel scheme on interfaces, and the number of sub-domains in computation.

Example 1. Consider the diffusion coefficients $a = b = 1$. The right side function, the boundary conditions and the initial values are given as

$$f(x,y,t) = e^t\Big(x(1-x)y(1-y) + 2by(1-y) + 2ax(1-x)\Big), \qquad (21)$$

$$u(0,y,t) = 0, \quad u(1,y,t) = 0; \quad u(x,0,t) = 0, \quad u(x,1,t) = 0, \qquad (22)$$

$$u_0(x,y) = x(1-x)y(1-y). \qquad (23)$$

Table 1. Numerical errors of the S-DDM with different local multilevel numbers K and m for the constant coefficient diffusion problem

Errors $\lambda =$		8	4	2	1	0.5
K=1 m=1	L_∞	DIV	DIV	DIV	8.4582e-5	4.2582e-5
	L_2	DIV	DIV	DIV	5.0211e-5	2.5165e-5
K=2 m=1	L_∞	DIV	DIV	5.9484e-3	7.8582e-5	4.2582e-5
	L_2	DIV	DIV	1.9845e-3	4.7604e-5	2.5165e-5
K=4 m=2	L_∞	4.5643e-4	2.7389e-4	1.4958e-4	7.8582e-5	3.9928e-5
	L_2	2.9505e-4	1.7189e-4	9.2108e-5	4.7638e-5	2.4175e-5

Numerical results in Table 1 show the effects of the multilevel numbers K and m on numerical errors at time $t = 0.2$. With $K > 1$ and $m > 1$ in the S-DDM scheme, it relaxes the stability condition and also improves the accuracy of the solution. Take the uniformly spatial step size as $h = 1/40$, choose the time step sizes as $\Delta t = 1/200, 1/400, 1/800, 1/1600$ and $1/3200$. The stability condition of the standard explicit scheme (one level scheme with $K = 1$ and $m = 1$) on the interfaces is determined by the ratios $\lambda = \frac{\Delta t \max\{a,b\}}{h^2} \leq \frac{1}{2}$. When λ is large, the stability condition of the standard explicit scheme will be broken and the method does not converge any more. However, from the discussion in the last section, by using the local multilevel explicit scheme on interfaces in the S-DDM scheme, we can relax the condition so that it is stable and works efficiently, where the stable condition is improved to $\bar{\lambda} = \frac{\lambda}{Km^2} \leq \frac{1}{2}$. In the example, we

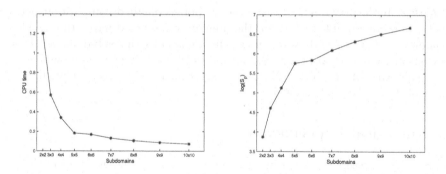

Fig. 2. The CPU times by the S-DDM with $K = 2$ and $m = 2$ over multiple sub-domains (left) and the logarithm of speedup ($\log S_P$) of the S-DDM with $K = 2$ and $m = 2$ (right)

divide the domain into 4 sub-domains, and take the final time to be $T = 0.2$. In Table 1, the first pair of $K = 1$ and $m = 1$ breaks the stable condition when $\lambda = 8, 4$, and 2, and the corresponding numerical results diverge. The second pair of $K = 2$ and $m = 1$ relaxes the stable condition such that for the case $\lambda = 2$, it is stable and then works well. But for the cases of $\lambda = 8$, and 4, they still do not work. Further relaxing the stable condition by choosing $K = 4$ and $m = 2$ in the last row, we can see that reasonable results are obtained since the corresponding local multilevel schemes are stable for all λ in the table.

Using $h = 1/100$ and $\Delta t = 1/2000$, the S-DDM with multilevel parameters $K = 2$ and $m = 2$ is applied. The CPU time and the speedup curve at $t = 1.0$ are given in Figure 2. We can see that CPU time decreases when domain is divided into more sub-domains and the speedup is increasing when more sub-domains are used.

References

[1] Aziz, K., Settari, A.: Petroleum Reservoir Simulation. Applied Science Publisher, Ltd., London (1979)
[2] Bear, J.: Hydraulics of Groundwater. McGraw-Hill, New York (1978)
[3] Chen, Z., Huan, G., Ma, Y.: Computational Science and Engineering Series. Computational Science and Engineering Series, vol. 2. SIAM, Philadelphia (2006)
[4] Clavero, C., Jorge, J.C., Lisbona, F.J., Shishkin, G.I.: An alternating direction scheme on a nonuniform mesh for reaction-diffusion parabolic problems. IMA J. Numer. Anal. 20, 263–280 (2000)
[5] Ewing, R.E. (ed.): The Mathematics of Reservoir Simulation, Frontiers in Applied mathematics, vol. 1, pp. 294–318 (1988)
[6] Dawson, C.N., Du, Q., Dupont, T.F.: A finite difference domain decomposition algorithm for numerical solution of the heat equation. Math. Comp. 57, 63–71 (1991)

[7] Douglas Jr., J., Peaceman, D.: Numerical solution of two dimensional heat flow problem. Am. Instit. Chem. Eng. J. 1, 505–512 (1955)

[8] Douglas Jr., J., Kim, S.: Improved Accuracy for Locally One-Dimensional Methods for Parabolic Equations. Math. Model Methods Appl. Sci. 11, 1563–1579 (2001)

[9] Du, Q., Mu, M., Wu, Z.N.: Efficient parallel algorithms for parabolic problems. SIAM J. Numer. Anal. 39, 1469–1487 (2001)

[10] Liang, D., Du, C., Wang, H.: A Fractional Step ELLAM Approach to High Dimensional Convection Diffusion Problems with Forward Particle Tracking. J. of Comput. Phys. 221, 198–225 (2007)

[11] Lions, P.L.: On the Schwarz alternating method I. In: Glowinskin, R., Golub, G.H., Meurant, G.A., Periaux, J. (eds.) Proceeding of the First International Symposium on Domain Decomposition Methods for Partial Differential Equations, Paris, pp. 1–42. SIAM, Philadelphia (1988)

[12] Portero, L., Jorge, J.C.: A generalization of Peaceman-Rachford fractional step method. J. Comput. Appl. Math. 189, 676–688 (2006)

[13] Rivera, W., Zhu, J., Huddleston, D.: An efficient parallel algorithm with application to computational fluid dynamics. J. Comput. Math. Appl. 45, 165–188 (2003)

[14] Shi, H.-S., Liao, H.-L.: Unconditional Stability of Corrected Explicit-Implicit Domain Decomposition Algorithms for Parallel Approximation of Heat Equations. SIAM J. Numer. Anal. 44, 1584–1611 (2006)

[15] Smith, B.F., Bjørst, P.E., Gropp, W.D.: Domain Decomposition Methods for Partial Differential Equations. Cambridge University Press, Cambridge (1996)

[16] Yanenko, N.: The method of fractional steps. Springer, Heidelberg (1971)

New Shock Detector for Shock-Boundary Layer Interaction

Chaoqun Liu and Maria Oliveira

University of Texas at Arlington, Arlington, TX 76019, USA
`cliu@uta.edu`

Abstract. Standard compact scheme or upwind compact scheme have high order accuracy and high resolution, but cannot capture the shock which is a discontinuity. This work developed a modified compact scheme by an effective shock detector to block compact scheme to cross the shock, a control function, and an adaptive scheme which uses some WENO flux near the shock. The new scheme makes the original compact scheme able to capture the shock sharper than WENO and, more important, keep high order accuracy and high resolution in the smooth area which is particularly important for shock boundary layer interaction and shock acoustic interaction. The scheme is robust and has no case-related coefficients.

Keywords: compact scheme, WENO, shock-capturing, boundary layer, discontinuity detector.

1   Introduction

The flow field is in general governed by the Navier-Stokes system which is a system of time dependent partial differential equations. However, for external flow, the viscosity is important largely only in the boundary layers. The main flow can still be considered as inviscid and the governing system can be dominated by the time dependent Euler equations which are hyperbolic. The difficult problem with numerical solution is the shock capturing which can be considered as a discontinuity or mathematical singularity (no classical unique solution and no bounded derivatives). In the shock area, continuity and differentiability of the governing Euler equations are lost and only the weak solution in an integration form can be obtained. The shock can be developed in some cases because the Euler equation is non-linear and hyperbolic. On the other hand, the governing Navier-Stokes system presents parabolic type behavior in and is therefore dominated by viscosity or second order derivatives. One expects that the equation should be solved by high order central difference scheme, high order compact scheme is preferable, to get high order accuracy and high resolution. High order of accuracy is critical in resolving small length scale in flow transition and turbulence process. However, for the hyperbolic system, the analysis already shows the existence of characteristic lines and Riemann invariants. Apparently, the upwind finite difference scheme coincides with the physics for a hyperbolic system.

W. Zhang et al. (Eds.): HPCA 2009, LNCS 5938, pp. 78–87, 2010.

History has shown the great success of upwind technologies. We should consider not only the eigenvalues and eigenvectors of the Jacobian system, but also non- linearity including the Rankine-Hugoniot shock relations. From the point of view of shocks, it makes no sense to use high order compact scheme for shock capturing which use all gird points on one grid line to calculate the derivative by solving a tri-diagonal or penta-diagonal linear system when shock does not have finite derivatives and downstream quantities cannot cross shock to affect the upstream points. From the point of view of the above statement, upwind scheme is appropriate for the hyperbolic system. Many upwind or bias upwind schemes have achieved great success in capturing the shocks sharply, such as Godunov [4], Roe [15], MUSCL [19], TVD [5], ENO [6,16,17] and WENO [7,12]. All these shock- capturing schemes are based on upwind or bias upwind technology, which is nice for hyperbolic system, but is not favorable to the N-S system which presents parabolic equation behavior. The small length scale is very important in the flow transition and turbulence process and thus very sensitive to any artificial numerical dissipation. High order compact scheme [10,20] is more appropriate for simulation of flow transition and turbulence because it is central and non-dissipative with high order accuracy and high resolution.

Unfortunately, the shock-boundary layer interaction, which is important to high speed flow, is a mixed type problem which has shock (discontinuity), boundary layer (viscosity), separation, transition, expansion fans, fully developed turbulence, and reattachment. In the case of shock-boundary layer interaction, there are elliptic areas (separation, transition, turbulence) and hyperbolic areas (main flow, shocks, expansion fans), which makes the accurate numerical simulation extremely difficult if not impossible. We may divide the computational domain to several parts: the elliptic, hyperbolic, and mixed. The division or detection can be performed by switch function automatically such as shock detectors which simply sets $\Omega = 1$ for the shock area and $\Omega = 0$ for the rest. The switch function may give good results for shock-boundary layer interaction, but it will have too many logical statements in the code which may slow down the computation. The switch function could also be case-related and very difficult to adjust. It would also slow down the convergence for steady problems.

A combination of compact scheme and WENO scheme should be desirable. There are some efforts to combine WENO with standard central [1,9] and WENO with upwind compact scheme [14,22]. Their mixing function is somewhat complex and has a number of case related adjustable coefficients.

In order to overcome the drawback of the CS scheme, we need to achieve local dependency in shock regions and recover the global dependency in smooth regions. This fundamental idea will naturally lead to a combination of local dependent scheme, e.g. WENO and global dependent compact schemes which we call "Modified Compact Scheme" (MCS).

This effort is to use WENO to improve 6th order compact scheme as we called as "modified compact scheme (MCS)" which uses a new shock detector to find the shock and a control function to mix the schemes (CS and WENO). The mixing function is designed in following ways: the new scheme automatically becomes bias when approaching the shock, but rapidly recovers to be upwind compact, with high order of accuracy and high resolution.

2   Modified Compact Scheme (MCS)

The compact scheme is great to resolve small length scales, but cannot be used for the cases when a shock or discontinuity is involved. Our new modified compact scheme is an effort to remove the weakness by introducing WENO flux when the computation is approaching the shock.

2.1   Effective New Shock Detector

A very effective shock detector [13] has been proposed by Liu. The detector has two steps. The first step is to check the ratio of the truncation errors on the coarse and fine grids and the second step is to check the local ratio of the left and right hand slopes. The currently popular shock/discontinuity detectors such as Harten's, Jameson's and WENO can detect shock, but mistake high frequency waves and critical points as shock and then damp the physically important high frequency waves. Preliminary results show the new shock/discontinuity detector is very delicate and can detect all shocks including strong, weak and oblique shocks or discontinuity in function and first, second, and third order derivatives without artificial case related constants, but never mistake high frequency waves and critical points, expansion waves as shock. This will overcome the bottle neck problem with numerical simulation for the shock-boundary layer interaction, shock-acoustic interaction, image process, porous media flow, multiple phase flow, detonation wave and anywhere the high frequency waves are important, but discontinuity exists and is mixed with high frequency waves. To introduce our new two step shock/discontinuity detector, we need to introduce some popular shock detectors first.

Harten's Switch Function and Jameson's Shock Detector. *Harten* defined an automatic switch function that is able to detect large changes in the variation of the function values f_i. It generates values between 0 and 1, where 0 is considered smooth and 1 is considered non-smooth. The switch is defined as

$$\theta_{j+1/2} = \max\left(\hat{\theta}_j, \hat{\theta}_{j+1}\right), \tag{1}$$

with

$$\hat{\theta}_i = \begin{cases} \left|\dfrac{|\alpha_{i+1/2}| - |\alpha_{i-1/2}|}{|\alpha_{i+1/2}| + |\alpha_{i-1/2}|}\right|^p, & \text{if } |\alpha_{i+1/2}| + |\alpha_{i-1/2}| > \varepsilon \\ 0, & \text{otherwise} \end{cases},$$

where $\alpha_{i+1/2} = f_{i+1} - f_i$ and ε is a suitably chosen measure of insignificant variation in f. *Jameson's* shock detector is similar, which can be described as

$$\theta_{i+1/2} = \frac{|p_{i-1} - 2p_i + p_{i+1}|}{|p_{i-1}| + 2|p_i| + |p_{i+1}|}, \tag{2}$$

is related to the second order derivative of the pressure.

WENO. The WENO weights use smoothness measurements that evaluate the changes in the variation of the function values f_i. Assuming that the three weights ω_i have equal contribution, we can determine that a function is smooth if all values are approximately $1/3$:

$$\omega_i = \frac{\alpha_i}{\sum_{j=0}^{2} \alpha_j}; \quad \alpha_i = \frac{1}{(IS_i + \varepsilon)^2}, \quad i = 0, 1, 2, \tag{3}$$

where

$$IS_0 = \frac{13}{12}\left(f_{i-2} - 2f_{i-1} + f_i\right)^2 + \frac{1}{4}\left(f_{i-2} - 4f_{i-1} + 3f_i\right)^2;$$

$$IS_1 = \frac{13}{12}\left(f_{i-1} - 2f_i + f_{i+1}\right)^2 + \frac{1}{4}\left(f_{i-1} - f_{i+1}\right)^2;$$

$$IS_2 = \frac{13}{12}\left(f_{i+2} - 2f_{i+1} + f_i\right)^2 + \frac{1}{4}\left(f_{i+2} - 4f_{i+1} + 3f_i\right)^2.$$

New Two Step Shock/Discontinuity Locator Proposed by C. Liu. This new shock detector consists of two main steps: a *multigrid truncation error ratio check* and a *local slope ratio check*.

Step 1. Determine the multigrid ratio of the approximation of the sum of the fourth, fifth and sixth truncation errors for $[F = f + \text{smooth sine wave of small amplitude}]$ and select the points where the ratio is smaller than 4. Theoretically, the ratio of the fourth order truncation error of coarse and fine grids should be 16, but any function that has a ratio of 4 will be considered smooth and passing the test. The points which have a ratio less than 4 will be picked out for the second left- and right-hand slope ratio check.

The multigrid truncation error ratio check is

$$MR(i, h) = \frac{T_C(i, h)}{T_F(i, h) + \varepsilon}, \tag{4}$$

with

$$T_C(i, h) = T_4(i, 2h) + T_5(i, 2h) + T_6(i, 2h) =$$
$$= \frac{\left|f_i^{(4)}\right|(2h)^4}{4!} + \frac{\left|f_i^{(5)}\right|(2h)^5}{5!} + \frac{\left|f_i^{(6)}\right|(2h)^6}{6!}$$

and

$$T_F(i, h) = T_4(i, h) + T_5(i, h) + T_6(i, h) =$$
$$= \frac{\left|f_i^{(4)}\right|(h)^4}{4!} + \frac{\left|f_i^{(5)}\right|(h)^5}{5!} + \frac{\left|f_i^{(6)}\right|(h)^6}{6!},$$

where $T_F(i, h)$ is the truncation error sum calculated at the fine grid with n points and $T_C(i, h)$ is the truncation error sum calculated at the coarse grid with $n/2$ points. $T_F(i, h)$ and $T_C(i, h)$ have fourth, fifth and sixth order derivatives which are calculated by the sixth order compact scheme.

Step 2. Calculate the local left and right slope ratio check only at the points which have frist ratio less than 4. The new local left and right slope ratio check is given by

$$LR\,(i) = \left| \frac{\left| \frac{f_R'}{f_L'} \right| - \left| \frac{f_L'}{f_R'} \right|}{\left| \frac{f_R'}{f_L'} \right| + \left| \frac{f_L'}{f_R'} \right| + \varepsilon} \right| = \left| \frac{(f_R')^2 - (f_L')^2}{(f_R')^2 + (f_L')^2 + \varepsilon} \right|, \tag{5}$$

where $f_R' = 3f_i - 4f_{i+1} + f_{i+2}$, $f_L' = 3f_i - 4f_{i-1} + f_{i-2}$, and ε is a small number to avoid division by zero.

(Optional) Step 3. Use a cutoff value of 0.8 to create a 0/1 switch function on the result of Step 2. If the value is zero, f is considered locally smooth, and if the value is one, f has a shock/discontinuity around that point.

Note that Liu's first step always checks $f + \sigma \sin(k\pi x + \phi)$ instead of f, where σ is a small number. Since all derivatives are calculated by a subroutine with standard compact scheme, the cost of two-step checks is relatively inexpensive.

For a universal formula, the data set is normalized between zero and one when used with the shock locator.

2.2   Control Function for Using WENO to Improve CS

Basic Idea of the Control Function. Although the new shock detector can provide accurate location of shock including weak shock, strong shock, oblique shock and discontinuity in function, first, second and third order derivatives, it is a switch function and gives one in shock and zero for other regions. A switch function cannot be directly used to mix CS and WENO, as the sudden change in schemes may generate non-physical oscillations; therefore, we must develop a rather smooth function to mix CS and WENO. A new control function Ω is defined, such that the mixed scheme is given by:

$$\Omega \cdot CS + (1 - \Omega) \cdot WENO. \tag{6}$$

The combination leads to a tri-diagonal matrix system for the solution of the derivatives of the primitive function H of f:

$$\frac{1}{3}\Omega H_{j-3/2}' + H_{j-1/2}' + \frac{1}{3}\Omega H_{j+1/2}' =$$

$$= \frac{\Omega}{h} \left[\frac{1}{36}\left(H_{j+3/2} - H_{j-5/2}\right) + \frac{7}{9}\left(H_{j+1/2} - H_{j-3/2}\right) \right] +$$

$$+ (1 - \Omega)\left[\omega_{0,j-1/2}\left(\frac{1}{3}f_{j-3} - \frac{7}{6}f_{j-2} + \frac{11}{6}f_{j-1}\right) + \right.$$

$$\left. + \omega_{1,j-1/2}\left(-\frac{1}{6}f_{j-2} + \frac{5}{6}f_{j-1} + \frac{1}{3}f_j\right) + \omega_{2,j-1/2}\left(\frac{1}{3}f_{j-1} + \frac{5}{6}f_j - \frac{1}{6}f_{j+1}\right) \right].$$

Construction of the Control Function. In the new shock detector we define the multigrid ratio $MR(i, h)$ as a ratio of coarse grid truncation over fine grid truncation. The ratio should be around 16 if the function has at least sixth order continuous derivatives. We define

$$\Omega = 1.0 - \min[1.0, 8.0/MR(i, h)] \cdot LR, \tag{7}$$

where MR is the multigrid global truncation error ratio and LR is the local ratio of the left and right side angles. If the shock is met, MR is small, LR is 1 and $\Omega = 0.0$. The WENO scheme is used and the CS is fully blocked. If the area is smooth, MR should be around 16.0 and LR is close to zero (left and right angles are similar). Additional requirement is set that any point must compare with left and right neighboring points and we pick the largest Ω among the neighboring points.

The value of 8.0 is chosen so that the fourth order continuous function is treated as a smooth function and only need half of LR for Ω. It is easy to find there are no case-related adjustable coefficients which is quite different from many other published hybrid schemes. The shock detector is very reliable and the new scheme is very robust.

3   Computational Results by MCS

To test the numerical scheme MCS for 2-D and 3-D shock-boundary layer interaction, a 2-D incident shock-boundary layer interaction case was studied (figure 1). The Reynolds number is 3×10^5, the Mach number is set to 3, and the attack angle is $32.24°$. A numerical grid of dimensions 257×257 is used (figure 2).

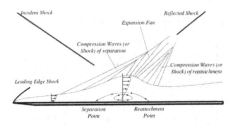

Fig. 1. Sketch of incident shock-boundary layer interaction

The pressure distribution with streamlines is observed in figures 3 and 4, while figure 5 shows the contour of the density. The distribution of the Ω calculated in the x-direction is in figure 6. The results show that the numerical scheme captures the shock sharply while maintaining high resolution in the boundary layer.

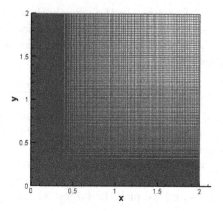

Fig. 2. Stretched grid (257×257)

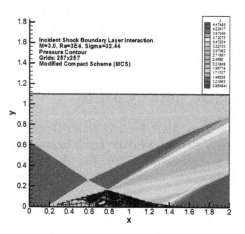

Fig. 3. Pressure distribution and streamlines

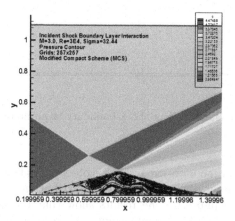

Fig. 4. Pressure distribution (locally enlarged)

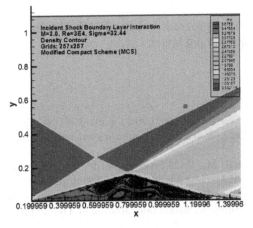

Fig. 5. Density distribution

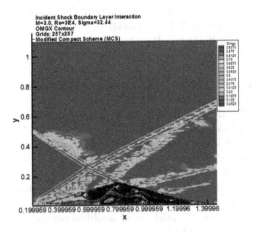

Fig. 6. Distribution of Ω calculated in x-direction

4   Conclusion

A new shock detector was developed and was utilized as part of a combination
of compact scheme and WENO scheme to create a modified compact scheme,
capable of capturing shocks sharply and at the same time maintaining high
resolution in smooth areas. The new scheme is robust and has no case-related
coefficients.

Acknowledgments. This work is supported by the AFRL Air Vehicles Sum-
mer Faculty Program. The authors thank Drs. Poggie, Gaitonde, and Visbal for

their support through the program and also TACC (Texas Advanced Computing Center) for the computational hours.

References

1. Costa, B., Dong, W.: High order hybrid central-WENO finite difference scheme for conservation laws. Journal of Computational and Applied Mathematics 204, 209–218 (2007)
2. Gaitonde, D., Visbal, M.: Padé-type high-order boundary filters for the Navier-Stokes equations. AIAA Journal 38(11), 2103–2112 (2000)
3. Gaitonde, D., Canupp, P.W., Holden, M.: Heat transfer predictions in a laminar hypersonic viscous/inviscid interaction. Journal of Thermophysics and Heat Transfer 16(4) (2002)
4. Godunov, S.K.: A difference scheme for numerical computation of discontinuous solution of hydrodynamic equations. Math Sbornik 47, 271–306 (in Russian); translated US Joint Publ. Res. Service, JPRS 7226 (1969)
5. Harten, A.: High resolution schemes for hyperbolic conservation laws. Journal of Computational Physics 49, 357–393 (1983)
6. Harten, A., Engquist, B., Osher, B., Charkravarthy, S.R.: Uniformly high order accurate essentially non-oscillatory schemes III. Journal of Computational Physics 71, 231–303 (1987)
7. Jiang, G.S., Shu, C.W.: Efficient implementation of weighted ENO scheme. Journal of Computational Physics 126, 202–228 (1996)
8. Jiang, L., Shan, H., Liu, C.: Weighted compact scheme for shock capturing. International Journal of Computational Fluid Dynamics 15, 147–155 (2001)
9. Kim, D., Kwon, J.: A high-order accurate hybrid scheme using a central flux scheme and a WENO scheme for compressible flowfield analysis. Journal of Computational Physics 210, 554–583 (2005)
10. Lele, S.K.: Compact finite difference schemes with spectral-like resolution. Journal of Computational Physics 103, 16–42 (1992)
11. Liu, C., Xie, P., Oliveira, M.: High order modified compact scheme for high speed flow. Technical Report to AFRL/RB
12. Liu, D., Osher, S., Chan, T.: Weighted essentially non-oscillatory schemes. Journal of Computational Physics 115, 200–212 (1994)
13. Oliveira, M., Lu, P., Liu, X., Liu, C.: A new shock/discontinuity detector. International Journal of Computer Mathematics (accepted, 2009)
14. Ren, Y., Liu, M., Zhang, H.: A characteristic-wise hybrid compact-WENO scheme for solving hyperbolic conservation laws. Journal of Computational Physics 192, 365–386 (2003)
15. Roe, P.L.: Approximate Riemann solvers, parameter vectors and difference schemes. Journal of Computational Physics 43, 357–372 (1981)
16. Shu, C.W., Osher, S.: Efficient implementation of essentially non-oscillatory shock-capturing scheme. Journal of Computational Physics 77, 439–471 (1988)
17. Shu, C.W., Osher, S.: Efficient implementation of essentially non-oscillatory shock-capturing schemes II. Journal of Computational Physics 83, 32–78 (1989)
18. Su, J., Xie, P., Oliveira, M., Liu, C.: Error analysis for weighted higher order compact finite difference scheme. Applied Mathematical Sciences 1(58), 2863–2881 (2007)

19. Van Leer, B.: Towards the ultimate conservative difference scheme. V. A second order sequel to Godunov's scheme. Journal of Computational Physics 32, 101–136 (1979)
20. Visbal, M., Gaitonde, D.: On the use of higher-order finite-difference schemes on curvilinear and deforming meshes. Journal of Computational Physics 181, 155–158 (2002)
21. Wadhams, T.P., Holden, M.S.: Summary of experimental studies for code validation in the LENS facility with recent Navier-Stokes and DSMC solutions for two- and three-dimensional separated regions in hypervelocity flows. AIAA Paper 2004-917 (2002)
22. Zhou, Q., Yao, Z., He, F., Shen, M.Y.: A new family of high-order compact upwind difference schemes with good spectral resolution. Journal of Computational Physics 227(2), 1306–1339 (2007)

Performance of Local Gauss Integration in Finite Element and Finite Volume Methods for the Navier-Stokes Equations

He Zhong[1] and Zhangxin Chen[2]

[1] Faculty of Science, Xi'an Jiaotong University, Xi'an 710049, P.R. China
[2] Department of Chemical and Petroleum Engineering, Schulich School of Engineering, University of Calgary, Calgary, AB T2N 1N4, Canada

Abstract. This paper is concerned with the application of new stabilized finite element and finite volume methods for solving the Navier-Stokes equations. These methods are based on local Gauss integration and equal-order conforming or nonconforming finite element pairs. Their performance is investigated through numerical experiments.

Keywords: Stabilized finite element, stabilized finite volume, nonconforming, Gauss integration, and numerical experiments.

1 Introduction

The development of stable mixed finite element methods is an important component in the simulation of the flow of incompressible fluids. The importance to ensure the compatibility of the approximation of velocity and pressure by satisfying the *inf-sup* condition is widely understood. However, while they do not satisfy the *inf-sup* condition, the equal-order pairs of mixed finite elements remain a popular practical choice in scientific computation. Their popularity results from the facts that these equal-order pairs have simple date structure and are computationally convenient and efficient in a parallel or multigrid context [1,4]. Therefore, the study of these pairs has recently attracted much attention.

In order to remedy the lack of satisfying the *inf-sup* condition, a new stabilization technique based on local Gauss integration has recently been proposed, which is a special case of local pressure projection approach and free of stabilization parameters. The central idea of this technique is to add a stabilized term that is constructed by the difference between consistent and under-integrated Gauss integrals. Unlike the penalty or other stabilization methods that uncouple the velocity and pressure, it aims to relax the continuity equation without requiring an approximation of derivatives, and it is completely local at the element level [4,8,10].

This paper will present the application of the local Gauss integration technique to the conforming and nonconforming finite element and finite volume methods for numerically solving the Navier-Stokes equations. The performance of these methods is investigated through numerical experiments.

W. Zhang et al. (Eds.): HPCA 2009, LNCS 5938, pp. 88–95, 2010.

2 Preliminaries

Consider the Navier-Stokes equations with a bounded open set Ω, with a Lipschitz boundary $\partial\Omega$:

$$-\nu\Delta u + (u\cdot\nabla)u + \nabla p = f \quad \text{in}\quad \Omega, \tag{1}$$

$$\operatorname{div} u = 0 \quad \text{in}\quad \Omega, \tag{2}$$

$$u = 0 \quad \text{on}\quad \partial\Omega, \tag{3}$$

where $u = (u_1, u_2)$ represents the velocity vector, p is the pressure, f prescribes the body forces, and $\nu > 0$ denotes the dynamic viscosity.

In what follows, we employ the standard definitions for the Sobolev spaces $H^s(\Omega)$ and their associated inner product $(\cdot,\cdot)_{s,\Omega}$, norms $\|\cdot\|_{s,\Omega}$, and seminorms $|\cdot|_{s,\Omega}$, $s \geq 0$. When $s = 0$ we will write $L^2(\Omega)$ instead of $H^0(\Omega)$ in which case the norm and inner product are denoted by $\|\cdot\|_\Omega$ and $(\cdot,\cdot)_\Omega$, respectively. As usual, $H_0^s(\Omega)$ will denote the closure of $C_0^\infty(\Omega)$ with respect to the norm $\|\cdot\|_{s,\Omega}$, and $L_0^2(\Omega)$ will denote the space of all square integrable functions with a vanishing mean on Ω. Spaces consisting of vector-valued functions will be denoted in bold face.

To introduce the variational formulation, set $\mathbf{X} = \left(H_0^1(\Omega)\right)^2$ and $M = L_0^2(\Omega)$, and define the continuous bilinear forms $a(\cdot,\cdot)$ and $d(\cdot,\cdot)$ and the trilinear form $b(\cdot;\cdot,\cdot)$ on $\mathbf{X}\times\mathbf{X}$, $\mathbf{X}\times M$, and $\mathbf{X}\times\mathbf{X}\times\mathbf{X}$, respectively, by

$$a(u,v) = (\nabla u, \nabla v), \quad d(v,q) = (\operatorname{div} v, q), \quad b(u;v,w) = ((u\cdot\nabla)v,w).$$

Then the weak formulation of (1)–(3) is to seek $(u,p) \in \mathbf{X}\times M$ such that

$$\mathcal{B}(u,p;v,q) + b(u;u,v) = (f,v) \qquad \forall (v,q) \in \mathbf{X}\times M, \tag{4}$$

where

$$\mathcal{B}(u,p;v,q) = \nu a(u,v) - d(v,q) + d(u,q).$$

The bilinear form $d(\cdot,\cdot)$ satisfies the *inf-sup* condition [2,5,6]

$$\sup_{0\neq v\in\mathbf{X}} |d(v,q)|/\|v\|_1 \geq C_0\|q\|_0, \tag{5}$$

where C_0 is a positive constant depending only on Ω.

3 The Finite Element and Finite Volume Approximation

3.1 The Stabilized Finite Element Method

For $h > 0$, let $\mathcal{T}_h$ is a regular, quasi uniform triangulation of Ω into triangles $\{K_j\}$ [2,3]: $\overline{\Omega} = \cup\overline{K}_j$. Associated with $\mathcal{T}_h$, we define the lower order conforming finite element space

$$\mathcal{P}_h = \left\{v \in H_0^1(\Omega) : v|_K \in P_1(K) \quad \forall K \in \mathcal{T}_h\right\},$$

and the nonconforming finite element space [2]:

$$\mathcal{NC}_h = \{v \in L^2(\Omega) : v|_K \in P_1(K) \quad \forall K \in \mathcal{T}_h, v(\xi_{jk}) = v(\xi_{kj}), \ v(\xi_j) = 0 \quad \forall j, k\},$$

where $P_1(K)$ is the space of linear polynomials on K, and ξ_{jk} and ξ_j represent the centers of an interior edge $e_{jk} = \partial K_j \cap \partial K_k$ and a boundary segment $e_j = \partial \Omega \cap \partial K_j$, respectively. For every $v \in \mathcal{NC}_h$, its norm and inner product are understood element-wise, e.g.,

$$\|v\|_{1,h} = \left(\sum_j |v|_{1,K_j}^2\right)^{1/2}.$$

We will approximate the velocity and pressure within $(\mathbf{X}_h, M_h) = ((\mathcal{P}_h)^2, \mathcal{P}_h \cap M)$ or $(\mathbf{X}_h, M_h) = ((\mathcal{NC}_h)^2, \mathcal{P}_h \cap M)$. In either case, the pair $\mathbf{X}_h \times M_h$ does not satisfy a discrete counterpart of the *inf-sup* condition (5). To remedy this defect, a simple local and effective perturbation $G_h(\cdot, \cdot)$ [4,8] is added to the weak formulation:

$$G_h(p,q) = \sum_{K_j \in \mathcal{T}_h} \left\{ \int_{K_{j,2}} pq \, d\mathbf{x} - \int_{K_{j,1}} pq \, d\mathbf{x} \right\}, \qquad p, q \in L^2(\Omega),$$

where $\int_{K_{j,i}} pq \, d\mathbf{x}$ indicates an appropriate Gauss integral over K_j that is exact for polynomials of degree i $(i = 1, 2)$, and pq is a polynomial of degree not greater than two. In such a manner, the incompressibility constraint will be relaxed.

Consequently, we define the L^2-projection operator $\Pi_h : L^2(\Omega) \to W_h$

$$(p, q_h) = (\Pi_h p, q_h) \qquad \forall p \in L^2(\Omega), q_h \in W_h, \tag{6}$$

where $W_h \subset L^2(\Omega)$ denotes the piecewise constant space associated with $\mathcal{T}_h$. Now, using (6), we define the bilinear form $G_h(\cdot, \cdot)$ as follows:

$$G_h(p,q) = (p - \Pi_h p, q - \Pi_h q) \qquad \forall p, q \in L^2(\Omega). \tag{7}$$

In the conforming case, the variational form of the finite element method reads: Find $(\mathbf{u}_h, p_h) \in (\mathbf{X}_h, M_h)$ such that

$$\mathcal{B}_h(\mathbf{u}_h, p_h; \mathbf{v}_h, q_h) + b(\mathbf{u}_h; \mathbf{u}_h, \mathbf{v}_h) = (\mathbf{f}, \mathbf{v}_h), \quad (\mathbf{v}_h, q_h) \in (\mathbf{X}_h, M_h), \tag{8}$$

where

$$\mathcal{B}_h(\mathbf{u}_h, p_h; \mathbf{v}_h, q_h) = \nu a(\mathbf{u}_h, \mathbf{v}_h) - d(\mathbf{v}_h, p_h) + d(\mathbf{u}_h, q_h) + G_h(p_h, q_h).$$

In the nonconforming case, we define the discrete bilinear and trilinear forms

$$a_h(\mathbf{u}_h, \mathbf{v}_h) = \sum_{K \in \mathcal{T}_h} \int_K \nabla \mathbf{u}_h : \nabla \mathbf{v}_h \, d\mathbf{x},$$

$$d_h(\mathbf{v}_h, p_h) = \sum_{K \in \mathcal{T}_h} \int_K p_h \nabla \cdot \mathbf{v}_h \, d\mathbf{x},$$

$$b_h(\mathbf{u}_h; \mathbf{v}_h, \mathbf{w}_h) = \sum_{K \in \mathcal{T}_h} \int_K (\mathbf{u}_h \cdot \nabla)\mathbf{v}_h \cdot \mathbf{w}_h \, d\mathbf{x}.$$

Then the discrete bilinear form becomes

$$\mathcal{B}_h(u_h, p_h; v_h, q_h) = \nu a_h(u_h, v_h) - d_h(v_h, p_h) + d_h(u_h, q_h) + G_h(p_h, q_h), \quad (9)$$

and the variational form becomes: Find $(u_h, p_h) \in (\mathbf{X}_h, M_h)$ such that

$$\mathcal{B}_h(u_h, p_h; v_h, q_h) + b_h(u_h; u_h, v_h) = (f, v_h). \quad (10)$$

3.2   The Stabilized Finite Volume Method

To introduce the finite volume method, we need to construct a dual partition T_h^* of T_h, consisting of dual elements of T_h usually called boxes or control volumes, which is arbitrary, but the choice of appropriate dual elements is crucial for the analysis of the underlying discretization method [7]. The dual mesh can be constructed by the following rule (see Fig. 1):

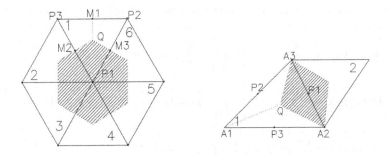

Fig. 1. The conforming and nonconforming finite element and their control volumes

1. The conforming case: For each element $K \in T_h$ with vertices P_j and edge midpoints M_j, $j = 1, 2, 3$, select its barycenter Q and connect Q to M_j to construct the dual partition T_h^*;
2. The nonconforming case: Similarly, for each element $K \in T_h$ with vertices A_j and midpoints P_j, select its barycenter Q and connect Q to A_j to obtain T_h^*.

Associated with the dual elements are the characteristic functions

$$\chi_j(\boldsymbol{x}) = \begin{cases} 1 & \text{if } \boldsymbol{x} \in K_j^* \in T_h^*, \\ 0 & \text{otherwise.} \end{cases}$$

Now, the dual finite element space is defined as

$$\mathbf{X}_h^* = \{\, \boldsymbol{v} = (v_1, v_2) \in (L^2(\Omega))^2 : v_i|_{K^*} \in \mathcal{P}_0(K^*) \quad \forall K^* \in T_h^*; \\ v_i|_{K^*} = 0 \text{ on any boundary dual element } K^*, i = 1, 2\}.$$

Furthermore, there exits an invertible linear mapping $\Gamma_h : \mathbf{X}_h \to \mathbf{X}_h^*$ [9] such that, if

$$v_h(x) = \sum_{j=1}^{N} v_h(P_j)\phi_j(x), \qquad v_h \in \mathbf{X}_h, \ x \in \Omega, \tag{11}$$

where N is the total number of the nodes in $\mathcal{T}_h$ and $\{\phi_j\}$ indicates the basis for the finite element space $\mathbf{X}_h$, then

$$\Gamma_h v_h(x) = \sum_{j=1}^{N} v_h(P_j)\chi_j(x), \qquad x \in \Omega, \ v_h \in \mathbf{X}_h, \tag{12}$$

where the conforming or nonconforming space $\mathbf{X}_h$ corresponds to its counterpart $\mathbf{X}_h^*$.

Multiplying equation (1) by $\Gamma_h v_h \in \mathbf{X}_h^*$ and integrating over the dual elements $K_h^* \in \mathcal{T}_h^*$, multiplying equation (2) by $q_h \in M_h$ and integrating over the primal elements $K \in \mathcal{T}_h$, and applying Green's formula for both equations, we obtain the following bilinear forms for the finite volume method:

$$A(u_h, v_h) = -\sum_{j=1}^{N} v_h(P_j) \cdot \int_{\partial K_j^*} \frac{\partial u_h}{\partial n} \, ds, \quad u_h, v_h \in \mathbf{X}_h,$$

$$D(v_h, p_h) = -\sum_{j=1}^{N} v_h(P_j) \cdot \int_{\partial K_j^*} p_h n \, ds, \quad v_h \in \mathbf{X}_h, p_h \in M_h,$$

$$(f, \Gamma_h v_h) = \sum_{j=1}^{N} v_h(P_j) \cdot \int_{K_j^*} f \, dx, \quad v_h \in \mathbf{X}_h,$$

where n is the unit normal outward to ∂K_j^*.

The conforming finite volume approximation for equations (1–3) is: Find $(u_h, p_h) \in (\mathbf{X}_h, M_h)$

$$C_h(u_h, p_h; v_h, q_h) + b(u_h; u_h, \Gamma_h v_h) = (f, \Gamma_h v_h), \quad (v_h, q_h) \in (\mathbf{X}_h, M_h), \tag{13}$$

where

$$C_h(u_h, p_h; v_h, q_h) = \nu A(u_h, v_h) - D(v_h, p_h) + d(u_h, p_h) + G_h(p_h, q_h),$$

and the counterpart in the nonconforming case is

$$C_h(u_h, p_h; v_h, q_h) + b_h(u_h; u_h, \Gamma_h v_h) = (f, \Gamma_h v_h), \tag{14}$$

where

$$C_h(u_h, p_h; v_h, q_h) = \nu A(u_h, v_h) - D(v_h, p_h) + d_h(u_h, p_h) + G_h(p_h, q_h).$$

4   Numerical Experiments

We present numerical results to show the convergence performance of the stabilized finite element and finite volume methods presented. In all experiments here, the viscosity is $\nu = 0.1$, and the Navier-Stokes equations are considered on $\Omega = [0,1] \times [0,1]$ with a body force $\boldsymbol{f}(\boldsymbol{x})$ such that the true solution is

$$p(\boldsymbol{x}) = 10(2x_1 - 1)(2x_2 - 1), \quad \boldsymbol{u}(\boldsymbol{x}) = (u_1(\boldsymbol{x}), u_2(\boldsymbol{x})),$$
$$u_1(\boldsymbol{x}) = 10x_1^2(x_1 - 1)^2 x_2(x_2 - 1)(2x_2 - 1),$$
$$u_2(\boldsymbol{x}) = -10x_1(x_1 - 1)(2x_1 - 1)x_2^2(x_2 - 1)^2.$$

The Newton iteration is terminated when the two-step difference is less than $1.0E - 5$. As the numerical results show in Table 1-4 and Fig. 2, the convergence

Table 1. The rate of the finite element method using the $P_1 - P_1$ pair

$\frac{1}{h}$	$\frac{\|u-u_h\|_0}{\|u\|_0}$	$\frac{\|u-u_h\|_1}{\|u\|_1}$	$\frac{\|p-p_h\|_0}{\|p\|_0}$		$\|u\|_0$ - rate	$\|u\|_1$ - rate	$\|p\|_0$ - rate
8	0.500759	0.915625	0.054460	/	/	/	
12	0.219490	0.506576	0.024897	2.0343	1.4599	1.9304	
16	0.122173	0.336016	0.014483	2.0365	1.4270	1.8834	
24	0.053584	0.190981	0.006915	2.0327	1.3934	1.8231	
32	0.029916	0.129766	0.004160	2.0260	1.3433	1.7664	
36	0.023577	0.111250	0.003390	2.0219	1.3071	1.7383	

Table 2. The rate of the finite volume method using the $P_1 - P_1$ pair

$\frac{1}{h}$	$\frac{\|u-u_h\|_0}{\|u\|_0}$	$\frac{\|u-u_h\|_1}{\|u\|_1}$	$\frac{\|p-p_h\|_0}{\|p\|_0}$		$\|u\|_0$ - rate	$\|u\|_1$ - rate	$\|p\|_0$ - rate
8	1.10078	1.67749	0.0813157	/	/	/	
12	0.478051	0.913630	0.0396967	2.0570	1.4986	1.7685	
16	0.265138	0.591110	0.0239170	2.0490	1.5136	1.7612	
24	0.116069	0.322773	0.0117717	2.0373	1.4922	1.7483	
32	0.0647919	0.212867	0.00715772	2.0266	1.4470	1.7294	
36	0.0510644	0.180202	0.00584909	2.0215	1.4144	1.7142	

Table 3. The rate of the finite element method using the $NCP_1 - P1$ pair

$\frac{1}{h}$	$\frac{\|u-u_h\|_0}{\|u\|_0}$	$\frac{\|u-u_h\|_1}{\|u\|_1}$	$\frac{\|p-p_h\|_0}{\|p\|_0}$		$\|u\|_0$ - rate	$\|u\|_1$ - rate	$\|p\|_0$ - rate
8	7.42961	17.2021	0.128198	/	/	/	
12	3.86647	12.4441	0.074954	1.6108	0.7986	1.3237	
16	2.32746	9.67349	0.048659	1.7643	0.8755	1.5018	
24	1.09515	6.64813	0.0253345	1.8593	0.9250	1.6097	
32	0.630693	5.04910	0.0156162	1.9182	0.9564	1.6819	
36	0.501812	4.50477	0.0127625	1.9408	0.9685	1.7133	

Table 4. The rate of the finite volume method using the $NCP_1 - P1$ pair

$\frac{1}{h}$	$\frac{\|u-u_h\|_0}{\|u\|_0}$	$\frac{\|u-u_h\|_1}{\|u\|_1}$	$\frac{\|p-p_h\|_0}{\|p\|_0}$	$\|u\|_0$ - rate	$\|u\|_1$ - rate	$\|p\|_0$ - rate
8	1.1861	1.77506	0.03607	/	/	/
12	0.510523	0.967564	0.0180991	2.0791	1.4966	1.7008
16	0.281497	0.627789	0.0109325	2.0693	1.5037	1.7524
24	0.122104	0.343784	0.00532302	2.0600	1.4852	1.7750
32	0.0676932	0.226366	0.00319048	2.0505	1.4525	1.7793
36	0.0532040	0.191321	0.00258863	2.0449	1.4281	1.7748

rates of order $O(h^2)$ and $O(h)$ for velocity in the L^2- and H^1-norm are obtained, and the convergence rate for pressure in the L^2-norm is close to an order of $O(h^{1.7})$. The numerical experiments indicate that the local Gauss integration method is simple and efficient in the stabilization.

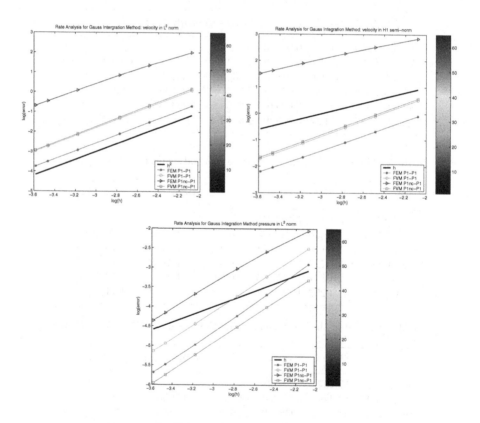

Fig. 2. The rate analysis for the velocity and pressure

References

1. Bochev, P.B., Dohrmann, C.R., Gunzburger, M.D.: Stabilization of low-order mixed finite elements for the Stokes equations. SIAM J. Numer. Anal. 44, 82–101 (2006)
2. Chen, Z.: Finite Element Methods and Their Applications. Springer, Heidelberg (2005)
3. Ciarlet, P.G.: The Finite Element Method for Elliptic Problems. North-Holland, Amsterdam (1978)
4. Li, J., He, Y., Chen, Z.: A new stabilized finite element method for the transient Navier-Stokes equations. Comput. Methods Appl. Mech. Engrg. 197, 22–35 (2007)
5. Girault, V., Raviart, P.A.: Finite Element Method for Navier-Stokes Equations: Theory and Algorithms. Springer, Heidelberg (1987)
6. Temam, R.: Navier-Stokes Equation, Theory and Numerical Analysis, 3rd edn. North-Holland, Amsterdam (1983)
7. He, G., He, Y., Chen, Z.: A penalty finite volume method for the transient Navier-Stokes equations. Applied Numer. Math. 58, 1583–1613 (2008)
8. Li, J., Chen, Z.: A new local stabilized nonconforming finite element method for the Stokes equations. Computing 82, 157–170 (2008)
9. Li, R.: Generalized difference methods for a nonlinear Dirichlet problem. SIAM J. Numer. Anal. 24, 77–88 (1987)
10. Zhu, L., Li, J., Chen, Z.: A new local stabilized nonconforming finite element method for the stationary Navier-Stokes equations (submitted for publication)

Performance Combinative Evaluation of Typical Virtual Machine Monitors*

Jianhua Che, Qinming He, Kejiang Ye, and Dawei Huang

College of Computer Science and Technology, Zhejiang University,
Hangzhou 310027, China
{chejianhua,hqm,yekejiang,davidhuang}@zju.edu.cn

Abstract. As one of pivotal components, the efficiency of virtual machine monitor(VMM) will largely impact the performance of a virtualization system. Therefore, evaluating the performance of VMMs adopting different virtualization technologies becomes more and more important. This paper selects three typical open source VMMs(i.e. OpenVZ, Xen and KVM) as the delegates of operating system-level virtualization, para-virtualization and full-virtualization to evaluate their performance with a combinative method that measures their macro-performance and micro-performance as a black box and analyzes their performance characteristic as a white box. By correlating the analysis results of two-granularity performance data, some potential performance bottlenecks come out.

Keywords: Virtualization; Virtual Machine; Virtual Machine Monitor; Performance Evaluation.

1 Introduction

Virtual machine(VM) has gained broad applications in high performance computing (HPC) [5] and server consolidation[3] for its numerous benefits. In a virtualization system, resource virtualization of underlying hardware and concurrent execution of virtual machines are in the charge of virtual machine monitor(VMM) or hypervisor[2]. By creating the same view of underlying hardware and platform APIs from different vendors, virtual machine monitor enables virtual machines to run on any available computer. However, virtual machine monitor also complicates the implementation of traditional computer architectures and depresses the performance of some specific operations, so it's significant to assess the performance of various virtual machine monitors.

This paper evaluates the effectiveness of three typical virtual machine monitors available for x86 platform-OpenVZ[6], Xen[4] and KVM[1], representing three popular virtualization technologies, i.e. *operating system-level virtualization, para-virtualization* and *full-virtualization*. Specifically, our contributions are listed as follows: First, we measure and analyze their performance characteristics of virtualized processor, virtualized memory, virtualized disk and java

---

* Research was supported by the State Key Development Program for Basic Research of China("973 project", No.2007CB310900).

W. Zhang et al. (Eds.): HPCA 2009, LNCS 5938, pp. 96–101, 2010.

server, and provide a quantitative and qualitative comparison of three virtual machine monitors. Second, we propose a combinative evaluation method that measures them as a black box to obtain their macro-performance and micro-performance and analyzes them as a white box to observe their performance characteristics. Through correlating two kind of analysis results, some potential performance bottlenecks are discovered. This combinative method presents a powerful artifice to identify the performance characteristics and flaws of those more and more intricate computer systems.

2   Virtual Machine Monitor

2.1   OpenVZ

OpenVZ[6] is an operating system container that requires the same kernels of host and guest operating systems. It includes a custom kernel and several user-level tools. The custom kernel is a modified Linux kernel with virtualization, isolation, checkpoint and resource management. The resource manager comprises three components: fair CPU scheduler, user beancounters and two-level disk quota. OpenVZ implements a two-level CPU scheduler that the OpenVZ scheduler see to the CPU time slice's assignment based on each container's CPU unit value, and the Linux scheduler decides the process to execute in this container. OpenVZ controls container operations and system resources with about 20 parameters in user beancounters.

2.2   Xen

Xen[4] is a para-virtualized hypervisor that needs kernel modifications of host and guest operating systems, but no change to application binary interface(ABI) so that existing applications can run without any modification. Guest domains can manage hardware page table with read-only privilege, but update operation should be validated by Xen. Regarding system calls, Xen allows guest domains to register fast handlers directly accessed by physical processor bypassing ring 0. From its 2.0 version, Domain0 hosts most unmodified Linux device drivers and controls resource allocation policies and guest domain management. To achieve I/O's virtualization, Xen designs a shared memory and asynchronous buffer-descriptor ring model and two communication mechanisms: synchronous call and asynchronous event.

2.3   KVM

KVM(Kernel-based Virtual Machine)[1] is a virtual machine monitor based on full-virtualization and hardware-assisted virtualization such as Intel VT or AMD-SVM. KVM implements virtualization by augmenting traditional *kernel* and *user* mode of Linux with a new process mode named *guest*. Guest mode has no privilege to access the I/O devices. KVM consists of two components: *kernel module* and *user-space*. Kernel module manages the virtualization of memory and other hardware through a character device */dev/kvm* and *kill* command. With */dev/kvm*, each virtual machine may have its own address space. A set of shadow page tables are maintained for translating guest address to host address. User-space takes charge the I/O's virtualization with a lightly modified QEMU.

3   Performance Measure and Analysis

To measure and analyze the performance of OpenVZ, Xen and KVM, a series of experiments have been conducted with SPECCPU 2006, RAMSPEED 3.4.4, Bonnie++ 1.03, NetIO126, and SPECJBB 2005. All experiments were run on Dell OPTIPLEX 755 with a 2.33GHz E6550 Intel Core2 DUO processor, 2GB DDRII 667 RAM, Seagate 250GB 7200 RPM SATA II disk. We adopted Ubuntu Linux 8.10 AMD64 with kernel 2.7.12 as host and guest operating system, and OpenVZ in patched kernel 2.7.12, Xen 3.3 and KVM-72 as virtual machine monitor. The memory allocated for each virtual machine was set to 1 GB.

3.1   Macro-performance Measure

The Macro-Performance mainly means the overall performance of a subsystem or whole system. We will measure the virtualization overhead of processor subsystem, file subsystem and java server in three virtual machine monitors.

Processor Virtualization. KVM displays a low score regardless of CINT2006 or CFP2006 especially on 410.bwaves benchmark(about 50% degradation), while OpenVZ and Xen are almost accordant to native environment as figure 1 and figure 2. 410.bwaves numerically simulates blast waves in three dimensions, which presumes amount of data exchange. Therefore, KVM spends many time to switch among *guest*, *kernel* and *user* when updating the nonlinear damped periodic system's matrix data. Although KVM still need to improve its efficiency for computing-intensive workloads, processor virtualization is not already the performance bottleneck of virtualization systems.

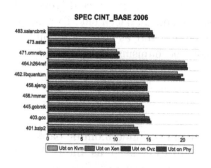

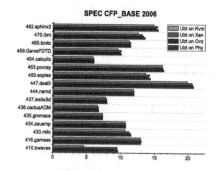

Fig. 1. The result of CINT2006 in four environments

Fig. 2. The result of CFP2006 in four environments

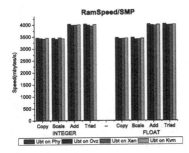

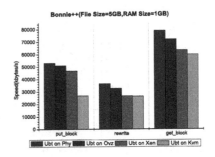

Fig. 3. The speed of memory access in RAMSMP

Fig. 4. The bandwidth of three disk I/O operations in Bonnie++

Memory Virtualization. The speed in four environments discloses a basic harmony on four memory access operations regardless of integer or float point number as figure 3. The result of four integer operations is almost the same as four float operations, but the speeds of *Copy* and *Scale* are lower than *Add* and *Triad*, which mainly because *copy* and *scale* involve more data moving. Generally, the presence of virtualization layer doesn't cumber the performance of memory access operations, especially their memory access speed or bandwidth.

Disk Virtualization. The bandwidth of three disk I/O operations in KVM is lowest as figure 4, mainly for KVM implements its virtualized disk I/O based on QEMU. Xen batches guest domains' I/O requests and accesses the physical device with relative driver. After being moved into physical memory with DMA, the I/O data will be transferred to guest domains by memory page flipping. OpenVZ's second level scheduler, i.e. the Jens Axboe's CFQ I/O scheduler allots all available I/O bandwidth according to each container's I/O priority, so it holds the best block *read* and *write* performance when only hosting one container.

Java Server. As for their capabilities of sustaining a virtual machine to act as java server, Xen wins the highest score when the number of warehouses is under 4 as figure 5. This because Xen deals with various java transactions using para-virtualization. But OpenVZ keeps a higher score than Xen when the number of warehouse exceeds 3, perhaps thanks to OpenVZ's nicer ability to support more concurrent processes. KVM exposes the worst score owing to its emulating manner to deal with java transactions. However, all their performance fall behind native environment, clarifying the need of further improvement on processing efficiency of these java transactions.

3.2 Micro-performance Measure

The Micro-Performance mainly means the fine performance of some specific operations or instructions. We will measure the virtualization overhead of some operations like *system call* and *context switch* in three virtual machine monitors.

System Operations Virtualization. As implementing common system operations with the host's APIs, OpenVZ holds a similar latency as native

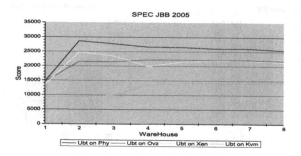

Fig. 5. The result of SPECjbb2005 test

environment except for process fork. KVM shows a latency close to native environment and better than OpenVZ and Xen in several system calls and signal install, but longer delay than OpenVZ and Xen in process create. As process fork involves memory allocation and hardware page table update, KVM has to wait for available address space and shadow page table update. It is a long trip to remap guest address to host address with shadow page table. Xen discards shadow page table and allows guest domain itself to register a local page table and some common signal or exception handlers with MMU. This enables guest domains to batch hardware page table updates with a single hypercall and less TLB flushing times.

Table 1. System operations time and context switch latency in μs

	Ubt	Ovz	Xen	KVM	Context Switch	Ubt	Ovz	Xen	KVM
syscall	0.1164	0.1165	0.5699	0.1179	2p0k	1.01	1.75	3.91	4.87
read	0.2237	0.2848	0.9219	0.2268	2p16k	1.67	2.29	4.7	6.39
write	0.2151	0.2722	0.8714	0.2162	2p64k	1.41	1.49	4.37	5.46
stat	0.9223	1.2904	1.835	0.9461	4p0k	1.29	1.78	4.43	5.55
fstat	0.2275	0.2304	0.8257	0.2314	4p16k	1.98	2.44	5.16	6.44
open/close	1.839	2.3595	4.1215	1.8672	4p64k	1.57	1.97	4.76	6.04
sigl insl	0.2404	0.2434	0.789	0.2487	8p0k	3.81	2.04	5.41	5.87
sigl hndl	1.5389	1.6534	3.6856	6.872	8p16k	2.28	2.65	6.17	6.77
pipe	4.7132	4.7898	14.959	12.522	8p64k	1.89	2.17	5.76	6.97
fork+exit	134.318	188.212	473.82	849	16p16k	2.38	2.83	6.4	7.95
fork+exec	490.727	481.364	1279	2203.3	16p64k	1.93	2.29	5.88	7.59
fork+sh	1065	1770.3	2731	4877	64p64k	4.47	8.26	8.58	15.11

Context Switch. OpenVZ switches a container's processor context by resorting to the host kernel, so it owns a proximal latency. Xen execute a hypercall at least to change the page table base, which incurs some extra overhead. As KVM need to remap the shadow page table for context switch, it cost the most time.

3.3 Correlation Analysis

Performance bottleneck usually means all key factors that block multiple facets of computer systems. Therefore, one needs to correlate all analysis results to identify the performance lagging factors. From the macro-performance data, we can find that the overhead of processor virtualization in relatively mature virtual machine monitors is minimal, but disk I/O appears a large performance lag. Hence, disk I/O should be a performance bottleneck of virtualization systems. From the micro-performance data, we can find that the latencies of process create and context switch in virtualized environment fall behind native environment with a huge degree, which implies two main factors that baffle the performance of virtualization systems. Therefore, we may preliminarily determine hardware page table update, interrupt request and I/O are three main performance bottlenecks for common virtualization systems. As most high-cost operations involve them, it's critical for researcher and developer to optimize the handle mechanism of hardware page table update, interrupt request and I/O. In addition, correlating analysis can be conducted in a finer granularity such as profiling the performance event log. With some profiling tools, e.g. OProfile, Xenoprof, *top* or *xentop* command, more details of the virtualization overhead may be discovered.

4   Conclusion and Future Work

Performance evaluation on virtual machine monitors plays an important role in improving their design and implementation. We make a quantitative and qualitative evaluation on three typical open source virtual machine monitors: OpenVZ, Xen and KVM, and present a combinative method to identify three potential performance bottlenecks. In the future, we will carry on correlative analysis and combinative evaluation on them with several profiling tools.

References

1. Kivity, A., Kamay, Y., Laor, D., Lublin, U., Liguori, A.: kvm: the Linux Virtual Machine Monitor. In: Linux Symposium, pp. 225–230 (2007)
2. Rosenblum, M., Garfinkel, T.: Virtual Machine Monitors: Current Technology and Future Trends. Computer, 39–47 (2005)
3. Apparao, P., Iyer, R., Zhang, X., Newell, D., Adelmeyer, T.: Characterization & analysis of a server consolidation benchmark. In: Proceedings of the 4th ACM SIGPLAN/SIGOPS International Conference on Virtual Execution Environments(VEE), pp. 21–30. ACM, New York (2008)
4. Barham, P., Dragovic, B., Fraser, K., Hand, S., Harris, T., Ho, A., Neugebauer, R., Pratt, I., Warfield, A.: Xen and the art of virtualization. ACM SIGOPS Operating Systems Review 37(5), 164–177 (2003)
5. Huang, W., Abali, B., Panda, D.: A case for high performance computing with virtual machines. In: Proceedings of the 20th annual international conference on Supercomputing, pp. 125–134. ACM Press, New York (2006)
6. Wiki. Welcome to OpenVZ Wiki, http://wiki.openvz.org/Main_Page

Lunar Crater Rims Detection from Chang's Orbiter Data Based on a Grid Environment

Shengbo Chen, Xuqing Zhang, and Shengye Jin

College of Geo-exploration Science and Technology, Jilin University,
Changchun 130026, China

Abstract. The surface of the moon is scarred with millions of lunar crater, which are the remains of collisions between an asteroid, comet, or meteorite and the moon with different sizes and shapes. With the launch of Chang's orbiter, it is available to detect the lunar crater at a high resolution. However, the Chang's orbiter image is combined by different path/orbit images. In this study, a batch processing scheme to detect lunar crater rims from each path image is presented under a grid environment. SGE (Sun Grid Engine) and OpenPBS (Open Portable Batch System) are connected by Globus and MPICH-G2 as Linux PC Cluster respectively. And the Globus GridFTP is used for parallel transfer of different rows of Chang's orbiter images by MPICH-G2 model. The detection algorithms on each node are executed respectively after the parallel transfer. Thus, the lunar crater rims for the experimental area are generated effectively.

1 Introduction

Lunar craters are craters on the Earth's Moon. The Moon's surface is saturated with craters, almost all of which were formed by impacts. They are the remains of collisions between an asteroid, comet, or meteorite and the Moon. Because of the Moon's lack of liquid water, and atmosphere, or tectonic plates, there is little erosion. These craters remain unchanged until another new impact changes it. They range in size up to many hundreds of kilometers, but the most enormous craters have been flooded by lava, and only parts of the outline are visible. When the crater was formed, the materials in surrounding area are splashed out of the ground. Craters typically will have raised rim, consisting of materials ejected but landing very close by crater wall, the downward-sloping portion of the crater. The rims of lunar craters are typically lighter in shade than older materials due to exposure to solar radiation for a lesser time [1].

The Chang's 1 orbiter, launched on 24 October 2007 at 10:05 UT, is the first of a planned series of Chinese missions to the moon. The primary science objectives are to obtain three-dimensional stereo images of the lunar surface, analyze the distribution and abundance of elements on the surface, survey the thickness of lunar soil, and to evaluate helium-3 resources and other characteristics, and to explore the environment between the Moon and Earth. The science payload comprises a stereo camera system to map the lunar surface in visible wavelengths. The camera operates by taking nadir (0 degrees), forward (+17 degrees), and backward (-17 degrees) images of the Moon and combining the overlapping frames to produce stereo images. The CCD array

W. Zhang et al. (Eds.): HPCA 2009, LNCS 5938, pp. 102–107, 2010.

consists of three parallel rows, one each for the nadir, forward, and backward views. Image spatial resolution is about 120 m and the swath width is 60 km [2].

The use of clusters and Grids for high-performance applications has become widespread lately. High-performance computing could afford the significantly expensive supercomputers of the time. A Grid based image processing system was designed and implemented with respect to the technology of middleware. And the results confirm the feasibility of the application of computational Grids to digital image processing [3] [4]. Different architectures have been presented for application on image processing [5] [6]. A distributed algorithm, able to run in a Grid system, was presented for change detection from MODIS spectral bands [7]. A distributed Grid computation-based platform and corresponding middleware for Grid computation was developed and a constrained power spectrum equalization algorithm and effective block processing measures were applied during the processing [8].

It is available to detect the lunar craters in Chang's orbiter images at spatial resolution of about 120 m. However, the Chang's orbiter image is combined by different path/orbit images. The detection of lunar craters on the whole image is so great challenged for the whole moon due to these mass data. In this study, a batch processing scheme is presented to detect lunar crater rims from each path image under a grid environment.

2   Grid Architecture

A computational Grid environment is different from standard parallel computing environments. It may incorporate nodes with different processor types, memory sizes, and so forth, and have highly heterogeneous and unbalanced communication network, comprising a mix of different intra-machine networks and a variety of Internet connections whose bandwidth and latency characteristics may vary greatly in time and space.

Such a Grid is comprised of application layer, collective layer, resource layer, and fabric layer (Figure 1). The Grid fabric layer provides the resources to which shared access is mediated by Grid protocols. The Globus Toolkit has been designed to use existing fabric components, including vendor-supplied protocols and interfaces. GRAM (Globus resource allocation manager) protocols defined by Globus Toolkit are used to access SGE (Sun Grid Engine), OpenPBS (Open Portable Batch System), and LSF (Load Sharing Facility). The connectivity layer defines core communication and authentication protocols required for Grid-specific network transactions. Communication protocols enable the exchange of data between Fabric layer resources. The resource layer builds on connectivity layer communication and authentication protocols to define protocols for the secure negotiation, initiation, monitoring, control, accounting, and payment of sharing operations on individual resources. Resource layer implementations of these protocols call fabric layer functions to access and control local resources. Collective layer build on the narrow resource and connectivity layer neck in the protocol hourglass, so they can implement a wide variety of sharing behaviors without placing new requirements on the resources being shared. Meta-scheduler CSF4 (Community Scheduler Framework 4) is applied in the collective layer. Applications are constructed in terms of, and by calling upon, services defined at any layer. At each layer, well-defined protocols provide access to some useful service: resource management, data access, resource discovery, and so forth. Batch processing of rims detection is implemented in the application layer.

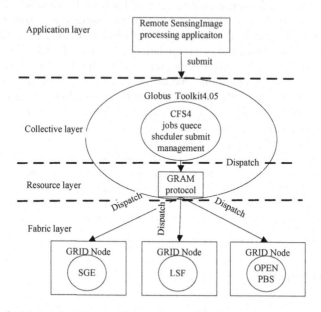

Fig. 1. A layered architecture for running application on a Grid environment

The deployment of each node as follows:

Hardware deployment: CPU 2.8GBMHz, RAM 512MB;
Network environment: 100M Intranet;
Operating System: Redhat linux 9.0.
Where SGE, LSF, OpenPBS are made up of two PC.

3   MPICH-G2 Programming Model

3.1   MPICH-G2

Computational Grids enable the compiling and coordinated use of geographically distributed resources for such purposes as large-scale computation, distributed data analysis, and remote visualization. In this study, we advocate the use of a well-known low-level parallel programming model, the Message Passing Interface (MPI), as a basis for Grid programming. MPICH-G2, a complete implementation of the MPI-1 standard that uses services provided by the Globus Toolkit, extends the popular Argonne MPICH implementation of MPI for Grid execution. MPICH-G2 hides heterogeneity by using Globus Toolkit services for such purposes as authentication, authorization, executable staging, process creation, process monitoring, process control, communication, redirection of standard input and output, and remote file access.

As a result a user can run MPI programs across multiple computers at different sites using the same commands that would be used on a parallel computer. MPICH-G2 enables the use of several different MPI features for user management of heterogeneity [9].

3.2 GridFTP

GridFTP has been used as a protocol to effectively transfer a large volume of data in Grid computing. GridFTP supports a feature called parallel data transfer that improves throughput by establishing multiple TCP connections in parallel and automatic negotiation of TCP socket buffer size. These features of GridFTP are realized by a new tranfer mode called extended block mode. GridFTP server and client software conforming to GridFTP is including in the Globus Toolkit, which is the standard middleware for Grid computing [10]. The protocol of GridFTP is implemented by the libraries, globus-ftp-control-library and globus-ftp-client-library. As an example, the parallelism is set to 4 for the transfer of every 4 orbital images from the client to the control.

3.3 Programming Model

Conventional MPI programs across multiple parallel computers within the same machine room can be run by using MPICH-G2, where MPICH-G2 is used primarily to manage startup and to achieve efficient communication via use of different low-level communication methods. Batch processing of rims detection is implemented under MPICH-G2 programming model.

Under the MPICH-G2 programming model, after the program in the client is submitted, the background begins to run with the help of Globusrun. Every orbital image will be transferred to Network File System (NFS) from the client. Every node will also run the program by Dynamically-Updated Request Online Collocator (DUROC), and the subprocess of every node will be managed by components of GRAM called by DUROC. The parameters are transferred to every process from the control process, and the images will be manipulated by the executable program of OpenCV (Open Computer Vision Library) and the transferred parameters called by the subprocess in every node. The results are returned to the client by the GridFTP after the images are processed.

4 Experiment Results

The whole moon is covered by every orbital image of Chang's orbiter with 120 m of spatial resolution. In order to detect the crater rims of the moon, every orbital image is batch-processed to be made up an image for the whole moon. Under such a Grid environment, the open computer vision libraries from OpenCV are used to compile the program for the rim detection. And every orbital image is manipulated in a process of every node. The returned results for every orbit are combined into the whole rims of the lunar crater.

As an example, every orbital image of Chang's Orbiter is transferred to NFS of every cluster from the client by GridFTP. These images are batch-processed by different Grid nodes. The image transfer and image processing are executed by different modules respectively. The I/O efficiency of MPICH-G2 is thus improved by the techniques. The detected rims from Chang's Orbiter image (6264*3955 pixels) (right) and its original image (left) are illustrated as Figure 2. The average consumed time for every node is 2.88s, and the longest time is just 3.40s. However, the average consumed time is 14.73s for a serial computing environment. Obviously, the computing efficiency is improving greatly under such a Grid environment. Most of the diameter sizes of the craters from the first open images of Chang's Orbiter are distributed in the size ranges of 300-500km.

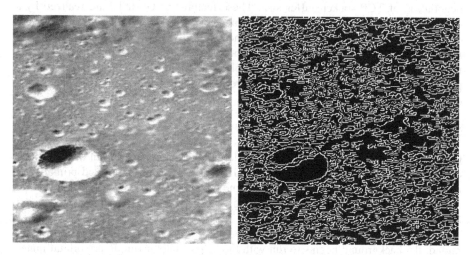

Fig. 4. The subset of Chang's Orbiter (6264*3955 pixels) and the detected rims of lunar craters

5 Conclusions

The Moon's surface is saturated with craters, almost all of which were formed by impacts. The rims of lunar craters are typically lighter in shade than older materials due to exposure to solar radiation for a lesser time. With the launch of Chang's Orbiter, it is available to detect these rims of lunar crater from the CCD images with the resolution of 120m. However, it will be a challenge to batch-process these mass data timely and efficiently.

In order to detect the rims of lunar craters, every orbital image is processed respectively by different nodes in a Grid environment based on MPICH-G2 and GridFTP techniques. Thus, the crater rims for the whole moon are detected by batch-processing every orbital image of Chang's Orbiter. From the distribution of lunar crater in the first open image of Chang's Orbiter, it is robust to batch process pieces of data cut from the mass data by different process in a Grid environment. And the efficiency can be improved greatly by the presented method.

References

1. Moore, H.J., Boyce, J.M., Schaber, G.G., Scott, D.H.: Lunar Remote Sensing and Measurements. United States Government Printing Office, Wahington (1980)
2. Huixian, S.: Scientific Objectives and Payloads of Chang'E-1 Lunar Satellite. J. Earth Syst. Sci. 114, 789–794 (2005)
3. Shen, Z., Luo, J., Zhou, C., et al.: System Design and Implementation of Digital-image Processing Using Computational Grids. Computers & Geosciences 31, 619–630 (2005)
4. Shen, Z., Luo, J., Huang, G., et al.: Distributed Computing Model for Processing Remotely Sensed Images Based on grid Computing. Information Sciences 177, 504–518 (2007)
5. Shen, Z., Luo, J., Zhou, C., et al.: Architecture Design of Grid GIS and its Applications on Image Processing Based on LAN. Information Sciences 166, 1–17 (2004)
6. Muresan, O., Pop, F., Gorgan, D., Cristea, V.: Satellite Image Processing Applications in MedioGrid. In: IEEE Computer Society-Fifth International Symposium on Parallel and Distributed Computing, ISPDC 2006 (2006)
7. Pop, F., Gruia, C., Cristea, V.: Distributed Algorithm for Change Detection in Satellite Images for Grid Environments. In: IEEE Computer Society-Sixth International Symposium on Parallel and Distributed Computing, ISPDC 2007 (2007)
8. Li, S., Zhu, C., Ge, P.: Remote Sensing Image Deblurring Based on Grid Computation. J. China Univ. of Mining & Tech. 6, 409–412 (2006)
9. Roy, A., Foster, I., Gropp, W., Karonis, N., Sander, V., Toonen, B.: MPICH-GQ: Quality-of-service for Message Passing Programs. In: Processings of Supercomputing 2000. IEEE Computer Society Press, Los Alamitos (2000)
10. Ito, T., Ohsaki, H., Imase, M.: GridFTP-APT: Automatic Parallelism Tuning Mechanism for GridFTP in Long-fat Networks. IEICE Trans. Commun. E91-B, 3925–3936 (2008)

Study on Parallel System Performance Modeling Based on TCPN

Bin Cheng[1,2], Xingang Wang[1,3], Ying Li[1], and Weiqin Tong[1]

[1] School of Computer Engineering and Science, Shanghai University,
Shanghai 200072, China
[2] College of Mathematics, Physics and Information Engineering,
Zhejiang Normal University, Zhejiang Jinhua 321000, China
[3] College of Information Engineering, Zhejiang University of Technology,
Hangzhou 310014, China
cb@shu.edu.cn, wxg@zjut.edu.cn,
bxyzly@163.com, wqtong@mail.shu.edu.cn

Abstract. Hierarchical TCPN model proposed in this paper describes the parallel program and the resources respectively to bring less effect to modify the program structure because of running environment changes. Performance analysis and validation of program correctness can be done based on this model.

1 Introduction

Although the skills in developing parallel algorithms and programs are growing with the use of parallel and massively parallel hardware, there are no general development rules or guidelines to get maximum performance from the hardware. It is clear at least today, there is a great gap between the peak performance and performance attainable by a practical application [1,4]. The performance of parallel systems (a parallel program executing on parallel hardware) is not only determined by the performance of the hardware itself but also by the structure of the parallel program and the assignment of program parts to resources [3].

In this paper we put forward a formal method to support for functional and temporal specification which can specify various aspects of parallel system like software, such as control flow, data flow, communication, synchronization and so on, and hardware, such as processors, memory, communication media etc. It is simple but expressive graphical means. This novel method can develop parallel software by performance engineering during the whole parallel development cycle.[1] It means the performance analysis begins at the early design phases and goes on until the completion of the application, not work during or after the running procedure like some test tools now. Otherwise, it happens often that a correct program is a program with lower performance and leads to the huge expenses to modify program.

---

[1] This work is supported in part by Shanghai Leading Academic Discipline Project, Project Number: J50103.

W. Zhang et al. (Eds.): HPCA 2009, LNCS 5938, pp. 108–113, 2010.
© Springer-Verlag Berlin Heidelberg 2010

2 Formal Model of Parallel System Based on TCPN

Formal methods are frequently applied in industries to build mission-critical systems where insufficient verification can cause human injury or large-scale financial loss. The topic of using the formal method to identify the correctness verification and performance analysis of the parallel program gains a lot of attention [5,6]. Through analyzing and comparison, the parallel system is modeled based on Timed Coloured Petri Net (TCPN) in this paper, which is expanded based on the basic Petri net.

2.1 Time Model of Parallel Program

The time factor of TCPN is the key factor to analyze the performance of parallel program. The execution time of parallel program (ET) is the time segment from the first task execution of the program to the last. Aim at the formal modeling of parallel program based on distributed memory architecture, the paper divides ET into 4 components. They are calculation time Tcal, communication time Tcom, synchronization time Tsyn and I/O access time TIO, that is

$$ET= T_{cal}+T_{com}+T_{syn}+T_{IO} \tag{1}$$

The equality (1) can represent the holding time of different kind of action visually, such as calculation, communication, synchronization and I/O access.

The parallel program (PPr) is composed of n tasks. Each task E_i is implemented with m phases, i.e. $E_i=< E_{p1}, E_{p2}, ..., E_{pm} >$. Each E_{pj} is a 4-tuple, $E_{pj}=<P_{id}, P_{type}, P_{interval}, P_{re}>$. P_{id} is the order number of phase in the task. P_{type} is the type of phase, such as calculation, communication, synchronization, I/O access. $P_{interval}$ is the execution period of phase. P_{re} is the dependent relationship between the phases, such as communication and synchronization. The whole execution process of parallel program is a ordered sequences PPr=<$E_1,E_2, ...,E_n$>. $E_1.E_{p1}$ is the first phase to execute and $En.E_{pm}$ is the last. All the phases of one same task are sequential. So PPr is the critical path of the parallel program execution. And each component of equality (1) can be defined as

$$T_x = \sum_{x=E_i.E_{pj}.P_{type}} E_i.E_{pj}.P_{interval} \quad (i=1, 2, ..., n; j=1, 2, ..., m) \tag{2}$$

Equality (2) means each component of equality (1) is the sum of execution time of corresponding action in the critical path.

2.2 PRM Model Based on TCPN

It's figured that the performance of parallel systems is not only determined by the performance of the hardware itself but also by the structure of the parallel program and the assignment of program parts to resources in this paper. It means the performance measures of interest are the run time of the parallel program and the degree of hardware utilization. With PRM[1] a modeling technique has been given considering hardware resources, parallel program and mapping between them as the performance influencing factors for the prediction of performance of parallel computations running on parallel hardware. The separation of the three specification elements should enable to vary each of them, as far as possible, independently from the other specifications. This approach can realize various mapping between the parallel program and the resource with minimal additional effort and compare the performance of program running on different resource.

Definition 1 S={P-TCPN, R-TCPN, M} is the model of parallel systems. **P-TCPN** is the model of parallel program based on TCPN. **R-TCPN** is the model of resource based on TCPN. And M is the mapping between **P-TCPN** and **R-TCPN**.

Definition 2 P-TCPN = $(P_p, T_p, A_p, C, \Phi, FT)$ satisfying the following requirements:

(1) P_p is a finite set of places. A place contains zero or more tokens. A token has 3 attributes $<p, v, tm>$ to denote a token in place p with value v and time tm. v is the colour of the token and tm is the time that token arrives at the p. P_{start} and P_{end} are $E_1.E_{p1}$ and $En.E_{pm}$ denote the start place and the end place of P-TCPN respectively.

(2) T_p is a finite set of transitions. $P_p \cap T_p = \varnothing$.

(3) A_p is a set of flow relations, $A_p \subseteq (P_p \times T_p) \cup (T_p \times P_p)$. It shows the track of tokens flowing in the net.

(4) C is a colour function. Each $p_i \in P_p$ has a set of colours attached to it, i.e. $v \in C(p_i)$.

(5) Φ is the set of functionalities of T_p. $\forall t_i \in T_p$ finishes partial function of the program, which is $\Phi(t_i)$.

(6) FT is the set of time functions of T_p. $FT(t_i)$ is the time delay to realize $\Phi(t_i)$ and also describes the interval that t_i occupies the related resources.

Definition 3 R-TCPN=$(\sum_r, P_r, T_r, A_r)$ satisfying the following requirements:

(1) $\sum_r$ is a finite set of resources. $\sum_r = (r_1, r_2...r_n)$.

(2) P_r is a finite set of home places for the resources $r \in \sum_r$. r is idle and available if there is a resource token in its home place. The token has 3 attributes $<p, v, tm>$ too, describing the token's home place p, the physical characteristics v and the time of resource occupied tm separately.

(3) T_r is a finite set of transitions.

(4) A_r is a set of flow relations, $A_r \subseteq (P_r \times T_r) \cup (T_r \times P_r)$. $\forall a_i \in A_r$ is the direction of resource flows and describes the interactions between resources.

Definition 4 $M \subseteq (P_r \times T_p) \cup (T_p \times P_r)$ is the mapping between **P-TCPN** and **R-TCPN**.

(1) $P_r \times T_p$ is the set of arcs leading from resource home to processes transitions. It is resource assignment.

(2) $T_p \times P_r$ is the set of arcs which is opposite to $P_r \times T_p$. It will happen only if the time of resources occupied by process is equal to the time of allowable service, or the process releases the resources after finishing the task.

2.3 Dynamic Behavior of TCPN

P-TCPN and R-TCPN specify the static structure of parallel system based on TCPN. In this section we define the behavior of P-TCPN.

(1) Enabled Transition

A transition is enabled if there are enough tokens, which are to be consumed, on each of its input places in P-TCPN and the required resources in R-TCPN can be assigned. Only the Enabled Transition can fire, i.e. finish some functions of the parallel program.

(2) Event

An event is a tuple $(t, p_{in}, p_{out}, time)$. It means the possible firing t will consume tokens from p_{in} and add the new tokens to p_{out} in P-TCPN. And $time$ is the happening time of event. $time$ is equal to the minimum of the timestamp of all tokens in p_{in}. An event is corresponding to some functions of the parallel program, i.e. it is $E_{pj} \in E_i$.

(3) State

Event happening will change the system state. The state notes the static status of the parallel system. S is the set of all possible states. And $s \in S$ is a set of tuples (p, v) which $p \in P_p$, $v \in C(p)$.

(4) Reachable State

An event may occur if it is enabled, i.e. $(t, p_{in}, p_{out}, time)$ occurs in state s and state changes into the state s'. It is $s' = s - p_{in} + p_{out}$ and s' is directly reachable from s by the occurrence of event $e=(t, p_{in}, p_{out}, time)$. It is described by $s_1 \xrightarrow{e} s_2$. So the firing sequence of the parallel system is a sequence of states and events, $s_1 \xrightarrow{e_1} s_2 \xrightarrow{e_2} s_3 \xrightarrow{e_3} \ldots \ldots$ and s_i is reachable from s_1 only if there exists a firing sequence of finite length from s_1 to s_i.

We can get a reachable graph which organizes all reachable state in a graph and answer any question of the parallel system performance based on the reachable graph. It is not discussed in this paper.

3 Example

MLFMA(multilevel fast multipole algorithm) is one of the most effective methods solving electromagnetic scattering problems from complex objects. And the parallelization of MLFMA can greatly reduce the solution time of large-scale electromagnetic scattering problems involving complicated three-dimensional objects. The basic data structure of parallel MLFMA is a distribute tree, i.e. assigning every branch of the tree to different processors. The scatterers finish the aggregation, translation and disaggregation based on the distribute tree. The bottom-to-up method is adopted to build the tree. So it is very important to build the finest level of the distributed tree. Whether the data of finest level is assigned equally or not will affect the load balancing and the parallel efficiency of the MLFMA. The data of the finest level in the distribute tree is the Geometric Data after scatterers' triangulation, which are vertices, facets and edges.

To keep the specification as clear and flexible as possible, a hierarchical model is applied throughout the parallel system specification. Fig.1 is the top model of the algorithm which is constructing the finest level of the distributed tree. It describes the information transmission among the submodels and the task execution flow. There are 3 substitution transitions in Fig.1 which are realized by relevant submodel in detail.

The place between the substitution transitions shows the information interaction and every place has a colour set. The substitution transition t_{adjust} is described in detail as Fig.2., which is the construction of finest level of the distributed tree. And Table 1 expresses the semantic of the transitions and places in Fig.2.

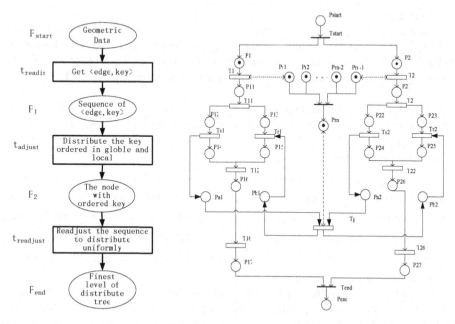

Fig. 1. Top model of the algorithm

Fig. 2. Construction of the finest level of distributed tree based on TCPN

Table 1. Semantic of the transitions and places in Fig.2

Transition	Semantic	Place	Semantic
T_1, T_2	Quick sorting key value of local node to get maximum and minimum	P_1, P_2	Entry of different processes
T_{11}, T_{21}	Beginning of the sending and receiving operation among the nodes	P_{11}, P_{21}	Beginning of process communication
$T_{si}(i=1,2)$	Sending operation of process i based on the maximun or minimum of key	$P_{12}, P_{22};$ P_{14}, P_{24}	Beginning/Ending of sending operation
$T_ri(i=1,2)$	Receiving operation of process i based on the maximun or minimum of key	$P_{13}, P_{23};$ P_{15}, P_{25}	Beginning/Ending of receiving operation
T_{12}, T_{22}	Ending of the sending and receiving operation among the nodes	P_{16}, P_{26}	Executing the equential statement of relevant process
T_g	Computing the massage from different processes and feeding back	$P_{a1}, P_{a2};$ P_{b1}, P_{b2}	Sending/Receiving buffer of process
T_{16}, T_{26}	Computing the key value and the amount of the key of each node	P_{17}, P_{27}	Global-ordering and local-ordering
		$P_{r1}....P_m$	Resources of the parallel system

Correctness verification of the model, as Fig.2., should be done first. Then build the limited reachable state graph of the model, find the critical path PPr and calculate ET and each component of ET, such as Tcal, in the path. The performance analysis will be easy now based on Amdahl's law. The detail to realize the performance analysis will be discussed in other paper.

4 Conclusions

Correctness and performance are the principal requirement of a program. The major challenges are to support the process of developing parallel software by effective performance analysis during the software development cycle now. Considering that the performance of parallel systems is not only determined by the performance of the hardware, but also by the structure of the parallel program, TCPN model proposed in this paper describes resource and parallel program respectively. Performance engineering activities based on TCPN model ranges from performance prediction in early development stages, performance analysis in the coding phase, to locate the performance bottleneck and modify it. Furthermore, based on the TCPN model, we can investigate on various levels of abstraction and analyze concerning performance, functional validity and correctness.

References

1. Ferscha, A.: Modelling Mappings of Parallel Computations onto Parallel Architectures with the PRM-Net Model. In: Girault, C., Cosnard, M. (eds.) Proc. of the IFIP WG 10.3 Working Conf. on Decentralized Systems, pp. 349–362 (1990)
2. Balbo, G., Chiola, G., Bruell, S.C., Chen, P.: An Example of Modelling and Evaluation of a Concurrent Program using Coloured Stochastic Petri Nets: Lamport's Fast Mutual Exclusion Algorithm. IEEE Transactions on Parallel and Distributed Systems 3(2), 221–240 (1992)
3. Ferscha, A., Kotsis, G.: Optimum Interconnection Topologies for the Compute-Aggregate-Broadcast Operation on a Transputer Network. In: Proceedings of the TRANSPUTER 1992 Conference, pp. 307–326. IOS Press, Amsterdam (1992)
4. Ferscha, A.: A Petri Net Approach for Performance Oriented Parallel Program Design. Journal of Parallel and Distributed Computing 15(3), 188–206 (1992)
5. Herzog, U.: Formal methods for performance evaluation. Springer Lectures on Formal Methods and Performance Analysis, 1–37 (2002)
6. Gesbert, L., Loulergue, F.: Semantics of an Exception Mechanism for Bulk Synchronous Parallel ML. In: Eighth International Conference on Parallel and Distributed Computing, Applications and Technologies, pp. 201–208 (2007)
7. Carter, J., Gardner, W.B.: A Formal CSP Framework for Message-Passing HPC Programming. In: 2006 Canadian Conference on Electrical and Computer Engineering, CCECE 2006, pp. 1466–1470 (2007)

A 3D Geological Modeling and Numerical Simulations of Near-Fault Endangered Field

Haiying Cheng[1], Huagang Shao[1], Hualin Wang[2], and Hongwei Wang[2]

[1] Department of Computer Science and Information Engineering,
Shanghai Institute of Technology, Shanghai 200235, PRC
{chenghaiying,hgshao}@sit.edu.cn
[2] Earthquake Administration of Shandong Province, Jinan 200072, PRC
david1978@126.com, hong2006@163.com

Abstract. It is very important to study the Near-fault endangered field for earthquake engineering, earthquake forecasting and reducing earthquake disaster. This paper is based on the correlative data and geology information of moderate and upwards earthquakes of Zibo City, Shandong, China. A 3D geology model of the main active fault of Zibo City (Zhangdian-Renhe Fault) is created. Numerical simulations of the near-fault disservice field have been performed, and numerical results are discussed with comparing the experiments.

Keyword: fracture; earthquake; near-fault; numerical simulation.

1 Introduction

Near-fault ground motion has been an active research field of Seismology and Earthquake Engineering in the recent ten years. In the 80th of 20 century, strong ground motion records were accumulated very much faster than before, especially during the Loma Prieta (1989, Ms=7.1), Northridge (1994, Ms=6.7), Kobe (1995, Ms=6.9) and Jiji (1999, Ms=7.3) earthquakes, there were tens or more than hundred pieces of accelerogram recorded in each event. Some significant engineering characteristics, such as near-fault rupture directivity effect, hanging wall effect, crystals wave guide effect and basin edge effect, were recognized from the recordings.

In many areas of the world, the threat to human activities from earthquakes is sufficient to require their careful consideration in the design of structures and facilities. So it is very important to study the Near-fault Endangered Field for earthquake engineering, earthquake forecasting and reducing earthquake disaster. The goal of earthquake-resistant design is to produce a structure or facility that can withstand a certain level of shaking without excessive damage. In urban active fault surveying project•research on the spatial data modeling based on earthquake geology and active tectonics is very important for interrelated application fields. In this paper, Explicit Lagrangian finite difference method is adopted to numerically reveal the characteristics of distortion field, stress field and displacement field of near-fault zone. The results can show the characteristics of mutual contact blocks' deformation, and because

W. Zhang et al. (Eds.): HPCA 2009, LNCS 5938, pp. 114–118, 2010.

of the stiffness puzzling equation in the computer easy to achieve, calculation is fast and taking up small storage space.

2 General Situation of the Project

Zibo City is a developer region in economy and culture of Shandong province. It locates at the important geotectonic situation, spans the East Hebei-Bosea fault zone, West Shandong fault zone and East Shandong fault zone, and lies in the combined part of uplift and depression. There are three main faults in Zibo City which are Zhangdian-Renhe fault, Wangmu Mountain fault and Wangmu Mountain offset fault. This paper mainly simulates the geologic condition of Zhangdian-Renhe fault. Zhangdian-Renhe fault is about 50 kilometers long, spread from south to north. The characteristic of faultage structure surface, the scrape on the faultage surface and the quartz chipping structure surface indicate that the rupture way is glue rupture mainly, and creep rupture partly.

3 Model Designing and Results Discussion

There are five experiment segments considered along the Zhangdian-Renhe fault. The location of the concealed fault, the burying depth of superior breakpoint and the delamination of medium are chosen according to the data provided by Earthquake Engineering Academe of Shandong Province. The choice of the experiment segments is based on the consideration of the influence of the concealed rupture to Zibo city zone.

In this paper we chose the results of the second segment as the examples to illuminate the simulation to Zhangdian-Renhe fault. The second segment has four layers, which are cultivated soil (cover layer), clay, weathered bedrock and integrated bedrock that are from the earth's surface down.

The inclination of the computing model is 45 degree, and there is 5 meters dislocation between the lower block and the upper block. The topside is cover layer. There are 100 meters to the left of the interface of the fault and 200 meters to the right, 120 meters thick of Z-direction and 1000 meters long of Y-direction.

The generated model has 83500 calculation elements and 105084 grid points. The interval between the grid points near interface is 5 meters, and the interval between the grid points far interface is 10 meters.

Here, the extracted figures are the group figure and the interface figure. The group figure is also called appearance figure, which is shown in Fig.1. The interface figure can indicate the location, incline and obliquity of the interface, which is shown in Fig.2.

After completely computing with the seismic wave (Ms=5.5) inputted, it outcomes the displacement contour of profile, which is shown in Fig.3, the displacement distributing of section plane in level direction, which is shown in Fig.4, and the displacement distributing of section plane in uprightness direction, which is shown in Fig.5.

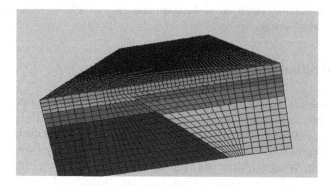

Fig. 1. Group

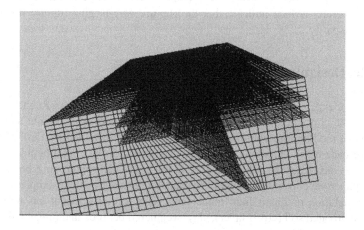

Fig. 2. Location of the interface

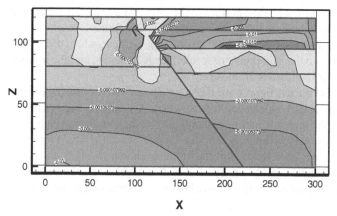

Fig. 3. Displacement contour of profile

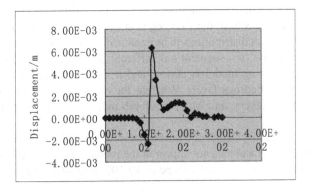

Fig. 4. Displacement distributing of section plane in level direction

We consider a consult line 300 meters long along the section plane of the rupture, compute the displacement of the consult points in X-direction, Y-direction and Z-direction. The difference between arbitrary two adjacent points' displacements is actually the distortion arisen between the two points on the earth's surface after the sudden displacement of the lie concealed earthquake fault happened.

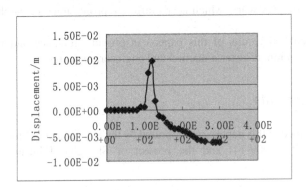

Fig. 5. Displacement distributing of section plane in uprightness direction

There are several characteristics of the final computing result.

(1) When the Ms is changeless, the model of 45 degree inclination and the model of 80 degree have different result. The displacement distributions in horizontal direction and in vertical direction of the 80 degree inclination model are 1 magnitude bigger than the 45 degree inclination model's. From the results of the numerical simulation, we can see that the earthquake destroy of the 80 degree inclination model is worse than the 45 degree inclination model's at the same earthquake conditions.

(2) As a specific model, its displacement distribution in vertical direction is more obvious than that in horizontal direction.

(3) At the same earthquake conditions, the results of different segments have more or less difference. Especially the first segment is more different from the other segments. Its displacement distributions in horizontal direction and in vertical direction are both tiny. Because the first segment has different geologic conditions from the other segments, its computing model is elastic, and it has two layers (weathered bedrock layer and integrated bedrock layer). Whereas the other segments all have cover layer and diversified soil layers, and Mohr-Coulomb model is adopted as their computing model.

(4) In view of the displacement distribution in vertical direction, the most deformation of the earth's surface does not appear at the projection of the fault's breakpoint on the surface, whereas appears at the scope of 10-100 meters from upper block.

4 Conclusions

(1) Explicit Lagrangian finite difference method can do well in the simulation of active faults and near-fault endangered field, and Mohr-Coulomb model can commendably reflect the properties of soil.

(2) It is needed to do more in 3-D seismic structural model. The rationality of the model directly constrains and affects the computing result, and any parameter changed, the results will change. Therefore, the prediction of the deformation of the earthquake zone is a very complex work, which needs different professional researchers to cooperate closely.

(3) The calculated results of this paper can provide guidance and reference for earthquake prevention, disaster reduction and engineering design.

Acknowledgements

The work described in this paper was supported by the key project of Shanghai Institute of Technology (KJ2009-14) and the project of Shanghai Education Committee (YYY08027).

References

1. Itasca Consulting Group, Inc. FLAC (Fast Lagrangian Analysis of Continua) User Manuals, Version 5.0, Minneapolis, Minnesota (May 2005)
2. Toro, G., Abrahamson, N.A., Schneider, J.F.: Model of strong ground motions from earthquakes in Central and Eastern North America: Best estimates and uncertainties. Seism Res. Lett. 68(1), 41–57 (1997)
3. Toro, G., McGuire, R.: An investigation into earthquake ground motion characteristics in Eastern North America. Bull. Seism Soc. Amer. 77(4), 468–489 (1987)
4. Wald, D.J., Heaton, T.H., Hudnut, K.W.: The slip history of the 1994 Northridge, California, earthquake determined from strongmotion, teleseismic, GPS, and leveling data. Bull. Seism Soc. Amer. 86(1B), S49–S57 (1996)

Fast ARFTIS Reconstruction Algorithms Using CUDA

Deqi Cui[*], Ningfang Liao, Wenmin Wu, Boneng Tan, and Yu Lin

Department of Optical and Electronical Engineering, Beijing Institute of Technology,
No.5 Zhongguancun South Street, Haidian District, Beijing, 100081, China
cuideqi@bit.edu.cn

Abstract. In order to realize the fast reconstruction processing of all-reflective Fourier Transform Imaging Spectrometer (ARFTIS) data, the authors implement reconstruction algorithms on GPU using Compute Unified Device Architecture (CUDA). We use both CUDA 1DFFT library and customization CUDA parallel kernel to accelerate the spectrum reconstruction processing of ARFTIS. The results show that the CUDA can drive hundreds of processing elements ('manycore' processors) of GPU hardware and can enhance the efficiency of spectrum reconstruction processing significantly. Farther, computer with CUDA graphic cards will implement real-time data reconstruction of ARFTIS alone.

Keywords: ARFTIS, Reconstruction, CUDA, Parallel.

1 Introduction

For hyperspectral Fourier transform imaging spectrometer (FTIS) the data have two distinct characteristics: one is a large quantity of original data; the other is a large amount of calculation for reconstruction algorithm [1, 2]. This type of imaging spectrometer has been adopted as optical payload in Chinese "Chang'e I" lunar exploration satellite and Chinese "Huanjing I" environmental satellite. For the specificity of processing hyperspectral data, it will consume a lot of time, one-track data takes one day, using the general-purpose computer currently. It is difficult to satisfy the demand of users, especially for emergency command (such as 5·12 Wenchuan earthquake). Therefore, improving processing speed is particularly important.

Graphics processing units (GPUs) originally designed for computer video cards have emerged as the most powerful chip in a high-performance workstation. Unlike multicore CPU architectures, which currently ship with two or four cores, GPU architectures are "manycore" with hundreds of cores capable of running thousands of threads in parallel [3]. From the above, we can see the powerful computational capability of the GPU. Moreover, as the programmability and parallel processing emerge, GPU begins being used in some non-graphics applications, which is general-purpose computing on the GPU (GPGPU).

The emergence of CUDA (Compute Unified Device Architecture) technology can meet the demand of GPGPU in some degree. CUDA brings the C-like development environment to programmers for the first time, which uses a C compiler to compile programs, and provides some CUDA extended libraries [4-6]. Users needn't map

---

[*] Corresponding author.

W. Zhang et al. (Eds.): HPCA 2009, LNCS 5938, pp. 119–126, 2010.

programs into graphics APIs anymore, so GPGPU program development becomes more flexible and efficient. Our goal in this paper is to examine the effectiveness of CUDA as a tool to express parallel computation in FTIS applications.

2 Interfere Data Reconstruction Theory

Firstly, introduce all-reflective Fourier transform imaging spectrometer (ARFTIS) designed by our team. ARFTIS works on FTIS imaging principle. The optical structure of ARFTIS is shown in Figure 1. It consists of an all-reflected three-mirror anastigmatic (TMA) telescope, an entrance slit, the Fresnel double mirror, the reflective collimating system, the reflective cylindrical system and the focal plane array (FPA) detector. The incidence beam is first imaged onto the entrance silt by the TMA telescope system, and then the wavefront is split by the Fresnel double mirror, and it is collimated by the collimating system, then through the cylindrical system to image the interference fringes onto the FPA [7].

Interfere data cube can be transformed to spectrum data cube by data reconstruction processing, which includes interference frame filtering, window filtering, spectral reconstruction and phase-corrected etc.[8-10]. Spectral reconstruction and window filtering are able to be accelerated befittingly. The following parts will introduce the basic theories of them separately.

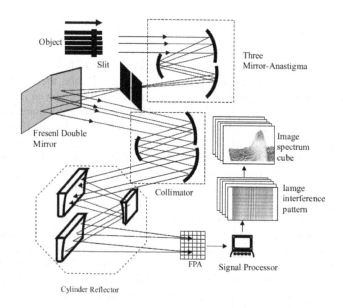

Fig. 1. All-Reflected Fourier Transform Imaging Spectrometer Principle

2.1 Spectral Reconstruction

The spectral cube can be obtained by using one-dimensional FFT transform to each line of each frame with in interference cube separately. The data must be symmetric processing in order to carry out FFT transform, if the original interference data is a single side acquisition. After symmetric processing we can obtained a double side interference data $I(l)$, then the modulus of the Fourier transform of $I(l)$ is the spectral of measurement $B(v)$.

$$B(v) = \mathcal{F}[I(l)] = \sum_{l=0}^{N-1} f(l)\exp\left(-j\frac{2\pi lk}{N}\right) \quad k=0, 1, 2, 3....N-1 \quad (1)$$

2.2 Window Filtering

Theoretically, the monochromatic spectra $B(v)$ (as impulse function) can be obtained by a Fourier transform from the interferogram $I(l)$ (as cosine function), which the optical path difference is from the negative infinity to positive infinity. But, in fact, the acquisition of FTIS $I'(l)$ is only a limited optical path difference $(-L \sim L)$ within the interferogram, which is equivalent to add a door function $T(l)$ to the cosine function, and the spectra will be $B'(v)$. After Inverse Fourier Transform in interferogram, it is no longer an impulse function, but a $\sin c$ function, which generates errors in spectral reconstruction. Therefore, window filtering is required before Fourier Transform. The window filtering function can be selected from Bartlett (triangular), Blackman, Hamming and Hanning etc.

3 Parallel Optimization

3.1 CUDA Introduction

The hardware architecture can be seen from Figure 2. CUDA-enable cards contain many SIMD stream multi-processors (SM), and each SM has also several stream processors (SP) and Super Function Unit (SFU). These cards use on-chip memories and cache to accelerate memory access.

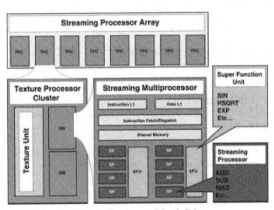
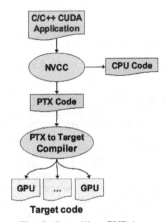

Fig. 2. CUDA Hardware Block Diagram   **Fig. 3.** Compiling CUDA

For software, CUDA mainly extended the driver program and function library. The software stack consists of driver, runtime library, some APIs and NVCC compiler developed by NVIDIA [11]. In Figure 3, the integrated GPU and CPU program is compiled by NVCC, and then the GPU code and CPU code are separated.

3.2 Implementation Spectral Reconstruction

For Fourier Transform, CUDA provide a library of CUFFT which contains many highly optimized function interfaces [12], we can call these APIs simply. Before using the CUFFT library, users just need to create a Plan of FFT transform, and then call the APIs. For FFT transform, device memory is needed to be allocated when creating the Plan and the device memory will not vary in succeeding computations. For window filtering we use customization CUDA parallel kernel to implementation matrix computing.

The framework designed is considered the two-dimensional irrelevance of reconstruction processing, that means the reconstruction processing is parallelizable in space-dimensional. We designed parallel optimization reconstruction arithmetic, which is parallel processing per frame interference data of a point spectral. The flow chart shows in Figure 4.

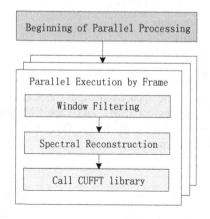

Fig. 4. Flow Chart of Parallel Optimization

Part Codes
```
// Allocate host memory for the signal
Complex* h_signal = (Complex*)malloc(sizeof(Complex) * SIGNAL_N * lines);
// Allocate device memory for signal
Complex* d_signal;
const unsigned int mem_size = sizeof(Complex) * SIGNAL_N * lines;
CUDA_SAFE_CALL(cudaMalloc((void**)&d_signal, mem_size));
// Copy host memory to device
CUDA_SAFE_CALL(cudaMemcpy(d_signal, h_signal,
sizeof(Complex)*SIGNAL_N*lines, cudaMemcpyHostToDevice));
```

```
// CUFFT plan
cufftHandle plan;
CUFFT_SAFE_CALL(cufftPlan1d(&plan, SIGNAL_N, CUFFT_C2C, 1));
Complex* p_signal = (Complex*)d_signal;
for (int line = 0; line < lines; line++)
{
    // Transform signal and kernel
    CUFFT_SAFE_CALL(cufftExecC2C(plan, (cufftComplex *)p_signal,
(cufftComplex *)p_signal, CUFFT_INVERSE));
    p_signal += SIGNAL_N;
}
//Destroy CUFFT context
CUFFT_SAFE_CALL(cufftDestroy(plan));
// Copy device memory to host
CUDA_SAFE_CALL(cudaMemcpy(h_signal, d_signal,
sizeof(Complex)*SIGNAL_N*lines, cudaMemcpyDeviceToHost));
// cleanup memory
free(h_signal);
CUDA_SAFE_CALL(cudaFree(d_signal));
```

4 Experiment Results and Analysis

We experiment with simulation data, which is generate by FTIS Simulation Software (developed by CSEL, Beijing Institute of Technology) The data parameters are as follows, the total pixel of each scene of interfere data cube is 512 (track through width) × 512 (track along width) × 512 (interference-dimensional, double side). The input data precision is 12-bit integer per pixel. The output spectral data is 115bands per point, saved as 16-bit float. Reconstruction processing includes window filtering and 512 points FFT.

We carried out parallel optimization using NVIDIA GTX 280. The hardware specifications show in table 1. Program development language is C++, and compiler is NVCC and the Microsoft Visual Studio 2008 compiler. The experiment environment is Intel Core 2 Duo E8500 CPU (dual-core, 3.16G), Windows XP 32bit OS.

Table 1. NVIDIA GTX 280 Hardware Specifications

Texture processor clusters (TPC)	10
Streaming multiprocessors (SM) per TPC	3
Streaming processors (SP) per SM	8
Super function units (SFU) per SM	2
Total SPs in entire processor array	240
Peak floating point performance GFLOPS	933

Experiment with one scene data (512 frames × 512 lines × 512 points × 12bit). Interference pattern shows in Figure 5; reconstruction image shows in Figure 6; spectral result shows in Figure 7;

Fig. 5. the Interference Pattern of One Scene

Fig. 6. Reconstruction Image, Left: Original Simulation Image; Middle: 510nm Reconstruction Band Image; Right: 890nm Reconstruction Band Image

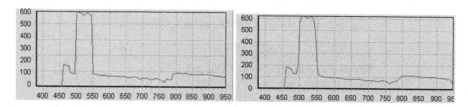

Fig. 7. Reconstruction Spectrum of Point A Left: Original Simulation Spectrum; Right: Reconstruction Spectrum

From Figure 6 and Figure 7 we can see that the reconstructed image matched with the original simulation image, and spectral characteristics is correct. However, there are some small difference between reconstructed spectra value and original simulation spectra value. We consider it impact by the sampling precision of simulation and computing precision of reconstruction, and it is in an acceptable error range.

The optimize results show in table 2. It can be clearly seen from Table 2 that the effect of speed-up on GPU processing is obvious. Large memory block on GPU is better to accelerate the speed of stream processor shared bus access than system memory.

Table 2. Optimize Results Compared CPU with GPU

Mode	Time(s)	Speed-up
CPU	116.8	1
CPU + GPU 1MB block	8.3	14.07
CPU + GPU 512MB block	5.5	21.24

5 Conclusions

In this paper, we introduced novel implementations of ARFTIS reconstruction algorithms based on a novel technology and new type hardware. Using CUDA programming and CUDA-enabled GPUs we can easily implement basic reconstruction algorithms. It has been proved that the algorithm can enhance the efficiency of the spectrum reconstruction processing significantly. However, the advantages in performance and efficiency on CUDA depend on proper memory block allocated. It provides a feasible example for parallel optimizing of ARFTIS data reconstruction by using CUDA, as well as providing a reference for using GPGPU computing effectively.

Future work includes implement more optional algorithms for ARFTIS. Another work is to optimize CUDA efficiency on multi-core CPU.

Acknowledgment

The authors gratefully acknowledge the support of National Natural Science Foundation of China, No.60377042; National 863 Foundation of China, No.2006AA12Z124; Aviation Science Foundation, No.20070172003 and Innovative Team Development Plan of Ministry of Education, No.IRT0606; National 973 Foundation of China, No.2009CB7240054.

References

1. Chu, J.: The Study of Imaging Fourier Transform Spectroscopy. Beijing Institute of Technology, Beijing (2002) (in Chinese)
2. John Otten III, L., Glenn Sellar, R., Rafert, B.: Mighty Sat II.1 Fourier-transform hyperspectral imager payload performance. In: Proc. SPIE, vol. 2583, p. 566 (1995)
3. Takizawa, H., Yamada, N., Sakai, S., et al.: Radiative Heat Transfer Simulation Using Programmable Graphics Hardware. In: Proceedings of the 5th IEEE/ACIS International Conference on Computer and Information Science (2006); 0-7695-2613-6/06
4. NVIDIA, GPU Computing Programming a Massively Parallel Processor (2006)
5. NVIDIA, NVIDIA CUDA Programming guide version 2.0,
   http://www.developer.download.nvidia.com

6. Tölke, J.: Implementation of a Lattice Boltzmann kernel using the Compute Unified Device Architecture. Submitted to Computing and Visualization in Science (2007)
7. Cui, D., Liao, N., Ma, L., et al.: Spectral calibration method for all-reflected Fourier transform imaging spectrometer. In: Proc. SPIE, 716022 (2008)
8. Ma, L.: The Study of Spectral Reconstruction for Imaging Fourier Transform Spectrometer. Beijing Institute of Technology, Beijing (2008) (in Chinese)
9. Griffiths, P.R.: Fourier Transform Infrared Spectrometry. Wiley Interscience Publication, New York (1986)
10. Villemaire, A.J., Fortin, S., Giroux, J., et al.: Imaging Fourier transform spectrometer. In: Proc. SPIE, vol. 2480, p. 387 (1995)
11. NVIDIA, The CUDA Compiler Driver NVCC,
    http://www.developer.download.nvidia.com
12. NVIDIA, CUFFT Library version 1.1,
    http://www.developer.download.nvidia.com

Numerical Methods for Nonequilibrium Solute Transport with First-Order Decay and Zero-Order Production*

Yazhu Deng and Ming Cui**

School of Mathematics, Shandong University, Jinan, China
yazhud@math.sdu.edu.cn, mingcui@sdu.edu.cn

Abstract. Solute transport in the subsurface is often considered to be a nonequilibrium process. Nonequilibrium during transport of solutes in porous medium has been categorized as either transport-related or sorption-related. For steady state flow in a homogeneous soil and assuming a linear sorption process, we will consider advection-diffusion-adsorption equations. In this paper, numerical methods are considered for the mathematical model for steady state flow in a homogeneous soil with a linear sorption process. The modified upwind finite difference method is adopted to approximate the concentration in mobile regions and immobile regions. Optimal order l^2- error estimate is derived. Numerical results are supplied to justify the theoretical work.

1 Introduction

Solute transport in the subsurface is often considered to be a nonequilibrium process. Nonequilibrium during transport of solutes in porous medium has been categorized as either transport-related or sorption-related. Transport nonequilibrium (also called physical nonequilibrium) is caused by slow diffusion between mobile and immobile water regions. These regions are commonly observed in aggregated soils [8, 12] or under unsaturated flow conditions [2, 13, 14, 15], or in layered or otherwise heterogeneous groundwater systems. Sorption-related nonequilibrium results from either slow intrasorbent diffusion [1] or slow chemical interaction [7]. In most of these models, the soil matrix is conceptually divided into two types of sites; sorption is assumed to be instantaneous for one type and rate-limited for the other type.

Solute transfer between immobile/mobile water regions or instantaneous/ rate-limited sorption sites is commonly described by a first-order rate expression or by Fick's law if the geometry of the porous matrix can be specified. Models that are based on well-defined geometry are difficult to apply to actual field situations, as they require information about the geometry of the structural units that are rarely available [6]. Hence, the first-order rate formulation has been extensively used to model underground contaminant transport.

---

* This work is supported by the National Natural Science Foundation of China (Grant No. 10271066). The Project-sponsored by SRF for ROCS, SEM.

** Corresponding author.

W. Zhang et al. (Eds.): HPCA 2009, LNCS 5938, pp. 127–132, 2010.

In this paper, the modified upwind difference method is considered for the two-region physical nonequilibrium models which were given in [16], where the two-region transport model assumed that the liquid phase can be partitioned into mobile and immobile regions and that the solute exchanges between two liquid regions can be modeled as a first-order process.

$$\beta R \frac{\partial C_1}{\partial T} = \frac{1}{P} \frac{\partial^2 C_1}{\partial X^2} - \frac{\partial C_1}{\partial X} - \omega(C_1 - C_2) - \mu_1 C_1 + \gamma_1(X) \tag{1}$$

$$(1 - \beta) R \frac{\partial C_2}{\partial T} = \omega(C_1 - C_2) - \mu_2 C_2 + \gamma_2(X) \tag{2}$$

where C_1 is the reduced volume-averaged solute concentration, C_2 is the reduced kinetically adsorbed concentration, μ is a first-order decay coefficient, γ is a zero-order production coefficient, X and T are space and time variables, respectively; β, R, P and ω are adjusted model parameters and subscripts 1 and 2 on μ and γ refer to equilibrium and nonequilibrium sites, respectively. We shall assume that ω and μ cannot be negative. Notice that zero-order production terms in (1) (2) are functions of position X, but that first-order rate coefficients are assumed to be constant. Subscripts 1 and 2 refer to mobile and immobile regions if dimensionless transport equations are interpreted in terms of the two-region model. The general initial and boundary conditions are given by:

$$C_1(X, 0) = C_2(X, 0) = C_i(X) \tag{3}$$

$$(-\frac{\delta}{P} \frac{\partial C_1}{\partial X} + C_1)|_{X=0} = C_0(T) \tag{4}$$

with $\delta = 0$ for a first-type and $\delta = 1$ for a third-type boundary condition and

$$\frac{\partial C_1}{\partial X}(\infty, T) = 0 \tag{5}$$

where C_i is the initial concentration and C_0 is the boundary concentration.

The organization of the paper is as follows. In section 2, the modified upwind difference methods is proposed to the dimensionless mathematical model for steady state flow in a homogeneous soil with a linear sorption process. Optimal order estimate in l^2- norm is derived. In section 3, numerical results were presented for the nonequilubrium transport model which was given in [16].

2   The Modified Upwind Finite Difference Method

There have been many numerical methods for miscible displacement in porous media. In [5] the finite difference method is proposed combining with the method of characteristic method for convection-dominated problems in porous media. An alternating direction method combined with a modified method of characteristic is presented in [4] for miscible displacement influenced by mobile water and immobile water. Yi-rang Yuan [17] formulated a modified upwind finite difference procedure for compressible two-phase displacement problems. The modified upwind finite difference method is efficient to treat the equation with significant convection and has the second-order accuracy in space variable.

We organize our regularity hypothesis on the solution c_1, c_2 of (1) (2) according to the results in which they are used.

$$c_1, c_2 \in W^{1,\infty} \cap L^\infty(W^{4,\infty}), \frac{\partial c_1}{\partial t}, \frac{\partial c_2}{\partial t} \in L^\infty(W^{1,\infty}), \frac{\partial^2 c_1}{\partial t^2}, \frac{\partial^2 c_2}{\partial t^2} \in L^\infty(L^\infty).$$
(6)

For convenience, we introduce the new parameters: $u = 1$, $D = 1/P$, $a = \beta R$ and $b = (1 - \beta)R$. For the sake of simplicity, denote the bounded domain $\Omega = [0,1]^2$, space step $h = \frac{1}{N}$, $x_{ij} = (ih, jh)$, $i, j = 0, 1...N$. Let Δt is the time step and $t^n = n\Delta t$, $w_{ij}^n = w(x_{ij}, t^n)$.

Let δ_x, δ_y and $\delta_{\bar{x}}, \delta_{\bar{y}}$ stand for forward and backward difference respectively. Define

$$D_{i+\frac{1}{2},j} = \frac{D_{i+1,j} + D_{i,j}}{2}, \quad D_{i-\frac{1}{2},j} = \frac{D_{i-1,j} + D_{i,j}}{2}$$

similarly, we can define $D_{i,j+\frac{1}{2}}, D_{i,j-\frac{1}{2}}$.

Now, assume $\{C_{1,ij}^n, C_{2,ij}^n\}$ are known. Then the modified upwind finite difference method for (1) (2) is given by: finding that $\{C_{1,ij}^{n+1}, C_{2,ij}^{n+1}\}$, for $1 \leq i, j \leq N - 1$ satisfying

$$a_{ij}\frac{C_{1,ij}^{n+1} - C_{1,ij}^n}{\Delta t} + b_{ij}\frac{C_{2,ij}^{n+1} - C_{2,ij}^n}{\Delta t} + \delta_{U^{n+1},x}C_{1,ij}^{n+1} + \delta_{W^{n+1},y}C_{1,ij}^{n+1}$$
$$- \left\{ \left(1 + \frac{h}{2}\frac{|U_{ij}^{n+1}|}{D_{ij}}\right)^{-1} \delta_{\bar{x}}(D\delta_x C_{ij}^{n+1}) + \left(1 + \frac{h}{2}\frac{|W_{ij}^{n+1}|}{D_{ij}}\right)^{-1}\delta_{\bar{y}}(D\delta_y C_{ij}^{n+1}) \right\}$$ (7)
$$+ \mu_{1,ij}C_{1,ij}^{n+1} + \mu_{2,ij}C_{2,ij}^{n+1} = \gamma_{1,ij} + \gamma_{2,ij}$$

$$b_{ij}\frac{C_{2,ij}^{n+1} - C_{2,ij}^n}{\Delta t} = \omega\left(C_{1,ij}^{n+1} - C_{2,ij}^{n+1}\right) - \mu_{2,ij}C_{2,ij}^{n+1} + \gamma_{2,ij},$$ (8)

where

$$\delta_{U^n,x}C_{1,ij}^n = U_{ij}^n\left\{H(U_{ij}^n)D_{ij}^{-1}D_{i-\frac{1}{2},j}\delta_{\bar{x}}C_{ij}^n + \left(1 - H\left(U_{ij}^n\right)\right)D_{ij}^{-1}D_{i+\frac{1}{2},j}\delta_x C_{ij}^n\right\},$$

$$\delta_{W^n,y}C_{1,ij}^n = W_{ij}^n\left\{H(W_{ij}^n)D_{ij}^{-1}D_{i,j-\frac{1}{2}}\delta_{\bar{y}}C_{ij}^n + \left(1 - H\left(W_{ij}^n\right)\right)D_{ij}^{-1}D_{i,j+\frac{1}{2}}\delta_y C_{ij}^n\right\}.$$

$$H(z) = \left\{ \begin{array}{ll} 1, & z \geq 0, \\ 0, & z < 0. \end{array} \right.$$ (9)

and initial values are given by:

$$C_{1,ij}^0 = c_{1,0}(x_{ij}), \ C_{2,ij}^0 = c_{2,0}(x_{ij}), \ 0 \leq i, j \leq N.$$

3   Convergence Analysis

Let $\pi = c_1 - C_1$ and $\xi = c_2 - C_2$, where c_1, c_2 are the solutions of (1) (2) and C_1, C_2 are numerical solutions of difference scheme (7) (8) respectively. Then we define the inner product and norm in discrete space $l^2(\Omega)$.

$$(f^n, g^n) = \sum_{i,j=1}^{N} f_{ij}^n g_{ij}^n h^2, \quad \|f^n\|^2 = (f^n, f^n)$$

By introduce the induction hypothesis

$$\sup_{0 \le n \le L} \max \{ \|\xi^n\|, \ \|\zeta^n\|, \ \|\delta_x \zeta^n\| + \|\delta_y \zeta^n\| \} \to 0, \quad (h, \Delta t) \to 0. \tag{10}$$

and some techniques and applying discrete Gronwall Lemma, the following theorem can be obtained.

Theorem 1. *Suppose that the solution of the problem (1) (2) satisfies the condition (6) and the time and space discretization satisfy the relations $\Delta t = O(h^2)$, then the following error estimate holds for the modified upwind difference scheme (7) (8):*

$$\begin{aligned} &\|c_1 - C_1\|_{\bar{L}^\infty([0,T];\ h^1)} + \|c_2 - C_2\|_{\bar{L}^\infty([0,T];\ l^2)} \\ &+ \|d_t(c_1 - C_1)\|_{\bar{L}^2([0,T];\ l^2)} + \|d_t(c_2 - C_2)\|_{\bar{L}^2([0,T];\ l^2)} \le M^* \{\Delta t + h^2\} \end{aligned} \tag{11}$$

where $\|g\|_{\bar{L}^\infty(J;X)} = \sup_{n\Delta t \le T} \|g^n\|_X$, $\|g\|_{\bar{L}^2(J;X)} = \sup_{n\Delta t \le T} \left\{ \sum_{n=0}^{L} \|g^n\|_X^2 \Delta t \right\}^{\frac{1}{2}}$ *and*
$M^* = M^* \left\{ \left\| \frac{\partial^2 C_1}{\partial t^2} \right\|_{L^\infty}, \ \left\| \frac{\partial^2 C_2}{\partial t^2} \right\|_{L^\infty}, \ \|C_1\|_{L^\infty(W^{4,\infty})}, \ \|C_1\|_{W^{1,\infty}} \right\}$.

4   Numerical Examples

For the nonequilubrium transport model in one dimension [7, 8, 16]

$$\beta R \frac{\partial c_1}{\partial t} = D \frac{\partial^2 c_1}{\partial x^2} - \frac{\partial c_1}{\partial x} - \omega(c_1 - c_2) - \mu_1 c_1 + \gamma_1(x) \tag{12}$$

$$(1 - \beta) R \frac{\partial c_2}{\partial t} = \omega(c_1 - c_2) - \mu_2 c_2 + \gamma_2(x) \tag{13}$$

Van Genuchten [7, 8, 16] presented the analytical solutions for different initial and boundary conditions. In Fig.1 and Fig. 2, the analytical solution and the solution of modified upwind finite difference method are compared. It is shown that the the modified upwind finite difference method(MUDM) is more accurate that upwind difference method(UDM).

Example 1. Initial Value Problem with Stepwise Initial Distribution. We choose $D = 0.1$, $\beta = 0.5$, $R = 2$, $\omega = 1$, $\mu_1 = \mu_2 = 0.2$, $\gamma_1 = \gamma_2 = 0$. $\Delta t = 0.0025$ and $h = 0.05$. Let

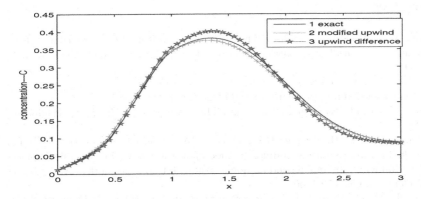

Fig. 1. Calculated resident equilibrium C_1 distribution versus distance x at $T = 1$

$$c_{1,0}(x) = c_{2,0}(x) = \begin{cases} 0.3, & 0 \leq x < 0.5, \\ 1, & 0.5 \leq x < 1. \\ 0.1, & 1 \leq x \end{cases} \tag{14}$$

Example 2. Boundary Value Problem with Stepwise Boundary Condition. We choose $D = 0.25$, $\beta = 0.5$, $R = 2$, $\mu_1 = \mu_2 = 0$, $\gamma_1 = \gamma_2 = 0$. and $\Delta t = 0.006$, $h = 0.08$. Assume that the initial concentration is zero. The boundary condition is given by

$$c_0(t) = \begin{cases} 1, & 0 < t \leq 3 \\ 0, & t > 3 \end{cases} \tag{15}$$

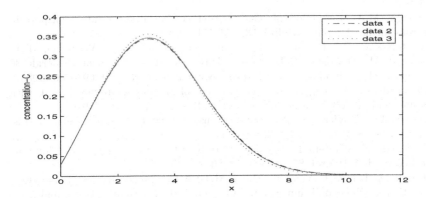

Fig. 2. Calculated resident equilibrium C_1 distribution versus distance x at $T = 3$

In Fig.2, *data* 2 is the analytical solution c_1 at $T = 3$. *data* 1 is obtained by modified upwind finite difference method and *data* 3 is obtained by upwind finite difference method.

References

[1] Ball, W.P., Roberts, P.V.: Long-term sorption of haloginated organic chemicals by aquifer material. 2. Intraparticle diffusion. Environ. Sci. Technol. 25, 1237–1249 (1991)

[2] Bond, W.J., Wierenga, P.J.: Immobile water during solute transport in unsaturated sand columns. Water Resour. Res. 26, 2475–2481 (1990)

[3] Chen, Z.: Finite Element Methods and Their Applications. Springer, Heidelberg (2005)

[4] Cui, M., Chen, H., Ewing, R.E., Qin, G.: An Alternating direction Galerkin method combined with a modified method of characteristics for miscible displacement influenced by mobile and immobile Water. Int. J. of Numerical Analysis and Modeling 5, 659–672 (2008)

[5] Douglas Jr., J., Russell, T.F.: Numerical Methods for Convection Dominated Diffusion Problems Based on Combining the Methods of Characteristics with Finite Element or Finite Difference Procedures. SIAM J. Numer. Anal. 19, 871–885 (1982)

[6] Fortin, J., Flury, M., Jury, W.A., Streck, T.: Rate-limited sorption of simazine in saturated soil columns. J. Contam. Hydrol. 25, 219–234 (1997)

[7] Van Genuchten, M.T., Davidson, J.M., Wierenga, P.J.: An evaluation of kinetic and equilibrium equations for the prediction of pesticide movement through porous media. Soil Sci. Soc. Am. J. 38, 29–35 (1974)

[8] Van Genuchten, M.T., Wierenga, P.J.: Mass transfer studies in sorbing porous media I Analytical solutions. Soil.Sci. Amer. J. 40, 473–480 (1976)

[9] Van Genuchten, M.T., Wagenet, R.J.: Two-site/two-region models for pesticide transport and degradation: Theoretical development and analytical solutions. Soil Sci. Soc. Am. J. 53, 1303–1310 (1989)

[10] Hornung, U.: Miscible Displacement in Porous Media Influenced by Mobile and Immobile Water, Nonlinear Partial Differential Equations. Springer, New York (1988)

[11] Maraqa, M.A.: Prediction of mass-transfer coefficient for solute transport in porous media. J. Conta. Hydrol. 53, 153–171 (2001)

[12] Nkedi-Kizza, P., Biggar, J.W., Van Genuchten, M.T., Wierenga, P.J., Selim, H.M., Davidson, J.M., Nielsen, D.R.: Modeling tritium and chloride 36 transport through an aggregated oxisol. Water Resour. Res. 19, 691–700 (1983)

[13] De Smedt, F., Wierenga, P.J.: A generalized solution for solute flow in soils with mobile and immobile water. Water Resour. Res. 15, 1137–1141 (1979)

[14] De Smedt, F., Wierenga, P.J.: Solute transfer through columns of glass beads. Water Resour, Res. 20, 225–232 (1984)

[15] De Smedt, F., Wauters, F., Sevilla, J.: Study of tracer movement through unsaturated sand. J. Hydrol. 85, 169–181 (1986)

[16] Toride, N., Leij, F.J., Van Genuchten, M.T.: A Comprehensive set of Analytical Solution for Nonequilibrium Solute Transport With First-Order Decay and Zero-Order Production. Water Resour. Res. 29, 2167–2182 (1993)

[17] Yuan, Y.-r.: The upwind finite difference method for compressible two-phase displacement problem. Acta Mathematica Applicatae Sinica 25(3), 484–496 (2002)

Parallel Computing of Catchment Basins in Large Digital Elevation Model

Hiep-Thuan Do*, Sébastien Limet, and Emmanuel Melin

LIFO – Univerité d'Orléans
Rue Léonard de Vinci, B.P. 6759 F-45067 ORLEANS Cedex 2
{hiep-thuan.do,sebastien.limet,emmanuel.melin}@univ-orleans.fr

Abstract. This paper presents a fast and flexible parallel implementation to compute catchment basins in the large digital elevation models (DEM for short). This algorithm aims at using all the specific properties of the problem to optimize local computations and to avoid useless communications or synchronizations. The algorithm has been implemented in MPI and the first benchmarks show the scalability of the method.

Keywords: Parallel implementation, Digital elevation model, Catchment basin, Image Segmentation.

1 Introduction

Geo-hydrology is an interdisciplinary domain dealing with the flow of water through aquifers and other shallow porous media. This domain is a branch of earth sciences relevant to many fields of soil science like agriculture or civil engineering. To study the flow of water one method consists in computing *catchment basins* only considering surface topography as if soil was impervious. The input information consists in a *Digital Elevation Model* (DEM).

Computing catchment basins is a problem very close to the well known *watershed transform* method in the field of mathematical morphology. This is a region-based segmentation approach widely studied in the area of *Image Analysis*. *Image Segmentation* is the process of partitioning the image into disjoint regions that are homogeneous with respect to some property such as gray value, altitude or texture. Indeed, a gray scale image can be viewed as a DEM where the lengths of the gradients between pixel values are considered as the altitude of the corresponding points. Catchment basins of the images denote the expected homogeneous regions of the images and ridges of land that separate catchment basins are called *watersheds*. As we see, the intuitive idea underlying watershed transform method comes from geography, indeed we propose to reverse this analogy by using watershed transform methods, wildly tuned for Image Analysis, to initial geographical catchment basin computing.

Watershed transform algorithms use two method classes based on flooding process [8, 1] or rain falling simulation [6, 5]. These methods are sequential

---

* Hiep-Thuan Do's PHD Thesis is funded by Conseil General of Loiret (France).

W. Zhang et al. (Eds.): HPCA 2009, LNCS 5938, pp. 133–138, 2010.

and need an extensive use and a careful management of the memory. Required memory size is a priori unknown, and the data are addressed in unstructured manner, causing performance degradation on virtual memory.

The parallelization of classical sequential algorithms based on an ordered queue proposed in [2] requires strong synchronizations between the processors maintaining local queues and repeated labeling of the same pixels performed for appropriately labeling parts of catchment basins. To compute watershed, some other parallel methods [3, 4] have been proved scalable, but are still computationally expensive for large images.

The quality of the results of catchment basin computing depends on the quality of the DEM in the one hand and on the surface it covers on the other hand. Since several years, very large high resolution DEM issued from satellite or air plane LIDAR scanning, are available. Then it becomes crucial to focus on fast scalable parallel methods being able to perform catchment basin computation on very large of datasets.

The goal of this paper is to present a SPMD parallel implementation onto MIMD architectures to efficiently computes catchment basins of large DEM. This approach is mainly based on local data analysis. This makes possible a very efficient parallelization. We use a *dependency graph*, which encapsulates results of local computations and reduces drastically the cost of communications related to global analysis steps. This method overcomes synchronizations and communication overheads due to no local information needed by nodes to take local decisions. Moreover we adapt the *path compression* part of algorithm *Union-Find* [7] in order to, first, compute connected components, and secondly, resolve the global dependency graph. Further tests on different large DEM have been performed to evaluate the efficiency and the scalability of the method.

The paper is organized as follows. We describe the detailed implementation of our new algorithm in Section 2. Experimental results are sketched in Section 3. Finally, we close with a conclusion.

2   The Parallel Watershed Algorithms

A *Digital Elevation Model* (DEM) is a regular square 2D grid of vertices representing geographic positions, with 4-connectivity or 8-connectivity where an altitude is associated to each vertex. Formally, the *grid* is a triple $G = (D, E, f)$, where (D, E) is a graph and f is the function giving the altitude of the nodes of D. The graph (D, E) consists of a set $D \subseteq Z^2$ of *vertices* (or *nodes*) and a set $E \subseteq D \times D$ of pairs of vertices describing the connectivity of the grid. Each node (x, y) represents a 2D geographic position. Each $p \in D$ has an altitude given by the function $f : D \longrightarrow \mathbb{R}$ assigning a float value to p. Therefore f denotes the topographic relief. We define a *neighboring* for each node p with respect to the grid G, denoted by $N_G(p) = \{p' \in D | (p, p') \in E\}$. In the case of 8-connectivity $E = \{((x, y), (x', y')) | (x, y) \neq (x', y') \text{ and } |x - x'| \leq 1 \text{ and } |y - y'| \leq 1\}$.

Our method to delimit catchment basins of a DEM is in the class of arrowing technique. It consists in exploring node neighborhood, choosing the lower neighbor and iterate the process. We follow the path of steepest downslope through the grid until reaching a final point that has no lower neighbor. This point is a local minimum and is called a *well*. Vertices having the same final well belong to the same catchment basins. We formalize *the steepest downslope* via the *parent* function. Each node $p \in D$, $parent(p)$ is the neighbor of lowest altitude. Note that $parent(p)$ may be p itself if all neighbors are upper. If two neighbors have the same altitude, we enforce an artificial strict order using the classical lexicographical order $\prec$ on pairs. This order eliminates *flat zone* without any specific processing. The practical results show that computed catchment basins are consistent with regard to hydro-geology. Figure 1(a) gives an example of a DEM, the arrows between nodes represents the function *parent*. In this DEM, the pixel $(6,5)$ and $(6,6)$ form a flat zone. Because of lexicographic order, $parent((6,6)) = parent((6,5)) = (6,5)$.

Formally, the parent q of the node p is the element of $N_G(p)$ that verifies: $\forall p' \in N_G(p) \cup \{p\}$ such that $p' \neq q$ either $f(q) < f(p')$ or $f(q) = f(p')$ and $q \prec p'$.

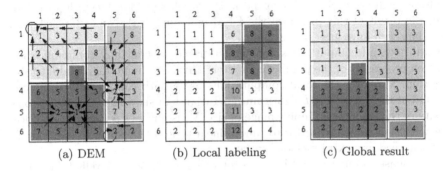

(a) DEM   (b) Local labeling   (c) Global result

Fig. 1. Example of DEM

We call *flow graph*, the graph $Flow = (D, \{(p, parent(p)\})$. This graph is partitioned into connected components (see Figure 1(a)) that are almost trees (to be real trees, the edges of the form (p, p) have to be removed). In Figure 1(a), the four connected components have different backgrounds. The root of a tree in *Flow* is such that $parent(p) = p$ and corresponds to a local minimum. In the example, the four wells are nodes $(1, 1)$, $(4, 5)$, $(5, 3)$ and $(6, 5)$. We define a *catchment basin CB* as a connected component in *Flow*. Then, a catchment basin contains all nodes of D that are in the same tree of *Flow*. The root rp of catchment basin CB is called *primary well*.

As in [4], our parallel approach maps data onto the processors of the parallel computer. The global domain D of a grid $G = (D, E, f)$ is partitioned into disjoint sub-domains D_i. In the example illustrated by Figure 1(a), the domain is split into four sub-domains symbolized by the thick lines in the grid. For example the sub-domain D_1 is the set $\{(x, y) \in Z^2 | 1 \leq x \leq 3 \text{ and } 1 \leq y \leq 3\}$.

Each sub-domain D_i is extended with a so-called *extension area* denoted $D_i{}^+$. The extension area consists of all neighbors of nodes belonging to D_i that are not included in D_i. It is defined as follows: $D_i{}^+ = \{p \in D | p \notin D_i \text{ and } \exists q \in D_i$ such that $p \in N_G(q)\}$. In the example of Figure 1(a), $D_1^+ = \{(4,1),(4,2),(4,3),(4,4),(1,4),(2,4),(3,4)\}$.

This data distribution has consequences when we want to locally compute catchment basins since the nodes of one basin can be distributed on several sub-domains as it can be seen in Figure 1(a). In such cases, it becomes impossible to compute the real tree without global data access. This kind of access is time consuming, so to avoid them our method computes a *partial tree* and postpones the problem to another phase of our algorithm. Among the local wells computed in a sub-domain, it is possible to locally detect primary wells of the global domain thanks to the extension area. Indeed a local well that has a parent in the extension area is not a primary well, it is then called *secondary well*. In Figure 1(b), the upper right sub-domain has four local wells $(1,4)$, $(3,4)$, $(3,5)$ and $(3,6)$, but all are secondary since their parents are in the extension area.

At this point, labels are locally given to both primary and secondary wells in a such way that labels of each sub-domains are disjoint. The method gives to all the nodes of each catchment basin the label of the local well. Figure 1(b) gives the result of this phase on the DEM of Figure 1(a). Nodes labeled with secondary well have gray background.

Until now, all computations can be performed without any communication between processors of the parallel computer. This is optimum for scalability and speed up. Moreover the local computations use a path compression technique inspired of the *Union-Find* algorithm [7]. Tarjan had shown that the time complexity of this step for an input image of size N_i, is quasi $O(N_i)$. So, in practice, this algorithm can be regarded to run in linear time with respect to its input. It does not need any extra memory space.

Next phase in our method leads to relabeling of secondary wells taking into account no local informations. During this phase each secondary well is coalesced into a primary well. We start with one to one communications in order to update pixel labels of the extension area. After this step we locally know in which catchment basin, pixels of the extension area belongs to. Then we introduce the *parent well* notion. A well pw is called *parent well* of a secondary well sw if $parent(sw)$ belongs to the catchment basin corresponding to well pw. We create a local dependency graph LDG_i which contains dependency informations between local catchment basins. We locally associate any secondary wells sw with its parent $parent(sw)$. In Figure 1(b), we get $LDG_1 = \{5 \to 10\}$, $LDG_2 = \{6 \to 1, 7 \to 3, 8 \to 3, 9 \to 3\}$, $LDG_3 = \emptyset$ and $LDG_4 = \{10 \to 2, 11 \to 2, 12 \to 2\}$.

The local dependency graphs are then broadcasted to all other processors for building of *global dependency graph* GDG=$\bigcup_1^{P_{nb}} LDG_i$, where P_{nb} is the number of processors. The GDG is a graph which connected components are trees rooted by primary wells. On each processor P_i, catchment basin CB_{sw} corresponding to secondary well $sw \in LDG_i$ is merged into the catchment basin CB_{rw} corresponding to root well rw. This is called the union of wells. The union of wells is then propagated on the path between the root well rw and the secondary well sw in the GDG. This step is continuously repeated until all secondary wells are labelled with the identifier of their their roots (primary wells). Note that this process is parallel since each processor works on resolution only for its own local secondary wells. Moreover we need only one communication phase involving data structures much more reduced compared to initial data size.

Finally, labels of nodes in the catchment basins corresponding to secondary well sw are replaced by label of its root well rw in GDG by the linear scan for all nodes in sub-domain D_i. This phase of our method is purely parallel without any communications. The global labeling of DEM is illustrated in Figure 1(c).

3   Experimental Results

This algorithm described in this paper has been implemented in C++ using Open MPI. It has been tested on the **MIREV platform** consisting of eight nodes linked with a gigabit ethenet network. Each node is a bi-pro with AMD Opteron Quad-Core 2376 2.3Ghz with 16G SDRAM DDR2-PC5300 EEC 667 Mhz. We tested up to 64 processors on different *Digital Elevation Models* (MNT_a with size 3,980 x 5,701; MNT_b with size 10,086 x 14,786; and MNT_c with size 36,002 x 54,002) which are provided by the Company Géo-Hyd in Orléans, France.

Let P_{nb} be number of processors used. The running time T(P) is the time elapsed between the moment that the first processor starts and the moment that the last processor finishes. The measured times excludes data loading, distribution, coalescence, and saving. The *relative speedup* of the parallel algorithm is measured by: $SP(P_{nb}) = \frac{T_{min}}{T(P_{nb})}$ where T_{min} is the execution time of our algorithm onto one processor. Note that, due to memory size limitation, it is not possible to run our program for MNT_c onto one sole node. In this case only, we choose to fix T_{min} as the execution time of our algorithm onto two processors. Then, in this case, the speedup linear curve start at coordinate (1,0) and is parallel to the classical speedup linear curve (Figure 2(b)).

Looking at Figure 2(a), for MNT_a and MNT_b, we remark that the relative speedup is close to linear speedup at the beginning of the curves. Of course, when number of processors grows, the speedup partially decreases, since cost

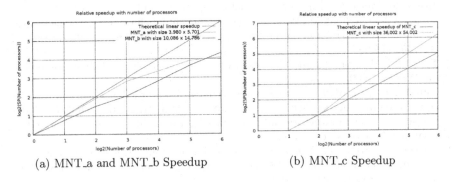

(a) MNT_a and MNT_b Speedup   (b) MNT_c Speedup

Fig. 2. Relative speedup with number of processors

of communications becomes more important compared to local computation gain. With a larger DEM (1.9 Gpoints for MNT_c) speedup increases linearly (Figure 2(b)) and the computation takes 92 seconds using 64 processors. This illustrates the good scalability of our approach. Note that MNT_c speedup is super linear. A possible reason is the cache effect resulting from the different memory hierarchies.

4   Conclusion

We presented an efficient and scalable parallel algorithm to compute catchment basins in large DEM. All computations are parallel and no complex data structures are constructed. Moreover, all data structures are distributed onto cluster nodes. Synchronizations and communications are localized between super steps of the algorithm to avoid time consuming during the core of the computation.

The algorithm described in this paper computes all catchment basins with regard to the DEM. Some of them are irrelevant from the hydro-geology point of view because they are too small or result of approximation of the elevation values. As in the area of *Image Segmentation* it is possible to create a hierarchy of catchment basins that would help to eliminate such problems.

Since principles of catchment basins computing in the field of geography is close to watershed transform method in the field of *Mathematical Morphology*, we think that our parallelizing method can be directly adapted to *Image Segmentation*. This would speed up segmentation for high resolution images.

References

[1] Beucher, S., Meyer, F.: The morphological approach to segmentation: The watershed transformation. In: Dougherty, E.R. (ed.) Mathematical morphology in image processing. Optical Engineering, ch. 12, vol. 34, pp. 433–481. Marcel Dekker, New York (1993)

[2] Moga, A.N.: Parallel Watershed algorithms for Image Segmentation. PhD thesis, Tampere University Technology (February 1997)

[3] Moga, A.N., Cramariuc, B., Gabbouj, M.: Parallel watershed transformation algorithms for image segmentation. Parallel Computing 24(14), 1981–2001 (1998)

[4] Moga, A.N., Gabbouj, M.: Parallel image component labeling with watershed transformation. IEEE Transactions on Pattern Analysis and Machine Intelligence 19(5), 441–450 (1997)

[5] Stoev, S.L.: RaFSi - A Fast Watershed Algorithm Based on Rainfalling Simulation. In: WSCG (2000)

[6] Sun, H., Yang, J., Ren, M.: A fast watershed algorithm based on chain code and its application in image segmentation. Pattern Recogn. Lett. 26(9), 1266–1274 (2005)

[7] Tarjan, R.E.: Data structure and Network Algorithms. SIAM - Society for Industrial and Applied Mathematics (1983)

[8] Vincent, L., Soille, P.: Watersheds in digital spaces: an efficient algorithm based on immersion simulations. IEEE Transactions on Pattern Analysis and Machine Intelligence 13(6), 583–598 (1991)

A Hybrid Parallel Evolutionary Algorithm Based on Elite-Subspace Strategy and Space Transformation Search

Xiaojian Dong[1], Song Yu[1,*], Zhijian Wu[1], and Zhangxing Chen[2]

[1] State Key Lab of Software Engineering, Wuhan University,
Wuhan 430072, P.R. China
yusong0926@gmail.com
[2] Department of Chemical and Petroleum Engineering, Schulich School of
Engineering , University of Calgary, Calgary 2500, Canada

Abstract. In this paper, we present a new Hybrid Parallel Evolutionary Algorithm. It is based on Elite-subspace Strategy and combined with Space Transformation Search strategy to solve systems of non-linear equations. Verified by numerical experiments, our algorithm present an outstanding universal characteristics and superior convergence as well. All of the solutions can be obtained within a short period of time.

Keywords: Space Transformation Search (STS), Elite-subspace Strategy, evolutionary algorithm, optimization.

1 Introduction

In the real life, many problems can be referred to as non-linear equation or system of non-linear equations. Considering the following system of non-line equations:

$$f_i(x_1, x_2, ..., x_n) = b_i, i = 1, 2, ..., m, \tag{1}$$

where $X = (x_1, x_2, ..., x_n) \in D \subset R^n$. Solving the above problem amounts to the discovery of $X^* = (x_1^*, x_2^*, ..., x_n^*) \in D \subset R^n$, which satisfies the system of equations (1). As for such a problem, there exist many conventional methods (such as simple iterative method, Newton method, conjugate gradient method, homotopies method, simplicial method etc.)[1] and some parallel algorithms[2]. But the methods available depend too much on the problem itself and always put on some powerful constraints on the function, for example, continuance, differentiable, unisolution and so on.

For the past few years, evolutionary algorithms have been increasingly utilized in many research areas. Their global optimization, parallelism, and effectiveness have been widely known. With the help of naturally evolutionary process, evolutionary algorithms have overcome the negative aspects represented by some conventional numerical methods. As multi-clue global optimal method rather than

---

* Corresponding author.

W. Zhang et al. (Eds.): HPCA 2009, LNCS 5938, pp. 139–145, 2010.

multi-clue one, the algorithms adopt both multi-individuals and random search tactics. This paper presents a Hybrid Parallel Evolutionary Algorithm (HPEA) for solving system of non-linear equations. By applying it to some problems, we find that our algorithm has an outstanding universal characteristics and superior convergence as well. All of the solutions can be obtained within a short period of time by our algorithm. For problem (1) we construct the following function:

$$F(X) = F(x_1, x_2, ..., x_n) = \sum_{i=1}^{m}(f_i(x_1, x_2, ...x_n) - b_i)^2. \tag{2}$$

Therefore, problem(1) is converted into a function optimization problem as follows:

$$\min_{x \in D} F(X) = 0, \tag{3}$$

where D is the solution space.

The rest of this paper is arranged as follows: Sction 2 is the description of our algorithm. The numerical experiments are given in Section 3. In Section 4 we come to the conclusions.

2   Hybrid Parallel Algorithm

2.1   Space Transformation Search (STS)

Many evolutionary optimization methods start with some initial solutions, called individuals, in the population, and try to improve them toward some optima solution(s). The process of searching terminates when some predefined conditions are satisfied. In some cases, the searching easily stagnates when the population falls into local optima. If the stagnation takes places too early, the premature convergence of search is caused. Under these circumstances, the current search space hardly contains the global optimum. So it is difficult for the current population to achieve better solutions. However, Space transformation search, based on opposition learning method[3], originally introduced by Hui Wang[4], has been proven to be an effective method to cope with lots of optimization problems. When evaluating a solution x to a given problem, we can guess the transformed solution of x to get a better solution x'. By doing this, the distance of x from optima solution can be reduced. For instance, if x is -10 and the optimum solution is 30, then the transformed solution is 40. But the distance of x' from the optimum solution is only 20. So the transformed solution x' is closer to the optimum solution. The new transformed solution X^* in the transformed space S can be calculated as follows:

$$x^* = k(a + b) - x, \tag{4}$$

where $x \in R$ within $[a, b]$ and k can be set as 0,0.5,1 or a random number within $[0, 1]$.

To be more specific, we put it in an optimization problem, let $X = (x_1, x_2, ..., x_n)$ be a solution in an n-dimensional space. Assume $f(X)$ is a fitness function which is used to evaluate the solution's fitness. According to the definition of the STS, $X^* = (x_1^*, x_2^*, ..., x_n^*)$ is the corresponding solution of X in the transformed search space. If $f(X^*)$ is better than $f(X)$, then update X with X^*; otherwise keep the current solution X. Hence, the current solution and its transformed solution are evaluated simultaneously in order to continue with the fitter one. The interval boundaries $[a_j(t), b_j(t)]$ is dynamically updated according to the size of current search space. The new dynamic STS model is defined by

$$X_{ij}^* = k[a_j(t) + b_j(t)] - X_{ij}, \tag{5}$$

$$a_j(t) = min(X_{ij}(t)), b_j(t) = max(X_{ij}(t)) \tag{6}$$

$$i = 1, 2, ..., PopSize, j = 1, 2, ..., n.$$

2.2 Elite-Subspace Strategy

Multi-parent crossover operators, where more than two parents are involved in generating offspring, are a more flexible version, generalizing the traditional two-parent crossover of nature. They have obtained great achievement in the field of evolutionary computation, and Guo[5] presents a simple, highly efficient operation of the evolutionary algorithm (GT). Based on this algorithm, a Elite-subspace Evolutionary Algorithm has been proposed by Wu(EGT)[6].

The EGT is described briefly as follows.

(1) Select M individuals $x_1, x_2, ..., x_k, x_{k+1}, ..., x_M$ from the population, $x_1, x_2, ..., x_k$ are k best individuals and $x_{k+1}, ..., x_M$ are the random individuals;

(2)M random real numbers $a_i(i = 1, 2, ..., M)$ are generated, subject to

$$\sum_{i=1}^{M} a_i = 1, -0.5 \le a_i \le 1.5; \tag{7}$$

(3)The offspring vector x is generated as follows:

$$V = x|x \in S, x = \sum_{i=1}^{M} a_i x_i. \tag{8}$$

In EGT, by adopting the elite-subspace strategy, good information in the solution space will be fully utilized and make the algorithm converge quickly. For the selection of elites, When k is too large, obviously, the solving information can be fully used, however, the larger k is, the smaller diversity of the subspace is. The selection of k is determined by the size of M.

Set X_{worst}^i and X_{best}^i are the worst individual and the best one respectively on processor i at time t_j, p is the number of processors, $P = \{X_1, X_2, ..., X_p\}$ are stored in the share memory. If $F(X_i) < 10^{-20}(i = 1, 2, ..., p)$, we take the X_i as the solutions to problem(1) or else we consider that the solution to problem (1) does not exist.

Table 1. The main steps of HPEA

```
Begin
  for all i = 1, 2, ..., p do in parallel;
  Initialize the population Pᵢ, Pᵢ(0) = (X₁ⁱ, X₂ⁱ, ..., X_Nⁱ), Xⱼⁱ ∈ D, j = 1, 2, ..., N;
  evaluate Pᵢ(0), tᵢ = 0, Xᵢ = X_best^i to form a population P = (X₁, X₂, ..., X_p);
  while(termination condition);
    if (rand(0, 1) < p_s);
      Execute STS operation and form TP(t);
      Evaluate the population TP(t);
      Calculate evaluation times;
      Add TP(t) to P(t);
      Sort(P(t), 2 * PopSize);
    else
      Execute EGT operation;
      Evaluate the population P(t);
      Calculate evaluation times;
      Sort(P(t), PopSize);
    end if;
  while end
  output X_best and f(x_best);
  for end;
End
```

3 Numerical Experiments

To verify the effectiveness of HPEA, we solve the following 5 problems.

All numerical experiments are simulated on PC with Intel C2.0G CPU.

In the following experiments, given that $p_s = 0.2, p = 2, N = 120, M = 10, K = 3, L = 2$, and the terminate condition is $F(X_{best}^i) < 10^{-20}$.

Problem 1

$$\begin{cases} -x_1^3 + 5x_1^2 - x_1 + 2x_2 = 3 \\ x_2^3 + x_2^2 - 14x_2 - x_1 = 19 \end{cases}, \tag{9}$$

where $x_i \in (0, 10), i = 1, 2$.

As for the above problem, we carried out the experiment 100 times, we obtained the following solution for each time:

$$\begin{cases} x_1 = 5.000000000000000 \\ x_2 = 4.000000000000000 \end{cases}. \tag{10}$$

It costs 0.11 second on the average for each run.

Problem 2

$$\begin{cases} 0.05x_1^2 - 0.05x_2^2 - 0.125x_1 + 0.1x_2 = 3.8 \\ 0.1x_1x_2 - 0.1x_1 - 0.125x_2 = -0.125 \end{cases}, \tag{11}$$

where $x_i \in (-100, 100), i = 1, 2$.

As for the above problem, we carried out the experiment 100 times, we obtained the following solution for each time:

$$\begin{cases} x_1 = 10.000000000000000 \\ x_2 = 1.000000000000000 \end{cases}. \tag{12}$$

It costs 0.15 second on the average for each run.

Problem 3

$$\begin{cases} sinx_1 + 2x_2 + e^{x_2} = 1 \\ -3x_1 + cosx_2 = -2 \end{cases}, \tag{13}$$

where $x_i \in (-100, 100), i = 1, 2$.

As for the above problem, we carried out the experiment 100 times. We obtained the following solution for each time:

$$\begin{cases} x_1 = 0.9860086056666499 \\ x_2 = -0.2807615979485714 \end{cases}. \tag{14}$$

It costs 0.17 second on the average for each run.

Problem 4

$$\begin{cases} sinxcosy + sinycosz + sinzcosx = 1 + \frac{\sqrt{6}}{2} \\ tanxtany + tanytanz + tanztanx = 1 + \frac{4\sqrt{3}}{3} \\ sinxtanytanz = \frac{1}{2} \end{cases}, \tag{15}$$

where $x, y, z \in (0, 10)$.

We carried out the experiment 100 times. We obtained the solution for each time:

$$\begin{cases} x = 4.000000000000000 \\ y = 3.000000000000000 \\ z = 1.000000000000000 \end{cases}. \tag{16}$$

It costs 0.23 second on the average for each run.

Problem 5

$$\begin{cases} \sum_{i=1}^{4} x_i = 18048 \\ \sum_{i=1}^{4} x_i cosy_i = 13657.36315298172 \\ \sum_{i=1}^{4} x_i siny_i = 5497.052905295088 \\ \sum_{i=1}^{4} x_i cos^2 y_i = 14508.29635946082 \\ \sum_{i=1}^{4} x_i cosy_1 siny_i = 3157.294805334107 \\ \sum_{i=1}^{4} x_i^2 = 105543794 \\ \sum_{i=1}^{4} x_i^2 cosy_i = 91598751.25016867 \\ \sum_{i=1}^{4} x_i^2 siny_i = 33470578.99613227 \end{cases}, \tag{17}$$

where $x_i \in R, y_i \in [0, 2\pi], i = 1, 2, 3, 4$.

By using our algorithm, we obtained two solutions within very short time. In runs of 100 times, we have got the following solution for 67 times:

$$\begin{cases} x_1 = 1357.000000000000000 \\ x_2 = 3234.000000000000000 \\ x_3 = 5567.000000000000000 \\ x_4 = 7890.000000000000000 \\ y_1 = 2.6433011521454106 \\ y_2 = 6.0583868995227146 \\ y_3 = 0.7719591281570915 \\ y_4 = 0.2153736296961017 \end{cases} \tag{18}$$

and got the following solution for 33 times:

$$\begin{cases} x_1 = 159.1926436024564000 \\ x_2 = 3568.7596021349145000 \\ x_3 = 4656.0337256900393000 \\ x_4 = 8294.0140285725902000 \\ y_1 = 2.5201349855577422 \\ y_2 = 0.6329200963034247 \\ y_3 = 6.0523415860612193 \\ y_4 = 0.4437806933535721 \end{cases} \tag{19}$$

The average time for each run is 2.12 seconds.

4   Conclusion

The idea of HPEA is based on space transformation search method and Elite-subspace Evolutionary Algorithm to help us obtain the solutions of systems of non-linear equation within a short period of time and at the same time, our algorithm can solve not only the system of non-linear equations but also other problems so long as the problems can be converted into an optimal problems, however, according to no free lunch theory[7], in some cases, our algorithm can still not avoid premature convergence, in some more complex problems. This will be an important work to continue.

Acknowledgment

This work was supported by the National Basic Research Program of China(973 program, No.: 2007CB310801).

References

1. Quarteroni, A., Sacco, R., Saleri, F.: Numerical Mathematics. Springer, New York (2000)
2. Alexander: A Globally Convergent Parallel Algorithm. Nonlinear Analysis Theory Application 3(1), 339–350 (1989)

3. Rahnamayan, S., Tizhoosh, H.R., Salama, M.M.A.: Opposition-Based differential evolution. In: Proceedings of IEEE Congress Evolutionary Computation, vol. 12, pp. 64–79 (2008)
4. Wang, H., Wu, Z., Liu, Y.: Space Transformation Search: A New Evolutionary Technique. In: Genetic and Evolutionary Computation (2009) (in press)
5. Tao, G.: A New Algorithm for Solving Function Optimization Problems with Inequality Constraints. J. Wuhan Univ. (Nat. Sci. Ed.) 45, 771–775 (1999)
6. Wu, Z.: An Elite-subspace Evolutionary Algorithm for Solving Function Optimization Problems. Computer Applications 23, 13–15 (2003)
7. Wolpert, D.H., Macready, W.G.: No free lunch theorems for optimization. IEEE Transaction on Evolutionary Computation 1, 67–82 (1997)

Surface Reconstruction Technology from Dense Scattered Points Based on Grid

Jianzhou Feng, Lingfu Kong, and Xiaohuan Wang

School of Information Science and Engineering,
Yanshan University, 066004 QinHuangDao, China
fjzwxh@ysu.edu.cn

Abstract. In order to improve the speed of surface reconstruction from densely scattered points, and reduce the application cost, this paper describes a new and fast surface reconstruction method based on grid computing. The proposed method converts large-scale unorganized 3D scanned datasets into layered datasets firstly. Then based on data parallel mechanism, a loosely coupled parallel reconstruction algorithm is designed; the algorithm has less inter-node communication, so that it is more suitable for grid computing. In order to realize load balance in grid, the priority preemptive scheduling strategy is designed based on two-level scheduling model. Finally, the grid environment is built by Globus Toolkit, and the parallel reconstruction and visualization are achieved based on mpich-G2 and the Visualization Toolkit (VTK), this experiment shows that the reconstruction time is reduced significantly.

Keywords: surface reconstruction, grid computing, parallel algorithm, job Scheduling, Visualization.

1 Introduction

In the past several decades, 3D scanners have greatly developed and been widely used in the field of surface reconstruction of complicated engineering. With the development of laser scanners, it has become possible to acquire the mass data that contains more details of detected objects and realize high-fidelity modeling. But it also brings some questions, for example, the reconfiguration speed is too slow to meet real-time requirements.

In order to improve the speed of surface reconstruction from densely scattered points, the easiest way is to adopt more advanced high-performance computing equipments, which will greatly increase the application cost. On the other hand, researchers have proposed several fast algorithms. Sergei Azernikov proposed a multiresolution volumetric method, which realized fast 3D reconstruction through reducing data [1]. Amit Mhatre and Piyush Kumar used projective clustering to design and implement a fast surface reconstruction algorithm, the method relied on two new approximation algorithms: fast projective clustering and parallel dynamic nearest neighbor searching based on shifted quad-trees [2]. Yi Fa-ling and Li Qing-hua also proposed a parallel Delaunay algorithm [3]. In these methods, a significant reduction

W. Zhang et al. (Eds.): HPCA 2009, LNCS 5938, pp. 146–152, 2010.

in the amount of data will affect the reconstruction accuracy; else a small amount of data reduction can not make a strong impact to the reconfiguration speed. These common parallel algorithms such as the parallel Delaunay algorithm are the tightly coupled algorithm facing to clusters. A large number of data communications occur between sub-tasks, which are not conducive to raising the reconstruction speed greatly.

The emergence of grid computing technology provides a new opportunity to solve this problem. Grid is a geographically distributed system that enables integration of heterogeneous resources needed for execution of complex, demanding scientific and engineering applications. This paper applies grid technology to the field of surface reconstruction. By integrating the decentralized computing resources to provide a unified service for surface reconstruction, the method improves reconstruction speed and reduces the application cost.

This paper is structured as follows: section 2 describes the design of parallel algorithm based on contour line and the realization of this algorithm in grid environment, including job scheduling, parallel reconstruction and rendering. Section 3 discusses the result and analysis of the experiment. Conclusion and future work are discussed in section 4.

2 Parallel Algorithm Design of Surface Reconstruction and Application in Grid Environments

2.1 Parallel Algorithm Design Based on Contour

Because grid resources are geographically distributed and heterogeneous, a loosely coupled parallel algorithm must be designed. The surface reconstruction algorithm based on contour lines is commonly used as 3D reconstruction which based on the layered data. Because the layered data can generate contour line independently, the algorithm has good parallelism and can be used to achieve loosely coupled data parallel mechanism easily. However, the datasets that come from laser scanners generally do not have layered structure, so that it is difficult to implement contour line algorithm. This paper designed a file format conversion algorithm that changes the scattered points file into a layered file format. Then based on the contour line reconstruction algorithm, this paper designed parallel contour line reconstruction algorithm. The figure 1 shows the basic principle.

By the data parallel mechanism [4], first of all, unorganized datasets must be converted into layered datasets. Then the layered datasets will be assigned to the fittest nodes by grid scheduler module. Take the Master-Slave model for instance, the nodes that own the datasets begin to carry out parallel computation according to the parallel contour reconstruction algorithm, the computing results will be back to the master node, the master node will merger the computing results that come from slave nodes and the master node itself in accordance with the merger rules, finally the master node finished the mapping task and the visualization on the display is done in this node.

In reconstruction process, this paper used distributed storage strategy; the complete data files will be distributed to each participating sub-process node by the main process. Therefore, when the main process distributed the tasks, it simply distributes the serial numbers of tasks information to sub-processes. Sub-processes will obtain the start position and end position information according to the serial numbers, and read the data blocks which will be deal with in these nodes. Because the computing result from each node will finally become a part of display images independently, there are not too many communications among the nodes. So the speed of parallel algorithms will become faster.

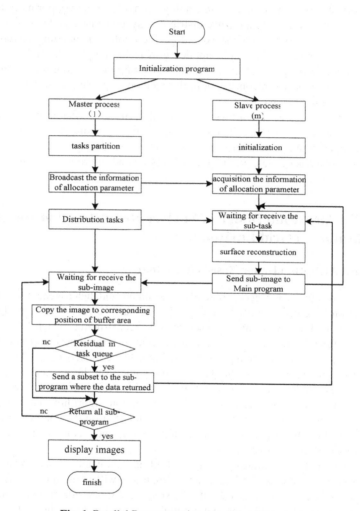

Fig. 1. Parallel Reconstruction Algorithm Flowchart

2.2 Realization of Parallel Algorithm in Grid Environment

In this paper, grid experimental platform was set up based on the Globus Tool-kit4.0.1[5], which contained one SMP cluster called Tsinghua Tongfang Explorer 108 (including 8 computing nodes and one management node) and one PC cluster with 26 personal computers. These computing resources form two grid domains.

Format Conversion of Scattered Point Files. In this paper, the unorganized scattered point data are stored as text files and have no internal links among the points. The files mainly record the three-dimensional coordinates of each data point, the format is (x y z). In order to convert unorganized datasets to layered datasets, this paper adopts VTK[6] (The Visualization Toolkit) developed by American Kitware Inc. With VTK's format conversion functions, the scattered point files can quickly be changed into layered files. First, the three-dimensional scattered point data is converted into volume data through vtkGaussianSplatter class.

```
profile->SetPoints(points);
vtkGaussianSplatter*popSplatter=vtkGaussianSplatter::
New(); popSplatter->SetInput(profile);
```

The "points" pointer is used to store three-dimensional coordinate values of scattered points. The three-dimensional coordinate values will be stored as vtkPolyData format by the "profile" pointer, and then further be converted into volume data by the vtkGaussianSplatter filter. At last, with vtkPDataSetWriter class, the volume data will be stored in a series of layered data file that own the same prefix.

```
vtkPDataSetWriter * dataslice=vtkPDataSetWriter::New();
dataslice ->SetInput(popSplatter->GetOutput());
dataslice -> SetFileName("/home/fjz/dataslice.pvtk");
dataslice ->SetNumberOfPieces(93);
dataslice ->Write();
```

Job Scheduling. In order to realize load balance in grid, this paper designs the priority preemptive scheduling strategy based on two-level scheduling model. The entire grid system is composed of two-level schedulers, which are the central scheduler (managing the entire grid) and the local grid schedulers (managing each sub-domain). Each job is submitted to the central scheduler firstly and then is unified scheduled by the central scheduler. After the jobs are allocated to each sub-grid domain, they are scheduled by the local scheduler for the second scheduling. Finally each job is distributed to the most appropriate node to implement. Priority refers to setting up priority to users, jobs and resources. The jobs submitted by different users are implemented in accordance with the priority order of the users. As to the different jobs of the same user, they are implemented in accordance with the priority order of the jobs. In addition, in the matching process about jobs and resources, it gives priority to the resources. For example, local resources often have a higher priority than the remote resources, and the resource of lower CPU occupancy rate is often given a higher priority than the resource of a higher CPU occupancy rate. It is to guarantee the best resource to match with the job. Finally it forms a job queue and a resource queue, the job that own (s) the higher user priority and the higher job priority matches with the resources that own the higher resource priority firstly.

The Condor-G technology is used to implement the scheduling strategy above. Condor-G[7] is a combination of condor and Globus. When the grid environment is composed of a number of grid domains that are managed by different types of local resources Manager, Condor-G comes in handy. In this system, the PC domain and the SMP cluster domain respectively use Condor and PBS as the local scheduler. The Condor-G is chosen as the central scheduler. Thus, the system forms a two-level scheduling model. By setting the user priority, job priority and resource priority, it makes full use of the Condor's advertisement (ClassAd) and match (MatchMaking) mechanism and implements the priority preemptive scheduling strategy. At the same time , Condor-G also has the capability of supporting the migration of job, that is, if the node running the process fails, user can monitor the situation through the central manager and then move the job to another available node to implement. The scheduling model shows in the figure 2.

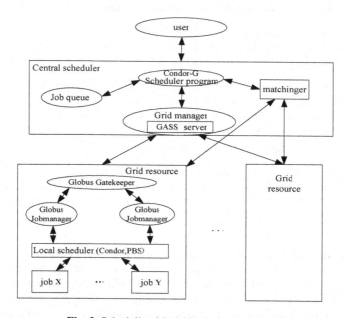

Fig. 2. Scheduling Model Based on Condor-G

Parallel Reconstruction and Visualization. In order to achieve the parallel reconstruction and visualization, this paper builds a parallel reconstruction environment based on VTK and Mpich-G2 [8].

Initialization. Through the vtkMPIController class, processes are allocated including the master-slave process information, process number, etc. Then the instance is created by using vtkParallelFactortory class and vtkObjectFactory class. The initialization of process finished.

The calculation of contour lines. The calculation of contour lines is achieved by vtkContourFilter class. After receiving the task information from the master process, the slave process reads the layered data and calls vtkContourFilter class. Then the calculation of contour lines finishes, the result will be returned to the master process through the port information.

Surface rendering. When there is no waiting tasks in task pool, the master process will render the image based on the returned information after slave processes finished all tasks and returned the results back to the master process. Rendering is realized by the class of vtkAppendPolyData and vtkPolyDataMapper. In this process, first of all, the master process merges image information by the class of vtkAppendPolyData in accordance with the task information returned from the slave processes. Then the image is drawn through vtkPolyDataMapper class. Finally, images realize remote visualization by using the VTK visualization library and VRML technology, including the setting of display window size, background and location parameters. The reconstruction images can be observed from a different angle by arbitrary spin.

3 Result and Analysis of the Experiment

The testing scattered point data of this paper all come from the Internet network. Figure 3 shows the reconstructed image of the bunny in different parallelism through the application of the above algorithm from 40,256 data points. With the increase in parallelism, the reconstruction speed has become faster. When the parallelism is 5, the time of reconstruction is only a half of that when the parallelism is 1. Obviously, the proposed algorithm is faster than sequential algorithms, and also faster than those tightly coupled parallel reconstruction algorithms because of less inter-node communication.

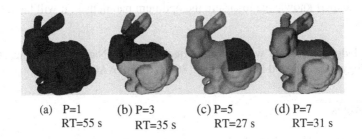

| (a) P=1 | (b) P=3 | (c) P=5 | (d) P=7 |
| RT=55 s | RT=35 s | RT=27 s | RT=31 s |

Fig. 3. Reconstructed Result in Different Parallelism (P: Parallelism, RT: Reconstructed time)

The speed-up ratio will increase in different rate with the increase of parallelism for the same dataset. When crossing a critical point, the speed-up ratio starts decreased, as shown in Figure 4.

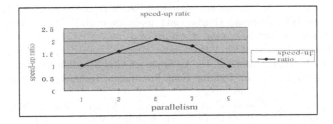

Fig. 4. Parallelism and Speed-up Ratio

It can be seen, the parallelism is not the higher the better. Although almost no communications among sub-nodes, the communications among master node and sub-nodes still exist. The communications will be more and more when the parallelism becomes higher, which will impact the speed of reconstruction. There is an optimum parallelism which makes the speed of reconstruction fastest.

4 Conclusion and Future Work

This paper has proposed a new fast method for surface reconstruction from dense scattered points. In this method, grid computing technology is applied to the field of surface reconstruction. In order to adapt to the characteristics of grid computing, a loosely coupled parallel contour reconstruction algorithm is designed based on lay-ered data and implemented with VTK and Mpich-G2. At the same time, a two-level scheduling model and the priority preemptive scheduling strategy are designed to realize load balance with Condor-G. Finally, by analyzing the speed-up ratio of the reconstruction speed in the case of different parallelism, the proposed algorithm is verified to improve the speed of reconstruction. Moreover, because of the impact of communication between the tasks, every dataset during the reconstruction has an optimum parallelism. Building an intelligent task decomposition mechanism based on agent and expert knowledge to ensure the optimum parallelism, it will be the focus of future work.

Acknowledgments. This work is supported by China National Programs for High Technology Research and Development (863, No.2006AA04Z212).

References

1. Azernikov, S., Miropolsky, A., Fischer, A.: Surface Reconstruction of Freeform Objects Based on Multiresolution Volumetric Method. In: Proceedings of the eighth ACM sympo-sium on Solid modeling and applications, Washington, USA, pp. 115–126 (2003)
2. Mhatre, A., Kumar, P.: Projective Clustering and its Application to Surface Reconstruction: Extended Abstract. In: Proceedings of Graphics Interface 2007, Canada, pp. 477–478 (2007)
3. Yi, F.-l., Li, Q.-h., Yang, W.-w.: Parallel Algorithm of Delaunay Triangulation Dividing. Mini-Micro Systems 22(4), 450–452 (2001)
4. Ahrens, J., Brisilawn, K., Martin, K., et al.: Large-Scale Data Visualization Using Parallel Data Streaming. IEEE Computer Graphics and Applications 21(4), 34–41 (2001)
5. The Globus Alliance, http://www.globus.org
6. The Visualization Toolkit, http://www.vtk.org
7. Imamagic, E., Radic, B., Dobrenic, D.: An Approach Grid Scheduling by Using Condor- G Matchmaking Mechanism. In: 28th Int. Conf. Information Technology Interfaces ITI 2006, pp. 625–631. Cavtat/Dubrovnik (2006)
8. Karonis, N., Foster, I.: MPICH-G2: A grid-enabled implementation of the Message Passing Interface. Journal of Parallel and Distributed Computing 63(5), 3–10 (2003)

Parallel Branch Prediction on GPU Platform

Liqiang He and Guangyong Zhang

College of Computer Science, Inner Mongolia University
Hohhot, Inner Mongolia 010021 P.R. China
liqiang@imu.edu.cn, zhang03_11@163.com

Abstract. Branch Prediction is a common function in nowadays microprocessor. Branch predictor is duplicated into multiple copies in each core of a multicore and many-core processor and makes prediction for multiple concurrent running programs respectively. To evaluate the parallel branch prediction in many-core processor, existed schemes generally use a parallel simulator running in CPU which does not have a real passive parallel running environment to support a many-core simulation and thus has bad simulating performance. In this paper, we firstly try to use a real many-core platform, GPU, to do a parallel branch prediction for future general purpose many-core processor. We verify the new GPU based parallel branch predictor against the traditional CPU based branch predictor. Experiment result shows that GPU based parallel simulation scheme is a promising way to faster simulating speed for future many-core processor research.

1   Introduction

Branch prediction is a common used function in nowadays superscalar or multi-core microprocessor. It uses the branch history (either local or global history or both) to predict whether a next branch instruction is taken or not taken. The accuracy of a branch predictor affects the control flow of a running program with more or less instructions executed along the wrong paths and then affects the final performance of the program. Lots of researches have done related to branch prediction [1, 2] in the past decades.

Branch prediction research generally needs a simulator. Existed schemes include cycle-by-cycle based simulator which runs a program in its simulating environment and uses the real executing flow to investigate the functionality of a branch predictor, and trace based simulator which is much simple and faster than the former but loses some run-time accuracy.

In multicore and many-core processor, branch predictor is duplicated into multiple copies in each core of the processor. Each predictor records its own branch history from the running program in the host core and makes the particular prediction respectively. There is a big design space that can be explored for branch predictors in a many-core system. For example, Branch predictors in different cores can (a) cooperate between each other to increase the prediction accuracies for multi-threaded program, or (b) dynamically combine into together

W. Zhang et al. (Eds.): HPCA 2009, LNCS 5938, pp. 153–160, 2010.
© Springer-Verlag Berlin Heidelberg 2010

to build a more powerful ones, or (c) switch off part of them to save power if their behaviors are same. Investigating or exploring the design space of the parallel branch prediction for a many-core processor needs a parallel branch predictor simulator. A general technique to build a parallel simulator in academic literature is to parallelize the traditional sequential simulator using *array* structure or *Pthread* programming. This technique may be suitable when doing research for multicore processor with less than sixteen cores but absolutely not useful or impossible for a multicore with more than thirty-two cores or a many-core cases.

In this paper, we try to use a real many-core platform, Graphic Processing Unit (GPU), to help faster simulating speed for massive parallel branch predictor research for future many-core general purpose processor. It is well known that GPU is original designed to target very regular massive parallel computing such as matrix operation, FFT, and lineal algebra. But the processor simulating, including branch prediction, cache accessing, pipeline processing, has a very irregular program behavior which GPU does not favor initially. To our best knowledge, this is the first work that tries to (a) map an irregular program to a regular organized GPU structure and (b) use the existed massive parallel GPU platform to do many-core microprocessor architecture research, especially parallel branch prediction in this paper.

We rewrite most of the code of the branch predictor component in a widely used superscalar processor simulator, SimpleScalar [3], and let them run in a real many-core platform, NVIDIA GeForce9600GT GPU processor [4]. We verify our result (including the control flow and branch predicting outputs of the simulated program) from GPU running against the one from the original CPU based running. Experiment results show that (a) the GPU based code can perform exactly the same functionality as the compared CPU based code which verifies the correctness of our code and proofs the ability of GPU to do irregular operations, and (b) the GPU code can potentially faster the simulating speed with its many-core structure when comparing with the serialized CPU code.

The rest of this paper is organized as follows. Section 2 presents GPU architecture. Section 3 simply introduces the rationale of the branch predictor in this paper and the organization of the parallel branch predictor in future many-core microprocessor. Section 4 describes the design and implementation of our GPU based parallel branch prediction simulator. Section 5 gives the experimental methodology and results. Section 6 discusses the related works, and Section 7 concludes this paper.

2   GPU Architecture

2.1   Hardware Model

The structures of CPU and GPU are shown in Figure 1. The more transistors on GPU are devoted to data processing rather than data caching and flow control. The GeForce 9600 GT architecture has 8 multiprocessors per chip and 8 processors (ALUs) per multiprocessor.

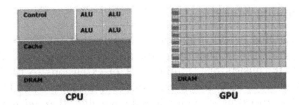

Fig. 1. The GPU Devotes More Transistors to Data Processing than CPU[5]

2.2   Memory Model

The memory model of NVIDIA GeForce 9600 GT is shown in Figure 2 (left). Each multiprocessor has on-chip memory of the following four types.

- One set of local 32-bit registers per processor. The total number of registers per multiprocessor is 8192.
- A shared memory that is shared by all the processors of a multiprocessor. The size of this shared memory per multiprocessor is 16 KB and it is organized into 16 banks.
- A read-only constant cache that is shared by all scalar processor cores and speeds up reads from the constant memory space, which is a read-only region of device memory. The size of the constant cache is 8 KB per multiprocessor.
- A read-only texture cache that is shared by all the processors in a multiprocessor, which speeds up reads from the texture memory space. The texture cache size is 8 KB per multiprocessor.

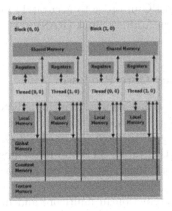
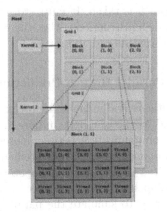

Fig. 2. CUDA Memory (left) and Programming (right) Model[5]

The local and global memory spaces are read-write regions of device memory and are not cached. A single floating point value read from (or written to) global memory can take 400 to 600 clock cycles. CPU and GPU transfer data through the global memory.

2.3 Programming Model

CUDA's programming model (Fig.2.right)assumes that the threads execute on a physically separate device that operates as a coprocessor to the host running the C program. It consists of a minimal set of extensions to the C language and a runtime library. GPU is a typical SIMD parallel model. The CPU implements parallel processing of multi-threads by calling **kernel** function which runs on GPU. A group of threads with multiple same instructions and different data streams form a **block**, different blocks can execute different instruction streams, and many *blocks* form a **grid**. *Thread, block* and *grid* form a three-dimensional-thread-space. For convenience, **threadIdx** is a 3-component vector, so that threads can be identified using a one-dimensional, two-dimensional, or three-dimensional thread index, forming a one, two, or three-dimensional thread block.

3 Rationale of Branch Predictor

3.1 2Bits Branch Predictor in Single Core

2Bits branch prediction is a simple and well known prediction scheme. Although the prediction accuracy is much less than many up-to-date complicated branch predictors like OGEHL [1] and L_TAGE [2], but it is sufficient to be an example to show how to realize a parallel branch predictor in GPU. In a 2Bits branch predictor, there is a table to record the local histories of different branches, and each entry of the table uses 2 bits to trace the recent branch history of one branch instruction. A set-associate cache, BTB, provides the branch target if the branch is taken. It must store the entire PC in order to accurately match the branch instructions. Also, there is a Return Address Stack (RAS) to be used for sub-routine call and return.

3.2 Parallel Branch Prediction in Many-Core Processor

In multicore and many-core processor, each core has its own branch predictor to be used by the program running in it. Cores are connected through crossbar or grid. Communication between cores can be done through the on-chip link. All the components in a branch predictor, predicting table, BTB and RAS, must be duplicated in each core. The operations in these separate predictors are parallel and independent on each other.

In order to simulate the parallel branch prediction in multicore and many-core processor, people can change the scalar data structure in original simulator with **array** and **for** loop structure, or using **Pthread** parallel programming technique. But these methods are only useful when the number of cores is less than thirty-two in our experiment. When the cores are more then thirty-two, the simulating speed is dropped dramatically, and sometime it is unacceptable for the researcher. In this paper, we try to use an existed many-core platform, GPU, to construct our massive parallel branch predictor. It is well known that

GPU is designed for massive regular operation. But processor simulating, including branch predicting, has very irregular program behaviors. How to map such irregular applications into the GPU platform is interest for us. To our best knowledge known, this is the first work that tries to map such irregular program, especially branch predictor, into GPU platform.

4   Parallel Branch Prediction in Many-Core Processor

We use SimpleScalar as our baseline implementation. It models a five-stage, out-of-order superscalar microprocessor. In this paper, we select 2Bits prediction scheme as an example to realize in GPU platform, but it is easy to port our method for other prediction schemes.

To do branch prediction, SimpleScalar uses two functions, *lookup()* and *update()*. The *lookup* function is to do predicting using the PC of branch instruction, and the *update* is to do updating predicting table using the actual branch result when the previous prediction is wrong.

To port the CPU codes to GPU, we need to do two steps. First, there are many *Static* variables in original code that can not be handled by GPU program. So we need redefine all these variables to global variables such that they can be ported into GPU code. Second, we rewrite the two functions, *lookup* and *update*, to GPU kernel fashion. To do this, (a) all the definitions of *Structure* need to change to *Array*, and the corresponding variables need to be redefined, (b) for the variables used as the interface of *kernel* we need define two same entities, one is for CPU, and the other is for GPU, and the values of GPU variables need to be transferred from the corresponding CPU ones, and (c) the prediction result needs to be copied back to CPU in order to be used by other part of the codes. The method to call the two GPU kernels in CPU part is as follows:

$$bpred\_lookup <<< 1, NUM >>> ( )$$

and

$$bpred\_update <<< 1, NUM >>> ( )$$

Where *NUM* is the number of predictors we want to parallel simulate. Through varying the value of *NUM*, we can model different number of parallel branch predictors in a multicore or many-core processor.

5   Experiment Setup and Result

Our experiment is conducted in Fedora Core 8 Linux system. The GPU chip is NVIDIA GeForce9600 GT, and we use CUDA 2.1 programming environment. Four benchmark programs, *mgrid, applu, apsi,* and *crafty,* are selected from SPEC CPU 2000 [7]. In our 2Bits branch predictor, branch history table has 2K entries, BTB is 4 way-associated and has 512 sets, and RAS has 8 entries. We validate our GPU based implementation against the CPU based one, and prove the correctness of the GPU one in logic semantics. Thus, in the following content, we only show and compare the running time of different implementations, and do not present the prediction results due to the meaningless of this work.

In our experiment, due to the hardware (global memory and register file) limitation we can only fork up to four parallel predictors in GPU. Although it is not desirable for our motivation of this work, it is acceptable for us at present time because this is our first step to target our final objective. The main task for us in this stage is to verify our thinking that GPU can handle irregular applications as the regular ones, and try to investigate the potential speedup of using GPU vs. CPU. Improving the parallelism will be our next work in the future. For the experiment, we construct two-threads, three-threads, and four-threads workloads using a same SPEC program, and compare the running time in GPU platform with the one in CPU platform. To be fairness, we run the same experiment four times and use the average number as the final result.

Table 1 shows the program running times in CPU and GPU respectively. It is clear to see that GPU based running time is much longer than the CPU based one, and it is not like the intuitively desired result. Through carefully analysis we know that it is because of the low parallelism (the maximum is four) of our experiments. When the kernels are called from CPU, lots of data need to be transferred to GPU, and the calling and returning also need time to finish, thus the communication between CPU and GPU takes most of the running time for our GPU based implementation which causes the performance degradation. If we can successfully increase the parallelism, then the GPU code will surpass the CPU one.

In another view, Figure 3 (left) shows the running times of four programs with different number of threads. When the number increases from one to four, the time does not change a lot, especially at 2, 3, and 4 threads cases. Compare with the data shown in Figure 3 (right), the running times in CPU increase

Table 1. Program running times in CPU and GPU

Benchmark	No. of Thread	1	2	3	4
mgrid	CPU	393.30	439.11	477.94	526.87
	GPU	8416.0	8445.28	8457.31	8428.12
	Ratio	21.39	19.23	17.69	15.99
applu	CPU	332.08	347.91	365.42	376.76
	GPU	2757.15	3243.70	3243.09	3237.75
	Ratio	8.30	9.32	8.87	8.59
apsi	CPU	379.29	421.45	453.84	492.92
	GPU	7072.14	8973.61	8942.55	8984.73
	Ratio	18.64	21.29	19.70	18.22
crafty	CPU	435.07	553.10	648.38	742.95
	GPU	18040.9	21757.1	21773.5	21748.8
	Ratio	41.46	39.33	33.58	29.27

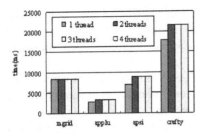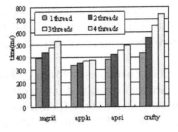

Fig. 3. Running times in GPU (left) or CPU (right) with different number of threads

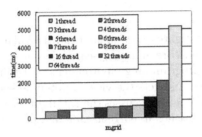

Fig. 4. Running times of *mgrid* in CPU with different number of threads

continuously with the number of threads increasing. For crafty, the times increase dramatically for four threads running vs. the single thread running. All the data shows that GPU has a good extendibility than CPU in terms of the parallel program running.

To further show the CPU limitation, we run mgrid in CPU platform with up to sixty-four threads. Figure 4 shows that when the number of parallel running program is greater than sixteen, the running time increases dramatically in CPU platform. Thus if we can improve the parallelism of our GPU based code, a big speedup can be obtained. To do this, we must take the hardware limitation into account when designing the software. As presented in section 2, the global memory, especially the register file, are very limited resources, so we must split out big kernel into small ones such that we can fork more parallel threads and let them run concurrently in GPU and get speedup over the CPU implementation.

6   Related Works

Branch prediction has got long time attention in industry and academic research literature. Most of the researches focus on how to improve the predicting accuracy [1, 2], and less work has been done on how to simulate massive parallel branch predicting for future large scale multicore and many-core processor.

GPU was announced initially for graphic process, but recently due to the highly parallel structure and powerful computing capability GPU has been widely used in massive scientific computing applications [8, 9], such as GPGPU [10]. Most of applications in GPGPU are regular computation, and very few works have been done for irregular application, microprocessor simulating for instance.

This work, to our best knowledge known, is the first work that targets the GPU on very irregular application, multicore and many-core processor simulating. Although we do not obtain performance speedup over CPU based code, we verify our idea of port CPU code to GPU platform, and know the potential speedup of GPU vs. CPU ones. The further improvement of our code will leave for our future work.

7   Conclusion

This paper, firstly, investigates how to map an irregular application, parallel branch predicting for multicore and many-core microprocessor in GPU platform using NVIDIA CUDA programming environment. It verifies the correctness of the GPU implementation and gets the view of potential speedup of GPU implementation over the CPU one. It discusses the details of the GPU implementation, and analyzes the existed issues in current code and presents the future work of this paper.

Acknowledgements

This work is supported by Inner Mongolia Natural Science Foundation Project No. 208091, and the Ph.D Research Startup Foundation of Inner Mongolia University No. 208041.

References

1. Seznec, A.: Analysis of the OGEHL predictor. In: Proceedings of the 32th International Symposium on Computer Architecture (IEEE-ACM), Madison (June 2005)
2. Seznec, A.: A 256 Kbits L-TAGE predictor, CBP-2 (December 2006)
3. Burger, D., Austin, T.M.: The SimpleScalar Tool Set, Version 2.0. ACM SIGARCH Computer Architecture News 25(3), 13–25 (1997)
4. NVIDIA GeForce 9600 GT,
   http://www.nvidia.com/object/product_geforce_9600gt_us.html
5. NVIDIA CUDA: Programming Guide. Version 2.2. (4/2/2009)
6. Lee, J.K.L., Smith, A.J.: Branch prediction strategies and branch target buffer design. Computer 17(1) (January 1984)
7. Henning, J.: SPEC CPU2000: Measuring CPU Performance in the New Millennium. IEEE Computer, Los Alamitos (2000)
8. Kerr, A., Campbell, D., Richards, M.: QR Decomposition on GPUs. In: Proceeding of 2nd Workshop on GPGPU 2009, Washington, D.C., USA, March 8 (2009)
9. Gulati, K., Croix, J.F., Khatri, S.P., Shastry, R.: Fast Circuit Simulation on Graphics Processing Units (IEEE) (2009)
10. GPGPU, http://www.nvidia.cn/object/cuda_home_cn.html

Calculation of TNT Equivalence of Composite Propellant and Visualized Software Development

Ning He[1], Cong Xiang[2], Bin Qin[2], and Qi Zhang[3]

State Key Laboratory of Explosion Science and Technology,
Beijing institute of technology, BJ 100081, PRC
HeNing@bit.edu.cn

Abstract. It is one of the main factors on safety researching that effective measures should be taken to determine the TNT equivalence of composite propellant. This paper based on the minimum free energy method, programmed composition with MATLAB for calculating equilibrium products of composite propellant detonation and TNT equivalence of composite propellant with different ratio, and developed visualized software. The results show that the higher mass fraction of aluminum powder was, the higher thermal damage to the environment was for the same mass of composite propellant. Meanwhile the increasing of the mass fraction of solid explosives in all the components will improve the explosive properties, which will provide some theoretical foundations for the risk assessment of composite propellant and provide foundations for the safety performance of composite propellant.

1 Introduction

Composite propellant is the power source of rockets and missile engines; it is difficult to distinguish the solid propellant from explosives by chemical natures. Its reaction heat and energy density can match those of conventional high efficiency explosives or even much higher. It is not only a burning material in accordance with some law, but also a material with potential danger of explosion or detonation. On the other hand, since high energy explosives adding is involved in all the processes of high energy composite propellant manufacturing, the danger classes and safe distance of building should be determine according to the actual dangerous when designing of its manufacturing workshop, processing workshop and storage warehouse. However systematic research has not yet been carried out on the safety of high energy composite propellant, which hinders the arming process of high performance weapons. This issue has become increasingly prominent with the increasing applications of high energy composite propellant in rockets, missiles and other high-tech weapons and equipments. Therefore it is a necessary task to carry out the TNT equivalence of composite propellant.

In previous studies, the determination of TNT equivalence of composite propellant is mainly based on experimental study i.e. researches are carried out to determine the TNT equivalence of explosive according to the actual explosion output. Simulation pressure consistent of the air explosion of TNT explosive and

W. Zhang et al. (Eds.): HPCA 2009, LNCS 5938, pp. 161–168, 2010.

composite propellant matching the experiment results can be got after air explosion experiments of some quantities of TNT explosive and composite propellant. But the affection to its explosive heat due to different ratio of composite propellant is neglected in experiment researches. Based on the minimum free energy method, the paper program composition with MATLAB to calculate the detonation balance products of composite propellant and determine the detonation heat of composite propellant, which can provide foundations for the risk assessment, improving the risk analysis awareness of composite propellant, and determine the danger classes of composite propellants, danger classes of the workshop and its external and internal safety distance.

2   Determination of the TNT Equivalent of Composite Propellant

Detonation is the extreme state of explosion. The physical parameters of composite propellant under detonation state should be considered as basic index for safety assessment when considering the system safety analysis. Composite propellant detonation parameters are the important indicators of its safety assessment. Since there are not yet experimental methods to determine C-J detonation products components, we can only determine them by theoretic calculation.

In 1958, W. B. White and some others presented to use minimum free energy method to calculate system chemical balance. After later scientists' deep study in accordance with the thermal dynamics theory, they found that assuming that the detonation gas as ideal gas, then the total free energy equals the total of each component's free energy. When the system reaches chemical balance, the total free energy is the minimum. Thus considering the detonation procedure of composite propellant, the components percentages which make the system's total free energy minimum is the detonation balance components under certain temperature and pressure. The system may also contain gaseous products and condensed products (for instanceincomplete combustion carbon particles). Assuming that there is a system consists of l kind of chemical elements, which will generate n kind of gaseous products and n-m kind of condensed products after combustion. Its free energy function is as follows:

$$G(n) = \sum_{i=1}^{m} [x_i^g \left(\frac{G_m^\theta}{RT}\right)_i^g + x_i^g \ln p + x_i^g \ln \frac{x_i^g}{\overline{x}^g}] + \sum_{i=m+1}^{n} x_i^{cd} \left(\frac{G_m^\theta}{RT}\right)_i^{cd}. \quad (1)$$

Where: $G(n)$ is the function of system total free energy; $G_i^g(x_i^g)$ is the free energy function of the ith gaseous component; $G_i^{cd}(x_i^{cd})$ is the free energy function of the ith condensed component; G_m^θ is the material standard free energy; x_i^g is the amount of the ith gaseous components; x_i^{cd} is the amount of the ith condensed component; n is the system amount of substance including all components; T is the system temperature; P is the system pressure.

Atomic conservation equation is:

$$n_j = \Sigma_{i=1}^{m} a_{ij} x_i^g + \sum_{i=m+1}^{n} d_{ij} x_i^{cd}. \qquad \text{J} = (1, 2, 3, l) \qquad (2)$$

where n_j is the jth amout of substance; a_{ij} is the jth amount of substance in the ith gaseous components; d_{ij} is the jth amount of substance in the ith condense components. The system free energy function (1) and atomic conservation equation (2) are the basic equations to calculating the balance components of the system. According to the basic equations, the iterative equation group (3)–(5) is as follows:

$$a_j(1+u) + \sum_{j=1}^{l} r_{jk}\pi_j + \sum_{i=m+1}^{n} d_{ij} x_i^{cd} = n_j + \sum_{i=1}^{m} a_{ij} y_i^g (C_i^g + \ln y_i^g - \ln \bar{y}^g). \quad (3)$$

$$\sum_{i=1}^{m} G_i^g(y) = \sum_{j=1}^{l} \pi_j a_j. \qquad (4)$$

$$C_i^{cd} - \sum_{j=1}^{l} \pi_j d_{ij} = 0. \qquad (5)$$

If negative value occurs during the equation iterative, damping factor λ can be adopted for correction, so as to make certain the iterative calculating works successfully. Assuming $\Delta_i^g = x_i^g - y_i^g$, then, $Z_i = y_i^g + \lambda \Delta_i^g = y_i^g + \lambda(x_i^g - y_i^g)$, Z_i will be the initiative value of next iterative.

Iterative partial code is as follows:

```
p1 = 1; t1 = 298.16;
while(1)
Gc = G(1) * C;
Gal2o3 = G(19) * Al2O3;
Y = [ CO CO2 H2O H2 Cl2 HCl F2 HF O2 N2 NO OH H O N Cl F ];
for i = 1 : 17
        if Y(i) == 0
        Gy(i) = 0;
    else
        Gy(i) = Y(i) * (G(i + 1) + log( p2 * Y ( i )/ sum( Y )));
    end
end

GY1 = sum(Gy) + Gc + Gal2o3;
r = zeros ( 7, 7);
for i = 1 : 7
   for j = 1 : 7
      for k = 1 : 17
         r(i , j) = r(i , j) + a(k , i) * (k , j) * Y(k);
```

```
      end
    end
  end
  for i = 1 : 7
    alpha(i) = sum( a( : , i)'. * Y);
  end

  GY201 = xc * G(1);
  GY219 = xal2o3 * G(19);
  for i = 1 : 17
    if x( i ) == 0
    else
      GY2 = GY201+ GY219 + x(i) * (G(i + 1) + log(p2 * x(i)/ sum(x)));
    end
  end
```

3   Results

In this paper, 1 *mol* of Four different formulations composite propellants are
used to calculate, the mass ratio of components for each composite propellant
see Table1.

Table 1. The mass ratio of each component

Groups	Ammonium perchlorate(%)	Aluminum(%)	HTPB(%)	RDX(%)
1	70	18	12	–
2	70	5	10	15
3	60	28	12	–
4	47.4	6	13.8	32.8

Table 2. Detonation balance products of each group[1]

Major product	Group 1	Group 2	Group 3	Group 4
H_2O	0.5455	1.3815	0.3146	1.1897
H_2	0.5134	0.2904	0.4943	0.8193
O_2	1.17e-16	1.05e-7	2.97e-21	7.09e-11
CO	0.0951	0.2594	0.0970	0.1981
CO	0.2700	0.3846	0.2637	0.4884
NO	2.60e-11	2.31e-5	2.133e-14	1.62e-7
N	0.202	0.458	0.144	0.6253
Cl	3.65e-8	1.6e-4	3.790e-10	4.43e-6
HCl	0.404	0.5358	0.288	0.3928
Al_2O	2.84e-25	3.48e-13	2.392e-33	2.73e-16
$Al_2O_3(s)$	0.2034	0.0783	0.2268	0.1171
$Al(s)$	0.0452	0.0174	0.1312	0.0261
$C(s)$	0.2388	0.4505	0.1409	0.7334

1) No reliable experimental data for C-J detonation balance
products till now, reference only.

Table 3. TNT equivalent of four groups of composite propellants

		Group 1	Group 2	Group 3	Group 4
Explosion Heat (MJ/kg)		3.616	4.36	4.05	6.74
TNT equivalent		0.798	0.95	0.89	1.48

Detonation balance products of each group see results in Table 2. Calculated with the explosion heat according to similar energy principle, the TNT equivalent of four different composite propellant groups see Table 3.

4   Visualized Software for TNT Equivalent Calculating

4.1   Introduction to Visualized Software

Operate the software mainly by setting the initial conditions and the distribution ratio of propellant group; Calculating; and the results outputting three steps. The software interface shown below, and an example was presented for introducing how to use the software.

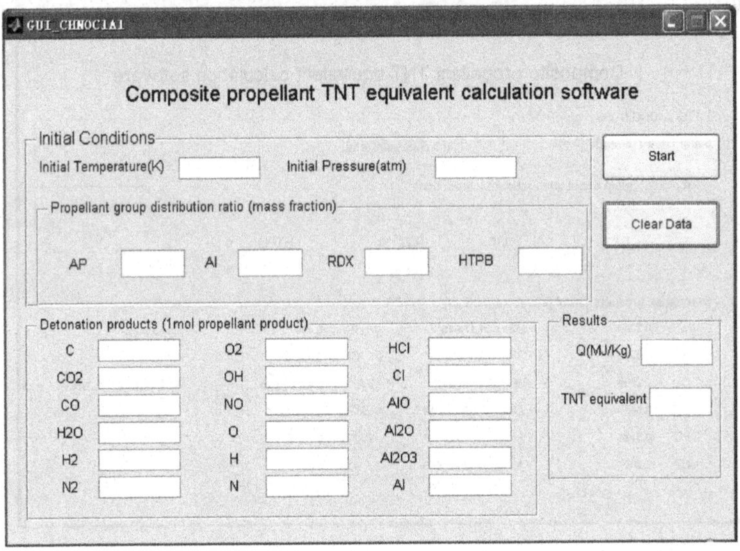

Fig. 1. The software interface. Setting the initial conditions and the distribution ratio of propellant group.

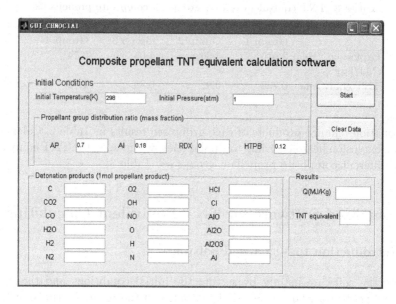

Fig. 2. Taken Group 1 for an example, input related data, clicks 'Start' to calculate

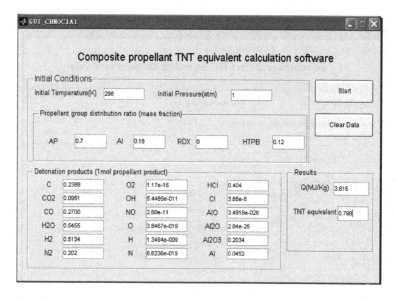

Fig. 3. Results show after the calculation. If a new calculation to be started, click 'Clear Data' to exit the last operate, then start a new calculation after return to the main interface of the software.

4.2   Features of Visualized Software

Simple operations and easy to use. Visualized software is developed with MATLAB, which interface is simple and easy to use. Those researchers familiar with MATLAB can master the software as easily as common office software and soon start calculation work. Usually, researchers can calculate the detonation balance products, explosion heat value and TNT equivalent of the composite propellant after inputting the initial values after the prompt of the interface labels. (Now the components of composite propellant applies to this software include AP, Al, RDX and HTPB. If needed, the software can be developed further for the application of other formula components.)

Higher accuracy. This software based on the minimum free energy method to calculate the balance components of detonation products, which can describe the state of detonation products very well, thus its results is close to the true values. For simple chemical reactions, equilibrium constant can be used to determine the balance components. But the complex products of propellant detonation may be as many as dozens, including C, H, O, N, Cl, F, Al and other elements. So the calculating to its chemical balance will involve in dozens of chemical reactions, and need to establish large non-linear equation group, which chemical balance equilibrium constant is difficult to be determined accurately, and the equation group is difficult to be solved. While the minimum free energy ignores the detailed chemical reaction processes, only take the final equilibrium state into consideration, which can establish linear equation group only for the conditions of element conservation and minimum free energy, so the calculation is simplified greatly.

5   Conclusions

The results shows that with the same initial conditions, same quantity composite propellant, the more the Al powder content is, the larger explosion heat is, that is, Al powder will improve the explosion heat of high energy composite propellant. With the increasing of solid explosive content, the explosive performance of the propellant will be improved.

Visualized software for the TNT equivalent calculating of composite propellant makes the determination of the product of propellant detonation and calculation of TNT equivalent much easier and more convenient, which can avoid lots of experiments cost, help to provide some theoretical foundations for the danger evaluation of composite propellant and acknowledgement of its safety performance.

References

1. Babuk, V.A., Vassiliev, V.A., Sviridov, V.V.: Propellant formulation factors and metal agglomeration in combustion of aluminized solid rocket propellan. Combustion science and technology 163, 261–289 (2001)

2. Sun, Y., Li, S.: Combustion Characteristics of Coated Nano Aluminum in Composite Propellants. Defence Science Journal 56 (2006)
3. Xinhua, C., Wansheng, N.: Research of Explosive Characteristic of Hypergolic Propellant. Theory and Practice of Energetic Materials 5, 300–304 (2003)
4. Jianhong, Y., Jinglong, X.: Calculation of TNT Equivalence of High Energy Propellant. Computer Simulation 23, 992–1003 (2006)
5. Qingzhong, C., Qingjie, J.: Design of the Ingredients of Black Powder Energtic Materials. IEEE Trans. Magn. 12, 214–217 (2004)
6. He, Z., Suozhang, C.: The OptimalMathematicsModel on Con stitution of Combustion Balance. Journal of North China Institute of Technology 24, 332–335 (2003)
7. Xue, W., Pan, G., Yi, L.: Minimum free energy method Pyrotechnic products balance calculation. Chinese Journal of Explosives and Propellants 4, 61–63 (1999)
8. Song, D., Pan, G., Wang, N.: Calculational Model of Pyrotechnical Combustion Products Based on Minimum Free Energy. Journal of Projectiles, Rockets, Missiles and Guidance 1, 61–63 (2006)
9. Wang, T., Li, S.: Free-Energy Minimization Investigation on Combustion of GAP Under Constant Pressure and Adiabatic Condition. Chinese Journal of Explosives and Propellants 4, 16–19 (2003)
10. Miccio, F.: Numerical modeling of composite propellant combustion. Symposium (International) on Combustion 2, 2387–2395 (1998)
11. Wang, X., Jackson, T.L., Massa, L.: Numerical simulation of heterogeneous propellant combustion by a level set method. Combustion, Theory and Modelling 8, 227–254 (2004)
12. Weidong, C., Piyush, T., Vigor, Y.: A model of AP/HTPB composite propellant combustion in rocket-motor environments. Combustion Science and Technology 180, 2143–2169 (2008)

The High Performance Computing on the Crash-Safety Analysis*

Lei Hou[1,2], Haiyan Ding[1], Hanling Li[1], and Lin Qiu[2]

[1] Dept. of Mathematics, Shanghai University, Shanghai 200444
[2] Division of Computational Science E-Institute of
Shanghai Universities at SJTU, China
houlei@staff.shu.edu.cn

Abstract. In this paper an application of angle variation boundary condition are discussed for the virtual test methods in the structure deformation safety analysis. The mathematical review and finite element simulations are given to yield further study on the theoretical model and practical testing standards with the statistical conclusion.

1 Introduction

By useful mathematical models and virtual tests (CAE, FEA) scientists and engineers have been studying in depth how to create a link between the crucial life saving virtual test and the celebrated dry honeycomb structure (phase1-P1) [LLS] with the visco-elastic plastic (phase2-P2) theory[HHa, LLu, CaCZ].

Several articles are useful sources of information; for example, [MCr, LLS, JSe] are standard texts giving mathematical and engineering perspectives upon the subject. Further more [H] gave specific computational method, in which the rate control of honeycomb strength is based on the non-recoverable crush densification. In this paper we introduce the development of recoverable controlled fluid-structure interaction soft solid conceptP2from 2 dimension [LLu] to 3 dimension [CaCZ, YX] in positive definite FEA schemes. Most non-Newtonian fluids are characterized by an underlying microstructure that is primarily responsible for creating the macroscopic properties of non-Newtonian fluids such as elongation [P, TTa].

Some of the effects of "visco elasticity" like Weissenberg effects [JSe] include die swell are non-Newtonian. Wherein fluid emerges from a pipe and then undergoes a subsequent and sudden radial expansion downstream. The first stable choice for three field Stokes equation without the Newtonian viscosity has been made in the work by [JSe]. After Marchal and Crochet [MCr, LLS] the research had been focused on the reformulation of the momentum equation[GN], so that it includes the contribution of the micro-scopic effects towards the FEA solution of the P-T/T equation in calculation of the macro-scopic non-Newtonian stress flow [LLu]. It is not possible to review all relevant studies here. In our

---

* The authors gratefully acknowledge the support of NSFC(10871225) and SLADP(J.50101).

W. Zhang et al. (Eds.): HPCA 2009, LNCS 5938, pp. 169–176, 2010.

framework, a simple numerical shift can introduce the contribution of the micro-scopic shell element model [H] towards the currently validated macro-scopic non-Newtonian models. The crash safety analysis is performed in the paper and the super-convergence results are presented in the figures according to the hermite interpolation on the rectanguler mesh for 2 and 3 dimension[LLS, LLu].

2 The Hermite Finite Element Model and Its Convergence Analysis

By use of standard rheologic term in material physics, we may analyze the spe-cial feature of the non-Newtonian P-T/T equation, for the resistance to the extensional and simple shear rate

$$\lambda \underline{\dot{\tau}} = [2\eta \underline{\underline{D}} - \exp\{\tfrac{\varepsilon \lambda}{\eta_0}(\tau_{xx} + \tau_{yy})\}\underline{\tau}] - \lambda[\underline{u} \bullet \nabla \underline{\tau} - \nabla \underline{u} \bullet \underline{\tau} - (\nabla \underline{u} \bullet \underline{\tau})^T$$
$$+\xi(\underline{\underline{D}} \bullet \underline{\tau} + (\underline{\underline{D}} \bullet \underline{\tau})^T], \quad in \quad \Omega$$

which gives best estimate of the stress over-shoot for the elongating element over-stretch known as non-slip impact hardening besides the simple shear. Here $\underline{\tau}$ is the stress field, $\underline{\underline{D}}$ is strain, μ is the deformation velocity field in e/p material, η is the viscosity, λ the relaxation constant, ε is the elongation rate, ξ is the shear rate, ρ is the density. The FEA calculation of the moving Maxwell type equation is at least 3rd-order of convergence by use of the Hermite bicubic elements.

For each element the interpolation shape function $\varphi_j^{(k,l)}(x,y)$ are defined as:

$$f(x,y) = \sum_{j=1}^{N} \sum_{0 \leq k,l \leq 1} f^{(k,l)}(x_j, y_j)\varphi_j^{(k,l)}(x,y) = \sum_{j=1}^{N} \sum_{0 \leq k,l \leq 1} f^{(k,l)}\varphi_j^{(k,l)}$$

Here $f^{(k,l)}(x,y) = \frac{\partial^{k+l} f}{\partial^k x \partial^l y}$, The interpolation shape functions are:

$$\varphi_i^{(0,0)}(\xi,\eta) = (1 + \xi_i\xi)^2(1 + \eta_i\eta)^2(2 - \xi_i\xi)(2 - \eta_i\eta)/16,$$

$$\varphi_i^{(1,0)}(\xi,\eta) = \xi_i(1 + \xi_i\xi)(\xi^2 - 1)(1 + \eta_i\eta)^2(2 - \eta_i\eta)/16,$$

$$\varphi_i^{(0,1)}(\xi,\eta) = \eta_i(1 + \eta_i\eta)(\eta^2 - 1)(1 + \xi_i\xi)^2(2 - \xi_i\xi)/16,$$

$$\varphi_i^{(1,1)}(\xi,\eta) = \xi_i\eta_i(1 - \xi^2)(1 - \eta^2)(1 + \xi_i\xi)(1 + \eta_i\eta)/16,$$

Here $\{\xi_i\} = \{-1, 1, 1, -1\}$, $\{\eta_i\} = \{-1, -1, 1, 1\}$, $i = 1, 2, 3, 4$.

On the other hand, we calculated the large e/p deformation resulting from stress rate $\dot{\tau}$ known as shear thinning. That is the Cauchy conservation equation subject to the P-T/T stress effects

$$\rho \underline{\dot{u}} = [\nabla \bullet \underline{\tau} - \rho \underline{u} \bullet \nabla \underline{u}], in \ \Omega - \Gamma_0$$

including the velocity field $\underline{u}$ in region Ω -Γ_0 . The initial boundary condition of stress is decided by static test $\underline{\tau}(0)$ in the impact experiment and the impact speed $\underline{\mu}(0)$ that is: $\underline{\tau}(0) = \underline{\tau}(static)$; $\underline{\mu}(0) = \mu_{x_0}$ on $\Gamma_0 \subset \Gamma$ where Ω is the material volume, Γ is the surface, Γ_0 is the contacted surface(along x moving boundary direction). We treat the boundary (usually singular) between the contacting and non-contacting surfaces as the free surface or flow from over-stretched. Extensional dominated flow of visco-elastic fluids are encountered in many practical situations (e.g. fiber spinning, spray and atomization, and extensional rheometry).

The positive definite semi-discretized form of the Runge-Kutta-Galerkin method is the simplified step of the coupled Cauchy P-T/T equations. The further higher order computation is based on the following analysis

$$\frac{\partial \underline{u}}{\partial t} = \frac{1}{\rho}\nabla \cdot \underline{\tau} - \underline{u} \cdot \nabla \underline{u}$$

With discrete component form[HQ, MCr, LLS]

$$\frac{\partial}{\partial t}\{u_x\}_{4N} = \frac{1}{\rho}\{A\}^{-1}_{4N\times 4N} \cdot (\{B_1\}_{4N\times 4N} \cdot \{\tau_{xx}\}_{4N} + \{B_2\}_{4N\times 4N} \cdot \{\tau_{xy}\}_{4N})$$

$$-\sum_{j=1}^{N} \sum_{0\leq k,l\leq 1} u_x^{(k,l)}(j)\,\{A\}^{-1}_{4N\times 4N} \cdot \{E1j(k,l)\}_{4N\times 4N} \cdot \{u_x\}_{4N}$$

$$-\sum_{j=1}^{N} \sum_{0\leq k,l\leq 1} u_y^{(k,l)}(j)\,\{A\}^{-1}_{4N\times 4N} \cdot \{E2j(k,l)\}_{4N\times 4N} \cdot \{u_x\}_{4N}$$

The 3rd order convergence is guaranteed with the 4 point bicubic elements in the Hemite finite element space domain; while keep the model geometry hence, the stiff matrix in a positive definite condition. Therefore it is a fixed time (0< t < t1≪∞) stable numeric scheme (transient LBB). Further more the 2nd and 3rd order Runge-Kutta method have been tested with geometric dimensional controlled time steps to yield the accurate stable solution (the 4th and 3rd order solution are identical) in a sense of evolutionary stability.

For contact thin-layer near boundary an anisotropic visco-elastic P-T/T equation is studied to analyse (an exponential impact term has been added to the UCM equation) the following semi-discrete equations, the Galerkin-Runge-Kutta (3rd order or higher) scheme

$$\{\dot{\tau}_{xx}^{n+1}\} = \frac{1}{2}(\{Fp_1\}^n + \{Fp_1\}_{pre}^{n+1})$$

$$\{\dot{\tau}_{yy}^{n+1}\} = \frac{1}{2}(\{Fp_2\}^n + \{Fp_2\}_{pre}^{n+1})$$

$$\{\dot{\tau}_{xy}^{n+1}\} = \frac{1}{2}(\{Fp_3\}^n + \{Fp_3\}_{pre}^{n+1})$$

where

$$Fp_1 = \frac{2\eta}{\lambda} \cdot \{A\}_{4N\times 4N}^{-1} \cdot \{B1\}_{4N\times 4N} \cdot \{u_x\}_{4N} + 2(1-\zeta) \cdot \sum_{j=1}^{N} \sum_{0\leq k,l\leq 1} \tau_{xx}^{(k,l)}(j)$$

$$\{A\}_{4N\times 4N}^{-1} \cdot \{E1j(k,l)\}_{4N\times 4N} \cdot \{u_x\}_{4N} - \frac{1}{\lambda} \cdot \{\tau_{xx}\}_{4N}$$

$$+ (2-\zeta) \cdot \sum_{j=1}^{N} \sum_{0\leq k,l\leq 1} \tau_{xy}^{(k,l)}(j) \{A\}_{4N\times 4N}^{-1} \cdot \{E2j(k,l)\}_{4N\times 4N} \cdot \{u_x\}_{4N}$$

$$- \zeta \cdot \sum_{j=1}^{N} \sum_{0\leq k,l\leq 1} \tau_{xy}^{(k,l)}(j) \{A\}_{4N\times 4N}^{-1} \cdot \{E1j(k,l)\}_{4N\times 4N} \cdot \{u_y\}_{4N}$$

$$- \frac{\varepsilon}{\eta_0} \cdot \sum_{j=1}^{N} \sum_{0\leq k.l\leq 1} [\tau_{xx}^{(k,l)}(j) + \tau_{yy}^{(k,l)}(j)] \{A\}_{4N\times 4N}^{-1} \cdot \{Cj(k,l)\}_{4N\times 4N} \cdot \{\tau_{xx}\}_{4N}$$

$$- \sum_{j=1}^{N} \sum_{0\leq k,l\leq 1} u_x^{(k,l)}(j) \{A\}_{4N\times 4N}^{-1} \cdot \{E1j(k,l)\}_{4N\times 4N} \cdot \{\tau_{xx}\}_{4N}$$

$$- \sum_{j=1}^{N} \sum_{0\leq k,l\leq 1} u_y^{(k,l)}(j) \{A\}_{4N\times 4N}^{-1} \cdot \{E2j(k,l)\}_{4N\times 4N} \cdot \{\tau_{xx}\}_{4N}$$

$$Fp_2 = \frac{2\eta}{\lambda} \cdot \{A\}_{4N\times 4N}^{-1} \cdot \{B2\}_{4N\times 4N} \cdot \{u_y\}_{4N} + 2(1-\zeta) \cdot \sum_{j=1}^{N} \sum_{0\leq k,l\leq 1} \tau_{yy}^{(k,l)}(j)$$

$$\{A\}_{4N\times 4N}^{-1} \cdot \{E2j(k,l)\}_{4N\times 4N} \cdot \{u_y\}_{4N} - \frac{1}{\lambda} \cdot \{\tau_{yy}\}_{4N}$$

$$+ (2-\zeta) \cdot \sum_{j=1}^{N} \sum_{0\leq k,l\leq 1} \tau_{xy}^{(k,l)}(j) \{A\}_{4N\times 4N}^{-1} \cdot \{E1j(k,l)\}_{4N\times 4N} \cdot \{u_y\}_{4N}$$

$$- \zeta \cdot \sum_{j=1}^{N} \sum_{0\leq k,l\leq 1} \tau_{xy}^{(k,l)}(j) \{A\}_{4N\times 4N}^{-1} \cdot \{E2j(k,l)\}_{4N\times 4N} \cdot \{u_x\}_{4N}$$

$$- \frac{\varepsilon}{\eta_0} \cdot \sum_{j=1}^{N} \sum_{0\leq k.l\leq 1} [\tau_{xx}^{(k,l)}(j) + \tau_{yy}^{(k,l)}(j)] \{A\}_{4N\times 4N}^{-1} \cdot \{Cj(k,l)\}_{4N\times 4N} \cdot \{\tau_{yy}\}_{4N}$$

$$- \sum_{j=1}^{N} \sum_{0\leq k,l\leq 1} u_x^{(k,l)}(j) \{A\}_{4N\times 4N}^{-1} \cdot \{E1j(k,l)\}_{4N\times 4N} \cdot \{\tau_{yy}\}_{4N}$$

$$- \sum_{j=1}^{N} \sum_{0\leq k,l\leq 1} u_y^{(k,l)}(j) \{A\}_{4N\times 4N}^{-1} \cdot \{E2j(k,l)\}_{4N\times 4N} \cdot \{\tau_{yy}\}_{4N}$$

$$Fp_3 = \frac{\eta}{\lambda} \cdot \{A\}_{4N \times 4N}^{-1} \cdot [\{B1\}_{4N \times 4N} \cdot \{\ddot{u}_x\}_{4N} + \{B2\}_{4N \times 4N} \cdot \{u_y\}_{4N}]$$

$$- \frac{1}{2}(2 - \zeta) \cdot \sum_{j=1}^{N} \sum_{0 \le k,l \le 1} \tau_{xx}^{(k,l)}(j) \{A\}_{4N \times 4N}^{-1} \cdot \{E1j(k,l)\}_{4N \times N} \cdot \{u_y\}_{4N}$$

$$- \frac{1}{2}\zeta \cdot \sum_{j=1}^{N} \sum_{0 \le k,l \le 1} \tau_{xx}^{(k,l)}(j) \{A\}_{4N \times 4N}^{-1} \cdot \{E2j(k,l)\}_{4N \times 4N} \cdot \{u_x\}_{4N}$$

$$- \frac{1}{2}(2 - \zeta) \cdot \sum_{j=1}^{N} \sum_{0 \le k,l \le 1} \tau_{yy}^{(k,l)}(j) \{A\}_{4N \times 4N}^{-1} \cdot \{E2j(k,l)\}_{4N \times 4N} \cdot \{u_x\}_{4N}$$

$$- \frac{1}{2}\zeta \cdot \sum_{j=1}^{N} \sum_{0 \le k,l \le 1} \tau_{yy}^{(k,l)}(j) \{A\}_{4N \times 4N}^{-1} \cdot \{E1j(k,l)\}_{4N \times 4N} \cdot \{u_y\}_{4N}$$

$$+ (1 - \zeta) \cdot \sum_{j=1}^{N} \tau_{xy}(j) \{A\}_{N \times N}^{-1} \cdot \{E1j\}_{N \times N} \cdot \{u_x\}_{N}$$

$$+ (1 - \zeta) \cdot \sum_{j=1}^{N} \tau_{xy}(j) \{A\}_{N \times N}^{-1} \cdot \{E2j\}_{N \times N} \cdot \{u_y\}_{N}$$

$$- \frac{1}{\lambda} \cdot \{\tau_{xy}\}_{N} - \frac{\varepsilon}{\eta_0} \cdot \sum_{j=1}^{N} [\tau_{xx}(j) + \tau_{yy}(j)] \{A\}_{N \times N}^{-1} \cdot \{Cj\}_{N \times N} \cdot \{\tau_{xy}\}_{N}$$

$$- \sum_{j=1}^{N} u_x(j) \{A\}_{N \times N}^{-1} \cdot \{E1j\}_{N \times N} \cdot \{\tau_{xy}\}_{N}$$

$$- \sum_{j=1}^{N} u_y(j) \{A\}_{N \times N}^{-1} \cdot \{E2j\}_{N \times N} \cdot \{\tau_{xy}\}_{N}$$

note that,

$$\{\mu_x\}_{4N} = \left[\left\{\mu_x^{(0,0)}\right\}_N, \left\{\mu_x^{(1,0)}\right\}_N, \left\{\mu_x^{(0,1)}\right\}_N, \left\{\mu_x^{(1,1)}\right\}_N \right]^T$$

$$\{A\}_{4N \times 4N} = [A(0,0), A(1,0), A(0,1), A(1,1)]_{4N \times 4N}$$

$$A(k,l) = \left(\iint_e \varphi_i^{(k,l)}(x,y)\varphi_j(x,y)dxdy \right)_{4N \times N}$$

$$\{B1\}_{4N \times 4N} = [B1(0,0), B1(1,0), B1(0,1), B1(1,1)]_{4N \times 4N}$$

$$B1(k,l) = \left(\iint_e \varphi_i(x,y)\frac{\partial \varphi_j^{(k,l)}(x,y)}{\partial x}dxdy \right)_{4N \times N}$$

$$\{B2\}_{4N \times 4N} = [B2(0,0), B2(1,0), B2(0,1), B2(1,1)]_{4N \times 4N}$$

$$B2(k,l) = \left(\iint_e \varphi_i(x,y) \frac{\partial \varphi_j^{(k,l)}(x,y)}{\partial y} dxdy \right)_{4N \times N}$$

$$\{Cj(k,l)\}_{4N \times 4N} = \left[C_j^{kl}(0,0), C_j^{kl}(1,0), C_j^{kl}(0,1), C_j^{kl}(1,1) \right]_{4N \times 4N}$$

$$C_j^{kl}(n,p) = \left(\iint_e \varphi_i(x,y) \varphi_j^{(k,l)}(x,y) \varphi_m^{(n,p)}(x,y) dxdy \right)_{4N \times N}$$

$$\{E1j\}_{4N \times 4N} = \left[E_{1j}^{(0,0)}, E_{1j}^{(1,0)}, E_{1j}^{(0,1)}, E_{1j}^{(1,1)} \right]_{4N \times 4N}$$

$$E_{1j}^{(k,l)} = \left(\iint_e \varphi_i(x,y) \varphi_j^{(k,l)}(x,y) \frac{\partial \varphi_m^{(n,p)}(x,y)}{\partial x} dxdy \right)_{4N \times N}$$

$$\{E2j\}_{4N \times 4N} = \left[E_{2j}^{(0,0)}, E_{2j}^{(1,0)}, E_{2j}^{(0,1)}, E_{2j}^{(1,1)} \right]_{4N \times 4N}$$

$$E_{2j}^{(k,l)} = \left(\iint_e \varphi_i(x,y) \varphi_j^{(k,l)}(x,y) \frac{\partial \varphi_m^{(n,p)}(x,y)}{\partial y} dxdy \right)_{4N \times N}$$

where the initial value (n=0) is from the test and documented in the FEA boundary condition data base.

The Runge Kutta-Galerkin method yields the higher precision solution with at least 3rd order of convergence. To solve the stability problem for the element over-stretch limite in the complex contacting boundary, we developed a technique with the combination of the cubic element and the shell element. It simulated large deformation successfully.

3   Examples of the Impact Simulation

Understanding the honeycomb (HC) only "dry" (shell element) case is the first step in the stable solution scheme in the P1 positive definite condition(see Fig. 1,2,3). For visco-elastic fluid "wet" filled (cubic element) case however, the situation is more complex.

Here also, visco-elastic fluids sometimes exhibit behavior quite different from Newtonian fluids whereas a viscous Newtonian thread tends to break as a result of necking instability. Furthermore we study the behavior of micro-capillary balancing that against gravity in multi-phase properties [HQ, MCr, LLS].

The 3-dimensional positive definite framework [HQ] assured the simulation with the preprocessor. The resolution of this type of rheologic problem is much clearly structured and to be solved in the positive scheme. Especially for the impact hardening and shear thinning (IHST) in 3-dimension is in a very sound theoretic background now.

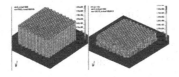

Fig. 1. (a) the P1 un-crushed HC ;   (b) the P1 crushed HC

In the numeric transient 3-D scheme, a nonlinear Riccati differential system is kept therefore to keep the LBB positive definite condition in time domain [HQ, MCr]. The spatial discretization is restrict to the Finite Element Method [HHa, LLu] with the direct application of the semi-Hermite method to equations $(1)or(2)$ and leads to the three field Stokes system in space. With the Newtonian contribution of stress, a lot of freedom to choose the approximation spaces for stress can be made (see [GN]).

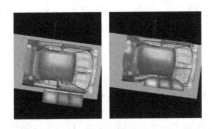

Fig. 2. Auto-crash side impact: (a) CAE before crash test; (b) CAE after crash test

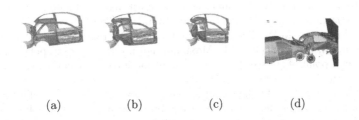

(a)   (b)   (c)   (d)

Fig. 3. CAE simulation of complex auto-crash front/rear impact case: (a),(b),(c) The crash-bumper structure deformation with the stochastic slip condition; (d) The complex non-Newtonian contact deformation in the crash simulation

The FEA simulation has been obtained by one of the authors for the crash safety analysis (Fig.2). The honeycomb blocks were made of cells. We are now extending the knowledge base into a new space that is the visco-elastic-plastic rate control concept. The bending of HC barrier gives flexibility of the blocks in the all angle impact and offering the new stable space for body crash confinement. The bending happens when the hinge get sufficient contact support (surface) with crush. The orthotropic impact angle in the specific dimension (a:diameter of HC cross section; b:length of HC; s:length of impact vector).

4   Conclusion

Apart from the hard protection (solid crash barrier) and skin contact protection (ie. airbag etc), we introduced the soft-solid non-Newtonian protection concept known as the recoverable crush. The mathematical simulation of the accurate prediction shows well assured quality for the impact defence scheme model by use of the bicubic Hermite element analysis. With the high performance computing platform (ARUP/Ls-dyna v.971) in the mathematics department, the auto-crash safety simulations have shown the feasibility of the finite element modelling process and the mathematical understanding of its engineering application. After intensive scientific and technical research since 2000 with ARUP/Ls-dyna [H], enable us to engage pre-/post-processing with complex boundary condition from the industrial problems. The explicit solver of LS-Dyna supplies the best stable impact solution for the nonlinear equation.

References

[CaCZ]   Cao, L.Q., Cui, J.Z., Zhu, D.C.: SIAM J. Numerical Analysis 40(5), 1683–1697 (2002)
[GN]   Giesekus, H.: J. Non-Newt. Fluid Mech. 11, 69 (1982)
[HHa]   Hou, L., Harwood, R.: Nonlinear properties in the Newtonian and Non-Newtonian Equations. Nonlinear analysis 30(4), 2497–2505 (1997)
[HQ]   Hou, L., Qiu, L.: Computation and asymptotic analysis in the impact problem. ACTA Math. Appl. Sin. 25(1), 117–127 (2009)
[H]   Hou, L.: Failure modes analysis in the crash barrier. In: Proc. 5th Euro LS-Dyna Conference, The ICC Birmingham, B-02 (2005)
[JSe]   Johnson Jr., M.W., Segalman, D.: J. Non-Newt Fluid Mech. 2, 225 (1977)
[LLS]   Lin, Q., lü, T., Shen, S.M.: Maximum norm estimate, extrapolation and optimal point of stresses for finite element methods on strongly regular triangulation. J. Comp. Math 1, 376–383 (1983)
[LLu]   Lü, T., Lu, J.: Splitting extrapolation for solving second order elliptic systems with cured boundary in R^3 by using d-quadratic isoparametric finite element. Appl. Numer. Math. 40, 467–481 (2002)
[MCr]   Marchal, J.M., Crochet, M.J.: A new mixed finite element for calculating viscoelastic flow. J. Non-Newt. Fluid Mech. 26, 77–114 (1987)
[P]   Petrie, C.J.: Elongational Flows. Pitman, London (1979)
[TTa]   Thien, N.P., Tanner, R.I.: A new constitutive equation derived from network theory. J. Non-Newt. Fluid. Mech. 2, 353–365 (1977)
[YX]   Young-Ju, L., Xu, J.: New formulations, positivity preserving discretizations and stability analysis for non-newtonian flow models, vol. 195, pp. 1180–1206 (2006)

A Heuristic Rule of Partitioning Irregular Loop for Parallelizing Compilers

Changjun Hu[1], Yali Liu[1,2], Jue Wang[1], and Jianjiang Li[1]

[1] School of Information Engineering, University of Science and Technology Beijing,
No. 30 Xueyuan Road, Haidian District, Beijing, P.R. China, 100083
huchangjun@ies.ustb.edu.cn, {necpu5,jianjiangli}@gmail.com
[2] School of Science and Technology, Beijing City University,
No. 269 BeisihuanZhonglu Road, Haidian District, Beijing, P.R. China, 100083
liuyali@bcu.edu.cn

Abstract. For irregular applications on distributed-memory systems, computation partition is an important issue on parallel compiling techniques of parallelizing compilers. In this paper, we propose a local optimal solution, called heuristic computes rule (HCR), which could be used for irregular loop partitioning. This rule considers both the iteration being partitioned and the iterations partitioned, which ensures that iterations are assigned so as to produce less communication costs. And HCR rule proposes that irregular loop partitioning should trade off the maximum message degrees of processors, the number of messages, the message sizes, and workload balance. In our experiments, we compare HCR with almost owner computes rule and least communication computes rule. The results show that the executing of irregular loop partitioned by HCR rule has much less communication cost and achieve better performance.

1 Introduction

Exploiting parallelism for irregular[1, 2] problems is a challenging task due to their irregular data access pattern. And there is no possibility of code optimization for irregular loop at compile time. On distributed-memory architecture, researchers presented the method of runtime libraries, which helps compilers to implement computation partitioning for irregular loops. For examples, Y.S. Hwang et al. described a runtime library called CHAOS, which uses the owner computes rule. R. Ponnusamy et al. proposed the almost owner computes rule[3]. M. Guo et al. proposed the least communication computes rule to partition irregular loop[4]. The owner computes specifies that each of iterations should be executed dividedly by the processor which possesses the left-hand side array reference of the assignment. However there are often two or much more irregular statements in a loop, therefore this rule is not very suitable. When almost owner computes rule is applied, the iteration is assigned to the processor that owns most of array references in the iteration. When the least communication computes rule is applied, the iteration should be assigned to a processor with minimum the number of messages.

In view of the fact that communication aggregation usually is used before and after processors executing assigned iterations (we consider the irregular loop body doesn't have loop-carried dependence), then it is more suitable that the implementation of

W. Zhang et al. (Eds.): HPCA 2009, LNCS 5938, pp. 177–182, 2010.

irregular loop iterations is divided into three phases. 1) Import phase: Processors send and receive messages to each other for exchanging data of data arrays. 2) Computation phase: Processors execute their iterations assigned. 3) Export phase: Processors send non-local data updated to other processors and received data from other processors. Because the three phases are implemented in sequence, therefore scheme for guiding partitioning of loop iterations should try to reduce the communication cost of import phase and that of export phase apart. Even the least communication computes rule focuses on communication, but it regards import phase and export phase as a whole, and only considers the communication brought by the iteration being partitioned. It is not best for partitioning irregular loops.

HCR rule uses communication coalescing[5, 6]. Our rule not only wants to reduce communication frequency and redundant data transfer, but also wants to decrease overload imbalance when computations of irregular loop are executed in runtime. HCR rule takes advantage of the communication information brought by those iterations which have been partitioned. HCR method has several major advantages:

1. HCR strives to reduce import and export communication times respectively.

2. When assigning an iteration, HCR rule tried to merge the message for fetching non-local data (required for executing this iteration) into those messages (required for executing iterations which have been assigned), so to achieve the goal of reducing the number of messages of import phase and that of export phase.

3. We proposed that there are three factors which influence communication cost of HCR rule, which are the messages degree of processors, the number of total messages and the maximum size of messages. We evaluates values of those three factors based on weights given according executing environment and computes the workload balance factor, and then, determines this iteration should be assigned to which processor.

The remainder of this paper is as follows. Section 2 describes the HCR algorithm. Section 3 analyzes the obtained results. Section 4 gives concluding remarks.

2   HCR Rule

In this section, we first give two assumptions, then we give six definitions, and lastly we introduce HCR rule.

Assumption 1. Iteration with index $k(0 \leq k < i)$ had been assigned to an processor.

Assumption 2. Iteration i will be assigned to processor P_j. Here we separate iteration $k(k > i)$ from all of iterations of a loop, which don not be considered when the iteration i is being partitioned.

Under these assumptions, we will have six definitions as follows:

Definition 1. $|Set|$ is defined as the number of elements of Set.

Definition 2. Under above assumptions, both directed graph $G_{Import}(P_j, i) = (V, E_{Import})$ and $G_{Export}(P_j, i) = (V, E_{Export})$ are called CPG (communication pattern graph[7]), which represent respectively the communication information of import phase and that of export phase. Each vertex in V represents a processor, a directed edge in E_{Import}

represents a message between processors in import phase, and E_{Export} represents messages in export phase. Fig. 1 shows examples of $G_{Import}(P_j,i)$ and $G_{Export}(P_j,i)$. Value on the directed edge represents the message size. We also define $G(P_j,i)=(V, E_{Import} \cup E_{Export})$, which represents CPG of both import phase and export phase.

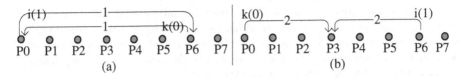

Fig. 1. The iteration (k=0) is executed on processors P0, and iteration (i=1) is on P6. (a) is CPG of $G_{Import}(P_6,1)$, and (b) is CPG of $G_{Export}(P_6,1)$.

Definition 3. In CPG the *messages degree* of a processor is defined as the degree of its vertex. $MaxD_{Import}(P_j,i)$, and $MaxD_{Export}(P_j,i)$ is defined as the maximum of degrees among all vertices in $G_{Import}(P_j,i)$ and in $G_{Export}(P_j,i)$. In Fig. 1 $MaxD_{Import}(P_6,1)$ is 2, and $MaxD_{Export}(P_6,1)$ is 2. So $MaxD_{Import}(P_j,i)$ and $MaxD_{Export}(P_j,i)$ represent the least communication steps (arose by iterations with index $k(0 \leq k \leq i)$) among all processors in import phase and export phase respectively(Here we temporarily don't consider the iteration with index $k(k>i)$). And we define $MaxDegrees(P_j,i)$ in $G(P_j,i)$ as such:

$$\frac{MaxD_{Import}(P_j,i) + MaxD_{Export}(P_j,i)}{2}$$. It represents the average value of communication steps needed in both two phases.

Definition 4. E_{Import} and E_{Export} have been used to represent the set of directed edges in $G_{Import}(P_j,i)$ and $G_{Export}(P_j,i)$. In Fig. 1 $E_{Import}=\{(P6,P0),(P0,P6)\}$ and $E_{Export}=\{(P0,P3),(P6,P3)\}$. In here we define $NumMes(P_j,i)$ in $G(P_j,i)$ as such:

$$\frac{|E_{Import}| + |E_{Export}|}{2}$$. $NumMes(P_j,i)$ is used to represent the average of *the number of messages* of import phase in $G_{Import}(P_j,i)$ and that of export phase in $G_{Export}(P_j,i)$.

Definition 5): $MaxMS_{Import}(P_j,i)$ and $MaxMS_{Export}(P_j,i)$ are defined as the *maximum message size* in $G_{Import}(P_j,i)$ and $G_{Export}(P_j,i)$. We define $MaxMS(P_j,i)$ in $G(P_j,i)$ as such: $$\frac{MaxMS_{Import}(P_j,i) + MaxMS_{Export}(P_j,i)}{2}$$.

Definition 6. In $G(P_j,i)$, $CompLoad(P_j,i)$ is defined as the maximum count of iterations assigned to processors, which means the maximum workload among processors.

Lastly we introduce HCR rule. We proposed that there are four factors affecting the performance of executing iterations of irregular loop on processors of distributed-memory systems. These factors are the maximum value of message degrees of processors, the number of total messages, the maximum size of messages, and the workload balance among processors. And these factors are respectively evaluated with $MaxDegrees(P_j,i)$, $NumMes(P_j,i)$, $MaxMS(P_j,i)$, and $CompLoad(P_j,i)$ defined above. Because those factors have different influence on performance of executing irregular loop, we use a weight set (W1, W2, W3, and W4) to represent the different impacting degrees. Weight values should be given in according to the specific running environment. Here we give equation(1), which formulates the communication and workload arose by iteration $k(0 \leq k \leq i)$ when iteration i will be assigned to processor P_j.

$$PValue(P_j,i) = MaxDegrees(P_j,i) \times W1 + NumMes(P_j,i) \times W2$$
$$+ MaxMS(P_j,i) \times W3 + CompLoad(P_j,i) \times W4 \qquad (1)$$

Then we assign iteration i to the processor which has minimum value of $PValue(P_j,i)$ among all processors. We give our algorithm for partitioning iterations as follow. The algorithm for partitioning iterations doesn't be parallelized in this paper. Comparing with the cost of communication among processors, the cost of partitioning iterations can be omitted. It has been proved in our experiments.

```
Algorithm_Partition(M, N)
  Input: M(the number of iterations),
         N(the number of processors)
  Output: results of partitioning iterations
  For i = 0 To (M-1)
    For j = 0 To (N-1)
          Calculate_MaxDegrees(P_j, i)
          Calculate_NumMes(P_j, i)
          Calculate_MaxMS(P_j, i)
          Calculate_CompLoad(P_j, i)
          PValue(P_j, i) = MaxDegrees(P_j, i)*W1
          PValue(P_j, i)+= NumMes(P_j, i)*W2
          PValue(P_j, i)+= MaxMS(P_j, i)*W3
          PValue(P_j, i)+= CompLoad(P_j, i)*W4
    End For
    FindMin(PValue)
    UpdateGraph_GI_GE()
  End For
```

3 Experiments and Analysis

We made the experiments respectively using almost owner computes rule (AOCR), least communication computes rule (LCCR) and our HCR rule. Same to M. Guo et al.[4], we also use one of irregular loops of ZEUS-2D[8] for our study. Its kernel codes have four index arrays. In our experiments we generated random number as the values of index arrays. All experiments described in this paper are carried out in an Ethernet switched cluster with 12 nodes. Each node has an Intel Xeon(3.0GHz with 1024KB Cache). The Operating-System is RedHat Linux with kernel 2.6.9. Nodes are interconnected with 1KMbps Ethernets. The MPI library used is MPICH-1.2.5.2. Programs are written in C, and use system call MPI_Wtime() for measuring execution time. We will present the experimental results, which are averages of 20 runs. The experiments are run on platforms with 4, 6, 8 and 12 nodes respectively. The values of W1, W2, W3 and W4 (see Section 2) are 5, 4, 0.01, and 1 respectively.

In Fig. 2 we can see that HCR rule reduce the messages degrees of processors and achieves the least communication steps, and even the number of messages increased very highly with increasing number of processors, but the number of messages is

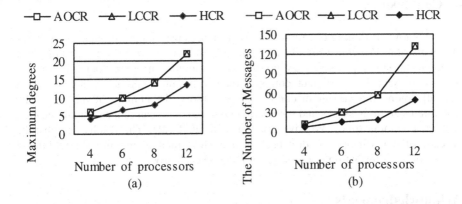

Fig. 2. (a) shows the maximum degrees, and (b) shows the number of messages in CPG

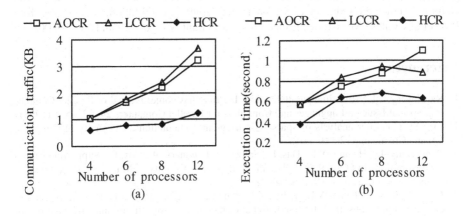

Fig. 3. (a) shows communication traffic (KB), and (b) shows execution times

lowest. Although all rules use message aggregation, but the communication traffic and execution time of HCR rule are lowest in Fig. 3. The reason is that HCR rule not only tries to reduce communication cost in import and export phases, but also tries to hold suitable workload balance.

From above experiments, we can see that AOCR and LCCR rules have similar experimental results. It is because two rules only consider the iteration being partitioned, but they do not take advantage of partition information of iterations which have been partitioned. But HCR rule not only take advantage of partition information of partitioned iterations, but also make a tradeoff among the maximum degrees of processors, the number of messages, the maximum size of messages, and the load balance factors. But a drawback of HCR rule is that it requires more memory to save CPG.

4 Conclusions

Computation partitioning of irregular loop influences parallel performance considerably on distributed-memory architecture. The almost owner computes rule and the least communication computes rule are not best to partitioning irregular loops. In this paper, we presented an efficient computation partitioning approach which makes a tradeoff among the maximum degrees of processors, the number of messages, the maximum size of messages and the overload balance, so it can reduce communication costs and running time. We have implemented HCR rule. The results demonstrate efficacy of our schemes. A drawback is that HCR method requires the additional storage of the information of messages of CPG on each processor.

Acknowledgements

The research is partially supported by the Hi-Tech Research and Development Program (863) of China under Grant No. 2006AA01Z105 and No. 2008AA01Z109, Natural Science Foundation of China under Grant No.60373008, and by the Key Project of Chinese Ministry of Education under Grant No. 106019 and No. 108008.

References

1. Rauchwerger, L.: Run-time parallelization: It's time has come. Journal of Parallel Computing, Special Issue on Languages and Compilers for Parallel Computers 24, 527–556 (1998)
2. Lin, Y.: Compiler analysis of sparse and irregular computations. University of Illinois at Urbana-Champaign (2000)
3. Ponnusamy, R., Hwang, Y.S., Das, R., Saltz, J., Choudhary, A., Fox, G.: Supporting irregular distributions in FORTRAN 90D/HPF compilers. University of Maryland, Department of Computer Science and UMIACS (1994)
4. Guo, M., Li, L., Chang, W.L.: Efficient loop partitioning for parallel codes of irregular scientific computations. In: Fifth International Conference on Algorithms and Architectures for Parallel Processing, pp. 60–70. IEEE Computer Society, Los Alamitos (2002)
5. Chakrabarti, S., Gupta, M., Choi, J.D.: Global communication analysis and optimization. ACM SIGPLAN Notices 31, 68–78 (1996)
6. Chavarría-Miranda, D., Mellor-Crummey, J.: Effective communication coalescing for data-parallel applications. In: Proc. the tenth ACM SIGPLAN symposium on Principles and practice of parallel programming, pp. 14–25. ACM, New York (2005)
7. Guo, M., Cao, J., Chang, W.L., Li, L., Liu, C.: Effective OpenMP Extensions for Irregular Applications on Cluster Environments. LNCS, pp. 97–104. Springer, Heidelberg (2004)
8. Stone, J.M., Norman, M.L.: ZEUS-2 D: A radiation magnetohydrodynamics code for astrophysical flows in two space dimensions: the hydrodynamic algorithms and tests. Astrophysical Journal Supplement Series 80, 753–790 (1992)

Numerical Simulation of Dimension Effect to Deformation in the Cataclastic Medium Goafs Using UDEC

Jianhua Hu[1,*], Dezheng Lao[1], Qingfa Chen[1], Keping Zhou[1], and Yingmen Huang[2]

[1] School of Resources and Safety Engineering of Central South University,
Changsha Hunan, 410083, China
Tel.: 0731-88879965 13787056402
hujh21@126.com
[2] Guangxi GaofengMining Co. L td.,
Hechi, Guangxi 547205, China

Abstract. In cataclastic rock medium, goafs are the potential security hidden troubles in the mining process. The sort of goafs has the characteristics of the large deformation in roof rock mass. In order to predict the deformation of roof, the numerical method was used under the mining goafs. Using the universal distinct element code (UDEC), three working condition goafs with different sizes were carried out the numerical simulation tests. For three structure sizes, the goafs surrounding rock all displayed the above deformation characteristics. According to the difference of goafs structure sizes, the roof displacements reached a 19.11mm, 26.78mm, and 47.35mm respectively. The analyses for plastic zone in the three conditions showed that the holistic span of plastic zones changed with the goafs size; the plastic zones transfixed gradually in roof, and formed the caving zones at last. Regarding to deformation characteristics of different sizes, these measures were provided, such as a network anchor injection, the lateral filling, cement grouting, and so on. The research results showed that in the cataclastic medium, the sizes of goafs' structure has an obvious impact on the deformation of surrounding rock; the deformation increases with the sizes gradually; the goafs treatment measures provided could effectively guarantee the safety of mine production.

Keywords: cataclastic medium, discrete element, deformation, goafs.

1 Introduction

Rock, especially the cataclastic rock is a discontinuous geological media, is a discontinuous, heterogenetic, anisotropic and non-linear natural geological body which is cut by a large number of bedding, joints and faults. As a result of the complexity of the cataclastic rock media, some numerical analysis methods, such as the finite difference

---

* Corresponding author.

W. Zhang et al. (Eds.): HPCA 2009, LNCS 5938, pp. 183–190, 2010.

method, finite element method and boundary element methods [1,2], are commonly used by L. Jing (2003) and HU Jianhua (2005). However, they are often limited by small deformation assumption. To address the engineering problems of the rich and the large deformation of cataclastic and jointed rock mass, the actual results differ materially from the project. Underground structure in cataclastic medium, such as mining stopes and underground excavation cavern and the mass transit railway and tunnel engineering, its stability and deformation are influenced by the discontinuous surface. Therefore, using the numerical methods based on the assumption of continuity to study, it is difficult to meet the requirements of the construction and design. Discrete element method is particularly suitable for weak joints-rich surface and engineering problems of large deformation by a recent survey by WANG Weihua (2005), X.B. Zhao(2008), Sotirios S(2007), Xiao-gang HE(2008) and Yao-She Xie(2009) [3-7]. To model the response of discontinuous rock masses, Cundall (1971) and Cundall and Hart (1985) developed the discontinuum approach [8,9]. Discrete element modeling (DEM) offers the advantage of simulating block interaction through individual joints, and is particularly suited to examining the behavior of fractured rock masses during excavation. So the discrete element method has been widely applied in order to provide a theoretical basis for the analysis of the deformation of cataclastic and jointed rock mass by Yuli XIA (2007), Shen, A. King (2008), MA Fenghai (2001), WANG Guijun (2004), and Zheng Yungming(2002) [10-14]. However, the mining engineering, as a result of the existence of a large number of goafs, which have different shapes and size, forms a major mining hazards. In order to handle reasonably and make good use of the goafs, it is necessary to study the size effect of different goafs and to analyze the deformation law of goafs in cataclastic medium and dispose the basic measures which are conducive to the project.

2 Project Description

Gaofeng mine, due to historical reasons and coyoting mines indiscriminately, destruction and all kinds of pillars and security isolation pillars, leaves a large number of irregular goafs which have been -179m level by YAN Rong-gui (2003) [15]. No.105 mine body is mainly shallow mined by indigenous people. As a result, the size of goafs is different. With the exception of a small amount of overlap and transfixion, the rest are not too large and straight. The structure of mining area develops well, including series of folds and faults and the associated cracks by ZHOU Zhihui (2004) [16]. Main faults are as follows: Barry- Sn Longtoushan fracture zone, fracture zone between layers, the fracture in the northwest(vertical), north-east fracture(horizontal) and north-south fracture by DENG JIngcan (2001) [17]. The northern ore body is cataclastic structure and the length of sliding surface in the rock is less than 0.5m. Calcite veinlets are the major joints. Its length is more than 10m and its width is 1-8cm.The interval is approximately 1.5m with 25-30°. It is believed in the survey that there is a group of joints whose inclination is 25°and space is 0.5m and there are three groups of intermittent joints whose inclination is 65°with about 1.5m space. These two kinds of joints are the main joints in cataclastic ore body.

3 Discrete Element Models

In cataclastic rock, the security and stability of mining operations are the main factors to be concerned. The factors impacting the stability of goafs in cataclastic medium are as follows: the size of goafs, depth of goafs, ground stress field, mechanics parameters and so on. It is important to research about dimention effect on the deformation of goafs in cataclastic medium. Three kinds of case conditions and their size of corresponding goafs model are shown in Table 1.

Table 1. Models table of dimension effect to goafs

	Size of goaf /m^2	Size of model /m^2
Case 1	18×6	200×160
Case 2	30×14	200×160
Case 3	60×22	200×160

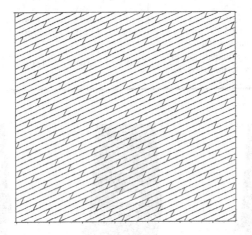

Fig. 1. Distribution forms of joint sets in the cataclastic medium

The mechanical parameters of ore body and the upper and lower plate are show in Table 2 by DENG JIngcan (2001) [17]. Two groups of main joints of different inclination, constituting the characteristics of cataclastic ore body, as shown in Figure 1. In the calculation process, two forms of false joints are set, that is, goaf's ore excavation boundary line and boundary line with the surrounding cement and mechanical parameters of all false joints are the same in simulation process. Mechanical parameters of joints are shown in Table 3.

Table 2. Mechanics parameters of mines and rocks

Rock	Elastic modulus ×10⁴MPa	Poisson's ratio	Cohesion (MPa)	Internal friction angle(°)	Unidirectional pressure(MPa)	Unidirectional tensile(MPa)	Bulk density /t m³
Ore body	1.62	0.22	2.11	42	34.04	1.64	4.41
Hanging edit reef limestone	1.84	0.25	2.52	46	38.07	2.01	2.58
Footwall reef limestone	2.18	0.26	2.80	45	47.76	2.24	2.58

Table 3. Mechanics parameters of joint sets

Groups of joint	Inclination (°)	Positive stiffness /Pa	Shear stiffness /Pa	Cohesion /Pa	Internal friction angle /°	Tensile strength /Pa
Real Joints	25	1.2e10	1.2e10	0.25e6	23	1e6
	65	1.2e10	1.2e10	0.25e6	23	1e6
	65	1.2e10	1.2e10	0.25e6	23	1e6
	65	1.2e10	1.2e10	0.25e6	23	1e6
False Joints	Boundary line 0° ~90° , Boundary line of ore body determined by the actual model	5e10	5e10	1e10		1e10

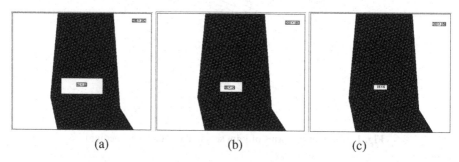

(a)   (b)   (c)

Fig. 2. Discrete element models of goafs to dimension effect

4   Analysis

4.1   Displacement Analysis

(1)   Analysis of vertical deformation

Figure 3 shows that the y direction deformation law of surrounding rock in three working conditions. It is seen from the chart that the overall strain, due to the orientation effect of main groups of joint, deformation in the y direction is a non-holonomic symmetrical shape and the roof subsides with floor raised. As a result of weight force of rock, it shows the subsidence volume of roof is greater than the raise of floor from the size of deformation values. From the size effect of goaf structure, it shows that deformation of surrounding rock increases as the expansion of goaf. The largest values of deformation are in the range of 20, 25 and 40mm respectively the corresponding working conditions. In addition, the range of deformation increases as the size of goaf expands, and the stability of goaf variates. The deformation of two sides rock in goafs is small, and the stability of cataclastic rock in two sides is better than the roof.

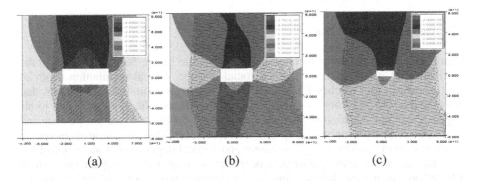

(a)   (b)   (c)

Fig. 3. Laws of displacement in the three goafs

(2) Analysis of roof settlement

Figure 4 shows the settlement law of all the points of roof in the three kinds of conditions. From the curves of the roof subsidence, we can see that under two major fracture groups, the settlement forms of the roof are basically the same, showing the asymmetric distribution. The settlement of joints which are tend to one side increase obviously, showing a quick non-continuous trend of sinking ,see Figure 4-a. There are two reasons for the settlement of roof. First, the tendentious settlement caused by the direction of joint groups, which is the main reason. In addition, subsidence of varying degrees caused by joints cracks or joints reversed in different parts of the roof in goafs. The largest subsidence values of the roof of goafs are on the left side of the centerline, and their values are 19.11mm, 26.78mm and 47.35mm respectively. It can be seen that the max settlement value of the roof increase linearly as the size of goaf increases, see Figure 4-b. Especially, for working condition 3, its maximum subsidence value is larger than that of underground space of intact rock. And it has also caused the disruption of joints and falling of rock, which makes the safety and Istability worse.

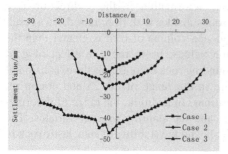 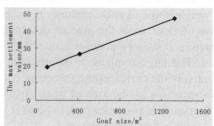

Fig. 4. Curves of settlement laws to goafs in the cataclastic medium

4.2 Analysis of Plastic Zone

Plastic zones in three working conditions are shown in Figure 5(a), (b), (c). From the distribution of plastic zones, it can be found that the vertical distribution depth of plastic zones of roof reaches 9.5m and depth of bottom is 7.5m. Its basic shape is that inserting the roof and floor along the tendency line. In the effect of cracks and joints staggered and embedded, it is stable. However, it cracks easily in the plastic zone and the loose ore in the zone may drop off, see Figure 5(a). The affected areas of plastic zones in working condition 2 grow bigger and vertical depth of roof and floor of the zone reaches about 15m. Transfixion occurs in local area of roof space. In vertical affected area of roof, its length is one half of that of exposed area and the overall stability is poor. To some extent, the roof may collapses, see Figure 5(b). In Figure 5(c), the scope of plastic zone further expands, but the basic law is consistent with working condition 2. The vertical depth of the plastic zone of roof is about 20m and transfixion has occurs. It may be happened to the large-scale collapse. Actually, No.2 goaf, corresponding to the working condition 3, loose rock collapsed is full of the goaf. As a result of the medium size of working condition 2, the plastic zone of roof has been connected, thus the stability is poor. It must be reinforced by bolt-grouting support or some other ways to improve stability and its safe environment. In working condition 3, as a result of large exposed area, it is difficult to reinforce to ensure its safety and stability.

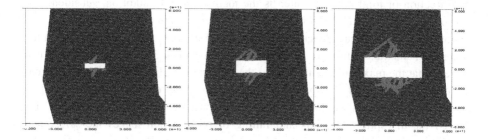

Fig. 5. Laws of plastic zone in the three goafs

4.3 Treatment Measures

To deal with goafs, the common measures are included filling, caving, blocking, support and their combined effect [10-13], as well as induced-caving [14-16]. Because the ore grade of Gaofeng Mine is high, it is necessary to implement the filling mining technology to protect it. Therefore, for the above mentioned goafs, it is feasible to use the corresponding control measures to promote safety and stability.

(1) For the small size goafs, using the application of shotcrete rockbolt mesh to control the local rock caves. And its follow-up space can be used as compensation for cutting space of mining.
(2) For the medium size goafs, because the stability of pillar between goafs is better the roof, both sides of pillars can be used for filling.
(3) For the large size goafs, because the roof is prone to cave and collapse, it is feasible to use mixed filling. After the complete filling of goafs, grouting and cementation can be carried out between ore and waste. Then ,recovers the local resource and improves the utilization of resources.

5 Conclusions

(1) There is certain positive correlation between the deformation of goafs and the structure and size of goafs. The deformation value of goafs increases as the size increases. In addition, the study shows that transfixion of plastic zone has occurred in the medium size goafs, obviously worsen the stability of stopes.
(2) The deformation of roof is under the effect of cataclastic characteristics, forming asymmetric settlement. The value of settlement increases sharply on the side of tendency. There is certain linear positive correlation between the maximum value of settlement and exposed area of goafs.
(3) Dispose measures of goafs in different size and achieve safety and stability standard of mining and the requirements of maximize of resources recovery.

Acknowledgements

The authors wish to acknowledge the collaborative funding supported by the National Key Technology R&D Program in the 11th five year plan period (2006BAB02B04-1-1). And supported by the Open Research Fund of State Key Laboratory of Geomechanics and Geotechnical Engineering, Institute of Rock and Soil Mechanics, Chinese Academy of Sciences, under grant NO. Z110703. Project supported by Hunan Provincial Natural Science Foundation of China,under Grant NO.09JJ4025.

References

1. Jing, L.: A review of techniques, advances and outstanding issues in numerical modeling for rock mechanics and rock engineering. International Journal of Rock Mechanics & Mining Sciences 40(3), 283–353 (2003)
2. Hu, J., Zhou, K., Li, X., Yang, N. (eds.): Numerical analysis of application for induction caving roof. Journal of Central South University of Technology 12(Supp.1), 146–149 (2005)
3. Wang, W., Li, X.: A Review on Fundamentals of Distinct Element Method and Its Applications in Geotechnical Engineering. Geotechnical Engineering Technique 19(4), 177–181 (2005)
4. Zhao, X.B., Zhao, J., Cai, J.G., Hefny, A.M.: UDEC modelling on wave propagation across fractured rock masses. Computers and Geotechnics 35(1), 97–104 (2008)
5. Vardakos, S.S., Gutierrez, M.S., Barton, N.R.: Back-analysis of Shimizu Tunnel No. 3 by distinct element modeling. Tunnelling and Underground Space Technology 22(4), 401–413 (2007)
6. He, X.-g., Zhang, R.-w., Pei, X.-d., Sun, Y. (eds.): Numerical simulation for determining three zones in the goaf at a fully-mechanized coal face. Journal of China University of Mining and Technology 18(2), 199–203 (2008)
7. Xie, Y.-S., Zhao, Y.-S.: Numerical simulation of the top coal caving process using the discrete element method. International Journal of Rock Mechanics and Mining Sciences (2009); Available online 5 May
8. Cundall, P.A.: A computer model for simulating progressive largescale movements in blocky rock systems. In: Proceedings of the Symposium of the International Society of Rock Mechanics, Nancy, France (1972); Paper No. II-8
9. Cundall, P.A., Hart, R.D.: Itasca report on: Development of generalized 2-D and 3-D distinct element programs for modeling jointed rock. US Army Engineering Waterways Experiment Station (1985); Paper SL-85-1, USACE
10. Xia, Y., Peng, S., Gu, Z., Ma, J.: Stability analysis of an underground power cavern in a bedded rock formation. Tunnelling and Underground Space Technology 22(2), 161–165 (2007)
11. Shen, A., King, H.: Displacement, stress and seismicity in roadway roofs during mining-induced failure. International Journal of Rock Mechanics and Mining Sciences 45(5), 672–688 (2008)
12. Feng-hai, M., Yang-Fan: Research On Numerical Simulation of Stratum Subsidence. Journal of Liaoning Technical University (Natural Science Edition) 20(3), 257–261 (2001)
13. Guijun, W.: Dem Analysis on Stability of Unsupported Tunnels in Jointed Rock Masses at Different Depths. Chinese Journal of Rock Mechanics and Engineering 23(7), 1154–1157 (2004)
14. Yungming, Z., Wensheng, C., Xiurun, G., Xiating, F.: Modelling of Ground Surface Subsidence at JinShanDian Underground Iron Mine by Discrete Element Method. Chinese Journal of Rock Mechanics and Engineering 21(8), 1130–1135 (2002)
15. Yan, R.-g., Fang, J.-q., Cao, Y., Deng, J.-c. (eds.): : Triggering Mechanism of Caved Mine Seism Arising from Disasterous Ground Pressure of Gaofeng Mining Area. Mining and Metallurgical Engineering 23(2), 7–10 (2003)
16. Zhou, Z.: Control Measures of Safety Hidden Danger in 100# Orebody of Gaofeng Mine. Ming Technology 4(2), 14–17 (2004)
17. Deng, J.: Analysis of Stability and Survey of Engineering Geological in the deep mining of Gaofeng. Ming. Ming Technology 1(2), 66–67 (2001)

A Parallel Implementation of the Hybrid Algorithm for Electromagnetic Scattering by Arbitrary Shaped Cavities

Jungao Hu, Hu Yue, Cui Yanbao, and Zhi Xiaoli

School of Computer Engineering and Science, Shanghai University,
Shanghai 200072, China

Abstract. The Cascading Segmentation Algorithm combined with IPO, FMM and Generalized Reciprocit Integral (GRI) can effectively solve the problem of electromagnetic scattering by arbitrary shaped cavities. A parallel algorithm based on the Hybrid algorithm is presented in this paper in an attempt to solve this problem when the scale is very large. Using different decomposition strategy for different steps and suitable approach in data preprocessing, computing tasks are distributed into each computing processor evenly, which can ensure the parallel implementation has better parallel efficiency and better memory scalability. Experimental results show good performance of this parallel algorithm with a parallel efficiency of nearly 90%.

1 Introduction

As a measure of the detection ability of a target in radar systems, radar cross section (RCS) has been an important subject in electromagnetic research. The particular importance of the RCS prediction for cavities is due to its dominance to the target's entire RCS. Because of its significant industrial and military applications, the cavity problem has attracted much attention recently. A variety of methods have been proposed for solving the arbitrary shaped cavity problems, such as IPO, FMM, Cascading Segmentation algothrim and Hybrid algorithm. Among these methods, the Hybrid algorithm has established itself as the most powerful one.

However, the Hybrid algorithm can't meet time requirement in the practical application when the number of unknowns become very large, and these large-scale problems can't be solved on a single computer due to huge memory requirement. Recently, in an attempt to extend the range of problems that can be solved by the Hybrid algorithm, the authors have developed a parallel algorithm using data decomposition approach with Message Passing Interface (MPI).

The paper is organized as follows: firstly, the characteristic of sequential algorithm is discussed, which may affect the design of parallel algorithm. Then, we shall follow it with a discussion of major issuers in the parallelization, such as data decomposition strategies, data preprocessing, and we shall also briefly discuss the load balancing and communication. Finally, some test cases are shown to verify the correctness and parallel efficiency of this parallel algorithm.

W. Zhang et al. (Eds.): HPCA 2009, LNCS 5938, pp. 191–197, 2010.

2 A Brief Review of the Hybrid Algorithm

Iterative Physical Optics approach [1] is proposed by F.O.Basteiro etc. in 1995 which iteratively applies physical optics to account for multiple reflections inside the cavity. The IPO algorithm is an efficient approach in analyzing electromagnetic scattering by large and complex cavities.

The fast multipole method (FMM) is proposed by Rokhlin at the University of Yale in the end of 80s. Then, C.C. Lu, W. C. Chew [6], [7] applied this method to efficiently and accurately compute magnetic scattering of the large and complex objects in the mid 1990s. The IPO method has a high computational complexity of O (N^2), where N is the number of unknowns. To accelerate the speed of computing, FMM is employed in the iterative process of IPO, and then the computational complexity is reduced from O (N^2) to O $(N^{1.5})$.

The Segmented approach for computing the electromagnetic scattering by large and arbitrary shaped cavities [3] is also proposed by F. O.Belleiro etc in 1998. The cavity, in this approach [3], is divided into two different parts: the front section (typically smooth) and the complex termination (see Fig.1 for an illustration). The front section is subdivided into several sections (see Fig.2 for an illustration), and each of them is analyzed independently from the rest of the cavity. Generalized Reciprocity Integral (GRI) is proposed by Pathak and Burkholder in 1993 [4], [5] which is used to analyze electromagnetic scatting of large cavity with complex termination.GRI is applied to the Segmented approach to avoid retracing back, which is quite time-consuming.

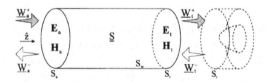

Fig. 1. Cavity geometry model

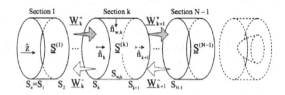

Fig. 2. Front part splitted into several sections

A note: in the following, the cover is denoted as the mouth of a cavity, which is a virtual surface as a part of total cavity (see Fig.1). The sequential version for Hybrid algorithm can be expressed with six main steps as follows.

- **Step 1:** In the Section k, equivalent electromagnetic currents on the cover are obtained, which are induced by incident wave from variable directions.
- **Step 2:** In the Section k, the incident magnetic field inside the cavity is obtained using Kirchh of approximation, which is induced by electromagnetic currents on the Section k cover.
- **Step 3:** In the Section k, an iterative solution is adopted to the magnetic field integral equation until the stable current on the inner cavity walls is reached, using multiple reflections inside the cavity.
- **Step 4:** In the Section k, the electromagnetic fields on the cover are obtained in this step, which are induced by the stable current on the inner cavity. Then, a simplified connection scheme based on the Kirchho of approximation is used to get electromagnetic fields on the Section k+1 cover induced by the electromagnetic fields on this cover. If (k<N) go to Step1, while the front section is subdivided into N sub-sections.
- **Step 5:** in the last section, just like **Step 4**, The Kirchhoff approximation is used again to get the electromagnetic fields on the last cover
- **Step 6:** The generalized reciprocity integral [5] is used to obtain the global response of the whole cavity at the termination.

This **Step 3** is the key process in the Hybrid algorithm, and also a process which we shall pay much attention in the parallelizing. The basic principle behind FMM [6], [7], [8] is to divide the interaction force into two parts: near-field force between nearby box and far-field force between well separated ones. To get such decomposition, the cavities are enclosed in many boxes with the same size (see Fig.3 for an illustration). The near-field force is directly calculated using IPO method while the computation of far-field force is divided into three stages called the upward phase or the aggregation phase, the translation phase and the downward phase or the disaggregation phase.

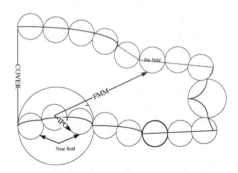

Fig. 3. Illustration the domain decomposition of cavity box

3 Parallelism Discussion

It is well known that the key to design a parallel algorithm is how to decompose the task. Domain decomposition and functional decomposition are two main methods to decomposition. As discussed in section 2, the Hybrid algorithm mainly focuses on the mutual action between the cover facets and cavity facets, or mutual action between the cavities boxes. Both of the two calculations are data related, so domain decomposition is chosen. Therefore, the design of our parallel algorithm mainly focuses on how to get a good data decomposition with good load balancing and minimal communication.

3.1 Domain Decomposition and Load Balancing

The computation of **Step 2** is similar to that of **Step 4** and **Step 5**. **Step 2** and **Step 5** are the reverse course. Hence, they use he same parallel strategy. The difference between **Step 4** and **Step 5** is that **Step 4** has to compute the electromagnetic fields for the cover of the next section, but this computation is so easy that it doesn't need to be paralleled. Take **Step 2** for example without loss of generality, this step focuses on the mutual action between the cover facets and cavity facets. The computational complexity is O (NM), where N is the number of cavity facets and M is the number of cover facets. The cavities facets are distributed equally to each processor .Why are not the cover facets? It is because that N is much larger than M. This will reduce the computational complexity to O (NM/P) and also excellent load balancing can be achieved if we do in this way.

Step 3 is the key process in this algorithm. In this step the computation mainly focuses on the mutual action between the cavities boxes. As discussed in section2, this step is divided into the near-field part and the far-field part. In the near-field, there are two ways to decompose data, one is by cavity box, and the other is by facets of cavity. The latter is chosen with the reason that the latter has a relative small parallel granularity, which may be good for load balancing. In the far-filed, we choose samples for partitioning. In the aggregation phase and the disaggregation phase, the calculation is based on part cavity fields and part samples. In the translation phase, the calculation is based on total far-filed cavity boxes and part samples. Since the cavity facets and the samples are distributed into each processor almost equally, the parallel algorithm can reach better parallel efficiency and better memory scalability.

3.2 Data Preprocessing Discussion

Although the data preprocessing is not a key step in parallel algorithm, inappropriate data preprocessing approach will increase the ratio of execution time of the sequential part of the program, which will seriously affect parallel efficiency. Data Preprocessing mainly includes reading geometric data, geometric modeling and electromagnetic modeling.

There are two ways to preprocess the geometric data. One is the master-slave model; the other is the peer-to- peer model. In the master-slave model (see Fig.4), the master reads geometric data, and completes geometric modeling and electromagnetic modeling, and then broadcasts the result to other computing nodes. This approach has two shortcomings: First, other computing nodes must wait for the completion of data preprocessing in the master node. Second, a large-scale intensive communications from the master node to the computing nodes impact the parallel efficiency significantly. In the peer-to-peer model (see Fig.5), each node does the same thing including geometric data reading, geometric and electromagnetic modeling. Although some storage and computation redundancy exist, the peer-to-peer method is feasible. Because the computation time is negligible comparing with the total algorithm and the memory required for geometric data is relatively small.

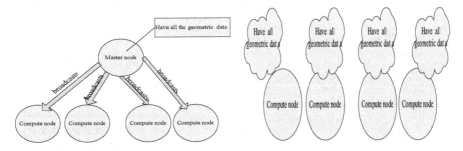

Fig. 4. The master- slave model l   **Fig. 5.** The peer-to-peer mode

3.3 Communication Discussion

Communication is not good for the parallel efficiency, so communication should be minimized, however, it is impossible to avoid communication. Now, some communication procedures used in our algorithm are discussed as follows.

(1) In the **Step 2**, each node only has N/P cavity facets, so after **Step 2**, only part of cavity facets have valid current on each node. But all of the cavity facets should have valid current for the next computation, so communication is required. This can be accomplished by an MPI_Allgatherv function. For the same reason, a communication using an MPI_Allgatherv is required in the **Step 4** and **Step 5**.

(2) For the far field, this is partitioned by samples. After the translation phase, result calculated by all samples is required for the disaggregation phase. In fact, each node only has 1/p samples of all cavity facets. Communication is required to resolve this problem. This can be accomplished by an all-to-all communication procedure, such as MPI_Alltoall. After an iterative process, only partly cavity fields have valid currents in each node. However, total value of currents in each node is required for the next iterative process. MPI_Allgatherv is used again to achieve this object in our approach.

4 Results and Discussion

This section will present some results to demonstrate the validity of the parallel algorithm proposed in this paper.

(1) The value of RCS obtained by the sequential Hybrid algorithm should be the same to that computed by the parallel algorithm. To verify the correctness of the parallel algorithm, the result of a test case with 2032 unknowns is presented at Fig.6. The degree is from 1 to 49 and the number of iterative is ten in this case, and the front cavity is divided into three sections.

We can see the correctness of parallel algorithm in accordance with the sequential Hybrid algorithm in Fig.6.

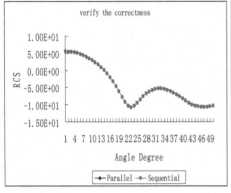
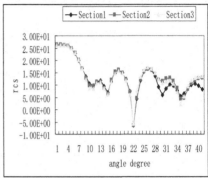

Fig. 6. Sequential and parallel result

Fig. 7. The cavity is divided into one, two and three sections

Another test case is present in Fig.7 .this test case is a cylindrical cavity with 1:6, N=43,632. We can see from Fig.7 that the rcs result is almost the same whether the cavity is divided into one, two or three sections.

(2) It is well known that the parallel efficiency is the key factor to assess the performance of a parallel algorithm

The parallel efficiency can be defined as $\quad \eta = \dfrac{BT_{B}}{PT_{p}} \times 100\%$

T_{B} is the execution time on B processors and T_{p} is the execution time on P processors. B is the minimal number of processors which can solve the problem. All the test cases reported in this paper are executed on ZiQiang3000 which is a supercomputer cluster at the Shanghai University.

Another two test cases are demonstrated to check the parallel efficiency. The first one is a small rectangle straight cavity with 1:1:3, N=27,134. Another is relatively big cylindrical cavity with 1:3, N =104,444. Both of them can be computed in two nodes and the front cavities are divided into three sections.

The parallel efficiency is shown in the Fig.8. In the two cases, nearly 90% efficiency is achieved, which shows efficiency of the parallel algorithm. The parallel efficiency decreases with the number of CPU increases, since the communication volume increases.

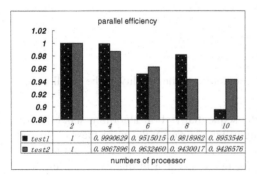

Fig. 8. Parallel efficiency

5 Summary

With the development of the high performance computer and parallel algorithms, parallel method has become an important way to solve the large-scale scientific computing problems. A parallel implementation of the Hybrid algorithm is presented in this paper, which can effectively extend the range of problems that can be solved by the sequential Hybrid algorithm. This method parallelizes all the key steps of the Hybrid algorithm, and we choose different decomposition strategy for different steps. For the near filed, we distribute cavity fields to each processor evenly, while samples are chosen in the far field. Through the node-based data and computation overlapping peer-to-peer model, large-scale intensive communication is avoided during data pre-processing. Experimental results show the high parallel efficiency and relatively high accuracy of this parallel algorithm by comparing with the sequential algorithm on distributed memory computers. A parallel efficiency of nearly 90% is achieved.

Acknowledgments

This work is supported in part by Aviation Industry Development Research Center of China and Shanghai Leading Academic Discipline Project, Project Number: J50103.

References

1. Obelleiro, F., Rodriguez, J.L., Burkholder, R.J.: An Iterative Physical Optics Approach for Analyzing the Electromagnetic Scattering by large Open-Ended Cavities. IEEE Transactions on antennas and propagation 43(4), 356–361 (1995)
2. Xiaoan, X., Xiaoli, Z.: Implementation of Parallel Computing for Electromagnetic Scattering by Large Cavities (September 2008)
3. Obelleiro, F., Campos-Nino, J., Rodrignez, J.L., Pino, A.G.: A segmented approach for computing the electromagnetic scattering of large and deep cavities. Progress In Electromagnetic Research, 129–145 (1998)
4. Ling, H., Kim, H.: On the Kirchhoff's approximation to scattering from discontinuities in large waveguide ducts. Microwave and Optical Technology Letters 7(4), 168–172 (1994)
5. Gao, L.W., Zhenping, Z., Wu, H.: Fast Calculate the RCS of Electrically Large Cavity by IPO+FMM Combined with the GRI and Connection Technology. Journal of Electronics& Information Technology (2007)
6. Lu, E.J., Okunbor, D.I.: A massively parallel fast multipole algorithm in three dimensions. In: The Proceedings of Fifth IEEE International Symposium on Parallel and Distributed Processing, pp. 40–48 (1996)
7. Lu, C.C., Chew, W.C.: Fast far-field approximation for calculating the RCS of large objects. Microwave Opt. Tech. Lett. 8(5), 238–241 (1995)
8. Velamparambil, S., Chew, W.C., Song, J.: On the Parallelization of dynamic Multilevel Fast Multipole Method on Distributed Memory Computers. Innovative Architecture for Future Generation High-Performance Processors and Systems, pp. 3–11 (2000)

A Fair Concurrent Signature Scheme Based on Identity

Xiaofang Huang[1,2] and Licheng Wang[2]

Department of Computer Science, Southwest University of Science and Technology
Mianyang, Sichuan 621000, China
National Engineering Laboratory for Disaster Backup and Recovery, Beijing
University of Posts and Telecommunications, Beijing 100876, China
tinahxf@gmail.com

Abstract. The concept of concurrent signatures was introduced by Chen, Kudla and Paterson at Eurocrypt 2004, which allows two parties to produce two ambiguous signatures until the initial signer releases an extra piece of information (called keystone). Once the keystone is released, both signatures are bound to their true signers concurrently. However, Susilo, Mu and Zhang pointed out the original concurrent signature is not ambiguous to any third party if both signers are known to be trustworthy, and further proposed perfect concurrent signatures to strengthen the ambiguity of concurrent signatures in ICICS 2004. Unfortunately, Susilo *et al.*'s schemes are unfair for the matching signer because they enable the initial signer to release a carefully prepared keystone that binds the matching signer's signature, but not the initial signer's. Therefore, we present a fair identity based concurrent signature in an effective way to correct these flaws in ambiguity and fairness. Moreover, our scheme is more efficient than other concurrent signature schemes based on the bilinear paring.

Keywords: concurrent signature, bilinear pairings, fairness, ambiguity.

1 Introduction

Fairness in exchanging signatures is a fundamental and well-studied problem in cryptography. At Eurocrypt 2004, Chen, Kudla and Paterson[1] introduced a novel concrete concurrent signature scheme, which allows two entities produce two ambiguous signatures until an extra piece of information (namely the keystone) is released by one of the parties, and the both signatures are bound to their true signers concurrently. In [1], Chen *et al.* pointed out that the *full* power of fair exchange is *not necessary* in many applications scenarios, including one party needing the service of the other, credit card payment transactions, secret information releasing, and fair tendering of contracts. So, the concurrent signature scheme can be used as a weak tool, which provides a more natural dispute resolution than the reliance on a TTP to realize practical exchanges. Later, Susilo, Mu and Zhang [2] pointed out that in Chen *et al.*'s concurrent

W. Zhang et al. (Eds.): HPCA 2009, LNCS 5938, pp. 198–205, 2010.
© Springer-Verlag Berlin Heidelberg 2010

signatures, if the two parties are known to be honest players, any third party can identify who is the true signer of both ambiguous signatures even before the keystone is released. Then Susilo *et al.* proposed a stronger notion called *perfect concurrent signatures* and presented two concrete constructions from Schnorr signature and bilinear pairing. In their schemes, any third party can not deduce the true signer of the signatures before the keystone is released even both signers are known to be trustworthy. Based on the idea of the *perfect concurrent signatures*, Susilo and Mu [3] proposed a tripartite concurrent signature scheme from bilinear pairings, and Chow and Susilo [4] constructed two identity-based perfect concurrent signature schemes. However, in [5,6], Wang *et al.* pointed out that Susilo *et al.*'s perfect concurrent signatures [2,4] are actually not concurrent signatures because the initial signer Alice can cheat the matching signer Bob, if she releases a carefully prepared keystone so that Bob's signature is binding, but not to her. And Wu *et al.* [7]presented an ID_based concurrent signature, which allows the two parties control their keystones respectively only if the two keystones are released the both signatures become binding to their true signers concurrently. However, this scheme is not a real concurrent signature, because the party who released his/her keystone later can gain the significant advantage over the other.

1.1   Our Contribution

In this paper, we provide a fair ID_based concurrent signature, which can offer more ambiguity and stronger fairness than previous schemes. In our construction, the signatures are verified without binding the public key of the signer in the phase of the signature verification before the keystone is released. Once the keystone is released, the signatures can be bound simultaneously. Moreover, our scheme is more efficient than other concurrent signature schemes based on the bilinear paring [2,5]. The rest of this paper is organized as follows. In section 2, we briefly review some of the previous and related works in this area. Then, in section 3, we propose a fair ID_based concurrent signature scheme and give a generic construction of fair exchange protocol without TTP. In section 4, we analyze the security and efficiency of our proposal. Finally, section 5 concludes the paper.

2   Related Work

2.1   Bilinear Pairing

Let G_1 be a cyclic additive group generated by P, whose order is a prime q, and G_2 be a cyclic multiplicative group with the same order q. Let $\hat{e} : G_1 \times G_1 \rightarrow G_2$ be a bilinear map [8][9]:

Definition 1 Co-Diffie-Hellman(Co-CDH) Problem
Given $P_1, P_2, aP_1, bP_2 \in G_1$ (for unknown randomly chosen $a, b \in Z_q$), compute $abP_2 \in G_2$.

Definition 2 Co-CDH Assumption

If IG is a Co-CDH parameter generator, the advantage $Adv_{IG,A}(l)$ that an algorithm A has in solving the Co-CDH problem for sufficiently large security parameter l is defined to be the probability:

$$\Pr \begin{bmatrix} < q, G_1, G_2, \hat{c} > \leftarrow G(1^l) \\ P_1, P_2 \leftarrow G_1^*; a, b \leftarrow Z_q^* \\ A(q, G_1, G_2, P_1, P_2, aP_1, bP_2) = abP_2 \in G_2 \end{bmatrix}$$

The Co-CDH assumption is that $Adv_{IG,A}(l)$ is negligible for all efficient algorithms A.

2.2 Review on Concurrent Signatures

As defined in [1], a concurrent signature consist of the following four algorithms:

SETUP: A probabilistic algorithm that on input a security parameter 1^l, outputs the descriptions of: the set of participants $\mathcal{U}$, the message space $\mathcal{M}$, the signature space $\mathcal{S}$, the keystone space $\mathcal{K}$, the keystone fix space $\mathcal{F}$, and a function $KGEN : \mathcal{K} \rightarrow \mathcal{F}$. The algorithm also outputs the public keys $\{X_i\}$ of all the participants, each participant retaining their private key x_i, and any additional system parameters π.

ASIGN: A probabilistic algorithm that on inputs $< X_i, X_j, x_i, h_2, M >$, where $h_2 \in \mathcal{F}$, X_i and $X_j \neq X_i$ are public keys, x_i is the private key associated with X_i, and $M \in \mathcal{M}$, outputs an ambiguous signature $\sigma = < s, h_1, h_2 >$ on M, where $s \in \mathcal{S}, h_1, h_2 \in \mathcal{F}$.

AVERIFY: A deterministic algorithm that takes as input S=$<\sigma, X_i, X_j, M>$ and outputs accept or reject, where $\sigma = < s, h_1, h_2 >$. If $\sigma = < s, h_2, h_1 >$ then AVERIFY(σ, X_i, X_j, M) = VERIFY(σ, X_j, X_i, M). This is the symmetry property of AVERIFY.

VERIFY: A deterministic algorithm which takes as input $< k, S >$ where $k \in \mathcal{K}$ is a keystone and S $= < \sigma, X_i, X_j, M >$, where $\sigma = < s, h_1, h_2 >$ with $s \in \mathcal{S}, h_1, h_2 \in \mathcal{F}, X_i$, and X_j are public keys, and $M \in \mathcal{M}$. The algorithm checks whether k is a valid keystone. If not, it terminates with output reject. Otherwise it runs AVERIFY(S).

In [1], it was claimed that both σ_i and σ_j provide identity ambiguity. After the keystone k is released by one of parties, the identity of the signers is revealed and the signatures become binding. Therefore, fairness in exchange of signatures is achieved.

3   Fair ID_Based Concurrent Signature Schemes

In this section, we design a fair ID_based concurrent signature scheme based on the ideas of the original notion of concurrent signature [1] and ID_based ring signature [10]. To illustrate it clearly, we divide it into five parts: Setup, Key generation, Asign, Averify and Verify.

3.1   Setup Algorithm

The private key generator (PKG) randomly chooses the $x \in Z_q^*$ and keeps it as the master secret key, and then sets $P_{pub} = xP$. It selects two cryptographic hash functions $H_1 : \{0,1\}^* \to G_1$, $H_2 : \{0,1\}^* \to Z_q^*$ and publishes system parameters $\{G_1, G_2, \hat{e}, q, P, P_{pub}, H_1, H_2\}$. The algorithm also sets $\mathcal{M} = \mathcal{K} = \mathcal{F} = Z_q$.

3.2   Key Generation Algorithm

The signer u submits ID_u to PKG, PKG sets the signer's public key $P_u = H_1(ID_u)$ and computes the signer's private key $s_u = xP_u = xH_1(ID_u)$. Then PKG sends the private signing key to the signer via a secure channel.

3.3   Asign Algorithm

The algorithm takes as inputs the parameters (P_i, P_j, s_i, f, m), where s_i is the secret key associated with the public key P_i, and $m \in \mathcal{M}$ is the message. The initial signer randomly choose $f = H_2(k), f \in \mathcal{F}$, and $\alpha \in Z_q^*$, outputs $\sigma = (C_1, C_2, V)$ as the ambiguous signature where $C_1 = f, h = H_2(m \| P_i \| P_j \| C_1), C_2 = \alpha P_i - C_1 - hP_j, V = (h + \alpha)s_i$.

3.4   Averify Algorithm

This algorithm takes as input $(m, \sigma, P_i, P_j, P_{pub})$, where P_i, P_j are public keys and $\sigma = (C_1, C_2, V)$ is the signature on m. The algorithm checks whether $\hat{e}(P, V) = \hat{e}(P_{pub}, C_1 + C_2 + hP_i + hP_j)$ holds with equality. If so, it outputs accept; Otherwise, it outputs reject.

3.5   Verify Algorithm

The **VERIFY** algorithm takes as input (k, S), where $k \in \mathcal{K}$ is the keystone and $S = (m, \sigma, P_i, P_j, P_{pub})$, where $\sigma = (C_1, C_2, V)$. The algorithm verifies whether k is valid. If the output of the verification is rejection, then it outputs **REJECT**. Otherwise, it runs **AVERIFY** and the output of this algorithm is the output of the AVERIFY algorithm.

Note that PKG as the private key distributor is trustworthy in our scheme, but it doesn't take party in the exchange of the signatures. So in point of the fair exchange, our scheme can provide the signatures exchange in a fair way without TTP. Then, on our signature scheme we will construct a fair exchange protocol without TTP running between parties A and B, as shown in Fig.1:

$A(ID_A)$

Key-pair$(P_A, s_A), m_A \in M$

$k \in K, f = H_2(k) \in F,$

$C_1 = f,$

$\sigma_A = \textbf{ASIGN}(P_A, P_B, s_A, f, m_A)$ $\xrightarrow{m_A, \sigma_A}$ $\textbf{AVERIFY}(m_A, \sigma_A, P_A, P_B, P_{pub})$

$\quad = (C_1, C_2, V)$

$B(ID_B)$

Key-pair$(P_B, s_B), m_B \in M$

$\xleftarrow{m_B, \sigma_B}$ $\sigma_B = \textbf{ASIGN}(P_A, P_B, s_B, f, m_B)$

$\quad = (C_1', C_2', V')$

VERIFY $C_1' = C_1$

AVERIFY $(m_B, \sigma_B, P_A, P_B, P_{pub})$

$\xrightarrow{k}$ $C_1 = H_2(k)$

Fig. 1. Fair Exchange Protocol without TTP

3.6   Performance Analysis

Table 1 gives the efficiency comparison for all known concurrent signature based on bilinear pairing. As for the computational overheads, we only consider bilinear mappings (denote by P_a) and multi-exponentiations on G_2(denote by M_uG_2).

Table 1. Efficiency Comparison

Concurrent Signature Schemes	Comp. Cost of A	Comp. Cost of B	Comp. Cost of Averifier	Comp. Cost of Verifer
Susilo-Mu-Zhang[2]	$2P_a + 1M_uG_2$	$3P_a + 1M_uG_2$	$3P_a + 2M_uG_2$	$4P_a + 2M_uG_2$
Chow-Susilo[4]'s scheme 1	$2P_a + 1M_uG_2$	$3P_a + 1M_uG_2$	$3P_a + 1M_uG_2$	$4P_a + 2M_uG_2$
Chow-Susilo[4]'s scheme 1		$1P_a$	$2P_a$	$3P_a$
Wang-Bao-Zhou[5]	$2P_a + 1M_uG_2$	$3P_a + 1M_uG_2$	$3P_a + 2M_uG_2$	$4P_a + 2M_uG_2$
Our scheme			$2P_a + 1M_uG_2$	$2P_a$

From Table 1, we can see that the cost of our scheme is less than the other concurrent signature schemes based on bilinear pairing.

4   Security Analysis

Based on the results in [1,10], it is not difficult to prove the security of our scheme. Formally, we have the following theorem.

Theorem 1. *If Co-CDH problem is hard, then our signature scheme is existentially unforgeable under a chosen message attack in the random oracle model.*

Proof. Suppose $\mathcal{A}$ is an adversary, who can break the signature scheme and achieve a forgery. Then we can construct an algorithm $\mathcal{S}$ that uses $\mathcal{A}$ to solve the Co-CDH problem with non-negligible probability. $\mathcal{S}$ will simulate the challenger by simulating all the random oracles with $\mathcal{A}$ to solve the Co-CDH problem. That is, a contradiction against the assumption in the theorem, so our signature scheme is secure.

Simulations: S gives the parameters $\{G_1, G_2, \hat{e}, q, p, P, P_{pub}, H_1, H_2\}$ and identity $ID^* \in R\{0,1\}^*$ to $\mathcal{A}$. During the game, $\mathcal{S}$ should perfectly respond to $\mathcal{A}$'s hash oracle and signing oracle queries in the simulation. Roughly speaking, these answers are randomly generated, but to maintain the consistency and to avoid collision, $\mathcal{S}$ keeps three lists to store the answers used. We assume $\mathcal{A}$ will ask for ID's private key before ID is used in any other queries.

H_1-Queries: To respond to $\mathcal{A}$'s H_1-queries, $\mathcal{S}$ maintain a list of $H_1^{List} = (ID_i, H_1(ID_i))$. If an entry for the query is found, the same answer will be given to $\mathcal{A}$; otherwise, $\mathcal{S}$ will pick a random value and return as the answer to $\mathcal{A}$, then add $< ID^*, h >$ to the H_1^{List}.

H_2-Queries: $\mathcal{A}$ can query the random oracle H_2 at any time. $\mathcal{S}$ simulates the H_2 oracle in the same way as the H_1 oracle by keeping the H_2^{List}.

Private Key Extract Queries: $\mathcal{A}$ can query the private key for any identities ID_i. If $ID_i = ID^*$, and then $\mathcal{S}$ terminates the game. Otherwise $\mathcal{S}$ find the respond (ID_i, h_i) from H_1^{List} and returns the appropriate private key $s_i = xh_i$.

KGen Queries: $\mathcal{A}$ can request a random keystone $k \in K$ and return a keystone fix $f = H_2(k)$. $\mathcal{S}$ maintains a and answers queries by choosing a random keystone $k \in K$ and computing $f = H_2(k)$, then adds $< k, f >$ to the K^{List}, which is the *sublist* of H_2^{List} but just used to answer KReveal queries.

Asign Queries: $\mathcal{A}$ can query the signature on m with ID. On input of $(P_i, P_j, P_{pub}, f, m)$, where P_i and P_j $(P_i \neq P_j)$ are public keys and $m \in \mathcal{M}$ is the message to be signed. $\mathcal{S}$ returns $\sigma = (C_1, C_2, V)$ as the signature, where $C_1 = f$ and $h = H_2(m\|P_i\|P_j\|C_1)$ which is added to the H_2^{List}, and $C_2 = \alpha P_i - C_1 - hP_j$.

Finally, $\mathcal{A}$ outputs a forged signature $\sigma' = (C_1, C_2', V')$ on some message m', which has not been queried on to signing oracle.

Solving Co-CDH: It follows from the forking lemma [11] that if $\mathcal{A}$ can outputs a valid forged signature with negligible probability, then we need to apply the rewind technology. So $\mathcal{A}$ finally outputs anther forged signature $\sigma' = (C_1, C_2', V')(C_2 \neq C_2')$ at the end of the second run.

After using the rewind technology twice, $\mathcal{S}$ could obtain two signatures (M, σ), (M, σ'), satisfying:
$$\hat{e}(P, V) = \hat{e}(p, V'),$$
$$V = (h + \alpha)s_i,$$
$$V' = (h' + \alpha)s_i.$$

Set $P_i = bP$, then $\mathcal{S}$ can deduce:
$$s_i = abP = (h - h')^{-1}(V - V')$$

Thus, $\mathcal{S}$ can use the two valid forged signatures to solve Co-CDH with non-negligible probability in polynomial time by forking lemma. This contradicts the hardness of Co-CDH problem. Hence, the proof completes. $\square$

Theorem 2. *Both signatures in our scheme are ambiguous to any third party before k is released.*

Proof. Ambiguity means that given a concurrent signature without the keystone, any third party cannot distinguish who is the true signer of this signature. Susilo *et al.* [2] provide four cases to strengthen the notion of ambiguity in [1], and this strengthened notion is called as perfect ambiguity. We'll provide a full formal specification via the following game between Adversary $\mathcal{A}$ and challenger $\mathcal{C}$.

Simulation, Queries: They are the same as in the game for unforgeability.

Challenge: Adversary $\mathcal{A}$ choose the challenge tuple (P_i, P_j, m_1, m_2), where P_i, P_j are public keys and m_1, m_2 are two messages to be signed. Then, $\mathcal{C}$ picks keystone $k \in K$ and compute $f = KGEN(k)$, and then though randomly choosing $b \in \{1, 2, 3, 4\}$ $\mathcal{C}$ outputs ambiguous signatures $\sigma_1 = (C_1, C_2, V)$ and $\sigma_2 = (C'_1, C'_2, V')$ as follows[13]:

$$\text{if } b = 1, \sigma \longleftarrow ASIGN(P_i, P_j, s_i, m_1, f), \sigma_2 \longleftarrow ASIGN(P_i, P_j, s_i, m_2, f)$$
$$\text{if } b = 2, \sigma \longleftarrow ASIGN(P_i, P_j, s_j, m_1, f), \sigma_2 \longleftarrow ASIGN(P_i, P_j, s_j, m_2, f)$$
$$\text{if } b = 3, \sigma \longleftarrow ASIGN(P_i, P_j, s_i, m_1, f), \sigma_2 \longleftarrow ASIGN(P_i, P_j, s_i, m_2, f)$$
$$\text{if } b = 4, \sigma \longleftarrow ASIGN(P_i, P_j, s_j, m_1, f), \sigma_2 \longleftarrow ASIGN(P_i, P_j, s_j, m_2, f)$$

$\mathcal{A}$ can repeat the above queries.

Output: Adversary $\mathcal{A}$ finally outputs a value $b' = \{1, 2, 3, 4\}$ as its guess for b. We say $\mathcal{A}$ wins the game if $b = b'$ and $\mathcal{A}$ has not requested on any of the following values: f, C_2 and C'_2. So the probability which $\mathcal{A}$ can win the above game can be defined as follows

$$|\Pr[b = b'] - 1/4|.$$

This means no polynomial bounded adversary can guess the correct signers with a probability greater than $1/4$ before k is released.

The original concurrent signature [1] has weaker ambiguity as pointed out in [2], because when the two signers are known to be honest, then the first two possibilities can be disregarded, and hence, the third party can identify who is the signer by verifying $h' + f \equiv (H_1((g^c y_i^{h'} y_j^f \mod p)\|m)) \mod q$ before the keystone is released. However, the flaw is improved in our scheme since the signatures needn't to be bound the f with the signer's public key in the phase of *averify*. Hence, the proof completes. □

Theorem 3. *Our scheme is fair if both signatures can be bound with their signer's identity simultaneously after the keystone is released.*

Proof. The proof is similar to the proof of fairness of the concurrent signatures in [1] and fairness can be obtained in a similar way as we do in Theorem 1 and Theorem 2, so we omit this proof due to space limitation.

5   Conclusion

We presented a fair ID-based concurrent signature scheme based on bilinear pairings. This scheme improves the weakness in ambiguity and fairness of the existing concurrent signatures to achieve truly fairness. Furthermore, our scheme is more efficient than the others based on the bilinear pairings. As for the future work, it is interesting to consider how to construct concurrent signature schemes in multi-party settings.

Acknowledgments

This work was supported by the Natural Science Foundation of China (No. 60673098, 60973159 and 90718001).

References

1. Chen, L., Kudla, C., Paterson, K.G.: Concurrent signatures. In: Cachin, C., Camenisch, J.L. (eds.) EUROCRYPT 2004. LNCS, vol. 3027, pp. 287–305. Springer, Heidelberg (2004)
2. Susilo, W., Mu, Y., Zhang, F.: Perfect concurrent signature schemes. In: López, J., Qing, S., Okamoto, E. (eds.) ICICS 2004. LNCS, vol. 3269, pp. 14–26. Springer, Heidelberg (2004)
3. Susilo, W., Mu, Y.: Tripartite Concurrent Signatures. In: The 20th IFIP International Information Security Conference (IFIP/SEC2005), pp. 425–441. Springer, Boston (2005)
4. Chow, S., Susilo, W.: Generic construction of (identity-based) perfect concurrent signatures. In: Qing, S., Mao, W., López, J., Wang, G. (eds.) ICICS 2005. LNCS, vol. 3783, pp. 194–206. Springer, Heidelberg (2005)
5. Wang, G., Bao, F., Zhou, J.: The Fairness of Perfect Concurrent Signatures. In: Ning, P., Qing, S., Li, N. (eds.) ICICS 2006. LNCS, vol. 4307, pp. 435–451. Springer, Heidelberg (2006)
6. Huang, Z.J., Huang, R.F., Lin, X.Z.: Perfect Concurrent Signature Protocol. In: SNPD 2007, Qingdao, China, pp. 467–472 (2007)
7. Wu, X.F., Wang, X.F., Wang, S.P., et al.: Efficient identity-based concurrent signature scheme. Computer Engineering and Applications 43(27), 127–129 (2007)
8. Boneh, D., Franklin, M.: Identity-based Encryption from the Weil pairing. In: Kilian, J. (ed.) CRYPTO 2001. LNCS, vol. 2139, pp. 213–229. Springer, Heidelberg (2001)
9. Joux, A.: A One Round Protocol for Tripartite Diffie-Hellman. In: Bosma, W. (ed.) ANTS 2000. LNCS, vol. 1838, pp. 385–394. Springer, Heidelberg (2000)
10. Chow, S.S.M., Yiu, S.-M., Hui, L.C.K.: Efficient Identity Based Ring Signature. In: Ioannidis, J., Keromytis, A.D., Yung, M. (eds.) ACNS 2005. LNCS, vol. 3531, pp. 499–512. Springer, Heidelberg (2005)
11. Pointcheval, D., Stern, J.: Security proofs for signature schemes. In: Maurer, U.M. (ed.) EUROCRYPT 1996. LNCS, vol. 1070, pp. 387–398. Springer, Heidelberg (1996)

Numerical Simulation of Rotating-Cage Bio-reactor Based on Dynamic Mesh Coupled Two-Phase Flow

Jiang Fan[1], Huang Chunman[2], Liang Zhongwei[1], and Wang Yijun[1]

[1] Mechanical and Electrical Engineering College of Guangzhou University,
Guangzhou Guangdong 510006
jiangfan2008@gzhu.edu.cn
[2] Mechanical and Electrical Engineering Department of Guangdong Baiyun University,
Guangzhou Guangdong 510450

Abstract. The cage bio-reactor is a new high-efficient sewage treatment reactor. The flowing inside of reactor influences the sewage treatment effect of reactor so numerical simulation is adopted to analyze the flowing inside of reactor in an attempt to identify the factors that influence the effect of sewage treatment, and provides the data for the following structure optimization of bio-reactor. In this paper, a coupled dynamic mesh with two-phase flow is used to analyze the hydrodynamic characteristic of the rotating-cage bio-reactor; the computation results show that the air flow enters into the bio-reactor, and then it rises toward right, bumps into the cage wall with the anti-clockwise rotation, scatters, and forms two back-flows in the upper of the bio-reactor. The backflow center has the tendency to form cavity; however, under the central shaft, the air flow does not disperse, where the volume fraction of the gas phase is low.

1 Introduction

The pollution of rivers is increasingly serious, and has caused wide attentions; thus many corresponding treatments were explored. At present, more sewage treatment equipments are the complete equipments for the sewage treatment plant in China and abroad and less treatment equipment system is used in the polluted rivers and lakes. The sewage treatment equipment used in the river and lake is mainly in the aeration ship and shore bio-reactor [1-3]. The latter is of low effect, high cost, complex operation, difficult management; moreover, the shore bio-reactor lacks flexibility; thus the system is very difficult to be widely applied. Chen Wei-ping, the professor of South China University of Technology, developed a new effective rotating-cage bio-reactor; the sewage treatment environment with suspended bio-carriers is based on the idea of initiative moving bed, and showed good water treatment effect [1,2] in the simulation. The flowing inside of reactor influents the sewage treatment effect of reactor, therefore, uses numerical simulation to analyze flowing inside of reactor, should find out the factors that influent the effect of sewage treatment, and provides the data for the following structure optimization of bio-reactor. In this paper, coupled dynamic mesh with two-phase flow the hydrodynamic characteristic of the rotating-cage bio-reactor is analyzed, and the detailed information of flow field in the bio-reactor could be obtained.

W. Zhang et al. (Eds.): HPCA 2009, LNCS 5938, pp. 206–211, 2010.

2 Control Equations and Calculation Parameters

The flow in rotating-cage is a complicated flow including three phase of gas, liquid and solid. Due to the large size, the simulation of three-phase flow in bio-reactor is quite difficult. To simplify the calculation, the flow field computation in rotating-cage reactor is only two phase flow of gas and liquid without the suspend bio-carriers. That's because the cross section of rotating-cage bio-reactor is equal everywhere in axial direction; only two-phase flow in center cross section is need to be analyzed; then the governing equation is simplified to be the two-dimension condition, as shown in Fig. 1.

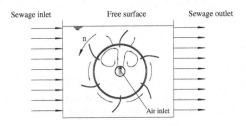

Fig. 1. Physical model of rotating-cage bio-reactor

Flow field governing equations of rotating-cage bio-reactor include the mass conservation equation and the momentum conservation equation, expressed as the following in general form:

$$\frac{\partial(\rho\phi)}{\partial t} + div(\rho u\phi) = div(\Gamma \, grad\,\phi) + S \tag{1}$$

Where, ρ is fluid density; t is computation time; ϕ is general variable, represents the solution variable v_x, v_y; Γ is general diffusion coefficient ; S is general source item.

The two-phase flow of rotating-cage should maintain that the sum of gas-liquid two-phase is 1. Since the inner flow is perturbation, the standard $k-\varepsilon$ turbulence transporting equation is closed.

The fixed shaft of the rotating-cage bio-reactor is simulated by dynamic mesh technology. For the influence of moving boundary needs to be considered, the flow control equations are improved; the general control equation [4-5] is shown as:

$$\frac{d}{dt}\int_{V_s}\rho\phi dV + \int_{L_s}\rho\phi(u-u_g)ndS = \int_{L_s}\Gamma\nabla\phi ndS + \int_{V_s}SdV \tag{2}$$

Where, ϕ is general variable; V_s is control volume; L_s is boundary of the control volume; u is average velocity; u_g is moving velocity of dynamics mesh; n is normal unit vector in surface directing outwards.

When the bio-reactor rotate angle is small, grids among of cage like spring [6], along with rotation of the cage, its deformation is small; when it is large, grids around the cage should distort, and when the distortion exceeds a certain limit, grids start to remesh locally until the distortion meets the limit. As shown in Fig.2, where the grids change as the cage rotates.

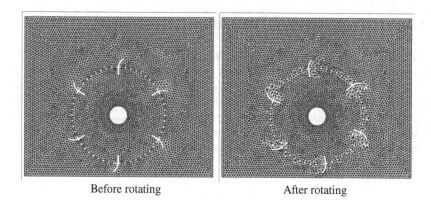

Before rotating   After rotating

Fig. 2. Dynamics mesh of rotating-cage bio-reactor

Boundary conditions are: the region considered is the single region around the single cage. The sewage inlet locates at lower left, the sewage outlet locates at lower right, the air inlet, is aeration holes on the centre shaft, the air outlet is the upper ones. The initial condition is that: some sewage is pre-filled in computation region, and the calculation step is decided by the minimum grid size, the calculation time cost is determined until the aeration flow arrives at the free surface.

The geometric parameter: the calculate region has the length of 800 mm, and the width of 650 mm; the inner wall of rotating-cage has the diameter of 368 mm, and the thickness of 8 mm; the outside blades have the maximum diameter of 470 mm; the inside blades have the length of 30 mm; the aeration shaft has the diameter of 75 mm; the center of rotating-cage has the height of 250 mm. The compute regions are triangle elements, which are consist of 26266 nodes and 50144 elements.

In computation, the gas phase is air, and the liquid phase is sewage; their physical parameters are: for air, the density is 1.225 kg/m^3, and the dynamic viscosity is 1.7894×10^{-5} Pa/s; for sewage, the density is 1000.35 kg/m^3, and the dynamic viscosity is 1.005×10^{-3} Pa/s. The boundary conditions: the influent velocity is 0.12 m/s, the aeration velocity is 0.66 m/s, and the rotation speed is 1.5 rpm.

3 Calculation and Analysis

Through numerical simulation computation, we have obtained many physical parameters of the calculation region, such as pressure, speed, gas phase distribution, and so on. These parameters are provided the detailed data to analyze multi-phase dynamic flow inside the bio-reactor.

The contour in the Fig.3 left is the whole pressure distribution in the reactor, it demonstrates that: the pressure distribution is nearly related to the sewage depth. That's because the sewage velocity is very low in the reactor, its pressure is almost the static pressure. There are two regions of small pressure above the central shaft, that's because the air flow leads the water flow rise, the fluid of the side has no (not) enough time to supplement so the low pressure forms, and in this location the cavity is easy to form, too. At the right of Fig. 3, the pressure curve shows the distribution on the fixed straight line (two point coordinates of this line is (-100, 80), (100, 80)); both sides of the central shaft have large trough; these troughs mean low pressure region in the contour.

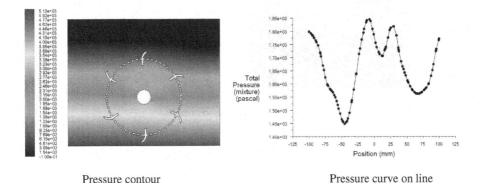

Pressure contour   Pressure curve on line

Fig. 3. Pressure results

The left of Fig. 4 is the velocity vector, it shows that the air flow comes from the aeration hole on the shaft centre; the upper air flow shrinks bundles; under the action of slow sewage flow, the flow rises to right, after bumped into the wall of rotating-cage bio-reactor with anti-clockwise rotation, it inclines to left, and disperse at the upper region of reactor; then it escapes out of the reactor. At the bottom of centre shaft, because of high pressure, the air flows to upper along the central shaft wall, then it confluences with the upper air flow. At the right of Fig. 4, it is the velocity distribution on the fixed straight line; there has two velocity peaks in both sides of the centre shaft and a velocity trough; it shows that the air flow trends to be divided into two parts. Contrary to the relation of pressure and velocity on the fixed straight line, at the place of low pressure, the velocity is also low; two regions of low pressure is up to the central shaft; at the close of cavity, the velocity is also very low; apparently, the place is the vortex center.

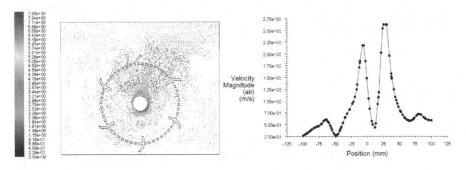

Volume fraction of air in bio-reactor   Air velocity of in bio-reactor

Fig. 4. Velocity results

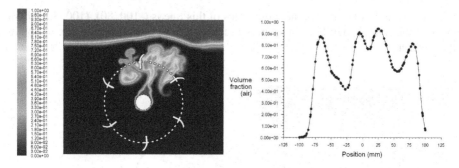

Fig. 5. Air volume fraction results

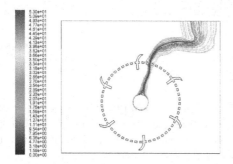

Fig. 6. Streamline

The contour in the left of Fig. 5 is the volume fraction distribution of gas phase at the calculating region; the aeration of central shaft collects that of upper shaft, which rises to the right, meets the cage wall by clockwise rotating; then the gas phase scatters; thus the volume fraction of gas phase becomes greater at the upper of the central shaft. Under of central shaft, the gas phase distribution becomes very small. At the right side of Fig. 5, it demonstrations the condition of gas phase distribution on the straight line; where, curves show that the region is full of the gas phase.

Fig. 6 shows streamline distribution, where the aeration entrance is taken as the beginning of the computation region; and it demonstrates that the direction of flow vector and the gas phase; it tends to flow from the shaft centre to its right, and then leave the calculation region.

4 Conclusions

The model of dynamic mesh has coupled two phase flow computation, it can simulate real flow condition of the rotating-cage bio-reactor, and can obtain the detailed information of flow field in the bio-reactor; thus it can reduce the cost and developing time of the rotate-cage bio-reactor.

The results of pressure, velocity, gas phase volume fraction distribution show that: the air flow enters into the bio-reactor from the aeration hole on the central shaft, then it rises toward right, bumps into the cage wall with anti-clockwise rotation, and scatters, forms two back-flow in the upper of bio-reactor; the backflow center has the tendency to be cavity; on the top, where is the aerobic region. But under the central shaft, the air flow doesn't disperse, thus there the volume fraction of gas phase is low, also it is an aerobic area. This division of reaction zone is advantage to the sewage treatment.

Acknowledgment

Thanks the support from the open fund of Guangdong key laboratory for advanced metallic materials processing (No.2007006).

References

1. Jiang, F.: Biological properties of material and structure of suspended bio-carriers and cage-type bio-reactor. Ph.D. Thesis. South China University of Technology, Guangzhou, Guangdong, China (2006)
2. Chen, W.P., Jiang, F., Wu, C.D., et al.: A rotating-cage and suspended carriers biology sewage treatment method and equipment. Chinese invention patent, Patent No. 200410077611.2
3. Jiang, F., Yu, Z.H., Wang, Y.J., et al.: Comparison of sliding grid and dynamics mesh of rotation-cage-type bio-reactor. Journal of Guangzhou University 6(3), 37–41 (2007)
4. Jiang, F., Chen, W.P., Li, Y.Y.: Dynamics Numerical Simulation of Cage-type Bio-reactor. In: Proceedings of the International Conference on Mechanical Engineering and Mechanics, November 2007, vol. 1, pp. 1015–1018 (2007)
5. Jiang, F., Chen, W.P., Mai, M.R., et al.: Numerical simulation on water and sediments two-phase flows in river. Progress in Safety Science and Technology V, 1634–1639 (November 2005)
6. Jiang, F., Chen, W.P., Wang, Y.J., et al.: Numerical simulation of flow field inside of micro-inline pump based on moving mesh. Fluid Machinery 35(7), 20–24 (2007)
7. Li, M., Wang, G.Q., Yu, G., et al.: Numerical simulation of hydrodynamic behaviors of internal circulation bio-fluidized bed reactor. Acta Scientiae Circumstantiae 24(3), 400–404

Energy-Efficient Intrusion Detection System for Wireless Sensor Network Based on MUSK Architecture

Surraya Khanum[1], Muhammad Usman[2], Khalid Hussain[3],
Rehab Zafar[1], and Muhammad Sher[1]

[1] Department of Computer Science, International Islamic University,
Islamabad, Pakistan
s_delhvi@yahoo.ca, rehab_zafar@yahoo.com,
m.sher@iiu.edu.pk
[2] University Institute of Information Technology, Pir Mehr Ali Shah,
Arid Agriculture University, Rawalpindi, Pakistan
manilasani@yahoo.com
[3] Faculty of Computing, Riphah University, Rawalpindi
khalidhussain@riphah.edu.pk

Abstract. Wireless Sensor Network (WSN) is usually deployed in hostile and uncontrollable environment. The WSN is vulnerable to security threats due to its hostile nature. There are several static security techniques in order to make WSN secure. These techniques are encryption keys, VPN, firewalls etc. All these techniques provide security from external threats. Additionally, these techniques do not provide strong security mechanism because of limited energy resources of WSN. There is a need of dynamic, real time and energy-efficient security mechanism for WSN. The existing real time security mechanisms are energy and time consuming. We have proposed a dynamic, real time and energy efficient Intrusion Detection System (IDS). Our proposed approach minimizes the security control messages and eliminates the need to update the signatures manually.

1 Introduction

Wireless Sensor Network (WSN) is an emerging technology [1, 2]. The WSN is usually deployed in a critical environment where the human labour is not involved. The WSN has a centralized control system called as Base Station (BS). Popular examples of WSN are fire response, traffic monitoring, military command etc. [1, 2]. The traditional security mechanisms for Ad hoc and other types of networks cannot be directly applied to WSN [1]. To minimize the potential attacks on WSN like any other network, there are two types of defensive approaches: Static and Dynamic [3]. Firewalls and encryption techniques are common examples. On the other hand, an Intrusion Detection System (IDS) is a dynamic monitoring system. A number of security techniques have been proposed for the security of WSN [4, 5]. Most of them are based on specific types of attacks (selective forwarding, sinkhole, and MAC) [6, 7, 8]. All these schemes are not energy efficient in nature. Therefore there is a need for dynamic real-time defensive system that fits in the security requirement for WSN.

In this paper we have proposed an energy efficient framework using IDS for WSN that not only minimizes the security control communication load over the network but

W. Zhang et al. (Eds.): HPCA 2009, LNCS 5938, pp. 212–217, 2010.
© Springer-Verlag Berlin Heidelberg 2010

also eliminates the need for writing the manual signature. The minimization of control messages save the battery time of sensors which enhance network lifetime. There exists a communication costs for each pair of sensor nodes so the reduction of control message gives energy-efficient framework for WSN. Our proposed IDS architecture is called as MUSK agent (MUSK is a shorten form of *M*uhammad *U*sman and *S*urraya *K*hanum, the first two authors of this research paper) is installed on each node of WSN that continuously monitors intrusion.

MUSK agent sends an Intrusion Report (IR) message to Cluster Header (CH) when an intrusion occurs. An IR contains intrusion activity in the form of report. When CH receives the IR message from any MUSK agent, it makes a vote scheme within that cluster. All MUSK agents cast a vote against that requested IR. If more than half votes are in favour of intrusion the CH assumes that a real intrusion has taken place. Then CH sends a True Detection (TD) message to Base Station (BS). True detection is the real confirmation of intrusion that is drawn from the vote scheme. The BS makes a decision called as TD ACTION against that TD report.

The remainder of the paper is organized as follows: Related works are reviewed in Section 2. The Section 3 discusses the architecture of MUSK agent. Section 4 highlights the basic advantages of our proposed architecture. Section 5 is about conclusions and future works. At the end of the paper references are given.

2 Related Work

The WSN is resource restricted in nature so the Intrusion Detection System (IDS) for Ad hoc and other types of networks cannot be directly applied on it [9]. The authors made a survey on wireless sensor networks security in [10]. In [10] authors have high lighted the obstacles and the requirements for WSN security like data authentication, data integrity, time synchronization, confidentiality etc. Also classify important threats and defensive measures against it.

The author uses a machine learning approach for intrusion detection in WSN in [11]. Detection agent is introduced and installed on each node. Though this approach is real time intrusion detection but it is not an energy efficient approach. In [12] the authors have highlighted layer wise security problems in WSN. The authors introduced a new idea called as Intelligent Security Agent (ISA) that uses the cross layer interaction by maintaining the inter layer communication at minimum level with high level of abstraction. This scheme is also very energy consuming as lot of computation is involved in ISA mechanism. The authors have discussed the deployment of IDS in [13]. The IDS are distributed in nature so deployed on some particular node. Energy consumption by the IDS is also discussed in the paper. This research paper provides a good base for having energy consumption parameter.

3 The MUSK Architecture and Its Working

This Section gives an overview of our proposed MUSK architecture, the MUSK agent communication structure with the CH, communication structure of CH with BS and rotation of new CH that takes place after a specific interval of time.

3.1 The MUSK Agent Architecture

In our proposed architecture, the MUSK agent is installed on each node in the network. There exists no trust association and collaboration between each pair of MUSK agents. It has to rely on its own intrusion detection mechanism as shown in Fig 1. Three functional units i.e. Monitoring Unit (MU), Management Unit (MGU) and Coordinating Unit (CU) are used in this architecture.

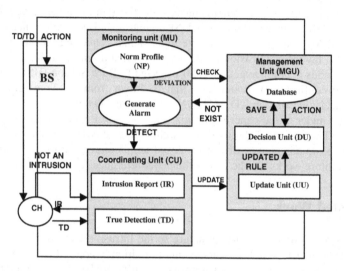

Fig. 1. MUSK Agent Architecture

The Monitoring Unit (MU) is used to monitor the intrusions. When MU detects an intrusion, it sends CHECK message to the Management Unit (MGU) in order to verify the occurrence of intrusion from the repository of pre-defined intrusions. If match occurs, the MGU informs its sub unit Decision Unit (DU) by sending an ACTION message to take a pre-defined action against that intrusion. If no match occurs against the intrusion entry which is stored in the database, the MGU sends NOT EXIST message to MU assuming that it is a novel intrusion. Then MU sends a DETECT message to Coordinating Unit (CU) in order to verify novel intrusion. That generates an Intrusion Report (IR) for every novel intrusion. The IR contains the information about an intrusion activity in the form of report. That is generated for the real detection of intrusion called as True Detection (TD). This IR message is then forwarded to Cluster Header (CH) for voting within that cluster. If more than half votes are in favour of intrusion then CH sends a TD message to the BS reporting for an occurrence of intrusion. Otherwise, NOT AN INTRUSION message sends to the requested IR. The BS makes a decision on that IR report called the TD ACTION that contains the decision in the form of report. Then it is forwarded to the requested CH. That broadcast the TD ACTION to all MUSK agent within its cluster and all CH's over the network. The CU collects TD ACTION from CH and sending an UPDATE message to the MGU informing about the decision of the novel intrusion. That sends TD ACTION to its sub unit Update Unit (UU) for generating a new rule against that novel intrusion. This unit generates a new rule along with the decision called as UPDATED RULE. This message is then forward to the DU for action. That performs an action and send SAVE message to the repository of database for storing this novel intrusion.

3.2 Communication Structure of MUSK Agent with CH

The communication structure of MUSK agent with the CH is shown in the figure 2. When MUSK agent discovers a novel intrusion it sends IR message to CH. The CH performs voting by collecting IR messages from all MUSK agents within its cluster domain. If more than half MUSK agents are against the requested IR the CH sends NOT AN INTRUSION message to the requested IR MUSK agent. Otherwise CH sends TD message to BS for the decision. The decision is taken by the BS which is a centralized decision making authority. The BS sends TD REPORT that contains the action against the IR to the requested CH. CH forward TD REPORT to all MUSK agents with in its cluster domain and all CH's over the network.

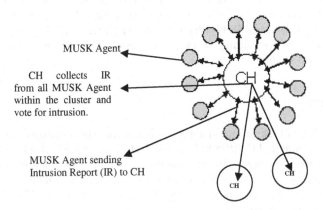

Fig. 2. Communication Structure of MUSK agent with CH

3.3 Communication Structure of CH with BS

The Communication structure of CH with BS is shown in the figure 3. The MUSK agent communicates with BS through CH. When MUSK agent discovers an intrusion, it sends an IR message to CH. Then CH performs voting on that IR request. If more than half MUSK agent votes in favour of requested IR then CH sends TD message to BS which is a centralized authority for decision making. The decision triggers an action against the requested IR i.e. drop the malicious packets, isolate the malicious node from rest of the network etc. The BS takes an appropriate action against the IR request which updates its database and sends TD REPORT to the requested CH.

3.4 Rotation of New CH

The Collaboration–based Intrusion Detection (CID) and Routing Tables Intrusion Detection (RTID) are the major types of technologies used to detect attacks [4]. The

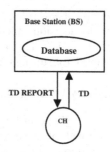

Fig. 3. Communication Structure of CH with BS

CID is an intrusion detection system which continuously monitors the intrusions during the cluster duty cycle. A cluster header (CH) is chosen from a cluster, assuming to be have large battery time as compare to the other nodes in the cluster. The cluster duty cycle performed after a specified interval of time for the selection of new CH. When there is a rotation of new CH, the base station (BS) takes all IR messages form all CH's in the network and save in its database. After the selection of new CH, the BS sends the previously saved IR reports to the newly elected CH. So that previously intrusions would not be lost during the election of new CH. which is a major advantage of our proposed scheme.

4   Advantages

One major advantage of our proposed approach is that the whole network becomes up to date with just a single TD REPORT to any CH. This framework eliminates the duplication of intrusion request to BS, minimizes the security control messages, reduces the network load and saves the sensor node resources. The reduction of communication load over the network enhances the network lifetime which makes the whole network energy efficient.

Another major advantage of this scheme is that the attacks from distant node are restricted. The CH has the Identities (ID's) of all MUSK agents within its cluster domain. The CH first checks the node ID before proceeding to response of IR request to any MUSK agent within its cluster domain. Moreover, only those nodes participate which are the members of that CH domain.

This scheme provides inter and intra cluster security mechanism. There exists no trust relationship between each pair of nodes. In our proposed security mechanism, if one or some (not all) nodes are compromised it will not compromise the whole network.

5   Conclusions and Future Works

In this paper, we have proposed MUSK architecture for intrusion detection. This scheme reduces the work load over the network by just sending the one request to BS and whole network is updated. All those MUSK agents that have not yet discovered the intrusion are also updated. The reduction of communication load enhances the network lifetime and saves the overall energy resource of WSN. In addition, the information related to previous intrusions is not lost during the formation of a new CH. The Performance evaluation of MUSK Architecture based on different attacks is the future work of this research work.

References

1. Kalantzis, S.: Security Models for Wireless Sensor Networks (2006)
2. Alemdar, A., Ibnkahla, M.: Wireless Sensor Networks: Applications and Chalenges. IEEE, Los Alamitos (2007)
3. Sun, B., Osborne, L.: Intrusion Detection Techniques In Mobile Ad Hoc And Wireless Sensor networks, The University of Alabama Sghaier Guizani, University of Quebec at Trois-Rivieres
4. Chen, R.-C., Hsieh, C.-F., Huang, Y.-F.: A New Method for Intrusion Detection on Hierarchical Wireless Sensor Networks. ACM, New York (2009)
5. Huai-bin, W., Zheng, Y., Chun-dong, W.: International Conference on Communications and Mobile Computing Intrusion Detection for Wireless Sensor Networks Based on Multi-Agent and Refined Clustering. In: IEEE International Conference on Communications and Mobile Computing (2009)
6. Ngai, E., Liu, J., Lyu, M.: On the Intruder Detection for Sinkhole Attack in Wireless Sensor Networks. In: IEEE International Conference on Communications, ICC 2006 (2006)
7. Ioannis, K., Dimitriou, T., Freiling, F.: Towards Intrusion Detection in Wireless Sensor Networks. In: 13th European Wireless Conference (2007)
8. Ren, Q., Liang, Q.: Secure Media Access Control (MAC) in wireless sensor networks: intrusion Detections and Countermeasures. In: 15th IEEE International Symposium on Personal, Indoor and Mobile Radio Communications (2004)
9. Lewis, F., Cook, D.J., Das, S.K., John, W.: Wireless Sensor Networks Smart Environments Technologies (2004)
10. Wei, Y., Paul, L., Havinga, J.M.: How to Secure a Wireless Sensor Network. In: ISSNIP. IEEE, Los Alamitos (2005)
11. Yu, Z.: A Framework of Machine Learning Based Intrusion Detection for Wireless Sensor Networks. In: International Conference on Sensor Networks, Ubiquitous, and Trustworthy Computing. IEEE, Los Alamitos (2008)
12. Kuldeep, K., Sharma Ghose, M.K.: Wireless Sensor Networks Security: A New Approach, Computer Science and Engineering Department, Sikkim Manipal Institute of Technology, India
13. Hai, T.H., Huh, E.-N.: Minimizing the Intrusion Detection Modules in Wireless Sensor Networks. IEEE, Los Alamitos (2008)

A Novel Parallel Interval Exclusion Algorithm[*]

Yongmei Lei, Shaojun Chen, and Yu Yan

School of Computer Engineering and Science, Shanghai University,
Shanghai 200072, China
ymlei@mail.shu.edu.cn

Abstract. The optimization algorithm based on interval analysis is a deterministic global optimization algorithm. However, Solving high-dimensional problems, traditional interval algorithm exposed lots of problems such as consumption of time and memory. In this paper, we give a parallel interval global optimization algorithm based on evolutionary computation. It combines the reliability of interval algorithm with the intelligence and nature scalability of mind evolution computation algorithm, effectively overcomes the shortcomings of Time-Consuming and Memory-Consuming of the traditional interval algorithm. Numerical experiments show that the algorithm has much high efficiency than the traditional interval algorithm.

1 Introduction

The interval optimization algorithm is the method that based on interval analysis to find the global optimal solution in a given search interval. Such kind of optimization algorithm usually use branch and bound strategy to exclude the part that does not contain the optimal solution and obtain the dependable results through continuously subdividing search interval and updating the approximation of the optimal solution.

Moore-Skelboe algorithm is the simplest B&B algorithm, when combing to the Mid-test accelerating tools, it can solve differentiable and Non-differentiable problems to obtain the global optimal solution [1]. Varies accelerating tools such as Mid-test, monotonic test, convex test are constructed to delete the invalid intervals [2]. However, when the objective function is non-differentiable, most accelerating tools are invalid [3]. Casado and Markot etc. propose a new multi-splitting technology which subdivides the interval into several numbers in one Iteration steps so as to speed up the similartaxis rate [4]. Casado and Martinez etc propose a new Heuristic select rule [5]. Sotiropoulos etc propose that combing the genetic algorithms to interval algorithms to reduce the current search intervals and update the upper and lower bounds of the objective functions [6].

This article proposes a parallel Interval Exclusion Algorithm (PIEA). The algorithm absorbed the similartaxis and dissimilation operation from the mind evolutionary computation to split or delete intervals. At the same time, interval algorithms give the bound of similartaxis and dissimilation operation so as to rapidly convergence to the reliable optimization.

---

[*] This work is supported by Shanghai Leading Academic Discipline Project J50103.

W. Zhang et al. (Eds.): HPCA 2009, LNCS 5938, pp. 218–223, 2010.

2 Interval Algorithm and Interval Arithmetic

2.1 Interval and Interval Arithmetic

The set of compact interval is denoted by:

$$X = [a,b] = \{x \in R \mid a \leq x \leq b\} \tag{1}$$

If $a = b$, $X = [a,b]$ is called the point interval.

For given intervals $X = [a,b], Y = [c,d] \in I(R)$:

$$
\begin{aligned}
X + Y &= [a+c, b+d] \\
X - Y &= [a-d, b-c] \\
X \cdot Y &= [\min(ac, ad, bc, bd), \max(ac, ac, bc, bd)] \\
X / Y &= [a,b][1/d, 1/c], 0 \notin [c,d]
\end{aligned}
\tag{2}
$$

X^n is defined by:

$$
X^n = \begin{cases}
[1,1] & \text{if } n = 0 \\
\left[a^n, b^n \right] & \text{if } a \geq 0 \text{ or } a \leq 0, n \text{ is odd} \\
[b^n, a^n] & \text{if } b \leq 0, n \text{ is even} \\
[0, \max(a^n, b^n)] & a \leq 0 \leq b, n \text{ is even}
\end{cases}
\tag{3}
$$

N-dimensional interval vector I^n is defined by:

$$X = (X_1, X_2, \ldots X_n)^T, X_i \in I \tag{4}$$

2.2 The Interval Optimization Problems

Consider the following global optimization problem:

$$\min_{x \in S} f(x) \tag{5}$$

N-dimensional interval vector $S \subseteq R^n$ is the first search interval. The function $f : R^n \to R$ is continuous. Define the global optimizer is f^*. The set of global optimizers is denoted by X^*, that is:

$$f^* = \frac{\min}{x \in S} f(x), \quad X^* = \{x \in S \mid f(x) = f^*\} \tag{6}$$

$F : I^n \to I$ is called interval function, if $f(X_1, X_2, \ldots X_n) \subseteq F(X_1, X_2, \ldots X_n)$, F is called the expansion of f .Nature interval expansion $F(X_1, X_2, \ldots X_n)$ replace the x which is in $f(x)$ by $(X_1, X_2, \ldots X_n)$.

3 Parallel Interval Algorithm Based On Evolution Computation

This paper proposes a parallel interval algorithm that integrates interval arithmetic and evolutionary Computation method. It can not only ensure interval splitting direction, but also can ensure the reliability. Similartaxis operation is used to select better direction of split so as to quickly achieve local minimum value. In this process, using branch and bound technology to delete or reduce intervals that does not contain the global minimum, make the dissimilation operation more efficient in smaller space.

The algorithm has the following characteristics:

(1) Did not use convex, Hessian matrix or derivative information.

(2) Use evolution algorithm to guide the split direction and use interval algorithm to reduce search space, accelerate speed of deleting invalid interval.

The main features of interval algorithm based on MEC are as follows:

Branch and Bound: This paper use nature expansion of interval function and divide search interval into several sub-intervals in each iterative step.

Interval selection rules: Use the dissimilation operation of MEC to have a current optimization and divide the interval which contains this optimum value. Meanwhile, the box which have the smallest lower bound should also been divided, this will help the dissimilation operation to jump out of local optimum value and make the similartaxis operation quickly get the global optimum value.

Delete rules: the delete rules in this paper use mid-test rule, if the objective function is differentiable, it can also combine to monotonic test to delete interval which is invalid.

Terminate rule: when the width of search interval $w(X) \le \varepsilon$, the algorithm is terminated.

4 Implementation of PIEA

The PIEA proposed in this paper is based on the mind evolution computation model [7, 8], and therefore has a good nature parallel characteristic and scalability. It can combine to the High-Speed parallel computer to improve efficiency, and the reasons mainly concentrated in the following 3 points: (1) The data is relatively independent and do not need data association. (2) There is little communication among all process and have no I/O communication. (3) It always been a state of cycling.

PIEA uses Master-Slave mode, filters and outputs the final results through block partition strategy and distributes the task to a number of nodes. In this way, it will effectively reduce the memory load, improve the convergence speed.

The framework of parallel algorithm is as followings:

In PIEA, the main process and each slave process do their similartaxis and dissimilation operation independently and they do not need any communications except for main process sending search space and parameter need a broadcast operation and retrieve the result from slave processes need a group-gather operation. In this way, it can save communication time and the algorithm will perform better.

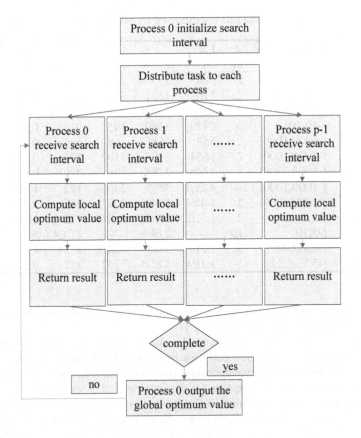

Fig. 1. PIEA framework

5 Numerical Experiment and Results

In order to test the search efficiency of PIEA and under what condition the algorithm will perform well, 13 functions have been tested. These functions all have strong deceptive or high dimensions. The machines that have been used in tests are the ZiQiang 3000 cluster environment of Shanghai University. Experiment 1 analysis the perform efficiency of PIEA. Among them, IA represents traditional interval algorithm, PIEA represents the name of parallel interval exclusion algorithm, FX represents the count number of expand function assessment, GX represents the count number of gradient expand function assessment, CPU represents the problem solving time, RandNumber represents the randomly scattered points number in interval, NodeNumber represents the number of nodes in parallel algorithm.

The numbers of assessment and calculation time in PIEA are all the average number of 10 times after test. The assessment of objection function and gradient expand function are directly impact on the problem solving time. In general, the more the number of assess, the more the time consume. It is generally believed that the time cost in FX and GX assessment is one times more than point assessment.

Table 1. The comparative data between PIEA and IA with the scatter number equals two

Function	Search inter-val(S)	dim	FX IA	PIEA	GX IA	PIEA	CPU(s) IA	PIEA
Deceptive	[-1000,1000]	2	304	295	202	184	0.005	0.005
Hump6	[-1000,1000]	2	1108	1521	738	210	0.024	0.019
Branin	[-1000,1000]	2	4.8E4	3.8E4	3.0E4	1.5E4	1.387	0.211
Beale	[-10,10]	2	2929	3399	1952	912	0.489	0.049
Booth	[-1000,1000]	2	553	1655	368	596	0.005	0.019
Hump3	[-1000,1000]	2	1654	1995	1102	376	0.024	0.019
Levy1	[-1000,1000]	1	1348	2185	898	320	0.019	0.024
Levy2	[-1000,1000]	1	4.2E4	3595	2.8E4	192	1.162	0.617
Sphere	[-1000,1000]	5	1.4E4	1.4E4	9022	912	0.149	0.058
Goldstein	[-2,2]	2	1.3E5	2.0E4	9.1E4	412	18.23	0.278
Rosenbrock	[-5,10]	10	------	2.6E6	------	1.3E4	>1h	30.97
Griewank 5	[-600,600]	5	1.2E6	3.E5	6.2E5	1724	113.9	4.924
Rastrigin	[-5.12,5.12]	5	1.1E4	1.8E4	7742	852	0.379	0.36

The comparison of function assessments and interval expand function assessments between PIEA and IA are shown in table 1.

As can be seen from the table 1 that only when test functions for Booth and Levy1 the traditional interval algorithm performs better than PIEA. When test functions for Deceptive and Rastrigin the two algorithms perform similar. In rest functions, PIEA is superior to IA, especially for function Goldstein, Griewank 5 and Branin.

In experiment 2, select the function Goldstein, Griewank and Rosenbrock to analysis the performance of PIEA, the results are shown in table 2. N represents the number of nodes, TT represents total time, CT represents communication time, and SU represents the Speed-Up.

Table 2. Parallel PIEA performance

N	Goldstein TT	CT	SU	Griewank5 TT	CT	SU	Rosenbrock TT	CT	SU
1	0.279	0	1	4.954	0	1	31.17	0	1
2	0.266	0.101	1.049	3.059	0.275	1.619	16.83	0.503	1.852
3	0.237	0.145	1.177	2.788	0.312	1.777	12.16	0.732	2.563
4	0.649	0.562	0.43	2.409	0.399	2.056	9.93	0.956	3.319
5	1.097	1.012	0.254	2.273	0.645	2.179	8.054	1.211	3.87
6	1.265	1.181	0.221	5.721	3.682	0.866	7.138	1.523	4.367

Table 2 shows that with the node number increase Speed-Up time first increase and then reduce, this phenomenon depend on the communication time proportion. When the node number is small, communication time can be neglected to the total time. However, it will largely influence the total time when the node number is big enough, because they need more communication.

Thus, following Features of PIEA can be seen from tables above:

(1) The scatter number in each box greatly affects the performance of the algorithm.
(2) PIEA generally performs better than traditional Interval algorithm, especially when the problem is much more complex or precise.
(3) The parallel Speed-Up is largely determined by the communication time proportion in total time.
(4) PIEA can quickly Convergence to global optimization without losing reliability.

6 Conclusions

A parallel Interval Exclusion Algorithm (PIEA) proposed in this paper is more efficiency than the traditional interval algorithm. Thus, use PIEA can significantly reduce the space and time complexity, even in the Non-Use of derivative instruments to accelerate the convergence speed. In general, PIEA belongs to interval optimization framework, so it can definitely meet the precision requirements to achieve the optimal solution.

References

1. Casado, L.G., Martinez, J.A., Garcia, I.: Experiment with a new selection criterion in a fast interval optimization algorithm. Journal of Global Optimization 19, 247–264 (2001)
2. Csendes, T., Laszlopal, J.O., Sendin, H.: The Global optimization method revisited. Optim. Lett. 2, 445–454 (2008)
3. Flouds, C.A., Gounaris, C.E.: A review of recent advances in global optimization. J. Glob. Opim. (2008), doi:10.1007/s
4. Hsirch, M.J., Meneses, C.N., Pardalos: Global Optimization by continuous GRASP. Optim. Lett. 1, 201–212 (2007)
5. Casado, L.G., Garcia, I., Csendes, T.: A new Multi-section technique in interval methods for global optimization. Computing 65, 263–269 (2000)
6. Sotiropoulos, D.G., Stavropoulos, E.C.: A new hybrid genetic algorithm for global optimization. Nonlinear Analysis, Theory, Methods and Applications 30, 4529–4538 (1997)
7. Chengyi, S., Yan, S.: Mind-Evolution-Based Machine Learning: Framework and the Implementation of Optimization. In: Kopacek, P. (ed.) Proc of IEEE Int. Conf on intelligent Engineering systems, September 17-19. IEEE Inc., Vienna (1998)
8. Chengyi, S., Jianqing, Z., Junli, W.: The analysis of efficiency of similartaxis searching. In: Joint 9th IFAS World Congress and 20th NAFIPS International Conference, pp. 35–48 (2001)

Parallel Numerical Solution of the Time-Harmonic Maxwell Equations

Dan Li

Computer Science
University of British Columbia
Vancouver, BC V6T 1Z4, Canada
danli@cs.ubc.ca

Abstract. We develop a parallel implementation of a scalable numerical solution to linear systems arising from finite element discretization of the mixed formulation of the time-harmonic Maxwell equations. We apply this method to complicated domains. Our approach is based on a recently proposed diagonal preconditioner, an algebraic multigrid method and a new auxiliary space preconditioning technique. Numerical experiments demonstrate the scalability of our implementation.

Keywords: time-harmonic Maxwell equations, finite element methods, saddle point linear systems, preconditioners, parallel solvers.

1 Introduction

We are interested in solving linear systems arising from finite element discretization of the mixed formulation of the time-harmonic Maxwell equations. The following model problem is considered: find the vector field u and the multiplier p such that

$$
\begin{aligned}
\nabla \times \nabla \times u - k^2 u + \nabla p &= f \quad \text{in } \Omega, \\
\nabla \cdot u &= 0 \quad \text{in } \Omega.
\end{aligned}
\tag{1}
$$

Here $\Omega \subset \mathbb{R}^3$ is a simply connected polyhedron domain with a connected boundary $\partial\Omega$. The datum f is a given generic source, and k is the wave number and $k^2 \ll 1$. On $\partial\Omega$, Dirichlet boundary conditions are applied, such that $u \times n = 0$ and $p = 0$, where n denotes the outward unit normal on $\partial\Omega$.

Finite element discretization using Nédélec elements of the first kind for the approximation of the vector field and standard nodal elements for the multiplier yields a saddle point linear system of the form

$$
\mathcal{K}x \equiv \begin{pmatrix} A - k^2 M & B^T \\ B & 0 \end{pmatrix} \begin{pmatrix} u \\ p \end{pmatrix} = \begin{pmatrix} g \\ 0 \end{pmatrix} \equiv b,
\tag{2}
$$

where now $u \in \mathbb{R}^n$ and $p \in \mathbb{R}^m$ are finite arrays representing the finite element approximations, and $g \in \mathbb{R}^n$ is the load vector associated with f. Denote the

W. Zhang et al. (Eds.): HPCA 2009, LNCS 5938, pp. 224–229, 2010.

finite element spaces for the approximations of the vector field and the multiplier as V_h and Q_h. The matrix $A \in \mathbb{R}^{n \times n}$ is symmetric positive semidefinite with nullity m, and corresponds to the discrete curl-curl operator on V_h; $B \in \mathbb{R}^{m \times n}$ is a discrete divergence operator with full row rank, and $M \in \mathbb{R}^{n \times n}$ is the scalar mass matrix on V_h.

A large variety of approaches to solving saddle point systems can be found in literature. Benzi, Golub, and Liesen [2] provide a comprehensive survey of numerical solution techniques used to solve general saddle-point systems. We are interested in solving (2) iteratively using Krylov subspace methods. Many difficulties in solving (2) arise from the large kernel of the discrete curl-curl operator A. Usually the matrix A can be regularized, to make it easier to invert. Greif and Schötzau [4] have investigated the augmentation of A with the scalar Laplacian and have derived preconditioners for the iterative solution. The Greif and Schötzau (GS) preconditioning approach was demonstrated to have mesh size independent salability, but it requires efficient solvers for Poisson problems and for $H(\mathrm{curl})$ problems, which we implement in this paper.

In this paper, simple domains are discretized with our parallel mesh generator and we provide an interface for general mesh generators for complicated domains. We develop an efficient parallel implementation of the GS preconditioner. We investigate the performance of the outer solver as well as the inner iterations associated with inversion of the preconditioner. We solve the associated Poisson and $H(\mathrm{curl})$ problems with the Conjugate Gradient (CG) method taking Algebraic Multigrid (AMG) and auxiliary space preconditioners, respectively. Our numerical results indicate that both the inner and outer solvers scales well with the mesh size, both on uniform and unstructured meshes.

2   Scalable Iterative Solvers

Efficient iterative solutions to (2) depend on efficient preconditioning techniques. We use MINRES with the block diagonal GS preconditioner as the outer solver. The GS preconditioner is defined as

$$\mathcal{P}_{M,L} = \begin{pmatrix} A + \gamma M & 0 \\ 0 & L \end{pmatrix}, \tag{3}$$

where $\gamma = 1 - k^2$, L is the scalar Laplace matrix on Q_h. The preconditioned matrix $\mathcal{P}_{M,L}^{-1}\mathcal{K}$ has strongly clustered eigenvalues with mesh size independent spectral bounds. The overall computational cost of the solution procedure depends on the ability to efficiently solve linear systems whose associated matrices are $A + \gamma M$ and L.

Linear systems associated with L are standard Poisson problems, for which many efficient solution methods exist. We chose to use CG iteration with the BoomerAMG preconditioner [6]. Solving $A + \gamma M$ efficiently is a key component in the inner iterations. The curl-curl operator has a high nullity, which makes it significantly more difficult to handle than general elliptic bilinear forms. Hiptmair and Xu (HX) proposed effective auxiliary space preconditioners for linear systems arising from conforming finite element discretizations of H(curl)-elliptic variational problems recently [7], based on fictitious or auxiliary spaces as developed in [5,10]. We use the following preconditioner discussed in [7] to solve linear systems associated with $A + \gamma M$:

$$\mathcal{P}_V^{-1} = \operatorname{diag}(A + \gamma M)^{-1} + P(\bar{L} + \gamma \bar{Q})^{-1} P^T + \gamma^{-1} C(L^{-1}) C^T, \qquad (4)$$

where $\bar{L}$ is the vector Laplace matrix on Q_h^3, $\bar{Q}$ is the vector mass matrix on Q_h^3, C maps gradients on Q_h to V_h and the matrix P is the matrix form of the nodal interpolation operator Π_h^{curl}, such that $\Pi_h^{\text{curl}} : Q_h^3 \to V_h$. For $0 < \gamma \le 1$ the spectral condition number $\kappa_2(\mathcal{P}_V^{-1}(A + \gamma M))$ only depends on the domain where the problem is defined and the shape-regularity of the mesh, but is independent of the mesh size [7].

Our parallel implementation is based on the above the GS, HX and AMG preconditioners. Note that we do not form L^{-1} and $(L + \gamma Q)^{-1}$ explicitly, since matrix inversion is expensive and the inverted matrices will be dense. We consider two approaches to approximate the inversion. In the first approach, one AMG V-cycle is used. The second approach is less accurate, but requires little computational effort: the inversion is approximated by reciprocals of diagonal entries. We will compare the results for these two different methods in Section 4.

3   Parallel Implementation

We are interested in solving the Maxwell equations based on the lowest order discretization with the first kind Nédélec elements of the lowest order and linear nodal elements. Our code employs PETSc [1] and Hypre [3] libraries. Some of the meshes are generated with TetGen [9]. The meshes are partitioned with METIS [8]. MPI is used for message passing.

Our meshes are composed of tetrahedra. The degrees of freedom in this discretization are associated with vertices and edges of the tetrahedra. Elements are partitioned as non-overlapping subdomains. Each processor owns the elements uniquely. Any degrees of freedom on the border between subdomains are owned by the processor of lowest global index. Once a partition is obtained, we reorder elements, vertices and edges such that the numbering is contiguous on the processor that owns them. This approach for assigning degrees of freedom to processors also fits well with the sparse matrix partitioning scheme employed in PETSc. This numbering is hard to implement in parallel. Currently, the reordering is done sequentially, starting with the processor with the lowest rank in the communicator. After the reordering, the assembly of matrices and vectors is done in parallel on the processor that holds them.

4   Numerical Experiments

This section is devoted to assessing the numerical performance and parallel scalability of our implementation on different test cases. The outer solver is MINRES with the GS preconditioner. There are two Krylov subspace solvers associated with inversion of the block diagonal preconditioner. The (1,1) block of

$\mathcal{P}_{M,L}$ is solved with CG method with the HX preconditioner. The (2,2) block is solved with CG iteration with the BoomerAMG preconditioner. In all experiments, the convergence tolerance is set to 10^{-5} for the outer iterations and 10^{-6} for the inner iterations. The wave number k is set to 0, unless specified explicitly. The code was executed on a cluster with 2.6GHz Intel processors.

We first consider a simple problem in a cubic domain, which is discretized with a structured tetrahedral mesh. We keep the problem size per processor approximately the same in our scaling tests, while increasing the number of processors. The initial mesh is shown in Figure 1. The scalability results are shown in Table 1. Table 1 also shows execution times for solving the Laplace operator with linear nodal finite elements on the same tetrahedral meshes, taking CG with the BoomerAMG preconditioner. The following notations are used to record the results: np denotes the number of processors in the run, Nel is the total number of elements, its is the number of outer MINRES iterations, its_{i_1} is the number of inner CG iterations for solving $A + \gamma M$, its_{i_2} is the number of CG iterations for solving L, while t_s and t_a denote the average times needed for solve and assemble phases in seconds respectively.

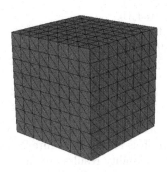
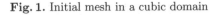
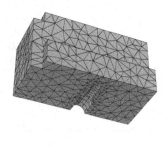

Fig. 1. Initial mesh in a cubic domain

Fig. 2. Initial mesh in a non-convex domain

Table 1 shows that the outer and inner iterations remain fixed when the mesh is refined. The time spent in assembling the linear system also scales well, but the time spend in numerically solving the system grows. This is because Boomer-AMG takes more time per iteration when np increases. As shown in Table 1, the Laplace operator is solved within roughly the same number of iterations while the mesh is refined, but the time spent in each iteration increases. Our implementation relies on efficient AMG methods. If the computation time of the AMG method is improved, the computation time for our method will be improved accordingly. Taking reciprocals of diagonal entries instead of performing V-cycles, the numerical results are show in Table 2. Even though the iteration counts are no longer independent of the mesh size, the solve time is reduced greatly. This is because the diagonal approximation is a much cheaper operation.

Table 1. Numerical results for the problem in a cube

np	Nel	its	its_{i_1}	its_{i_2}	t_s	t_a	Laplace its	t_s
1	3,072	5	26	3	0.34s	1.20s	3	0.01s
2	6,000	5	26	4	0.68s	1.24s	4	0.02s
4	13,182	5	26	3	1.27s	1.44s	4	0.03s
8	24,576	4	25	4	1.05s	4.44s	4	0.05s
16	48,000	4	25	3	8.90s	5.09s	5	0.35s
32	93,750	4	25	4	22.29s	5.68s	5	0.91s
64	196,608	4	24	4	48.13s	5.95s	4	1.72s

Table 2. Numerical results for the problem in a cube. Iterations and solve time spend, taking reciprocals of diagonal entries as matrix inversion.

np	Nel	its	its_{i_1}	its_{i_2}	t_s	t_a
1	3,072	5	43	3	0.18s	1.20s
2	6,000	5	51	4	0.26s	1.24s
4	13,182	5	67	3	0.37s	1.44s
8	24,576	4	77	4	0.39s	4.44s
16	48,000	4	99	3	1.19s	5.09s
32	93,750	4	123	4	3.01s	5.68s
64	196,608	4	158	4	5.51s	5.95s

The second problem considered is in a non-convex domain, discretized with an unstructured tetrahedral mesh. The initial mesh is shown in Figure 2. This model came from TetGen example files [9]. The scalability results are shown in Table 3, for $k = 0$ and $k = 0.125$. In both cases, the iteration counts (both inner and outer) are mesh size independent, which demonstrates the scalability of our method.

Table 3. Numerical results for the problem in a non-convex domain

np	Nel	$k = 0$					$k = 0.125$				
		its	its_{i_1}	its_{i_2}	t_s	t_a	its	its_{i_1}	its_{i_2}	t_s	t_a
4	3,633	20	28	4	1.02s	0.18s	24	28	4	1.13s	0.19s
8	7,763	21	29	4	1.96s	0.19s	19	29	4	1.82s	0.19s
16	14,511	21	27	5	18.77s	0.19s	23	30	5	22.08s	0.16s
32	35,523	20	31	5	79.49s	0.32s	21	31	5	80.01s	0.30s

5   Conclusion

We have developed a parallel implementation of fully scalable numerical solutions to linear systems arising from finite element discretizations in mixed formulation of the time-harmonic Maxwell equations. Our implementation is based on the GS block diagonal preconditioner. Taking the GS preconditioner, MINRES converges within a small number of iterations, independent of the mesh size, as demonstrated in our numerical experiments. The GS preconditioner is inverted as two decoupled problems: one with HX-CG, and the other with AMG-CG. The inner Krylov subspace iterations are not sensitive to the mesh size. The assembly time also demonstrates very good scalability with the number of processors. The performance of our implementation depends on AMG solvers. Improvement of AMG methods will improve the efficiency of our approach.

Acknowledgment

The author would like to thank Dr C. Greif and Dr D. Schötzau, University of British Columbia, for their help and support. This work was the outcome of fruitful discussions with them.

References

1. Balay, S., Buschelman, K., Eijkhout, V., Gropp, W.D., Kaushik, D., Knepley, M.G., McInnes, L.C., Smith, B.F., Zhang, H.: PETSc users manual. Technical Report ANL-95/11 - Revision 3.0.0, Argonne National Laboratory (2008)
2. Benzi, M., Golub, G.H., Liesen, J.: Numerical solution of saddle point problems. Acta Numerica 14, 1–137 (2005)
3. Falgout, R., Cleary, A., Jones, J., Chow, E., Henson, V., Baldwin, C., Brown, P., Vassilevski, P., Yang, U.M.: Hypre webpage (2009), http://acts.nersc.gov/hypre/
4. Greif, C., Schötzau, D.: Preconditioners for the discretized time-harmonic Maxwell equations in mixed form. Numerical Linear Algebra with Applications 14(4), 281–297 (2007)
5. Griebel, M., Oswald, P.: On the abstract theory of additive and multiplicative schwarz algorithms. Numerische Mathematik 70(2), 163–180 (1995)
6. Henson, V.E., Yang, U.M.: BoomerAMG: a parallel algebraic multigrid solver and preconditioner. Applied Numerical Mathematics 41, 155–177 (2000)
7. Hiptmair, R., Xu, J.: Nodal auxiliary space preconditioning in H(curl) and H(div) spaces. SIAM Journal on Numerical Analysis 45(6), 2483–2509 (2007)
8. Karypis, G.: METIS webpage (2009), http://glaros.dtc.umn.edu/gkhome/views/metis/
9. Si, H.: TetGen webpage (2009), http://tetgen.berlios.de/
10. Xu, J.: The auxiliary space method and optimal multigrid preconditioning techniques for unstructured grids. Computing 56(3), 215–235 (1996)

The Semi-convergence of Generalized SSOR Method for Singular Augmented Systems

Jianlei Li and Tingzhu Huang

School of Applied Mathematics,
University of Electronic Science and Technology of China,
Chengdu, Sichuan, 611731, P.R. China
hnmaths@163.com, tzhuang@uestc.edu.cn

Abstract. Recently, Zhang and Lu proposed the generalized symmetric SOR (GSSOR) method for solving the nonsingular augmented systems and studied the convergence of the GSSOR method. In this paper, we prove the semi-convergence of the GSSOR method when it is applied to solve the singular augmented systems, which is the generalization of the GSSOR iteration method.

Keywords: semi-convergence, singular augmented systems, generalized symmetric SOR method, iterative method.

1 Introduction

We consider the following augmented systems of the form:

$$\begin{pmatrix} A & B \\ B^T & 0 \end{pmatrix} \begin{pmatrix} x \\ y \end{pmatrix} = \begin{pmatrix} f \\ g \end{pmatrix}, \tag{1}$$

where $A \in \mathbb{R}^{m \times m}$ is a symmetric positive definite matrix, $B \in \mathbb{R}^{m \times n}$ is a matrix of rank r with $n \leq m$, i.e., rank $B = r$, $0 < r \leq n$. $f \in \mathbb{R}^m$ and $g \in \mathbb{R}^n$ are two given vectors. Denote B^T as the transpose of the matrix B. When $r = n$, note that the coecient matrix is nonsingular and the linear systems (1) have a unique solution. When $r < n$, the coefficient matrix is singular, in such case, we assume that the linear systems (1) are consistent. Such systems are also referred to as saddle point problems or Karush-Kuhn-Tucker (KKT) systems. The augmented systems (1) are important and arise in a large number of scientific and engineering applications, such as the field of computational fluid dynamics [2], constrained and weighted least squares problems [3], interior point methods in constrained optimization [4], mixed finite element approximations of elliptic partial differential equations (PDEs) [5]. Especially, see [1] for a comprehensive survey.

For the nonsingular augmented systems (1), many efficient iterative methods based on matrix splitting as well as their numerical properties have been studied in the literature. The preconditioned iterative methods [8,9], the inexact Uzawa methods [6,10], the SOR-like method [7], the general SOR (GSOR) method [13],

W. Zhang et al. (Eds.): HPCA 2009, LNCS 5938, pp. 230–235, 2010.

the symmetric SOR (SSOR) method [15,16] and the modified SSOR (MSSOR) method [17] for solving the nonsingular augmented systems (1) were proposed and analyzed, respectively. Furthermore, the general symmetric SOR (GSSOR) method [18] was presented. In most cases, the matrix B is full column rank in scientific computing and engineering applications, but not always. If $r < n$, the augmented systems become the singular linear systems. When the linear systems are consistent, Zheng, Bai and Yang [12] show that the GSSOR method proposed in [13] can be used to solve the singular augmented systems (1), and it is semi-convergent.

In this paper, the GSSOR method for solving singular linear augmented systems (1) is further investigated and the semi-convergence conditions are proposed, which generalize the result of Zhang and Lu [18] for the nonsingular augmented systems to the singular augmented systems.

2   Main Result

Before the semi-convergence of the GSSOR method is discussed, we first review the GSSOR method presented in [18].

The augmented systems (1) can be written as the following equivalent form

$$\begin{pmatrix} A & B \\ -B^T & 0 \end{pmatrix} \begin{pmatrix} x \\ y \end{pmatrix} = \begin{pmatrix} f \\ -g \end{pmatrix}. \tag{2}$$

Considering the following matrix splitting:

$$\mathcal{A} = \begin{pmatrix} A & B \\ -B^T & 0 \end{pmatrix} = D - \mathcal{A}_L - \mathcal{A}_U, \tag{3}$$

where

$$D = \begin{pmatrix} A & 0 \\ 0 & Q \end{pmatrix}, \ \mathcal{A}_L = \begin{pmatrix} 0 & 0 \\ B^T & 0 \end{pmatrix}, \ \mathcal{A}_U = \begin{pmatrix} 0 & -B \\ 0 & Q \end{pmatrix},$$

and $Q \in \mathbb{R}^{n \times n}$ is a nonsingular symmetric matrix. Denote I as an identity matrix with appropriate dimension. Let

$$L = D^{-1}\mathcal{A}_L, \ U = D^{-1}\mathcal{A}_U, \ \Omega = \begin{pmatrix} \omega I_m & 0 \\ 0 & \tau I_n \end{pmatrix},$$

where ω and τ are two nonzero real numbers. The GSSOR method is defined as follows:

$$\begin{pmatrix} x_{(i+1)} \\ y_{(i+1)} \end{pmatrix} = \mathcal{H}(\omega, \tau) \begin{pmatrix} x_i \\ y_i \end{pmatrix} + \mathcal{M}(\omega, \tau) \begin{pmatrix} f \\ -g \end{pmatrix}, \tag{4}$$

where

$$\mathcal{H}(\omega, \tau) = \mathcal{U}(\omega, \tau)\mathcal{L}(\omega, \tau) = \begin{pmatrix} \mathcal{H}_{11} & \mathcal{H}_{12} \\ \mathcal{H}_{21} & \mathcal{H}_{22} \end{pmatrix}$$

$$= \begin{pmatrix} (1-\omega)^2 I - \frac{\omega\tau(2-\tau)(1-\omega)}{1-\tau}[A^{-1} & [-\omega(2-\omega)I + \frac{\omega^2\tau(2-\tau)}{1-\tau} \\ \times BQ^{-1}B^T] & \times A^{-1}BQ^{-1}B^T]A^{-1}B \\ \frac{\tau(2-\tau)(1-\omega)}{1-\tau}Q^{-1}B^T & I - \frac{\omega\tau(2-\tau)}{1-\tau}Q^{-1}B^T A^{-1}B \end{pmatrix}, \tag{5}$$

and

$$\mathcal{M}(\omega,\tau) = (I - \Omega U)^{-1}(2I - \Omega)(I - \Omega L)^{-1}D^{-1}\Omega,$$

$$\mathcal{U}(\omega,\tau) = (I - \Omega U)^{-1}[(I - \Omega) + \Omega L],$$

$$\mathcal{L}(\omega,\tau) = (I - \Omega L)^{-1}[(I - \Omega) + \Omega U].$$

Thus, the GSSOR method takes the following iterative scheme ($\tau \neq 1, k = 0, 1, 2, \ldots$):

$$\begin{cases} y_{i+1} = y_i + \frac{\tau(2-\tau)}{(1-\tau)}Q^{-1}B^T[(1-\omega)x_i - \omega A^{-1}By_i + \omega A^{-1}f] - \frac{\tau(2-\tau)}{(1-\tau)}Q^{-1}, \\ x_{i+1} = (1-\omega)^2 x_i - \omega A^{-1}B[y_{i+1} + (1-\omega)y_i] + \omega(2-\omega)A^{-1}f. \end{cases}$$

Here Q is an approximate matrix of the Schur complement matrix $B^T A^{-1}B$.

Next, some basic concepts and lemmas are given for latter use.

For a matrix $A \in \mathbb{R}^{m \times m}$, the splitting $A = M - N$ is a nonsingular splitting if M is nonsingular. Denote $\rho(A)$ as the spectral radius of a square matrix A. Let $T = M^{-1}N$, $c = M^{-1}b$, then solving linear systems $Ax = b$ is equivalent to considering the following iterative scheme

$$x_{k+1} = Tx_k + c. \tag{6}$$

It is well known that for nonsingular (singular) systems the iterative method (6) is convergent (semi-convergent) if and only if T is a convergent (semi-convergent) matrix. On the semi-convergence of the iterative method for solving general singular linear systems $Ax = b$, one can see [11,14,19,20,21]. When A is singular, the following two lemmas give the semi-convergence property about the iteration method (6).

Lemma 1. *[12,14] Let $A = M - N$ with M nonsingular, $T = M^{-1}N$, $c = M^{-1}b$. Then for any initial vector x_0, the iterative scheme (6) is semi-convergent to a solution x of linear equations $Ax = b$ if and only if the matrix T is semi-convergent.*

Lemma 2. *[11,12] Let $H \in \mathbb{R}^{l \times l}$ with positive integers l. Then the partitioned matrix*

$$T = \begin{pmatrix} H & 0 \\ \tilde{L} & I \end{pmatrix}$$

is semi-convergent if and only if either of the following conditions holds true:

(1) $\tilde{L} = 0$ and H is semi-convergent;
(2) $\rho(H) < 1$.

When the augmented systems (1) are nonsingular, the convergence of GSSOR method is studied in [18]. When $r < n$, the matrix $\mathcal{A}$ is singular. The following theorem describes the semi-convergence property when the GSSOR method is applied to solve the singular augmented systems (1).

Theorem 1. *Assume that $r < n$, Q is a symmetric positive definite matrix, denote the maximum eigenvalue of $Q^{-1}B^T A^{-1}B$ by μ_{max}, then the GSSOR method (4) is semi-convergent to a solution x of the singular augmented systems (1) if ω satisfies $0 < \omega < 2$ and τ satisfies the following condition:*

$$0 < \tau < min\{\tau_1, 1\} \quad or \quad 2 < \tau < \tau_1 + 2, \tag{7}$$

where $\tau_1 = \frac{2+2(\omega-1)^2}{\omega(2-\omega)\mu_{max}}$.

Proof. By Lemma 1, we only need to describe the semi-convergence of the iteration matrix $\mathcal{H}(\omega, \tau)$ defined by equation (5) of the GSSOR method.

Let $B = U(B_r, 0)V^*$ be the singular value decomposition of B, where $B_r = (\Sigma_r, 0)^T \in \mathbb{R}^{m \times r}$ with $\Sigma_r = \text{diag}(\sigma_1, \sigma_2, ..., \sigma_r)$, U, V are unitary matrices. Then

$$P = \begin{pmatrix} U & 0 \\ 0 & V \end{pmatrix}$$

is an $(m+n)$-by-$(m+n)$ unitary matrix. Define $\widehat{\mathcal{H}}(\omega, \tau) = P^*\mathcal{H}(\omega, \tau)P$, here P^* denote the conjugate transpose of P, then the matrix $\mathcal{H}(\omega, \tau)$ has the same eigenvalues with matrix $\widehat{\mathcal{H}}(\omega, \tau)$. Hence, we only need to demonstrate the semi-convergence of the matrix $\widehat{\mathcal{H}}(\omega, \tau)$.

Define matrices

$$\widehat{A} = U^*AU, \ \widehat{B} = U^*BV \ and \ \widehat{Q} = V^*QV.$$

Then it holds that $\widehat{B} = (B_r, \ 0)$ and

$$\widehat{Q}^{-1} = \begin{pmatrix} V_1^*Q^{-1}V_1 & V_1^*Q^{-1}V_2 \\ V_2^*Q^{-1}V_1 & V_2^*Q^{-1}V_2 \end{pmatrix}$$

with appropriate partitioned matrix $V = (V_1, \ V_2)$. Denote $Q_1 = (V_1^*Q^{-1}V_1)^{-1}$ and $Q_2 = (V_2^*Q^{-1}V_1)^{-1}$. By simple computation, we have

$$\widehat{\mathcal{H}}(\omega, \tau) = \begin{pmatrix} U^*\mathcal{H}_{11}U & U^*\mathcal{H}_{12}V \\ V^*\mathcal{H}_{21}U & V^*\mathcal{H}_{22}V \end{pmatrix},$$

$$U^*A^{-1}BQ^{-1}B^T U = (U^*A^{-1}U)(U^*BV)(V^*Q^{-1}V)(V^*B^T U)$$
$$= \widehat{A}^{-1}(B_r, 0)\widehat{Q}^{-1}(B_r, 0)^T$$
$$= \widehat{A}^{-1}B_r Q_1^{-1}B_r^T,$$

$$U^*A^{-1}BV = (U^*A^{-1}U)(U^*BV) = \widehat{A}^{-1}(B_r, 0) = (\widehat{A}^{-1}B_r, 0),$$

$$V^*Q^{-1}B^T U = (V^*Q^{-1}V)(V^*B^T U) = \begin{pmatrix} Q_1^{-1}B_r^T \\ Q_2^{-1}B_r^T \end{pmatrix},$$

and

$$V^*Q^{-1}B^T A^{-1}BV = (V^*Q^{-1}V)(V^*B^T U)(U^*A^{-1}U)(U^*BV)$$
$$= \widehat{Q}^{-1}(B_r,\ 0)^T \widehat{A}^{-1}(B_r,\ 0)$$
$$= \widehat{Q}^{-1}\begin{pmatrix} B_r^T \widehat{A}^{-1}B_r & 0 \\ 0 & 0_{n-r} \end{pmatrix}. \tag{8}$$

Thus

$$\widehat{\mathcal{H}}(\omega,\tau) = \begin{pmatrix} \widehat{\mathcal{H}}_1(\omega,\tau) & 0 \\ \widehat{L}(\omega,\tau) & I_{n-r} \end{pmatrix},$$

where

$$\widehat{\mathcal{H}}_1(\omega,\tau) = \begin{pmatrix} (1-\omega)^2 I_m - \frac{\omega\tau(2-\tau)(1-\omega)}{1-\tau}[\widehat{A}^{-1} & [-\omega(2-\omega)I + \frac{\omega^2\tau(2-\tau)}{1-\tau} \\ \times B_r Q_1^{-1}B_r^T] & \times \widehat{A}^{-1}B_r Q_1^{-1}B_r^T]\widehat{A}^{-1}B_r \\ \frac{\tau(2-\tau)(1-\omega)}{1-\tau}Q_1^{-1}B_r^T & I_r - \frac{\omega\tau(2-\tau)}{1-\tau}Q_1^{-1}B_r^T\widehat{A}^{-1}B_r \end{pmatrix}$$

and

$$\widehat{L}(\omega,\tau) = \begin{pmatrix} \frac{\tau(2-\tau)(1-\omega)}{1-\tau}Q_2^{-1}B_r^T, & -\frac{\omega\tau(2-\tau)}{1-\tau}Q_2^{-1}B_r^T\widehat{A}^{-1}B_r \end{pmatrix}.$$

As $\widehat{L}(\omega,\tau) \neq 0$, From Lemma 2 we know that the matrix $\widehat{\mathcal{H}}(\omega,\tau)$ is semi-convergent if $\rho(\widehat{\mathcal{H}}_1(\omega,\tau)) < 1$.

When the GSSOR method is applied to solve the following nonsingular saddle point problem

$$\begin{pmatrix} \widehat{A} & B_r \\ B_r^T & 0 \end{pmatrix}\begin{pmatrix} \widehat{x} \\ \widehat{y} \end{pmatrix} = \begin{pmatrix} \widehat{f} \\ \widehat{g} \end{pmatrix}, \tag{9}$$

with the preconditioning matrix Q_1, and vectors $\widehat{y},\ \widehat{g} \in \mathbb{R}^r$, the iterative matrix of the GSSOR method is $\widehat{\mathcal{H}}_1(\omega,\tau)$. By (8), μ_{max} is also the maximum eigenvalue of $Q_1^{-1}B_r^T\widehat{A}^{-1}B_r$. From Theorem 3.2 of [18], we know that $\rho(\widehat{\mathcal{H}}_1(\omega,\tau)) < 1$ if $0 < \omega < 2$ and τ satisfy (7). By the above analysis, the proof of the theorem is completed.   □

3   Conclusion

In this paper, the GSSOR method for solving singular linear augmented systems (1) is further investigated and the semi-convergence conditions are proposed, which generalize the result of Zhang and Lu [18] for the nonsingular augmented systems to the singular augmented systems.

Acknowledgments. This research was supported by the Scientific and Technological Key Project of the Chinese Education Ministry (107098), the Specialized Research Fund for the Doctoral Program of Chinese Universities (20070614001), 973 Programs (2008CB317110), NSFC (10771030), Sichuan Province Project for Applied Basic Research (2008JY0052).

References

1. Benzi, M., Golub, G.H., Liesen, J.: Numerical solution of saddle point problems. Acta. Numerical. 14, 1–137 (2005)
2. Elman, H.C., Silvester, D.J., Wathen, A.J.: Finite Elements and Fast Iterative Solvers. In: Numerical Mathematics and Scientific Computation. Oxford University Press, Oxford (2005)
3. Björck, Å.: Numerical Methods for Least Squares Problems. SIAM, Philadelphia (1996)
4. Bergamaschi, L., Gondzio, J., Zilli, G.: Preconditioning indefinite systems in interior point methods for optimization. Comput. Optim. Appl. 28, 149–171 (2004)
5. Brezzi, F., Fortin, M.: Mixed and Hybrid Finite Element Methods. Springer Series in Computational Mathematics, vol. 15. Springer, New York (1991)
6. Elman, H.C., Golub, G.H.: Inexact and preconditioned Uzawa algorithms for saddle point problems. SIAM J. Numer. Anal. 31, 1645–1661 (1994)
7. Golub, G.H., Wu, X., Yuan, J.-Y.: SOR-like methods for augmented systems. BIT Numer. Math. 41, 71–85 (2001)
8. Rusten, T., Winther, R.: A preconditioned iterative method for saddle point problems. SIAM J. Matrix. Anal. Appl. 13, 887–904 (1992)
9. Bramble, J., Pasciak, J.: A preconditioned technique for indefinite systems resulting from mixed approximations of elliptic problems. Math. Comp. 50, 1–17 (1988)
10. Bramble, J., Pasciak, J., Vassilev, A.: Analysis of the inexact Uzawa algorithm for saddle point problems. SIAM J. Numer. Anal. 34, 1072–1092 (1997)
11. Chen, Y.-L., Tan, X.-Y.: Semiconvergence criteria of iterations and extrapolated iterations and constructive methods of semiconvergent iteration matrices. Appl. Math. Comput. 167, 930–956 (2005)
12. Zheng, B., Bai, Z.-Z., Yang, X.: On semi-convergence of parameterized Uzawa methods for singular saddle point problems. Linear. Algebra. Appl. 431, 808–817 (2009)
13. Bai, Z.-Z., Parlett, B.N., Wang, Z.-Q.: On generalized successive overrelaxation methods for augmented linear systems. Numer. Math. 102, 1–38 (2005)
14. Berman, A., Plemmons, R.J.: Nonnegative Matrices in the Mathematical Sciences. SIAM, Philadelphia (1994)
15. Darvishi, M.T., Hessari, P.: Symmetric SOR method for augmented systems. Appl. Math. Comput. 183, 409–415 (2006)
16. Zheng, B., Wang, K., Wu, Y.-J.: SSOR-like methods for saddle point problems. Inter. J. Comput. Math. 86, 1405–1423 (2009)
17. Wu, S.-L., Huang, T.-Z., Zhao, X.-L.: A modified SSOR iterative method for augmented systems. J. Comput. Appl. Math. 228, 424–433 (2009)
18. Zhang, G.-F., Lu, Q.-H.: On generalized symmetric SOR method for augmented system. J. Comput. Appl. Math. 219, 51–58 (2008)
19. Cao, Z.-H.: Semiconvergence of the extrapolated iterative method for singular linear systems. Appl. Math. Comput. 156, 131–136 (2004)
20. Song, Y.-Z., Wang, L.: On the semiconvergence of extrapolated iterative methods for singular systems. Appl. Numer. Math. 44, 401–413 (2003)
21. Song, Y.-Z.: Semiconvergence of nonnegative splittings for singular systems. Numer. Math. 85, 109–127 (2000)

A Scientific Workflow System Based on GOS

Lei Li, Bin Gong*, and Yan Ma

School of Computer Science and Technology, Shandong University,
Jinan 250101, P.R. China
windfire@mail.sdu.edu.cn, gb@sdu.edu.cn, yanpony@126.com

Abstract. With the advent of grid and application technologies, domain scientists are building more and more complex applications on distributed resources. In order to enable scientists to conduct application scenarios conveniently, scientific workflow is emerging as one of the most important and challenging grid application classes. GOS (Grid Operating System) is a novel grid middleware and can provide various scientific applications for scientists. In this paper, a grid-oriented scientific workflow management system is designed and integrated into GOS. Workflow engine uses light-weight threading techniques and event-driven mechanism to instantiate and dispatch jobs. Some important components will be discussed, and the main implements of the system are also introduced.

1 Introduction

In the past years, grid computing[1] has been developed as a powerful resource to compute, restore and solve scientific problems. Scientific communities are utilizing grids to share, manage, process large data sets. However, developing scientific applications for these large-scale collaborative grid infrastructures is a difficult task. Many e-scientists lack the necessary low-level expertise to utilize the current generation of Grid toolkits.

Workflow in grid environment has received much attention lately. Grid workflow [2] can be defined as the composition of grid applications which execute automatically on heterogeneous and distributed resources in a well-defined order to accomplish a specific goal[3]. With the advances in e-Sciences and the growing complexity of scientific analyze, such as climate modeling, astrophysics, biology and chemistry, researchers require the creation of a collaborative workflow management system as their sophisticated problem solving environment.

In GOS grid environments, various agora organizations provide a great deal of scientific applications. In most cases, researchers complete an experiment always needs lots of sophisticated activities. Moreover, there are dependencies between one activity and others that form a graph called Non-DAG (Directed Acyclic Graph). Scientific workflow management system has emerged to concerns the automation of scientific processes.

The remainder of this paper is structured as follows: The related work is in Sect. 2 that review some existing workflow system. Section 3 gives an overview of

---

* Corresponding author.

W. Zhang et al. (Eds.): HPCA 2009, LNCS 5938, pp. 236–241, 2010.
© Springer-Verlag Berlin Heidelberg 2010

GOS and its main features. Section 4 discusses the architecture of the workflow system and Sect. 5 implements a biologic sequence experiment to test the system. At last, the conclusion and future work are in Sect. 6.

2   Related Work

There have been a number of efforts within the Grid community to develop various purpose workflow management systems. We will talk some typical systems that relate to ours.

Condor[4] is a specialized resource management system for compute-intensive jobs. DAGMan works as a meta-scheduler for Condor system. It aims to discover available resources for the execution of jobs. But it lacks dynamic features such as iteration and automatic intermediate data movement.

Kepler[5] and Taverna[6] are open-source workflow systems. They all provide a user-friendly graphical interface. Kepler is unique in that it seamlessly combines high-level workflow design with execution and runtime interaction, access to local and remote data, and local and remote service invocation. Taverna is a workbench for workflow composition and enactment developed as part of the myGrid project, the focus of which is bioinfomatic applications.

Compared with the work listed above, this paper provides a decentralized, just-in time workflow system and integrated it into GOS grid project. In addition, many efforts have been made on the structured workflow language to support sequence, parallelism, choice and loop.

3   GOS System

Grid operating system, GOS for short, is part of China National Grid (CN-Grid) project[7]. It is a new grid middleware that provides transparent access to distributed computing resources. As a test bed for the new generation of information infrastructure by integrating high performance computing and process transaction capacity, it deploys multidisciplinary scientific application.

Now, GOS v3 deploys on CNGrid, includes 10 grid nodes locating in 8 cities. GOS framework is composed by grid portal, grid system software and grid resources. Grid portal faces to end-users and system administrator. Grid system software based on operating system, tomcat, axis, and so on, provide grid/web service to shield the heterogeneous and dynamic environment. Grid resources are local applications which encapsulate as a secure grid service.

GOS provides a single entry sign for users to use and manage resources based on the web portal. The basic functions it supports are: a) User management: user register, authentication & authorization, user mapping. b) Resource management: cluster info, job queue info, application encapsulation. c) Batch job management: job submission, job info, job monitor. d) File system management: upload, download, directory and file manage, etc.

4   System Architecture

A scientific workflow management system should at least implements: a model for describing workflows, an engine for executing/managing workflows, last but not least, different levels for users to compose, control and analyze workflows.

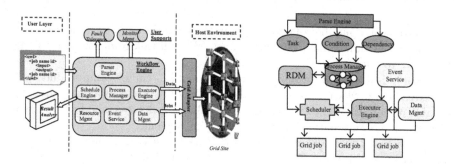

Fig. 1. Architecture of the Workflow System **Fig. 2.** Information Flow of the Engine

With the requirements of workflow system, the three layer architecture for workflow system is proposed and shows it in Fig.1. The user layer offers a workflow language for describing and submitting workflow instances. Some user interface like result analyze, workflow monitor are also contained. Workflow enactment engine is in system layer for executing and managing workflows. The host environments are physical grid resources for computing.

4.1   Structured Workflow Language

Workflow language is the basis of a workflow system. In order to allow users to model their workflows, a structured and xml-based user workflow language (UWL) is defined. Unlike other existing workflow language, UWL is a Non-DAG supported language. The control structures like sequence, parallel, choice and loop are exhibited. The language is comprised of basic job activity, some compound control activities and data link relations. The description of workflow can be abstract or concrete. Users can specify the tasks without referring to specific grid resources when they do not concern where the jobs run. It provides a high level of construction and users need not concern the concrete execution.

The *uwl* is the root of the language element. It represents the start of the workflow. The *job* element describes an activity of a workflow. It includes attributes of id, name, host and so on for the detail info. Users may specify the particular resource with host or leave it to workflow engine. The *input* and *output* elements depict the data type and location between jobs. They may be a file, a directory or a parameter value.

The language also provide compound structures to helps users to build complex control activities like choice and loop. We use if-else and switch elements to describe choice and multi-cases respectively. Meanwhile, the for and while elements describe the loop structure until they reach the setting values. Their attribute condition controls when and how often the job is executed. In order to improve the reusability of the system, subworkflow element is used to extract the existing workflows to construct a new model.

The link element and its attributes specify the data dependencies between the workflow jobs. The attributes from and to identify the source and destination of the datasets. And its value must be the job id or compound control activity id defined before.

4.2   Workflow Enactment

The workflow enactment is build to parse, manage and execute the workflow in the dynamic environment. Figure 2 shows the information flow of the enactment engine. Up to now, the main implements of the workflow enactment engine includes parse engine, resource management, event service, execute engine and data engine. They cooperate mutually for the execution of a user workflow[8].

Parse Engine: The user workflow language is in the logical layer. Parse engine is provided to parse the xml based language into objects that can be invoked and accessed by workflow scheduler. The engine first reads the elements and attributes of user's workflow description, and then stores them into corresponding objects. After this process, the engine can find the order of workflow tasks, the condition statement of control structures, the data flow and other useful information. Parse engine extracts information from xml based language and provides it to the succeeding component for the workflow management.

RDM: In a grid environment, many applications have the same functionality and may be provided by different organizations. From a user's perspective, it is better to use the application that offers a higher performance at a lower cost. Resource discovery & management (RDM) module will find all the applications provided by different grid nodes. When a user's abstract workflow is submitted, the workflow engine can query RDM to find the appropriate applications for every job at run time.

Execute engine: Execute engine, which using light-weight threading techniques and event-driven mechanism to instantiate and dispatch tasks, is an important component for managing the run-time environment of workflow. It controls the execution order of workflows, submits jobs to remote grid nodes, communicates between threads of execution, etc. In GOS, the execution of a job must be in grip mode. Grip is a particular trait of GOS, it provides the user info and sets operate context at run-time.

At runtime, the execution threads need communicate between jobs and their successors. Taking account of this, an event-driven mechanism with subscription-notification model has been developed to control and manage execution activities. We use TSpace as an event-driven tool. When a job's status changes, it will generate an event and send to tuple space. Then the system will take action automatically depending on the event.

Data Engine: In scientific workflows, data movement is the basic process for job execution. Data engine is responsible for transferring the data between user workstation and grid site. Therefore, a mediated transfer approach is used for data management. The intermediate data generated at every step is registered in a data center service. So that input files of every task can be obtained by querying the data center. GOS also provides the file management module and some user APIs for programming.

4.3 Fault Tolerance

Workflow runs in dynamic and unstable grid environments. Task level retry will run a failed job once again. It just reruns the job on the same resource. This may be simple but efficient to improve efficiency and save resource. Alternate resource will find a new resource and submit the failed job on it. When the job reruns and still fail over, the run-time system find and match a new resource, then the job will be submitted on it.

5   Implementation

The Epigenomics workflow shown in Fig.3 is essentially a data processing pipeline to automate the execution of the various genome sequencing operations. The DNA sequence data generated by the Illumina-Solexa Genetic Analyzer system is split into several chunks that can be operated on in parallel. The data in each chunk is converted into a file format that can be used by the Maq system[9].

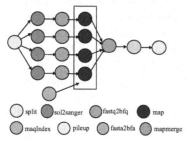

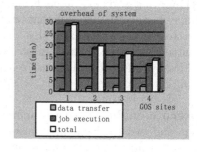

Fig. 3. Epigenomics workflow   **Fig. 4.** The process time over various nodes

The real world application epigenomics mapping and assembly is implemented as the test of feasibility for the system based on the GOS. The latest GOS version 3.1 is deployed for the experiments. In our experiment, we split the sequence data into 8 chunks, and the impact of number of grid sites is shown in Fig.4. The most time-consumed processes are data transfer and job execution. As can be seen from the statistics, data transfer time is increasing with more grid sites because of the input and output data between different jobs. On the other hand, the computation intensive jobs can execute on different GOS sites in parallel, thus will improve the efficiency. The whole speed up rate is about 50 percents. It demonstrates that the performance of the workflow management system can be significantly improved by using GOS grid.

6 Conclusion and Future Work

In this paper, a workflow prototype is proposed to help domain scientists modeling and executing scientific workflows in GOS environment. An XML-based workflow language is proposed to describe the workflow. The event-driven communication mechanism and subscription-notification approach make the workflow execution loosely-coupled and flexible. This work takes advantage of the features provided by GOS to implement a scalable, prompt workflow system. The epigenomics workflow experiment has been applied on it successfully and demonstrates that it can solve many domain problems.

Moreover, the prototype system implemented now is not perfect. The intending work will focus on workflow execution optimization. In addition, there are some defects to be improved in the future. The work should continue to improve the usability, functionality, and scalability of the system.

Acknowledgement

This work is supported by a grant from the National High Technology Research and Development Program of China (863 Program) (No.2006AA01A113).

References

1. Foster, I., Kesselman, C., Tuecke, S.: The Anatomy of the Grid: Enabling Scalable Virtual Organizations. International Journal of Supercomputer Applications 15(3) (2001)
2. Zhao, Y., Raicu, I., Foster, I.: Scientific Workflow Systems for 21st Century, New Bottle or New Wine? IEEE Congress on Services 2008 - Part I (2008)
3. Yu, J., Buyya, R.: A Novel Architecture for Realizing Grid Workflow using Tuple Spaces. In: Proceedings of the 5th IEEE/ACM International Workshop on Grid Computing (2004)
4. Thain, D., Tannenbaum, T., et al.: Condor and the Grid. In: Grid Computing: Making the Global Infrastructure a Reality. John Wiley & Sons, NJ (2003)
5. Ludäscher, B., et al.: Scientific Workflow Management and the Kepler System. Concurrency and Computation: Practice & Experience 18(10), 1039–1065 (2006)
6. Li, P., Brass, A., et al.: Taverna workflows for systems biology. In: International Conference on Systems Biology (2006)
7. China National Grid, http://www.cngrid.org
8. Li, F., Gong, B., et al.: An Adaptive System of Service-Oriented Visualization on the Grid. In: ChinaGrid Annual Conference (August 2008)
9. Bharathi, S., et al.: Characterization of Scientific Workflows. In: Third Workshop on Workflows in Support of Large-Scale Science, 2008, pp. 1–10 (2008)

Performance Optimization of Small File I/O with Adaptive Migration Strategy in Cluster File System*

Xiuqiao Li, Bin Dong, Limin Xiao, and Li Ruan

School of Computer Science and Engineering
BeiHang University 100191 Beijing, P.R. China
{xiuqiaoli,bdong}@cse.buaa.edu.cn, {xiaolm,ruanli}@buaa.edu.cn

Abstract. While cluster file systems exploit data striping scheme to boost large file I/O throughput, small file performance is impaired and neglected. Common metadata-based optimizations introduce obstacles such as metadata server overload and migration latency. In this paper, a novel adaptive migration strategy is incorporated into metadata-based optimization to alleviate these side effects by migrating file dynamically. Guided by proposed adaptive migration threshold model, two types of file migration are applied to reduce metadata server load without degrading current performance of file system obviously. Schemes of latency hiding and migration consistency are also introduced to reduce overhead induced by small file optimization. Our results indicate that proposed optimization can substantially improve file creation and deletion performance, and boost small file I/O throughput by more than 20%. Moreover, side effects on overall performance produced by file migration are slight and can be absorbed by improvements.

1 Motivation

Recently, small file I/O performance of cluster file system has aroused wide concern [1–3] in high performance computing area. Current design of cluster file systems, which mainly caters for large file I/O, distributes files among multiple I/O server nodes in order to exploit access parallelism. However, network overhead is induced as clients are required to connect metadata server first to retrieve data distribution of requested file before transferring file data. Compared with large file I/O, gains saved by accessing small files in parallel cannot cover initial network overhead, making small file I/O poor performance. According to study [4] on access patterns in scientific computing, small requests account for more than 90% of all requests but only contribute to less than 10% of total I/O data. Although referred I/O amount is small, those requests include many accesses on immediate and final result files. Thus, topologies among files in cluster file system restrict I/O performance of computing applications.

---

* This paper is supported by Hi-tech Research and Development Program of China (863 Program, No. 2007AA01A127).

W. Zhang et al. (Eds.): HPCA 2009, LNCS 5938, pp. 242–249, 2010.
© Springer-Verlag Berlin Heidelberg 2010

In single-node file system, metadata-based optimizations [2] are common techniques being used to reduce disk accesses and improve small file I/O performance. This type of optimizations store small file as extended attribute in file's metadata and fetch file data in a single disk access. Cluster file system can also apply similar idea to eliminate small file I/O bottleneck. Compared with situations in single-node file system, however, several obstacles will be introduced when lots of small files are placing on metadata servers (MDSs) and file sizes are increasing.

1) MDS overload

Metadata-based optimizations store small files as metadata attribute on MDSs in order to reduce network operations by piggybacking file data with response for get-ting attribute. When lots of small files are placed on MDSs, this method will definitely increase server load and degrade performance of metadata operations. According to study on file system traces, requests targeting for metadata can account for up to 83 percent of the total number of I/O requests [4]. Thus large scale of small files will make MDS overload and become bottleneck of the whole file system.

2) Migration overhead

Another problem induced by metadata-based optimizations is that small files need to be migrated to IOSs as file size is increasing. Clients are required to wait for the completion of migration to perform other requests. Moreover, files on migration can be concurrently accessed by multiple clients, making migration effects even worse. And to the best of our knowledge, no substantial research is conducted on this problem currently.

In this paper, we improved metadata-based small file I/O optimization by incorporating a novel adaptive migration strategy, which alleviates side-effects induced by common metadata-based optimizations. The main feature of our improvements is that file migration can be performed adaptively and dynamically, considering both characteristic of I/O requests on files and metadata server status, such as disk capacity and I/O load. Thus MDS overload and effects on metadata requests can be reduced. Moreover, migration overhead can be reduced and hidden by proposed optimization schemes, such as latency hiding and migration response.

2   Architecture and Design Objectives

The optimization was designed and implemented on PVFS2 [5], a well-known open source cluster file system. Current design of PVFS2 emphasizes on improving large file I/O while performance related to small file is not good. File metadata in PVFS2 contains three types of attributes: common attributes, file type related attributes and extended attributes. Common attributes refers to listed information similar with unix file, such as create time, file type, and credentials. The second one includes special attributes related to file objects, such as data distribution and datafile handles. In order to increase feasibility of requests and implementation, our method stores file data as this type of attributes on MDS.

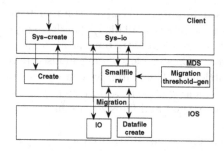 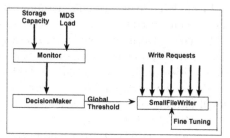

Fig. 1. Architecture of optimization   **Fig. 2.** Architecture of threshold model

The proposed adaptive migration strategy is implemented by two modules in this design. Figure 1 describes the architecture of proposed optimization. First, a migration threshold generation module is added on every metadata server node. This module aims to compute migration threshold dynamically based on collected information about MDS and requested files. Another module is responsible for migration issues, such as migration data between MDSs and I/O servers (IOSs) and migrating files response. File accesses include creation, deletion, read/write and attributes operations, etc. Our optimization mainly targets for small file performance improvements on the first three operations. Otherwise, another optimization objective is to reduce migration effect both on MDSs load and overall performance. The main design objectives of our optimization can be summary as follows:

1) Improve file creation and deletion performance

File creation in original PVFS2 needs to create datafile handles on IOSs, which spend valuable time [6]. As we optimize small file by storing data on MDS, there is no need to create these handles at file creation stage. Thus our optimization bypasses handle creation at file creation stage and defers it to migration stage. We also propose a latency hiding scheme to reduce overhead on datafile creation. Latency on deleting a small file in our method is rather small, since there is no need to remove datafiles on IOSs except redundant handles created during latency hiding.

2) Boost read and write throughout

Our optimization needs only one network round for reading small file, and another round for storing file data into metadata. It is metadata server's responsibility to modify and store small file data.

3) Adjust migration threshold adaptively

It is critical to decide proper migration threshold for small files on MDSs. A dynamic migration threshold model was proposed to guarantee overall performance by dynamically migrating files.

4) Reduce migration overhead

Migration of small files will introduce overhead and effect I/O performance of concurrent accesses. We intends to propose several optimization schemes to reduce overhead of small files migration.

3   Adaptive Migration Strategy

3.1   Dynamic Migration Threshold Model

In order to implement adaptive migration, we need to decide when small files should be migrated. A dynamic migration threshold model is responsible for this work. There are four factors considered to maintain threshold model: (1) Spare capacity on MDS; (2) Load of MDS; (3) Frequency of file migration; (4) Maximum threshold. The out-put threshold of specific file depends on two parameters, namely global threshold and fine tuning parameter. The first two factors contribute to the global threshold and the third one is considered to tune threshold for specific file with the purpose to avoid frequent migration. The fourth factor limits upper threshold of small files storing on MDS that can be considered as large files. Architecture of proposed model is described in figure 2.

The model needs three steps to decide the final migration threshold. First, meta-data server collects information of spare capacity and load of MDS dynamically. This is achieved by running a performance updater state machine on MDS periodically. The spare capacity P_{sg} is calculated by the proportion of available space in total storage capacity. Similarly, the load of MDS P_{ld} can be computed by the proportion of current throughput in predefined theoretical value of maximum throughput of MDS.

Then global threshold can be computed by following formula

$$Th_{global} = \begin{cases} (1-p)Th_{old} & \text{if } P_{sg} \geq Th_{sg} \\ max((1+q)Th_{old}, Th_{max}) & P_{ld} < Th'_{ld}, P_{sg} < Th_{sg}, \\ (1-q)Th_{old} & P_{sg} < Th_{sg} \end{cases} \quad (1)$$

where Th_{global} is the global migration threshold, p and q are adjustment parameters depending on P_{sg} and P_{ld} respectively, $Th_{sg}, Th_{ld}, Th'_{ld}$ are the predefined thresholds of spare capacity and load of MDS, Th_{old} is the final threshold of last cycle and Th_{max} is the given maximum threshold.

Finally, the final migration threshold of specific file is figured out by choosing the larger one between threshold limit and fine-turned threshold. Formula 2 gives this calculation:

$$Th_{final} = max(Ft \bullet Th_{global}, Th_{max}), \quad (2)$$

where Ft is fine tuning factor of specific file, which is stored in non-negative decimal value as a common attribute.

In our model, spare capacity is given the highest priority, as MDS must guarantee available storage for file metadata. The second important factor considered is whether MDS is overload. There are two load parameters specified to make decision on how to adjust migration threshold. One named Th_{ld} defines overload threshold and another one named Th'_{ld} decides whether migration threshold can be increased. Only when current load of MDS exceeds Th'_{ld} , files can be migrated to MDS, avoiding frequent migration. Considering above priorities of factors, rules for selected files to be migrated are listed as follows:

*1)*Lower global threshold by p percent when the spare capacity of MDS reached the predetermined value Th_{sg} and give priority to migrate less frequently accessed files.

2) Lower global threshold by percent q when MDS load reached the predetermined value Th_{ld} and give priority to migrate most frequently accessed files.

3) Increase global threshold by q percent when MDS load is below the predetermined value Th'_{ld} and give priority to migrate most frequently accessed files.

4) Fine tuning thresholds of frequently migrated files.

5) Migrate file whose size exceeds its migration threshold.

3.2   File Migration

Considering network efficiency tradeoff, two types of migrations, namely, active and passive migrations, are implemented in our method. Active migration means that MDS migrates file to IOSs when file size exceeds current threshold. Passive migration is that clients can take the initiative to trigger file migration on MDS when amount of writing data exceeds current threshold. This way could avoid large amount of data being transferred more than one time. Client will transfer request data to IOSs in parallel after received acknowledgement of migration completion from MDS.

3.3   Latency Hiding

Our optimization defers datafile creation to file migration instead of file creation stage. This is because creation of datafile handles spends valuable time [7] and file migration creates extra overhead for clients. In order to reduce above side-effects, a latency hiding scheme is introduced to solve the problems.

1)Latency hiding for datafile creation

A pre-migration threshold parameter is added into threshold model and always smaller than current migration threshold. When small file size exceeds this threshold, datafile creation is performed on IOSs to overlap file writing. By setting this threshold carefully, overhead can be hidden perfectly.

2)Migration latency hiding for clients

In our optimization, clients need to wait for the completion of migration on MDS before completion. As figure 3b shows, file migration in PVFS2 requires an extra network round to get file size of datafiles. However, this step can be omitted as all datafiles are empty when we do file migration. In this way, one more network round can be saved compared with unoptimized write operation.

3.4   Migration Response

Cluster file systems support concurrent accesses from multiple clients. It is possible that files on migration are accessed by other clients. To guarantee consistency of small file, file will be locked by setting flag in metadata attributes, which definitely effects performance of concurrent accesses. In this paper, we propose three response strategies depending on analysis of different request types.

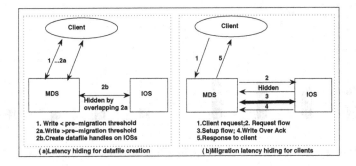

Fig. 3. Latency hiding schemes

1) Revoke file migration when client requests involve modification or deletion of small files in order to avoid unnecessary files migration.

2) Notify clients to retry at a reasonable interval for read or write requests. One of reasons of this way is that file migration in our optimization spends less time than one normal write request before optimization. Another one is founded on the "non-conflicting write" semantics established in PVFS2 that most of applications do not write the same file from different clients at the same time [8].

3) Respond without delay to other requests that do not refer to small file data.

4   Experiments

Several experiments were conducted to evaluate the performance of proposed optimization. The experiments used 5 Lenovo X86 server nodes to d stock and optimized PVFS2 separately. Each node has four Intel Xeon5160 processors with 4Gb DDR2 memory and connects with other nodes with 1Gbps Ethernet. In order to demonstrate general performance of proposed optimization, four configurations described in table 1 are designed to cater for evaluation.

Table 1. Configuration of experiments

Configuration	MDS	IOS	Client
#1	1	1	1
#2	1	2	2
#3	2	1	2
#4	2	2	1

Postmark [9], which was designed for small I/O performance measurement, was selected as the benchmark to measure performance of proposed optimization. Figure 4 depicts the comparison of file create and delete throughout between

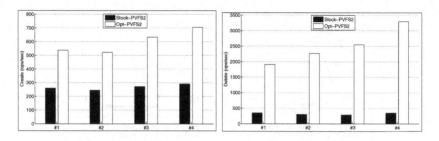

Fig. 4. Create and delete throughout under different configurations

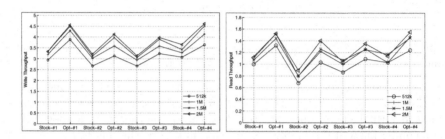

Fig. 5. Read and write throughput under different configurations

stock and optimized PVFS2 under different configurations. Our experiments show the distinct advantage of proposed optimization over stock PVFS2. This can be explained by datafile handle creation bypassing in our optimization.

Figure 5 shows the comparison of read and write throughput between stock and optimized PVFS2 in the function of different configurations. Initially a given threshold was designated by server configuration file and then adaptive threshold model adjust it dynamically in order to maintain MDS performance. Maximum file size was set up to 3M in order to evaluate small files performance. As the figure shows, our optimized PVFS2 outperforms stock version by more 20% and initial threshold has no significant effects on throughput. This is because our adaptive threshold model was adjusting it dynamically during the experiments.

Figure 6 shows the migration effects on read and write throughput under proposed optimization. In this experiment, minimum and maximum of file size was set to 1.9M and 2.1M respectively, and the migration threshold was set to 2M file in order to measure migration cost. Besides, file was written by block size of 512k each time. As we can see from above figures, file migration did not affect the overall performance of file system under all four configurations, and optimized version outperforms stock one as usual. Proposed latency hiding scheme and migration optimization contribute to this effort. Throughput under configuration 4 was better than other ones as it had more IOS to boost file transferring in parallel. From Figure 6, we can learn that our optimization has slight migration side-effects on throughput, which can be ignored, and overall performance of file system can still outperforms stock PVFS2 more than 10%.

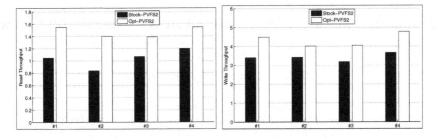

Fig. 6. Migration effects on read and write throughput

5   Conclusion

Common metadata-based optimizations of small file performance in cluster file system do not take MDS load and migration side-effects into consideration. The pro-posed optimization can boost small file performance more than 20% while guarantee overall performance by adaptively migrating small files. With the presented latency hiding scheme and optimizations on migration, overheads induced by storing small files on MDS are reduced as expected.

Optimization can still be improved in the future as we do not consider cache effects currently. However, it is tricky to cache small files on client-side because of design complexities of both memory mangement and concurrent consistency.

References

1. Hildebrand, D., Ward, L., Honeyman, P.: Large Files, Small Writes, and pNFS. In: Proceedings of the 20th Annual International Conference on Supercomputing, Queensland, Australia, pp. 116–124 (2006)
2. Shaikh, F., Chainani, M.: A Case for Small File Packing in Parallel Virtual File System (PVFS2). In: Advanced and Distributed Operating Sytems (2007)
3. Kuhn, M., Kunkel, J., Ludwig, T.: Directory-based Metadata Optimizations for Small Files in PVFS2. In: Luque, E., Margalef, T., Benítez, D. (eds.) Euro-Par 2008. LNCS, vol. 5168, pp. 90–99. Springer, Heidelberg (2008)
4. Wang, F., Xin, Q., Hong, B., Brandt, S.A., Miller, S.L.: File System Workload Analysis For Large Scale Scientific Computing Applications. In: 12th NASA Goddard Conference on Mass Storage Systems and Technologies, USA, pp. 139–152 (2004)
5. Roselli, D., Lorch, A.T.E.: A Comparison of File System Workloads. In: Proceedings of the 2000 USENIX Annual Technical Conference, Berkeley, CA, USA, pp. 41–54 (2000)
6. A. N. Laboratory. PVFS2 Online Document (2008), http://www.pvfs.org/
7. Devulapalli, A., Wyckoff, P.: File Creation Strategies in a Distributed Metadata file System. In: Parallel and Distributed Processing Symposium, USA, pp. 1–10 (2007)
8. Sebepou1, Z., Magoutis, K., Marazakis, M., Bilas, A.: A Comparative Experimental Study of Parallel File Systems for Large-Scale Data Processing. In: First USENIX Workshop on Large-Scale Computing, Berkeley, CA, USA (2008)
9. Katcher, J.: PostMark: A New File System Benchmark (2008), http://www.netapp.com

Efficiently Packing Circles into a Larger Containing Circle

Jingfa Liu[1,*], Yali Wang[2], and Jinji Pan[1]

[1] School of Computer and Software
Nanjing University of Information Science and Technology Nanjing 210044, China
jfliu@nuist.edu.cn, panjinji@nuist.edu.cn
[2] School of Electronic & Information Engineering,
Nanjing University of Information Science and Technology, Nanjing 210044, China
boldwyl@gmail.edu.cn

Abstract. The circles packing problem consists in placing a set of circles into a larger containing circle without overlap. The objective is to determine the smallest radius of the containing circle as well as the coordinates of the center of each given circle. Lacking powerful optimization method is the key obstacle to solve this problem. A novel heuristic global optimization method, energy landscape paving (ELP) which combines core ideas from energy surface deformation and taboo search, is introduced. By giving some critical revisions to the ELP method and incorporating new configuration update strategy into it, an improved energy landscape paving (IELP) algorithm is put forward for the circles packing problem. The effectiveness of the algorithm is demonstrated through a set of typical instances taken from the literature.

1 Introduction

The packing problem has a wide spectrum of applications [1]. It is encountered in a variety of real world applications including production and packing for the textile, apparel, naval, automobile, and food industries. Many various optional features exist on this problem, e.g., the container can be circle, rectangle or polygon, and the packed items can be circular, rectangular or irregular. This paper addresses the circles packing problem (CPP) where the items and container are circles.

The CPP consists in packing n circles c_i of known radius r_i, $i \in N = \{1, 2, \ldots, n\}$, into the smallest containing circle c_0. The objective is to determine the radius r_0 of c_0 as well as the coordinates (x_i, y_i) of the center of c_i, such that $d(c_i, c_j) \geq r_i + r_j$, and $d(c_i, c_0) \leq r_0 - r_i$, where $d(c_i, c_j)$ denotes that the Euclidean distance between circles c_i and c_j, $i, j \in N$ and $i \neq j$.

The CPP is surprisingly difficult and has been proven to be NP-hard. For packing identical circles in a larger containing circle, Birgin et al. [1], and Mladenović et al. [2] developed various heuristics to generate approximate solutions. Some authors have studied the problem of packing unequal circles as well. Huang et al. [3] and Wang et al.

* This work is supported by the Natural Science Foundation of Education Committee of Jiangsu Province (09KJB52008), the Foundation of Nanjing University of Information Science and Technology and Qing Lan project.

W. Zhang et al. (Eds.): HPCA 2009, LNCS 5938, pp. 250–256, 2010.

[4] developed quasi-physical quasi-human algorithms inspired from human packing strategies. Huang et al. [5] presented two greedy algorithms which use a maximum hole degree rule (which is a strategy of selecting and packing the circles one by one) and a self look-ahead search strategy. Lü et al. [6] incorporated the strategy of maximum hole degree into the PERM scheme. The basic idea of their approach is to evaluate the benefit of a partial configuration (where some circles have been packed and others outside) using the principle of maximum hole degree, and use the PERM strategy to prune and enrich branches efficiently. Akeb et al. [7] gave an adaptive beam search algorithm that combines the beam search, the local position distance and the dichotomous search strategy.

This paper uses a novel global optimization algorithm, the energy landscape paving (ELP) [8, 9], to solve the CPP. By giving some critical revisions to the ELP and incorporating new configuration update strategy into it, an improved energy landscape paving (IELP) algorithm is put forward. The experimental results show that the proposed algorithm is very effective for the circles packing problem.

2 Conversion of the Problem

We call the coordinates of the center of all the n circles a configuration, and denote it by $X=(x_1, y_1, x_2, y_2, \ldots, x_n, y_n)$.

By the quasi-physical strategy [3, 4], we imagine that all n circles and the larger containing circle as smooth elastic solids. When two different circles are imbedded into each other, the extrusive elastic potential energy between them is proportional to the square of the depth of their mutual embedment according to elasticity mechanism. Thus, the circles packing problem is converted into an optimization problem "minimize $E(X)$" with the following potential energy function:

$$E(X)=\sum_{i=0}^{n-1} \sum_{j=i+1}^{n} u_{ij} ,$$

where u_{ij} is the extrusive elastic potential energy between circles i and j.

$$u_{ij} =\frac{1}{2}d_{ij}^2 , \ i<j, \ i, j=0, 1, 2, \ldots, n.$$

Here d_{ij} is the embedding depth between circles i and j. Obviously, $E(X) \geq 0$. For a given radius r_0 of the larger containing circle, if there exists a configuration $X^*=(x_1^*, y_1^*, \ldots, x_n^*, y_n^*)$ subject to $E(X^*)=0$, then X^* is a feasible solution to CPP, whereas if $E(X^*)>0$, then X^* is not a feasible solution to CPP.

3 Algorithm

The energy landscape paving (ELP) method [8, 9] is an improved Monte Carlo (MC) global optimization method. As all good stochastic global optimizers, it is designed to explore low-energy configurations while avoiding at the same time entrapment in local minima. This is achieved by performing low-temperature MC simulations, but with a modified energy expression designed to steer the search away from regions that have already been explored. This means that if a configuration X is hit, the energy $E(X)$ is increased by a "penalty". In the present paper we choose $\overline{E}(X)=E(X)+kH(E, t)$ as the replacement of the energy E, where $H(E, t)$ is the histogram in energy at MC sweep t and k is a constant. The sampling weight for a configuration X is defined as $\omega(\overline{E}(X))=\exp(-\overline{E}(X)/k_BT)$, where k_BT is the thermal energy at the (low) temperature T, and k_B is Boltzmann constant.

Within ELP the sampling weight of a local minimum configuration decreases with the time that the system stays in that minimum, and consequently the probability to escape the minimum increases. The accumulated histogram function $H(E, t)$ from all previously visited energies at the MC sweeps helps the simulation escape local entrapments and surpass high-energy barrier easier. However, in ELP, there exists a technical flaw. Consider an attempted move in ELP which yields a new lower energy minimum that has never been visited before and happens to fall into the same bin which contains other energies previously visited in the earlier steps. Undesirably, the likelihood of accepting this new energy minimum X_2 becomes small as the result of the penalty term $kH(E, t)$, i.e., the ELP minimization may miss this new lower energy configuration X_2 near X_1. To overcome this shortcoming, we give an improvement on ELP. In the improved ELP, the acceptability of the new configuration X_2 is determined by a comparison between $E(X_1)$ and $E(X_2)$, where two cases are possible: (a) $E(X_2)<E(X_1)$ and (b) $E(X_2)\geq E(X_1)$. For case (a), the simulation unconditionally accepts the new configuration X_2 and starts a new round of iteration; for case (b), if the new configuration X_2 satisfies the condition expression random$(0,1)<\exp\{[\overline{E}(X_1, t)-\overline{E}(X_2, t)]/k_BT\}$, then the simulation accepts X_2 and starts a new round of iteration, otherwise does not accept X_2 and restores X_1 as the current configuration.

In the configuration $(x_1, y_1, ..., x_i, y_i, ..., x_n, y_n)$, we define the relative energy RE_i of the circle c_i as E_i/r_i^2, where $E_i=\sum_{j=0, j\neq i}^{n} d_{ji}^2$. Suppose that the circle c_i is the next circle to be picked and moved. Define the taboo region as the region where all packed circles (except the circle c_i) occupy at this moment in the larger containing circle, and the vacant region as the remainder except the taboo region at this moment in the larger containing circle.

In ELP minimization, each iterative step must update the current configuration. In order to update configuration X_1, the original ELP simulation picks out the circle c_i with the maximum extrusive elastic potential energy in X_1 with the positions of the other circles unchanged. Then, randomly determine the position of the center of the circle c_i in the larger containing circle and gain a new configuration X_2. At last, the system decides whether to accept X_2 according to a comparison between $E(X_1)$ and $E(X_2)$. These strategies of updating configurations are not efficient enough to solve the CPP. We give the following new configuration update strategy.

◆ For the current configuration X_1, we pick out the circle c_i with the maximum RE_i and randomly put the center of c_i into the vacant region in the larger containing circles c_0, and gain a new configuration X'.

◆Once producing new configuration X', we execute the gradient descent procedure based on adaptive step length to locate its nearest local or global energy minimum configuration $\bar{X}$.

◆ If a circle c_i with maximum RE_i has been put randomly five times within the vacant region in the larger containing circle and every time after executing the gradient descent method the updated configuration $\bar{X}$ is not accepted, we take its RE_i as zero in the next jumping time, i.e., the circle c_i is forbidden one time.

By incorporating new configuration update strategy into the ELP method, an improved energy landscape paving (IELP) algorithm is put forward. The details of the algorithm IELP are described as follows:

Program IELP

Process:

1) Randomly give the initial configuration X_1. Set $T:=5$, $k \in [20, 50]$. Let $t:=1$ and initialize $H(E, t)$.
2) Compute $E(X_1, t)$ and $\bar{E}(X_1, t)$.
3) Pick out the circle c_i with maximum RE_i in the current configuration, set $j:=1$.
4) Randomly put the center of c_i into the vacant region of c_0, and gain a new configuration X'.
5) Let $h:=1$, $\bar{X} := X' - \text{Grad } E(X') \times h$, and compute $E(X')$ and $E(\bar{X})$.
   //Grad $E(X')$ denotes the gradient vector of $E(X)$ at X'.
6) **If** $E(\bar{X}) < E(X')$ **then** $X':=\bar{X}$, $\bar{X}:=X'-\text{Grad } E(X') \times h$, compute $E(\bar{X})$, and go to 8);
   Else $h:=h \times 0.8$, go to 7).
7) **If** $h < 10^{-2}$ **then** go to 9);
   Else $X':=\bar{X}$, $\bar{X}:=X'-\text{Grad } E(X') \times h$, compute $E(\bar{X})$ and go to 8).
8) **If** $E(\bar{X}) < 10^{-8}$, **then** stop with success;
   Else go to 6).
9) Let $X_2 := \bar{X}$, compute $E(X_2, t)$ and $\bar{E}(X_2, t):=E(X_2, t)+ kH(E(X_2), t)$.
10) **If** $E(X_2, t) < E(X_1, t)$ **then** accept X_2, go to 12);

Else If random(0,1)<exp{[$\bar{E}$ (X_1, t) - $\bar{E}$ (X_2, t)]/$k_B T$} **then** accept X_2, go to 12);

   Else do not accept X_2, and restore X_1 as the current configuration, $j:=j+1$, go to 11).

11) **If** $j>5$ **then** set RE$_i$:=0, go to 3);

    Else go to 4).

12) **If** $t<1,000,000$ **then** $t:=t+1$, go to 3);

    Else stop with failure.

4   Experimental Results

To evaluate the performance of the proposed algorithm, we implement the algorithm IELP coded in Java and run on a Pentium IV 1.6GHz and 512M RAM. We test all 14 instances listed in [6]. These benchmark instances, which include 5 equal circle packing instances and 9 unequal ones, are typical representatives. For each instance, the number n of circles to be packed, the radius r_i of each of the n circles, and the best known solution are reported in Table 1.

Table 1. 14 instances and their current best known solutions

No.	n	Instance r_i, $i=1, 2, ..., n$	Best solution
1	7	$r_i=20$, $i=1, 2, ..., 7$	60
2	9	$r_1=...=r_4=10$, $r_5=...r_9=4.1415$	24.143
3	10	$r_1=50$, $r_2=40$, $r_3=32$, $r_4=31.5$, $r_5=r_6=r_7=20$, $r_8=11$, $r_9=r_{10}=10$	98.9
4	10	$r_1=50$, $r_2=40$, $r_3=r_4=r_5=30$, $r_6=21$, $r_7=20$, $r_8=15$, $r_9=12$, $r_{10}=10$	99.8851
5	11	$r_1=10$, $r_{i+1}=r_i+1$, $i=1, 2, ..., 10$	57.17
6	12	$r_1= r_2= r_3=100$, $r_4=r_5= r_6=48.26$, $r_7=...=r_{12}=23.72$	215.47
7	15	$r_1=1$, $r_{i+1}=r_i+1$, $i=1, 2, ..., 14$	38.8380
8	16	$r_1=21$, $r_{i+1}=r_i+1$, $i=1, 2, ..., 15$	128.0539
9	17	$r_1=25$, $r_2=20$, $r_3= r_4=15$, $r_5= r_6= r_7=10$, $r_8=...=r_{17}=5$	49.20
10	17	$r_1=...= r_4=100$, $r_5=...= r_9=41.415$, $r_{10}=...=r_{17}=20$	241.43
11	37	$r_1=r_2=...=r_{37}=20$	135.176
12	50	$r_1=r_2=...=r_{50}=20$	159.32
13	61	$r_1=r_2=...=r_{61}=20$	173.226
14	91	$r_1=r_2=...=r_{91}=20$	211.334

For each instance, IELP is run for five times independently. The obtained minimal radius of the larger containing circle over five independent runs and the running time under this minimal radius are listed in Table 2, in comparison with those obtained by the improved quasi-physical (IQP) algorithm [3], the hybrid algorithm based on simulated annealing and taboo search (SATS) [10], the beam search algorithms BS1 and BS2 based on the different diversification strategies [7], and the PERM algorithm [6], respectively. In Table 2, r_0^{IQP}, r_0^{SATS}, r_0^{BS1}, r_0^{BS2}, r_0^{PERM}, and r_0^{IELP} indicate the minimal containing circle radius obtained by IQP, SATS, BS1, BS2, PERM and IELP, respectively. "_" denotes that the corresponding algorithms do not report the results. Time (s) denotes the running time (in second) of IELP under r_0^{IELP}.

Table 2 shows that we find new smaller radius (which are reported in **boldface**) of the larger containing circle missed in previous literatures for four unequal circle packing instances 3, 5, 9, 10, and two equal circle packing ones 11 and 12. For instances 1, 2, 4, 6, 7, 8, and 13, we find the smallest radii as reported in [6, 7]. For instance 14, SATS gains better result than IELP, but the precision of the former is 10^{-6} and the precision of the latter is 10^{-8}. So, for all 14 instances in [6], IELP either finds better solutions missed in previous literature or obtains the best known precise solutions. Moreover, the runtime of IELP for each instance is also comparable to other algorithms.

Table 2. Results of IELP for 14 instances listed in Table 1, in comparison with those by IQP [3], SATS [10], BS1 [7], BS2[7], and PERM [6], respectively

No.	r_0^{IQP}	r_0^{SATS}	r_0^{BS1}	r_0^{BS2}	r_0^{PERM}	r_0^{IELP}	time (s)
1	_	60	_	_	60	60.0000	0.07
2	_	_	_	_	24.143	24.1430	0.10
3	_	_	_	_	98.9	**98.8358**	59.46
4	99.92	_	99.8851	99.8851	99.89	99.8851	27.03
5	57.65	_	_	_	57.17	**57.0954**	200.33
6	215.47	215.47	_	_	215.47	215.4700	0.50
7	_	39.37	38.8407	38.8380	39.00	38.8380	597.47
8	_	_	128.0539	128.5826	130.00	128.0539	1070.46
9	50	50	49.3029	49.2069	49.20	**49.1876**	1707.21
10	241.43	241.43	_	_	241.43	**241.4214**	1.35
11	_	135.176	_	_	135.176	**135.1754**	0.29
12	159.32	159.32	_	_	159.32	**158.9503**	158.95
13	_	173.226	_	_	173.226	173.2260	1.77
14	_	211.334	_	_	216.45	211.3354	26.33

5 Conclusions

This paper solves the CPP using an effective global optimization algorithm, the improved energy landscape paving method, which incorporates new configuration update strategy into the ELP method, and with some critical revisions to the latter. We evaluate our approach on 14 representative equal or unequal circles packing instances. The experimental results show the effectiveness of the proposed algorithm.

References

1. Birgin, E.G., Martinez, J.M., Ronconi, D.P.: Optimizing the packing of cylinders into a rectangular container: a nonlinear approach. European Journal of Operational Research 160, 19–33 (2005)
2. Mladenović, N., Plastria, F., Urosević, D.: Reformulation descent applied to circle packing problems. Computers and Operations Research 32, 2419–2434 (2005)
3. Huang, W.Q., Kang, Y.: A short note on a simple search heuristic for the disk packing problem. Annals of Operations Research 131, 101–108 (2004)
4. Wang, H.Q., Huang, W.Q., Zhang, Q.A., Xu, D.M.: An improved algorithm for the packing of unequal circles within a larger containing circle. European Journal of Operational Research 141(2), 440–453 (2002)
5. Huang, W.Q., Li, Y., Li, C.M., Xu, R.C.: New heuristics for packing unequal circle into a circular container. Computers and Operations Research 33, 2125–2142 (2006)
6. Lü, Z.P., Huang, W.Q.: PERM for solving circle packing problem. Computers and Operations Research 35(5), 1742–1755 (2008)
7. Akeb, H., Hifi, M., M'Hallah, R.: A beam search algorithm for the circular packing problem. Computers and Operations Research 36(5), 1513–1528 (2009)
8. Hansmann, U.H.E., Wille, L.T.: Global optimization by energy landscape paving. Physical Review Letters 88(6), 068105 (2002)
9. Liu, J.F., Huang, W.Q.: Studies of finding low energy configuration in off-lattice protein models. Journal of Theoretical and Computational Chemistry 5(3), 587–594 (2006)
10. Zhang, D.F., Deng, A.S.: An effective hybrid algorithm for the problem of packing circles into a larger containing circle. Computers and Operations Research 32(8), 1941–1951 (2005)

Heterogeneous Database Integration of EPR System Based on OGSA-DAI

Xuhong Liu[1], Yunmei Shi[1], Yabin Xu[1], Yingai Tian[1], and Fuheng Liu[2]

[1] Computer School, Beijing Information Science and Technology University,
Beijing 100101, China
[2] College of Information Science and Engineering, Qingdao Agricultural University,
Qingdao 266109, China

Abstract. In this paper, we describe a service-oriented middleware architecture based on OGSA-DAI which integrates heterogeneous database distributed in different electronic patient record (EPR) system. OGSA-DAI provides uniform access to heterogeneous databases that have heterogeneous DBMSs by web service. We solve data heterogeneity on information expressed by specifying the criteria of information description and then mapping physical data to a virtual table. Users retrieve data from virtual table by SQL query.

1 Introduction

Along with the development of information technology, almost all the hospitals have established electronic patient record system to help doctors to improve work efficiency [1]. Most recently, people focus on integrating the information of patients that distributed at different hospitals which always have their own electronic patient record system [2]. These electronic patient record systems are not only allocated at different nodes, but high heterogeneous for each other. On the one hand, the data resources in these electronic patient record systems have heterogeneous storage and operating systems. On the other hand, the data are heterogeneous on information expressed due to lacking of a uniform criterion for the same conceptual entities.

Heterogeneity existed in electronic patient record system hinders the share of the clinical information, thus brings about repetitive works and high medical expenses [3]. So, it is necessary to design a middleware to integrate heterogeneous medical databases allocated at different nodes. Grid-based technologies, like OGSA-DAI are emerging as potential solutions for managing and collaborating distributed and heterogeneous resources in the clinical domain[4][5]. OGSA-DAI has mainly addressed the issue of data access, with much less effort spent on data integration [6]. The OGSA-Distributed Query Process (DQP) Project has been adding data integration functionality using OGSA-DAI services [7]. However, it is too complex to be widely used[8].

We design a middleware architecture based on OGSA-DAI to solve the problem introduced before. In our architecture, OGSA-DAI provides uniform access to heterogeneous data sources. We solve the data heterogeneity on information expressed by information mapping.

W. Zhang et al. (Eds.): HPCA 2009, LNCS 5938, pp. 257–263, 2010.

2 OGSA-DAI

The OGSA-DAI, namely Open Grid Services Architecture - Data Access and Integration, has produced grid enabled middleware presently based on the GGF defined OGSI interfaces, which will migrate to use the recently proposed WSRF as well as possibly investigating layering on top of other standards, to allow access to, and integration of, data resources in an OGSA Grid environment[9]. The currently defined OGSA-DAI services are:

• Data Access and Integration Service Group Registry (DAISGR) - allows resource discovery to take place. A client can use one of these services to identify a resource provider that best meets its requirements.

• Grid Data Service Factory (GDSF) - acts as a persistent access point to a data resource and contains additional related metadata that may not be available at the DAISGR.

• Grid Data Service (GDS) - is the service used by the client to access a data resource. These are created by a GDSF and generally are not persistent services.

3 System Architecture

On the basis of OGSA-DAI, We design a Grid Data Services to encapsulate data with different schema distributed across multiple databases within a group of clinical partners. The system exposes several heterogeneous databases to users as a single virtual table without affecting the current system. Users query the virtual table through data service and the query is transformed into a series of physical queries that dispatched to different physical databases by query parsing. The results returned by physical databases are integrated according to information mapping. This platform can help to integrate electronic patient record system that partitioned and distributed across multiple nodes which belong to different medical institutions. The framework is illustrated as Fig.1.

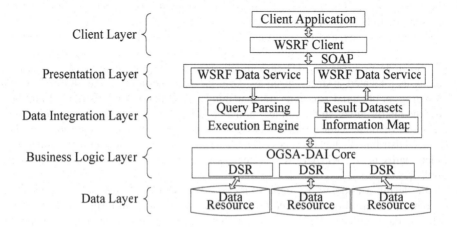

Fig. 1. Heterogeneous data integration platform architecture overview

The system consists of data layer, business logic layer, data integration layer, presentation layer and client layer. Data layer exposes several heterogeneous databases including relational database, XML database and file system through OGSA-DAI. Only relational database is taken into account in this system for the moment. The business logic layer consists of a set of data service resources (DSR) that act as a front-end to a data resource. Each DSR implements the core DAI functionality which includes overseeing the coordination of the activities for a specific data resource. Data integration layer converts the data between virtual table and physical database by query parsing according to the information map table. The presentation layer consists of a set of WSRF data services that accepts query from the client to create a perform document that implies a set of activities to be performed. The client layer provides interfaces for users to access WSRF data service.

4 Implementation

4.1 Information Map Table

Information mapping is the most important function of data integration layer. The data converted between physical databases and virtual table is performed by query parsing according to information map table. The information map table registers information criterion, details of physical databases and mapping between physical databases and virtual tables as so on. The mapping shows the relationship between the columns in physical tables and those in virtual tables that are loosely coupled. There always exist several information map tables corresponding to different data service. We demonstrate an information map table of electronic patient record system as follows.

```
<dataServiceResource >
  <normativeResource>
    <normativeField>ID</normativeField>
    <normativeField>Department </normativeField>
    <normativeField>MedicalHistory </normativeField>
    <normativeField>PatientInformation </normativeField>
    <normativeField>Diagnoses</normativeField>
  </normativeResource>
  <sourceFieldsMap>
    <PatientName value="MediRecord.PatientID"/>
    <PatientName value="EMRecord.PatientIdentifier"/>
    <Department value="MediRecord.Office"/>
    <Department value="EMRecord.Department"/>
    <MedicalHistory value="MediRecord.MedicalCase"/>
    <PatientInformation value="MediRecord.PatientInfo"/>
    <PatientInformation value="EMRecord.PatientExam"/>
    <Diagnoses value="MediRecord.Diagnose"/>
    <Diagnoses value="EMRecord.Diagnosis"/>
  </sourceFieldsMap>
  <sourceTables>
    <table> MediRecord</table>
    <table> EMRecord </table>
  </sourceTables>
```

```
<sourceTableRelation> MediRecord.IDNO= EMRecord.no
</sourceTableRelation>
</dataServiceResource >
```

The *normativeResource* element includes the information criterion and each *normativeField* element describes a normal property. The *sourceFieldsMap* element shows the matching between normal property and column in physical databases. A normal property can map with no or several columns. The *sourceTables* element demonstrates the physical databases while the *sourceTableRelation* element describes their relationship.

4.2 Virtual Table

Virtual table is a uniform view that encapsulates physical databases which have different schema and DBMSs. The details of physical databases are transparent to users and users can only perform SQL queries across virtual table. The virtual table is established according to information map table when users access the corresponding data service.

According to information map table, the data in physical databases is mapped to virtual table. The columns in virtual table are normal properties described in information map table. The data is translated from several physical databases by query parsing module according to the relationship between normal property and physical column defined in information map table. Fig.2 illustrates the map between the columns in virtual table and that in physical databases in electronic patient record system.

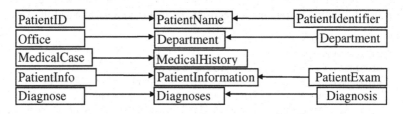

Fig. 2. The left and right columns in the figure are properties in physical table MediRecord and EMRecord respectively. The middle columns are normal properties in information map table.

The Information map table is different according to different data service, and so is the Virtual table. Although several data services maybe access the same physical database, they don't influence each other.

4.3 Performing Steps

The steps of the whole system are as follows.

Step 1 Data Service Discovery and Resource Selecting. User telnets information portal by authentication firstly, then checks the data services that is offered by the system and selects the corresponding virtual table. Consequently, user looks at the metadata and selects data space for result data. When user fills out SQL query finally, a perform document is produced.

Step 2 Extracting Virtual Activities. Data Integration layer extracts virtual activity by parsing the perform document to produce a task list of virtual activities.

Step 3 Conversion Activity. Execution Engine converts the task list of virtual activities into a task list of physical activities. The sequence of activity execution within a single request is defined by associating the input of one activity with the output of another activity to define a data flow.

Step 4 Performing Activities. Execution Engine dispatches the task list of physical activities to OGSA-DAI core that interactive with physical databases.

Step 5 Returning Results. A sequence result datasets are delivered to execution engine after OGSA-DAI core has accomplished a query request. Execution engine converts the columns of the result datasets to normal properties that described in information map table. The converted datasets are saved in a temporary database. The user retrieves the data by using an SQL query that is performed on the temporary database.

Step 6 Delivering Results. The final results are transferred to user's data space by delivery activities when all query tasks are accomplished.

4.4 Experiment Result

The experiments have been conducted on the heterogeneous collection of machines with installation of different DBMSs. We set up a virtual Grid environment including two servers and one client. All machines are installed with Globus Toolkit 4.0 [10] and OGSA-DAI. Other development tools include J2sdk1.4.2_13, Apache Tomcat 5.0, Apache ANT1.6, Mysql4.0, and Oracle9.0.2 and so on. Two electronic patient record systems, which use Mysql and Oracle respectively, are distributed at two severs. Users submit SQL query by web portal that locates at client node.

For the sake of privacy, all the medical data information we used is simulated including basic personal data information, basic health data information. They are stored, respectively, in different database management systems located at two server nodes. Fig.3 shows the query result of the instance. It can be seen from the results that

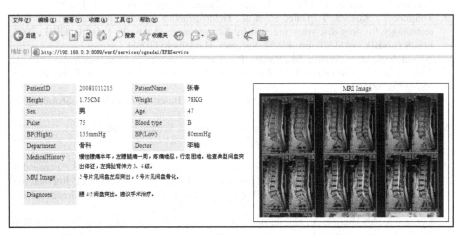

Fig. 3. Experiment result illustrates medical information in different database management systems located at two server nodes

our system integrates distributed, heterogeneous databases in a seamless way, so that medical data information can be highly shared and accessed very conveniently.

5 Conclusion

This paper offers a platform based on OGSA-DAI for transparent resource management in electronic patient record system. The platform allows the virtualization and sharing of heterogeneous data resources connected to the platform. OGSA-DAI provides a unified and transparent access to distribute heterogeneous storage resources and we adopt information mapping to solve the data heterogeneity on information expressed. The platform we introduced provides a uniform view for distributed and heterogeneous electronic patient record system. Future work is to perform data mining and data analysis on this view, which is one of the key topics of study work recently [11][12].

Acknowledgments

This work are supported by funded project in *Study of Internet key technologies about distributed and heterogeneous data integration* under the Grant KM200910772014 and *Study Of EPR System Construction And Knowledge Discovery Based On XML* under the Grant KM200810772007 from Beijing Municipal Education Commission, China. We would like to thank the funding agency in supporting this research.

References

1. Yuzhong, C.: Designing and Application of Electronic Medical Record Based on Middleware. China Digital Medicine 3, 32–34 (2008)
2. Benggong, Y., Na, L.: Research on Information Integration Platform for Electronic Health Records Based on the Third Party. Computer System & Applications 3, 2–5 (2008)
3. Tohsato, Y., Kosaka, T., Date, S., et al.: Heterogeneous database federation using Grid technology for drug discovery process. In: Konagaya, A., Satou, K. (eds.) LSGRID 2004. LNCS (LNBI), vol. 3370, pp. 43–52. Springer, Heidelberg (2005)
4. Antonioletti, M., Atkinson, M., Baxter, R., et al.: The design and implementation of Grid database services in OGSA-DAI. Concurrency Computation Practice and Experience 17, 357–376 (2005)
5. Hai, G.: Distributed Heterogeneous Data Integration Based on OGSA-DAI, Shandong Jinan (2007)
6. Interoperability of Virtual Organizations on a Complex Semantic Grid,
   http://www.inteliGrid.com/data/works/att/
   d51_2.content.03243.pdf
7. Alpdemir, M.N., Mukherjee, A., Gounaris, A., Paton, N.W., Watson, P., Fernandes, A.A.A.: OGSA-DQP: A Service for Distributed Querying on the Grid. In: International Conference on Extending Database Technology 2004, Heraklion, Crete, Greece (2004) (in press)
8. Lynden, S., Mukherjee, A., Hume, A.C., et al.: The design and implementation of OGSA-DQP: A service-based distributed query processor. Future Generation Computer Systems 25, 224–236 (2009)

9. Towards Open Grid Services Architecture (OGSA),
   `http://www.globus.org/ogsa/`
10. Foster, I.: Globus Toolkit Version 4: Software for Service-Oriented Systems. In: IFIP International Federation for Information Processing 2005. Springer, Heidelberg (2005)
11. Stankovski, V., Swain, M., Kravtsov, V., et al.: Grid-enabling data mining applications with DataMining Grid: An architectural perspective. Future Generation Computer Systems 24, 259–279 (2008)
12. Congiusta, A., Talia, D., Trunfio, P.: Service-oriented middleware for distributed data mining on the grid. Journal of Parallel and Distributed Computing 68, 3–15 (2008)

RTTM: A New Hierarchical Interconnection Network for Massively Parallel Computing*

Youyao Liu[1,2], Cuijin Li[1], and Jungang Han[1,2]

[1] Xi'an University of Post and Telecommunications, Xi'an, 710121, China
[2] Microelectronics School, XIDIAN University, Xi'an, 710071, China
{lyyao2002,hjg}@xupt.edu.cn, licuijin@yahoo.com.cn

Abstract. Since reducing the diameter is likely to improve the performance of an interconnection network, the problem of designing interconnection network with low diameter is still a current research topic. Another important issue in the design of interconnection networks for massively parallel computers is scalability. A new hierarchical interconnection network topology, called Rectangular Twisted Torus Meshes (RTTM network), is proposed. At the lowest level of RTTM network, the Level-1 sub-network, also called a Basic Module, consists of a mesh connection of $2^m \times 2^m$ nodes. Successively higher level networks are built by recursively interconnecting $a \times 2a$ next lower level sub-networks in the form of a Rectangular Twisted Torus. An appealing property of the RTTM network is its smaller diameter and shorter average distance, which implies a reduction in communication delays. The RTTM network allows the exploitation of computational locality as well as easy expansion up to a million processors.

1 Introduction

Advances in hardware technology, especially VLSI circuit technology, have made it possible to build a large-scale multiprocessor system that contains thousands or even tens of thousands of processors [1]. One crucial step on designing such a multiprocessor system is to determine the topology of the interconnection network (network for short), because the system performance is significantly affected by the network topology [2,3].

In current network research, some basic regular network topologies, such as 2D Mesh and 2D Torus, have been proposed. Among these topologies, the 2D Torus is the most studied (in over 50% of the cases) [4,5]. Each dimension of a 2D Torus network may have a different number of nodes, leading to rectangular topology. The topology is denoted as mixed-radix networks (i.e. Rectangular Torus) [4]. However, Rectangular Torus has two important drawbacks: 1) it is not edge-symmetric, and 2) the distance-related network parameters (diameter and average distance) are quite far from the optimum values of square topology. The edge asymmetry introduces load imbalance in this network, and for many traffic patterns the load on the longer dimension is larger than the load on the shorter one [4]. In addition, maximum and average packet delays are relatively long since they depend on the poor values of diameter and average distance exhibited by this network.

---

* The paper supported by National Science Foundation of China (90607008) and the national high technology research and development program of China (2007AA01Z111).

W. Zhang et al. (Eds.): HPCA 2009, LNCS 5938, pp. 264–271, 2010.

Therefore, Rectangular Twisted Torus (RTT) networks was proposed in [7] to reduce maximum and average distance among their nodes, and avoid the edge-asymmetry problem of rectangular Torus. RTT network has aspect ratios of 2: 1 (the longer dimension has twice the number of nodes than the shorter one). However, RTT network suffers from the limitation of scalability because of insufficient node degree.

A new hierarchical network topology, called Rectangular Twisted Torus Meshes (RTTM network), is proposed in this paper. The RTTM is a topology suitable for scalable massively parallel computer system. An RTTM network allows for exploitation of computational locality as well as modular future expansion. Further, it has a regular structure which makes node addressing and message routing straightforward. Specifically, an RTTM network has smaller diameter and shorter average distance than those of 2D Mesh, 2D Torus, and TESH networks. The lowest level sub-network of RTTM is called a Basic Module (BM). A BM consists of a mesh connection of $2^m \times 2^m$ nodes. Successively higher level networks are built by recursively interconnecting $a \times 2a$ next lower level sub-networks in the form of a Rectangular Twisted Torus. This topology, together with the small number of ports per node, makes the network amenable to efficient VLSI realization.

The rest of the paper is organized as follows. Section 2 describes the topology architecture and the properties of RTTM. In section 3, we present a routing algorithm for RTTM. Section 4 gives performance evaluation using OPNET. Section 5 concludes the paper.

2 Architecture of RTTM Interconnection Network

2.1 Preliminaries

Definition 1. A 2-dimensional (2D) Mesh topology is an $N_1 \times N_2$ array with $2N_1 \times N_2 - N_1 - N_2$ links and $N_1 \times N_2$ nodes. The address of each node is labeled by a pair of integers (n_1, n_2), where $0 \le n_1 \le N_1-1$ and $0 \le n_2 \le N_2-1$. There is a link between node $u = (u_1, u_2)$ and $v = (v_1, v_2)$ if $|u_1 - v_1| + |u_2 - v_2| = 1$. If we also require that there are wrap-around links that connect nodes of the first column (respectively row) to those at the last column (respectively row), then it is called a 2D Torus.

A 2D Mesh has $N_1 \times N_2$ nodes and $(N_1-1) \times N_2 + (N_2-1) \times N_1$ links. A 2D Torus has $N_1 \times N_2$ nodes and $N_1 \times N_2$ links. The diameter k and average distance $\bar{k}$ of a 2D Torus of $a \times 2a$ nodes are: $k = \frac{3}{2}a$; $\bar{k} = \left(\frac{2a}{4} + \frac{a}{4}\right) \cdot \frac{2a^2}{2a^2 - 1} \approx \frac{3}{4}a$ [7,8]. Therefore, It is interesting to note that in this $a \times 2a$ 2D Torus under uniform traffic the average number of hops on X will be twice as many as those on Y. If every X link is 100% busy, Y links will be at most 50% busy and the maximum average link utilization will be 75%.

Definition 2. A Rectangular Twisted Torus (RTT) of size $a \times 2a$ consists of a rectangular array of a rows and $2a$ columns. This topology has $4a \times a$ links. Each node (i,j) is connected to the four neighbor nodes as follows: i. for $j=0$, four neighboring nodes are $((i\pm1) \bmod 2a, 0)$, $(i,1)$, $((i+a) \bmod 2a, a-1)$; ii. for $1 \le j \le a-2$, four neighboring nodes are $((i\pm1) \bmod 2a, j)$, $(i,1)$, $(i, (j\pm1))$); iii. for $j=a-1$, four neighboring nodes are $((i\pm1) \bmod 2a, a-1)$, $(i, a-2)$, $((i+a) \bmod 2a, 0)$.

The diameter k and average distance $\bar{k}$ of a RTT of $a \times 2a$ nodes are: $k=a$; $\bar{k} = \frac{4a^2-1}{3(2a^2-1)} a \approx \frac{2}{3}a$ [4,7]. Thus, adding a twist to $2a$ links in a $a \times 2a$ RTT results in a significant reduction of the diameter and average distance.

Specifically, the diameter is reduced by 33.3% and average distance by 11.1%. Furthermore, a very important property is regained in the RTT: the symmetry in dimensions X and Y. This means that under uniform traffic, both X and Y links can be fully utilized (100%), leading to a 33.3% increase in link utilization with respect to 2D rectangular Torus.

2.2 Topology of RTTM Network

Rectangular Twisted Torus Meshes (RTTM) is a hierarchical interconnection network, which consists of Basic Modules (BM) where the BMs are hierarchically interconnected for higher level networks. RTTM can be constructed by adopting the construction procedure of TESH networks [3]. The BM, also referred to as Level-1 network, consists of a 2D Mesh network, which could be of any size $2^m \times 2^m$ with m being a positive integer. Figure 3 shows a 4×4 BM, for which $m=2$. Successively higher level networks are built by recursively interconnecting $a \times 2a$ next lower level sub-networks in a RTT network. A second level sub-network, for example, can be formed by interconnecting $a \times 2a$ BMs. As shown in Figure 4, each BM is connected to its logically adjacent BMs using 4×8 RTT scheme. Similarly, a third level sub-network can be formed by interconnecting $a \times 2a$ second level sub-networks, and so on. Thus, Level-L is interconnected as a $a \times 2a$ RTT network, where Level-$(L-1)$ is used as subnets of Level-L. We will use the notation (L, a, m)-RTTM to denote a network with L levels in its hierarchy. As seen in Figure 3, all ports of the interior nodes are used for intra-BM interconnection. The exterior nodes have either one or two free ports. These free ports are used for inter-BM interconnections to form higher level networks.

It is useful to note that for each higher level interconnection, a BM must spend 4 of its free links. Since the total number of links available for higher level interconnections is $2^m \times 2^m+4$, the highest possible level L is $L_{max}=(2^m \times 2^m+4)/4=4^{m-1}+1$. For example, the highest possible level is $L_{max}=5$ when $m=2$. Since a (L, a, m)-RTTM has $(a \times 2a)^{(L-1)} \times 2^{2m}$ nodes, the maximum number of nodes which can be interconnected by a RTTM network is $(a \times 2a)^{(L_{max}-1)} \times 2^{2m}$ nodes. RTTM has lower wiring complexity than most other interconnection networks and the same wiring complexity as TESH

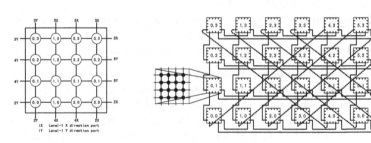

Fig. 2. A 4×4 Basic Module   **Fig. 3.** (2, 4, 2)-RTTM network

network. However, RTTM provides full interconnection of nodes within a BM, but it has less wiring for interconnecting nodes located in different BMs. The rationale for this arises from the principle of locality of computations.

2.3 Properties of RTTM Network

We now compare the (L, a, m)-RTTM with other topologies such as 2D Mesh, 2D Torus [4], RTT [7], TESH. Their topological properties are shown in Table 1. In terms of scalability, all networks except RTT can be easily scaled up by adding additional rows and columns.

(L, a, m)-RTTM has the following characteristics: i. (L, a, m)-RTTM network has smaller diameter and shorter average distance, which implies a reduction of network communication delays; ii. (L, a, m)-RTTM has better capability of fault tolerance, any single faulty link or any single faulty node can be bypassed by only two additional hops as long as the node is neither the source nor the destination for any message.

$$diameter:\ k = 2(2^m - 1) + 2(L-2)a + a \tag{1}$$

$$average\ distance:\ \overline{k} = \frac{\left((2L-3)\sum_{i=1}^{a} i \bullet N_i + 2\sum_{i=1}^{2^{m+1}-2} i \bullet N_i\right)}{\left(2a^2 \bullet (2L-3) - 3\right) + \left(2^{2m+1} - 2\right)} \tag{2}$$

$$= \frac{((2L-3)(2a^2 - 1)\overline{k}_{RTT} + 2(2^{2m} - 1)\overline{k}_{Mesh})}{(2a^2(2L-3) - 3) + (2^{2m+1} - 2)}$$

$$where\ \overline{k}_{RTT} = \frac{4a^2 - 1}{3(2a^2 - 1)},\ \overline{k}_{Mesh} = \frac{k_1 + k_2}{3}$$

3 Routing in RTTM Network

Now, we introduce a routing algorithm which computes the shortest path between any pair of nodes by applying simple operations on their coordinates.

As seen in Fig. 2, nodes in a basic module are addressed by two digits, the first representing the column index and the next representing the row index. More generally, in an L level network, the node address is $A = (a_{2L-1}, a_{2L-2})(a_{2L-3}, a_{2L-4}) \ldots (a_3, a_2)(a_1, a_0)$. Here, the total number of digits is $2L$, and pairs of digits run from pair number L for Level-L, to pair number 1 for the first level, i.e., the BM. Specifically, the i-th pair (a_{2i-1}, a_{2i-2}) indicates the position of the Level-(i-1) sub-network within the i-th level to which the node belongs; $i = 1, \ldots, L$. In a two level network, for example, the address becomes $(a_3, a_2)(a_1, a_0)$. The first pair of digits (a_3, a_2) identifies the BM (that the node belongs to) and the last pair of digits (a_1, a_0) identifies the node within that BM.

Routing of messages in a RTTM network is performed from the top level to the bottom level. That is, it is first done at the highest level network. After the packet reaches its highest level sub-destination, routing continues within the sub-network to the next lower level sub-destination. This process is repeated until the packet arrives at its final destination. When a packet is generated at a source node, the node checks its destination. If the packet is destined to the current BM, routing is performed within the BM only. If the packet is addressed to another BM, the source node sends the packet to the outlet node which connects the BM to the higher level at which routing should be performed. Suppose a packet is to be transported from a source node 000000 to destination node 231121. In this case, we see that routing should first be done at level-3, therefore the source node sends the packet to the level-3 outlet node 000030, whereupon the packet is routed at level-3. After the packet reaches the (2,3) level-2 network, routing within that network is continued until the packet reaches BM (1,1). Finally, the packet is routed to its destination. It is important to note that the links within the RTTM are assumed to be bidirectional full-duplex links. Further, we adopt the convention that the direction of communication of the higher level vertical links is from bottom to top, and for horizontal links it is from left to right.

We use the deterministic strategy: at each level, horizontal routing is performed first. Once the packet reaches the destination column, vertical routing begins. With this strategy, routing can be performed with the help of a routing tag.

The pseudo-code of routing algorithm for a (L, a, m)-RTTM network

```
Routing();
source: S = (s_{2L-1}, s_{2L-2}) (s_{2L-3}, s_{2L-4}) ... (s_3, s_2) (s_1, s_0);
destination: D = (d_{2L-1}, d_{2L-2}) (d_{2L-3}, d_{2L-4}) ... (d_3, d_2) (d_1, d_0);
begin
for i = L down to 2;
DO IN PARALLEL:begin
```

$$
\begin{cases} \Delta x_0 := d_{2i-1} - s_{2i-1}; \\ \Delta y_0 := d_{2i-2} - s_{2i-2}; \end{cases} \begin{cases} \Delta x_1 := d_{2i-1} - s_{2i-1} - a; \\ \Delta y_1 := d_{2i-2} - s_{2i-2} - a; \end{cases} \begin{cases} \Delta x_2 := d_{2i-1} - s_{2i-1} + a; \\ \Delta y_2 := d_{2i-2} - s_{2i-2} - a; \end{cases} \begin{cases} \Delta x_3 := d_{2i-1} - s_{2i-1} + 2a; \\ \Delta y_3 := d_{2i-2} - s_{2i-2}; \end{cases}
$$

$$
\begin{cases} \Delta x_4 := d_{2i-1} - s_{2i-1} - 2a; \\ \Delta y_4 := d_{2i-2} - s_{2i-2}; \end{cases} \begin{cases} \Delta x_5 := d_{2i-1} - s_{2i-1} + a; \\ \Delta y_5 := d_{2i-2} - s_{2i-2} + a; \end{cases} \begin{cases} \Delta x_6 := d_{2i-1} - s_{2i-1} - a; \\ \Delta y_6 := d_{2i-2} - s_{2i-2} - a; \end{cases} \quad \text{end}
$$

```
(t_{2i-1}, t_{2i-2}) := (Δx_j, Δy_j) such that |Δx_j| + |Δy_j| is minimum;
endfor; tag: T = (t_{2L-1}, t_{2L-2}) (t_{2L-3}, t_{2L-4}) ... (t_3, t_2);
for i = 2L-1 down to 2;
    while (t_i ≠ 0) do
        if i is odd, outlet_node_address=horizontal outlet of
        Level-(⌊i/2⌋+1); endif;
        if i is even, outlet_node_address=vertical outlet of
        Level-(⌊i/2⌋+1); endif;
        send packet to next BM; t_i = t_i - 1 mod 2^m;
    endwhile;
endfor; BM_tag (t_1, t_0)= D (d_1, d_0) -receiving node address;
while (t_1 ≠ 0) do
    if t_1 > 0, move packet to right node;   t_1= t_1 - 1; en-
dif;
    if t_1 < 0, move packet to left node;   t_1= t_1 + 1; endif;
endwhile;
while (t_0 ≠ 0) do
    if t_0 > 0, move packet to upper node;   t_0= t_0 - 1; en-
dif;
    if t_0 < 0, move packet to lower node;   t_0= t_0 + 1; en-
dif;
endwhile;
end
```

Table 1. Comparison of topology of 4-degree (where $L \geq 2$, $\lceil \bullet \rceil$ ceiling function)

Topology	Number of Links	Network diameter	Average Distance
2D Mesh $N=k_1 \times k_2$	$2k_1k_2-k_1-k_2$	k_1+k_2-2	$\dfrac{k_1+k_2}{3}$
2D Torus $N=k_1 \times k_2$	$2k_1k_2$	$\left\lceil \dfrac{k_1}{2}\right\rceil+\left\lceil \dfrac{k_2}{2}\right\rceil$	$\left(\dfrac{k_1}{4}+\dfrac{k_2}{4}\right)\dfrac{k_1k_2}{k_1k_2-1}$
RTT $N=a \times 2a$	$4a^2$	a	$\dfrac{4a^2-1}{3(2a^2-1)}$
TESH $N=2^{2mL}$	$2^{2m(L-1)}(2^{2m+1}-2^{m+1})+$ $2^{2m+1}(1-2^{2m(L-1)})/(1-$ $2^{2m})$	$(2L+1)2^m-4$	$\dfrac{(2L-3)(2^{2m+1}-2^m)+12((2^{2m}-1)(2^m-1))}{3((2^{2m}(2L-3)-3)+(2^{2m+1}-2))}$
RTTM $N=(a \times 2a)^{(L-1)} \times 2^{2m}$	$(2a^2)^{L-1}(2^{2m+1}-2^{m+1})+$ $4(1-(2a^2)^{L-1})a^2/(1-$ $2a^2)$	$(2L-3)a+$ $2^{m+2}-4$	$\dfrac{(2L-3)(4a^3-a)+12((2^{2m}-1)(2^m-1))}{3((2a^2(2L-3)-3)+(2^{2m+1}-2))}$

4 Performance Evaluation

Performance evaluation is an important aspect of network design. Two prominent performance parameters are the average latency and the average throughput. In order to probe into the performance of the RTTM network, the structures of RTTM, 2DMesh, 2DTorus were modeled and simulated in this research. The routing algorithm introduced in section 2 was utilized for evaluating RTTM while the X-Y routing algorithm was utilized for evaluating 2D Mesh and 2D Torus. Both the X-Y routing algorithm and the routing algorithm introduced in section 2 are the shortest deterministic routing algorithm, which ensures the fire of these four structures. Four kinds of networks are modeled by OPNET Modeler. By using packet-switched mechanism, every node has an external network interface connecting the Processing Element (PE) with the router node. External PE can be source or information sink based on different conditions of modeling. The datagram generated by a source PE is 64bits, and the traffic rate and destination are configurable. The clock frequency is 1GHz. The proceeding rate of every PE is the same, generated data packets content according to uniform distribution, data links using full-duplex channels.

4.1 Performance Comparisons of Four Kinds of Networks

We simulated and analysed the performance of RTTM, 2D Mesh, 2D Torus and TESH structures in a network of 512 nodes.

The networks generate data streams from source nodes to destination nodes which are chosen according to uniform distribution. when the datagram sending rates are all 80 packets/s, the average latency, average throughput, and average utilization rate of links are shown in figure 4. Figure 4 (a), shows that the network average latency of RTTM is shorter than 2D Mesh、 2D Torus and TESH, and nearly half of the 2D Mesh. Figure 4 (b) shows the average throughput of RTTM structure increases slower than 2D Mesh and 2D Torus in a short time. But, with the increasing period of the simulation, the average throughput of RTTM structure keeps increasing till saturation and tends to stay in a stable state and higher than TESH, while 2D Mesh and 2D Torus decrease sharply to almost zero. The average utilization of links of the RTTM structure (see figure 4 (c)) also increases higher than TESH with the increasing period of simulation. From the foregoing analyses, performances of these four kinds of networks will all be lower as time progresses. But under the same scenarios, performance of RTTM is better than 2D Mesh, 2D Torus and TESH.

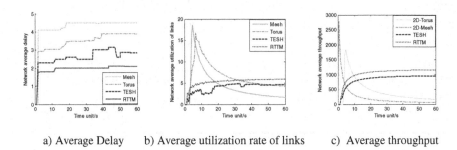

a) Average Delay   b) Average utilization rate of links   c) Average throughput

Fig. 4. Performance comparisons of these three kinds of network

4.2 Performance Comparisons of Same Links in the RTTM

For the same source node and destination node scenario, we simulated and analysed the performance of same links in RTTM by changing datagram sending frequency of every source node in the same clock periods as following.

For the ease of data analysis, the clock period is counted by the seconds, and the simulation lasted 60 seconds. Figure 5 shows the average latency, average utilization and average throughput of the same link with injection rates of 4 packets/s, 8packets/s, 40 packets/s, and 80 packets/s. The higher is the rate of datagram sending, the shorter is the network average latency with the increasing period of simulation (see figure 5 (a)). Figure 5 (b) shows the higher is the rate of datagram sending, the higher is the average utilization rate of links. The average utilization rate of links keeps increasing till saturation and tends to stay in a stable state with the increasing period of simulation. From figure 5 (c), it may be deduced that the rate of datagram

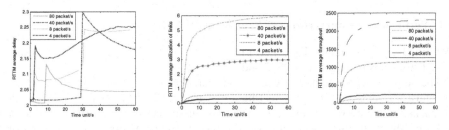

a) Network Average Delay   b) Average utilization rate of links   c) Average throughput

Fig. 5. Comparisons of same links in the RTTM network

transmission is inversely proportional to the average network throughput. Moreover, the average throughput keeps increasing till saturation and tends to stay in a stable state with the increasing period of simulation. Thus it is clear that under the communication of same links, network performance is not only related to topological structure and also related to the rate of sending datagrams.

5 Conclusion

We have presented an interconnection network, called RTTM, suitable for implementing massively parallel systems. The key, attractive features of the proposed network include smaller diameter, shorter average distance and higher average link utilization while it is feasible to interconnect thousands of processors at an adequate performance level. The RTTM network allows for exploitation of computational locality as well as modular future expansion. And, it has a regular structure which makes node addressing and message routing straightforward. These features make the RTTM is a topology suitable for scalable massively parallel system. The communication performance with a real application is under evaluation.

References

1. Wu, R.-Y., Chang, J.G., Chen, G.-H.: Node-disjoint paths in hierarchical hypercube networks. In: 20th International Parallel and Distributed Processing Symposium, April 25-29, p. 5 (2006)
2. Yang, Y., Funahashi, A., Jouraku, A., et al.: Recursive Diagonal Torus: An Interconnection Network for Massively Parallel Computers. IEEE Transactions on Parallel and Distributed Systems 12(7), 701–715 (2001)
3. Vijay, K., Jain, S., Horiguchi, S.: VLSI Considerations for TESH: A New Hierarchical Interconnection Network for 3-D Integration. IEEE Transactions on Very Large Scale Integeration (VLSI) Systems 6(3), 346–353 (1998)
4. Dally, W., Towles, B.: Principles and Practices of Interconnection Networks. Morgan Kaufmann Press, San Francisco (2004)
5. Salminen, E., Kulmala, A., Hamalainen, T.D.: Survey of Network-on-chip Proposals. White Paper, OCP-IP, March, pp. 1–12 (2008)
6. Cvetanovic, Z.: Performance Analysis of the Alpha 21364-based HP GS1280 Multiprocessor. In: Proceedings of the 30th Annual International Symposium on Computer Architecture, pp. 218–228 (2003)
7. Caimara, J.M., Moreto, M., Vallejo, E., et al.: Mixed-radix Twisted Torus Interconnection Networks. IEEE International HYPERLINK, Los Alamitos (2007),
http://ieeexplore.ieee.org/xpl/RecentCon.jsp?punumber=4203121

Benchmarking Parallel I/O Performance for a Large Scale Scientific Application on the TeraGrid

Frank Löffler[1], Jian Tao[1], Gabrielle Allen[1,2], and Erik Schnetter[1,3]

[1] Center for Computation and Technology
[2] Department of Computer Science
[3] Department of Physics and Astronomy,
Louisiana State University, Baton Rouge LA, USA

Abstract. This paper is a report on experiences in benchmarking I/O performance on leading computational facilities on the NSF TeraGrid network with a large scale scientific application. Instead of focusing only on the raw file I/O bandwidth provided by different machine architectures, the I/O performance and scalability of the computational tools and libraries that are used in current production simulations are tested as a whole, however with focus mostly on bulk transfers. It is seen that the I/O performance of our production code scales very well, but is limited by the I/O system itself at some point. This limitation occurs at a low percentage of the computational size of the machines, which shows that at least for the application used for this paper the I/O system can be an important limiting factor in scaling up to the full size of the machine.

1 Introduction

The rapid increase of computational resources available for science and engineering provides a great opportunity as well as a great challenge for computational scientists. Highly efficient and scalable scientific applications that can fully leverage the computational power of the supercomputers are seen to be crucial for new scientific discoveries in many fields, for instance Gamma Ray Burst modeling [14] in astrophysics. Developing and optimizing such large scale scientific applications for current resources benefits from well-defined and standardized benchmarks that can provide a basis for measuring and understanding performance. Such benchmarks also importantly help define and describe the application scenario making it easier to engage computer scientists and HPC consultants in further optimization strategies. Such benchmarks for numerical relativity are being defined through the NSF XiRel project [1, 16].

Many existing benchmarks for HPC systems focus on measuring the performance and scaling of only the compute power provided (e.g. [10]), with only some exceptions (e.g. [13]). However, in practice most production codes also generate large amounts of data output that typically is written to a network filesystem. If this is not done efficiently the performance and scaling of the whole simulation suffers.

W. Zhang et al. (Eds.): HPCA 2009, LNCS 5938, pp. 272–279, 2010.

There are several reasons why large data output is needed. First, analysis and visualization of simulation data typically occurs after the simulation completes, and particularly for 3D-visualization the amount of data which has to be stored for this can already easily reach hundreds of GiB. This type of output can typically be controlled by parameters and it might be possible to reduce the data size by e.g. down-sampling. This is different for the second reason to write large amounts of data. It is common that simulations take many days, even weeks or months to run, even on large and powerful supercomputers. However, the maximum queue walltime is typically on the order of some days at most. This means that the simulation has to have a way to save all the necessary data (*checkpoint*) and then be able to continue later, by reading in these data (*restart*). This paper focuses only on benchmarking I/O using the checkpoint scenario, since it is well-defined and practically unavoidable for large scale scientific applications.

This paper concentrates on understanding the time spent writing such checkpoint files within the typical environment of a production simulation. This does not necessarily aim for the largest possible files or the most optimized use of provided bandwidth, but focuses on the typical use of the facilities by scientists performing production simulations. The Cactus-Carpet computational infrastructure on which our application code is built in introduced in section 2. Section 3 provides details on the Cactus I/O layer. The I/O benchmark specifications and computational resources are described in section 4 and 5 respectively. Finally the benchmark results are provided in section 6 and summarized in 7.

2   Cactus-Carpet Computational Infrastructure

In the Cactus-Carpet computational infrastructure [11, 8, 15, 9] the simulation domain is discretized using high order finite differences on block-structured grids employing a Berger-Oliger block-structured AMR method [7] which provides both efficiency and flexibility. The time integration schemes used are explicit Runge-Kutta methods. The basic recursive Berger-Oliger AMR algorithm is implemented by the Carpet library. The Cactus framework hides the detailed implementation of Carpet from application developers and separates application development from infrastructure development. Time integration is provided by the Method of Lines time integrator.

Cactus is an open source software framework consisting of a central core, the *flesh*, which connects many modules (*thorns* in Cactus terminology) through an extensible interface. Cactus is highly portable and runs on all variants of the Unix operating system as well as the Windows platform. Carpet acts as a driver layer of the Cactus framework providing adaptive mesh refinement, multi-patch capability, as well as memory management, parallelization, and efficient I/O.

3   Cactus I/O Layer

One of the aims of the Cactus computational toolkit is to provide common infrastructure that is needed by scientific simulation codes across different disciplines. This approach emphasizes code reusability, and leads naturally to well constructed interfaces, and well tested and supported software. By providing I/O infrastructure scientists can concentrate more on their science problems and at the same time it creates a de-facto standard which helps to compare or exchange data much more easily. The number of people involved in writing and using such a complex infrastructure is large which makes it necessary to divide it into separate thorns and a clearly specified interface between them.

This paper focuses on one of the typically largest I/O operations: writing checkpoint files. Because these data is usually quite large it is important to choose an appropriate file format. The most used format for this within Cactus is the Hierarchical Data Format, version 5 (HDF5) [12]. It was designed to store and organize large amounts of numerical data, stores these data in binary form and supports compression and parallel reading and writing.

Cactus itself does not include thorns which handle the low-level I/O itself because the flesh does not have access to information describing the actual data structures used to store the grid variables. Because this paper focuses on simulations using the Carpet mesh refinement driver, the thorn which provides the low-level checkpoint routines is provided by the Carpet code: CarpetIOHDF5. This thorn can handle different ways to write checkpoint files. The option which is most often used in production simulations is to write in parallel to one file per MPI process, which is why this setting was chosen for our tests.

4   Benchmark Specifications

These benchmarks have been set up with an emphasis on the I/O operations of a typical production simulation. The chosen configuration evolves a stable Tolman-Oppenheimer-Volkoff (TOV) star together with the underlying relativistic spacetime. The focus of this paper lies primarily on the I/O scaling, which is why we only pick one particular numerical relativity application that uses the CCATIE [5, 4] and Whisky [6, 17] codes. Using another Cactus application is not expected to change the overall I/O scaling much, but will be part of future investigations.

The fluctuation of the I/O results is quite high, because unlike for the CPU scaling runs, the benchmarked part of the system is fundamentally shared among all users. The only way to exclude fluctuations from this error source would be to run on the systems exclusively. Even if this would be easily possible, it would not reflect the typical user environment. Our approach to minimize this error is to perform more than a single checkpoint in one simulation and to perform more than one such simulation for each core count, choosing the fastest of those simulations for the analysis of the results. For this paper each of three identical simulations for each core count wrote ten checkpoint files.

The chosen benchmark saves 151 three-dimensional arrays, 148 of double precision floating point type and 3 of integer type. In addition, various one-dimensional arrays and scalar values are saved, together with the complete set of parameters. The three-dimensional arrays are by far the largest part of the saved data. This amounts to an average size of a checkpoint file per core of

205 MiB to 255 MiB. For the largest simulations using 2048 cores this sums up to about 650 GiB per complete checkpoint and about 6.4 TiB in total (for 10 checkpoints).

5 Computational Resources

The benchmarks were run as specified above on three different clusters which the numerical relativity group at Louisiana State University use for production type simulations: QueenBee (LONI), Ranger (TACC) and Kraken (NICS). QueenBee is about an order of magnitude smaller than the other two clusters, in both the number of CPUs available as also in the size of the I/O system. Especially the effect of the different number of file servers (OSSs, OSTs) is clearly visible in the results.

Table 1. This table shows some specifics of the tested clusters as of May 2009. It can be seen very clearly that Ranger and Kraken are roughly comparable in both the number of cores and the specifics of the I/O system, and that QueenBee is smaller by an order of magnitude. OSS and OST are functional units in Lustre file system, where OSS stands for the object storage server, and OST stands for object storage targets. In a given Lustre file system, more OSSs and OSTs give larger I/O bandwidth.

	QueenBee	Ranger	Kraken
number of nodes	668	3,936	8,256
number of cores per node	8	16	8
total number of cores	5,344	62,976	66,048
peak performance (TFlop/s)	50.7	579.3	608.0
disk size (TiB)	192	1,700	2,400
number of OSSs	4	50	48
number of OSTs	16	300	336
default stripe count	1	4	4
expected peak I/O (GiB/s)	≈0.9	≈25	≈30

All resources used for this paper utilize Lustre [2] as the parallel scratch filesystem. The performance for parallel operations on Lustre is not only limited by the type of used fileservers and the interconnect between them and the compute nodes, but also by the number of used fileservers. Most of the data is stored on one type of Lustre server, the object storage server (OSS). These OSSs have a number of physical devices attached which are used to store the data, the so called object storage targets (OST). Lustre can spread files across a number of those OST in a RAID 0 like fashion, which is called *striping*.

The maximum number of OSTs used to store one file is called *stripe count*. Using this parallel operation can significantly increase performance. A typical setting for the stripe count is 4. The optimal setting of this parameter depends on the number of I/O processes, the size of the files and the specifics of the used cluster. Some important specifics of each cluster can be found in table 1.

The expected peak I/O bandwidth assumes a benchmark specifically designed to maximize the I/O throughput. However, the goal of the benchmarks done for this paper is to measure the total time needed for the whole application to save its state. This also includes the time to structure the data in the right way for I/O and compressing the data for smaller files. This is why it is not expected to reach the expected peak I/O bandwidth of the clusters.

6   Parallel I/O Benchmark Results

The benchmarks have been run from 1 to 2048 cores on Ranger and Kraken and up to 1024 cores on QueenBee (see fig. 1). Higher core counts could not be used on Ranger and Kraken because the application itself shows scaling problems at these sizes. On QueenBee the tests ran to 1024 cores only, since it was apparent from both the theoretical limits and the results for 1024 cores that the available I/O bandwidth is already saturated. Each simulation used the default stripe settings (see table 1). It is important that this amount of data can be written

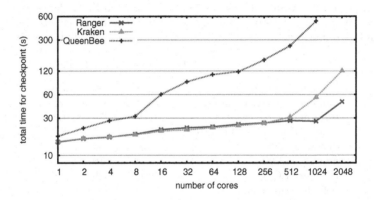

Fig. 1. Plotted is the time which is needed to write one single checkpoint on all cores of the simulation. This time should stay below 10 minutes which is the case for Ranger and Kraken. On QueenBee, this is reached for a simulation using 1024 cores. The almost constant line for Ranger and Kraken for simulations up to 512 cores shows that the I/O system of these systems scales very well up to that point, while the I/O system of QueenBee does not scale well already beginning with 16 cores.

to disk in a time very short compared to the maximum wallclock time, which typically is one or two days. However, this is not the only limitation. The larger supercomputer systems grow, the more they are subject to failure. Even if the maximum walltime is set to more than a day it might be interesting to checkpoint much more often to avoid the risk of loosing a large amount of time of a large simulation. Practically this means that writing a checkpoint should not need more than ≈ 10 minutes.

Figure 2 plots the time which the different systems needed to write a complete set of checkpoint files for a given number of cores writing in parallel. As can be seen, the time for all three systems is well below 10 minutes, except for QueenBee and very large numbers of cores where is comes close already for 1024 cores. However, it is important to keep in mind that 1024 cores are already a substantial part of the QueenBee system, while the same amount of cores is still small for the Ranger and Kraken systems. Figure 2 shows the total average

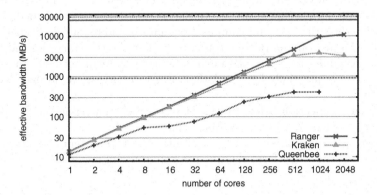

Fig. 2. This shows the total bandwidth of all cores within one simulation, writing to the I/O system in parallel. This is measured as the total written size of the files divided by the time to finish the complete checkpoint and includes application overhead. For each cluster, the expected peak bandwidth is plotted as horizontal line.

bandwidth used during the write of the checkpoint files. The total bandwidth scales linear for Kraken and Ranger up to 512 cores and reaches its maximum on Ranger just above 10 TiB/s. The results on QueenBee seem to be worse, but they are just as good given that the whole system is much smaller than the other two and that the application still reaches about 50% of the expected maximum peak I/O bandwidth without optimizing the benchmark towards that goal. Another difference between the results on Ranger and Kraken on one side and QueenBee on the other side is the deviation from a linear scaling on QueenBee above 16 cores. The reason is here that the results were not measured on an empty system. The I/O system on a cluster is a shared resource and medium size jobs on QueenBee (16 to 64 cores) are still negligible compared to the total size of Ranger or Kraken.

The results obtained so far indicate that the Cactus-Carpet I/O layer scales well for the size of current production runs (256-2048 cores). However, even for this scale of simulation a large percentage of the available I/O bandwidth is used, leading to potential contention for resources for other applications (e.g. on the remaining 58,000 cores of Ranger). The benchmarking team were in close contact with the administrative personnel of all three sites to avoid impact on the work of other users as much as possible, which is of interest to both sides.

Current work in increasing the CPU scaling of our parallel application code to around 16,000 cores for production simulations will require I/O capabilities that are one order larger than achieved in our results. This becomes harder and harder to achieve while retaining an acceptable level of availability. Another possibility would be to find better ways to use a given I/O system on the application level. For example, potential ways to improve on that level include:

- Use downsampling (e.g. write only every second data point) or hyperslabbing (e.g. write data of only a smaller region). This strategy would not however be possible for checkpointing where the complete data set is needed.
- Overlap the write I/O with computation. This would require additional work in the Cactus framework to automatically describe the start and end times in the schedule tree where data can be written and will not be changed.
- Write I/O sequentially for simulations which otherwise would overload the I/O system.
- Tune data collection before writing it to disk, e.g. changing the chunk size which is written to disk in one operation.
- Optimize the use of contented bandwidth, the I/O system could be monitored choosing to perform checkpointing at times of low load.

7   Conclusions

I/O write performance and scalability of a large scale scientific application, which is built upon the Cactus-Carpet computational infrastructure, has been tested on some of the leading computational facilities of the NSF Teragrid and LONI networks. It has been shown that the I/O component of the tested application scales very well but the overall I/O performance is limited by the I/O system itself. For production simulations on Ranger and Kraken which typically use less than 1024 cores no problems are expected in the immediate future, but our infrastructure will need to be improved for larger simulations. For this it will be important to have continuing direct access to system level experts on the relevant machines.

Acknowledgments

This work is supported by the XiRel project via NSF awards 0701566/0653303, the CyberTools project via NSF award 701491, and the NSF Blue Waters project via NSF award 0725070. The development of performance measurement tools in Carpet is supported by the Alpaca project via NSF award 0721915.

This work used the *SimFactory* [3] for job management and the computational resources Kraken at ORNL and Ranger at TACC via the NSF TeraGrid allocation TG-MCA02N014. It also used the computational resources QueenBee at LSU/LONI. Thanks also go to the system level experts at each supercomputer center used for this work for their support and advice: Ariel Martinez, Jr. for QueenBee, Yaakoub El Khamra for Ranger and Heo Junseong for Kraken.

References

[1] XiRel: Next Generation Infrastructure for Numerical Relativity, http://www.cct.lsu.edu/xirel/

[2] The Lustre file system, http://www.lustre.org

[3] SimFactory, http://www.cct.lsu.edu/~eschnett/SimFactory/

[4] Alcubierre, M., Brügmann, B., Diener, P., Koppitz, M., Pollney, D., Seidel, E., Takahashi, R.: Gauge conditions for long-term numerical black hole evolutions without excision. Phys. Rev. D 67, 084023 (2003); eprint gr-qc/0206072

[5] Alcubierre, M., Brügmann, B., Dramlitsch, T., Font, J.A., Papadopoulos, P., Seidel, E., Stergioulas, N., Takahashi, R.: Towards a stable numerical evolution of strongly gravitating systems in general relativity: The conformal treatments. Phys. Rev. D 62, 44034 (2000); eprint gr-qc/0003071

[6] Baiotti, L., Hawke, I., Montero, P.J., Löffler, F., Rezzolla, L., Stergioulas, N., Font, J.A., Seidel, E.: Three-dimensional relativistic simulations of rotating neutron star collapse to a Kerr black hole. Phys. Rev. D 71, 024035 (2005); eprint gr-qc/0403029

[7] Berger, M.J., Oliger, J.: Adaptive mesh refinement for hyperbolic partial differential equations. J. Comput. Phys. 53, 484–512 (1984)

[8] Cactus Computational Toolkit home page, http://www.cactuscode.org/

[9] Mesh Refinement with Carpet, http://www.carpetcode.org/

[10] Dongarra, J., Bunch, J., Moler, C., Stewart, P.: Linpack, http://www.netlib.org/linpack/index.html

[11] Goodale, T., Allen, G., Lanfermann, G., Massó, J., Radke, T., Seidel, E., Shalf, J.: The Cactus framework and toolkit: Design and applications. In: Palma, J.M.L.M., Sousa, A.A., Dongarra, J., Hernández, V. (eds.) VECPAR 2002. LNCS, vol. 2565. Springer, Heidelberg (2003)

[12] Hierarchical Data Format Version 5 (HDF5) Home Page, http://hdf.ncsa.uiuc.edu/HDF5

[13] HPC challenge benchmark, http://icl.cs.utk.edu/hpcc/

[14] Ott, C.D., Schnetter, E., Allen, G., Seidel, E., Tao, J., Zink, B.: A case study for petascale applications in astrophysics: simulating gamma-ray bursts. In: Ott, C.D., Schnetter, E., Allen, G., Seidel, E., Tao, J., Zink, B. (eds.) MG 2008: Proceedings of the 15th ACM Mardi Gras conference, pp. 1–9. ACM, New York (2008)

[15] Schnetter, E., Hawley, S.H., Hawke, I.: Evolutions in 3D numerical relativity using fixed mesh refinement. Class. Quantum Grav. 21(6), 1465–1488 (2004); eprint gr-qc/0310042

[16] Tao, J., Allen, G., Hinder, I., Schnetter, E., Zlochower, Y.: XiRel: Standard Benchmarks for Numerical Relativity Codes Using Cactus and Carpet, Tech. report, Louisiana State University, Baton Rouge, LA 70803 (May 2008)

[17] Whisky, EU Network GR Hydrodynamics Code, http://www.whiskycode.org/

Reliability and Parametric Sensitivity Analysis of Railway Vehicle Bogie Frame Based on Monte-Carlo Numerical Simulation

Yaohui Lu[1,2], Jing Zeng[1], Pingbo Wu[1], Fei Yang[1], and Qinghua Guan[1]

[1] Traction Power State Key Laboratory, Southwest Jiaotong University,
Chengdu 610031, China
[2] School of Mechanical Engineering, Southwest Jiaotong University,
Chengdu 610031, China
yhlu2000@swjtu.edu.cn

Abstract. In order to study the structure reliability more exactly, the probability analysis method, instead of the traditional constant value analysis method, can be applied to overcome the uncertainty problem of the strength model. The reliability of railway vehicle bogie frame is influenced by many factors. In order to ensure the high reliability of bogie frame design, the precondition is found to be the dominating factor. In this paper, the parametric finite element model of bogie frame was established using the probability analysis method. The plate thicknesses, the service loads and material constants of bogie frame were set as the random variables and the distributed parameter values were obtained by statistics. The functions of failure state were established by allowed fatigue strength value and maximum principle stress of parent material or weld location of welded bogie frame. The reliability and parametric sensitivities of the random variables were simulated by Monte Carlo Method. Based on the analysis results, the random variables which are sensitive to the reliability of bogie frame can be controlled and optimized in practice so as to design high reliable bogie frame. The method applied in this paper provided an efficient way to evaluate the reliability and parametric sensitivity of the load bearing structure of high speed trains.

1 Introduction

In the process of designing the bogie frame in China, the method of safety factor which is a constant value method is still adopted to evaluate the strength of structure. In fact, the material characteristics, geometry dimension and loads of the bogie frame have uncertainties after manufacture or during operation. These uncertainties will result in errors in analysis, which causes difference between analysis results and actual events. Required by the national standard GB50153-92 "The uniform standard for designing of engineering structure reliability", the limit state design method based on probability theory which is expressed by partial factors should be used for the design of engineering structure. Probability analysis means that the influence of model input parameters and the supposed uncertainties is analyzed. And to improve the quality

W. Zhang et al. (Eds.): HPCA 2009, LNCS 5938, pp. 280–287, 2010.

and reliability of products, the uncertainties of input parameters can not be eliminated [1]. Therefore, in order to research the effects of uncertainties to the reliability of bogie frame, the probability analysis method instead of the traditional constant value method is utilized.

Monte Carlo method can deal with the structure reliability problem without direct integral. For the complex structure like the bogie frame, it is difficult to give the explicit expression of limit state function. But to use Monte Carlo method with the finite element method, the result of reliability can be obtained. Based on the probability analysis function of the finite element software ANSYS[2,3,4,5], the finite element model of railway vehicle bogie frame is established, in which the shell thickness, loading and material features are regarded as random variables, and the reliability and sensitivity of parameters of bogie frame are investigated.

2 Model Establishment for Bogie Frame

2.1 Finite Element Model

Firstly the solid model using CAD software is set up, and then the model is converted via the data interface of ANSYS and the finite element model is obtained through meshing, in which the element SHELL63 adopted, and the load and boundary conditions applied. The check for the convergence of mesh is conducted through the contrast analysis. The calculation results are convergent when the element size is 20, and the total number of nodes is 75010, the number of elements is 75358. The finite element model and the boundary condition of constraint are shown in Fig1. The spring element at the boundary of bogie frame is also meshed, the total number is 128. The nodes located at the bottom of spring element possess full constraints in order to simulate the actual boundary conditions. The parametric finite element model of bogie frame that takes the real constant of shell as a variable is used to inspect the influence of shell thickness to the bogie frame reliability.

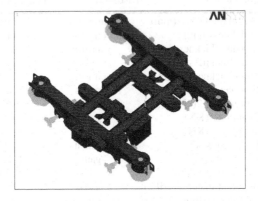

Fig. 1. Finite element model of bogie frame

2.2 Random Variable Selection and Distribution Parameter Determination Finite Element Model

The upper cover, bottom cover and web plate of side beam and the lateral beam of the bogie frame are selected as the investigation objects, and the shell thickness, taken as a random variable, is supposed to obey the uniform distribution. In table 1, the distribution parameter 1 of shell thickness variables represents the lower limit of shell thickness, and the distribution parameter 2 represents the upper limit of shell thickness. It is decided by the machining geometric tolerance for the load random variables. The loads on air spring, lateral bump stop, motor hanger and gear box are selected as investigation objects. Among these variables, the load on lateral bump stop obeys the exponential distribution, and the other variables obey the gauss distribution. For the gauss distribution, the parameter 1 expresses the mean value of load distribution, and the parameter 2 is the standard deviation of load distribution. The load applied refers to the standard UIC615-4[6]. The vertical load on air spring and the load on lateral bump stop are obtained by the statistic processing of dynamic simulation results in actual operating conditions. The mean values for the other loads are obtained by calculations according to the standard, and the standard deviations are 1/10 of mean values. As to the material property of bogie frame, the fatigue strength of parent material and fillet welding and Young's modulus of material are selected as the random variables. These variables obey the Gauss distribution, the parameter 1 indicates the mean value of load distribution, and the parameter 2 is the standard deviation of load distribution. The bogie frame material SMA490 is the same as specified in the standard JISE4207:2004 "railway vehicle bogie frame design general rule". Referring to this standard, the fatigue strength of bogie frame parent material is 155MPa, and the mean value of fatigue strength for fillet welding is 110 MPa, the mean value of Young's modulus is 210GPa, and the standard deviation of the material property is 1/20 of mean value, that are shown in table 1.

Table 1. Bogie frame random variable distribution types and parameters

Name of variables	Distribution type	Parameter 1	Parameter 2
upper cover of side beam thickness (mm)	uniform	11.5	12.5
lateral beam thickness(mm)	uniform	11.5	12.5
bottom cover of side beam thickness(mm)	uniform	15.5	16.5
web plate of side beam thickness 1(mm)	uniform	11.5	12.5
web plate of side beam thickness 2(mm)	uniform	15.5	16.5
the load on motor hanger 1(kN)	gauss	22	2.2
the load on motor hanger 2(kN)	gauss	2.2	2.2
the load on gear box 1(KN)	gauss	40.95	4.095
the load on gear box 2(KN)	gauss	40.95	4.095
the load on lateral stop (kN)	exponent	311.53	311.53
the left load on air spring(kN)	gauss	119.98	26.828
the right load on air spring (kN)	gauss	119.98	26.828
the allowable stress of parent material (MPa)	gauss	155	7.75
the allowable stress of fillet welding (MPa)	gauss	92	4.6
elastic modulus(GPa)	gauss	210	10.5

2.3 Limit State Function

Determination of the limit state function is the premier work for the bogie frame reliability and sensitivity analysis. Assuming the random variables denoted by $x_1, x_2, \cdots, x_n$, that are the main factors influencing the failure of bogie frame. Thus the limit state function of bogie frame can be expressed as:

$$G(x_1, x_2, \cdots, x_n) = [\sigma] - \sigma_{\max} \tag{1}$$

where, $[\sigma]$ indicates the allowable fatigue strength for the bogie frame parent material or fillet welding, and $\sigma_{\max}$ is the calculation stress. Then, we have

$G(x_1, x_2, \cdots, x_n) > 0$: bogie frame safe.

$G(x_1, x_2, \cdots, x_n) < 0$: bogie frame unsafe. $\tag{2}$

$G(x_1, x_2, \cdots, x_n) = 0$: bogie frame on critical state.

When the bogie frame is under normal operating condition, the fatigue strength reliability is mainly affected by the random variables selected in this paper. The limit state function for the fatigue strength reliability of bogie frame is decided by the maximal nominal stress $\sigma_{\max}$ on the parent material or welding joints and the allowable fatigue strength $[\sigma]$. If the maximal stress is smaller than the allowable fatigue strength, the bogie frame is safe, otherwise, is unsafe.

3 Monte Carlo Numerical Simulation

The Monte Carlo method is a random simulation method[2,7], which is based on the theory of probability and the theory of mathematical statistics, and is widely used to deal with the random fatigue problem. This method assures its reliability and accuracy by the central limit theory in the probability theory, and can be used to calculate the probability of failure. The Monte Carlo method has the advantages of good convergence in simulation, no need to linearize the limit state function and to normalize the random variables. Therefore, this method avoids the mathematical difficulties in the reliability analysis, and is the most effective method to deal with the nonlinear problems.

In this paper, the parametric finite element model of bogie frame and the limit state function are established, and the probability problem is analyzed by applying the Probabilistic Design System function of the software ANSYS combined with the Monte Carlo method. Then the reliability of bogie frame is studied and the sensitivity of parameters obtained [7,8,9]. Because the direct Monte Carlo method is based on large number of determinate finite element calculations, it is not practical in use. The larger the structure, the more the calculations. In this paper, the Latin Hypercube Sampling of Monte Carlo method is adopted, which can avoid the repeated sampling. The Latin Hypercube Sampling [10,11] has the ability to reduce the number of simulations needed to obtain reasonable results. In this method, the range of possible values of each random input variable is partitioned into strata, and a value from each stratum is randomly selected as a representative value. The representative values for each random variable are then combined so that each representative value is considered only once in the simulation process. In this way, all possible values of the random variables are represented in the simulation. For a set of random variables like , if correlated, they should be transformed into independent random variables at first by using Nataf transform referring to correlative document[12,13,14]. Then the random value corresponding to the distribution can be acquired for each random variable. The random variables are required to generate a corresponding set of uniformly distributed random values between 0 and 1.

4   Calculation Results of Reliability and Parametric Sensitivity

4.1   Reliability Analysis Results

The deterministic analysis of the bogie frame is carried out in advance to generate the parametric probability files, and then the distribution types of input variables and their distribution parameters are decided. The Monte Carlo Latin hypercube sampling is adopted, and total 1000 samples are taken in the analysis. The dominant factor to guarantee the results reliable is the sampling numbers. The sampling numbers can be judged by the aid of the failure function of random sampling and the trend of the sampling mean. If the sampling converges, the sampling numbers is enough. Fig.2 shows that 1000 sampling numbers is enough for failure functions of the parent material and the welding.

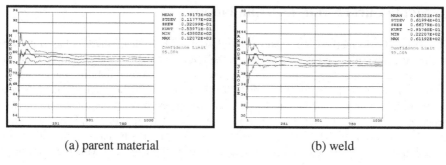

(a) parent material   (b) weld

Fig. 2. Mean value sample trend of failure possibility of bogie frame

The probability results of bogie frame parameters listed in table 2. It is seen that the random distribution of failure function is depended on the distribution type of random variables from the probabilistic results of bogie frame. The random variables are subjected to uniform and Gaussian distributions, except that the variable of the bearing load of lateral bump stop is subjected to exponent distribution. The distribution of sampling results of random variables is the failure function distribution that is subjected to flat Gaussian distribution. It is also known that the distribution type of random variables has significant effects on the results. Thus, the distribution types and parameters should be determined carefully based on experiments. The probability of bogie frame shows that the fatigue strength possesses considerable margin. Therefore, variables should be optimized to lighten the bogie frame on the precondition of allowed reliability.

Table 2. Probability results of response parameters of bogie frame

Name	Parent Material	Weld	Simulation Method
Mean (Average) Value	76.83	40.32	
Standard Deviation	14.04	6.20	Monte Carlo with
Skewness Coefficient	-5.02E-2	6.64E-2	Latin Hypercube Sampling
Kurtosis Coefficient	-6.02E-2	-9.58E-2	Number of Samples = 1000
Minimum Sample Value	31.22	22.21	
Maximum Sample Value	123.13	61.19	
Reliability	1.0	1.0	

NOTE: The confidence bounds are evaluated with a confidence level of 95%.

4.2 Results of Parametric Sensitivity

The calculation results are illustrated in Fig.3. The significant variables that affect the probabilistic sensitivities of parent material and weld seams are listed in Table3 and the insignificant variables listed in Table4. Among the variables that affect the fatigue probability of parent material, some of the bearing loads and the allowed fatigue strength of material are sensitive. For instance, the sensitivity factor of the bearing load of the air spring takes 41.95% of the total sensitivity factor, while that of the parent material fatigue strength possesses 28.48% of the total sensitivity factor. Similarly, the influences of some of the bearing loads and the allowed fatigue strength of weld seam are significant. Among the investigated variables, the sensitivity factors of the bearing load of air spring and the allowed fatigue strength of weld seam take 37.08% and 29.83% of the sensitivity factor. The plate thickness and local load variables have less effects on the probabilistic sensitivities of bogie frame. Therefore, the plate thickness can be optimized in the design period to avoid redundancy. In order to guarantee the probability of bogie frame under operation, the significant influencing factors such as the variables of the parent material and the weld seam fatigue strength should be improved in material selection and weld control process, it is also necessary to take the bearing loads of the air-spring base, the lateral bump-stop and gear box into account to increase the fatigue strength of bogie frame.

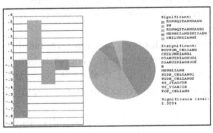
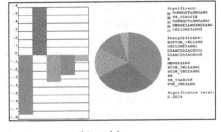

(a) parent material   (b) weld

Fig. 3. Sensitivity plot between all random input variables and a particular random output parameter

Table 3. Random input significant variables for the random output parameter

Variables	Sensitivity Coefficient			
	Parent material		Weld	
left load on air spring	-0.801	41.95%	-0.741	37.08%
allowed stress	0.544	28.48%	0.596	29.83%
right load on air spring	-0.335	17.54%	-0.331	16.54%
load on lateral stop	-0.141	7.36%	-0.252	12.62%
the load on gear box 2	-0.009	4.67%	-0.079	3.93%

Table 4. Random input insignificant variables for the random output parameter

variables	Sensitivity	
	weld	Parent material
bottom cover of side beam thickness	0.024	0.007
the load on gear box 1	0.013	0.047
the load on motor hanger 1	-0.029	-0.016
the load on gear box 2	0.012	0.007
elastic modulus E	-0.007	-0.031
lateral beam thickness	0.037	0.029
web plate of side beam thickness 1	0.037	0.013
web plate of side beam thickness 2	-0.039	0.019
upper cover of side beam thickness	7.26E-4	-3.80E-3

5   Conclusions

The parametric finite element model of bogie frame is setup based on the Monte Carlo numerical simulation method. Taking the plate thickness, material property and operational load as random variables, and giving the distribution types and parameters, the functions of failure state are established by allowed fatigue strength value and maximum principle stress of parent material or weld location of welded bogie frame. The reliability and the parametric sensitivity of the bogie frame are analyzed by the aid of the hybrid simulation of Monte Carlo and FEM with ANSYS. The conclusions are drawn as follows:

(1)   The work of the paper shows that it is feasible to use Monte Carlo method to analyze the probability and parametric sensitivity of complicated structures with many variables which has no explicit failure functions.

(2)   The distribution types and parameters of random variables for probability and parametric sensitivity analysis need considerable experiments. The distribution parameter of load is acquired by statistical treatment according to the UIC standard, and other parameters are based on the practical data from workshop, the distribution types are from the references.

(3)   Based on the analysis results, the random variables which are sensitive to reliability of bogie frame will be controlled and optimized in practice so as to avoid redundant design. In order to ensure the probability of bogie frame under operation, it is necessary to improve the structure material and weld process to increase the al-

lowed fatigue strength; and the influence of the bearing loads of air-spring, lateral bump-stop and gear box must be taken into consideration in design period to improve the fatigue strength of bogie frame.

(4)　The method of probability design instead of traditional design based on certain values provides an efficient way to evaluate reliability and parametric sensitivity of the load bearing structure of high speed train.

Acknowledgement

This research was performed by the supports of the National Basic Research Program of China (973 program) under grant 2007CB714700, the New Century Excellent Talent Foundation (NCET-07-0717) in China and doctoral innovation fund of Southwest Jiaotong University.

References

1. The standard of China GB50153-92: The Uniform Standard for Designing of Engineering Structure Reliability
2. Reh, S., Beley, J.-D., Mukherjee, S., Khor, E.H.: Probabilistic Finite Element Analysis using ANSYS. Structural Safety 28, 17–43 (2006)
3. Wei, W., Yujun, X.: Reliability Analysis on the Head of Blind Plate Based on Ansys. Petro-Chemical Equipment Technology 28(2), 9–10 (2007)
4. Zhen, F., Tao, Y., Pei-Yan, G., Dong, L.: Probabilistic Design of Cylinder Using ANSYS/PDS. Coal Mine Machinery 27(11), 21–23 (2006)
5. Sheng-min, Z.: Structure analysis based on ANSYS. Tsinghua University Press, Beijing (2003)
6. UIC615-4 code, Motive Power Units–Bogies and Running Gear –Bogie Frame Structure Strength Tests. International Union of Railways (2003)
7. Wei, Z.: Structure Reliability Theory and Application. Science Press, Beijing (2008)
8. Haug, E.B.: Mechanical Probability Design. China Machine Press, Beijing (1985)
9. Shi-wei, W.: Structure Reliability Analysis. China Communications Press (1990)
10. Ditlevsen, O., Madsen, H.O.: Structure Reliability Method. Tongji University Press (2006)
11. Nowak, A.S., Collins, K.R.: Reliability of Structures. The McGraw-Hill Companies, Inc., New York (2000)
12. Shipeng, W., Yimin, Z., Yancai, X.: Reliability Sensitivity to the Correlation Coefficients among Variables in Generalized Random Space. China Mechanical Engineering 18, 2782–2785 (2007)
13. Hongni, H., Zhenzhou, L.: Variance Analysis of Line Sampling-based Reliability Sensitivity. China Mechanical Engineering 28, 9–10 (2007)
14. Lu, Z., Song, S., Yue, Z., Wang, J.: Reliability sensitivity method by line sampling. Structural Safety 30, 517–532 (2008)

SVG-Based Interactive Visualization of PSE-Bio

Guoyong Mao[1,2] and Jiang Xie[3]

[1] Department of Electronic Information and Electric Engineering,
Changzhou Institute of Technology, Changzhou 213002
[2] Changzhou Key lab for research and application of software technology,
Changzhou 213002
[3] School of Computer Engineering and Science,
Shanghai University, Shanghai 200072

Abstract. PSE-Bio is a web service-based PSE for bioinformatics. To facilitate users to analyze various service invocation results with the web browser, a uniform visualization data object to encapsulate returned information is designed. SVG is used to implement visualization, and Ajax is adopted to make the visualization results interact with service again directly from the SVG page. The experiment is done in the end to indicate that this solution is suitable for visualization of bioinformatics.

1 Introduction

PSE-Bio is a web service-based PSE (Problem Solving Environment) for bioinformatics [1,2]. There are three layers in PSE-Bio, including GUI Front, Server and LIB, The GUI Front is implemented using JSP, user can submit their tasks from the JSP (Java Server Pages) page and download the result file after the service invocation is finished. Visualization of the result can be implemented by importing the file into CytoScape or some other visualization tools.

Nowadays, web services technology becomes very popular [3]; many biology database providers use it and offer WSDL (Web Service Description Language) files for users to query their database. To enrich the function of PSE-Bio, the LIB of PSE-Bio has been updated into a WSDL-based LIB: it is a virtually distributed library. It consists of many WSDL files, some are for invoking services deployed from self-developed algorithms like INPM [4], some are for invoking services deployed from open-source algorithms like Cap3 and Blast [5,6], and some are for invoking public bioinformatics databases, like Intact and NCBI [7,8]. With these WSDL files, users can also develop their own client applications to invoke remote services. To make PSE-Bio be used and accepted by more and more people, the visualization part is needed to be developed and integrated into PSE-Bio, if visualization can be implemented using the web browser, it will be much convenient for researchers in bioinformatics to use PSE-Bio, as they can submit their jobs, get the results and analyze the results with only the web browser.

With the development of Internet, XML-based graphics have been widely used in Internet visualization. Also, XML is the foundation of grid technology,

W. Zhang et al. (Eds.): HPCA 2009, LNCS 5938, pp. 288–294, 2010.

to make the visualization consistent with the trend of grid, the visualization approach using XML-based technology will be implemented,so as to develop a fully web browser enabled grid PSE for bioinformatics.

2   Visualization Data object

The new version of PSE-Bio contains several Web Service clients to invoke different services; the information returned from the server may be different in formats. For example, NCBI and IntAct are services of message type, the returned information are strings; BioServer service is deployed from INPM algorithm, it is RPC (Remote Procedure Call) type service; the returned information is Java object. To visualize different returned information using the same web browser page, it is needed to convert the return information into the same format.

Let us start by analyzing the returned information. Take IntAct service for an example, if the query string inputted in the JSP page is "brca", the message returned will be as follows:

```
Q8R4X4 (EBI-1639884) EBI-1639774
Q8R4X4(EBI-1639901) EBI-1639774
Q9BXW9-2 (EBI-1639830) P51587
P51587 (EBI-297231) EBI-539895
```

The first item in each line is the name of the start point; the third item in each line is the name of end point. While the item in semicolon is the relation between start point and end point, the formats of returned information in other services are the same. From the above messages we also find out that multiple lines may exit between start point and end point, like Q8R4X4 and EBI-1639774 in line 1 and line 2. Hence, the returned information can be treated as a directed graph with multiple edges between two vertices. So we developed a Java object named *"ReturnInf"* to encapsulate all returned messages, as shown in the following code segment.

```
public class ReturnInf implements java.io.Serializable{
public String[] StartNode; //name of start node
public String[] EdgeName; //name of edge
public String[] EndNode; //name of end node
public int LineNumber; //number of edges
public int NodesNumber; //number of nodes
public String[] NodesName; //name of nodes
public ReturnInf(){}
}
```

The meaning of each variable is commented in the code segment. For the returned message, it is needed to make some conversion before we can put them into data members of *ReturnInf* object. The conversion is simple: the start node, end node and name of each edge can be got by separate each line using space; the number of lines is the number of edges; while the number and name of all nodes can be got if we add all start nodes with end nodes and delete the repeated nodes. Though the *ReturnInf* object is relatively simple, it contains all returned information.

For services deployed from self-developed algorithms or from open-source algorithms, the returned information is just the *ReturnInf* object and no conversion is needed, as it is consistent with java bean criterion, such beans can be used as parameters to invoke services of RPC type, after the service invocation, this bean will be instanced to carry all the returned information.

3   Visualization

3.1   SVG Technology

Nowadays, the visualization tools that can be integrated into web browser mainly include Java3D-based Applet ,SVG (Scalable Vector Graphics) and X3D (extensible 3D) [9,10,11]. For security reasons, the Java3D-based Applet has been abandoned gradually. While SVG and X3D have become the industrial standards recently. SVG is a language for describing 2D graphics and graphical applications in XML.SVG builds upon many other successful standards such as XML (SVG graphics are text-based and thus easy to create), JPEG and PNG (Portable Network Graphic) for image formats, DOM (Document Object Model) for scripting and interactivity, SMIL (Synchronized Multimedia Integration Language) for animation and CSS (Cascade Style Sheet) for styling. SVG has a strong industry support, and many web browsers like Firefox, Opera and IE support it. The visualization result of PSE-Bio is 2D graphics, X3D is another XML-based graphics, but it aims at 3D, so we implement the visualization using SVG.

SVG graphics can be unlimitedly panned and zoomed without any additional work; also content-based image search can be implemented. SVG supports Java Script, there are lots of open source java script resources, Though there may be large number of nodes and edges in visualization graphics of PSE-Bio, it is not a tough job for SVG to implement visualization with its native virtues and powerful scripting and event support.

3.2   Build SVG Graphics

As mentioned in section 2, the final graphics is the directed graph with multiple edges between two nodes. It is not easy to distinguish edges if most of them are located between a few nodes. To display the information of nodes and edges in the graphics correctly, the function of it to zoom, pan and change view is not enough, if function of drag & drop of edges and nodes can be implemented, then the nearly overlapped edges can to dragged apart; Also, As the visualization results can interact with the server again and returned with new nodes and edges, we should be able to add them to the graphics. With this idea, the graph object is designed, as indicated in figure 1.

The graph object can be viewed as a binary tree. The node object and edge object are children of root object, which contains *Addpoint* and *AddLine* methods;

The *X* (*x* coordinates of node), *Y* (*y* coordinate of node), *Label* (label of node), *ID* (id of node) and *Links* (to which the node connects) are children of node object, which contains many methods, including *click, mouseup, mouseover, Links.push* (new node connects to current node) and *draglinks* (drag the connected edges); The *Start* (start point of node), *End* (end point of node) and *Name* (name of edge) are children of the edge object, which contains many methods, including *exist*(if the edge exists),*same*(name of two edges are the same), *overlap*(two edges with the same start point and end point but have different names) and *makeline*(build edges). From the information in *ReturnInf* object, the key step of build the final graphics is shown below.

1. Layout all the nodes in grid format based on the number of nodes in *ReturnInf* object, get *X* and *Y* coordinates of each node in the grid, and get nodes' name and number directly from *ReturnInf* object.

2. Traverse all edges in *ReturnInf* object to get some information, like if edge exists between two nodes, the overlapped times of one edge, and the start node and end node of each edge; Then use *makeline* method to draw edges, use *Links.push* method to add start node into the link list of end point, and add end node into the link list of start node. If the number of edges between two nodes is bigger than 1, then connect the two nodes with arcs of different radian.

3. Add mouse down property to node object; If the mouse is clicked only, then the information of node will be displayed; if the mouse is pressed down and moved, then drag the node into the location where the mouse is released, all the edges connected to this node will also be dragged.

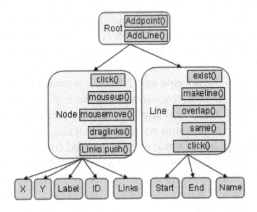

Fig. 1. Design of Graph Object

If the query string "Q8I486" is inputted to invoke IntAct web service, the SVG graphics in the web browser is shown in figure 2.

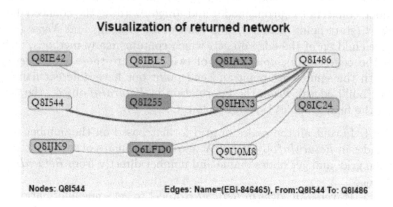

Fig. 2. The visualization graphics

In figure 2, all nodes are arranged in a grid, there are 9 edges from node Q8I486. The edge between node "Q8I544" and "Q8I486" is selected and highlighted; the name of the selected edge "EBI-846465" is displayed in the status message part, which located in the bottom of the graphics.

3.3   Interact with Web Service

For visualization of bioinformatics, the graphics shown above is not enough, as people may still want to find other neighbors of nodes in this graph, so as to expand the graph and find relations between these two graphs. For example, if we still want to find the connected edges of node "EBI-1639774" in figure 2, then we should use "EBI-1639774" as the query string to invoke the service again to expand the graph. Notice that if the service invocation here is redirected to the JSP page again, we can only get a graph related to value "EBI-1639774", we cannot get the expanded graph. It is necessary to invoke web service directly from the SVG page.

Ajax (Asynchronous JavaScript and XML) is a group of interrelated web development techniques used to create interactive web applications or rich Internet applications [12]. With Ajax, web applications can retrieve data from the server asynchronously in the background without interfering with the display and behavior of the existing page. The use of Ajax has led to an increase in interactive animation on web pages. Data is retrieved using the *XMLHttpRequest* object or through the use of Remote Scripting in browsers. JavaScript is supported very well in SVG, so we use Ajax to implement interaction between SVG and web service to update the graphics. The workflow of this interaction is shown in figure 3.

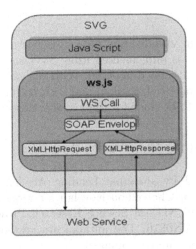

Fig. 3. Interaction between SVG and Web Service

In figure 3, *Ws.js* is the JavaScript, while the kernel of it is the *WS.call* object, which provides method to call web service and responsible for interacting with *XMLHttpRequest* object and handling SOAP response.

After service invocation, the returned information will be analyzed to get new nodes and edges, and then they will be added to the original graph using *Addpoint* and *MakeLine* method.

Actually, we can select every node in figure 3 to invoke IntAct web service; if node named "Q8I544" is selected, the expanded graph is shown in figure 4, we can see that 5 nodes and 5 edges are added to the original graph. The expanded graph is still in grid layout and can still be expanded in the same way. Therefore, this SVG and Ajax-based solution is suitable for visualization of bioinformatics.

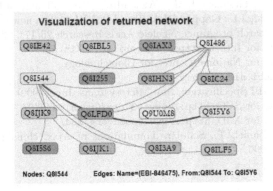

Fig. 4. Visualization result after Intact Web Service is called again

4 Conclusion

In this paper, a uniform visualization data object is designed, the interactive visualization of PSE-Bio is implemented using SVG and Ajax, and related implementation issues are discussed in detail. With the emerging of new web technologies like GWT (Google web toolkit) and with the development of the grid, there is still a lot work to be done for the visualization of PSE-Bio.

Acknowledgement

This work is supported by shanghai Leading Academic Discipline Project, Project Number: J50103, Changzhou Key lab for research and application of software technology, and Natural Science Research Project of Changzhou Institute of Technology: YN0816, The authors are grateful for the anonymous reviewers who made constructive comments.

References

1. Xie, J., Zhang, X.B., Zhang, W.: PSE-Bio: A Grid Enabled Problem Solving Environment for Bioinformatics, e-science. In: Third IEEE International Conference on e-Science and Grid Computing (e-Science 2007), pp. 529–535 (2007)
2. Xie, J., Zhang, Y., Zhang, W., Mao, G., Mei, J.:Studies of Agent Composition Model of PSE-Bio Workflow, escience. In: 2008 Fourth IEEE International Conference on eScience, pp. 743–748 (2008)
3. SOAP and Web Services, http://www-136.ibm.com/developerworks/webservices
4. Xie, J.: Numerical simulation of protein interaction network. Doctoral thesis of shanghai university, ch. 6 (2008)
5. Huang, X., Wang, J., Aluru, S., Yang, S.-P., Hillier, L.: PCAP: A Whole-Genome Assembly Program. Genome Research 13, 2164–2170 (2003)
6. Stephen, F.A., Thomas, L.M., Alejandro, A.S., Zhang, J.H., Zhang, Z., Miller, M., David, J.L.: Gapped BLAST and PSI-BLAST: a new generation of protein database search programs. Nucleic Acids Research 25(17), 3389–3402 (1997)
7. Official website for Intact, http://www.ebi.ac.uk/intact/
8. Official website for National Center for Biotechnology, http://www.ncbi.nlm.nih.giv
9. The Java 3D API Specification, Sun Microsystems, Inc. (2000)
10. Official website for SVG, http://www.w3.org/Graphics/SVG/
11. Official website for X3D, http://www.web3d.org/x3d/
12. Ryan, A., Nathaniel, T., Schutta :Foundations of Ajax. china posts & telecom press, Beijin, 2006

A Modification of Regularized Newton-Type Method for Nonlinear Ill-Posed Problems*

Ze-hong Meng[1], Zhen-yu Zhao[2], and Guo-qiang He[3]

[1] School of Mathematics and Statistics,
Zhejiang University of Finance and Economics, 310018
zehongmeng78@163.com
Tel.: +86-571-8755-7158; Fax: +86-571-8755-7158
[2] College of Science, Guangdong Ocean University, Zhanjiang, 524088
[3] Department of Mathematics, Shanghai University, 200444

Abstract. A Modification of regularized Newton-type method for nonlinear ill-posed problems is considered. Using an *a posteriori* stopping rule proposed by Kaltenbacher, the convergence of the method is proved under certain conditions on the nonlinear operator. Optimal convergence rates are also shown under appropriate closeness and smoothness assumptions on the difference of the starting value and the solution. Some special cases of the method are also given. Numerical results confirm the corresponding theoretical statements.

1 Introduction

In this paper, we consider the following nonlinear ill-posed operator equation

$$F(x) = y, \tag{1}$$

where $F : D(F) \subset \mathcal{X} \mapsto \mathcal{Y}$ is a nonlinear operator between Hilbert spaces $\mathcal{X}$ and $\mathcal{Y}$. We assume throughout that (1) has a (not necessarily unique) solution, which in general does not depend continuously on the right-hand side data y. Since in practice only measured data y^δ with

$$\|y - y^\delta\| \leq \delta \tag{2}$$

are available, where δ is a known error bound, equation (1) becomes

$$F(x) = y^\delta. \tag{3}$$

Because of ill-posedness of (1) and (3), they have to be regularized [1,2].

Presently, variational method and iterative method are the main methods for nonlinear ill-posed problems [1,3]. We all know Newton-type iterative methods for well-posed problems are effective and have been applied with success in many applications. However, only comparatively fewer rigorous theoretical treatments

---

* Project supported by the National Natural Science Foundation of China (No.10871168) and supported by the Education of Zhejiang Province (No.Y200804144).

W. Zhang et al. (Eds.): HPCA 2009, LNCS 5938, pp. 295–304, 2010.

of Newton-type methods for ill-posed problems can be found in the literature(see, e.g, [1,3] and references therein). The aim of this paper is to develop a new regularization method based on a modification of Newton iteration and to analyze its convergence properties.

The paper is arranged as follows. Section 2 gives the new method and some assumptions. Section 3 yields some basic estimates and section 4 is devoted to the convergence and convergence rates analysis of the new method. Section 5 gives the numerical results and finally in section 6, some special cases of the method and remarks are given.

2   Algorithm and Assumptions

Consider the Newton linearization of equation (3) at a current iterate x_n

$$F'(x_n)(x - x_n) = -(F(x_n) - y^\delta), \tag{4}$$

whose solution x can be assumed to be a better approximation than x_n for a solution $x^\dagger$ of (3). Since (4) is usually ill-posed, some regularization technique has to be used. If the Tikhonov regularization is used to solve (4), then we have

$$(A_n^* A_n + \alpha_n I)(x - x_n) = A_n^*(y^\delta - F(x_n)), \tag{5}$$

where $A_n = F'(x_n)$ and parameters $\alpha_n > 0$. If the Samanskii idea of combining one Newton iteration with several other simplified Newton iterations is used in the solution process([4],also see[5]), (5) becomes

$$\begin{cases} x_{n,k+1} = x_{n,k} + (A_n^* A_n + \alpha_n I)^{-1} A_n^*(y^\delta - F(x_{n,k})), \ 0 \le k < k_n, \\ x_{n,0} \text{ given}, \ x_{n+1} = x_{n,k_n}. \end{cases} \tag{6}$$

If $F(x_{n,k})$ is replaced by its first-order expansion $F(x_n) + F'(x_n)(x_{n,k} - x_n)$, iteration (6) can be simplified further and we derive the following algorithm.
   Method 1
$$\begin{cases} x_{n,k+1} = x_{n,k} - (A_n^* A_n + \alpha_n I)^{-1} A_n^*(F(x_n) - y^\delta + A_n(x_{n,k} - x_n)), \ \ 0 \le k < k_n \\ x_{n,0} = x_0, \ x_{n+1} = x_{n,k_n} \end{cases}$$

Although it seems to be more natural to take $x_{n,0} = x_n$ in the process, it is not clear how to prove convergence rates for the resulting method. The parameters α_n and the inner iteration steps k_n in method 1 are taken to satisfy

$$0 < q \le \frac{\alpha_{n+1}/k_{n+1}}{\alpha_n/k_n} \le 1, \quad \lim_{n \to \infty} \frac{\alpha_n}{k_n} = 0. \tag{7}$$

It is not difficult to show method 1 is equivalent to

$$x_{n+1} = x_0 - g_{k_n}(A_n^* A_n) A_n^*(F(x_n) - y^\delta - A_n(x_n - x_0)) \tag{8}$$

with

$$g_k(\lambda) = \frac{1}{\lambda}(1 - \alpha_n^k(\lambda + \alpha_n)^{-k}).$$

To analyze the convergence and convergence rates for the approximation solutions of any numerical method for ill-posed problems, an important assumption is the source conditions on the difference between an initial estimate x_0 and an unknown solution $x^\dagger$[1,3,6]. In the nonlinear situation it has the form

$$x_0 - x^\dagger = (F'(x^\dagger)^* F'(x^\dagger))^\nu w, \quad w \in \mathcal{N}(F'(x^\dagger))^\perp \tag{9}$$

with $\nu \geq 0(\mathcal{N}$ denotes the nullspace of an operator). This condition usually can be interpreted as smooth condition. Assume the initial guess x_0 and $x^\dagger$ is sufficiently close:

$$x^\dagger \in \mathcal{B}_\rho(x_0) := \{x \in \mathcal{X} \mid \|x - x_0\| \leq \rho\}. \tag{10}$$

And an assumption on F' which will be used in the convergence analysis of the paper is[1,3,6]

$$\begin{aligned} F'(\bar{x}) &= R(\bar{x}, x)F'(x) + Q(\bar{x}, x), \\ \|I - R(\bar{x}, x)\| &\leq C_R, \qquad\qquad \bar{x}, x \in \mathcal{B}_{2\rho}(x_0). \\ \|Q(\bar{x}, x)\| &\leq C_Q\|F'(x^\dagger)(\bar{x} - x)\|, \end{aligned} \tag{11}$$

The following estimate can be derived by (10) and (11)

$$\|F(x) - F(x^\dagger) - F'(x^\dagger)(x - x^\dagger)\| \leq \zeta\|F'(x^\dagger)(x - x^\dagger)\|, \quad x \in \mathcal{B}_\rho(x_0) \tag{12}$$

with $\zeta = C_R + \rho C_Q$.

We stop the outer iteration by using an a *posteriori* stopping rule proposed by Kaltenbacher [6]

$$\max\{\|F(x_{N-1}) - y^\delta\|, \hat{v}_N\} \leq \tau\delta < \max\{\|F(x_{n-1}) - y^\delta\|, \hat{v}_n\}, \quad 0 \leq n < N, \tag{13}$$

which is a modification of Morozov's discrepancy prinsiple. In (13), $\tau > 1$ and

$$\begin{aligned} \hat{v}_n &:= \|r_{k_{n-1}}(A_{n-1}A_{n-1}^*)(F(x_{n-1}) - y^\delta + A_{n-1}(x_0 - x_{n-1}))\| \\ &= \|F(x_{n-1}) - y^\delta + A_{n-1}(x_n - x_{n-1})\| \end{aligned} \tag{14}$$

with

$$r_k(\lambda) = 1 - \lambda g_k(\lambda) = \alpha_n^k(\lambda + \alpha_n)^{-k}.$$

3   Basic Estimates

Notate $A = F'(x^\dagger)$, $e_n = x_n - x^\dagger$. From [6], we know the stopping rule (13) is equivalent to the stopping rule

$$\max\{\|F(x_{N-1}) - y^\delta\|, \|F(x_N) - y^\delta\|\} \leq \tilde{\tau}\delta < \max\{\|F(x_{n-1}) - y^\delta\|,$$

$$\|F(x_n) - y^\delta\|\}, \ 0 \leq n < N, \tag{15}$$

where $\tilde{\tau} > 1$.

Lemma 1. The following conclusions about $g_k(\lambda)$ and $r_k(\lambda)$ hold:

i) for all nonnegative integer k, g_k is continuous with respect to λ, and for fixed $\lambda > 0$, $g_k(\lambda)$ converges to $\frac{1}{\lambda}$ as $k \to \infty$;

ii) $\sup_{\lambda>0} |\sqrt{\lambda} g_k(\lambda)| \le (\frac{k}{\alpha_n})^{\frac{1}{2}}$, $\forall k$, $\alpha_n > 0$;

iii) for fixed $\nu \ge 0$ and any $k, \alpha_n > 0$, $\sup_{\lambda \in [0,\bar{\lambda}]} |r_k(\lambda)\lambda^\nu| \le c_0(\frac{\alpha_n}{k})^\nu$, where

$$c_0 = c_0(\nu) = c_0(k,\nu;\bar{\lambda}) = \begin{cases} \nu^\nu \bar{\lambda}^{(k-\nu)}, & \text{if } k \le \nu, \\ \nu^\nu, & \text{if } k > \nu. \end{cases}$$

The verification of the lemma is trivial. By virtue of the spectral theory, Hölder inequality and lemma 1, for any selfadjoint positive semidefinite linear operator A, we have

$$|g_k(A)\sqrt{A}| \le (\frac{k}{\alpha_n})^{\frac{1}{2}}, \quad \forall k, \ \alpha_n > 0. \tag{16}$$

Lemma 2. Assume B_1, $B_2 \in L(\mathcal{X}, \mathcal{Y})$. Then for all nonnegative integer k, there exists some constant $\bar{d}$ such that

$$\|B_1(r_k(B_2^* B_2) - r_k(B_1^* B_1))\| \le \bar{d}\|B_1 - B_2\|;$$

$$\|r_k(B_2^* B_2) - r_k(B_1^* B_1)\| \le \bar{d}(\frac{k}{\alpha_n})^{\frac{1}{2}}\|B_1 - B_2\|. \tag{17}$$

Lemma 3. [6]   Assume $B \in L(\mathcal{X}, \mathcal{Y})$, $R \in L(\mathcal{Y}, \mathcal{Y})$ with $\|I - R\| < 1$. Then for any $\nu \in [0, \frac{1}{2}]$

$$\|((B^* R^* RB)^\nu)^\dagger (B^* B)^\nu\| \le \left(\frac{1}{1 - \|I - R\|}\right)^{2\nu}.$$

Lemma 4. For any $B \in L(\mathcal{X}, \mathcal{Y})$, $R \in L(\mathcal{Y}, \mathcal{Y})$ with $\|I - R\| < 1$, we have

$$\|RBr_k(B^* R^* RB)(B^* B)^\nu\| \le \tilde{r}(\frac{\alpha_n}{k})^{(\nu+\frac{1}{2})}, \quad k \in \mathbb{N}, \tag{18}$$

where $\tilde{r} = \bar{r}\left(\frac{1}{1-\|I-R\|}\right)^{2\nu}$ with $\bar{r} = c_0(k,\nu; \|RB\|^2)$.

Lemma 5.   Assume $x_n \in \mathcal{B}_\rho(x^\dagger)$ and (2), (11) hold. Then

$$\|F(x_n) - y^\delta - A_n e_n\| \le C_T \|A e_n\| + \delta \tag{19}$$

with $C_T = C_R(1 + C_R + \rho C_Q) + \frac{1}{2}\rho C_Q$.

Lemma 6.   Let N be determined by the stopping rule (13), $n < N - 1$ and $x_n \in \mathcal{B}_\rho(x^\dagger)$. Assume (2), (10) and (11) with $C_R < 1$ hold. Then

$$\delta \le c_1\|A e_n\| + c_2 v_{n+1} \tag{20}$$

with

$$c_1 = \max\{\frac{1 + C_R + \frac{1}{2}\rho C_Q}{\tau - 1}, \frac{C_T + \rho C_Q}{\tau - 1}\},$$

$$c_2 = \frac{1 + C_R}{\tau - 1}, \quad v_{n+1} = \|A r_{k_n}(A_n^* A_n)(x_0 - x^\dagger)\|. \tag{21}$$

4   Convergence Analysis

Lemma 7 [8]. Assume $\{\gamma_n\}$ is a sequence satisfying $0 \leq \gamma_{n+1} \leq a_n + b\gamma_n + c\gamma_n^2$, $n \in \mathbb{N}$, $\gamma_0 \geq 0$, here $b \geq 0$, $c \geq 0$ and $\{a_n\}$ satisfy $0 \leq a_n \leq a$, $\lim_{n \to \infty} a_n = \hat{a} \leq a$. Let $\underline{\gamma}$ and $\overline{\gamma}$ be defined as

$$\underline{\gamma} := \frac{2a}{1 - b + \sqrt{(1-b)^2 - 4ac}}, \quad \overline{\gamma} := \frac{1 - b + \sqrt{(1-b)^2 - 4ac}}{2c}.$$

If $b + 2\sqrt{ac} < 1$ and $\gamma_0 \leq \overline{\gamma}$, then $\gamma_n \leq \max\{\gamma_0, \underline{\gamma}\}$, $n \in \mathbb{N}$. If $\hat{a} < a$, then

$$\limsup_{n \to \infty} \gamma_n \leq \hat{\gamma} = \frac{2\hat{a}}{1 - b + \sqrt{(1-b)^2 - 4ac}}.$$

The following is one of the main results of the paper.

Theorem 1. Assume (2), (10), (11) hold, and (9) holds for $0 \leq \nu \leq \frac{1}{2}$. Let the iteration sequence $\{x_n\}$ be defined by method 1 with real sequences $\{k_n\}$ and $\{\alpha_n\}$ fulfilling (7). Moreover, let $\|x_0 - x^\dagger\|$, $\|w\|$, C_R be sufficiently small and τ be sufficiently large. Let $N = N(\delta)$ be chosen by (13). Then

$$\|x_{N(\delta)} - x^\dagger\| = O(\delta^{\frac{2\nu}{2\nu+1}}).$$

Proof. The proof consists of three steps.

(i) Assume $x_n \in \mathcal{B}_\rho(x^\dagger)$ as $n < N - 1$. With the notation

$$\tilde{A}_n = R(x_n, x^\dagger)A, \quad \tilde{v}_{n+1} := \|\tilde{A}_n r_{k_n}(\tilde{A}_n^* \tilde{A}_n)(x_0 - x^\dagger)\|, \tag{22}$$

we get by (18) that

$$\|\tilde{v}_{n+1}\| \leq \tilde{r}(\frac{\alpha_n}{k_n})^{(\nu + \frac{1}{2})}\|w\|. \tag{23}$$

By (17), we derive

$$\begin{aligned}|v_{n+1} - \tilde{v}_{n+1}| &\leq \|A r_{k_n}(A_n^* A_n)(x_0 - x^\dagger) - \tilde{A}_n r_{k_n}(\tilde{A}_n^* \tilde{A}_n)(x_0 - x^\dagger)\| \\ &\leq \|(I - R(x_n, x^\dagger))A r_{k_n}(A_n^* A_n)(x_0 - x^\dagger)\| + \\ &\quad \|\tilde{A}_n[r_{k_n}(A_n^* A_n) - r_{k_n}(\tilde{A}_n^* \tilde{A}_n)](x_0 - x^\dagger)\| \\ &\leq C_R v_{n+1} + \bar{d} C_Q \|x_0 - x^\dagger\|\|A e_n\|.\end{aligned} \tag{24}$$

Hence,

$$\begin{aligned}v_{n+1} &\leq \frac{1}{1 - C_R}\tilde{v}_{n+1} + \frac{\bar{d} C_Q \|x_0 - x^\dagger\|}{1 - C_R}\|A e_n\| \\ &\leq \frac{1}{1 - C_R}\tilde{r}(\frac{\alpha_n}{k_n})^{(\nu + \frac{1}{2})}\|w\| + \frac{\bar{d} C_Q \|x_0 - x^\dagger\|}{1 - C_R}\|A e_n\|.\end{aligned} \tag{25}$$

And by (20), (23), (25) we derive

$$\delta \leq (c_1 + c_2 \frac{\bar{d} C_Q \|x_0 - x^\dagger\|}{1 - C_R})\|A e_n\| + c_2 \frac{\tilde{r}\|w\|}{1 - C_R}(\frac{\alpha_n}{k_n})^{(\nu + \frac{1}{2})}. \tag{26}$$

Rewrite the iteration error e_{n+1} as

$$e_{n+1} = r_{k_n}(A_n^*A_n)(x_0 - x^\dagger) - g_{k_n}(A_n^*A_n)A_n^*(F(x_n) - y^\delta - A_n(x_n - x^\dagger)). \quad (27)$$

With $R_n = R(x_n, x^\dagger)$, $Q_n = Q(x_n, x^\dagger) = A_n - \tilde{A}_n$, we obtain by (11) and (27) that

$$\begin{aligned}
R_n A e_{n+1} = &\ \tilde{A}_n r_{k_n}(\tilde{A}_n^*\tilde{A}_n)(x_0 - x^\dagger) + \tilde{A}_n[r_{k_n}(A_n^*A_n) - r_{k_n}(\tilde{A}_n^*\tilde{A}_n)](x_0 - x^\dagger) \\
&- A_n g_{k_n}(A_n^*A_n)A_n^*(F(x_n) - y^\delta - A_n(x_n - x^\dagger)) \\
&+ Q_n g_{k_n}(A_n^*A_n)A_n^*(F(x_n) - y^\delta - A_n(x_n - x^\dagger)).
\end{aligned}$$

Therefore, by (11), (16), (17), (19) and (23),

$$\|Ae_{n+1}\| \leq \frac{1}{1 - C_R}\|R_n A e_{n+1}\| \leq \frac{1}{1 - C_R}[\tilde{r}(\frac{k_n}{\alpha_n})^{-(\nu+\frac{1}{2})}\|w\| +$$

$$\bar{d}\|x_0 - x^\dagger\|C_Q\|Ae_n\| + (C_T\|Ae_n\| + \delta) + C_Q\|Ae_n\|(\frac{k_n}{\alpha_n})^{\frac{1}{2}}(C_T\|Ae_n\| + \delta)].$$

Hence with the notation $\gamma_n^\delta := \|Ae_n\|(\frac{k_n}{\alpha_n})^{(\nu+\frac{1}{2})}$, (26) and the above estimate yield

$$\gamma_{n+1}^\delta \leq a + b\gamma_n^\delta + c(\gamma_n^\delta)^2, \quad n < N - 1, \quad (28)$$

where

$$a = q^{-(\nu+\frac{1}{2})}\frac{\tilde{r}\|w\|}{1 - C_R}(1 + \frac{c_2}{1 - C_R}),$$

$$b = q^{-(\nu+\frac{1}{2})}\frac{1}{1 - C_R}[\bar{d}\|x_0 - x^\dagger\|C_Q + (C_T + c_1 + c_2\frac{\bar{d}C_Q\|x_0 - x^\dagger\|}{1 - C_R})$$

$$+ C_Q c_2(\frac{k_0}{\alpha_0})^{-\nu}\tilde{r}\frac{\|w\|}{1 - C_R}],$$

$$c = q^{-(\nu+\frac{1}{2})}\frac{1}{1 - C_R}C_Q(\frac{k_0}{\alpha_0})^{-\nu}(C_T + c_1 + c_2\frac{\bar{d}C_Q\|x_0 - x^\dagger\|}{1 - C_R}).$$

(ii) Assume $\|x_0 - x^\dagger\|$, $\|w\|$, C_R and $\frac{1}{\tau}$ are sufficiently small such that

$$b + 2\sqrt{ac} < 1, \quad \|F'(x^\dagger)(x_0 - x^\dagger)\|(\frac{k_0}{\alpha_0})^{\nu+\frac{1}{2}} \leq \frac{1 - b + \sqrt{(1 - b)^2 - 4ac}}{2c}, \quad (29)$$

$$C_\theta = \max\{\|F'(x^\dagger)(x_0 - x^\dagger)\|(\frac{k_0}{\alpha_0})^{\nu+\frac{1}{2}}, \frac{2a}{1 - b + \sqrt{(1 - b)^2 - 4ac}}\}, \quad (30)$$

$$\|x_0 - x^\dagger\| + (\frac{k_0}{\alpha_0})^{-\nu}[C_\theta(C_T + c_1 + c_2\frac{\bar{d}C_Q\|x_0 - x^\dagger\|}{1 - C_R}) + c_2\frac{\tilde{r}\|w\|}{1 - C_R}] \leq \rho. \quad (31)$$

By lemma 7 and (29)-(30), we obtain

$$\|Ae_n\| \le C_\theta (\frac{k_n}{\alpha_n})^{-(\nu+\frac{1}{2})}, \ 0 \le n \le N. \tag{32}$$

And (26) and (32) yield

$$\delta \le C(\frac{k_n}{\alpha_n})^{-(\nu+\frac{1}{2})}, \qquad \text{for } n < N, \tag{33}$$

where C is a constant. With (16), (19) and (26),(27) yields

$$\|e_{n+1}\| \le \|x_0 - x^\dagger\| + (\frac{k_n}{\alpha_n})^{\frac{1}{2}} \left[(C_T + c_1 + c_2 \frac{\bar{d}C_Q \|x_0 - x^\dagger\|}{1 - C_R}) \|Ae_n\| \right]$$

$$\left[+c_2 \frac{\tilde{r}\|w\|}{1 - C_R} (\frac{k_n}{\alpha_n})^{-(\nu+\frac{1}{2})} \right].$$

Then by (31)and (32) , we derive that

$$x_{n+1} \in \mathcal{B}_\rho(x^\dagger), \ 0 \le n < N.$$

(iii) Since $\|F(x_{N-1}) - y^\delta\| \ge \|Ae_{N-1}\| - \|F(x_{N-1}) - F(x^\dagger) - Ae_{N-1}\| - \delta$, (13) with (12) implies

$$\|Ae_{N-1}\| \le \frac{(\tau+1)\delta}{1 - (C_R + \rho C_Q)}. \tag{34}$$

And hence (34) and (13) yield

$$v_N \le \frac{1}{1 - C_R} \left(\tau + (C_T + \rho C_Q) \frac{\tau+1}{1 - (C_R + \rho C_Q)} + 1 \right) \delta. \tag{35}$$

On the other hand, by Hölder inequality and lemma 3, we derive

$$\|r_{k_n}(\tilde{A}_n^* \tilde{A}_n)(x_0 - x^\dagger)\| = \|(\tilde{A}_n^* \tilde{A}_n)^\nu r_{k_n}(\tilde{A}_n^* \tilde{A}_n)((\tilde{A}_n^* \tilde{A}_n)^\nu)^\dagger (A^*A)^\nu w\|$$
$$\le \|r_{k_n}(\tilde{A}_n^* \tilde{A}_n)((\tilde{A}_n^* \tilde{A}_n)^\nu)^\dagger (A^*A)^\nu w\|^{\frac{1}{2\nu+1}}$$
$$\|(\tilde{A}_n^* \tilde{A}_n)^{\nu+\frac{1}{2}} r_{k_n}(\tilde{A}_n^* \tilde{A}_n)((\tilde{A}_n^* \tilde{A}_n)^\nu)^\dagger (A^*A)^\nu w\|^{\frac{2\nu}{2\nu+1}} \tag{36}$$
$$\le ((\frac{1}{1 - C_R})^{2\nu} \tilde{r}\|w\|)^{\frac{1}{2\nu+1}} \tilde{v}_{n+1}^{\frac{2\nu}{2\nu+1}}.$$

Now from the error representation (27) and (11), (16)-(17),(19), (24), (33)-(36),we can derive

$$\|x_N - x^\dagger\| = \|r_{k_{N-1}}(\tilde{A}_{N-1}^* \tilde{A}_{N-1})(x_0 - x^\dagger)$$
$$+ \left[r_{k_{N-1}}(A_{N-1}^* A_{N-1}) - r_{k_{N-1}}(\tilde{A}_{N-1}^* \tilde{A}_{N-1}) \right] (x_0 - x^\dagger)$$
$$- g_{k_{N-1}}(A_{N-1}^* A_{N-1})A_{N-1}^* (F(x_{N-1}) - y^\delta - A_{N-1}(x_{N-1} - x^\dagger))\|$$
$$\le \left((\frac{1}{1 - C_R})^{2\nu} \|w\| \right)^{\frac{1}{2\nu+1}} \tilde{v}_N^{\frac{2\nu}{2\nu+1}} + \bar{d}\|x_0 - x^\dagger\|(\frac{k_{N-1}}{\alpha_{N-1}})^{\frac{1}{2}} C_Q \|Ae_{N-1}\|$$
$$+ (\frac{k_{N-1}}{\alpha_{N-1}})^{\frac{1}{2}} (C_T \|Ae_{N-1}\| + \delta)$$
$$\le M_1 \delta^{\frac{2\nu}{2\nu+1}} + M_2 (\frac{M_3}{\delta})^{\frac{1}{2\nu+1}} \delta,$$

where M_1, M_2, M_3 are constants independent of δ. Then the assertion is proved.

The next theorem will give the convergence for the case of $\nu = 0$.

Theorem 2. Assume (2) (11) (10) and $x_0 - x^\dagger \in \mathcal{N}(F'(x^\dagger))^\perp$. Let the iterates $\{x_n\}$ be defined by method 1 with real sequences $\{k_n\}$ and $\{\alpha_n\}$ satisfying (7). Assume $\|x_0 - x^\dagger\|$, $\|w\|$, C_R are sufficiently small and τ is sufficiently large, and $N = N(\delta)$ is determined by (13). Then

$$\|x_{N(\delta)} - x^\dagger\| \to 0, \quad \text{as } \delta \to 0.$$

5   Numerical Results

Example 1. Consider the problem of identifying the coefficient c in the one-dimensional elliptic equation

$$\begin{cases} -u_{xx} + cu = 0, & x \in [0,1], \\ u(0) = 2, \; u(1) = 2e^1, \end{cases}$$

from measurements u^δ with $\|u^\delta - u^\dagger\|_{L_2} \le \delta$.

We will consider the following example $u^\dagger = 2e^x$, $c^\dagger = 1$. In the computation, the perturbed data is taken as

$$u^\delta = u^\dagger + \delta\sqrt{2}\cos(10\pi x)$$

with $\|u^\delta - u^\dagger\|_{L_2} = \delta$. The outer stopping rule is (15). In the computation, $k_n = [1.1^n]$, $\alpha_n = \alpha_0(\frac{1}{2})^n$ with $\alpha_0 = 0.1$ and $\frac{\alpha_{n+1}/k_{n+1}}{\alpha_n/k_n} \approx \frac{1}{2.2}$.

The problem is solved by finite difference schemes on $[0,1]$. Table 1 shows the iteration errors of the iteration c_n with $\delta = 0$ and $c_0 = 1 + 4x(1 - x)$. The local convergence is in fact the one predicted in the theoretical results of Sec.4, namely $O((\sqrt{\frac{k_n}{\alpha_n}})^{-1})$ (third column), but obviously slower than $O((\frac{k_n}{\alpha_n})^{-1})$ (fourth column).

We take the initial value $c_{0(\delta)} = 1 + 4x(1-x)$ with $\nu = \frac{1}{2}$ in table 2. In table 2, we have listed the stopping indices (second column), the errors (third column) and the numerical rates (forth column) of the regularized solutions generated by the method 1 with stopping rule (15) $\tilde{\tau} = 2.5$. Moreover we compared the stopping index N to the estimate $O(\log_{2.2}^{(\frac{1}{\delta})})$ in the last column. The results seem to approximately confirm the corresponding theoretical statements - especially the convergence rates $\|c_{N(\delta)} - c^\dagger\| = O(\delta^{\frac{1}{2}})$.

6   Some Specific Algorithms and Remarks

The results obtained in the previous sections show that not single α_n or k_n but the ratio $\frac{\alpha_n}{k_n}$ plays the role of the regularization parameter for method 1. Therefore, different choices of α_n and k_n yield different specific regularized Newton type algorithms. Below are some examples,

Method 2. Newton-Tikhonov method. When $k_n = 1$, $\forall n \in \mathbb{N}$, and $\{\alpha_n\}$ satisfies

$$0 < q \le \frac{\alpha_{n+1}}{\alpha_n} \le 1, \quad \lim_{n \to \infty} \alpha_n = 0, \tag{37}$$

Table 1. $(\delta = 0)$

n	$\|c_n - c^\dagger\|$	$\|c_n - c^\dagger\|\sqrt{\frac{1.1^n}{0.5^n}}$	$\|c_n - c^\dagger\|\frac{1.1^n}{0.5^n}$
1	0.29204	0.43316	0.64248
5	0.06254	0.44899	3.22328
10	0.00392	0.20177	10.3987
15	2.18e-4	0.08060	29.8216
20	2.07e-4	0.05511	146.377
25	2.00e-4	0.38181	7280.06

Table 2. $(c_{0(\delta)} = 1 + 4x(1-x))$

δ	$N(\delta)$	$\|c_{N(\delta)} - c^\dagger\|$	$\frac{\|c_{N(\delta)} - c^\dagger\|}{\sqrt{\delta}}$	$\frac{N(\delta)}{-\log_{2.2}^{(\delta)}}$
1.0e-2	5	0.06560	0.65602	0.85606
5.0e-3	6	0.04569	0.64617	0.89288
1.0e-4	9	0.00318	0.31821	0.77045
5.0e-5	10	0.00529	0.74810	0.79614
1.0e-6	14	4.38e-4	0.43847	0.79899
5.0e-7	15	2.04e-4	0.28882	0.81516
1.0e-7	16	1.17e-4	0.36857	0.78268
1.0e-8	19	2.40e-5	0.23953	0.81325

method 1 becomes

$$x_{n+1} = x_0 - (A_n^* A_n + \alpha_n I)^{-1} A_n^* (F(x_n) - y^\delta + A_n(x_0 - x_n)), \quad n \geq 0. \quad (38)$$

Method 3. Newton-iterative Tikhonov method. When $k_n = m > 1$, $\forall n \in \mathbb{N}$, $\{\alpha_n\}$ satisfies (37), method 1 is now

$$\begin{cases} x_{n,k+1} = x_{n,k} - (A_n^* A_n + \alpha_n I)^{-1} A_n^* (F(x_n) - y^\delta + A_n(x_{n,k} - x_n)), & 0 \leq k < m \\ x_{n,0} = x_0, \; x_{n+1} = x_{n,m}. \end{cases}$$

Method 4. Newton-implicit iteration method. When $\alpha_n = \alpha$, $\forall n \in \mathbb{N} \cup \{0\}$, $\{k_n\}$ satisfies

$$1 \leq \frac{k_{n+1}}{k_n} \leq \frac{1}{q}, \quad \lim_{n \to \infty} k_n = \infty,$$

the corresponding method becomes

$$\begin{cases} x_{n,k+1} = x_{n,k} - (A_n^* A_n + \alpha_n I)^{-1} A_n^* (F(x_n) - y^\delta + A_n(x_{n,k} - x_n)), & 0 \leq k < k_n \\ x_{n,0} = x_0, \; x_{n+1} = x_{n,k_n}. \end{cases}$$

Method 2 and method 3 are already discussed by some authors (see,e.g.,[6,8,10]). Method 4 is a new one, which can also be considered as applying the stationary implicit iterative method[11] to the following equivalent form of Newton equation (4)

$$F'(x_n)(x - x_0) = -(F(x_n) - y^\delta + F'(x_n)(x_0 - x_n))$$

Certainly, we can obtain other specific algorithms by choosing appropriate parameters α_n and k_n. One may even use different algorithms in different (outer) iteration steps, provided condition (7) is satisfied.

We give two remarks to conclude the paper.

i) The theorems show that in order to obtain the convergence and convergence rates, some severely restrictive assumptions have to be imposed on the derivative operator $F'(x)$ and the initial iterate x_0. In practice, these assumptions are hard to verify and even not to be satisfied. Unfortunately, this kind of assumptions are typical at present and no better assumptions for Newton-type methods with Kaltenbacher's stopping rule can be found in the literatures [1,3,6,8]. On the other hand, numerical experiments show that the regularized Newton type methods can also give satisfactory results in some cases for which these restrictive assumptions are not fulfilled [12].

ii) Theorem 1 only derives the optimal convergence rates for $\nu \in (0, \frac{1}{2}]$. In order to obtain the optimal convergence rates for $\nu > \frac{1}{2}$, the assumption (11) has to be strengthened further, for example, as $Q(\bar{x}, x) = 0$ in (11). We omit the details(refer to [6]).

References

1. Engl, H.W., Hanke, M., Neubauer, O.: Regularization of Inverse Problems. Kluwer, Dordrecht (1996)
2. Groetshch, C.W.: Inverse Problems in Mathematical Sciences. Vieweg, Braunschweig (1993)
3. Engl, H.W., Scherzer, O.: Convergence rates results for iterative methods for solving nonlinear ill-posed problems. In: Colton, D., et al. (eds.) Survey on Solution Methods for Inverse Problems, Wien, pp. 7–34. Springer, Heidelberg (2000)
4. Samanskii, V.: On a modification of the Newton method. Ukrain Mat. Z. 19, 133–138 (1967) (in Russian)
5. Otega, J.M., Rheinboldt, W.C.: Iterative Solution of Nonlinear Equations in Several Variables. Acad. Press, New York (1970)
6. Kaltenbacher, B.: A posteriori parameter choice strategies for some Newton type methods for the regularization of nonlinear ill-posed problems. Numerische Mathematik 79, 501–528 (1998)
7. Zhao, Z., He, G.: Reconstruction of High Order Derivatives by a New Mollification Method. Applied Mathematics and Mechanics 29, 352–373 (2008)
8. Blaschke, B., Neubauer, A., Scherzer, O.: On convergence rates for the iteratively regularized Gauss-Newton method. IMA Journal of Numerical Analysis 17, 421–436 (1997)
9. Kaltenbacher, B.: Some Newton-type methods for the regularization of nonlinear ill-posed problems. Inverse Problems 13, 729–753 (1997)
10. Bauer, F., Hohage, T.: A Lepskij-type rule for regularized Newton methods. Inverse Problems 21, 1975–1991 (2005)
11. He, G., Liu, L.: A kind of implicit iterative methods for ill-posed operator equations. J. Comput. Math. 17, 275–284 (1999)
12. He, G., Meng, Z.: A Newton type iterative method for heat-conduction inverse problems. Applied Mathematics and Mechanics 28, 531–539 (2007)
13. Kaltenbacher, B., Neubauer, A.: Convergence of projected iterative regularized methods for nonlinear problems with smooth solutions. Inverse Problems 22, 1105–1119 (2006)

An Improved Technique for Program Remodularization

Saeed Parsa[1] and Mohammad Hamzei[2]

[1] Computer Engineering Department
Iran University of Science and Technology, Tehran, Iran
parsa@iust.ac.ir
[2] Computer Engineering Department
Iran University of Science and Technology, Tehran, Iran
m_hamzei@comp.iust.ac.ir

Abstract. There has been a tremendous shift towards using clusters and networks of low-cost computers for high performance computing. High performance can be achieved by appropriate remodularization of computationally intensive programs. An appropriate modular structure of program exploits the inherent concurrency in the execution of the program. In this article a new relation to determine suitable modular structure for distributing programs across the network is presented. The relation is built automatically by analyzing the program call flow graph. The proposed relation outperforms the existing relation for computing the amount of concurrency in a distributed code by considering, situations in which more than one method are supposed to be executed on a single computational node.

Keywords: Program remodularization, Performance evaluation, Automatic parallelization.

1 Introduction

With regard to the high price and un-scalability of supercomputers, there has been a tremendous shift to using clusters and networks of low-cost computers. To speed up the execution of computationally intensive programs, the programs code could be partitioned and distributed over the networks and clusters of low cost computers. In order to remove the burden of developing distributed programs, automatic approaches to translate sequential code into corresponding distributed code has been presented[1][2][3].

Automatic translation of sequential programs into corresponding distributed code is mainly aimed at shortening the execution time of the programs[4][5]. The distribution policy underlying the automatic distribution approaches is mainly to minimize the communication cost. However, it is shown that minimization of the communication cost does not necessarily results in the highest degree of concurrency in the execution of the distributed modules of programs [4]. In addition to the communication cost the amount of concurrency resulted from

W. Zhang et al. (Eds.): HPCA 2009, LNCS 5938, pp. 305–310, 2010.

converting a local call to a corresponding remote asynchronous call has to be considered. Apparently, by maximizing the amount of concurrency in the execution of distributed modules the overall execution time of the modules will be reduced. The Actor model [6] is applied for distributing the modules across the network. According to the Actor model, distributed modules interact asynchronously with each other while the communications within a module are performed synchronously.

In reference [7] a new relation to compute the execution time of distributed programs is presented. A major difficulty with this relation is that it does not consider the situations in which two different methods are supposed to be on a same network node. To resolve the difficulty, in this article a new extension of the relation is presented. This new relation considers the reduction in the amount of concurrency in the execution of a module whenever two or more methods within the module are supposed to be executed simultaneously.

The remaining parts of this paper are organized as follows: In Section 2 program remodularization techniques to achieve high performance in terms of speedup are described. Section 3, presents a new parametric relation for determining the most appropriate modular structure to distribute a computationally intensive program. In Section 4 , two case studies are applied to evaluate the applicability of the proposed relation for determining suitable modular structure for distributing programs is presented. Finally, concluding remarks are the topic of Section 5.

2   Program remodularization

In order to improve the performance of a distributed program, the program could be restructured using a high performance model such as Actor model[8]. Therefore, in order to speedup the execution of a distributed program the program may be remodularized in such a way that the maximum amount of concurrency is achieved through asynchronous invocations. The modular structure of a distributed program determines which invocations should be transformed to asynchronous invocations. Accordingly, the amount of concurrency in a distributed program depends on the modular structure of the program. To achieve the maximum amount of concurrency, a suitable modular structure should be devised for the distributed program. A genetic clustering algorithm could be best applied to search for a suitable modular structure for a distributed program. The clustering algorithm looks for the smallest set of the program method calls to be replaced with remote asynchronous calls.

3   Performance Evaluation Relation

The execution time of a distributed program is affected by the amount of the concurrency in the execution time of the program modules. The amount of concurrency in the execution time of each remote call depends on the execution time of the callee and the time it takes the caller to execute the very first instruction which depends on any value affected by the callee. To resolve the difficulty the following parametric relation can be applied [7]:

$$EET_m(r) = T_d + \Sigma a_i * EET_{I_i}(r) + \Sigma(1 - a_i) * T(S_i) \qquad (1)$$

$$T(S_i) = max((EET_{I_i}(r) + 2t_{c_i}) - t_i, 0) \qquad (2)$$

$EET_m(r)$ calculates a value which is an estimation of the execution time of method m with respect to modular structure r.In the above relation, T_d is the total execution time of all the instructions excluding call instructions within the method m, $T(S_i)$ is the time elapsed to wait at synchronization point S_i where the results from I_i are required, t_i is the estimated execution time of the program statements located between I_i and corresponding synchronization point S_i and t_{c_i} is the communication time. The values of the parameters a_i in this relation are determined considering the remodularization, r, of the program classes. If in a given remodularization, r, of the program classes, I_i is an inter-module invocation then the value of a_i will be set to zero otherwise a_i will be 1.

A major difficulty with the above relation is that it does not consider the situation in which two or more methods are executed simultaneously on the same computational node in a network. Concurrent execution of method calls on a same computational node has a reverse effect on the speedup.

In Figures 2.a and 2.b, two different modular structures for the code in Figure 1, are presented. The *Estimated Execution Time EET* relation generated for these two modular structures is as follows:

$$EET(fa) = S_0 + S_1 + (max(S_3 + S_4 + max(S_6 + 2t_c - S_4, 0) + S_5 + 2t_c - S_1, 0)) + S_2 \qquad (3)$$

It is observed that despite having two different execution times for these two different modularizations, the EET relation for both of them is the same. The main reason is that both the methods fa and fc are executed simultaneously as two threads on the same computational node and the EET does not consider these cases. Therefore, since the two methods fa and fc are on the same computational node their execution overlaps and these two methods have to be

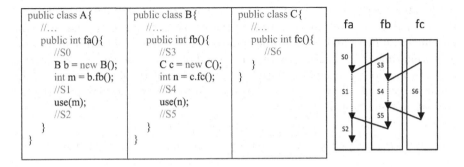

Fig. 1. A sample program and its program flow graph

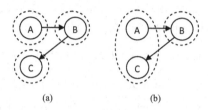

Fig. 2. Two modular structure of the program call graph

executed as different threads, concurrently. Therefore, the total execution time of fa and fc will be more than the time required to execute these methods, independently. The EET relation considers these two methods execute in parallel on two different computational nodes.

Suppose, the execution of the methods fa and fb, in Figure 2.b, overlaps for x units of time. Therefore, the execution of both the methods is delayed for at least x units of time. Considering this delay, the modular structure in Figure 2.a is preferred to the one presented in Figure 2.b.

Figure 3, Illustrates all possible relative executions of any two methods:

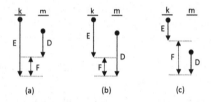

Fig. 3. All possible relative executions of any two methods

Considering different relative execution times of any two methods, the time in which the execution of any two methods overlaps could be estimated as follows:

$$max((T_m - max(ET(m) - ET(k), 0)), 0) \qquad (4)$$

In the above relation $T_m = EET(m)$ indicates the estimated execution time of the method m, The termination time of the methods m and k are shown by the parameters $ET(m)$ and $ET(k)$. The value of the $ET(m) - ET(k)$ is equal to the execution time of instructions between the end of method m and k. Considering any two methods overlap, overall methods overlap of the distributed program equals to sum of all two methods overlap. Accordingly, the new performance evaluation function is as follows:

$$NEET_p(r) = EET_p(r) + OTT_p(r)$$
$$OTT_p(r) = \Sigma_m \Sigma_k b_{mk} c_{mk} * max(T_m - max(ET(m) - ET(k), 0), 0) \qquad (5)$$

In this relation, if method i directly invoke method j or vice versa, then the value of b_{ij} will be set to 0 otherwise will be 1. The values of the parameters c_{ij}

are determined considering the remodularization, r, of the program classes. If in a given remodularization, r, of the program classes, methods i and j are in the same module then the value of c_{ij} will be set to 1 otherwise will be 0.

4   Evaluation

In this Section, two case studies are applied to evaluate the applicability of the proposed relation in comparison with the one presented in reference [7]. The performance evaluation relation is automatically constructed while traversing the program call flow graph. In order to automatically generate the *New Estimated Execution Time NEET* function for a program, the execution time of each instruction is computed in terms of CPU cycles according to the JOP microinstruction definition[9][10].

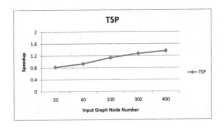
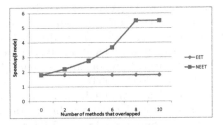

Fig. 4. Estimated speedup for TSP   **Fig. 5.** Estimated speedup for Test program

To evaluate our proposed relation two different case studies are used. In the first one a TSP program, including 18 classes and 129 method calls is remodularized by applying the *NEET* relation. In Figure 4 the estimated speedup using our proposed performance evaluation relation to remodularize the TSP program is presented.

The second case study uses a benchmark program, Test (m), including 10 method calls. In this test program the execution time of each method is 5000ms and the parameter m is the number of methods that may overlap at the execution time. In order to produce different overlaps in the execution of the methods, the method calls and their synchronization points, or in the other words the positions where the results of the method calls are used, are reordered.

As shown in Figure 5, as the number of overlapped method increases the speedup resulted from the modular structures resulted from *NEET* increases while no variations is considered in the execution times of the modular structure resulted from the *EET* relation.

5   Conclusion

The modular structure of a distributed program affects the degree of the concurrency in the execution of the program modules, when each module is considered as a separate distribution unit. It is a difficult task to find a suitable modular structure for a distributed program. The problem is to estimate the execution time of each method of the program while it is not clear whether the method calls are local or remote asynchronous. The difficulty is further aggravated when two invoked methods are supposed to execute concurrently on the same computational node. To resolve the difficulty a parametric relation to estimate the execution time of the distributed program can be extracted from the program. The extracted parametric relation could be applied as an objective function to look for the most suitable modular structure for the program in a genetic clustering algorithm.

References

1. Chen, M.K., Olukotun, K.: The jrpm system for dynamically parallelizing java programs. In: ISCA 2003: Proceedings of the 30th annual international symposium on Computer architecture, pp. 434–446. ACM, New York (2003)
2. Bal, H.E., Kaashoek, M.F.: Object distribution in orca using compile-time and run-time techniques. In: OOPSLA 1993: Proceedings of the eighth annual conference on Object-oriented programming systems, languages, and applications, pp. 162–177. ACM, New York (1993)
3. Deb, D., Fuad, M., Oudshoorn, M.: Towards Autonomic Distribution of Existing Object Oriented Programs. In: International Conference on Autonomic and Autonomous Systems, 2006, p. 17 (2006)
4. Parsa, S., Bushehrian, O.: Performance-driven object-oriented program re-modularisation. IET Software 2, 362–378 (2008)
5. Chan, B., Abdelrahman, T.S.: Run-time support for the automatic parallelization of java programs. J. Supercomput. 28, 91–117 (2004)
6. Astley, M., Agha, G.: Modular construction and composition of distributed software architectures. In: PDSE 1998: Proceedings of the International Symposium on Software Engineering for Parallel and Distributed Systems, Washington, DC, USA, p. 2. IEEE Computer Society, Los Alamitos (1998)
7. Parsa, S., Bushehrian, O.: On the Optimal Object-Oriented Program Re-modularization. In: Shi, Y., van Albada, G.D., Dongarra, J., Sloot, P.M.A. (eds.) ICCS 2007. LNCS, vol. 4487, pp. 599–602. Springer, Heidelberg (2007)
8. Tahvildari, L., Kontogiannis, K., Mylopoulos, J.: Quality-driven software re-engineering. J. Syst. Softw. 66, 225–239 (2003)
9. Schoeberl, M.: A time predictable Java processor. In: Proceedings of Design, Automation and Test in Europe, 2006. DATE 2006, vol. 1 (2006)
10. Schoeberl, M.: Jop: A java optimized processor for embedded real-time systems. Technischen Universität Wien, Fakultät für Informatik (2005)

Task Merging for Better Scheduling

Saeed Parsa, Neda Reza Soltani, and Saeed Shariati

Department of Computer Engineering,
Iran University of Science and Technology, Tehran, Iran
parsa@iust.ac.ir, soltani_n@comp.iust.ac.ir,
saeed_shariati@comp.iust.ac.ir

Abstract. This paper proposes a new algorithm to restructure task graphs for suitable scheduling. The algorithm reduces communication costs by merging those tasks within a task graph whose communication costs exceeds their execution time. Task duplication techniques are applied before the merge, to avoid any delay in the execution of the tasks dependent on the merged tasks. Our experiments with a number of known benchmark task graphs demonstrate the distinguished scheduling results provided by applying our task merging algorithm before the scheduling.

1 Introduction

The aim has been to restructure task graphs such that when applying any task scheduling algorithm to the restructured task graph, the minimum possible completion is obtained. Task merging and clustering are two well known techniques to restructure task graphs for suitable scheduling [1-4].

When merging a task node with its parent nodes any one of its siblings in the task graph, could be delayed. To resolve the difficulty, it is suggested to duplicate the parent nodes before the merge, subject to the condition that their execution times is less than the maximum time required to communicate with their successors [2]. However, this condition does not always necessitate the merge. In the approach presented in this paper, a node is merged with a subset of its parents only if the merge operation reduces its earliest time to start. If the merge postpones the execution of the other children of the parent node, the parent node is duplicated. If after the duplication, the number of independent tasks gets above the number of available processors, the duplication is considered as an opposing factor.

The remaining parts of this paper are organized as follows: In Section 2, a new task merging algorithm is presented. In Section 2.1, a relation for computing the earliest start time of tasks within a task graph is presented. In Section 2.1, a relation to compute the effect of merging each parent of a child node on the earliest start time of the child is offered. Section 2.2 presents a new relation to compute the benefits of merging a task node with any subset of its parents. In section 3, the results of applying our task merging algorithm to some benchmark task graphs is compared with the results of applying a number of known task merging and scheduling algorithms.

W. Zhang et al. (Eds.): HPCA 2009, LNCS 5938, pp. 311–316, 2010.
© Springer-Verlag Berlin Heidelberg 2010

2   A New Task Merging Algorithm

When combining a node v with one of its parents, p, the start time of the siblings of v may be increased. To resolve the difficulty, the parent node, p, could be duplicated before the merge. However, if there are not enough processors to execute the duplicated tasks in parallel, the merge may not be beneficial. Therefore, in the task merging quality function, Q, presented in section 2.2, the number of available processors, the total execution time of the tasks to be duplicated and the amount of reduction in earliest start time are considered as the three main factors in deciding whether to merge a task v with a subset, P_k, of its parents. Our new task merging algorithm is presented In Figure 1.

2.1   The RTM Algorithm

In this Section a new task merging algorithm, RTM (Redundant aware Task Merging), is presented. The algorithm is presented in Figure 1. The algorithm attempts to increase parallelism in the execution of a given task graph by reducing the earliest start time of the tasks within the task graph. As shown below in relation (1), to compute the earliest start time, EST_v, of a task, v, the earliest start time and the execution time of its parent nodes and the time it takes to receive the results from its parent, $\tau(p_i)$, the size of the data to be received by the task nodes, $c(p_i\ v)$, the latency, L, and the bandwidth, B, of the communication lines are required.

$$EST_v = \begin{cases} 0 & Parent(v) = \phi \\ MAX_{p_i \in Parents(v)}(EST(p_i) + \tau(p_i) + L + \dfrac{c(p_i,v)}{B}) & Parent(v) \neq \phi \end{cases} \quad (1)$$

A node v is merged with the subset of its parents, which reduce its earliest start time the most, EST_v. To achieve this, the time, $R_{p_i,v}$, at which the outputs of each parent node, p_i, can be collected by the child, v, is computed as follows:

$$R_{p_i,v} = EST(p_i) + \tau(p_i) + L + \frac{c(p_i,v)}{B}. \quad (2)$$

After $R_{p_i,v}$ are computed, the parents are sorted in decreasing order of R_{p_i}. Starting with the node with the highest value of $R_{p_i,v}$, the benefit of merging v with each of the parents, pi, on the earliest start time of v is computed. The node v is then merged with the subset of its parents, which reduce its earliest start time, and their number does not exceed the number of available processors.

As an example, in Figure 2, the earliest time to collect data from the parent nodes is computed by considering the execution time, τ, earliest start time, EST, of each parent node, p_1 to p_4, and the communication costs the earliest start time of node v. Also, applying relation (3), it is decided to merge v with p_1 and p_2. To avoid any increase in the earliest start time of the node c, the node p_2 is duplicated.

In the above relation EST $_{(p)}$ is the earliest start time of the task p, EST$_{Before}$(v) is the earliest start time before merging, EST$_{After}$(v) is the earliest start time after merging and $\tau(p)$ is the execution time of p.

Algorithm RTM (G)   // Redundancy aware Task Merging (RTM) Algorithm

Input: a task graph G (V, E, τ, c) where:

      V: Set of tasks, E: Set of task inter-connection lines

      τ: A function to compute the execution cost of each task

      c: A function to compute the communication costs

Output: $G'(V', E', \tau', c')$ = the modified task graph

Method:

  For each v in V **do** apply relation (1) to compute $EST(v)$

  End For;

$L1$: **For each** v in V **do**

    For each p_i in *Parents (v)* **do**

      Apply relation (2), below, to compute the earliest time, $R_{p_i,v}$, to collect data

            From parent, p_i, on v

      Sort the parents, p_i, on the value of $R_{p_i,v}$, descendingly,

            Giving the sequence $P = (p_1, p_2, ..., p_n)$;

    End for;

    Apply relation (3) to compute the benefit $Q_{v,k}$, of merging v with its parents

          p_1 to p_k in P for $1 \le k \le n$;

    If there are no $Q_{v,k} > 0$ **then** it is not possible to merge v with any subset of its parents

               go to $L1$;   **End if;**

    Find the subsequence $P_k = \{ (p_1, p_2, .., p_k)$ in P, $1 \le k \le n\}$ Such that $Q_{v,k}$ is maximum;

    Let $\Psi_{v,Pk}$ be the set of siblings of v whose earliest start time increases

    Let $D_{v,pk}$ be the set of parent nodes p_i in P_k with at least one child in $\Psi_{v,Pk}$

    For each node p in $D_{v,pk}$ **do**

      Let p' be a copy of p

      Remove any edges from p to nodes in $\Psi_{v,Pk}$

      Remove any edges from p' to nodes that not in $\Psi_{v,Pk}$

    End For;

  End For;

End.

Fig. 1. The RTM Algorithm

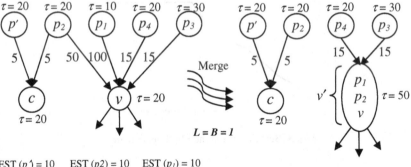

EST $(p') = 10$ EST $(p2) = 10$ EST $(p_1) = 10$

EST $(p4) = 10$ EST $(p3) = 10$

$R_{p',c} = 35$ $R_{p2,c} = 35$ EST$(c) = 35$ EST $(v') = 55$

$R_{p1,v} = 120$ $R_{p2,v} = 80$ EST$_{\text{Before}}(v) = 120$ EST$_{\text{After}}(v) = $ EST$(v') + \tau(p_1) + \tau(p_2) = 85$

$R_{p3,v} = 55$ $R_{p4,v} = 45$

Fig. 2. Efficacy of earliest start time

2.2 Task Merging Benefits

In order to decide whether to merge a task with a subset or all of its parents, relation (3) can be applied. This relation computes the benefit, Q, of combining a task with a subset of its parents considering the amount of reduction in earliest start time of the task, the execution time of the duplicated nodes and the number of parallel processors.

$$Q = \alpha \times \Delta T - (1 - \alpha) \times \Delta E.$$

(3)

In the above relation ΔT indicates the amount of reduction in the earliest start time of the node v, ΔE is the sum of the execution time of the duplicated parents of v and α is a parameter. The value of the parameter α depends on the maximum number of tasks to be executed in parallel, CT, and the number of available processors, Ω. To estimate the value of CT, the task graph is topologically sorted. Our experiments with different FFT task graphs have resulted in the following relation for computing the value of α:

$$\alpha = \begin{cases} \dfrac{\Omega - 1}{CT - 1} & \Omega < CT \\ 1 & \Omega \geq CT \end{cases}$$

(4)

The above relation was built when applying relation (3) to decide whether to merge each node of the FFT4 benchmark graph with different subsets of its parents. As shown in Figure 3, in order to apply relation (3), we gave 20 different values between 0 and 1 to α. The amount of reduction in parallel execution time for each value of α was computed. The value of α resulting in the maximum reduction in parallel execution time of the task graph was selected. Considering the value of α for different number of available processors, it was concluded that α can be estimated by applying relation (4).

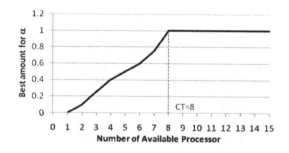

Fig. 3. Best fit for α in the FFT4 benchmark

3 Experimental Results

We have applied two known algorithm, FFT [5] and IRR [6], to generated five task graphs, FFT1, FFT2, FF3, FFT4 and IRR. Applying RTM and a known task merging algorithm, GRS [1],[2],[7], to restructure these benchmark task graphs, the restructured graphs where scheduled by a simple genetic algorithm [8] and another algorithm called LC [9]. The parallel execution times of the resultant scheduling were compared with the execution times resulted by applying 7 known scheduling algorithms: CLANS[10], DSC[11], MCP[12],[9][9] LAST[13], SR[6], LC[9] and Genetic[8]. Below, in table 3 and table 4, the comparison results are presented.

First of all, assume that the execution environment has more than eight processors, the inter-processors communication baud rate is 1 and the communication latency equals zero. In this case, applying equation 4, the value of α for the FFT4 task graph will be 1. Comparing the modified graph with the original FFT4 graph, it is observed that the critical path length is reduced about 82%. Also, the parallelism of the modified graph is about 880% higher than the original one. The parallel execution time of this scheduling is 125.

Table 1. A camparition of schedulings resulted before and after applying RTM

Graph	CLANS	DSC	MCP	LC	LAST	SR	Genetic	RTM+ Genetic
FFT1	124 / 4	124/4	148/8	127/8	146/1	146	173/3	**120/10**
FFT2	200 /8	205/8	205/8	225/8	240/8	215	225/20	**180/8**
FFT3	1860/4	1860/4	2350/8	2838/8	2220/2	--	1992/2	**1640/8**
FFT4	405/2	710/12	710/8	710/8	170/8	160	160/8	**125/8**
IRR	725/7	605/12	605/7	710/8	840/3	680	730/3	**555/10**

Assuming that the execution environment has just two processors and the inter-processors communication baud rate is 1 and the communication latency equals zero the value of α for the FFT4 task graph will be 0.2.

Table 2. A camparition of RTM and GRS

Graph	LC	GRS+LC	RTM+LC	Genetic	GRS +Genetic	RTM+ Genetic
FFT1	172	123	**120**	173/3	123/10	**120/10**
FFT2	225	180	**180**	225/20	180/10	**180/8**
FFT3	2838	1848	**1640**	1992/2	1848/8	**1640/8**
FFT4	710	130	**125**	160/8	135/8	**125/8**
IRR	710	590	**545**	730/3	641/10	**555/10**

4 Conclusions

This paper suggests a task graph restructuring step before applying any scheduling algorithm to the task graph. To exploit the parallelism inherent in the execution of tasks in a task graph the tasks could be merged by applying the algorithm presented in this paper. The algorithm attempts to exploit the inherent parallelism by minimizing the earliest start time of each task within the task graph. The earliest start time could be reduced by merging the task with some or all of its parent nodes. To avoid any delay in the execution time of the siblings of the task, their parents are duplicated before being merged with the task. When duplicating a parent node, the number of tasks apparently increases. Therefore, there should be enough number of available processors to execute the parallel tasks, otherwise the duplication and thereby the merge will not be beneficial. Our experimental results demonstrate the applicability of our proposed task merging algorithm to restructure task graphs for better scheduling.

References

1. Aronsson, P., Fritzson, P.: ATask Merging Technique for Parallelization of Modelica Models. In: 4th International Modelica Conference, Hamburg (2005)
2. Aronsson, P., Fritzson, P.: Task Merging and Replication using Graph Rewriting. In: 2nd International Modelica Conference, Germany (2003)
3. Ayed, M., Gaudiot, J.: An efficient heuristic for code partitioning. Parallel Computing 26(4), 399–426 (2000)
4. Kwok, Y., Ahmad, I.: Static scheduling algorithms for allocating directed task graphs to multiprocessors. ACM Computing Surveys (CSUR) 31(4), 406–471 (1999)
5. McCreary, C., et al.: A comparison of heuristics for scheduling DAGs on multiprocessors. In: Proceedings of International Parallel Processing Symposium (1994)
6. Sheahan, A., Ryan, C.: A transformation-based approach to static multiprocessor scheduling. ACM, New York (2008)
7. Aronsson, P., Fritzson, P.: Multiprocessor Scheduling of Simulation Code from Modelica Models (2002)
8. Parsa, S., Lotfi, S., Lotfi, N.: An Evolutionary Approach to Task Graph Scheduling. In: Beliczynski, B., Dzielinski, A., Iwanowski, M., Ribeiro, B. (eds.) ICANNGA 2007. LNCS, vol. 4431, pp. 110–119. Springer, Heidelberg (2007)
9. Kim, S., Browne, J.: A General Approach to Mapping of Parallel Computation upon Multiprocessor Architectures. In: International Conference on Parallel Processing (1988)
10. McCreary, C., Gill, H.: Automatic determination of grain size for efficient parallel processing. Communications of the ACM 32(9), 1073–1078 (1989)
11. Yang, T., Gerasoulis, A.: DSC: scheduling parallel tasks on an unbounded number of processors. IEEE Transactions on Parallel and Distributed Systems 5(9), 951–967 (1994)
12. Wu, M., Gajski, D.: Hypertool: a programming aid for message-passing systems. IEEE Transactions on Parallel and Distributed Systems 1(3), 330–343 (1990)
13. Baxter, J., Patel, J.: The LAST algorithm- A heuristic-based static task allocation algorithm. In: International Conference on Parallel Processing (1989)

The Closure Temperature Fields and Shape Optimization of Arch Dam Based on Genetic Algorithms

Hui Peng, Wei Yao, and Ping Huang

College of Civil and Hydroelectric Engineering
China Three Gorges University, Yichang 443002, Hubei Province, China
hpeng1976@163.com

Abstract. The optimization of arch dams is complex because its objective function and constraint conditions appear non-linear. Although many conventional optimization methods already applied to arch dam shape optimization, these methods impose lots of disadvantages on optimal results at last. A Genetic algorithm(GA)based on float-encoding is presented and applied to closure temperature field and Shape optimization of arch dams. The results of a practical project indicate that GA has an advantage over that by multi-objective non-linear programming method.

1 Introduction

Arch dam optimization design belongs to complex optimization problems. In general, the object function and constraint conditions are non-linear functions[1]. So far sequential quadratic programming method and multi-objective non-linear programming method are comparatively good optimization methods. However, there are great deal of previous preparations needed to make and the process of calculating is complex. Genetic algorithms(GA) is a kind of global optimization method which is created according to natural evolution. The obvious advantages of GA include no need of gradient information and functional continuity. At the same time, GA can be parallel processing large sets of complex optimization problems with powerful searching ability. The application of GA is wide and can resolve many kinds of engineering problems. In this paper, a Genetic algorithm(GA)based on float-encoding is presented and applied to closure temperature field and shape optimization of arch dams. The results of a practical project indicates that GA has an advantage over that by multi-objective non-linear programming method[2,3].

2 The Comprehensive Optimization Method of Closure Temperature Fields and Shape of Arch Dam

In this paper, the design variables involve in arch dam shape parameters and closure temperature field parameters. The constraint conditions are also related to foregoing

W. Zhang et al. (Eds.): HPCA 2009, LNCS 5938, pp. 317–324, 2010.

two aspects. When choosing objective function, we want to reach the goal that the total project construction fee is least under condition of present technology. So the cost of project is selected as objective function which includes concrete construction fee and artificial cooling fee [4,5,6].

2.1 Design Variables

Design variables corresponding to closure temperature fields of arch dam. The closure temperature fields can be expressed by uniform temperature fields Tm_0 and equivalent linear temperature differences Td_0 which value changes with elevation Z. Value of Tm_0, Td_0 changing with elevation Z has two types of formation. The first one is continuous function type and another one is stepladder type. Through comparison we find that stepladder type is more viable and easily performed. This paper selects stepladder function to express closure temperature field distribution. Suppose that arch dam is divided into $n-1$ sections along the height. The elevation at intersection points between each section is Z_i (i=1,2,....n). Between the scope of $(Z_{i-1}+Z_i)/2$ and $(Z_i+Z_{i+1})/2$ the corresponding uniform temperature and equivalent linear temperature are Tm_{0i}, Td_{0i} respectively. As a result, the total design variables of closure temperature fields are 2n. These variables can be written as follows:

$$x_1 = \{ Tm_{01}, Td_{01}\ Tm_{02}, Td_{02}, \ldots\ldots, Tm_{0n}, Td_{0n} \} \tag{1}$$

Design variables corresponding to arch dam shape. Under condition of given dam height and river valley, the hybrid model which uses both discrete and continuous function to describe arch dam shape is introduced. In figure one, thickness of each plane arch is T_a (m) and half central angle is Φ(degree). The upstream face of crown cantilever of arch dam can use up-convex quadratic curves to describe. In this quadratic curve two parameters β_1, β_2 will be used.

Here y is horizontal coordinate of upstream curves of crown cantilever at different elevation, z is elevation and H is dam height. When the arch dam is divided into n layers along height, the total $2n+2$ shape design variables including (T_{ai}、ϕ_i i=1,2,......n) and β_1, β_2 will be confirmed. Here x_2 stands for arch dam shape design variables:

2.2 Objective Function

In practical dam construction, artificial cooling fee occupies main part of concrete temperature control fee. It is difficult to accurately calculate artificial cooling fee C_t. But we can use empirical formulas to compute.

$$y = -\beta_1\left(\frac{z}{H}\right) + \beta_2\left(\frac{z}{H}\right)^2 \tag{2}$$

$$x_2 = \{ T_{a1}、\ \phi_2, T_{a2}、\ \phi_2\ ,\ldots\ T_{ai}、\ \phi_i\ \ldots, T_{an}、\ \phi_n、\ \beta_1、\ \beta_2 \} \tag{3}$$

$$C_t = C_0 \sum_{i=1}^{n} (Tm_{1i} - Tm_{oi})V_i \qquad (4)$$

Here Tm1i is the mean annual temperature. V_i is the dam volume between the elevation scope from $(Z_{i-1} + Z_i)/2$ to $(Z_i + Z_{i+1})/2$, C_0 is the unit price of artificial cooling(yuan/ $m^3 \cdot {}^0C$).

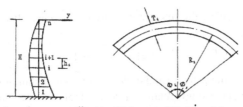

(a) Cross section of crown cantilever   (b) Layout of No.i i arch layer

Fig. 1. Sketch map of arch dam

Foundation excavation fee calculation is not only related to dam shape design variables but also related to river valley. The experiences of arch dam optimization tell us that if we do not consider this part of construction fee the optimized results will make the arch dam shape look like a broom. So we have to consider this part of excavation fee. In order to both taking account foundation excavation fee and dam body construction fee, in this paper a method of convert is used to combine with excavation fee and concrete pouring fee. Now the indiscrete fee calculating formula C_c covering foundation excavation fee and concrete pouring fee can be expressed as follows:

$$Cc = \sum_{i=1}^{n} C_{0i} V_i \qquad (5)$$

Here C_{0i} (yuan/ m^3) is comprehensive unit price of concrete pouring fee and foundation excavation fee between the elevation scope from $(Z_{i-1} + Z_i)/2$ to $(Z_i + Z_{i+1})/2$.

2.3 Constraint Conditions

Constraint conditions for temperature control. The temperature control constraint conditions come from the feasibility of implementation. According to present design codes and engineering practice, the maximum and minimum value of Tm_0, Td_0 (i=1,2,....,n) and temperature difference between upper and lower layer of each horizontal arch can be written as follows:

$$\begin{cases} A \leq T_{m0i} \leq B \\ C \leq T_{d0i} \leq D \end{cases} i=1,2,\cdots,n \text{ and } \begin{aligned} |T_{m0i} - T_{m0i+1}| \leq \Delta T_{m0} \\ |T_{d0i} - T_{d0i+1}| \leq \Delta T_{d0} \end{aligned} i=1,2,...,n-1 \qquad (6)$$

A, B are allowable minimum and maximum temperature value of T_{m0} respectively. C, D are allowable minimum and maximum temperature value of T_{d0} respectively.

Constraint conditions for arch dam shape. 1) Thickness of each horizontal arch. According to traffic needs the crest width is not less than $T_{a\,min}$ (the allowable minimum crest width according to design codes):

$$T_{an} > T_{a\,min} \tag{7}$$

According to general rules, the thickness of arches increases from up to down along arch dam height.

$$T_{ai+1} \leq T_{ai} \ (\text{i=1, 2, ...n-1}) \tag{8}$$

2) Degree of overhang in upstream and downstream of arch dam. In order to make dam construction convenient, the upstream and downstream of overhang degree should be limited:

$$m_1 \leq [m_1] \quad \text{and} \quad m_2 \leq [m_2] \tag{9}$$

Here $[m_1]$ and $[m_2]$ are allowable maximum overhang degree in upstream and downstream respectively. m_1 and m_2 are maximum overhang degree in upstream and downstream respectively.

3) The central angle of arch dam. According to general laws, the central angles decrease gradually from up to down along dam height. Another important reason is to guarantee the stability of abutment. As a result we need to limit the maximum central angle in each arch layer.

$$\phi_i \leq \phi_{i+1} \ (\text{i=1, 2...n-2}) \quad \text{and} \quad \phi_i \leq [\phi_i] \ (\text{i=1, 2...n}) \tag{10}$$

Here $[\phi_i]$ is the allowable maximum central angle in No.i arch layer.

Constraint conditions for arch dam safety. For the sake of guarantee safety of arch dam during construction and operation processes, the stress pattern should be limited. Under different loads imposed on arch dam the maximum stress in dam body should not surpass the allowable stress. When using arch crown cantilever method to analyze arch dam, the stresses in dam body should be meet some requirements listed as follows:

$$-[\sigma_{al}] \leq \sigma_{a\,min} ; \sigma_{a\,max} \leq [\sigma_{ar}] ; -[\sigma_{bl}] \leq \sigma_{b\,min} ; \sigma_{b\,max} \leq [\sigma_{br}] \tag{11}$$

When application of arch cantilever method or FEM to calculate arch dams, some stress conditions also need to be satisfied:

$$-[\sigma_l] \leq \sigma_3 \quad \text{and} \quad \sigma_1 \leq [\sigma_r] \tag{12}$$

Here σ_1, σ_3 are maximum and minimum principal stresses respectively. In order to ensure safety during the course of dam concrete pouring process, the tensile stresses in upstream face and downstream face of arch dam caused by dam gravity should be not very large. So,

$$-[\sigma_{gl}] \leq \sigma_{bg\,min} \tag{13}$$

Here we specify that if the compressive stress is positive and tensile stress is negative. The symbol of [σ]stands for allowable stress. a means the direction of arch(horizontal direction) and b means the direction of cantilever(vertical direction). l stands for tension and r stands for compression. g is defined as gravity effect. $[\sigma_{al}]$ is allowable tensile stress along arch direction, $\sigma_{a\min}$ is minimum stress along arch direction. $[\sigma_{ar}]$ is allowable compressive stress along arch direction, $\sigma_{a\max}$ is maximum compressive stress along arch direction. $[\sigma_{bl}]$ is allowable tensile stress along cantilever direction, $\sigma_{b\min}$ is minimum stress along cantilever direction, $\sigma_{b\max}$ is maximum compressive stress along cantilever direction, $[\sigma_{br}]$ is allowable compressive stress along cantilever direction. $[\sigma_{gl}]$ stands for allowable tensile stress under condition of dam cantilever gravity. $\sigma_{bg\min}$ is minimum stress under condition of cantilever gravity. The unit of stress is MPa.

3   Construction of GA

In order to simulate the process of life evolution, an initial population is produced by GA through random procedures. Each individual in initial population is called chromosome which is corresponded to a point in design variables space. Chromosomes consist of different elements called genes which are corresponded to each design variables. The fitness of genes can reflect the advantages and disadvantages of possible solutions. According to natural selection, large fitness of genes has more opportunities to be chosen and after continuous genetic operations new populations will be produced. After several generation evolutions, optimal individuals may be appeared. If we want to apply GA to arch dam optimization, we must solve some key problems listed as follows:

3.1   Parameters Coding

For the sake of directly simulating genetic evolution, standard genetic algorithm(SGA) usually doesn't deal with real numbers in optimal solution spaces directly. However, through coding operation the real numbers in optimal solution spaces can be converted into genotype bit string data structure in genetic spaces. At present, binary coding is often used and binary coding has some advantages in operation. But binary coding is complicated in coding and decoding. For arch dam optimization problems, real coded genetic algorithm shows with high accuracy and easy operations compared with SGA. Value of design variables can be taken as genes of chromosomes when coding. A group of   design   variables   can   be   arranged   as   a   chromosome   code. $x = \{x_1 \quad x_2\} = \{ T_{m01}, T_{d01}, T_{m02}, T_{d02}, \ldots\ldots, T_{m0n}, T_{d0n}, T_{a1} \setminus \phi_2, T_{a2} \setminus \phi_2, \ldots T_{ai} \setminus \phi_i \ldots, T_{an} \setminus \phi_n, \beta_1 \setminus \beta_2 \}$,there are total $4n+2$ design variables.

3.2   Fitness Functions and Constraint Conditions

GA needs that the fitness function should be nonnegative and the optimal result must be maximum value. In this paper, the upper and lower limits of design variables can be

confirmed when coding. Other constraints conditions can be decided by penalty function. So a new objective function should be set up here[7]:

$$g_0 = C - objF(x) + \sum_{j=1}^{N_c} M_j \quad \text{and} \quad g_0 = C - (C_c + C_t) + \sum_{j=1}^{N_c} M_j \qquad (14)$$

Here C is the positive number which is larger than $objF(x)$. N_c is number of constraint conditions(4n-2). When the No. j constraint condition is satisfied, then $M_j =0$,
otherwise a large number will be given to M_j (here the large number is 10^{11}).The
fitness functions can be constructed here: $g = 0, g_0 \geq 10^{11}$; $g = g_0, g_0 < 10^{11}$.

3.3 Genetic Operations

Genetic operations include selection operation, crossover operation and mutation operation. In this paper, a non-uniform mutation operation is applied. A individual is
selected at random.

$$x_{ib} = x_i + (b_{i2} - x_i)g(N_g) \quad k_1 \geq 0.5 \quad \text{and} \quad x_{ib} = x_i - (x_i - b_{i1})g(N_g)$$
$$k_1 < 0.5$$

$$g(N_g) = \left[k_2(1 - \frac{N_g}{N_{max}}) \right]^d$$

Here b_{i1} is lower limit of variable x_i . b_{i2} is upper limit of variable x_i . k_1, k_2 are uniform random numbers in interval (0,1). N_g is current generation number. N_{max} is
maximum evolution generation numbers. d is formal parameter. x_{ib} is random individual and $g(N_g)$ is fitness function.

4   Example

The arch dam shape parameters are showed in figure two, the arch dam locates in the
central area of China. During the process of calculation, the scale of population is 200
and crossover probability is 0.65. The total genetic evolution generations are 20. Here,
$A =5°C$, the value of B is mean annual maximum temperature, $C =-5°C, D =5°C$,
$\Delta T_{m0} =3 °C$, $\Delta T_{d0} =3 °C$,[σ_r]=5Mpa , [σ_l]=1.5Mpa , $C_0 =$1yuan/ m^3 ,
$C_{0i} =$100yuan/ m^3 . In the process of operation, mean annual temperature fields and
equivalent linear temperature differences and corresponding optimal results are listed
in table one below.

Notice: After optimization the total dam volume is 403,900 m^3 and artificial
cooling fee is RMB 1,709,200 yuan.

Under the condition of same calculating parameters and dam sizes, the results of
traditional multi-objective nonlinear optimization method are listed in table two as
follows:

Table 1. The optimization results based on GA

z(m)	Tmo (°C)	Tdo (°C)	T(m)	y(m)	Φ(°)	R(m)
120.000	15.824	2.142	6.93	0.00	63.98	159.15
100.000	15.020	4.951	9.18	7.63	63.66	158.71
80.000	13.919	4.985	10.19	13.17	61.43	153.11
60.000	11.594	4.833	10.71	16.61	51.79	148.64
40.000	7.548	4.864	18.94	17.96	37.92	154.11
20.000	12.458	4.709	27.86	17.22	30.04	143.65
.000	17.252	4.854	37.19	14.39	19.35	134.44

Table 2. Results of traditional method

z(m)	Tmo (°C)	Tdo (°C)	T(m)	y(m)	Φ(°)	R(m)
120.000	15.824	2.142	7.71	0.00		
100.000	15.020	4.951	9.35	7.63		
80.000	13.919	4.985	10.24	13.17	64.85	157.43
60.000	11.594	4.833	10.92	16.61	63.46	156.49
40.000	7.548	4.864	19.14	17.96	61.86	152.59
20.000	12.458	4.709	28.06	17.22	52.09	147.73
.000	17.252	4.854	37.71	14.39	38.62	153.10
					30.54	142.09
					20.69	133.57

Notice: Through traditional method optimization the total dam volume is $418,800 \, m^3$ and artificial cooling fee is RMB 1,748,000 yuan.

5 Conclusions

(1) The application of GA to the comprehensive optimization of closure temperature fields and shape of arch dam is viable.(2) Compared with traditional optimization methods, under the condition of same calculating parameters and dam sizes, the total dam body concrete volume can be saved 3.6% and artificial cooling fee can be saved

2.21% by means of GA.(3) The computing process is stable and doesn't need gradient information of objective function. Furthermore, GA needs not continuous objective function and it can search optimal results in the specified spaces powerfully. GA is suitable for dealing with parallel and large complex optimization problems and the written program based on GA has the character of generality.

Acknowledgement

This research was supported by National Natural Science Foundation of China (NSFC: 50679036) and Natural Science Foundation of Hubei Province(granted number: 2008CDZ069).

References

[1] Bo-fang, Z., Zhan-mei, L., Bi-cheng, Z.: The theory and application of structural optimization, pp. 259–270. Water Conservancy and Power Press, Beijing (1984)
[2] Zhong-hou, Y., Hai-xia, Y., Qing-wen, R.: The program system of stress analysis and shape optimization of high arch dam. In: The modern computation methods and programs, pp. 160–173. Hohai University Press, Nanjing (1992)
[3] Goldberg, D.E.: Genetic algorithms in search,optimization and machine learning, pp. 120–124. Addison-Wesley, New Yok (1989)
[4] Schnitter, N.J.: The Evolution of the Arch. Dam. Water Power & Dam Construction, 10–11 (1979)
[5] Serafim, J.L.: Four Decades of Concrete Arch Dam Design. In: Water Power & Dam Construction Handbook, pp. 180–186 (1989)
[6] Graham, J.R., et al.: Half Century of USBR Arch Dam Construction. In: Proceeding of ASCE, pp. 101–102 (1975)
[7] Hai-xia, Y.: Shape optimization of arch dams based on genetic algorithm. Journal of Nanjing Hydraulic Research Institute (2), 14–17 (2000)

Parallel Computing for Option Pricing Based on the Backward Stochastic Differential Equation

Ying Peng, Bin Gong*, Hui Liu, and Yanxin Zhang

School of Computer Science and Technology, Shandong University,
Jinan 250101, P.R. China
pengy@sdu.edu.cn, gb@sdu.edu.cn,
amyliuhui@sdu.edu.cn, zhangyanxintongxue@yahoo.com.cn

Abstract. The Backward Stochastic Differential Equation (BSDE) is a robust tool for financial derivatives pricing and risk management. In this paper, we explore the opportunity for parallel computing with BSDEs in financial engineering. A binomial tree based numerical method for BSDEs is investigated and applied to option pricing. According to the special structure of the numerical model, we develop a block allocation algorithm in parallelization, where large communication overhead is avoided. Runtime experiments manifest optimistic speedups for the parallel implementation.

1 Introduction

Over the past two decades, an increasing number of complex mathematical models have been applied in financial engineering. As most of these models can not be solved by analytical formulas, we must use numerical methods, which need much more computing efforts. Moreover, time constraints should be respected in financial trade-off, therefore effective parallel implementations are in great demand. To decrease the computation time, many parallelization works are presented for solving various numerical models in financial computing area [2,3,4,5,8].

The BSDE was firstly introduced to solve the problem of derivative pricing by El Karoui in [6]. Since then, the BSDE theory was applied in financial area more and more frequently. Comparing with the Black-Scholes formula [1], the BSDE is more robust to fit in the situation of probability model uncertainty, thus can be used to perform more approximated calculations in financial derivatives pricing and risk analysis.

In this paper, we develop a parallel algorithm for the BSDEs with application to option pricing. Though many efforts have been made in the numerical methods for solving BSDEs, few work has been done for the parallel implementation until now. The reminder of this paper is structured as follows: In Sect. 2 we present the application of BSDE in financial engineering. In Sect. 3, we describe the numerical algorithm for BSDE and apply it to option pricing. The parallel implementation is discussed in Sect. 4. Section 5 shows the experimental results. Finally we give the conclusion in Sect. 6.

---

* Corresponding author.

W. Zhang et al. (Eds.): HPCA 2009, LNCS 5938, pp. 325–330, 2010.

2 BSDEs in Financial Engineering

The general form of a BSDE is shown as following:

$$-dY_t = g(Y_t, Z_t, t)dt - Z_t dW_t, \ t \in [0, T] \ ,$$
$$Y_T = \xi \ , \tag{1}$$

where W_t is a d-dimensional Brownian motion. $Y_T = \xi$ is the terminal condition of the BSDE and ξ is a F_T measurable random variable. The solution of a BSDE is a couple of variables (Y_t, Z_t), and $g(\cdot)$ is a function of (Y_t, Z_t). In the following we give an example for the application of BSDEs in option pricing and risk hedging. Assuming a bond and a stock traded in a stock market. The bond price p_t and the stock price S_t, respectively, obey:

$$p_t = e^r t \ , \tag{2}$$
$$S_t = S_0 \exp(bt + \sigma W_t - \frac{1}{2}\sigma^2 t) \ , \tag{3}$$

where r is the return rate of the bond, b is the expected return rate of the stock, σ is the volatility of the stock, and $\{W_t\}_{t \geq 0}$ is a standard Brownian motion. S_t follows the geometric Brownian motion.

Now consider a call (or put) option with strike price X on time period $[0, T]$, where the option holder has the right to buy (or sell) a stock of equation (3) from the seller at time T. Then we can use the BSDE of equation (1) to calculate the price Y_0 of the option, which correspond to the value of Y_t at time 0. The terminal condition is given by:

$$\begin{aligned} Y_T = \xi &= \phi(W_T) \\ &= \max(S_T - X, 0) \text{ for a call } , \\ &= \max(X - S_T, 0) \text{ for a put } , \end{aligned} \tag{4}$$

where $\phi(\cdot)$ is a function of the Brownian motion W_T and represents the payoff of the option holder at time T.

Furthermore, the BSDE of equation (1) helps to determine the risk hedging strategy. For example, as at time T the option holder get the payoff Y_T, the seller of the contract should pay for the lost. In order to hedge the risk, he can use the Y_0 money to do investment at time 0, where Z_0 money is used to buy the stock and $Y_0 - Z_0$ is used to buy the bond. The function $g(\cdot)$ is given as following:

$$g(Y_t, Z_t, t) = -(rY_t + (b - r)Z_t + (R - r)(Y_t - Z_t)^-) \ . \tag{5}$$

Generally, the rate R is larger than r, thus we get a non-linear BSDE, i.e. the function $g(\cdot)$ is non-linear, while the Black-Scholes model can only deal with the linear case when $R = r$.

3   Numerical Algorithm

We study the algorithm of [7] based on time discretization and scaled random walk for non-linear BSDEs solving. We apply it in option pricing, as mentioned in Sect. 2.

In the numerical algorithm, the time period $[0, T]$ is devided into n time steps with interval $\delta = T/n$. Then we backwardly calculate Y_t.

As the state of the Brownian motion at time j can be approximated with scaled random walk:

$$W_t^j = \sqrt{\delta} \sum_{i=1}^{j} \varepsilon_i \,, \tag{6}$$

where $\{(\varepsilon_m)_{1 < m < n}\}$ is a Bernoulli sequence, we can use a binomial tree to represent the Brownian motion W_t, as shown in Fig.1.(a). The upper-triangular form of it is shown in Fig.1.(b) for better description, where for a node labeled (i, j), i and j represent respectively the space step and the time step the node locates on.

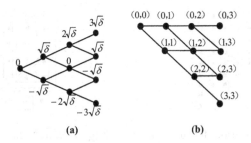

(a)   (b)

Fig. 1. Movement Approximation of the Brownian Motion

With the binomial tree model, we first calculate all the possible state of Y_T on level n with equation (4) and (6). In the following, an explicit scheme is performed iteratively from level $n - 1$ to level 0 of the tree to get the solution (Y_0, Z_0), as shown in equation (7). The total number of nodes to be computed is $(n + 1)(n + 2)/2$.

$$\begin{cases} Y_{i,\, j} = \frac{1}{2}(Y_{i,\, j+1} + Y_{i+1,\, j+1}) \\ \qquad + g(\frac{1}{2}(Y_{i,\, j+1} + Y_{i+1,\, j+1}), \frac{1}{2\sqrt{\delta}}(Y_{i,\, j+1} + Y_{i+1,\, j+1}), t_j) \,, \\ Z_{i,\, j} = \frac{1}{2\sqrt{\delta}}(Y_{i,\, j+1} - Y_{i+1,\, j+1}). \end{cases} \tag{7}$$

4   Parallel Implementation

Parallelization works for option pricing with traditional binomial tree model are discussed in [4] and [5]. According to the numerical model for non-linear BSDEs, we develop a block allocation algorithm by combining [4] and [5] to avoid large communication overhead.

We assume the number of time steps n and the number of processors p to be power of two. According to the structure of the binomial tree, the number of leaf node is $n+1$. All rows of nodes are distributed evenly among processors but the last processor receives an additional row. Thus each processor except the last one is in charge of $m = n/p$ rows of nodes. Initially option price of the leaf nodes are calculated simultaneously with equations (3), (4), (6) on each processor. For calculating the nodes of other levels, we only need to send the values of boundary nodes to the neighbor processor to perform equation (7). Thus large amount of data transfer is avoided. Furthermore, we introduce a parameter L so that the data transfer is performed every L levels to avoid frequent communication operation. In this way, the computation process is performed with $n/(L - 1)$ iterations. During each iteration, every processor operates on a block of $m * L$ nodes except the last one, which has $(m+1)*L$ nodes. Without loss of generality, we assume L to be power of two plus one so that n can be divided by $(L - 1)$. Figure 2 shows the block allocation for $n = 8, p = 2, L = 3$.

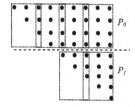

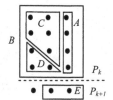

Fig. 2. Block Allocation for n=8, p=2, L=3

Fig. 3. Node Valuation in a Block

For the iteration valuating an arbitrary block B on processor P_k , we decompose block B into three regions: the inner regions A, C and the outer region D, as shown in Fig.3. The node value of the inner regions can be calculated only with the local data, while that of the outer region depends not only on local data, but also on the data of the neighbor block located on processor P_{k+1}. At the beginning of each iteration, data in A are already calculated before updating B. Thus C nodes can be updated only with local data according to equation (7). In the following, as the calculation of D nodes needs not only A nodes, but also the nodes of the first row (region E) on processor P_{k+1}, the corresponding data are transferred from processor P_{k+1} so that D nodes can be calculated.

To measure the performance of the parallel algorithm, the computation time and the communication time are evaluated. Overall, we obtain the total computing time of $O(n^2/p)$ for the parallel algorithm, with the communication time of $(O(n))$. Low communication overhead is achieved, as for large problem size the parallel communication time seems insignificant.

5   Experimental Results

We implement the parallel program by using C and MPI. Runtime experiments are performed on a LANGCHAO TIANSUO 10000 cluster with 2 Intel Xeon DP 2.8GHZ cpu and 2GB memory on each node. We use 16 nodes with 1 cpu per node for the experiment. The source code is compiled with the -O3 option set for gcc compiler. Table 1 shows the timing results for various number of time steps $n = 8192, 16384, 32768, 65536, 131072$. The block parameter L is fixed to 9.

Table 1. The Parallel Runtimes (in seconds) with the TIANSUO 10000 Cluster

n	$p = 1$	$p = 2$	$p = 4$	$p = 8$	$p = 16$
8192	2.33	1.52	0.85	0.74	0.7
16384	12.02	7.99	4.28	2.97	1.98
32768	51.35	35.7	18.27	8.72	5.35
65536	211.73	136.72	79.28	38.18	19.2
131072	864.19	575.65	338.94	160.71	83.71

The results in Table 1 seem optimistic. We can see that with a single processor, the running time increases greatly when the number of time steps n grows up. And the parallel runtime for $n = 131072$ decreases much more sharply than that with small n when the number of processors increases. For better analysis of the parallel runtime results, we use the data in Table 1 to produce speedup plots in Fig. 4.

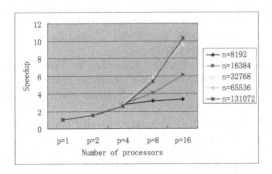

Fig. 4. Speedup Graph with the TIANSUO 10000 Cluster

As observed from Fig.4., for small number of time steps, the speedups increase very slowly while augmenting the number of processors, especially when $n = 8192$, the speedup only achieves 3.33 for $p = 16$. This could be explained that for small problem size, the parallel overhead is relatively large comparing with the computation time. Then for larger number of time steps, as the amount of computation increase quadratically when n grows up, the parallel overhead tends to be insignificant. Hence with the augmentation of p, the speedups increase much more rapidly for $n = 32768, 65536, 131072$ and achieve respectively 9.60, 11.02, 10.32 when $p = 16$. Therefore large number of time steps offers a better problem for parallel computing.

6   Conclusion

In this paper, a binomial tree based numerical algorithm for non-linear BSDEs is applied in option pricing and studied for parallelization. A parallel algorithm with block allocation is proposed according to the inherent structure of the numerical model. Large communication overhead is avoided on considering both the communication frequency and the amount of data transfer. Parallel run time analysis is performed on a cluster with 16 nodes and shows promising results.

Acknowledgement

This work was supported by a grant from the National High Technology Research and Development Program of China (863 Program) (No. 2006AA01A113).

References

1. Black, F., Scholes, M.: The pricing of options and corporate liabilities. Journal of Political Economy 81, 637–654 (1973)
2. Wan, J.W.L., Lai, K., Kolkiewicz, A.W., et al.: A Parallel Quasi-Monte Carlo Approach to Pricing American Options on Multiple Assets. International Journal of High Performance Computing and Ne tworking 4, 321–330 (2006)
3. Sak, H., Ozekici, S., Boduroglu, I.: Parallel computing in Asian option pricing. Parallel Computing 33, 92–108 (2007)
4. Huang, K., Thulasiram, R.K.: Parallel Algorithm for Pricing American Asian Options with Multi-Dimensional Assets. In: Proceedings of the 19th International Symposium on High Performance Computing Systems and Applications, pp. 177–185 (2005)
5. Gerbessiotis, A.V.: Architecture independent parallel binomial tree option price valuations. Parallel Computing 30, 301–316 (2004)
6. El Karoui, N., Peng, S., Quenez, M.C.: Backward Stochastic Differential Equations in Finance. Mathematical Finance 7, 1–71 (1997)
7. Peng, S., Xu, M.: The Numerical Algorithms and simulations for BSDEs (2008), ArXiv: math.PR/08062761
8. Surkov, V.: Parallel Option Pricing with Fourier Space Time-stepping Method on Graphics Processing Units. In: IEEE International Symposium on Parallel and Distributed Processing (2008)

Dynamic Turbulence Simulation of Ceramic Roller Kiln Based on Particle Systems

Wenbi Rao and Weixia Shi

Dept. Computer Science and Technology, Wuhan University of Technology,
Wuhan, China
{raowenbi,swx19832003}@yahoo.com.cn

Abstract. Particle systems are an effective way for visualizing "fuzzy" objects in a variety of context and the simulation of flame spreading is very useful in the combustion research of ceramic roller kiln. This paper introduces a dynamic turbulence model which can impact the flame spreading. According to the model, the flame spreading and temperature field of ceramic roller kiln are simulated in order to better understand the combustion of ceramic roller kiln. To strengthen the effect of three-dimensional visual simulation, two mechanisms are provided, one is particle collision and detection, and another is the temperature-color mapping table. It's shown that this visual model is feasible and of high performance.

Keywords: visualization, particle system, turbulence, ceramic roller kiln.

1 Introduction

Ceramic roller kiln is a new type of continuous industrial kiln which represents the trend of modern industrial kiln. As we know, energy saving is very important, so it is necessary to make the best of ceramic roller kiln.

In the process of combustion research, either experimental or numerical calculation will produce a large amount of data. It contains large and complex information which is not easy to understand and analyze. So how to account for a large number of complex data and analyze them in an intuitionist, simple and intelligible way is necessary, that is the visualization.

As a computer technology, visualization plays an important role in many research areas, therefore, it is also an available method for more intuitionist, in-depth analyzing in the combustion research of ceramics roller kiln [1]. However, as we know in our knowledge, there are hardly relevant literatures about the visual simulation of ceramic roller kiln now.

The structure of this paper is as follow: Section 2 we will introduces the ceramic roller kiln. basicprinciple of particle system will expatiate how to visualize the dynamic spreading process of turbulence. At last, some concluding remarks are given in Section 5.

W. Zhang et al. (Eds.): HPCA 2009, LNCS 5938, pp. 331–336, 2010.
© Springer-Verlag Berlin Heidelberg 2010

2 Ceramic Roller Kiln

Ceramic roller kiln is a tunnel-shaped kiln. Its cross-section is long and narrow. Unlike car tunnel kiln, it does not load products with the kiln car to move, but by an array of parallel rollers which have high-temperature and cross the cross-section of kiln working zone. Ceramic products on the rollers are delivered into the kiln along with the roller's rotation and their firing process is completed in the kiln, so call this type of kiln "ceramic roller kiln" [2]. This kind of kiln is mainly composed of the preheating zone, the firing zone and the cooling zone. In the firing zone, each section has a couple of burners which are staggered, symmetrical and alternately upward and downward. The combustion products of ceramic roller kiln directly contact with the ceramic products which could improve the heat transfer efficiency and form well-proportioned temperature fields [3]. Fig. 1 is the delineation of ceramic roller kiln.

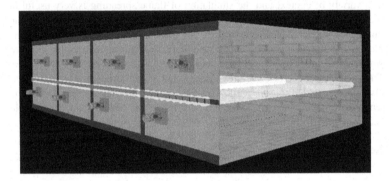

Fig. 1. The three-dimensional space of ceramic roller kiln

3 The Basic Principle of Particle System

Particle system is a collection of many minute particles that together represent a fuzzy object. Over a period of time, particles are generated into a system, move and change from within the system, and die from the system. To compute each frame in a motion sequence, the following sequence of steps is performed:

(1) New particles are generated into the system and each new particle is assigned its individual attributes.

(2) Any particles that have existed within the system past their prescribed lifetime are extinguished.

(3) The remaining particles are transformed and moved according to their dynamic attributes.

(4) An image of the living particles is rendered in a frame buffer.

The particle system can be programmed to execute any set of instructions at each step. Because it is procedural, this approach can incorporate any computational model that describes the appearance or dynamics of the object.

The original particle systems method was based on stochastic processes [4]. There was no interaction among particles. Now, the interactions among particles in a particle system and among particle systems are very important for simulating some phenomena [5].

4 The Visualization of Turbulence and Temperature Field of Ceramic Roller Kiln

4.1 Particle Collision and Detection on Chamber Wall

The general collision and contact problem is difficult. Fortunately, here we only consider the simplest case of particles colliding with plane. Even these simple collision models can add significant interest to the simulation.

There are two parts to the collision problem: detecting collisions, and responding to them in ceramic roller kiln, we need test if any particle contact with the chamber wall, if it's position match with any one of the conditions following, the particle collides with the chamber wall.

$$XWallef \leq x \leq XWalright$$
$$YWallup \leq y \leq YWalldow \qquad (1)$$
$$ZWallefro \leq z \leq ZWallback$$

Where $XWallef$ and $XWalright$ are the boundary positions of ceramic roller kiln on the x axis, the others seem like that.

Set the particle's lifetime zero is the response to collision in our model.

4.2 The Simulation of Turbulence

Turbulences are composed of a variety of different vortexes, the large vortexes are the main carriers of puissant energy, they are energetic, but the small vortex is the one which dissipates energy [6]. The transport and interaction of a variety of vortexes, lead to the convection, diffusion, agglomeration and dissipation of vortex- size in the flow field. In this paper, the turbulence was simulated according to analyze the characters of vortexes.

In order to achieve realism of flame motion, dynamic vortex was presented in the paper. The data structure of this vortex is a seven-dimensional vector of the real domain, the formula is:

$$Dvort = (Pv, Radi, Rainc, Angl, Ainc, Velo, Vac) \qquad (2)$$

where $Pv = \{Pv_x, Pv_y, Pv_z\}^T$ and $Radi$ are the central position and the radius of vortex, $Rainc$ is the disturbance quantity, $Angl$ and $Ainc$ are the rotation Angle and Angle increment of particle, $Velo$ and Vac are the vortex 's velocity and acceleration.

Vortex field is simulated by the particle system. In the beginning, all attributes of vortex have been initialized; their values will change over time.

If a particle comes into the vortex field at frame i, at the next frame $i+1$ (*Timef* is the time from one frame to the next), the value of *Angl is:*

$$Angl_{i+1} = Angl_i + Ainc \times Timef \tag{3}$$

The position and velocity of vortex are:

$$Pv_{i+1} = Pv_i + Velo_i \times Timef$$
$$Velo_{i+1} = Velo_i + Vac_i \times Timef \tag{4}$$

If the particles circumrotate in the *x-z* plane of its coordinate system, the position of a particle at frame $i+1$ is:

$$\begin{bmatrix} P'_x \\ P'_y \\ P'_z \end{bmatrix} = \begin{bmatrix} Pv_x \\ Pv_y \\ Pv_z \end{bmatrix} + \begin{bmatrix} \cos\theta & 0 & \sin\theta \\ 0 & 1 & 0 \\ -\sin\theta & 0 & \cos\theta \end{bmatrix} \cdot \begin{bmatrix} P_x - Pv_x \\ P_y - Pv_y \\ P_z - Pv_z \end{bmatrix} \tag{5}$$

Considering the mobility and randomness, disturbance quantity *Rainc* is inducted, According to (5), we obtain the expression:

$$P'_x = Pv_x + (P_x - Pv_x)\cos\theta + (P_z - Pv_z)\sin\theta + Rainc$$
$$P'_y = P_y + Rainc \tag{6}$$
$$P'_z = Pv_y - (P_x - Pv_x)\sin\theta + (P_z - Pv_z)\cos\theta + Rainc$$

Where $P' = \{P'_x, P'_y, P'_z\}^T$ is the particle's position at frame $i+1$, $P = \{P_x, P_y, P_z\}^T$ is its position at frame i, $\theta = Angl_{i+1}$.

If the particle has departed from vortex field, according to Newton second law, because of the resultant force, the particle's position and velocity will change over time, so at frame $i+1$, its velocity and position are:

$$(Spe_x)_{i+1} = (Spe_x)_i + HoriF * \cos\beta$$
$$(Spe_y)_{i+1} = (Spe_x)_i + \int_0^{Timef} (f/m - g)dt \tag{7}$$
$$(Spe_z)_{i+1} = (Spe_z)_i + HoriF * \sin\beta$$

$$P'_x = P_x + \int_0^{Timef} (Spe_x)_i dt$$
$$P'_y = P_y + \int_0^{Timef} (Spe_y)_i dt \tag{8}$$
$$P'_z = P_z + \int_0^{Timef} (Spe_z)_i dt$$

Where $Spe = \{Spe_x, Spe_y, Spe_z\}^T$ is the velocity of particle, *HoriF* is the horizontal flow speed, β is its angle, f is the thermal buoyancy, m and g are the mass and gravity.

4.3 Temperature - Color Mapping Table

To facilitate the expression of temperature in the process of flame spreading, we need to create a temperature-color mapping table. To reduce the complexity of the real-time calculations, we also need to establish a palette which contains all the colors we need, if the temperature known, according to corresponding index value of temperature, we can easily get the color value through searching.

In the palette, each temperature index contacts with a color's RGB values, the corresponding relation is:

$$Color = (R, G, B, Tempindex) \qquad (9)$$

According to relevant function, any temperature can associate with a color, when particles moving, the change of colors can express the change of temperatures.

The three-dimensional space of ceramic roller kiln was simulated with OpenGl. Fig. 2 shows the firing zone of ceramic roller kiln. The turbulence is shown in Fig. 3 around the ceramic product. It shows the dynamicity of vortex, Fig. 4 represents the temperature field of ceramic roller kiln. In the left of the figure, we can see a Temperature-Color comparison table.

Fig. 2. The firing zone of ceramic roller kiln

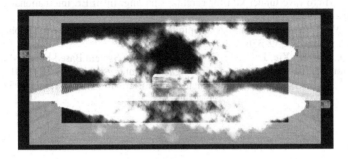

Fig. 3. The dynamic turbulence

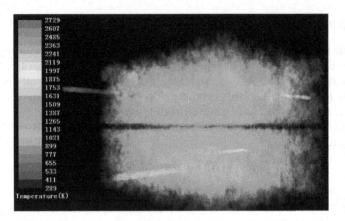

Fig. 4. The temperature field of ceramic roller kiln

5   Conclusion

A turbulence model based on particle system was presented in this paper, and it showed how to represent the dynamicity of flame. The mechanism of particle collision and detection to control the flame behavior accordingly was also provided. To display temperature field, we established a temperature-color mapping table. Therefore, the visualization of turbulence and temperature field of ceramic roller kiln can provide developers with direct insight to the combustion process.

Motion blur, texture mapping, and other techniques in computer graphics were also employed to achieve better results. The work is a useful addition to many applications.

References

1. Xiangge, Q.: Three-dimensional simulation of sintering of ceramics. Materials science Forum, 1287–1290 (2005)
2. Hu, G.: Ceramic Industrial Roller Kiln. China Light Industry Press, Beijing (1998)
3. Sato, M.: Microwave tunnel kiln for ceramic sintering. In: IEEE International Conference on Plasma Science (2002)
4. Revees, W.T.: Particle systems—A technique for modeling a class of fuzzy objects. ACM Computer Graphics, 359–376 (1983)
5. Zhang, Q., Wu, H., Xie, J., Zhang, Z.: Study of Particle System Based Flame Modeling and Realization. Journal of computer-aided design&computer graphics, 78–82 (2001)
6. Cheng, C.: Roller kiln gas flow and structural characteristics. Foshan ceramics 59(2), 17–20 (2002)

Rate Allocation in Overlay Networks Based on Theory of Firm Consumer

Mohammad Hossein Rezvani and Morteza Analoui

Department of Computer Engineering, Iran University of Science and Technology (IUST)
16846-13114, Hengam Street, Resalat Square, Narmak, Tehran, Iran
{Rezvani,Analoui}@iust.ac.ir

Abstract. We have designed a competitive market model for the overlay network in which each offered service is thought of as a commodity and the users can be viewed as consumers. The origin servers and the users who relay the service to their downstream nodes can thus be thought of as firms of the economy. Considering the high dynamics of the network due to joining and leaving of the nodes, the mechanism tries to regulate the price of each service in such a way that general equilibrium holds. For this property to hold in all generality, it tries to find a vector of prices such that demand of each service becomes equal to its supply.

Keywords: Overlay Networks, Multi-service Multicasting, Resource Allocation, Firm-Consumer Theory.

1 Introduction

The reason for node selfishness in overlay networks lies in the fact that the nodes belong to different administrative domains. The end-user nodes seek the complete freedom to choose the best line of action that maximizes their utilities. If their self-interests are not satisfied, they may not accept any proposed global optimization algorithm. In this context, the most important question is the following; "how should we exploit the inherent selfishness of the end-user nodes, so that the aggregate outcome of the activity of individual nodes behaving toward their own self-interests still leads to the network's overall utility maximization?"

To address node selfishness in the information collection step some works has employed game theory [1, 2, 3, 4, 5, 6]. Also, a few proposals exist in which node selfishness in tree construction step has been investigated [6, 1]. However, due to inherent limitations of game theory, the above proposals have to unrealistically assume that some global information about the network is available by the overlay nodes. A few other works has also been proposed to regulate the node selfishness by means of distributed pricing [7, 8].

We believe that the so called problem could be examined by microeconomics theory. Since each consumer in the economy is in fact a selfish utility maximizer, the behavior of the end-user node in the overlay network could be mapped to that of a consumer. From microeconomic theory point of view, the service provided by each

W. Zhang et al. (Eds.): HPCA 2009, LNCS 5938, pp. 337–343, 2010.

multicast server, plays the role of the "commodity" in an economy. Hence, we can model the overlay network as the *"overlay economy"* in which several commodities (multicast services) are provided. The overlay economy has two types of firm for each commodity: one is the origin server that provides the service (commodity) for the first time, and the other is the relaying nodes which relay the service to their downstream nodes. Also, by means of "equilibrium" concept from microeconomics theory, we can tune the allocated rates of the overlay nodes in such a way that welfare can be maximized in the overlay economy.

The original contributions of our work, differing from the aforementioned priced-based approaches is that we present an economical framework in which each node is provided with an income. Based on demand-supply theory, an exchange economy is formed in which the firms are either origin servers or end-users nodes who forward the media content to other nodes. We also take into account the price of underlying physical links in economical transactions.

The remainder of this paper is organized as follows: Section 2 introduces the network model. Section 3 presents the formulation of the competitive overlay economy. Finally, we conclude in Section 4.

2 Network Model

We consider an overlay network consisting of V end-hosts denoted as $\mathcal{V} = \{1, 2, ..., V\}$. Let us suppose that the overlay network consists of N media services, denoted as $\mathcal{N} = \{1, 2, ..., N\}$. So, there are N servers among V hosts $(N < V)$, each serve a distinct type of media service. We denote $S = \{s_1, s_2, ..., s_N\}$ as a set containing N servers. Suppose the network is shared by a set of N multicast groups. Any multicast group (multicast session) consists of a media server, a set of receivers, and a set of links which the multicast group uses. Any server belongs to anyone multicast group. Note that the links are the physical connections between nodes and routers, and routers and routers.

Let us suppose that the overlay network consists of L physical links, denoted as $\mathcal{L} = \{1, 2, ..., L\}$. The capacity of each link, that is the bandwidth of each physical link $l \in \mathcal{L}$ is denoted as c_l. We collect these capacities into a link capacity vector $\mathbf{C} = (c_l, l \in \mathcal{L})$.

Fig. 1-a shows an overlay network which consists of two multicast groups. In this example there is $S = \{s_1, s_2\}$ in which s_1 (node 0) indicates one group and s_2 (node 3) indicates second group. Solid lines indicate one group and dashed lines indicate the second group.

The overlay tree is built by formation of the multicast group gradually. The initial flow in each tree originates from a server and terminates in its downstream nodes. Fig. 1-b shows two trees each of which has been constructed by joining the nodes to multicast groups. All the nodes, except the server and leaf nodes, relay the multicast stream via unicast in a peer-to-peer fashion.

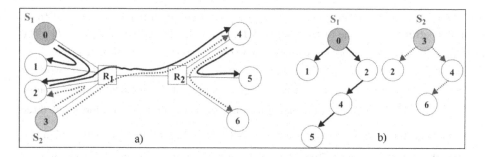

Fig. 1. a) Overlay network with two multicast groups b) of each multicast group

Each multicast session $n \in \mathcal{N}$ consists of F^n unicast end-to-end flows, denoted as set $\mathcal{F}^n$. The flows of each multicast group of Fig. 1-b can be obtained as follows

$$\mathcal{F}^1 = \{f^1_{01}, f^1_{02}, f^1_{24}, f^1_{45}\} \quad , \qquad \mathcal{F}^2 = \{f^2_{32}, f^2_{34}, f^2_{46}\}$$

Each flow f^n_{ij} of the multicast group n passes a subset of physical links, denoted as

$$\mathcal{L}(f^n_{ij}) \subseteq \mathcal{L}. \tag{1}$$

Fig. 1. a can be used to see the links used by each flow.

$$\mathcal{L}(f^1_{24}) = \{l_3, l_5, l_6\} \qquad \mathcal{L}(f^2_{34}) = \{l_4, l_5, l_6\}$$

Each flow $f^n_{ij} \in \mathcal{F}^n$ in multicast group n has a rate x^n_{ij}. We collect the rate of all flows of multicast group n into a rate vector $X^n = (x^n_{ij}, \; f^n_{ij} \in \mathcal{F}^n)$.

Finally, at the end of this section, we define the sets $Buy(i)$ and $Sell(i)$ for each overlay node i. $Buy(i)$ specifies all multicast groups in the overlay network from which node i receives (buys) services. Similarly, $Sell(i)$ specifies all multicast groups in the overlay network to which node i provides (sells) services.

3   Formulation of Competitive Overlay Economy

Now, we describe the competitive market system to include production as well as consumption. We name this system as *"competitive overlay market system."* In accordance with the notations presented in section 2, we will suppose throughout the paper that there is a fixed and finite number $n \in \mathcal{N}$ of each commodity.

Let $I = \{1,...,I\}$ index the set of consumers. Each consumer $i \in I$ is endowed with a nonnegative vector of the N commodities $\mathbf{e}_i = (e^1_i,...,e^N_i)$. Let $\mathbf{e} \equiv (\mathbf{e}_1,...,\mathbf{e}_I)$ denote the economy's endowment vector, and define an "allocation" as a vector $\mathbf{X} \equiv (X_1,...,X_I)$, where $\mathbf{X}_i = (x^1_i,...,x^N_i)$ denotes consumer i's bundle according to the allocation.

To describe the production sector, we suppose there are a fixed number J of firms in the current state of the overlay network that we index by the set $J = \{1,...,J\}$. The *competitive overlay economy* includes two sources of firms. The firms can be either the origin servers (i.e., $j \in S$) which originally offer the service to the network or can be the end-user nodes who relay the services to their downstream nodes. We now let $y_j \in R^N$ be a production plan for some firm. If, for example, there are three services in the overlay economy and $y_j = (7,0,13)$, then the production plan implies that firm j produces 7 units of service number 1 and 13 units of service number 3 but does not produce service number 2 at all. To summarize the technological possibilities in production, we suppose each firm j possesses a "production possibility set" Y_j, $j \in J$.

It is common in microeconomic literature to describe each market by a function named as "excess demand". Then, the whole of system may be described compactly by a single N-dimentional *"excess demand vector"*, each of whose elements is the excess demand function for one of the N markets. We can define a real-valued aggregate excess demand function for each service market and a vector-valued aggregate excess demand function for the competitive overlay economy as a whole. Aggregate excess demand for service $k \in S$ is

$$z_k(P) \equiv \sum_{i \in I} x_i^k(P, m_i(P)) - \sum_{j \in J} y_j^k(P) - \sum_{i \in I} e_i^k .$$ (2)

And the aggregate excess demand vector is

$$Z(P) \equiv (z^1(P),...,z^N(P)) .$$ (3)

A *Walrasian equilibrium* price vector $P^* >> 0$ clears all markets. That is $Z(P^*) = 0$.

The utility function u_i consists of an economic part and an empirical part. The former component, namely u_i^{eco} can be simply expressed as a function of allocated bandwidths of each service. The latter, namely u_i^{emp} accounts for the node's empirical utility for receiving certain services, which may be characterized by various characteristics arising from the underlying physical network routings such as loss rate, and delay. So, we have

$$u_i(t) = \alpha u_i^{eco}(t) + (1-\alpha) u_i^{emp}(t) .$$ (4)

The economic part of the consumer's utility function is the weighted sum of his benefit earned from the allocated bandwidth of each service. The economic utility function of consumer i can be expressed as follows

$$u_i^{eco}(t) = \sum_{n \in Buy(i)} \beta_n \ln(1 + \frac{x_{ki}^n(t)}{B^n}) . \tag{5}$$

Where $\sum_{n \in \mathcal{N}} \beta_n = 1$. As mentioned earlier in the section 2, $x_{ki}^n(t)$ is the rate at which

consumer i receives service n from its parent node k at time slot t. Also B^n denotes maximum allowed bandwidth of service n. The empirical utility function of consumer i can be expressed as follows

$$u_i^{emp}(t) = - \sum_{n \in Buy(i)} \beta_n \ln(1 + \frac{l_{ki}^n(t)}{D_i^n}) - \sum_{n \in Buy(i)} \beta_n \ln(1 + \frac{d_{ki}^n(t)}{L_i^n}) . \tag{6}$$

Where $\sum_{n \in \mathcal{N}} \beta_n = 1$. Negative sign in equation (6) indicates the utility loss that is

incurred by consumer i due to the delay and the loss rate of each of services he receives. Here, D_i^n and L_i^n are node-specific or application-specific parameters which represent the maximal tolerable delay and maximal tolerable loss rate of service n respectively.

Now, let's define the optimization problem of consumer i in the competitive overlay economy. Each consumer i on joining the overlay economy is endowed with an endowment vector $e_i = (e_i^1, ..., e_i^N)$. Each element e_i^k in this vector indicates the amount of service k which is endowed to user i. This endowment in actually is the amount of credit that enables the consumer i to enter the economy and take share in future transactions. The amount $P.e_i$ can be thought as "budget" for consumer i. So, one can imagine that each node in the overlay economy is provided with a budget, but in the form of the commodity, i.e., in the form of the amount of service. In optimizations which are based on consumer theory, only the economic part of the utility functions matters. The empirical part of the utility function serves to distinguish among appropriate locations of the overlay tree to be used on joining a new node. The utility maximization problem of each consumer i in the economy at each time slot t is as follows

$$\max_{\{x_{ki}^n(t) \mid n \in Buy(i)\}} u_i^{eco}(t) \tag{7}$$

$$\text{s.t.} \sum_{n \in Buy(i)} \left(p_n(t) x_{ki}^n(t) + \sum_{l \in \mathcal{L}(f_{ki}^n)} q_l(t) \right) \le \sum_{k=1}^N p_k(t).e_i^k + \Pi_i(P,t) \tag{8}$$

$$\sum_{n \in Buy(i)} x_{ki}^n(t) \le CD_i \tag{9}$$

$$b^n \le x_{ki}^n(t) \le B^n, \quad \forall n \in Buy(i) \tag{10}$$

Condition (8) implies the budget constraint of node i as a consumer in the overlay economy. The sum on left-hand side of (8) is just the expenditure of node i in which the first part includes the prices of different demanded services and the other part (the inner sigma) is the summation of prices of all links that f_{ki}^n goes through, or in other words, the underlying physical network prices that f_{ki}^n has to pay. The right-hand side of (8) simply is consumer's budget plus his share in the profit of his corresponding firm. Constraint (9) implies that the summation of rates of all services demanded by consumer i should be equal or less than his downlink capacity CD_i. Constraint (10) is an application-specific constraint and states that the receiving rate of each service should be in the interval between its minimum and maximum allowed bandwidth. The feasible region of constraints (8) to (10) is compact. So, by non-linear optimization theory, there exists a maximizing value of argument $\{x_{ki}^n(t) | n \in Buy(i)\}$ for the above optimization problem, which can be solved by Lagrangian method [9]. We denote the solution to consumer i's problem at time slot t by :

$$x_{ki}^n(t, P, P.e_i, \Pi_i(P), \sum_{l \in L(f_{ki}^n)} q_l(t), CD_i, b^n, B^n), \quad \forall n \in Buy(i) \tag{11}$$

The allocation set $\{x_{ki}^n(t), \quad \forall n \in Buy(i)\}$ is in fact the *Walrasian demand function of consumer i* in the overlay economy.

Now, we turn to the optimization problem of firms in our model of competitive overlay economy.

Due to the dual role of such overlay nodes, one can think that they are acting as both consumers and firms in the economy. We already investigated the consumer-related aspects of such intermediate nodes of the overlay tree in (7) to (11). In fact, each end-user $j \in J$ who relays the available services to his downstream nodes can be considered as firm j. Here, each firm j seeks to solve the following problem

$$\max_{y_j(t) \in Y_j} \sum_{n \in Sell(j)} p_n(t).y_j^n(t) \tag{12}$$

S.t.

$$\sum_{n \in Sell(j)} y_j^n(t) \le CU_j \tag{13}$$

$$y_j^n(t) \le x_{kj}^n(t), \qquad \forall n \in Sell(j) \tag{14}$$

$$y_j^n(t) = \sum_{k \in Chd(j)} x_{jk}^n(t) \tag{15}$$

Since for each firm of this class, all the required input services are present by its corresponding consumer node, we consider no cost of production for it in (12). Constraint (13) simply states that the sum of productions of all services produced by the firm j should not be greater than j's uploading capacity. Constraint (14) implies that in the firm j, the rate of each supplied service cannot exceed the rate at which it is provided to j. This constraint is unique in the overlay multicast, mainly due to the dual role of end-user nodes as both receivers and senders and is referred to as "data constraint." Constraint (15) states that y_j^n should be equal to the sum of the rates of the service type n that is supplied by the firm j to be used by its downstream nodes in the economy. Altogether, we can say that the solution to (12) is in fact the production plan of the firm j as introduced before in the section 3.2. With respect to the aforementioned constraints, we can represent this production plan by

$$y_j(t, P, CU_j, \{x_{kj}^n(t) \mid n \in Sell(j)\}, \{x_{jk}^n(t) \mid k \in Chd(j)\}). \qquad (16)$$

Each element $y_j^n(t, P, CU_j, x_{kj}^n(t), \{x_{jk}^n(t) \mid k \in Chd(j)\})$ of this production plan represents the amount of service type n which the end-user node j sells to his downstream nodes in the overlay economy. If node j does not provide a given service type, the corresponding element in the production plan y_j will be equal to zero. Due to space limitation, we omit the experimental results as well as algorithms of nodes' joining and leaving in this paper.

4 Conclusion

We have modeled the interactions of the overlay multicast network using the competitive exchange economy with production. In this model we have targeted the multi-service multi-rate allocation mechanism based on the Firm-Consumer theory.

References

1. Li, D., Wu, J., Cui, Y., Liu, J.: QoS-aware Streaming in Overlay Multicast Considering Selfishness in Construction Action. In: Proc. of IEEE INFOCOM 2007, Anchorage, Alaska (2007)
2. Habib, A., Chuang, J.: Incentive Mechanism for Peer-to-Peer Media Streaming. In: Proc. of IWQOS 2004, Montreal, Canada (2004)
3. Yuen, S., Li, B.: Strategyproof Mechanisms for Dynamic Multicast Tree Formation in Overlay Networks. In: Proc. of IEEE INFOCOM 2005, Miami, Florida, USA (2005)
4. Wang, W., Li, X., Suny, Z., Wang, Y.: Design Multicast Protocols for Non-Cooperative Networks. In: Proc. of IEEE INFOCOM 2005, Miami, Florida, USA (2005)
5. Liang, J., Nahrstedt, K.: RandPeer: Membership Management for QoS Sensitive Peer-to-Peer Applications. In: Proc. of IEEE INFOCOM 2006, Barcelona, Spain (2006)
6. Tan, G., Jarvis, S.A.: A Payment-based Incentive and Service Differentiation Mechanism for Peer-to-Peer Streaming Broadcast. In: Proc. of IWQOS 2006. Yale University, New Haven (2006)
7. Cui, Y., Xue, Y., Nahrstedt, K.: Optimal Resource Allocation in Overlay Multicast. IEEE Transactions on Parallel and Distributed Systems 17(8), 808–823 (2006)
8. Wang, W., Li, B.: Market-Based Self-Optimization for Autonomic Service Overlay Networks. IEEE J. on Selected Areas in Communications 23(12), 2320–2332 (2005)
9. Bertsekas, D.: Nonlinear Programming, 2nd edn. Athena Scientific, Belmont (1999)

Retraction: Synthesizing Neural Networks and Randomized Algorithms

Yonghong Shao[1], Qingyue Kong[2], and Yingying Ma[3]

[1] Department of Art and Design, Yiwu Industrial and Commercial College,
Yiwu, China
[2] Department of Information Engineering, Hebei Chemial & Pharmaceutical College,
Shijiazhuang, China
[3] College of Business Administration, South China University of Technology,
Guangzhou, China
shaoyonghong3046@163.com, Kongqingyue@163.com,
mayingying@163.com

Several conference proceedings have been infiltrated by fake submissions generated by the SCIgen computer program. Due to the fictional content the chapter "Synthesizing Neural Networks and Randomized Algorithms" by "Yonghong Shao, Qingyue Kong, and Yingying Ma" has been retracted by the publisher. Measures are being taken to avoid similar breaches in the future.

W. Zhang et al. (Eds.): HPCA 2009, LNCS 5938, pp. 344–349, 2010.
© Springer-Verlag Berlin Heidelberg 2010

A Dynamic Update Framework for OSGi Applications*

Fei Shen, Siqi Du, and Linpeng Huang

Department of Computer Science and Technology, Shanghai JiaoTong University
Shanghai, 200240, People's Republic of China
emmelle_0@sjtu.edu.cn, siqi.du@gmail.com,
huang-lp@cs.sjtu.edu.cn

Abstract. Dynamic software update is very meaningful for the downtime-critical applications to reduce the downtime during the software evolution phase. Nowadays more and more complicated applications are developed on the OSGi platform. In this paper, we present a dynamic software update framework for OSGi applications, known as DSUF. DSUF can provide component-level dynamic update. It works automatically and programmers do not need to change many codes for the existing codes to fit in the framework. Experiments show that DSUF will only cost reasonable extra computer resources.

1 Introduction

In the maintenance phase, the software might needs to be changed to fixing bugs, adding more functionality, improving performance, distributing to the new environment, etc. For normal situation, developers update the software by shutting down the executing programs, applying the patches and restarting the programs. We call this 'static update'. In some situation, the software has downtime limit, such as banking system, telephone system, etc. Shutting down these applications will cost huge loss even serious accidents.

So 'Change on the fly' [1], as known as dynamic software update, is proposed to solve the above problems. In Fabry's definition, when users adapt the dynamic software update: the whole software system should not have to be stopped at all, individual instances of objects may be momentarily unavailable while they are updated; the user will not detect that the system is being updated, i.e., the updating process is transparent to the users. [1]

In this paper, we will present a new dynamic update framework DSUF for Java-written OSGi [2] applications. Our dynamic update framework can update OSGi applications at bundle (component) level. DSUF has the following characters. (1) Automatic Update Process. When users initiate the update, the framework will automatically perform the whole update process. After the update, the data concurrency is

---

* Supported by the National Natural Science Foundation of China under Grant No.60673116 and the National High-Tech Research and Development Plan of China under Grant No. 2006AA01Z166.

W. Zhang et al. (Eds.): HPCA 2009, LNCS 5938, pp. 350–355, 2010.

preserved to ensure the correctness of the program execution. (2) Little Extra Computer Resources Consumption. The framework behaves as an ordinary OSGi bundle. It need only cache the service provider objects so the amount of extra memory and CPU consumption is very limited. (3) Easy Using. The usage of the framework is also very similar to the using of normal OSGi framework. So programmers need not modify a lot of codes to fit in our framework.

Researchers have proposed several mechanisms to tackle the dynamic update problems.[1][3][4][5][6][7][8]. But as far as we know, our DSUF is the only OSGi dynamic update solution with full state transfer function.

The rest of this paper is organized as follows. Section 2 gives an overview of the infrastructure for our DSUF framework. Section 3 explores the detail of DSUF. The performance evaluations and conclusions are given in section 4.

2 Infrastructure

The Java Language: Java is a dynamic programming language which provides reflection mechanism for programmers to load and retrieve runtime information about objects in a program. This mechanism is very useful for us to perform state transfer in dynamic software update.

OSGi framework: OSGi is a dynamic service-oriented, component-based framework for Java applications. It is widely used to build complex applications like IDEs, application servers, application frameworks, etc. [2] In OSGi, bundles (components) can be installed, started, stopped, uninstalled and updated dynamically. Bundles can provide services by binding specific interfaces with their implementations in the framework registry. Any bundles which need to use this service can ask the framework registry for the implementation of that interface. In our DSUF, we assume that bundles are only interacts with each other by providing and using services.

3 DSUF

3.1 The Update Unit

Conceptually, the dynamic update can be performed in the method level, class level, component level, etc. To perform method level update, the runtime context, including register, local variable in methods and so on, should be preserved and transformed to the new codes. But in java, these contexts are managed by the Java Virtual Machine and can not be accessed by other user defined classes. So it is almost impossible to achieve method level dynamic update for Java applications.

Class level dynamic update can be achieved, but it will cost too much computer resources, as explained in the section 3.3. This disadvantage makes it inapplicable.

In OSGi, an application is composed of several bundles. The OSGi framework provides a mechanism to install, start, stop, uninstall a bundle dynamically. So the dynamic update provided by DSUF is bundle-based.

3.2 The Architecture and Update Process

The architecture of DSUF is shown in Fig 1.

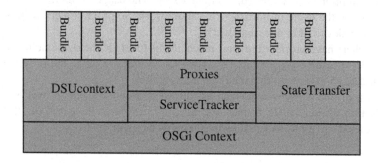

Fig. 1. The Architecture

DSUF itself is encapsulated as an OSGi bundle and registers the update service to the OGSi framework. It should be started before any other bundles excluding the system bundle. DSUF mainly has four modules: DSUcontext, Proxy, ServicesTracker and StateTransfer module. When a bundle is installed, the ServicesTracker will capture this event and create proxies for each service registered. The proxies will also be registered in the DSUcontext, which is a module that manages the relationships between proxies and their implementation objects and controls the dynamic update process. This step is automatic and programmers need not to change any code as they do for normal service registrations. To use a registered service, the user should acquire the service object from DSUcontext rather than OSGi BundleContext as usual. The StateTransfer module is in charge of the state transfer from the old bundles to the new bundles, so as to keep the data concurrency of the dynamic update process.

The update process of DSUF can be divided into the following steps (the word 'related' below means something in the bundles to be updated): (1) The proxies block any new coming invocation requests to the related services and wait for all current running service invocations to stop. (2) The DSUcontext stops the old bundles and starts the new bundles. (3) The DSUcontext performs state transfer if the state transfer mapping file exists. (4) Old bundles are uninstalled from the OSGi framework. (5) The proxies release the lock to the blocked invocation requests.

3.3 Proxy

To update software dynamically, we must substitute the old objects for the new ones. Also, all the references that were pointing to the old objects should be redirected to the new ones. Unfortunately, the redirecting job is not an easy task because the Java Virtual Machine does not provide APIs for programmers to get the objects that have a reference to a certain object.

One method to enable Java object reference redirecting is proxy. An updatable class is transformed into 3 classes, an implementation class, an interface class, and a proxy class.

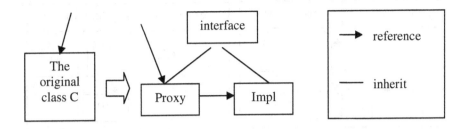

Fig. 2. Class transformation

The key point is that the class transformation separates the implementation object from the referencing objects by adding a proxy for each class. The proxy shares the same interface with the original class C. But it does not contain the actual implementation of the interface. The proxy class maintains a list of the actual implementation objects for C and redirects all method invocation towards the implementation objects. The external objects only hold the proxy class's reference.

So we just need to replace the object references in the proxy's implementation lists, if we want to substitute the old objects for the new ones in the dynamic update processes. [4] suggested that in order to provide class level update, all classes should be transformed in such way. This brings a large sum of memory consumption (about 6.36% for average and 18.92% for maximum).

For our framework, we do not transform all classes because the update unit we provide is the component level. Only the service implementation objects should be interacted with the objects outside the component and any other objects should only be accessed in the component. Thus, what we need to transform are the component objects and that will save a lot of memory consumption.

3.4 State Transfer

The components to be updated can contain states. According to Yves VANDE-WOUDE's definition, the state of a component is its internal structure and information content. Components can either be stateful or stateless, depending on whether they are required to maintain state between different operations in order to guarantee their working. [9] In stateful components, we must keep this states concurrency after the software update.

Because we assume that no objects other than the service implementation objects have interaction with other components, we can conclude that all objects in a component serve for the service implementation objects. Thus, the runtime objects in a component can be organized into several trees, the roots of which are the service implementation objects, as shown in fig. 3.

Apparently, the states of a component are all contained in these objects as themselves or their fields. So we can represent the 'location' of a component state by specifying the path from the service implementation objects to this field. For example, the path of state C in the old component can be represented as ro.ao.co. So we can retrieve any state from the root object if we know the path.

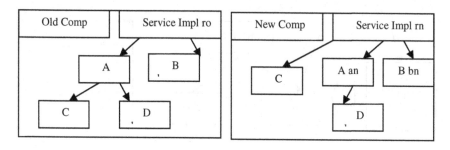

Fig. 3. The Component Objects Tree

According to this strategy, we can define a XML-based state mapping file to map the old component states to the new component states.

4 Performance Evaluation and Conclutions

To evaluate the performance impact DSUF brings to the application, we uses an OSGi-based FTP client called OGFTP. It is a command line FTP client program that can record the transfer time and memory consumed. Our test case is to transfer 512M bytes of data in a LAN that is composed of only 2 computers. The test case involves 771 service invocations. Our goal is to compare the running time and the heap memory consumption between the standard OGFTP (uses normal OSGi) and the updatable OGFTP (uses DSUF). The test result is shown below.

Table 1. The running time difference

	Maximum Diff	Minimum Diff	Average Diff
Total Diff / Each invocation (Absolute, ms)	608 / 0.79	188 / 0.24	375 / 0.48

We should not consider the time difference in percentage. Because the extra time spent for proxy is just at the very beginning of the service invocation rather than influencing the whole service invocation process. The extra time consumption by DSUF depends on the number of the service invocations and does not depend on the whole program running time. From table 1, we know that each invocation time is about 0.79 milliseconds for maximum and 0.48 milliseconds for average in our case.

Like the running time, we should not only consider the total heap memory difference, because each service would have its own proxy, the extra heap memory depends on the number of services registered. In our case, OGFTP only has one service, so we can easily find out the memory needed for a service. From table 2, we know that the memory consumption of each service is about 5.37% more than standard for maximum and 1.02% more for average in our case.

Table 2. The heap memory difference

	Maximum Diff	Minimum Diff	Average Diff
Standard OGFTP (bytes)	3011232	2967312	2949712
Diff(bytes / percentage)	161624 / 5.37%	17803 / 0.60%	30087 / 1.02%

In this paper, we proposed and implemented a dynamic software update framework for OSGi applications, DSUF. DSUF can determine the proper update time and perform state transfer if the user provides the state mapping file. The existing OSGi code can be ported to the DSUF very easily. Experiments show that the performance reduction the DSUF brings is not large.

References

1. Fabry, R.S.: How to design a system in which modules can be changed on the fly. In: Proceedings of the 2nd International Conference on Software Engineering, pp. 470–476. IEEE Computer Society Press, Los Alamitos (1976)
2. The OSGi Alliance, http://www.osgi.org
3. Goullon, H., Isle, R., Löhr, K.-P.: Dynamic restructuring in an experimental operating system. IEEE Transactions on Software Engineering 4(4), 298–307 (1978)
4. Orso, A., Rao, A., Harrold, M.J.: A Technique for Dynamic Updating of Java Software. In: Proceedings of the International Conference on Software Maintenance (ICSM 2002), October 03-06, p. 649 (2002)
5. Hicks, M., Moore, J., Nettles, S.: Dynamic software updating. In: Norris, C., Fenwick, J.J.B. (eds.) Proceedings of the ACMSIGPLAN 2001 Conference on Programming Language Design and Implementation, N.Y., June 20–22. ACM SIGPLAN Notices, vol. 36.5, pp. 13–23 (2001)
6. Hjálmtýsson, G., Gray, R.: Dynamic C++ classes. In: Proceedings of the USENIX 1998 Annual Technical Conference, June 15-19, pp. 65–76. USENIX Association (1998)
7. Segal, M.E., Frieder, O.: On-the-fly program modification: Systems for dynamic updating. IEEE Software 10(2), 53–65 (1993)
8. Plasil, F., Balek, D., Janecek, R.: SOFA/DCUP Architecture for Component Trading and Dynamic Updating. In: Proc. Fourth Intl Conf. Configurable Distributed Systems (ICCDS 1998), pp. 43–52 (1998)
9. Yves VANDEWOUDE. Dynamically updating component-oriented systems. Doctor thesis, http://www.cs.kuleuven.ac.be/~yvesv/Files/PhD.pdf

Multiscale Stochastic Finite Element Method on Random Boundary Value Problems

Lihua Shen[1] and X. Frank Xu[2]

[1] Institute of Mathematics and Interdisciplinary Science,
College of Mathematical Science, Capital Normal University,
Beijing 100048, China
shenlh@lsec.cc.ac.cn

[2] Department of Civil, Environmental, and Ocean Engineering,
Stevens Institute of Technology, Hoboken, NJ 07037, USA
x.xu@stevens.edu
http://personal.stevens.edu/~xxu1

Abstract. In this paper, we present a novel Multiscale Stochastic Finite Element Method (MSFEM) to solve boundary value problems involving random heterogeneous materials. The Green-function-based MSFEM decomposes a boundary value problem into three subproblems at three length scales with each being solved with reduced computational cost. A numerical example is provided to illustrate the MSFEM.

Keywords: multiscale stochastic finite element method, random heterogeneous materials, boundary value problems, Green function.

1 Introduction

Multiscale and stochastic modeling is becoming an emerging interdiscplinary research field. In dealing with elliptic partial differential equations involving highly fluctuating coefficients, novel multiscale stochastic computational methods are desired. In this paper, following the work presented in [2][3] , a Green-function-based multiscale stochastic finite element method is introduced to solve random boundary value problems involving multiple length scales.

2 Multiscale Stochastic Formulation

In engineering failure and reliability analysis, one essential task is to probabilistically evaluate stress in a boundary value problem (BVP) of random heterogeneous materials.

It is impractical and unnecessary to simulate every part of the BVP in detail, as engineering interest typically focuses on the area surrounding a crack (Fig.1). In the model problem there are three length scales: x, $y = \frac{x}{\epsilon_y}$ and $z = \frac{x}{\epsilon_y \epsilon_z}$ where ϵ_y depends on the correlation length of the particles and the radius of the section geometry and ϵ_z depends on the crack geometry. The stress can be expressed as $\sigma^\epsilon(x, \omega) = \sigma(x, \frac{x}{\epsilon_y}, \frac{x}{\epsilon_y \epsilon_z}, \omega)$. Here we introduce a multiscale stochastic formulation to decompose the original problem into the following three BVPs:

W. Zhang et al. (Eds.): HPCA 2009, LNCS 5938, pp. 356–361, 2010.

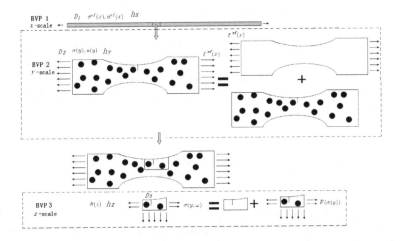

Fig. 1. Multiscale stochastic method: the BVP of the whole random heterogenous material are decomposed into three boundary value problems on different scales

- **BVP 1** *Solve the first BVP in the original domain D_1 using effective moduli:*

$$\begin{cases} \operatorname{div}\sigma^{ef}(x) + f(x) = 0 & \text{in} D_1, \\ \sigma^{ef}(x) = L^{ef}(x)e^{ef}(x), \ e^{ef}(x) = \frac{1}{2}(\nabla u^{ef}(x) + u^{ef}(x)\nabla) \ \text{in} D_1 \\ u^{ef}(x) = u(x) \ \text{on}\partial D_1^u, \quad \sigma^{ef}(x) \cdot n = t(x) \ \text{on}\partial D_1^t. \end{cases} \quad (1)$$

- **BVP 2** *Solve the second BVP in a sub-domain D_2 including geometric features and the crack:*

$$\begin{cases} \operatorname{div}\sigma(y,\omega) = 0 & \text{in} D_2, \\ \sigma(y,\omega) = L(y,\omega)e(y,\omega), \ e(y,\omega) = \frac{1}{2}(\nabla u(y,\omega) + u(y,\omega)\nabla) \ \text{in} D_2 \\ u(y,\omega) = u^{ef}(\epsilon_y y) \ \text{on}\partial D_2^u, \quad \sigma(y,\omega) \cdot n = t^{ef}(\epsilon_y y) \ \text{on}\partial D_2^t. \end{cases} \quad (2)$$

- **BVP 3** *Solve the third BVP in a smaller sub-domain D_3 surrounding the crack:*

$$\begin{cases} \operatorname{div}\tilde{\sigma}(z,\omega) = 0 & \text{in} D_3, \\ \tilde{\sigma}(z,\omega) = L(\epsilon_z z,\omega)\tilde{e}(z,\omega), \ \tilde{\sigma}(z,\omega) = \frac{1}{2}(\nabla \tilde{u}(z,\omega) + \tilde{u}(z,\omega)\nabla) \ \text{in} D_3, \\ \tilde{u}(z_a,\omega) = 0, \ \tilde{u}_1(z_b,\omega) = 0, \ \tilde{\sigma}(z,\omega) \cdot n = \sigma(\epsilon_z z,\omega) \cdot n \ \text{on}\partial D_3. \end{cases}$$
$$(3)$$

In these problems, we write the random heterogeneous elastic moduli $L(x, \frac{x}{\epsilon_y}, \omega)$ as $L(y,\omega)$ or $L(\epsilon_z z,\omega)$ to indicate the scales we consider. The variable n is the outer normal vector, ω is a sampling point in the probability space $(\Omega, \mathcal{F}, P)$ with Ω the sampling space, $\mathcal{F}$ the $\sigma-$algebra and P the probability measure. The body force $f(x)$ and the boundary conditions $u(x)$, $t(x)$ are deterministic and independent of microstructure. The mesh size for the three BVPs is denoted as h_x, h_y,h_z, respectively, with relations $\epsilon_y = \frac{h_y}{h_x}$, $\epsilon_z = \frac{h_z}{h_y}$. Points z_a and z_b are artificially given to ensure the uniqueness of the solution of **BVP 3**. In Equation

(2), the displacement boundary conditions are prescribed for two-dimensional cases.

For **BVP 1**, the finite element method to obtain the effective stress and strain is standard in engineering analysis. This can be done on a large scale with low computational cost. **BVP 2** is a random boundary value problem. It can be further decomposed into two coupled boundary value problems[2]. One is a deterministic BVP as follows

$$\begin{cases} \operatorname{div}\sigma^{(0)}(y) = 0 \quad \text{in } D_2, \\ \sigma^{(0)}(y) = L^{(0)}e^{(0)}(y), \; e^{(0)}(y) = \frac{1}{2}(\nabla u^{(0)}(y) + u^{(0)}(y)\nabla) \text{ in } D_2, \\ u^{(0)}(y) = 0 \quad \text{on } \partial D_2^u, \quad \sigma^{(0)}(y)\cdot n = t(\epsilon_y y) \quad \text{on } \partial D_2^t. \end{cases} \tag{4}$$

where the elastic moduli can be written as $L(y,\omega) = L^{(0)} + L^*(y,\omega)$[3] with $L^{(0)}$ corresponding the constant matrix field and $L^*(y,\omega)$ the particles. The other is a random BVP as follows

$$\begin{cases} \operatorname{div}\sigma^*(y,\omega) + \operatorname{div}p(y) = 0 \quad \text{in } D_2, \\ \sigma^*(y,\omega) = L^{(0)}e^*(y,\omega), \; e^*(y,\omega) = \frac{1}{2}(\nabla u^*(y,\omega) + u^*(y,\omega)\nabla) \text{ in } D_2, \\ u^*(y,\omega) = 0 \text{ on } \partial D_2^u, \quad \sigma^*(y,\omega)\cdot n = 0, \; p\cdot n = 0 \text{ on } \partial D_2^t. \end{cases} \tag{5}$$

To quantify the probabilistic moments of strain/stress, the random BVP (5) can be transformed into the following Fredholm integral equation of second kind [2]:

$$\begin{cases} (\Delta L^{(s)})^{-1}p^{(s)}(y)c_s + \sum_{r=1}^{M}\int_{D_2}\Gamma(y,y')c_{rs}(y',y)p^{(r)}(y')dy' = c_s e^{(0)}(y), \\ p^{(s)}(y)\cdot n = 0 \quad \text{on } \partial D_2, \quad s = 1, 2, \cdots, M. \end{cases} \tag{6}$$

Here $p(y,\omega) = \sigma(y,\omega) - \sigma^{(0)}(y) - \sigma^*(y,\omega)$ and has a series expansion as $p(y,\omega) = \sum_{r=1}^{M} p^{(r)}(y)\mathcal{M}_r(y,\omega)$ with $\mathcal{M}_r(y,\omega)$ the morphological random field for phase-$r(r = 1, 2, \cdots, M)$ in the M phases field. $\Gamma(y,y')$ is the modified Green function defined as

$$\Gamma_{ijkl}(y,y') = \frac{1}{2}\left(\frac{\partial^2 G_{ik}(y,y')}{\partial y_j \partial y_l'} + \frac{\partial^2 G_{jk}(y,y')}{\partial y_i \partial y_l'}\right)$$

and $G(y,y')$ is the Green function corresponding to Equation (4). The mean stress can be obtain by

$$\bar{\sigma}^{(r)}(y) = c_r L^{(r)}(y)(\Delta L^{(r)})^{-1}(y)p^{(r)}(y), \quad \bar{\sigma}(y) = \sum_{r=1}^{M}\bar{\sigma}^{(r)}(y),$$

$$\Delta L^{(r)}(y) = L^{(r)}(y) - L^{(0)}, \quad L(y,\omega) = \sum_{r=1}^{M}L^{(r)}(y)\mathcal{M}_r(y,\omega).$$

Different from **BVP 2**, the traction boundary conditions of **BVP 3** are random. The method to solve **BVP 3** is similar to **BVP 2**. It can be decomposed into two coupled problems. One is a deterministic BVP as follows

$$
\begin{cases}
\operatorname{div}\tilde{\sigma}^{(0)}(z) = 0 \quad \text{in } D_3, \\
\tilde{\sigma}^{(0)}(z) = L^{(0)}\tilde{e}^{(0)}(z), \ \tilde{e}^{(0)}(z) = \frac{1}{2}(\nabla\tilde{u}^{(0)}(z) + \tilde{u}^{(0)}(z)\nabla) \quad \text{in } D_3, \\
\tilde{u}^{(0)}(z_0) = 0, \ \tilde{u}_1^{(0)}(z_1) = 0, \ \tilde{\sigma}^{(0)}(z)\cdot n = 0 \quad \text{on } \partial D_3.
\end{cases}
\tag{7}
$$

and the other is

$$
\begin{cases}
(\Delta L^{(s)})^{-1}\tilde{p}^{(s)}(z)c_s + \sum_{r=1}^{M}\int_{D_3}\tilde{\Gamma}(z,z')c_{rs}(z',z)\tilde{p}^{(r)}(z')dz' \\
= c_s\tilde{e}^{(0)}(z) + F(p^{(1)},\cdots,p^{(M)},\sigma^{(0)}), \\
\tilde{p}^{(s)}(z)\cdot n = 0 \quad \text{on } \partial D_3, \quad s = 1,2,\cdots,M.
\end{cases}
\tag{8}
$$

where the volume fraction of phase-s $c_s(z) = \int_\Omega \mathcal{M}_s(z,\omega)dP(\omega)$, the correlation function $c_{rs}(z,z') = \int_\Omega \mathcal{M}_r(z,\omega)\mathcal{M}_s(z',\omega)dP(\omega)$, function $\Gamma(z',z)$ is the modified Green function corresponding to Equation (7) and

$$
\begin{aligned}
F(p^{(1)},\cdots,p^{(M)},\sigma^{(0)}) &= \tfrac{1}{2}\int_{\partial D_3}(\nabla G + G\nabla)F_1(p^{(1)},\cdots,p^{(M)},\sigma^{(0)})ds'', \\
F_1(p^{(1)},\cdots,p^{(M)},\sigma^{(0)}) &= \sum_{r=1}^{M}p^{(r)}(z')c_{st}(z',z)\cdot n + c_s(z)\sigma^{(0)}(z')\cdot n \\
-L^{(0)}\int_{D_2}\Gamma(z'',z')&\sum_{r=1}^{M}p^{(r)}(z'')c_{rs}(z'',z)dz''\cdot n.
\end{aligned}
\tag{9}
$$

3   MSFEM to Resolve the y-Scale and the z-Scale BVPs

In this section, we discuss the numerical approaches of MSFEM to resolve **BVP 2** and **BVP 3**. Particularly, we focus on the higher order Galerkin finite element method to solve the integral equation (6) and (8).

We use the standard notation for Sobolev spaces $W^{s,p}(D)$, see, e.g., [1] . For $p = 2$, we denote $H^s(D) = W^{s,2}(D)$.

Let $T_h = \{\tau\}$ consist of shape-regular simplices of D with mesh-size function $h(x)$ whose value is the diameter h_τ of the elements τ containing x. For any $\tilde{D} \subset D$, let $h_{\tilde{D}} = \max_{x\in\tilde{D}} h(x)$ be the (largest) mesh size of $T_h|_{\tilde{D}}$. Sometimes, we drop the subscript in $h_{\tilde{D}}$, writing h for the mesh size on $\tilde{D}$ that is clear from the context. In this paper, we also use h_x, h_y and h_z to denote the mesh sizes of domains on different scales. Let n be the dimension of the domain, we define $V = \{v \in (H^1(D_2))^n : v|_{\partial D_2^t} = 0\}$, the finite element spaces $S^{r,h_y}(D_2) = \{v \in (H^1(D_2))^n : v|_\tau \in (P^r(\tau))^n, v|_{\partial D_2^t} = 0, \forall\tau \in T_{h_y}\}$ and denote $S^{h_y}(D_2) = S^{1,h_y}(D_2)$ when $r = 1$.

3.1   Higher Order Galerkin Finite Element Method

We use the standard quadratic order finite element method with 9-node quadrilateral elements to solve Equation (4) with mesh size h_y. Once we obtain the approximation of the Green function and $e^{(0)}(y)$, we can resolve $p^{(r)}(y)$ in Equation (6) with mesh size h_y. The variational form is

$$\begin{cases} \int_{D_2} \Delta(L^{(s)})^{-1} c_s p^{(s)}(y) v(y) dy + \sum_{r=1}^{M} \int_{D_2} \int_{D_2} \Gamma_{h_y}(y,y') c_{rs}(y',y) p^{(r)}(y') v(y) dy dy' \\ \qquad = \int_{D_2} c_s e_{h_y}^{(0)}(y) v(y) dy, \quad \forall v \in V, \\ p^{(s)}(y) \cdot n = 0 \quad \text{on } \partial D_2^t, \quad s = 1, 2, \cdots, M \end{cases}$$

and the discretization form is

$$\begin{cases} \int_{D_2} \Delta(L^{(s)})^{-1} c_s p_{h_y}^{(s)}(y) v(y) dy + \sum_{r=1}^{M} \int_{D_2} \int_{D_2} \Gamma_{h_y}(y,y') c_{rs}(y',y) p_{h_y}^{(r)}(y') v(y) dy dy' \\ \qquad = \int_{D_2} c_s e_{h_y}^{(0)}(y) v(y) dy, \quad \forall v \in S^{h_y}(D_2), \\ p_{h_y}^{(s)}(y) \cdot n = 0 \quad \text{on } \partial D_2^t, \quad s = 1, 2, \cdots, M \end{cases}$$

with

$$(\Gamma_{h_y})(y,y') = \sum_{i,j=1}^{N} \nabla \phi_i(y) (A^{-1})_{ij} \nabla \phi_j(y').$$

where N is the degree of freedoms and $\phi_i(i = 1, 2 \cdots, N)$ is the shape function. The boundary conditions can be implemented by using the Lagrangian multipler method. **BVP 3** can be solved similarly.

4 Numerical Experiment

In this section, we present numerical results for the model problem. Due to the space limite, we only give the results of **BVP 2** using the quadratic order finite element method.

Our example is of a plane-stress tension problem for a two-phase composite with its geometry close to practical testing problems(see Fig. 2). Since the solutions of BVP 2 are only used to provide the boundary conditions for BVP 3, the crack is not considered in BVP 2. In **BVP 1** of this example, the traction on the left and right boundaries of the domain (thickness-1mm) is prescribed as 100KN/mm and on the top and bottom traction free. The effective stress is uniformly distributed and therefore the traction is 100KN/mm for **BVP 2**.

In our computation, we choose $L_0 = L_2$. Therefore $p^{(2)}(y) = 0$ and Equation (6) reduced to one equation with $s = 1$. The Poisson's ratio for both phases is $\nu_1 = \nu_2 = 0.2$. The Young's moduli for the matrix and the particles are chosen to be $E_1 = 200$GPa and $E_2 = 400$GPa. The correlation function we use is the exponential covariance function

$$c_{11}(y,y') = c_1 c_2 \rho(y,y') + c_1^2, \quad \rho(y,y') = \exp(-\frac{|y-y'|^2}{l_c^2})$$

where we choose $c_1 = c_2 = 0.5$. Here l_c indicates the correlation length.

Fig. 2 shows the numerical results of the mean value of $\sigma_{12}^{(1)}$ and $\sigma_{12}^{(2)}$ with mesh 16×56. Fig. 3 shows the mesh convergence of $p_{11}^{(1)}$.

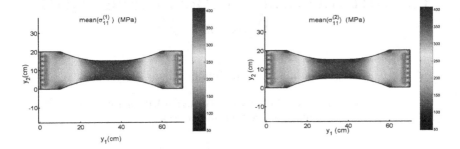

Fig. 2. The mean stress $\sigma_{11}^{(1)}$ and $\sigma_{11}^{(2)}$ with correlation length $l_c = 2$mm and mesh size $h_y = 1.25$mm(16×56)

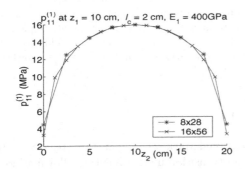

Fig. 3. The value of $p_{11}^{(1)}$ with $l_c = 2$mm, mesh size $h_y = 2.5$mm(8×28) and 1.25mm(16×56)

Acknowledgements. The material is based upon work supported by the US Department of Energy under Award No. DE-FG02-06ER25732 of Early Career Principal Investigator Program in Applied Mathematics. Dr. Lihua Shen would also like to acknowledge the support provided by the Grant No. 10801101 of the National Science Foundation of China and Outstanding Scholars Development Program of Beijing.

References

1. Adams, R.A.: Sobolev spaces. Academic Press, New York (1975)
2. Xu, X.F., Chen, X., Shen, L.: A Green-function-based multiscale method for uncertainty quantification of finite body heterogeneous materials. Comput. Struct. (2009) (in press), doi:10.1016/j.compstruc.2009.05.009
3. Xu, X.F.: A multiscale stochastic finite element method on elliptic problems involving uncertainties. Comput. Methods Appl. Mech. Engrg. 196, 2723–2736 (2007)

The BRI Algorithm for Double-Sides QBD Process

Dinghua Shi and Hongbo Zhang

Department of Mathematics, Shanghai University,
Shanghai 200444, P.R. China

Abstract. In this paper, we study the two-dimensional tri-diagonal quasi-birth-and-death (QBD) process with infinite blocks and the blocks are infinite double sides tri-diagonal matrices, which has an important application in queue theory such as joining the shortest queue problem. Our objective is to develop an accurate and easily implementable algorithmic approach to compute the stationary probabilities of the process. We also give the computational complexity for the algorithm and some numerical examples.

1 Introduction

Consider a two-dimensional Markov chain on state space $S = \{(i,j), i = 0, 1, \cdots, j = 0, \pm 1, \pm 2, \cdots\}$, its transition matrix has the following block structure

$$
\mathbf{P} = \begin{pmatrix} \mathbf{B_0} \ \mathbf{A} & & \\ \mathbf{C} \ \mathbf{B} \ \mathbf{A} & & \\ & \mathbf{C} \ \mathbf{B} \ \mathbf{A} & \\ & & \ddots \ \ddots \ \ddots \end{pmatrix}. \tag{1}
$$

where the block $\mathbf{B_0}$ and the repeat blocks $\mathbf{A}, \mathbf{B}, \mathbf{C}$ are infinite double-sides tri-diagonal matrices, for example

$$
\mathbf{B_0} = \begin{pmatrix} \ddots & \ddots & & \ddots & & \\ & b^{(0)}_{-1,-1} & b^{(0)}_{-1,0} & b^{(0)}_{-1,1} & & \\ & & b^{(0)}_{0,-1} & b^{(0)}_{00} & b^{(0)}_{01} & \\ & & & b^{(0)}_{1,-1} & b^{(0)}_{10} & b^{(0)}_{11} \\ & & & & \ddots & \ddots & \ddots \end{pmatrix},
$$

$$
\mathbf{A} = \begin{pmatrix} \ddots & \ddots & & \ddots & & \\ & a_{-1,-1} & a_{-1,0} & a_{-1,1} & & \\ & & a_{0,-1} & a_{00} & a_{01} & \\ & & & a_{1,-1} & a_{10} & a_{11} \\ & & & & \ddots & \ddots & \ddots \end{pmatrix}.
$$

W. Zhang et al. (Eds.): HPCA 2009, LNCS 5938, pp. 362–368, 2010.

and block $\mathbf{B}$ and $\mathbf{C}$ have the same structure and the similar notations. Such Markov chain is called double-sides QBD process, and has an important applications in queue models, especially for joining the shortest queue[8] or the generalized joining the shortest queue[4].

For the QBD process with both infinite levels and phases, the computation of the stationary distribution is usually very difficult. Although there are many numerical methods to compute the stationary distribution, for example, the compensation method[1], the power series algorithm[3], the dimension-reduction method[5] and the numerical method for level-dependent QBD process introduced in [2]. Wether they can be applied in double-sides QBD process or not, is not clear up to now.

In this paper, we propose an efficient algorithm to compute the stationary probabilities for the double-sides QBD process. Our method is based on two observations. First, given the transition probability matrix $\mathbf{P}$ and any initial probability vector $\boldsymbol{\pi}_0$ of a Markov chain, the vector sequence $\{\boldsymbol{\pi}_0 \mathbf{P}^n, n \geq 0\}$ of transient distributions converges to the stationary probability vector $\boldsymbol{\pi}$, provided that the process is ergodic[6]. The difficulty for implementing this idea is that the elements of the matrix $\mathbf{P}$ as show in (1) are themselves infinite matrices. On the other hand, we observe that we can only compute and will only need a finite number of the elements of the probability vector π (e.g., without the tail) in any numerical computation. Thus, what remains is to find a convergent computational scheme that only involves a finite portion of $\mathbf{P}$ during the computation process. The rectangle iterative(RI) algorithm that proposed for computing the stationary distribution of GI/M/1 Markov chains in [7] was largely motivated by this observation. With the above two observations, we can extend the RI algorithm to handle matrices with infinite blocks as in (1). This method does not require sophisticated analytical skills and can be implemented easily.

The rest of this paper is organized as follows. In Section 2, we give the block rectangle iterative(BRI) algorithm and its computing complexity. Section 3 gives some numerical results for the algorithm, and in section 4 we consider some open problem which is worthy of further study.

2 BRI Algorithm

Now we extend the RI algorithm pioneered in [7] to double-sides QBD processes. Let us first rearrange block matrices $\mathbf{P}_1, \mathbf{P}_2, \cdots$ based on the matrix $\mathbf{P}$ in (1) as follows:

$$\mathbf{P}_1 = \left(\mathbf{B}_0^{(1)} \ \mathbf{A}^{(1)} \right).$$

where

$$\mathbf{B}_0^{(1)} = \left(b_{0,-1}^{(0)} \ b_{00}^{(0)} \ b_{01}^{(0)} \right), \quad \mathbf{A}^{(1)} = \left(a_{0,-1} \ a_{00} \ a_{01} \right).$$

$$\mathbf{P}_2 = \begin{pmatrix} \mathbf{B}_0^{(2)} & \mathbf{A}^{(2)} \\ \mathbf{C}^{(2)} & \mathbf{B}^{(2)} & \mathbf{A}^{(2)} \end{pmatrix}.$$

where

$$\mathbf{B}_0^{(2)} = \begin{pmatrix} b_{-1,-1}^{(0)} & b_{-1,0}^{(0)} & b_{-1,1}^{(0)} \\ & b_{0,-1}^{(0)} & b_{00}^{(0)} & b_{01}^{(0)} \\ & & b_{1,-1}^{(0)} & b_{10}^{(0)} & b_{11}^{(0)} \end{pmatrix}, \quad \mathbf{A}^{(2)} = \begin{pmatrix} a_{-1,-1} & a_{-1,0} & a_{-1,1} \\ & a_{0,-1} & a_{00} & a_{01} \\ & & a_{1,-1} & a_{10} & a_{11} \end{pmatrix},$$

$$\mathbf{C}^{(2)} = \begin{pmatrix} c_{-1,-1} & c_{-1,0} & c_{-1,1} \\ & c_{0,-1} & c_{00} & c_{01} \\ & & c_{1,-1} & c_{10} & c_{11} \end{pmatrix}, \quad \mathbf{B}^{(2)} = \begin{pmatrix} b_{-1,-1} & b_{-1,0} & b_{-1,1} \\ & b_{0,-1} & b_{00} & b_{01} \\ & & b_{1,-1} & b_{10} & b_{11} \end{pmatrix}.$$

and matrices $\mathbf{P}_3, \mathbf{P}_4, \cdots$ are defined similarly. We note that for $n \geq 1$, $\mathbf{P}_n$ are $n \times (n+1)$ block matrices and the corresponding blocks are $(2n-1) \times (2n+1)$ matrices, so the actual sizes of matrix $\mathbf{P}_n$ is $n(2n-1) \times (n+1)(2n+1)$. To see the structural pattern more clearly, we illustrate the structures of $\mathbf{P}_1$ and $\mathbf{P}_2$ in Figure 1.

Now, let

$$\boldsymbol{\pi}^{(0)} = \left(\pi_0^{(0)} \right) = (1),$$

$$\boldsymbol{\pi}^{(1)} = \boldsymbol{\pi}^{(0)} \mathbf{P}_1 = \left(\boldsymbol{\pi}_0^{(1)}, \boldsymbol{\pi}_1^{(1)} \right).$$

Obviously, we have

$$\boldsymbol{\pi}^{(1)} = \left(\left(\pi_{0,-1}^{(1)}, \pi_{00}^{(1)}, \pi_{01}^{(1)} \right), \left(\pi_{1,-1}^{(1)}, \pi_{10}^{(1)}, \pi_{11}^{(1)} \right) \right),$$

$$= \left(\left(b_{0,-1}^{(0)}, b_{00}^{(0)}, b_{01}^{(0)} \right), (a_{0,-1}, a_{00}, a_{01}) \right),$$

$$= \mathbf{P}_1.$$

Similarly, let

$$\boldsymbol{\pi}^{(2)} = \boldsymbol{\pi}^{(1)} \mathbf{P}_2 = \left(\boldsymbol{\pi}_0^{(2)}, \boldsymbol{\pi}_1^{(2)}, \boldsymbol{\pi}_2^{(2)} \right).$$

where

$$\boldsymbol{\pi}_0^{(2)} = \left(\pi_{0,-2}^{(2)}, \pi_{0,-1}^{(2)}, \pi_{00}^{(2)}, \pi_{01}^{(2)}, \pi_{02}^{(2)} \right),$$

$$\boldsymbol{\pi}_1^{(2)} = \left(\pi_{1,-2}^{(2)}, \pi_{1,-1}^{(2)}, \pi_{10}^{(2)}, \pi_{11}^{(2)}, \pi_{12}^{(2)} \right),$$

$$\boldsymbol{\pi}_2^{(2)} = \left(\pi_{2,-2}^{(2)}, \pi_{2,-1}^{(2)}, \pi_{20}^{(2)}, \pi_{21}^{(2)}, \pi_{22}^{(2)} \right).$$

Then

$$\boldsymbol{\pi}^{(2)} = \mathbf{P}_1 \mathbf{P}_2.$$

In general, we have

$$\boldsymbol{\pi}^{(n)} = \boldsymbol{\pi}^{(n-1)} \mathbf{P}_n = \left(\boldsymbol{\pi}_0^{(n)}, \boldsymbol{\pi}_1^{(n)}, \cdots, \boldsymbol{\pi}_n^{(n)} \right), \tag{2}$$

$$= \mathbf{P}_1 \cdots \mathbf{P}_n, \quad n = 1, 2, \cdots. \tag{3}$$

where

$$\boldsymbol{\pi}_k^{(n)} = \left(\pi_{k,-n}^{(n)}, \cdots, \pi_{k0}^{(n)}, \cdots, \pi_{kn}^{(n)} \right), \quad k = 0, 1, \cdots, n.$$

Based on the above analysis, we have the following theorem

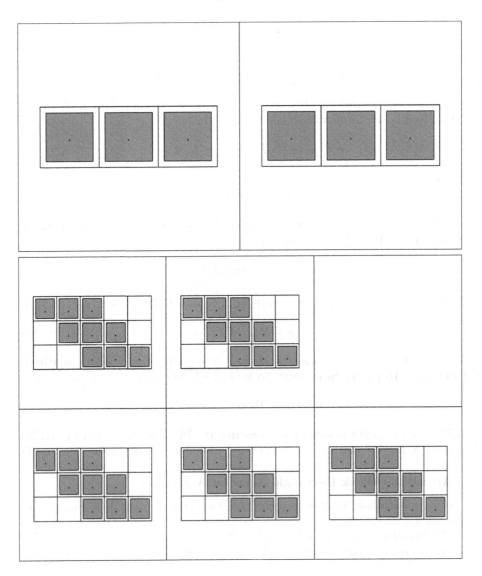

Fig. 1. The structures of block matrices $\mathbf{P}_1$ and $\mathbf{P}_2$

Theorem 1. *Consider the QBD process defined by (1). If it is ergodic, then the block vector sequence $\{\boldsymbol{\pi}^{(n)}, n \geq 1\}$ defined by (3) converges to the stationary distribution $\boldsymbol{\pi}$ of the process.*

Proof. Without loss of generality, let

$$\bar{\boldsymbol{\pi}}^{(0)} = (\cdots, \mathbf{0}, \bar{\pi}_0^0, \mathbf{0}, \cdots) = (\cdots, \mathbf{0}, (\cdots, 0, 1, 0, \cdots), \mathbf{0}, \cdots).$$

be the initial distribution, then by $\bar{\boldsymbol{\pi}}^{(1)} = \bar{\boldsymbol{\pi}}^{(0)} \mathbf{P}$ we can verify that

$$\bar{\pi}^{(1)} = \left(\bar{\pi}_0^{(1)}, \bar{\pi}_1^{(1)}, \bar{\pi}_2^{(1)}, \mathbf{0}, \cdots\right).$$

where

$$\bar{\pi}_k^{(1)} = (\cdots, 0, \pi_{k,-1}^{(1)}, \pi_{k0}^{(1)}, \pi_{k1}^{(1)}, 0, \cdots), \quad k = 0, 1, 2.$$

So the non-zero elements in the vector $\bar{\pi}^{(1)}$ are only determined by $\pi^{(1)}$, and so determined by $\mathbf{P}_1$. Similarly, in general we have

$$\bar{\pi}^{(n)} = (\bar{\pi}_0^{(n)}, \bar{\pi}_1^{(n)}, \cdots, \bar{\pi}_n^{(n)}, \mathbf{0}, \cdots).$$

where

$$\bar{\pi}_k^{(n)} = \left(\cdots, 0, \pi_{k,-n}^{(n)}, \cdots, \pi_{k0}^{(n)}, \cdots, \pi_{kn}^{(n)}, 0, \cdots\right).$$

and the non-zero elements of $\bar{\pi}^{(n)}$ are determined by $\pi^{(n)}$, and so by the matrices product $\mathbf{P}_1 \cdots \mathbf{P}_n$ only. Therefore we have

$$\lim_{n \to \infty} \pi^{(n)} = \lim_{n \to \infty} \bar{\pi}^{(n)} = \pi.$$

Remark 1. By the proof of theorem 1, for a ergodic QBD process, we find that

$$\pi = \mathbf{P}_1 \cdots \mathbf{P}_n \cdots. \tag{4}$$

is in fact the exact solution of stationary probabilities, we call it as **Block Rectangle-Iterative Solutions**. So for large N, we have

$$\pi^{(N)} = \mathbf{P}_1 \cdots \mathbf{P}_N \approx \pi.$$

Based on theorem 1, now we can describe the Block rectangle iterative(BRI) algorithm for calculating the stationary probabilities of double-sides QBD process:

Algorithm: Block Rectangle Iterative Algorithm

(1). *Initialization*: Give a stopping condition (the number of iterations) N, and set $\pi^{(0)} = 1$, $n = 1$;

(2). *Iteration*: Compute $\pi^{(n)} = \pi^{(n-1)}\mathbf{P}_n$;

(3). *Stopping condition*: If $n > N$ goto (4), otherwise, $n = n + 1$ and goto step (2);

(4). *Output*: When computation is stopped at $n = N$, use

$$\pi^{(N)} = \left(\pi_0^{(N)}, \pi_1^{(N)}, \cdots, \pi_N^{(N)}\right).$$

where

$$\pi_k^{(N)} = \left(\pi_{k,-N}^{(N)}, \cdots, \pi_{k0}^{(N)}, \cdots, \pi_{kN}^{(N)}\right), \quad k = 0, 1, \cdots, N.$$

as an approximation of the stationary distribution π.

When the BRI algorithm stops after N iterations, we will obtain the first $(N + 1) \times (2N + 1)$ values of the joint stationary probabilities as above, these numerical values are our main results.

Theorem 2. *When the number of iterations is N, the computation complexity of the BRI algorithm is $O(N^3)$.*

Proof. By the structure of $\mathbf{P}_n$, see color blocks in Figure 1, $(3n-1) \times (6n-3)$ multiplications and at most the same number of additions are needed to compute $\boldsymbol{\pi}^{(n-1)}\mathbf{P}_n$. So the number of operations is $O(n^2)$ for the n-th iteration. Therefore, it is clearly when we stop after the N-th iteration, the total number of operations is $O(N^3)$.

3   Numerical Examples

We take joining the shortest queue model considered in [8] as an example (the detail description for the model are omitted here), let parameters take values as: $\lambda = 0.6$, $\mu_1 = 0.6$, $\mu_2 = 0.4$ and $p = 0.5$. Take maximum iterative number $N = 3000$, the computing time are shown in table 1.

Table 1. CPU time with an increasing number of iterations

Iterative Number(n)	300	600	900	1200	1500
CPU Time(min.)	2.011	4.870	10.576	20.546	36.203

Iterative Number(n)	1800	2100	2400	2700	3000
CPU Time(min.)	58.964	90.306	131.947	184.563	250.046

4   Conclusion Remark

In this paper, we develop the BRI algorithm to compute the joint stationary probabilities of the double-sides QBD process.

Our method can be extended in a number of ways. For example, we can apply the BRI algorithm to process more than two dimensions. In this case, the storage of the mass data and how to improve to iterative speed, are very important problems and are worthy of to be further study. For instance, we can consider the parallel computing technique.

References

1. Adan, I.J.B.F., Wessels, J., Zijm, W.H.M.: Analysis of the asymmetric shortest queue problem. Queueing Systems 8, 1–58 (1991)
2. Bright, L.W., Taylor, P.G.: Calculating equilibrium distribution in level dependent quasi-birth-and-death process. Stochastic Models 11, 497–526 (1995)
3. Hooghiemstra, G., Keane, M., van de Ree, S.: Power series for stationary distributions of coupled processor models. SIAM J. Appl. Math. 48, 1159–1166 (1988)
4. Li, H., Miyazawa, M., Zhao, Y.Q.: Geometric decay in a QBD process with countable background states with applications to a join-the-shortest-queue model. Stochastic Models 23, 413–438 (2007)

5. Lian, Z.T., Liu, L.M.: A tandem network with IMAP inputs. Oper. Res. Lett. 36, 189–195 (2008)
6. Ross, S.M.: Stochastic process. John Wiley and Sons Inc., Chichester (1981)
7. Shi, D.H., Guo, J.L., Liu, L.M.: SPH-distributions and the rectangle iterative algorithm. In: Matrix-Analysis Methods in Stochastic Models, pp. 207–224. Marcel Decker, New York (1997)
8. Takahashi, Y., Fujimoto, K., Makimoto, N.: Geometric decay of the steady-state probabilities in a quasi-birth-and-death process with countable number of phases. Stochastic Models 1, 1–24 (2001)

The Multi-dimensional QoS Resources Optimization Based on the Grid Banking Model

Guo Tang, Hao Li, and Shaowen Yao

School of Software, Yunnan University, Kunming, China
tangguo001@gmail.com, Lihao707@ynu.edu.cn,
yaosw@ynu.edu.cn

Abstract. Grid is to provide exceptional service quality. But the quality of service (QoS) in grid cannot be guaranteed because of the complexity and diversity of grid environments. QoS parameters should be described for solving the QoS issues in grid. At present, a lot of works have been done on resources optimization on the grid, but less on the optimization of multi-dimensional QoS and the analysis of the multi-dimensional QoS optimization of resources. In this paper, we put forward a QoS-based grid banking model based on the idea of stratification. It is divided into the application-layer, the virtual organization layer, and the physical resources and facilities layer[1]. At each layer, the consumer agent, service agent, and resource provider agent optimize the multi-dimensional QoS resources. The optimization is done within the framework of the grid banking model and the hierarchical constraints in their respective conditions so that it can maximize the utility function. The optimization algorithm at all levels has been presented. It uses the principle of market economy about the price of constant iteration and the interaction among all levels to carry out the Service Level Agreement.

1 Introduction

In recent years, grid services studies have become a hot issue and QoS, which is the primary objective of the Service Grid study, has become the focus in grid. "To provide the extraordinary QoS"[1] is one of the three criteria to determine whether it is the grid or not. However, most of the grid application involves heterogeneous resources. In practice, a variety of types of resources are involved so more collaboration is required among various tasks, which makes the scheduling of resources distribution and the implementation of mission to be more complicated.

At present, the implementations of the network infrastructure are set up on the basis of "try one's best". Therefore, it can not guarantee the QoS. The performance and efficiency are also easily leading to a reduction in collaboration with a number of services even though the user has a diversity of needs. To solve these problems it is needed to address QoS in grid, i.e. the introduction of QoS mechanisms. Specifically, there must be a corresponding resource reservation protocol and resource scheduling

---

[1] This work is supported by the National Natural Science Foundation of China (Grant No.60763008).

W. Zhang et al. (Eds.): HPCA 2009, LNCS 5938, pp. 369–376, 2010.

algorithm, QoS parameter of QoS description and maintenance, QoS downgrade, etc. This paper proposes and sets up a bank under the grid structure of the model-level QoS based on different object's needs of QoS parameters on the classification at different aspects of QoS description.

This paper is organized as follows: In Section 2, we describe previous works regarding grid QoS. In section 3, we introduce the architecture of QoS-based grid banking model. In section 4, we analyze optimization solutions in detail under banking model. In section 5, we describe an algorithm. Finally, we conclude the paper in section 6.

2   Research of Grid QoS

In recent years, IETF has put forward two different Internet QoS Architectures: IntServ (integrated services)[2] and DiffServ (differentiated services)[3]. IntServ program required all routers on the path of treatment in the control signaling for each message stream and maintain for each flow path and the status of resource reservation. DiffServ program gathers the quality of the provision of specific scheduling services on the border of the network.

Ian Foster and Alain Roy and others had set up GARA[4] (General-purpose Architecture for Reservation and Allocation) model at Globus, GARA is composed of APIs (Application Program Interfaces) and RM (Resource Manager) from all levels, providing advanced and immediate reservation through a unified interface.

Rashid Al-Ali brought forward the G-QoSM (Grid QoS Management Architecture)[5] in Cardiff University, United Kingdom. It is an adaptive resource reservation and the QoS management architecture in OGSA grid environment.

Buyya, from an economic point of view, put forward GRACE(Grid Architecture for Computational Economy) [6]. GRACE mainly considers the deadline and budget constraints, it can control the allocation of resources, supply and demand of resources effectively. More literature [7-10] applied to put the principles of economics in grid resource scheduling and optimization.

3   QoS-Based Grid Banking Model

A grid bank is a grid mechanism that references to the economy grid [6], through simulating the bank's business process to manage and allocate the grid resource. Buyya mentioned QBank and GBank in the GRACE but it is only used to account. Paper [11] divides grid environment into three roles in grid bank: Grid Resources Consumer, Grid Bank, and Grid Service Provider. Banking activities as a transaction coordinator, it puts all the basic resources information into the grid resource manager (GMR). GMR sends information to the Resource Classify Center (RCC). RCC can classify different resources and keep it in a virtual pool (VP). VP is similar to the bank vault and all available resources are in dynamic storage.

We make a number of improvements based on the literature [11] in this paper and refine the function of grid banks. Grid bank is just about relying on the operating mechanism from business bank to classify and quantify the grid resources using QoS, similar to "currency" in our daily life, we call it Grid Dollar. In this paper, we use the Grid Dollar to quantify the parameters of the grid resources, in the meantime, we consider supply and demand of grid resources in the market, and the resource transaction is occurred inside the grid bank using price leverage.

The new grid bank model consists of three levels: the application layer, VO layer and physical resources and facilities layer. It is mainly composed of: the grid resource consumer agent, the overall allocation of resources agent, service agent, resource provider agent and other modules. Model structure is shown in Figure 1.

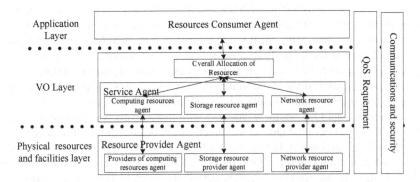

Fig. 1. Grid bank model and its interaction

The main role of application-layer is the resources consumer agent. It deals with interactive business between resource users and internal part of the grid bank. Connecting the middle layer is the VO level. The QoS requirements put forward by the consumer agent will be mapped to a particular type of grid QoS by the service agent in VO layer and it will be provided to the appropriate sub-agents. It is the physical resources and facilities layer at the bottom. The resources provider agent captures the various QoS attributes about physical resources to support the various types of QoS from VO layer. End-use of resources occurs in the physical resources and facilities layer. VO layer mainly resolves the overall situation problems. Application layer mainly solves the problem of easy use.

When we optimize the multi-dimensional QoS, from the physical resources and facilities layer, VO layer to the application layer, QoS parameters are changeable. The whole process is organized by three types of agents: resource provider agent, service agent and resources consumer agent under the coordination from the banking model. Resource provider agent acts on behalf of the potential resources' economic interests of the physical resources and facilities layer. Consumer agent acts on behalf of consumers who use the grid to achieve the interests in application layer. Service agent in the VO layer not only acts as a resources buyer from the aspect of resource provider agent, but also acts as a seller from the consumer agent. The three types of agents interact through the operation of the market mechanism. The object of market behavior is to pursue its own interests in economic field. The supply and demand situation in the market will be reflected in the price fluctuations on the resources.

In market economy, there are multiple service agents in consultation with the consumer agents at the same time. Grid resource allocation is adapted according to the price-oriented algorithm in the model. Although there is a hierarchical structure model, but given that the resources are shared at different levels, the main function of the model is to inquire the appropriate services which meet the QoS standards, manage local and remote resources, combine and match resources in a distributed environment and ultimately, complete the transaction.

4 Optimization Solutions

The research of QoS must distinguish the levels [12] because there are different representations of QoS at different levels. In order to quantify the parameters of QoS, Li Chunlin and Li Layuan, who put forward a three-dimensional (cost, time, reliability) QoS formula, respectively, optimized the task agent and resource agent [13,14,15]. In this paper, the quantitative dimensions have been expanded, the optimization on the three types of agents is done at the same time, the QoS needs is expressed more carefully at different levels and interaction between levels.

Each dimensional QoS vector interacting with three levels is expressed by a utility function, Multi-dimensional QoS utility function can be constructed through weighing one-dimensional QoS utility function at each level. Global QoS utility function at all levels is a linear combination of QoS utility function at each level. The ultimate goal of optimization is maximizing $U_{Grid}(Q_{global})$, at the limit of respective conditions at three levels[13].

$$MaxU_{Grid}(Q_{global}) = \sum (SP_i^j \log x_i^j + NP_i^k \log y_i^k + PP_i^l \log z_i^l) + \sum_m AP_m^i \log v_m^i + \frac{g}{f}$$

$$s.t. \sum_i z_i^l \le PC_l \ , \ \sum_i y_i^k \le NC_k \ , \ \sum_i x_i^j \le SC_j \ , \ \sum_j SD_i^j \le LS_i \ , \ \sum_k BD_i^k \le LN_i \ , \ \sum_i PD_i^l \le LP_i \ ,$$

$$\sum_{n=1}^N t_m^n \le T_i \ , \ \sum_i AP_m^i \le E_m \ , \ \sum_j SP_i^j + \sum_k NP_i^k + \sum_l PP_i^l \le SE_i$$

Above is a non-deterministic polynomial problem, which is a NP problem. To solve such problems one can use tabu search algorithm, simulated annealing algorithm, genetic algorithm, etc., Lagrange method is introduced to solve this problem in this paper. It finds the extreme on multi-equation on the restrictions of one or more variables and converts the problem which contains n variables and k restricted conditions into a more easy solution of $n + k$ variables of the equation. The variable is not subject to any constraint. This approach introduces a new scalar: Lagrange multiplier, which is the coefficient of each vector on linear combination of the constraint equations.

According to the ultimate goal to be achieve, Lagrangian function is constructed as following [15]:

$$L = \sum (SP_i^j \log x_i^j + NP_i^k \log y_i^k + PP_i^l \log z_i^l) + \lambda(SE_i - (\sum_j SP_i^j + \sum_k NP_i^k + \sum_l PP_i^l))$$

$$+ \sum_m AP_m^i \log v_m^i + \beta(E_m - \sum_i AP_m^i) + \gamma(T_i - \sum_{n=1}^N t_m^n) + \frac{g}{f} \ . \tag{1}$$

To solve (1) directly is very difficult. The maximum of the Lagrange problem can be decomposed into three questions at different layer [15]:

$$F_1 = Max \sum \left(SP_i^j \log x_i^j + NP_i^k \log y_i^k + PP_i^l \log z_i^l \right) \quad s.t. \sum_i z_i^l \leq PC_l \ , \sum_i y_i^k \leq NC_k \ , \sum_i x_i^j \leq SC_j$$

$$F_2 = Max \left\{ \left(SE_i - \sum_j SP_i^j - \sum_k NP_i^k - \sum_l PP_i^l \right) + \sum_m AP_m^i \log v_m^i + \frac{g}{f} \right\}$$

$$s.t. \sum_j SD_i^j \leq LS_i \ , \sum_k BD_i^k \leq LN_i \ , \sum_i PD_i^l \leq LP_i \ , \sum_m v_m^i \leq S_i$$

(2)

$$F_3 = Max \left\{ \left(E_m - \sum_i AP_m^i \right) + \left(T_i - \sum_{n=1}^N t_m^n \right) \right\} \quad s.t. \sum_{n=1}^N t_m^n \leq T_i \ , \sum_i AP_m^i \leq E_m \ .$$

Physical resources and facilities layer is to resolve F_1 with constraint conditions in (2). In order to obtain x_i^j, in accordance with F_1, we get Lagrangian function [15]:

$$L_{phy}\left(x_i^j, y_i^k, z_i^l \right) = \sum \left(SP_i^j \log x_i^k + NP_i^k \log y_i^k + PP_i^l \log z_i^l \right) + \lambda \left(SC_j - \sum_i x_i^j \right) + \beta \left(NC_k - \sum_i y_i^k \right) + \gamma \left(PC_l - \sum_i z_i^l \right)$$

$$= \sum \left(SP_i^j \log x_i^k + NP_i^k \log y_i^k + PP_i^l \log z_i^l - \lambda x_i^j - \beta y_i^k - \gamma z_i^l \right) + \lambda SC_j + \beta NC_k + \gamma PC_l \ .$$

(3)

VO layer must resolve F_2 with constraint conditions in (2). Construct Lagrangian utility function of service agent i [14]:

$$L_{VO}\left(SP_i^j, NP_i^k, PP_i^l, v_m^i \right) = SE_i - \sum_j SP_i^j - \sum_k NP_i^k - \sum_l PP + \sum_m AP_m^i \log v_m^i + \frac{g}{f}$$

$$+ \delta \left(S_i - \sum_m v_m^i \right) + \lambda \left(LS_i - \sum_j SD^j \right) + \eta \left(LN_i - \sum_k ND_i^k \right) + \beta \left(LP_i - \sum_i PD_i^l \right) \ .$$

(4)

To solve (4) directly is more complicated, according to service agent acting as the two roles: consumer to the physical resources and facilities layer, provider to application layer, the corresponding Lagrange (4) can break down into the following two functions [15]:

$$L_{VO\_1} = SE_i - \sum_j SP_i^j - \sum_k NP_i^k - \sum_l PP_i^l + \lambda \left(LS_i - \sum_j SD_i^j \right) + \eta \left(LN_i - \sum_k ND_i^k \right) + \beta \left(LP_i - \sum_i PD_i^l \right)$$

$$= SE_i - \sum_j SP_i^j - \sum_k NP_i^k - \sum_l PP_i^l + \lambda \left(LS_i - \sum_j \frac{px_j}{SP_i^j SC_j} \right) + \eta \left(LN_i - \sum_k \frac{py_k}{NP_i^k NC_k} \right) + \beta \left(LP_i - \sum_i \frac{pz_l}{PP_i^l PC_l} \right) \ ; (5)$$

$$L_{VO\_2} = \sum_m AP_m^i \log v_m^i + \frac{g}{f} + \delta \left(S_i - \sum_m v_m^i \right) \ .$$

(6)

The two functions can be implemented in parallel. In (5), in order to simplify the study, let the allocation delay of storage resource j : $SD_i^j = px_j/(SP_i^j SC_j)$. Similarly, the allocation delay of network resources k : $ND_i^k = py_k/(NP_i^k NC_k)$; the distribution delay of computing resources l : $PD_i^l = pz_l/(PP_i^l PC_l)$.

Application layer is to resolve F_3 with constrained conditions in (2). Where t_m^n is the time of the grid resource consumer agent m complete the nth job, in order to simplify the study, let $t_m^n = GT_{mn}/v_m^i = (GT_{mn} \bullet ps_i)/(S_i \bullet AP_m^i)$.

Combined with its constraints, construct Lagrange utility function of consumer agent as following [15]:

$$L_{APP}\left(AP_m^i\right) = \left(E_m - \sum_i AP_m^i\right) + \left(T_m - \sum_{n=1}^N \frac{GT_{mn} \bullet ps_i}{S_i \bullet AP_m^i}\right) + \lambda\left(T_m - \sum_{n=1}^N t_m^n\right)$$

5   Algorithm Implementation

Algorithm is based on the principle of economics: The agent at each layer obtains input from other layers, when consults with agents at other layer, it studies the supply and demand changes of resources. This algorithm has been modified and expanded on the basis of literature [13, 14, 15]. In accordance to the best utility function calculated in section 4, it then calculated out the price expressed in the grid dollars. Finally, the feedback is outputted to other relevant agents. Continuous iterative process is repeated until all participants have reached a common solution. The resource allocation and calculation of the price iteration algorithm from each agent described as follows:

5.1   Resource Provider Agent

1. To receive storage resource prices $x_i^{j(n)}$; network resource price $x_i^{k(n)}$; computing resource price $x_i^{l(n)}$ from service agent;
2. To maximize F_1 in (2), computing

$$x_i^{j*} = \frac{SP_i^j \bullet SC_j}{\sum_{i=1}^n SP_i^j} \quad ; y_i^{k*} = \frac{NP_i^k \bullet BC_k}{\sum_{i=1}^n NP_i^k} \quad ; z_i^{l*} = \frac{PP_i^l \bullet PC_l}{\sum_{i=1}^n PP_i^l}$$

3. If meeting $\sum_i z_i^{l*} \leq PC_l$, $\sum_i y_i^{k*} \leq NC_k$, $\sum_i x_i^{j*} \leq SC_j$

then calculate new price of storage resource j [15] :
$$px_i^{j(n+1)} = \max\{\varepsilon, px_i^{j(n)} + \eta(\sum_i x_i^{j*} - SC_j)\}$$

(Note: $\eta > 0$, it is a smaller step size of price, n is the number of iterations, ε is a protected price after considering the cost of a variety of revenue. This formula takes into account supply and demand law in market: If demand exceeds supply of the resources, the result of parentheses is positive. Then the final price will rise; if the demand is less than supply, the result is negative, and then the final price will fall. At the same time, calculating the maximum price between the protected price and the new price ensure the largest benefit of the resource provider agent [13].)

New price of network resource k [15]: $py_i^{k(n+1)} = \max\{\varepsilon, py_i^{k(n)} + \eta(\sum_i y_i^{k*} - NC_k)\}$;

New price of computing resource l [15]: $pz_i^{l(n+1)} = \max\{\varepsilon, pz_i^{l(n)} + \eta(\sum_i z_i^{l*} - PC_l)\}$;

4. Return to the storage resource agent the new price: $px_i^{j(n+1)}$; Return to the network resource agent the new price: $py_i^{k(n+1)}$; Return to the computing resource agent the new price: $pz_i^{l(n+1)}$.

5.2 Service Agent

1. To receive demand $v_m{}^i$ from consumer agent m;

2. Maximize sub-formula of L_{VO_2} in (6), calculate: $v_m^{i*} = AP_m^i \bullet S_i / \sum_m AP_k^i$

3. If $\sum_m v_m^{i*} \leq S_i$, calculate new services prices[15]:

$$ps_i^{(n+1)} = \max\{\varepsilon \quad , \quad ps_i^{(n)} + \eta(\sum_m v_m^{i*} - S_i)\} \quad ;$$

Return $ps_i^{(n+1)}$ to all consumer agent;

4. To receive the the new price $px_i^{j(n)}$ from storage resource provider j, $px_i^{k(n)}$ from network resource provider k, $px_i^{l(n)}$ from computing resource provider l;

5. Maximize sub-formula of L_{VO1} in (5), calculate [15]

$$SP_i^{j*} = \left(\frac{px_j}{SC_j}\right)^{\frac{1}{2}} \bullet \frac{\sum_j \left(px_j / SC_j\right)^{\frac{1}{2}}}{LS_i}, SP_i^{j*} = \left(\frac{py_k}{NC_j}\right)^{\frac{1}{2}} \bullet \frac{\sum_k \left(py_k / NC_j\right)^{\frac{1}{2}}}{LN_i}, PP_i^{j*} = \left(\frac{pz_l}{PC_j}\right)^{\frac{1}{2}} \bullet \frac{\sum_l \left(pz_l / PC_j\right)^{\frac{1}{2}}}{LP_i}$$

6. If meeting $\sum_j SP_i^{j*} + \sum_k NP_i^{k*} + \sum_l PP_i^{l*} \leq SE_i$,

then calculate the new price of storage resources : $x_i^{j(n+1)} = SP_i^{j*(n)} / px_i^{j(n)}$;

New price of network resources : $x_i^{k(n+1)} = NP_i^{k*(n)} / px_i^{k(n)}$;

New price of computing resources : $z_i^{l(n+1)} = PP_i^{l*(n)} / pz_i^{l(n)}$;

7. Return the new price $x_i^{j(n+1)}$, $x_i^{k(n+1)}$, $x_i^{l(n+1)}$, to the resource provider agent.

5.3 Consumer Resources Agent

1. To receive $ps_i^{(n)}$ from service agent i;

2. Maximize F_3 in (2), calculate [15]

$$AP_m^{i*} = \left(\frac{GT_{mn} \bullet ps_i}{S_i}\right)^{\frac{1}{2}} \bullet \frac{\sum_{n=1}^{N} \left(\frac{GT_{mn} \bullet ps_i}{S_i}\right)^{\frac{1}{2}}}{T_m} \quad ;$$

3. If $\sum_i AP_m^i \leq E_m$, calculate the demand of services[15]: $v_m^{i(n+1)} = AP_m^{i*(n)} / ps_i^{(n)}$;

Return $v_m^{i(n+1)}$ to the service agent i.

6 Summary

Based on the research of existing grid QoS, by using hierarchical thinking, we put forward the QoS-based grid bank model, and the model is divided into three layers. Resource consumer agents, service agents, and resource provider agent optimize resource among the layers and the interaction between the various agents may be done through the SLA. Optimization algorithm is based on the principle of economic. Continuous iterative process is repeated until all participants have reached a common solution. The proposition that multi-dimensional QoS resources are optimized based on the grid banking model will be a useful theoretical study to explore in grid resources quantifying. Research results can be widely used for grid QoS control strategy evaluation, selection and optimization.

Grid QoS control strategy is used to quantify the overall performance, meets many performance targets and the best integrated quantify, and leads to the corresponding implementation strategy. But there are still remain many issues to study, we will study these issues further under the framework of grid bank.

References

1. Foster, I., Kesselman, C.: The Grid: Blueprint for a New Computing Infrastructure (1999)
2. http://www.ietf.org/html.charters/OLD/intserv-charter.html
3. http://www.ietf.org/html.charters/OLD/diffserv-charter.html
4. Foster, I., Roy, A., Sander, V.: A Quality of Service Architecture that Combines Resource Reservation and Application Adaptation. In: Proceedings of the Eight International Workshop on Quality of Service, June 2000, pp. 181–188 (2000)
5. Al-Ali, R.J., Rana, O.F., Walker, D.W.: G-QoSM: Grid Service Discovery Using QoS Properties. Comput. Informatics J., Special Issue on Grid Computing 21, 363–382 (2002)
6. Buyya, R.: Economic-based distributed resource management and scheduling for Grid computing, in Thesis (2002)
7. Subramoniam, K., Maheswaran, M., Toulouse, M.: Towards a micro-economic model for resource allocation in Grid computing systems. In: Proceedings of the 2002 IEEE Canadian Conference on Electrical & Computer Engineering (2002)
8. Stuer, G., Vanmechelena, K., Broeckhovea, J.: A commodity market algorithm for pricing substitutable Grid resources. Future Generation Computer Systems 23, 688–701 (2007)
9. Wolski, R., Plank, J.S., Brevik, J., et al.: Analyzing Market-based Resource Allocation Strategies for the Computational Grid. International Journal of High-performance Computing Applications 15 (2001)
10. Kenyon, C., Cheliotis, G.: Architecture Requirements for Commercializing Grid Resources. In: Proceeding of the 11th IEEE International Symposium on High Performance Distributed Computing (HPDC), pp. 215–224 (2002)
11. Li, H., Zhong, Y., Lu, J., Zhang, X., Yao, S.: A Banking Based Grid Recourse Allocation Scheduling. In: GPC Workshops, pp. 239–244 (2008)
12. Chatterjee, B.S.S., Sydir, M.D.J.J., Lawrence, T.F.: Taxonomy for QoS specifications. In: Proc.of the 3rd Intel Workshop on Object-oriented Real-Time DependableSystems, pp. 100–107 (1997)
13. Chunlin, L., Layuan, L.: QoS based resource scheduling by computational economy in computational grid. Information Processing Letters 98, 119–126 (2006)
14. Chunlin, L., Layuan, L.: A distributed multiple dimensional QoS constrained. Journal of Computer and System Sciences, 706–726 (2006)
15. Chunlin, L., Layuan, L.: Cross-layer optimization policy for QoS scheduling in computational grid. Journal of Network and Computer Applications 31, 258–284 (2008)

A Cellular Automata Calculation Model Based on Ternary Optical Computers

Liang Teng[1], Junjie Peng[1], Yi Jin[1], and Mei Li[2]

[1] School of Computer Engineering and Science,
Shanghai University,Shanghai 200072, China
cabbage812@163.com, {jjie.peng,yijin}@shu.edu.cn
[2] College of Computer Science & Engineering,
Northwestern Polytechnical University, Xi'an 710072, China
plumlee@nwpu.edu.cn

Abstract. This paper proposes a novel CACM (Cellular Automata Calculation Model)[1], which has two advantages: the high controllability and the parallelism of computing. The former advantage means that: the transformation rules of every cell and a cell at different time can be different. And the latter guarantees that it is possible to construct a large-scale CA efficiently, for the reason that the CA is computed in parallel. The computing platform is TOC (Ternary Optical Computer) and the algorithm is superposition in dislocation, which are both the bases of the CACM. Using the CACM, it is valid to construct more complicated and powerful CA.

1 Introduction

CA (cellular automata) has been applied to a considerable variety of purposes, such as Parallel Computing Model, Simulation Model for Natural, Encryption System[1], Built-In Self-Test[2] and so on, in which the rules are not changed in the whole transformation process. In order to solve more complicated problems, it is need to transform the CA with different transformation rules and to be able to change the transformation rules arbitrarily. For example, when we construct an adaptive feedback control system, it is need to modify the transformation rule based on the result of the pre-step. The other problem is the computational speed. CA is parallelism in natural, so it is possible to compute large-scale CA in parallel.

In 2001, Prof. Yi Jin from Shanghai University proposed the framework of TOC [3] [4] [5]. Since then, several key theories of TOC have pushed the TOC to be a reality. Nowadays an experimental system of Tri-valued Logic Hundred-Bit Optical Calculator has been made [6] [7] [8], on this basis, the paper proposes a method that can be used to design a large-scale and high-controllability CACM. The method has

---

[1] This work is supported by the innovation project of Shanghai University (No. A.10-0108-08-901), the research project of excellent young talents in the universities in Shanghai (No. B.37-0108-08-002) and the Shanghai Leading Academic Discipline Project under Grant (No.J50103).

W. Zhang et al. (Eds.): HPCA 2009, LNCS 5938, pp. 377–383, 2010.

combined the CA's natural parallelism and TOC's parallelism of computing, the CACM also makes use of the advantage that calculation unit of TOC [9]which could be reconstructed to realize the high-controllability.

The Paper is organized as follows: In Section 2, the computing platform which is TOC and the theory of CA are simply reviewed. Then the method of implementing the large-scale and high-controllability CACM is explained in Section 3. Section 4 is an example and Section 5 is the systems analysis.

2   Basic Concept

2.1   Ternary Optical Computer

TOC is a opto-electronic hybrid parallel computer which makes use of the polarization of light to express information and uses the liquid crystal to change the state of the light. As light has the character of giant parallelism in space. The TOC can process the logic operation of giant tri-value data in parallel.

In 2008, Dr. Junyong Yan and others discovered the decrease-radix design principle [9] which indicates a normative method to reconstruct calculate unit, therefore TOC could be used to calculate all the tri-value logic operations.

2.2   Cellular Automata

In the 1950s, John Von Neumann [10][11] first introduced some kinds of CAs which are discrete dynamical systems, with simple construction but complex and varied behaviors. In order to research the CA by mathematical tools, people use the symbol vector (L_d, S, N, f) to describe CA. L expresses the space of cells and the d is the number of the dimension of the space, All of the possible states of one cell construct the sets S, and then the N is an arrange of cells and forms the parameters of function $f = (S_1, S_2, \cdots, S_{|N|})$, in which $|N|$ means the number of elements in N.

Nowadays, there are mainly two methods to implement the CA, one is to use VLSI and the other is to simulate it by software. The advantage of VLSI method is speed. However, if the f is fixed and the VLSI has been made, it is substantially difficult to change the f for constructing the other kind of CA. The second method is a serial process, it is need to calculate the f of all cells step by step, therefore when the scale of the CA become bigger, the efficiency of CA will linearly decrease.

3   CACM on TOC

3.1   Tri-value Logic Operations Between Matrices

The S of the CA which is implemented on TOC is tri-value, such as the sets{0, 1, 2}, so there are 19683 kinds of tri-value logic operation in all. In order to index it quickly, every tri-value logic operation is distributed a decimal number. The principle is described below:

Table 1. The Binary Tri-value Truth Talbe. The $a_0, a_1, a_2, a_3, a_4, a_5, a_6, a_7, a_8$ are the nine values of the tri-value truth table, therefore we can use the tri-value sequence $a_8 a_7 a_6 a_5 a_4 a_3 a_2 a_1 a_0$ as the index of the True-Value-Table

Ψ_n	0	1	2
0	a_0	a_1	a_2
1	a_3	a_4	a_5
2	a_6	a_7	a_8

For convenience, the tri-value sequence can be transformed into decimal number which is $k = \sum_{i=0}^{8} a_i 3^i$. Ψ_n expresses a tri-value logic operation whose index is n, all the tri-value logic operations constitute the set M, so $\Psi_n \in M$. From now on, it is valid to define the tri-value logic operation between matrices.

Definition 1: A, B are both m×n dimension matrices, $a_{i,j}, b_{i,j}$ are the elements of matrices. $a_{i,j}, b_{i,j} \in \{0,1,2\}$, $i \in \{0,1,\cdots,m-1\}$, $j \in \{0,1,\cdots,n-1\}$, so the tri-value logic operation between matrices can be defined as blow:

$$A\Theta B = \begin{bmatrix} a_{o,o} \Psi_{(0,0)} b_{o,o} & a_{o,1} \Psi_{(0,1)} b_{o,1} & \cdots & a_{o,n} \Psi_{(0,n)} b_{o,n} \\ a_{1,o} \Psi_{(1,0)} b_{1,o} & a_{1,1} \Psi_{(1,1)} b_{1,1} & \cdots & a_{1,n} \Psi_{(1,n)} b_{1,n} \\ \vdots & \vdots & \ddots & \vdots \\ a_{m,0} \Psi_{(m,0)} b_{m,o} & a_{m,1} \Psi_{(m,1)} b_{m,1} & \cdots & a_{m,n} \Psi_{(m,n)} b_{m,n} \end{bmatrix}. \tag{1}$$

In which, $\Psi_{(0,0)}, \Psi_{(0,1)}, \cdots, \Psi_{(m,n)} \in M$, furthermore they can be any tri-value logic operations and all different with each other.

If there are u matrices to do Θ logic operation, there will be an operation sequence $A_1 \Theta_1 A_2 \Theta_2 \cdots A_{u-1} \Theta_{u-1} A_u$, and every element of the matrices has its own operation sequence, such as the cell indexed by (a,b) of the CA has his own operation sequence which is $(\Psi_{(a,b)_1} \Psi_{(a,b)_2} \cdots \Psi_{(a,b)_{u-1}})$, $0 \leq a < m, 0 \leq b < n$.

The Θ calculation between giant-scale matrices can be completed in one clock cycle using TOC, so it can be used to calculation CA in parallel.

3.2 Construction of CACM for Tri-value and Two-Dimension CA

For the parameter d of the CA is two, it can be considered that the cells are placed on plain as matrix. Because of CA is a discrete dynamical system, the states of all cells in time t_i of the plain will change to the states t_{i+1} and the changing principles of every cell are different with each other, cell indexed by (a,b) has the principle

$f_{(a,b)} = \left(S_1, S_2, \cdots, S_{|N|}\right)$, we can call the discrete changing of all cells as One-Step. In One-Step, the N must be the same, but the f can be different for every cell, for reason that the parameters of f is same, but between which the operation sequence $(\Psi_{(a,b)_1}, \Psi_{(a,b)_2}, \cdots, \Psi_{(a,b)_u}), 0 < u < |N|$ could be different. In next steps, the N could also be changed. In summary, the transformation rules of every cell and one cell in different time are different which is the high controllability of this CACM. Therefore, it is important to define the N and f for the CA.

Table 2. The index of neighborhood cells

...	1	2
7	0	3
6	5	4

If we want to calculate the next state of the cell which is indexed by (a,b), we focus it as the centre of the table2 which is indexed by No.0. For example, the No.1 is the up neighborhood of the cell(a,b). The first step is to fix the N , thanks to the neighborhood cells have been indexed, it is easy to describe it ,such as N (0, 3, 7)means that the next state of the cell is determined by itself, right and left neighborhood cells. Because, the N of every cell in one-step is the same, it is valid to use the table2 to fix every cell. At last, there will be boundary problem, for example if the right neighbor of one cell is beyond the boundary ,there are two methods, one is simply set 0 to the state of her neighbor ,the other is cycle boundary.

At present the N has been fix, the other is f ,but there are m×n different f in One-Step, the cell indexed by (a,b) has its unique $f_{(a,b)}$ .thanks to the N is the same ,so we define the operation sequence $(\Psi_{(a,b)_1}, \Psi_{(a,b)_2}, \cdots, \Psi_{(a,b)_u}), 0 \leqslant u < |N|$ to represent $f_{(a,b)}$. It can be easily inserted into the vector $\left(S_1, S_1, \cdots, S_{|N|}\right)$ to construct the $f_{(a,b)}$,   for   example   there   will   be   the   equation $q_{(a,b)}^{t+1} = q_{(a,b)_0}^t \Psi_{(a,b)_1} q_{(a,b)_3}^t \Psi_{(a,b)_2} q_{(a,b)_7}^t$ which means the state of cell index by (a,b) in time t+1 is calculate by (himself $\Psi_{(a,b)_1}$ right-neighbor $\Psi_{(a,b)_2}$ left-neighbor). The $(q_{(a,b)_0}^t, q_{(a,b)_3}^t, q_{(a,b)_7}^t)$ is the state of the N , $q \in S$. For example in Equation(2), it is 4×4 CA whose N is (0,7,1) and the transfer rules are (Θ_1, Θ_2), these fix the One-Step computing of the CA. It is the same method to fix the next One-Step.

The symbol vector $\left(L_d, S, N, f\right)$ of CA has been fixed, so the CACM would be constructed ,then the next step is to compute the CACM.

3.3 Superposition in Dislocation

Superposition in dislocation is a novel method to compute the CA at the next state in parallel. Firstly we can store the state of every cell of the CA to a matrix A, and the $a_{i,j}$ is the value of the cell in the i th row and j th column.

$$(N:\Theta_1,\Theta_2) = \begin{pmatrix} (0,5,7): \begin{bmatrix} 17139 & 9328 & 19540 & 15693 \\ 10578 & 17347 & 12985 & 18781 \\ 18063 & 10786 & 12241 & 18123 \\ 15792 & 10057 & 11503 & 19599 \end{bmatrix}, \\ \begin{bmatrix} 15693 & 19540 & 9328 & 17139 \\ 12985 & 17347 & 10578 & 18781 \\ 10786 & 18063 & 18123 & 12241 \\ 15492 & 19599 & 11503 & 10057 \end{bmatrix} \end{pmatrix} \quad (2)$$

In this paper, we choose the second method to deal with the boundary problem Therefore, as it is showed in the figure 1, the matrix A is translated to the left in cycle and become the matrix B. the third step is to calculate $A\Theta B$. It is easy to see that the matrix C is result of the every cell of A calculated with his right neighbor. Then it is the same to do the next, such as we can translate A in cycle to the right and acquire D, do the calculate $C\Theta D$, the result is every cell of A calculated with its right neighbor and then calculated with his left neighbor. In this way, it is simply to complete the One-Step as the (L_d, S, N, f), then we can change the (N, f) to do the next One-Step.

In order to validate the method proposed in the paper, an experiment is demonstrated in section 4.

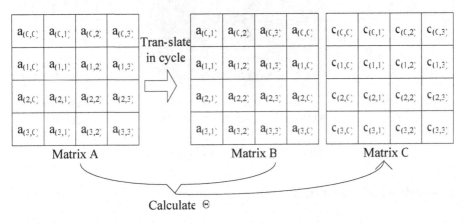

Fig. 1. The method of superposition in dislocation

4 Experiment

The CACM computing can be divided into several One-Step, in One-Step there is a circle, and every step of the circle is the calculation $A\Theta B$. Let's do only One-Step, the other is the same.

Table 3. The state of one CA

$d = 2\,;S = \{0,1,2\}$			
1	0	2	1
2	0	0	1
1	2	1	0
0	2	0	2

Step 1: fix the states of all cells of the CA as the Table 3 showed

Step 2: fix the (L_d, S, N, f) as the Equation(2) showed

Step 3: do the calculate Θ as what is showed in fig 2

Step 4: if the One-Step completed, go to Step 5,otherwise do Step 3

Step 5: the One-Step has been completed, go to Step 2 to do the next computing, If all the computing is over , go to the Step 6

Step 6: the result of the CA

The result is
$$\begin{bmatrix} 2 & 2 & 0 & 1 \\ 1 & 0 & 1 & 2 \\ 1 & 0 & 0 & 2 \\ 1 & 2 & 0 & 1 \end{bmatrix}$$

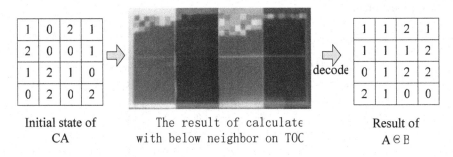

Initial state of CA　　The result of calculate with below neighbor on TOC　　decode　　Result of A ⊝ B

Fig. 2. The process of A ⊝ B on TOC

4　Analysis of the System

Time complexity of the system based on TOC relate to the N , it is $O(|N|)$, therefore the Time complexity has nothing to do with the scale of the CACM . Furthermore, the transformation rules of every cell and one cell in different step are different. These characters improve computing speed and increase the complexity of the CACM. therefore this kind of CACM can be used to simulate more complicated system.

References

1. Wolfram, S.: Cryptography with Cellular Automata. In: Williams, H.C. (ed.) CRYPTO 1985. LNCS, vol. 218, pp. 429–432. Springer, Heidelberg (1986)
2. Peter, D.: Cellular Automata-Based Signature Analysis for Built-in Self-Test. IEEE Transactions on Computers 39(10) (October 1990)
3. Jin, Y., He, H., Lu, Y.: Ternary Optical Computer Principle. Science in China (Series F) 46(2), 145–150 (2003)
4. Jin, Y., He, H., Lu, Y.: Ternary Optical Computer Architecture. Physical Script T118, 98–101 (2005)
5. Jin, Y., He, H., Ai, L.: Lane of parallel through carry in ternary optical adder. Science in China (Series F) 48(1), 107–116 (2005)
6. Bao, J., Jin, Y., Cai, C.: An Experiment for Ternary Optical Computer Hundred-Bit Encoder. Computer Technology and Development 17(2), 19–22 (2007)
7. Huang, W., Jin, Y., Ai, L.: Design and Implementation of the 100-Bit Coder for Ternary Optical Computers. Computer Engineering & Science 28(4), 139–142 (2006)
8. Jin, Y.: Management Strategy of Data Bits in Ternary Optical Computer. Journal of Shanghai University(Natural Science Edition) 13(5), 519–523 (2007)
9. Yan, J., Jin, Y., Zuo, K.: Decrease-radix design priciple for carrying/borrowing free multi-valued and application in ternary optical computer. Scinence in China Series F: Information Sciences 51(10), 1415–1426 (2008)
10. Wolfram, S.: Statistical Mechanics of Cellular Automata. Reviews of Modern Physics 55(3), 601–644 (1983)
11. Wolfram, S.: Theory and Applications of Cellular Automata. World Scientific, Singapore

Performance Evaluation of Authentication Certificate Based Seamless Vertical Handoff in GPRS-WLAN

Muhammad Usman[1], Surraya Khanum[2], Wajahat Noshairwan[1],
Ehtsham Irshad[1], and Azeem Irshad[1]

[1] University Institute of Information Technology, Pir Mehr Ali Shah,
Arid Agriculture University, Rawalpindi, Pakistan
manilasani@yahoo.com, wajahat.noshairwan@gmail.com
[2] Department of Computer Science, International Islamic University,
Islamabad, Pakistan
s_delhvi@yahoo.ca

Abstract. Authentication is an important security aspect in integrated wireless networks. Different protocols are currently used for first and second authentication in integrated wireless networks. Authentication Certificates (AC) are used by Mobile Node (MN) for seamless roaming between integrated wireless networks. AC's are helpful for seamless & secure second authentication in integrated wireless networks. This research paper is intended to evaluate the performance of AC based seamless vertical handoff. The Test-bed for this evaluation is comprises of NS-2 based GPRS-WLAN environment. We performed several experiments and the results proved that the AC based vertical handoff is seamless, it reduces network load and it ensures less time consumption for authentication at the time of vertical handoff. The results validates that AC based vertical handoff is seamless as compare to some of the other existing authentication protocols.

1 Introduction

Currently there is a trend to integrate cellular and computer networks in order to get complementary features of ubiquitous connectivity and better data rate. GPRS-WLAN integration [1] is an example of integrating heterogeneous networks. During rapid roaming between integrated networks, the security is a main concern for network entrepreneurs [2]. Authentication of each MN at the time of vertical handoff is important for secure integrated environment. Different authentication approaches such as single and dual authentication uses different protocols like, Extensible Authentication Protocol (EAP) [3] and Public Key Infrastructure (PKI) Cryptography based schemes [4] in integrated wireless networks. In single time authentication schemes, MN performs authentication only once. Using this scheme an unauthorized MN can get illegal access to the network's services. In dual authentication schemes, re-authentication is mandatory when user switches its network. This scheme causes delay for re-authentication in already established session of MN.

W. Zhang et al. (Eds.): HPCA 2009, LNCS 5938, pp. 384–389, 2010.

One of the better solutions is proposed in [5]. It is a hybrid scheme implemented in GPRS-WLAN tightly coupled integrated wireless network. In this scheme, MN gets an Authentication Certificate (AC) at the time of first authentication for seamless vertical handoff. Issuing server of AC updates partner network's authentication server about issuance of AC. The AC is encrypted by private key of issuing server. At the time of vertical handoff, MN just shows AC to the authentication server of target network which verifies it from its certificate repository and then authenticates only authorized MN. In this research paper we have evaluated the performance of AC based vertical handoff. We simulated AC based seamless vertical handoff scheme using different scenarios and then compared it with existing schemes.

The rest of the paper is organized as; section 2 describes the related work. The Mathematical Analysis is discussed in section 3. In Section 4 we have discussed Simulation environment and results. Section 5 concludes the contribution of this research paper. At the end of this paper references are given.

2 Related Work

Vertical handoff approaches such as trust delegation, local trust based approach and certificate based approach are discussed in [6]. The idea of most of them is at very abstract level. Particularly, in certificate based fast vertical handoff scheme, due to Certificate Authority's (CA) role, certificate based approach may not be practicable. WLAN_Centric authentication in integrated GPRS-WLAN network is discussed in [7]. This approach is based on loosely coupled architecture. It requires GPRS operator to install AAA server. This approach has a major draw back that how a cellular user can get initial authentication from WLAN centric authentication. In [8] Authors have introduced a mechanism using which an Inter-Base Station Protocol (IBSP) message can be transmitted between two heterogeneous networks. The Authorizations, Authentication, and Accounting (AAA) processes are only performed at early stage of connecting MN to Internet. This approach is more feasible for homogeneous networks. [9] Gives an authentication mechanism in IEEE 802.16e and CDMA2000 Networks for performing vertical handoff. This approach is secure but it does not provide seamless mobility. [10] Gives an interesting contribution in context of our proposed work. This article describes authentication and billing problems and proposed two protocols that provide both authentication and billing services. Although these protocols are efficient both in computation time and authentication but the contribution is not concern about the mobility.

3 Mathematical Analysis Using Efficiency Function

In this section, we have performed a mathematical analysis of AC based vertical handoff scheme. For this purpose, we have derived a linear mathematical function. We have called this linear mathematical function as an efficiency function. The proposed efficiency function has four equations which are given below.

Equation 1 gives us the total number of messages exchange between MN and network for dual authentication using EAP. Second equation gives us the total number of messages exchange between MN and network using EAP for initial and AC for second authentication.

Where, $y = a + b$ and $y = 5 + 3 = 8$. K is number of nodes. The value of K starts from 1 and it goes to n number of nodes in integrated wireless networks.

$$\sum_{K=1}^{n} k(y+2) = 10 + 20 + 30 + 40 + \ldots\ldots\ldots n \tag{1}$$

$$\sum_{K=1}^{n} k(y) = 8 + 16 + 24 + 32 + 40 + \ldots\ldots\ldots n \tag{2}$$

Equation 3 gives us the total number of messages exchange between MN and network for dual authentication using PKI cryptography. Equation 4 gives us the total number of messages exchange between MN and network using PKI cryptography based initial and AC based second authentication.

The proposed efficiency function is given below. Where, $z = c + d$ and $z = 13 + 3 = 16$ and K is number of nodes. The value of K starts from 1 and it goes to n number of nodes in integrated wireless networks.

$$\sum_{K=1}^{n} k(z+10) = 26 + 52 + 78 + 104\ldots\ldots\ldots n \tag{3}$$

$$\sum_{K=1}^{n} k(z) = 16 + 32 + 48 + 64 + 80\ldots\ldots\ldots n \tag{4}$$

4 Simulations

We have performed simulation on Network Simulator-2 (NS-2). The topology of scenario consists of four GPRS and two WLAN nodes which are interconnected with a single Protocol Translation Gateway (PTGW) node. The scenario also contains a mobile node represented by 7. The GPRS nodes are 0, 1, 2 and 3, which shows Base Station (BS), Home Subscriber Server/Authentication Centre (HSS/AUC) server, Serving GPRS Support Node (SGSN) and Gateway GPRS Support Node (GGSN) respectively. Similarly, WLAN nodes are 5 and 6 which shows Authentication, Authorization Accounting (AAA) server and Access Point (AP) respectively. Node 4 represents PTGW which interconnect GPRS and WLAN networks. All links have 1 MB bandwidth. We used User Datagram Protocol (UDP) as a transport protocol.

The EAP authentication is a 5-way handshake process. EAP ID request and response are each 128 bits in length. Similarly, EAP USIM challenge and response are each 1024 bits long. Finally, EAP success message has 128 bits length. Total single EAP based authentication messages size is 2432 bits. Similarly, the first message of PKI cryptography authentication scheme is attach request send by MN to network which is 128 bits long. MN also sends Hello message to the network which comprises of protocol version, supported ciphers, compression, random number and session ID which are collectively 128 bits long. Then network replies with same hello message of 128 bits strength. It also sends SGSN certificate, SGSN key exchange and

MN certificate request + hello done messages to the MN which are 1024, 1024 and 160 bits long respectively. MN replies with MN certificate, MN key exchange message, certificate verify message, and change cipher spec + finished message which are 1024, 256, 1024 and 192 bits long respectively. Then network send change cipher spec + finished message and attach accept + packet – Temporary Mobile Subscriber Identity (TMSI) message which are 192 and 72 bits in length respectively. Finally, MN send attach complete message to the network which has 128 bits length. Total single PKI cryptography based authentication messages size is 5480 bits. AC based authentication is a 3-way handshake process. At the time of vertical handoff network sends identity request message to the MN which has 128 bits length. Then MN shows AC to the network which has 1024 bits length. Finally, network grants authentication to the MN. This message is 128 bit long. Total Authentication Certificate based vertical handoff authentication messages size is 1280 bits.

4.1 Downwards and Upwards Vertical Handoff Simulation Scenarios

Our simulation model is based on eight scenarios, four among them are upwards vertical handoff scenarios and four are downwards vertical handoff scenarios. First downwards vertical handoff scenario shows dual authentication in GPRS-WLAN tightly coupled integrated wireless networks using EAP authentication scheme. Second downwards vertical handoff scenario shows EAP based initial authentication in GPRS network and AC based second authentication in WLAN. Third downwards vertical handoff scenario shows PKI cryptography based initial authentication in GPRS network and AC based second authentication that is in WLAN. Fourth downwards vertical handoff scenario shows the dual authentication using PKI cryptography based authentication scheme. Similarly, First upwards vertical handoff scenario shows dual authentication in GPRS-WLAN tightly coupled integrated wireless networks using EAP authentication scheme. Second scenario shows EAP based initial authentication in WLAN network and AC based second authentication in GPRS. Third scenario shows the dual authentication using PKI cryptography based authentication scheme. Fourth scenario shows PKI cryptography based initial authentication in WLAN network and AC based second authentication that is in GPRS network.

4.2 Summarized Results

In this section, we have summarized the results of simulations. We have summed up results on the basis of three parameters. These parameters are time for second authentication, number of messages for dual authentications and network load (i.e. size of messages for dual authentication).

4.2.1 Time for Second Authentication

The simulation results shows that AC based scheme is 77%, 49%, 72% and 49% (round off) efficient with respect to the time consumption of second authentication in integrated environment as compare to the other existing schemes in four scenarios which are discussed in section 4.1.

4.2.2 Number of Messages for Dual Authentication

The simulation results shows that AC based schemes is 39%, 20%, 39% and 20% (round off) efficient with respect to the number of messages as compare to the other existing schemes. This is also shown by a graph which is given in Figure 1.

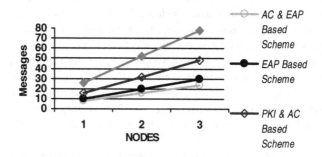

Fig. 1. Number of Messages Comparison between AC, PKI and EAP base VHO

4.2.3 Network Load

AC based schemes is 38%, 24%, 38% and 24% (round off) efficient with respect to the network load (i.e. size for messages for dual authentication) as compare to the other existing schemes. This is also shown by a graph which is given in Figure 2.

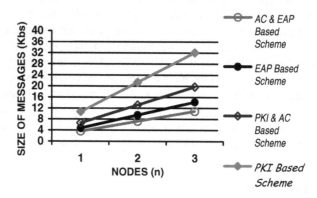

Fig. 2. Network Load Comparison between AC, PKI and EAP base VHO

5 Conclusions

In integrated environment, authentication is a basic security requirement. Different protocols like EAP, PKI and AC are used for second authentication. In this research paper, we have discussed the simulation environment, simulation scenarios; mathematical function and simulation results which validate the efficiency of AC based seamless vertical handoff in GPRS-WLAN tightly coupled integrated wireless networks. The validated results show that the AC based seamless vertical handoff approach not only reduces the number of messages it also make sure only authorized entry of MN from one network to other network. Results also validates that the AC based scheme cost less bandwidth for vertical handoff as it needs fewer messages of less size to be transferred between MN and network.

References

1. Salkintzis, A.K., Fors, C., Pazhyannur, R.: WLAN-GPRS integration for next generation mobile data networks. IEEE Wireless Communication, 112–124 (2004)
2. Shin, M., Mishra, J., Arbaugh, A.: Wireless Network Security and Interworking, pp. 455–466. IEEE, Los Alamitos (2006)
3. Extensible Authentication Protocol (EAP) progress in IETF time "06:00 PM" December 16 (2007), http://tools.ietf.org/html/draft-ietf-eap-keying-22
4. Kambourakis, G., Rouskas, A., Gritzalis, S.: Performance Evaluation of Public Key Based Authentication in Future Mobile Communication Systems (2004)
5. Usman, M., Noshairwan, W., Gilani, M., Irshad, A., Irshad, E.: Seamless Vertical handoff Using Authentication Certificate in GPRS-WLAN Tightly Coupled Integrated Wireless Networks. IEEE ICET (2008)
6. Wang, H., Prasad, A., Schoo, P.: Research Issues for Fast Authentication in Inter-Domain Handover. In: Wireless World Research Forum, WWRF (2004)
7. Jiang, M.-C., Chen, J.-C., Liu, Y.-W.: WLAN Centric authentication in integrated GPRS-WLAN networks. In: Vehicular Technology Conference (VTC), pp. 2242–2246. IEEE, Los Alamitos (2003)
8. Kim, P.S., Kim, Y.J.: New Authentication Mechanism for Vertical Handovers between IEEE 802.16e and 3G Wireless Networks. IJCSNS International Journal of Computer Science and Network Security (2006)
9. Park, S., Kim, S., Cho, J.: A Performance Evaluation of Vertical Handoff Scheme between IEEE 802.16e and cdma2000 Networks, project of: School of Electronics and Information, KyungHee University, Korea (2005)
10. Tseng, Y.M., Yang, C.C., Su, J.H.: Authenticationand Billing Protocols for the Integration of WLAN and 3G Networks. In: Wireless Personal Communications, pp. 351–366. Kluwer Academic, Dordrecht (2004); Printed in the Netherlands

Design and Implementation of Parallelized Cholesky Factorization

Bailing Wang[1,2], Ning Ge[3], Hongbo Peng[3],
Qiong Wei[3], Guanglei Li[3], and Zhigang Gong[3]

[1] School of Electronic Engineering and Computer Science,
Peking University, Beijing 100871, China
[2] Research Center of Computer Network and Information Security Technology,
Harbin Institute of Technology, Harbin 150001, China
wbl@hit.edu.cn
[3] IBM China System and Technology Lab, Beijing 100000, China
{gening,penghb,weiqiong,liguangl,gongzhig}@cn.ibm.com

Abstract. The bottleneck of most data analyzing systems, signal processing systems, and intensive computing systems is matrix decomposition. The Cholesky factorization of a sparse matrix is an important operation in numerical algorithms field. This paper presents a Multi-phased Parallel Cholesky Factorization (MPCF) algorithm, and then gives the implementation on a multi-core machine. A performance result shows that the system can reach 85.7 Gflop/s on a single PowerXCell processor and bulk of computation can reach to 94% of peak performance.

1 Introduction

The LAPACK software library represents a de factorization standard for high performance dense Linear Algebra computations and has served the HPC and Computational Science community remarkably well for twenty years. Cholesky factorization is one of the elementary matrix decompositions. Given a real symmetric positive definite matrix A, Cholesky factorization factors A into the form A=LL', where L is a real lower triangular matrix with positive diagonal elements, L' means the transpose of L.

Sequential scalar code has worse efficient in current multi-cores machines and block based parallel algorithms are developed to solve this problems. The adoption of block based algorithms can cut down the algorithm complexity for Cholesky factorization from $O(n^3)$ to $O((n/n_b)^3)$ (n_b is elementary processing block size). And combined with parallel processing amongst multiple processors, the computation capability of Cell/B.E.-like machine can be fully utilized. There are two kinds of mainstream block based parallel algorithm for Cholesky factorization: left looking and right looking[1]. A left looking block based (LLVB) algorithm is given out in [2]. A right looking block based (RLVB) algorithm implementation is presented in [3] The third parallel algorithm is mentioned as row Cholesky factorization algorithm in [4], but this is not a mainstream algorithm. There is no open paper indicates the performance of this algorithm on real machines.

W. Zhang et al. (Eds.): HPCA 2009, LNCS 5938, pp. 390–397, 2010.

Algorithm-1 shows the algorithm used in the LAPACK 3.1 library and implemented by the routine DPOTRF. Step-3, step-4 operations can be computed on multiple processors simultaneously. Step-3(the dominant operation) in this algorithm yields 1-D array of O (n) tasks in each panel computation. In the k-th panel computation, there are (processor num - k modulo processor num) processors are idle. This will cause poor load balance among processors especially at the end of large matrix computation (For DGEMM task computation operations increase with the processed panel length growing and the latter panel computation have the more idle time). The idle time for 1 processor is (k-1) tiles updating time at most.

Algorithm 1. Block based left looking Cholesky factorization

```
for k=1;k<=n/nb;k++
do
```
    1. DSYRK: Update the diagonal block

$$\tilde{A}_{kk} = A_{kk} - \begin{pmatrix} L_{k1} & \cdots & L_{k,k-1} \end{pmatrix}\begin{pmatrix} L_{k1} & \cdots & L_{k,k-1} \end{pmatrix}^T$$

    2. DPOTF2: Perform the unblocked Cholesky factorization of symmetric positive definite matrix

$$\tilde{A}_{kk} = L_{kk}L_{kk}^T$$

    3. DGEMM: Update the column panel

$$\begin{pmatrix} \tilde{A}_{k+1,k} \\ \vdots \\ \tilde{A}_{pk} \end{pmatrix} = \begin{pmatrix} A_{k+1,k} \\ \vdots \\ A_{pk} \end{pmatrix} - \begin{pmatrix} L_{k+1,1} & \cdots & L_{k+1,k-1} \\ \cdots & \cdots & \cdots \\ L_{p1} & \cdots & L_{p,k-1} \end{pmatrix}\begin{pmatrix} L_{k1} & \cdots & L_{k,k-1} \end{pmatrix}^T$$

    4. DTRSM: Compute the (n'-nb)*nb column panel of L by solving

$$L_{jk}L_{kk}^T = \tilde{A}_{jk}, (j = k+1,...,p)$$

```
End
```

The right looking algorithm is described in *Algorithm-2*. Step-2 step-3 operations can be compute on multiple processors in parallel. Step-3(the dominant operation) in this algorithm yields 2-D array of O (n^2) fine grain tasks in each panel computation. It will bring good balance among processors. In each panel computation, the idle time for 1 processor is a tile update time at most.

Algorithm 2. Block based right looking Cholesky factorization

```
for k=1;k<=n/nb;k++
do
```
    1. **DPOTRF2:** Perform the unblocked Cholesky factorization of symmetric positive definite matrix

$$\tilde{A}_{kk} = L_{kk}L_{kk}^T$$

    2. **DTRSM:** Compute the (n'-nb)*nb column panel of L by solving

$$L_{jk}L_{kk}^T = \tilde{A}_{jk} , \quad j=k+1, \ldots, p$$

3. **DGEMM**: Update the tail sub-matrix

$$\tilde{A}_{ij} = \tilde{A}_{ij} - L_{ik}L_{jk}^T, (i, j = k+1, \ldots, p \quad and \quad i \neq j)$$

End

These two algorithms have similar total loading and storing operations ($\sim O((1/3)*(n/n_b)^3*n_b^2)$).The right looking has equal tile loading and tile storing operations ($O((1/6)*(n/n_b)^3*n_b^2)$). The left looking has dominant loading operations ($O((1/3)*(n/n_b)^3*n_b^2)$) and few storing operations ($O(n^2)$). And 2 algorithms both have same computation operations ($O((1/3)*n^3)$).

Generally to say, modern machines have higher I/O read speed than write speed. The traditional left looking algorithm can achieve higher peak I/O speed (for its dominant load operation can utilize higher read I/O speed), but it has load-unbalance problem especially at end of large matrix. The traditional right looking algorithm can provide better load balance (for its 2-D sub-matrix updating way) but much more store operation limits the peak I/O speed which will constraints the peak computation performance achievable. In theory, a left looking algorithm that improves load balance problem can achieve best performance on multi-cores machine. Such an algorithm will be given in next section.

We have parallelized SVD algorithm in [5], and we will continue to illustrate how to parallelize Cholesky factorization on multi-core platform. In this paper, section 2 gave a new MPCF algorithm for Cholesky factorization to avoid the problem of traditional algorithms; section 3 proposes how to implement the system on PowerXCell processor and performance results for this system are also shown; and conclusions are given at last.

2 MPCF Algorithm for Multi-core platform

In order illustrate the mechanism clearly, we give the symbols and terms used in the following sections first.

Table 1. Symbols and terms used in the following sessions

Symbol	Description
K	Processor number
n_b	Fixed block size
N	Matrix size
N_{block}	Matrix size divided by block size (i.e. n/n_b).
N_{total}	$N_{block}*(N_{block}+1)/2$
Panel	One block column with n_b Elements column in one panel
Update Operations	Including DGEMM and DSYRK tile operations
Calculate Operations	Including DPOTF2 and DTRSM tile operations

MPCF Algorithm is a multi-phased cholesky factorization algorithm which adopts improved balanced left looking and right looking algorithms at different phases. The motivation of proposing MPCF algorithm is to utilize traditional algorithm advantage and avoid their disadvantage. MPCF algorithm combines balanced left looking algorithm and right looking algorithm to achieve both good load balance and high performance. And the performance data of MPCF implementation also approved this point. The MPCF algorithm is fit for $N_{block} > K$ situation. If $N_{block} <= K$, a right looking algorithm will be used on whole area.

The elementary operations in section-3 and section-4 refer to Fig 1. DGEMM, DSYRK, DTRSM and DPOTF2 are used to stand for these operations. The size of tiles is $n_b \times n_b$.

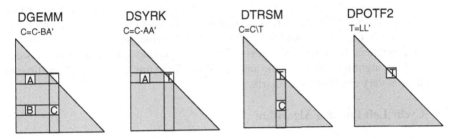

Fig. 1. Elementary Tile Operations in Block based Cholesky factorization

2.1 Matrix Area Partition

In the new algorithm, the triangular matrix A is divided into 3 areas (Area-1, Area-2 and Area-3) which are shown in Fig 2.

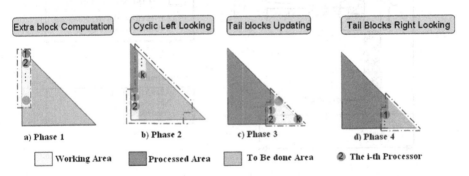

Fig. 2. Computation Phase Division. Phase 1: Working on area 1; Phase 2: Updating area 2; Phase 3: Working on area 3; Phase 4: Working on area 3 with right looking algorithm

Area-1 includes (N_{total} modulo K) blocks in the first column (Assume $N_{block} > K$). The purpose of area-1 is to ensure the left blocks number is multiple of K and is easy to distribute evenly over K processors. Area-3 includes tail (K*(K+1)/2 − K*(K+1)/2 modulo K) blocks. Blocks in each panel in this area is less than K and is difficult to load balance for left looking algorithm. The right looking algorithm has better load balance for this area. The blocks number of Area-3 is multiple of K also so that the accumulated updating operation from Area-1 Area-2 computed results can be scheduled onto K processors averagely. Except Area-1 and Area-3, the left area is called Area-2. This area covers bulk area of large matrix and a cyclic left looking algorithm is adopted.

There are 4 phases while working on the 3 matrix areas. Phase-1 is used to process extra blocks. All processors wait for DPOTRF on diagonal block at panel 1 and then (N_{total} modulo K)-1 processors can do DTRSM simultaneously. Phase-2 can be decomposed into ($N_{block} - K$) steps. Each step includes 2 parts: Updating and calculating of the current panel; Updating and calculating on some of the blocks in the next panel (the detail refer to section 3.3). Phase-3 updates the area-3 blocks. This is a transitional phase in which the updating operations (from 1st panel to (N_{block}-K)-th panel total (N_{block}-K) DGEMM/DSYRK is needed for each blocks in area-3) are processed in balance on K processors. And after phase-3 computation, the area-3 can be looked as an independent K panels sub-matrix. Phase-4 computes on area-3 with K steps right looking algorithm. Because the amount of blocks in this area is small, the time in this phase is very small in large matrix.

2.3 Cyclic Left Looking Algorithm

Cyclic left looking algorithm will take major time in large matrix. The i-th step works on i-th panel and $(i+1)$-th panel. The i-th step of the cyclic left looking algorithm is shown at Fig 3.

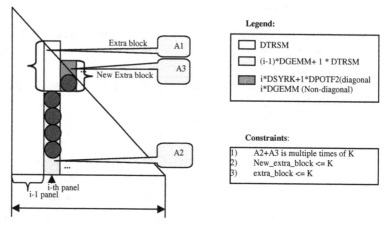

Fig. 3. The i-th Step in Cyclic Left Looking Algorithm

Firstly DTRSM tile operation is executed on A1 area (except diagonal block). Then DGEMM tile and DTRSM tile operations on A2 area + DSYRK tile and DPOTF2 tile operation on diagonal block in $(i+1)$-th panel are executed. Last, DGEMM tile updates the blocks in A3 (Not include diagonal block). In this algorithm, Operations on $(i+1)$-th panel depends on computing results of left neighbor blocks in i-th panel and should wait until the neighbor is done (The wait time is 1 DTRSM tile computation at most). The extra block and new extra_block calculation can refer to Algorithm-3: This algorithm is designed so that updating operations in each step is balanced scheduled on K processors and at most K status variables is enough to track dependencies between blocks in 1st panel and 2nd panel in 1 step.

3 Design and Implementation on PowerXCell

3.1 MPCF System Design

The MPCF system on PowerXCell^{TM} 8i is composed of 4 parts: PPE component, SPE main component, computation kernels, common utilities, and synchronization component, refer to Fig 4 to get the relation.

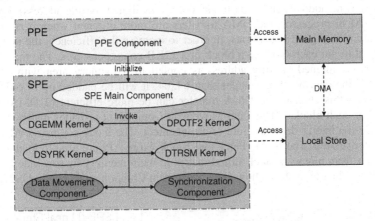

Fig. 4. MPCF System Architecture: PPE component, SPE main component, computation kernels, common utilities, and synchronization component

1) PPE Component: The PPE component provides the standard LAPACK API to applications. For most LAPACK routines, this component will do the real computation on PPE side. For the selected routines (DPOTRF), it will do parameter checks then make decision whether it is necessary to run components on SPEs. If it is necessary, they will create a new task which will then send the request to SPE module. After the SPE component finishes the task, the PPE component will write result and return to user's application.

2) SPE Main Component: It receives the request from PPE side. Then it will execute the optimized DPOTRF which will do the real computation. The MPCF algorithm is implemented in this component.

3) Computation Kernels: The SPE computing kernel component contains pure code for matrix operation on $n_b x n_b$ tiles (n_b is 64). It will process the data prepared by SPE Main component. Then it returns the result. The computation kernels include most float point operations of whole routine and their performances are critical to overall Cholesky factorization performance. They are highly optimized with multiple techniques including SIMD, loop unrolling, SPU intrinsic, assemble language (if necessary), etc.. The computation kernels for DPOTRF include DGEMM kernel, DSYRK kernel, DTRSM kernel and DPOTF2 kernel.

4) Common Utilities: Data Movement Component: help library developer to load and store data block from main memory; It also provides column major store into block by block store conversion function and reverse conversion function.

5) Synchronization Component: SPU programming helper routines, it's used to simplify synchronization, barrier and atomic support.

3.2 Data Movement Component

Tile based algorithm required fixed-size block transfer (64x64) from system memory to local store. If the matrix were stored in column by column manner, then computation would require numerous small DMA transfer (64 transfers of 64x8 bytes for aligned starting address, and 3x64 transfers for nonaligned starting address). For PowerXCellTM 8i processor, the DMA transfers are more efficient when performed on 128B naturally aligned boundaries. In order to increase the efficiency, the matrix was rearranged to put each 64x4 data block in a 32KB contiguous area. The matrix without 16 bytes aligned starting address is copied to a memory area with 16 bytes aligned. If the data block is smaller than 64x64, it will be padded up to 64x64 data block. With this change, the DMA transfer can be more efficient (2 DMA transfer request for each blocks). The Data Movement Component provides matrix_to_block API to do the matrix data structure re-arrangement. The block_to_matrix API do the reverse conversion. The Block_Fetch and Block_Store API are used to load and store data block from block by block stored matrix in main memory by row index and column index. The Fig. 5 shows how Data Movement Component works on QS22.

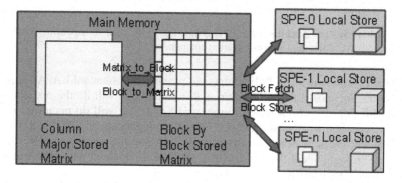

Fig. 5. Data movement among components while using new algorithm on QS22 platform

3.3 Performance of MPCF Algorithm

Fig. 6 shows performance of the double precision Cholesky factorization calculated as the ratio of execution time to the number of floating point operations calculated as n3/3, where n is the matrix size of the input matrix. The performance data of MPCF on QS22 machine is shown in Table-3. The whole lapack DPOTRF routine time is measured, and includes computation time, environment initialization/finalization and matrix to block/block to matrix conversion time. So the pure Cholesky factorization has higher Gflop/s number. The test data is from a QS22 machine with 2 PowerXCell processor @3.2GHz, 8GB Memory (Total 2x8 SPEs with 204Gflops DP theoretic peak performance). Compare with the left looking algorithm, the performance of MPCF is higher 23.8% at 10Kx10K matrix 16 SPEs.

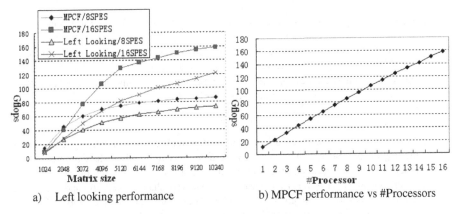

a)   Left looking performance   b) MPCF performance vs #Processors

Fig. 6. MPCF performance analysis

4   Conclusions

MPCF shows the better load balance and the higher performance of Cholesky decomposition on multi-cores system. It improves the performance of large scale scientific computation which depends on matrix decomposition. Much more matrix decomposition should be parallelized in the future.

References

1. Dongarra, J.J., Duff, L.S., Sorensen, D.C., Van der Vorst, H.A.: Numerical Linear Algebra for High Performance Computers. SIAM, Philadelphia (1998)
2. Kurzak, J., Dongarraa, J.J.: Implementing linear algebra routines on multi-core processors with pipelining and a look-ahead. In: Kågström, B., Elmroth, E., Dongarra, J., Waśniewski, J. (eds.) PARA 2006. LNCS, vol. 4699, pp. 147–156. Springer, Heidelberg (2007)
3. Buttari, A., Langou, J., Kurzak, J., Dongarra, J.: A Class of Parallel Tiled Linear Algebra Algorithms for Multicore Architectures, UT-CS-07-600, September 7 (2007) (also as LAPACK Working Note #191)
4. Michael, T.: Heath Prof. Parallel Numerical Algorithms. Cholesky Factorization, ch. 7, http://www.cse.illinois.edu/courses/cs554/notes/ 07_Cholesky.pdf
5. Bai-Ling, W., Jia-Ming, P., et al.: Parallel SVD of Bidiagonal Matrix on PowerXCell[TM] 8i Processor. In: Workshop on Cell Systems and Applications, Beijing, June 21- 22 (2008)

Network Coding for Creating Replica in Grid Environments

Banghai Wang[1,2], Jiangshou Hong[1], Lingxiong Li[1], and Dongyang Long[1]

[1] Department of Computer Science, Sun Yat-sen University, Guangzhou 510275, China
issldy@mail.sysu.edu.cn
[2] Faculty of Computer, Guangdong University of Technology, Guangzhou 510006, China
wbh@gdut.edu.cn

Abstract. We propose a new scheme for creating replica based on network coding in grid environments. For creating replica with network coding, there are two models: encoding between blocks of a replica and encoding between blocks of different replicas. The former is based on a butterfly-shaped topology, and the latter, in theory, based on any topology with a node more than one degree. Based on the latter model, furthermore, in practice, we propose a double-funnel-shaped topology. To evaluate our models, we extend NS2 by improving functions, modifying and adding classes. Compare to traditional strategies of creating replica, our experiment showed the strategy with network coding can improve data access time and I/O bottlenecks, low bandwidth consumption, or improve load balancing, increase robustness for being in support of departure of nodes.

Keywords: Data Grid; Replication; Network coding; NS2.

1 Introduction

A Data Grid connects a collection of hundreds of geographically distributed wide variety of resources including supercomputers, storage systems, data sources, and special classes of devices located in different parts of the world to facilitate sharing of data and resources. The size of the data that need to be accessible to users in various locations on the Data Grid is on the order of Petabytes, such as about 15 petabytes in 2008 for LHC(the Large Hadron Collider), a high energy particle physics community [2]. Ensuring efficient access to such huge and widely distributed data is a serious challenge to network and Grid designers [8]. Replication strategy is considered as one of the most effective way to deal with the challenge. Replication is used in data grids to help the grid to improve performance and to reduce blocking of communication between users, by reducing users' access latency and bandwidth consumption. Replication also helps in load balancing and can improve reliability by creating multiple copies of the same data [1]. The replication strategy had been investigated by several algorithms in several ways [8, 11, 9]. The replication strategies, however, could use the results of other technologies, such as the network coding and BitTorrent system [19], which is somewhat application of the idea of the grid. Network coding is the new results of information theory, in the model of which network nodes can not only store and forward data, but also encode the data received[3,14,12]. Our study

W. Zhang et al. (Eds.): HPCA 2009, LNCS 5938, pp. 398–403, 2010.
© Springer-Verlag Berlin Heidelberg 2010

investigates the usefulness and effectiveness of creating replicas with network coding. To address the scalability, we replicate data with network coding in the mesh topology. Since most datasets in the scientific data grid scenario are read-only [9], we do not consider the overhead of updates.

To evaluate our model we use the network simulator NS2 to generate assigned network topologies, and we use different dataset sizes to study the impact of replication on the data access cost on the overall grid. The paper is organized as follows. Section 2 gives an overview of previous work on network coding and grid replication. In Section 3, we introduce our replication topologies and algorithms with network coding. Section 4 describes the extending of NS2, the simulation framework and the results. Finally, we present brief conclusions and future directions in Section 5.

2 Related Work

A substantial amount of work has been done on data replication in grid environments, most of it has focused on single user, although Adam et al. considered the all over grid[1], the approach of creating replica is similar to the others. Based on the Globus resource management architecture, a co-allocation architecture is proposed. Sudharshan and Vazhkudai developed several co-allocation mechanisms to enable parallel downloading [16]. The most interesting one is called Dynamic Co-Allocation. The dataset that the client wants is divided into "k" disjoint blocks of equal size. Each available server is assigned to deliver one block in parallel. Based on the co-allocation architecture and the prediction technique, Ruay-Shiung Chang et al. improved the Dynamic Co-Allocation [13]. To prevent the drawback of Dynamic Co-Allocation, R. S. Chang et al. proposed (1) abort and retransfer, (2) one by one co-allocation [15]. In all of the studies presented in this section, the improving of performance is limited, especially when the order of replicas is large enough.

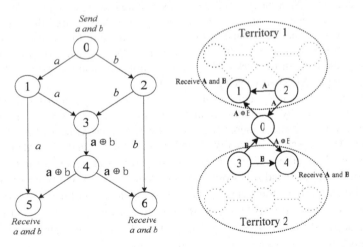

Fig. 1. The Butterfly-shaped Topology   **Fig. 2.** The Double-funnel-shaped Topology

Based on the idea of network information flow, Ahlswede et al. put forward the concept of network coding in 2000. Fig.1 demonstrates the network encoding model: a, b, said the source node 0 packets generated, corresponds separately to two symbols on some field being encoded; the encoding operation on the input a and b in the intermediate node (inter-node) 3 results in a new package (a⊕b), forwarding to the next node. As shown, each target node can decode the available information (a and b) from the information received. Since the network coding was put forward in 2000, it has rapidly developed and aroused the widespread interest in many fields. The new application based on the network coding technique in many fields, such as Ad-hoc net [4,17], P2P[10], network management, the error correction and so on have been appeared. The strategy of creating replica with network coding can improve I/O bottlenecks of source node, decrease bandwidth consumption and increase robustness of network.

3 The Strategy of Creating Replica with Network Coding

Practically, since the network resources involved in transferring the data are becoming increasingly faster and more efficient disk service time is becoming increasingly important in grid data retrieval. *The electromechanical nature of storage devices limits their performance at orders of magnitude lower than microprocessors and memory devices and, thereby, creates I/O bottlenecks* [1]. Disk I/O is a critical component of service time for data grid requests. Our strategy can improve I/O bottlenecks by network coding. Traditional network nodes had only the function of store-and-forward, but nodes with network coding can compute (encode). The computing in nodes is in exchange for bandwidth consumption and load balance in overall grid system. In our strategy, replication is assumed to be a server side phenomenon. A server decides when and where to create two or more copies (replicas) of one of its files according to the character of network [9] and decides when and where to encode. Some inter-nodes are selected to encode replica blocks, and the nodes required to create replica decode the codes in proper methods in our replication strategy. It is easy to find the inter-nodes because it is easy to find the butterfly sub-topological structure for the use of network coding in mesh topology. Fig.3 is the early grid projector, e-science topology [6]. Ho etc. proposed the random network coding scheme in galois field designated[7]. As an example for simple, XOR(⊕) is acted as the encoding way, so does in the Section 4.

The advantage of creating replica with network coding between different replicas can be well illustrated by the double-funnel topology. As shown in fig. 2, there are a source file A in node 2 and a source file B in node 3, and the replicas of A and B are created in node 1 and node 4. Usually, A and B are all stored and forwarded in node 0, but only (A⊕B) is store and forward in node 0 with network coding. First of all, A is from node 2 to node 0 and B is from node 3 to node 0, then A and B are encoded to (A⊕B), and then (A⊕B) is transferred to node 1 and node 4, and finally (A⊕B) and A from node 2 are decoded to B by (A⊕A⊕B) in node 1, as well as (A⊕B) and B from node 3 are decoded to A by (B⊕A⊕B) in node 4. In this way, we only need creating (A⊕B) in node 0.It is more importantly that the recourses of A and B exist in the grid once the departure of node 2 or node 3, thus increasing the robustness of the grid. Regarding as the network inside the dotted ellipse a territory, exchanging data with network coding between territory 1 and territory 2, the advantage is obviously. It is easier to find the inter-nodes like node 0 to encode, because the network coding, theoretically, is possible for each node more than one degree. For the star topology, the replica could be created on the central node with network coding. For Hierarchical or tree topology, which is one of the most important common architecture in current use [18], except the leaf nodes, all nodes have the possibility of coding.

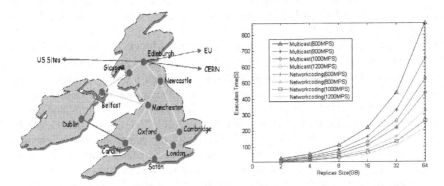

Fig. 3. The E-science Topology   **Fig. 4.** Simulation Results for Scenario 1

4 Experimental Evaluation

NS2 is a commonly network simulator, therefore we use it to make the simulation for our model. However, the original architecture of NS2 itself does not support the function of network coding, for which the original function of NS2 must be modified to meet our requirements. Our extending of NS2 includes five parts: i) Expanding packet header to distinguish network coding protocol packets and other protocol packets. ii)Adding classifier and replicator. A new classifier is inserted at the entrance of node. It separates the network coding packets from other packages, which will be forwarded by traditional way. iii) Adding encoding buffer and timer. A buffer queue is used to buffer packets from different links. These packets are encoded and sent under the control of the timer. Together with classifier, they enable the packets from different links to be encoded. iv) Adding encoding and decoding modules. v) Adding network coding agent. The agent has sealed the classifier and replicator, encoding buffer and timer queue, and encoding and decoding module to support the procedure of decoding.

   In general, there are two scenarios with network coding to create replica: single source multicast, multiple sources multicast. For scenario 1, more than one replica will be created in different places in grid, the original file of replica will be divided into a number of pieces similar to BT, with which are encoded. For scenario 2, different replicas belonged to different nodes would be created when be encoded between different replica. For more efficient simulate, a real network topology, early grid e-science topology (fig.3), was selected. Supposed the delay of the message transmission between nodes is directly proportional to the distance between two points and the delay about 20 ms/units, and supposed error free in the process of transmission. For scenario 1, we assume that a file in note Dublin, and replicas are created in note London and note Glasgow. We could find the notes Dublin, Belfast, Cardiff, Manchester, Newcastle, Glasgow and London constitutes a butterfly-shaped topology, and are encoded in node Manchester. The multicast could be viewed as the unicasts: Dublin to Glasgow, Dublin to London. The original file in Dublin was divided into even-numbered disjoint data blocks of equal size 1, 2, ..., 2k-1, 2k, the router of the even blocks 2, 4, ..., 2k is Dublin-Belfast and is broadcasted to Glasgow and Manchester, the router of the odd blocks 1, 3, ..., 2k -1 is Dublin-Cardiff and is broadcasted to Manchester and London by Satan, and the two adjacent blocks 1 and 2, 3 and 4, ..., 2k-1 and 2k, and finally the encoded k blocks $0 \oplus 1$, $2 \oplus 3$,..., $2k-1 \oplus 2k$ in Manchester and forward to Glasgow and London. The simulated data are in four groups: 64G, 32G, 16G, 8G, 4G, and 2G. The bandwidths are between 600MPS-1800MPS. For scenario 2, in double-funnel-shaped topology, as shown in fig. 2, the simulated data of file A and file B are in four groups: 8.8G, 9.1G; 3.2G, 5.1G; 2.7G, 12.3G; 800M, 800M. When the size of the two original files is not the same, the size of encoded blocks is the size of the small original file, and the remainder of the big file is not encoded and transported as the ordinary way(without network coding).

The result of first experiment showed that the efficiency of creating replica with network coding technology is much higher than that without network coding technology. The time with network coding technology is half of without it. As shown in Fig. 4, the curve of Multicat-1200MB and the curve of Networkcoding-600MB nearly overlap. Moreover, the larger is the replica, the higher the efficiency. The result of the second experiment showed that the technology of network coding doesn't improve the efficiency of creating replica. However once any node leaves, the two replicas are keeping available, thus increasing the robustness of the grid.

5 Conclusions and Further Directions

We have addressed the strategy of replication in Data Grid environments by investigating the algorithms of creating replica using the technology of network coding that can be used to improve data access time, bandwidth consumption, and scalability of the overall system. Our results show that using replication with network coding improves data access performance and bandwidth consumption of overall system as measured by the response time (scenario 1) and improve load balancing and increase the robustness of the over system (scenario 2). Our results also show that performance increases as the size of data increase. This discipline is also proved by C. Gkantsidis and P. R. Rodriguez [5]. These results are very promising, but they are based on further development of network coding. In future work, we will investigate realistic scenarios, and real user access patterns. We are also interested in exploring different topologies that select replica placement dynamically depending on current conditions.

Acknowledgments. This work was partially sponsored by the Natural Science Foundation of China (Project No. 60273062, 60573039).

References

1. Villa, A.H., Varki, E.: Co-allocation in Data Grids: A Global, Multi-user Perspective. In: Wu, S., Yang, L.T., Xu, T.L. (eds.) GPC 2008. LNCS, vol. 5036, pp. 152–165. Springer, Heidelberg (2008)
2. Cho, A.: Large Hadron Collider: The Overture Begins. Science 321(5894), 1287–1289 (2008)
3. Cohen, B.: Incentives build robustness in bittorrent. In: P2P Economics Workshop, Berkeley, CA (2003)
4. Fragouli, C., Widmer, J., LeBoudec, J.Y.: A network coding approach to energy efficient broadcasting: from theory to practice. In: Infocom 2006 (March 2006)
5. Gkantsidis, C., Rodriguez, P.R.: Network coding for large scale content distribution. In: Proc. IEEE Infocom 2005, March 2005, vol. 4, pp. 2235–2245 (2005)
6. E-science Topology,
   `http://www.e-science.ox.ac.uk/oxford/griduk.gif`
7. Ho, T., Koetter, R., Medard, M., et al.: A random linear network coding approach to multicast. IEEE Transactions on Information Theory 52(10), 4413–4430 (2006)
8. Lamehamedi, H., Szymanski, B., Shentu, Z., Deelman, E.: Data replication strategies in grid environments. In: Proceedings of 5th International Conference on Algorithms and Architecture for Parallel Processing, pp. 378–383 (2002)
9. Ranganathan, K., Foster, I.: Identifying dynamic replication strategies for a high-performance data grid. In: Proceeding of the Second International Workshop on Grid Computing, Denver, November 2001, pp. 75–86 (2001)
10. Ma, G., Xu, Y., Lin, M., Xuan, Y.: A Content Distribution System based on Sparse Linear Network Coding. In: Third Workshop on Network Coding, Netcod 2007 (2007)
11. Madi, M.K., Hassan, S.: Dynamic Replication Algorithm in Data Grid: Survey. In: International Conference on Network Applications, Protocols and Services 2008 (NerApps 2008), Malaysia (November 2008)
12. Chou, P., Wu, Y., Jain, K.: Network coding for the internet. In: IEEE Communication Theory Workshop, Capri. IEEE, Los Alamitos (2004)
13. Chang, R.-S., Wang, C.-M., Chen, P.-H.: Replica selection on co-allocation data Grids. In: Cao, J., Yang, L.T., Guo, M., Lau, F. (eds.) ISPA 2004. LNCS, vol. 3358, pp. 584–593. Springer, Heidelberg (2004)
14. Ahlswede, R., Cai, N., Li, S.R., Yeung, R.W.: Network information flow. IEEE Transactions on Information Theory (2000)
15. Chang, R.S., Chen, P.H.: Complete and fragmented replica selection and retrieval in Data Grids. Future Generation Computer Systems 23, 536–546 (2007)
16. Vazhkudai, S.: Enabling the Co-allocation of Grid data transfers. In: Proceedings of International Workshop on Grid Computing, Phoenix, Arizona, USA, November 17, pp. 44–51 (2003)
17. Katti, S., Rahul, H., Katabi, D., Hu, W., Médard, M., Crowcroft, J.: XORs in the Air:Practical Wireless Network Coding. In: SIGCOMM (2006)
18. Lin, Y.F., Wu, J.J., Liu, P.: A List-Based Strategy for Optimal Replica Placement in Data Grid Systems. In: ICPP 2008. 37th International Conference on Parallel Processing, 2008, Portland, Oregon, September 9-12, pp. 198–205 (2008)
19. Zissimos, A., Doka, K., Chazapis, A., Koziris, N.: GridTorrent: Optimizing data transfers in the Grid with collaborative sharing. Presented at 11th Panhellenic Conference on Informatics, PCI 2007, Patras, Greece (May 2007)

A Binary Method of License Plate Character Based on Object Space Distribution Feature

Mei Wang[1], Guang-da Su[2], and Sheng-lan Ben[2]

[1] Laboratory of Image Processing, Yantai Vocational College, Yantai 264670, China
wangmei336@163.com
[2] Department of Electronic Engineering, Tsinghua University, Beijing 100084, China

Abstract. For the problem of the difficult object-extraction in transition region and noise-effect in binary processes, the vehicle license plate characters binary method based on object space distribution feature is proposed. Considering the spatial distribution of object and background, the method with less false-dismissal and more false-alarm can extract more perfect object shape than conventional method. And then the morphology operation is used to throw away noise-isolated point. Actual vehicle images from traffic station are used to test the performance of different binary methods and the experimental results indicate that our algorithm achieved better binary results than other methods in object shape extraction and noises reduction.

1 Introduction

Binary processing is conventional image segmentation technology to separate object from background [1-3]. Vehicle License plate (VLP) character binary processing is its practical application. The traditional method of object binary processing is that the binary threshold is selected to identify the pixel-point whose gray-value more than the threshold as object and to identify the pixel-point, which gray-value is lower than the threshold as the background. In fact, binary processing equals two-classis decision. Gray-value is eigen-value and the threshold is break point. Up to now, principal object binary categories includes: (1) texture analysis binary method [2], its processing produce is shown as: firstly, to extract and analysis image texture; secondly, to identify object or background pixel-points depending on texture feature and their distribution feature is given; at last, object gray segmentation threshold is achieved by mini-max sense of pattern recognition. (2) Statistic binary method [6]. Statistic feature and prior knowledge as eigen-value are used to segment object and background. Its advantage is that the time-consuming is lower than other method. (3) bi-peak histogram binary method [7]. Gray histogram is the gray-scale function and it describes the pixel number of every gray-scale in the gray image. The gray-scale of the trough between two peaks is the threshold of object binary; (4) Classic Otsu optimization threshold method [1]. The method is the most commonly object binary method [1-3]. And, it is an effective classification method using the ration of inter-class variance, in-class variance and the total variance. Its disadvantage is that pixels space correlation isn't considered. Its performance of object segmentation is bad when there are lots noises in the actual image. For example, actual vehicle license

W. Zhang et al. (Eds.): HPCA 2009, LNCS 5938, pp. 404–409, 2010.

plate image character segmentation requires that character binary result keep perfect character shape and no noises. But Otsu character binary result isn't satisfactory.

This paper presents an object binary approach based on object space distribution feature. The object binary threshold is improved by the method with less false-dismissal and more false alarm. Increasing object area sharing probability, as, less false-dismissal can extract more precise object pixels in transition region [4] to perfect object shape than conventional method. And the morphology small area deletion operation, as, less false alarm is used to throw away noise-isolation point which can't be separated from background by single threshold. The performance of the object binary is well for transition region object pixel extraction and noise-isolation reduction. Actual vehicle license plate images from traffic station are used to test the performance of different binary methods and the experimental results show the method is suitable for the application of image segmentation with perfect object shape feature and less noises. Another point, the method solves the problem that character can't be segmented after object binary processing because of vehicle license plate character linking.

2   Plate Character Binary Based on Space Distribution Feature

The purpose of image segmentation is to separate image space into meaningful regions. If the object binary threshold is chosen, the object will be separated from the background. As, suppose $\forall (x, y) \in I$, $g(x, y)$ is the gray value of pixel-point (x, y) in image I , the object binary processing is described as:

$$Binary(x, y) = \begin{cases} 1, \text{ while } g(x, y) >= T \\ 0 \qquad\quad g(x, y) < T \end{cases} \tag{1}$$

here, T is the binary threshold. Since there is gray overlap region between object and background, only one selected threshold can't segment every object from background precisely. But the better method is to extract more object pixels regarded as background and get rid off isolation noises to improve binary performance.

2.1   NLPF Function and Object Gray Histogram Analysis

Considering the space distribution feature of object and background, the gray histogram is near to gray probability function $p(z)$ [7]. In fact, the gray probability function is sum of two single-peak probability functions of object and background. If the probability function is given, the optimization threshold as minimum error is computed to separate two categories regions from one image. Depending on the companion feature, suppose the prior probability of background and object is P_b, P_o, respectively. Then the relationship between them is $p_o = 1 - p_b$. The negative log-probability function (NLPF) of P_b and P_o is defined as,

$$\begin{cases} NLPF_b = -\log(P_b) \\ NLPF_o = -\log(P_o) = -\log(1 - P_b) \end{cases} \tag{2}$$

NLPF function is shown in Fig.1. There, the threshold optimization position is in the overlap between background and object, the optimization position is marked in Fig.1(a). Some pixel-points in the transition region can't be identified as object or background by one binary threshold easily. In practical application, some noises, whose eigen-value is higher than background, are identified as object. This is called as false alarm. And some object pixel-points in the transition boundary region, whose eigen-value is between object and background is identified as background. This is called false-dismissal alarm. In order to keep perfect object shape, the idea is to keep less false-dismissal and more false alarms. Depending on the companion and compensation feature between object and background region, to improve object area probability from $p_o^{'}$ to $p_o + \varepsilon$ (ε is the change latitude) implies to regard more pixel-points in transition region as object. And the relationship between them is $p_b^{'} = p_b - \varepsilon$. NLPF of object and background is described as,

$$\begin{cases} NLPF_b = -\log(P_b^{'}) = -\log(P_b - \varepsilon) \\ NLPF_o = -\log(P_o^{'}) = -\log(1 + \varepsilon - P_b) \end{cases} \tag{3}$$

The improved threshold optimization position is marked in Fig.1 (b).

Improved threshold method can identify some pixel-points in transition region as object to perfect object shape. But some background pixel-points as false alarm are identified as object too. Because some noises, which spatial distribution is unorganized and isolated, morphology small area deletion operation can remove them. To copy with this problem is next work.

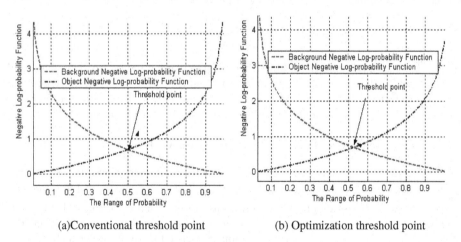

(a)Conventional threshold point   (b) Optimization threshold point

Fig. 1. Threshold point position of object and background NLPF

Usually some pixel-points with similar eigen-value and adjacent spatial location are regarded as object or background. The pixel-points of space distribution isolate can't form segmentation object region and they are usually identified as background.

In this paper, Object Gray-scale Histogram (OGH) is designed to analysis the spatial distribution feature of object and background boundary in overlap region, As,

OGH helps us find precise object binary threshold point, OGH overlap region threshold computing procedure is described as,

Firstly, the classic Otsu binary model $B_{ostu}(x, y)$ is designed as,

$$B_{ostu}(x, y) = \begin{cases} 1 \\ 0 \end{cases} if \begin{matrix} f(x, y) > T_{ostu} \\ f(x, y) < T_{ostu} \end{matrix} \tag{4}$$

here, T_{ostu} is binary threshold computed by classic Otsu. $f(x, y)$ is the gray-value in point (x, y). The result of binary processing shows the object pixel-point is 1 and the background pixel-point is 0.

Secondly, the result of object gray image $G_{ostu}(x, y)$ is achieved by logic AND between original gray image and its binary model $B_{ostu}(x, y)$. The result of $G_{ostu}(x, y)$ is that the object pixel-points keep original image value and background pixel-points gray-value is 0. The processing is shown as,

$$G_{ostu}(x, y) = f(x, y).and.B_{ostu}(x, y) \tag{5}$$

Above all, $G_{ostu}(x, y)$, which is gray image result of the object extracted by Otsu binary method. Corresponding object gray histogram *OGH* reflects the object gray distribution feature. And *OGH* is the statistics parameter of selection object too. To give an actual license plate example 鲁K 54746, OGH forming procedure is described in Fig.2. No.1 is OGH result using Otsu binary model. Fig.2 No.2 is OGH result after removing some noises.

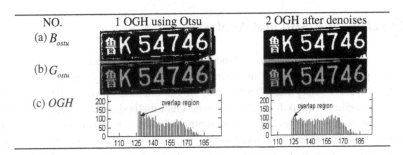

NO.	1 OGH using Otsu	2 OGH after denoises
(a) B_{ostu}	鲁K 54746	鲁K 54746
(b) G_{ostu}	鲁K 54746	鲁K 54746
(c) *OGH*	overlap region	overlap region

Fig. 2. The Histogram of object feature in overlap region between object and background

The object gray image computed by Otsu binary model is shown in Fig.2(a). Fig.2(c) shows that the optimization Otsu threshold is 126.29. Because of the shortage of incomplete object boundary and high noises, we increase the object probability ε to improve the performance of object binary processing. For example, $\varepsilon = 0.01$ is used in formulae(3), the improved threshold is 123.715. In the result images Fig.2(b), the shapes of letter "k" and number "4" and "6" are more complete than the result computed by Otsu binary method. From here we can found that some points in overlap region, whose gray value is between 123.715-126.29 belong to object or background. We can't separate them by Otsu optimization threshold. But these points have the common space distribution feature: object points are near to the object boundary, background points are far to object region and noises distribution are isolated and unorganized. In order to improve object binary result, the improved binary method based on space distribution feature of object and background is described as,

(a) The rule of regarding as more object pixel-points as possible is used for the pixel-points in overlap region. As, now allowing more false-alarm, those pixel-points which are false-dismissal using threshold segmentation will be regarded as object pixel-points to perfect object shape by improving object probability ε.

(b) The space distribution feature of background pixel-points is unorganized and isolated. Small area deletion of morphology operation can remove noises influence to segment single character object without adhesion.

2.2   The Procedure of Object Binary Processing Based on Space Distribution

In order to simple the computing, in practical, the binary processing is shown as,

Step1. Otsu threshold θ_1 is computed by Formula.(1). The eigen-values of object and background are f_o, f_b and $f_o \geq \theta_1 \geq f_b$.

Step2. To improve the threshold θ is used to perfect object shape. $\theta = \theta_1 - \varepsilon'$. For example, ε' is 0.01×255. To repeat binary processing and the result is I_{binary};

Step3. small area deletion of morphology operation is used to denoise and the result image is achieved as $I_{b-result}$.

3   Experiment Result and Analysis

In this paper, all experimental Chinese vehicle actual images with the size of 288×768 pixel in RGB model are from the Tongsan highway traffic station, Shandong province.To verify the effectiveness of our method, several difference binary methods including bi-peak histogram, classic Otsu method, license plate prior threshold selection method in Ref.[6] and the method in this paper were tested to compare the binary performance. The comparison result is shown as Fig.3.Experimental result showed that bi-peak histogram in Ref.[7], classic Otsu, prior threshold selection method in Ref.[6] all can extract object region accurately, but classic Otsu method can extract more object edge feature than bi-peak histogram method and it take high noises in object binary result. Prior threshold selection method can limit object pixel number but it can't throw off the noises effect, too. The object binary method in this paper can extract object feature including the overlap region. Experimental result showed that the object shape is more perfect. The small area deletion of morphology operator can help to get rid of the isolation noises pixel-points. The method can solve the problem of high-noising in character segmentation processing and it separates character from background with low sensitivity, such as plate disrepair, dirt, rivet and characters juncture, and detects precise break-point from projection histogram.

(a)Original image

(b)Ref.[6] method

(c)Ref.[7] method

(d)Otsu method

(e)The paper method

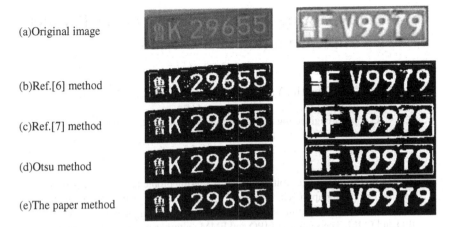

Fig. 3. The comparison result of different binary methods

4 Conclusion

In this paper, the improved object binary method based on spatial distribution feature is proposed. Experimental results show that the method achieved better binary results than other methods in object shape extraction and noises reduction. And the method solves the problem that license characters can't be segmented after vehicle license plate binary processing for characters linking. The object binary method can be used to segment actual vehicle license plate character.

Reference

1. Otsu, N.: A threshold selection method from gray-level histograms. IEEE Trans on System, Man and Cybernetics 9(1), 62–66 (1979)
2. Sahoo, P.K., et al.: A Surrey of thresholding technique. Computer Vision Graphics Image Process (41), 233–260 (1988)
3. Zhong-liang, F.: Image threshold selection method-Otsu method application. Computer Application 20(5), 37–39 (2000) (in Chinese)
4. Yu-jin, Z.: Transition region and image segmentation. ACTA Electronic SINICA 24(1), 12–17 (1996)
5. Nomura, S.: New methods for image binarization and character segmentation applied to an automatic recognition system of number plates. M.S. Thesis, Faculty of Electrical Engineering, Federal University of Uberlândia, Uberlândia City, Brazil (2002) (in Portuguese)
6. Hong, Z., Li-min, W., Gong-yi, W.: Research on binarization method of license plate recognition in automatic recognition. Applied Science and Technology 31(3), 15–19 (2004)
7. Hua-wei, L.: Determine dual threshold from double peak value directly. Pattern Recognition and Artificial Intelligence 2(15), 253–256 (2002)

The Load Balancing Algorithm Based on the Parallel Implementation of IPO and FMM

Ting Wang, Yue Hu, Yanbao Cui, Weiqin Tong, and Xiaoli Zhi

Computer engineering and science college, Shanghai University,
Shanghai 200072, China

Abstract. The large scale arbitrary cavity scattering problems can be tackled by parallel computing approach. This paper proposes a new method to distribute cavity scattering computing tasks on multiprocessors computer based on the IPO and FMM. The samples of IPO and FMM pattern can be divided into eight blocks, and this paper just analyzes the load balancing of the block in the lower-left corner using the invariability of angle. So this problem can be transformed into how to equally distribute an N*N matrix on P processors. Two matrix partitioning algorithms are introduced, and experimental results show that the optimal sub-structure algorithm is able to balance the load among multiprocessors effectively, thereby, improving the performance of the entire system.

1 Introduction

The Iterative Physical Optics (IPO) method considering multiple scattering based on the physical optical current is adopted to solve the magnetic field integral through iterative approach, which settles the scattering problem of the relatively large and arbitrary shaped cavity. The solving process of iterative integral has a high time complexity of O (N^2), where N is the number of unknowns. Fast Multipole Method (FMM) is a feasible strategy to reduce the time complexity from O (N^2) to O $(N^{1.5})$, so that IPO and FMM methods can be used to solve the scattering problem of the large scale cavity. Currently, IPO and FMM methods have been able to accurately solve small scale arbitrary shaped cavity scattering problem. However, with the continuous expansion of the practical application, how to resolve the medium and large scale cavity scattering problem has become a challenging problem, which can not be re-solved on a single processor. The parallel computing technology, which can use the large memory resources and the parallel computing capacity of multiprocessors com-puter, provides a feasible way to solve the large scale cavity scattering problem ef-fectively [1], [2]. In the high performance computing system for Linux, we have de-veloped a parallel Fast Multipole Method with the Message Passing Interface (MPI) and experimental results show that the parallel algorithm gets great speedup rate and good load balancing.

This paper is organized as follows. Section 2 discusses the computational models for the arbitrary shaped cavities, and then two algorithms and its examples are presented in Section 3. Section 4 illustrates the experiment results and discussion, comparing row-column partitioning algorithm with optimal sub-structure algorithm.

W. Zhang et al. (Eds.): HPCA 2009, LNCS 5938, pp. 410–417, 2010.

2 Models for the Arbitrary Shaped Cavities

The sketch map of general cavity is shown in Fig. 1. The adjoining cavity facets are directly formed into groups. As shown in Fig. 2, cavity facets 1, 2, 3, 4, 5 and 6 constitute one group, and cavity facets 22, 23, 24, 25 and 26 constitute another one. This method has significant advantages to calculate the typical cylindrical cavities and rectangular cavities: first, there are no empty groups; second, the number of the sub-scattering cavities in a group is same; third, the geometric symmetry is used to optimize the computation of transfer factors for the typical cavities. Unfortunately, for the particularly complicated cavities, all the far-field force transfer factors must be computed because of losing the symmetry relation when grouped [3], so both the computational complexity and memory space occupancy are enormous.

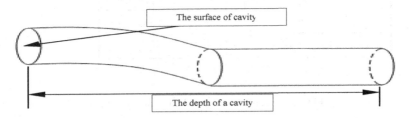

Fig. 1. The representation of general cavity

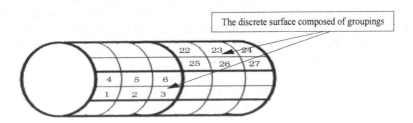

Fig. 2. The discrete surface composed of groupings

The cube structured grouping approach for the surface of a cavity is shown in Fig. 3. When using the cube structured grouping approach, the length of their edges depends on the maximum length of the cavity, and so this structured grouping approach creates a lot of empty groups. Thus, when using the invariability of the angle and translation to optimize the computation and storage space of the transfer factors, it needs to expand the whole cube (including the empty groups), so this method will cause the waste of a large amount of storage space and the declination of computational efficiency. However, when using the cuboids structured grouping approach to do that, it avoids this problem by adjusting the length, width and height according to the shape of the cavity, and then the empty groups is reduced to a minimum [4], [5]. This is shown in Fig. 4.

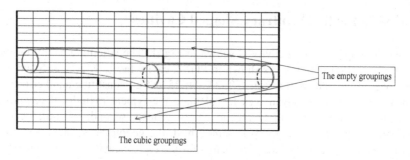

Fig. 3. The cube structured grouping of a cavity

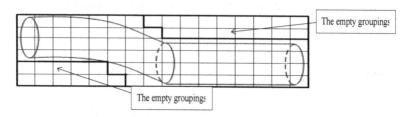

Fig. 4. The cuboids structured grouping of a cavity

As shown in Fig. 5, we assume that the number of groups along the cuboids' length, width, and height directions is N_x, N_y and N_z respectively, and then take a vertex grid as an original point which is extended to N_{x-1}, N_{y-1} and N_{z-1} grids along the cuboids' length, width, and height directions respectively. Thus a nearly eight times amplification of the cube [6] is created and finally the transfer factor array of the entire extended cube is filled using the invariability of the angle.

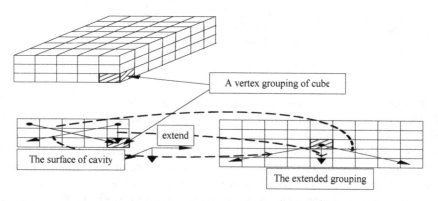

Fig. 5. The translation fixity of the transfer factor

The $2L^2$ angular spectrums are divided into eight blocks, as is shown in Fig. 6, where L is the FMM model number. The one in the lower-left corner (0~L/2, 0~L/2) is subdivided and then put in the same computation node as the counterpart of the other seven blocks. The load balancing of the lower-left corner one is transformed into how an N*N matrix is divided into P blocks running on P processors respectively and the P processors is ensured to maximize the load balancing, where N is L/2. In the following part of the paper, we will focus on the implementation of two matrix partitioning algorithms, and analyze the efficiency of the two methods based on the experiments.

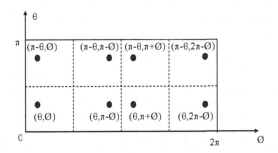

Fig. 6. The symmetry relation of the angular spectrum

3   Algorithm Design and Examples

Due to the uncertainty of N and P, two conditions should be discussed as follows:

1) In the case of N*N<=P: If a matrix of N*N needs P processors, each processor is assigned a sub-matrix block but the rest P-N*N processors are idle.

2) In the case of N*N>P: If a matrix of N*N needs N*N processors, each processor is at least assigned a sub-matrix block. So how to balance the load among multiprocessors is the key issue, and the following two algorithms effectively solve this problem.

3.1   Row-Column Partitioning Algorithm

The basic idea of partitioning is based on whether N is divisible by P, if so, the partitioning is performed dynamically according to row; otherwise, two important instances are fulfilled as depicted in the following:

● If N is greater than P, the matrix is directly divided according to row;

● If N is less than P, the partitioning is implemented by two steps. First this matrix is divided into P/N+1 blocks according to row, and then P/（P/N+1）
* （P/N+1）blocks according to column. If P is greater than the number of the divided blocks, a recursive operation is done as follows: the biggest piece is selected from the divided ones to continue dividing until P is equal to the number of the divided blocks.

3.2   Optimal Sub-structure Algorithm

Before presenting the parallel algorithm, it is necessary to define the basic theory: a problem is divided into several sub-problems which may be not independent to each other, so the results of the sub-problems should be saved in the solving process in order to directly reuse them when the same sub-problems are encountered in the follow-up problems, finally the undivided matrices are divided by a non-optimal method [7]. In this section we analyze this problem using a flow chart and then give an instantiation of this algorithm. The flow chart of the optimal sub-structure algorithm is shown in Fig. 7.

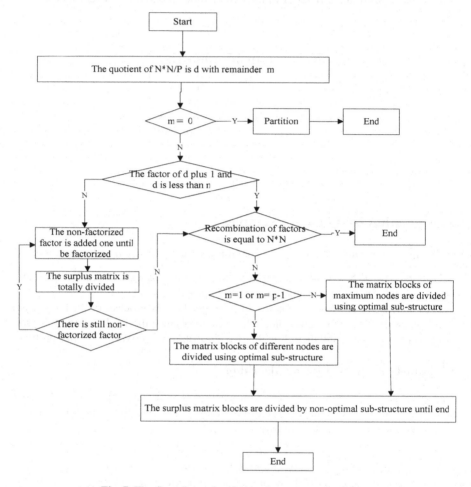

Fig. 7. The flow chart of optimal sub-structure algorithm

According to the row-column partitioning algorithm discussed above, it is directly divided into eight 1*8 matrices when an 8*8 matrix is divided into eight sub-matrices.

If the 8*8 matrix has to be divided into six sub-matrices, the following steps are executed:

1. The quotient of 8*8/6 is 10 and the remainder is 4, resulting in 11, 11, 11, 11, 10, 10.
2. 11 is factorized into 1*11 where 11 is greater than 8, so it needs to be revised to 12.

3. 12 is factorized into 2*6, 6*2, 3*4, 4*3, where no factors are greater than 8. Thus fifty-two nodes are left, and need to be divided into five sub-matrices.
4. The quotient of 52/5 is 10 and the remainder is 2, resulting in 11, 11, 10, 10, 10.
5. As step 2, 11 is revised to 12. Now there are forty nodes needing to be divided into four sub-matrices.
6. The quotient of 40/4 is 10 and 10 is factorized into 2*5, 5*2. Thus, the six blocks is 12, 12, 10, 10, 10, and 10.
7. As shown in Fig. 8, these factors are successfully recombined into 3*4+3*4+5*2+5*2+5*2+5*2=8*8 using the enumeration technique.

Let's further consider that this matrix is divided into fifteen blocks. The quotient of 8*8/15 is 4 with the remainder 5. And 4 is factorized into 1*4, 4*1, 2*2 and 5 into 1*5, 5*1, as shown in Fig. 9, these factors are successfully recombined into 1*5+1*5+1*5+1*5+4*1+4*1+4*1+4*1+4*1+4*1+4*1+4*1+4*1+4*1+4*1=8*8 using the enumeration technique.

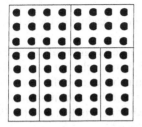

Fig. 8. Instantiation of 8*8/6

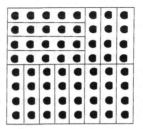

Fig. 9. Instantiation of 8*8/15

4 Results and Discussion

This paper proposes the row-column partitioning algorithm and optimal sub-structure algorithm to optimize the load balancing of the entire parallel program. In order to demonstrate the performance of the two algorithms, this paper uses a model where N is equal to eight. The experimental results take (MAX-AVG)/AVG as the standard, where MAX stands for the maximum number of vertices in the sub-matrices and AVG stands for the value of N*N/P [8]. The most important factor to restrict the efficiency of the parallel program is often the value of MAX, which impacts the load balancing of the multiprocessors computer; especially the overload machines severely restrict the efficiency of the entire parallel program [9].

The experiments are executed on a high performance cluster computer called "Ziqiang 3000"at Shanghai University. There are one hundred and ninety six nodes in this cluster computer whose parallel environment is MPICH 1.2.5 and the configuration of each node is Xeon3.06GHZ, 2G memories. In the experiments, the available maximum number of nodes is fifteen.

The results of (MAX-AVG)/AVG in two algorithms are shown in Fig. 10 where N is eight and P ranges from one to fifteen. The results of (MAX-AVG)/AVG in optimal sub-structure algorithm are always less than or at most equal to that in row-column partitioning algorithm. This means that the number of sub-matrices divided by optimal

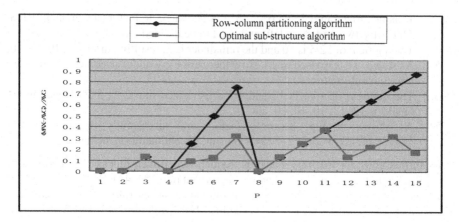

Fig. 10. The value of （MAX-AVG）/AVG

sub-structure algorithm is relatively well-proportioned, leading to the better load balancing on multiprocessors computer.

And as shown in Fig. 11, the runtime of the entire program represents the same meaning as that of the (MAX-AVG)/AVG value. Ultimately, we can safely draw a conclusion that the optimal sub-structure algorithm is better than the row-column partitioning algorithm. So the optimal sub-structure algorithm can improve the parallel efficiency of large scale arbitrary shaped cavity scattering problem effectively.

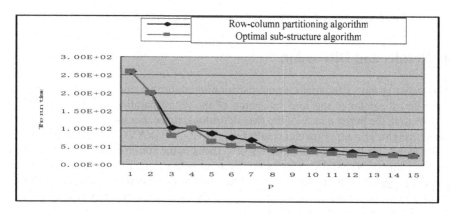

Fig. 11. The runtime of the parallel program in two algorithms

Though this paper uses the model where N is equal to eight, and the two algorithms can be applied to solve the model where N is arbitrary value. Because the maximal number of nodes in some sub-matrices is twice as much as that of the minimal ones using the row-column partitioning algorithm, the disadvantage of this algorithm becomes increasingly evident when N is larger. Optimal sub-structure algorithm is independent of the model size, so it improves the parallel efficiency of the entire program to a certain extent. However, the disadvantage of this algorithm is that it has some limitations when using non-optimal partitioning approach for the undivided matrices parts.

5 Conclusions

In this paper, we studied the modeling process of arbitrary shaped cavities, and proposed two efficient partitioning algorithms (row-column partitioning algorithm and optimal sub-structure algorithm) according to this model. Experimental results show that the optimal sub-structure algorithm divides equally matrices and obviously improves the efficiency of the entire parallel program. However, this algorithm has a certain limitation for some specific problems and needs to be further optimized. Currently we are focusing on this problem to get better load balancing so as to improve the entire performance.

Acknowledgements

This work is supported in part by Aviation Industry Development Research Center of China and Shanghai Leading Academic Discipline Project, Project Number: J50103.

References

1. Reinefeld, A., Gehring, J., Brune, M.: Communicating across parallel message-passing environments. Journal of Systems Architecture, 261–272 (1997)
2. Dembart, B., Yip, E.: A 3D fast multipole method for electromagnetic with multiple levels. Applied Computational Electromagnetic Society, 621–628 (1995)
3. Xiaoyan, X., Xiaoli, Z., Hailin, G., Xingang, W., Weili, N.: Implementation of Parallel Computing for Electromagnetic Scattering by Large Cavities. In: China-Japan Joint Microwave Conference (2008)
4. Sawley, M.L., Tenger, J.K.: A Comparison of Parallel Programming Models for Multiblock Flow Computations. Journal of Computational Physics, 280–290 (1995)
5. Obelleiro, F., Rodriguez, J.L., Burkholder, R.J.: An Iterative Physical Optics Approach for Analyzing the Electromagnetic Scattering by large Open-Ended Cavities. IEEE Transactions on antennas and propagation, 356–361 (1995)
6. Oliker, L., Biswas, R.: PLUM: Parallel load balancing for adaptive unstructured meshes. J. Parallel Distrib. Comput., 150–177 (1998)
7. Burkholder, R.J.: A Fast and Rapidly Convergent Iterative Physical Optics Algorithm for Computing the RCS of Open-Ended Cavities. Applied Computational Electromagnetics Society Journal, 53–60 (2001)
8. Ramme, F., Romke, T., Kremer, K.: A distributed computing center software for efficient use of parallel computer systems. In: High-Performance Computing and Networking, vol. 2, pp. 129–136. Springer, Heidelberg (1994)
9. Velamparambil, S., Chew, W.C., Song, J.: On the Parallelization of dynamic Multilevel Fast Multipole Method on Distributed Memory Computers. In: Innovative Architecture for Future Generation High-Performance Processors and Systems, pp. 3–11 (2000)

Sparse Matrix and Solver Objects for Parallel Finite Element Simulation of Multi-field Problems

Wenqing Wang[1,*] and Olaf Kolditz[1,2]

[1] Helmholtz Centre for Environmental Research - UFZ, Leipzig, Germany
wenqing.wang@ufz.de
[2] Technical University of Dresden, Dresden, Germany

Abstract. In this paper, we present an object-oriented concept of sparse matrix and iterative linear solver for large scale parallel and sequential finite element analysis of multi-field problems. With the present concept, the partitioning and parallel solving of linear equation systems can be easily realized, and the memory usage to solve coupled multi-field problems is optimized. For the parallel computing, the present objects are tailored to the domain decomposition approach for both equation assembly and linear solver. With such approach, the assembly of a global equation system is thoroughly avoided. Parallelization is realized in the sparse matrix object by the means of (1) enable the constructor of the sparse matrix class to use domain decomposition data to establish the local domain sparse pattern and (2) introduce MPI calls into the member function of matrix-vector multiplication to collect local results and form global solutions. The performance of these objects in C++ is demonstrated by a geotechnical application of 3D thermal, hydraulic and mechanical (THM) coupled problem in parallel manner.

1 Introduction

Finite element analysis of many engineering and science problems is computational intensive. Therefore, there is a tremendous demand for high performance computing in finite element analysis. In addition to the way of improving numerical algorithms, the parallel computing plays a key role in high performance of finite element analysis for decades (e.g. [1, 2, 3, 4, 5, 6]). However, for a long time, the parallel computing did save computational expense but raised even more costs because it could only be executed on expensive super computers and Linux clusters. Nowadays computer hardware is available at reasonable prices and thus the parallel computing becomes very attractive for scientific computing community. One can even run parallel simulations on a personal computer with a dual or quad core CPU.

Linear equation system is a fundamental part of the finite element method, and the solving of it is also one of the most time consuming parts of the finite element analysis in addition to the part of global assembly of equation system. The discretization of the weak form of an initial-boundary-value problem in the finite element space results in linear equation systems with sparse matrices. Larger grid posed to the finite element analysis means a more large sparse stiffness matrix, and also definitely means

---

* Corresponding author.

W. Zhang et al. (Eds.): HPCA 2009, LNCS 5938, pp. 418–425, 2010.

more computational expense. There are many references about the algorithms to solve sparse linear equation systems. Readers are referred to books by [7, 8, 9] for detailed guidance. For the parallel linear solver, there are popular standalone and portable packages available such as PETsc [10], Aztec [11], PSBLAS [12], AMG (specifically for multigrid method) [13].

Despite the availability of these packages, there are still good reasons to develop specific solvers: (1) memory management: Instead of importing additional memory and data transfer by using external linear solver packages, a 'light' parallel linear solver is necessary for one's own finite element code so that the solver can share the memory and data of the other parts of the code, and the efficiency is maintained in a high level; (2) hardware and software are improving, code needs maintain and develop in an easy way; (3) we may need to develop new parallel algorithm and implement it in a fairly cheap style. The most important point driving us to develop the present objects of sparse matrix and iterative solver is due to the reason: if existing linear packages are applied to parallel finite element applications, a global equation system has to be established. The present work is thoroughly avoiding this shortcoming in order to develop a concept of parallel finite element analysis on computer clusters with distributed memory.

In this paper, we present an object-oriented concept for sparse matrices and the associated iterative linear solvers for parallel and sequential finite element simulation of multi-field problems. The sparse matrix objects and linear solver object are designed for parallel and sequential finite element analysis of general multi-field coupled problems, and they are realized by C++ and MPI is used for inter-processor communication. The idea of this concept is to handle sparse pattern of matrix, sparse matrix and linear solver by three different C++ classes, respectively, and to restrict the assembly and solving of equations at the sub-domain level.

2 Concept of Sparse Matrix and Linear Solver Objects

The sparse matrix pattern arising from the finite element method is resulting from mesh topology. For multi-field problems, however, the individual time dependent partial differential equations (PDEs) may have different degree of freedom of the unknowns (i.e. scalar or vector quantities). Moreover, finite elements with different interpolation order are necessary for each field problem in order to guarantee numerical accuracy and stability. This type of multi-field problems leads to more complex sparse pattern of the derive stiffness matrix. The idea is to simply use the number of element nodes as a shift to access sparse matrix entries through the sparse table of degree of freedom (DOF) =1. This prompts that the sparse matrix is better to be abstracted into two individual data objects: (1) for sparse matrix structure and (2) for matrix data entries as well as related algebraic operations. To this purpose, the data and their associated methods of sparse matrix and solver are encapsulated into the following three classes:

- `SparseTable`: holds the sparse pattern of the stiffness matrix.
- `SparseMatrix`: contains values of matrix entries according to sparsity and degree of freedom per node, as well as provides methods algebraic matrix operations,
- `Solver`: Krylov-type subspace solver using the matrix operations provided by `SparseMatrix`.

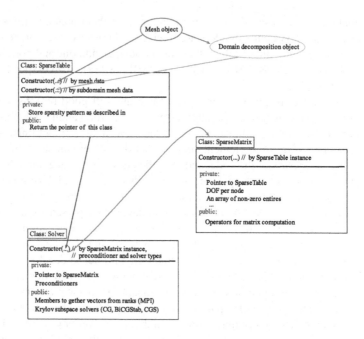

Fig. 1. Concept of matrix and solver objects and their relationships

Fig. 1 depicts basic functions of the objects and the relationships among these three objects.

SparseTable has two overloaded constructors, for sequential and parallel simulations, respectively. For a sequential run, the topological mesh data of whole domain are used as a parameter to construct the sparse table. For a parallelized run, the topological mesh data of all sub-domains are relevant to construct the sparse tables of the local sub-domains provided by the domain decomposition method, e.g. [14, 15]. We apply the domain decomposition method to partition the computational tasks of both equation system assembly and linear solver, and a priori decomposition of the finite element mesh into sub-domains is conducted by using METIS [16].

An instance of SparseTable together with the number of unknowns of the PDE, i.e. DOF per element node, is used to create the corresponding instance of SparseMatrix. This process is completed through the constructor of class SparseMatrix. Among the object data of SparseMatrix there are several pointer type members, which are referring to addresses of memory blocks of the sparse pattern data owned by the corresponding SparseTable. Moreover, the instance of SparseTable, as one of the constructor arguments, is only used to assign addresses to the these pointer type members of class SparseMatrix. This is done in order that any instance of SparseMatrix can access the members of SparseTable directly. Among the data members of SparseMatrix only the array member for values of non-zero entries needs additional memory allocation. As a consequence an instance of Solver can be created by referring the address of the existing SparseMatrix instance for algebraic matrix operations. To solve a coupled multi-field problem, a single instance of Solver can be used by different physical processes with different numerical controls to configure the type, the tolerance of accuracy and the preconditioner of the solver. The configuration of different numerical controls is performed by a single member function of `Solver`.

3 Parallelization

Regard to parallelization, we adopt the domain decomposition method to partition the computational task of the global matrix assembly and solution of the linear equation system. We do not need to build up a global equation system with the Krylov subspace solvers, which keeps the stiffness matrix untouched during solving iterations. Therefore, the parallel assembly of element matrices only takes place at sub-domain level, and the Krylov subspace solvers use the collection of the sub-domain matrix-vector product to update solution until a converged solution being obtained. During parallel simulation, each computer processor (i.e. CPU) assembles and manages matrices and vectors of each individual sub-domain by itself as shown in Fig. 2 on a local level. This means the domain decomposition of the global finite element assembly results in a priori partitioning of the global linear system of equations.

$$\mathbf{M}_0, \mathbf{K}_0, \mathbf{f}_0 \to A_0, b_0 \qquad \mathbf{M}_1, \mathbf{K}_1, \mathbf{f}_1 \to A_1, b_1 \qquad \cdots\cdots \qquad \mathbf{M}_m, \mathbf{K}_m, \mathbf{f}_m \to A_m, b_m$$

Fig. 2. Parallel assembly scheme of local equation systems [17]

The parallelization of the Krylov subspace solvers then becomes straightforward in the following two local and global steps:

1. Local CPU level: Perform matrix-vector products for each sub-domain by the related computer processor simultaneously, and then collect norms of such products from all involved processors to update local solutions and check solver convergence;
2. Global level with CPU communication: Collect solutions from all involved processors to obtain the global solution. While the collection of scalar norms is performed by MPI functions, i.e. using **MPI_Allreduce** a member function `CollectVector` of `Linear_EQS` is used to collect the solution vector. Moreover, all inter-node communication is restricted on the borders of the subdomains.

The schematic of the solver parallelization is illustrated in Fig. 3.

Concerning the creation of sparse matrices for each sub-domain, now we can use the full advantages of the object-oriented concept. For each sub-domain, the local sparse matrix is created as an instance of class `SparseTable` using the sub-domain mesh topology from the corresponding mesh object `a_dom`

```
SparseTable dom_spTable = new SparseTable(a_dom, true);
```

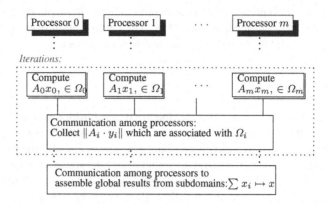

Fig. 3. Schematic of the parallelized linear solver

Thereafter, the local system of equations for each sub-domain is created by the overloaded constructor from Linear_EQS as

Linear_EQS a_LinSolver = **new** Linear_EQS(*dom_spTable, dof);

The creation of all instances of sparse classes is assigned to individual processors concurrently. Therefore the computer memory used for the global system of equations is also divided by processors accordingly.

4   Application Example

4.1   Model Set-Up

The application example comes from geotechnical engineering. Fig. 4 represents a near field model for safety assessment of nuclear repositories in crystalline rock using bentonite buffers to isolate the radioactive waste. The repository is built in the deep fully water saturated rock mass. We conduct parallel simulation of the thermal hydraulic and mechanical (THM) coupled processes in porous media of the repository in order to demonstrate the performance of the software design for the sparse matrix and solver objects SparseTable, SparseMatrix, and Linear_EQS. The 3D finite element mesh of a specified block containing the nuclear repository is depicted in Fig. 4 (right). The mesh has 66900 tetrahedra with 12485 nodes for linear and 94215 nodes for quadratic element interpolations. The partitioning of the mesh into sixteen sub-domains is also illustrated in Fig. 4 (right). Concerning to the FEM applied, we use linear elements for thermal (T) as well as hydraulic (H) processes, whereas quadratic element are adopted for the mechanical (M) process. Therefore, we have to create two different instances of class SparseTable for T and H processes, and for M processes, respectively. More details on the test example, e.g. material properties and function, can be found in the reference by [18].

Near field of repository   Grid and sub-domains

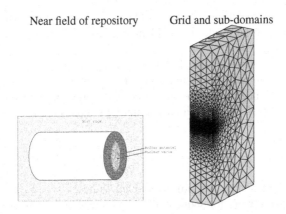

Fig. 4. Near field of repository, finite element mesh and domain decomposition

The hardware platform we use for the tests is a SUN X4600 cluster consisting of AMD x86_64 based processor nodes, each equipped with 8 × Opteron 885 with 8 GB of RAM per CPU.

4.2 Parallel Performance

To evaluate the parallel performance of the sparse solver object Linear_EQS we examine the parallel speed-up. To this purpose, we compare parallel simulations by partitioning the example mesh (Fig. 4) from 1 up to 16 sub-domains. For domain decomposition we use METIS. The speedup achieved on the SUN X4000 platform is given in Fig. 5.

The sudden drop of the speed-up with 10 sub-domains is caused by an unbalance of elements and nodes of among these sub-domains, in other words by the difference in local sub-domain sparse patterns. Unbalanced domain decomposition and a

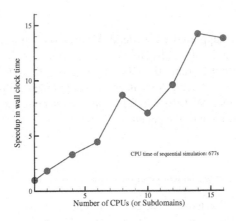

Fig. 5. Speedup of parallel computing using SparseMatrix object (measured in wall-time)

corresponding loss of speed-up is a typical feature if more complex (i.e. real world) model domains have to be used, i.e. the element mesh is adaptively refined near the canister area (Fig. 4).

Beginning from 16 sub-domains, the inter-processor communication time by using MPI collection function becomes visible and start to flatten the speed-up curve. In this case the saturation of speed-up is simply related to the problem size (i.e. 175945 tetrahedral elements). Therefore, an optimal parallel CPU configuration for this problem size is 16.

5   Conclusions

In this paper we presented an object-oriented concept of sparse matrices and corresponding linear solvers for sequential and parallel finite element simulations of multi-field (multi-physics) problems. The method is demonstrated for thermo-hydro-mechanical (THM) coupled multi-field problems.

In fact, the sparse matrix concept is nothing really new. Our literature review, however, revealed that there is still little work done concerning the concept and implementation of sparse matrix concepts in to scientific software codes, particularly for coupled multi-field problems with different types of partial differential equations (elliptic: mechanical, parabolic: hydraulic, mixed parabolic-hyperbolic: heat transport processes). A novel aspect of the present work is the development of sparse objects, i.e. sparse pattern, matrix, solver, for the finite element method in order to solve coupled multi-field problems. Moreover, a large flexibility for coupling schemes is introduced based on the object-oriented concept. Monolithic and partitioned (staggered) coupling algorithms as well as combinations of them can be used for strong and weak couplings, respectively. The key to this flexibility is the class hierarchy SparseTable ⇒ SparseMatrix ⇒ SparseSolver objects. Based on the implemented sparse objects concept the computational performance of multi-field finite element simulations could be improved significantly, i.e. memory consumption is reduced drastically and fast data access to matrix entries is guaranteed.

Acknowledgements

This research work is supported by Federal Ministry of Education and Research (BMBF) under grant 02C1114 and by the Federal Institute for Geosciences and Natural Resources (BGR) under grant 207-45000-38020. We are grateful to the excellent technical support by Thomas Schnicke concerning the parallel computer hardware. Especially we thank Jens-Olaf Delfs for careful manuscript reading and many constructive suggestions about the content of the paper.

References

[1] Law, K.: A parallel finite element solution method. Computer & Structure 23, 845–858 (1986)
[2] Farhat, C., Roux, F.: A method of finite element tearing and interconnecting and its parallel solution algorithm. International Journal for Numerical Methods in Engineering 32, 1205–1227 (1991)

[3] Salinger, A.G., Xiao, Q., Zhou, Y., Derby, J.J.: Massively parallel finite element computations of three-dimensional, time-dependent, incompressible flows in materials processing systems. Computer Methods in Applied Mechanics and Engineering 119, 139–156 (1994)

[4] Topping, B.H.V., Khan, A.I.: Parallel finite element computations. Saxe-Coburg Publications, Edinburgh (1996)

[5] Schrefler, B.A., Matteazzi, R., Gawin, D., Wang, X.: Two parallel computing methods for coupled thermohydromechanical problems. Computer-Aided Civil and Infrastructure Engineering 15, 176–188 (2000)

[6] Tezduyar, T.E., Sameh, A.: Parallel finite element computations in fluid mechanics. Computer Methods in Applied Mechanics and Engineering 195, 1872–1884 (2006)

[7] Ortega, J.M.: Introduction to Parallel & Vector Solution of Linear Systems. Plenum Press, New York (1988)

[8] Saad, Y.: Iterative Methods for Sparse Linear Systems, 2nd edn. (2003)

[9] Braess, D.: Finite Elements: Theory, Fast Solvers, and Applications in Solid Mechanics, 3rd edn. (2007)

[10] Balay, S., Buschelman, K., Gropp, W., Kaushik, D., McInnes, L.C.B.F.: PETSc users manual. PETSc home page (2007),
http://www-unix.mcs.anl.gov/petsc/petsc-as/

[11] Tuminaro, R., Heroux, M., Hutchinson, S., Shadid, J.: Official Aztec user's guide: Version 2.1 (1999)

[12] Filippone, S., Colajanni, M.: PSBLAS: a library for parallel linear algebra computation on sparse matrices. ACM Transactions on Mathematical Software 26, 527–550 (2000)

[13] Henson, V.E., Yang, U.M.: BoomerAMG: a parallel algebraic multigrid solver and preconditioner. Applied Numerical Mathematics 41, 155–177 (2002)

[14] Przemieniecki, J.S.: Theory of Matrix Structural analysis. McGraw Hill Book Co., New York (1986)

[15] Farhat, C., Roux, F.: An unconventional domain decomposition method for an efficient parallel solution of large-scale finite element systems. SIAM Journal on Scientific and Statistical Computing 13, 379–396 (1992)

[16] Karypis, G., Schloegel, K., Kumar, V.: Parallel graph partitioning and sparse matrix ordering library. University of Minnesota (1998)

[17] Wang, W., Kosakowski, G., Kolditz, O.: A parallel finite element scheme for thermo-hydro-mechanical (THM) coupled problems in porous media. Computers & Geosciences 35(8), 1631–1641 (2009)

[18] Wang, W., Kolditz, O.: Object-oriented finite element analysis of thermo-hydro-mechanical (THM) problems in porous media. International Journal for Numerical Methods in Engineering 69, 162–201 (2007)

Vector-Matrix Multiplication Based on a Ternary Optical Computer[*]

Xianchao Wang[1,2], Junjie Peng[1], Yi Jin[1], Mei Li[3],
Zhangyi Shen[1,4], and Shan Ouyang[1]

[1] School of Computer Engineering and Science, Shanghai University, Shanghai 200072, China
wxcdx@126.com, {jjie.peng,yijin}@shu.edu.cn,
{william_shen1,ou-yang-shan}@163.com
[2] School of Mathematics and Computational Science,
Fuyang Normal College, Fuyang 236041, China
[3] College of Computer Science and Engineering,
Northwestern Polytechnical University, Xi'an 710072, China
plumlee@nwpu.edu.cn
[4] Computer Science Department, Luoyang Normal University, LuoYang 471022, China

Abstract. This paper implements Optical Vector-Matrix Multiplication (OVMM) completely in parallel on a novel optical computing architecture, Ternary Optical Computer (TOC), by use of the Modified Signed-Digit (MSD) number system. For high efficiency, partial products (PPs) are generated in parallel and the vector inner products (VIPs) are produced by a binary-tree algorithm, and then the OVMM is implemented. The experimental result validates the feasibility and correctness of VMM on TOC. In this system, it is not necessary to gauge light intensities, but judge whether there is light during decoding.

1 Introduction

Optical vector-matrix multiplication (OVMM) was proposed by Lee et al. in 1970 [1]. Since then, some optical means have been put forward to implement OVMM [3-5]. In 2009, Li et al realized binary OVMM on ternary optical computer (TOC) [9]. In Li's work, all elements are only one bit. Meanwhile, several redundant representation schemes such as modified signed-digit (MSD) number [2,4], have been studied to perform carry-free addition and other arithmetic operations in the past several decades. We will implement OVMM on TOC by use of MSD number system.

The remainder is organized as follows. Section 2 primarily highlights some technological base. In section 3, we discuss several optical processors based on MSD and TOC. We generate all partial products in parallel, then add them up by a binary-tree algorithm, obtaining their products and vector inner products (VIP's) to

---

[*] Supported by the Shanghai Leading Academic Discipline Project under Grant (No.J50103), the National Natural Science Foundation of China under Grant (No.60473008), the Innovation Project of Shanghai University (No. A.10-0108-08-901) and the Research Project of Excellent Young Talents in the Universities in Shanghai (No. B.37-0108-08-002).

W. Zhang et al. (Eds.): HPCA 2009, LNCS 5938, pp. 426–432, 2010.

accomplish OVMM. Section 4 mainly gives an experiment to verify the correctness and feasibility of the OVMM on TOC. The last section is a summary.

2 Technological Base

2.1 Ternary Optical Computer and Decrease-Radix Design

In 2000 Prof. Jin proposed the principle and architecture of TOC [5,6]. He uses three steady light states, no intensity light (NI), horizontal polarization light (HPL), and vertical polarization light (VPL) to represent information. In the architecture there are 7 polarizers (VP1, VP2, VP3, VP4, VP5, HP1, and HP2), 3 monochromatic LCAs (L1, L2 and L3) and one photoreceptor array (D), as shown in Fig. 1, where S is the light source, E is the encoder, which is made up of VP1, L1, VP2 and L2, O is the optical processor, which contains VP3, HP1, L3, VP4, HP2, VP5 and L3, and it is divided into four equal parts, VV, VH, HH and HV, and D is the decoder. The VPi are clarity to VPL, but opacity to HPL, and the HPi are the reverse.

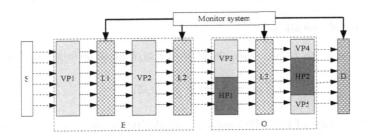

Fig. 1. Architecture of the optical part in TOC

In 2007, the decrease-radix design principle (DRDP) [7,8] was proposed by Yan et al. The principle indicates any binary tri-valued logic processors within 19683 can be reconfigured by some of 18 basic operating units (BOUs) [8]. The TOC experiment system was constructed in Shanghai University.

2.2 MSD Number System

MSD was proposed by A. Avizienis in 1961 [2], and was first used to optical computing by B. L Draker [4]. In MSD a numeral X is represented by equation (1).

$$X=\sum_i x_i 2^i, \ x_i \in \{\bar{1}, 0, 1\}, \tag{1}$$

where $\bar{1}$ denotes -1. There are redundancy representations in MSD. For example, $(4)_{10}=(100)_{2 \text{ or MSD}}=(1\bar{1}00)_{\text{MSD}}=(1\bar{1}\bar{1}00)_{\text{MSD}}$ and $(-4)_{10}=(\bar{1}100)_{\text{MSD}}=(\bar{1}1100)_{\text{MSD}}$.

Table 1. Truth tables of four transformations used in MSD addition

T	$\bar{1}$	0	1	W	$\bar{1}$	0	1	T'	$\bar{1}$	0	1	W'	$\bar{1}$	0	1
$\bar{1}$	$\bar{1}$	$\bar{1}$	0	$\bar{1}$	0	1	0	$\bar{1}$	$\bar{1}$	0	0	$\bar{1}$	0	$\bar{1}$	0
0	$\bar{1}$	0	1	0	1	0	$\bar{1}$	0	0	0	0	0	$\bar{1}$	0	1
1	0	1	1	1	0	$\bar{1}$	0	1	0	0	1	1	0	1	0

The redundancy provides the possibility of limiting carry propagation in an adder [2].

3 Processors Based on MSD and TOC

3.1 MSD Addition

In a MSD system an adder consists of four logic operators called the T, W, T', and W' transformations. Table 1 shows the truth tables of these operations' model [8]. The addition is performed by T, T', W, and W', keeping to the following three steps:

step 1: $x_i + y_i = 2t_{i+1} + w_i$; step 2: $t_i + w_i = 2t'_{i+1} + w'_i$; step 3: $t'_i + w'_i = s_i$.

3.2 MSD Multiplication

For $a = a_{n-1} \ldots a_1 a_0$ and $b = b_{n-1} \ldots b_1 b_0$, the product P is obtained by following formula:

$$p = ab = \sum_{0}^{n-1} p_i = \sum_{0}^{n-1} ab_i 2^i . \tag{2}$$

The multiplication of two MSD number includes two basic processes: generate all partial products (PPs) p_i and accumulate them. Consequently, to improve the speed, we must reduce the time spent in generating PPs and speed up the accumulation. Each p_i can be generated in parallel by the M transformation, whose truth table is shown in Table 2. Adding up all PPs can be completed by binary-tree algorithm [10].

Table 2. Truth table of the M transformation

M	$\bar{1}$	0	1
$\bar{1}$	1	0	$\bar{1}$
0	0	0	0
1	$\bar{1}$	0	1

The binary-tree algorithm is described as follows. Assuming that all p_i are available and the total n of p_i is even. Adding p_i and p_{i+1}, $(i=0,2,4,\ldots,n-2)$ produces the partial-sum ps^1_j, $j=0, 1,\ldots, n/2$. Similarly, adding ps^1_j and ps^1_{j+1}, produces the partial-sum ps^2_k, $k=0, 1,\ldots, j/2$. This process is repeated until the product p is produced. An example is as follows: $(14)_{10} \times (9)_{10} = (1110)_{MSD} \times (101\bar{1})_{MSD}$ as shown by

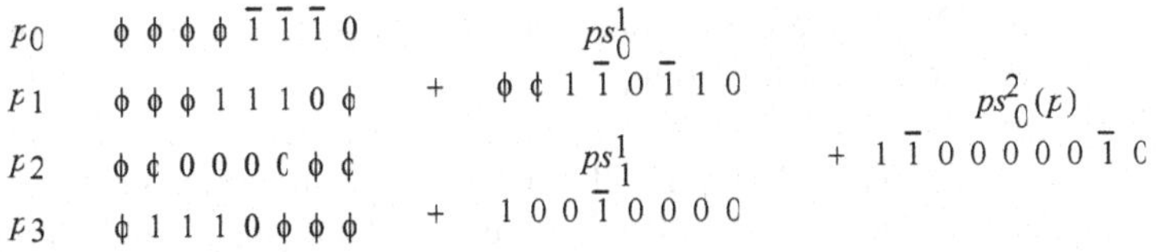

F_0 $\phi\ \phi\ \phi\ \phi\ \bar{1}\ \bar{1}\ \bar{1}\ 0$ ps^1_0

F_1 $\phi\ \phi\ \phi\ 1\ 1\ 1\ 0\ \phi$ $+$ $\phi\ \phi\ 1\ \bar{1}\ 0\ \bar{1}\ 1\ 0$ $ps^2_0(P)$

F_2 $\phi\ \phi\ 0\ 0\ 0\ \phi\ \phi\ \phi$ ps^1_1 $+$ $1\ \bar{1}\ 0\ 0\ 0\ 0\ 0\ \bar{1}\ 0$

F_3 $\phi\ 1\ 1\ 1\ 0\ \phi\ \phi\ \phi$ $+$ $1\ 0\ 0\ \bar{1}\ 0\ 0\ 0\ 0$

Fig. 2. An example of multiplication of two 4-bits MSD numbers

The computing process is shown in Fig. 2, where ϕ denotes a padded zero. At the left there are four p_i, each 8 bits. Then ps^1_0 and ps^1_1 are obtained by adding p_0 and p_1, p_2 and p_3, respectively. Finally, their product P, ps^2_0, is produced in the same way. We can see that the computations of p_i, ps^1_j and ps^2_0 are parallel, respectively.

3.2 MSD Vector-Matrix Multiplication

Consider a multiplication of vector α with matrix M given as follows:

$$\alpha_{1\times N}\ M_{N\times N} = \beta_{1\times N} . \tag{3}$$

All element digits in α and M are n. Every element β_i in β is computed by equation (4), and β_i is, generally, called vector inner product (VIP).

$$\beta_j = \sum_{i=1}^{N} \alpha_i m_{ij},\ j=1,\cdots N \cdot \tag{4}$$

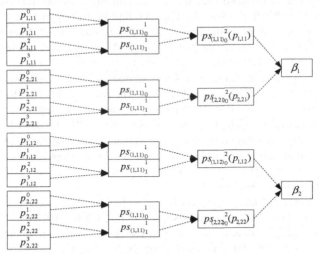

Fig. 3. An example of vector-matrix multiplication by use of binary-tree algorithm

The process of computing β_j is similar to the multiplication of two numbers. Firstly, all PPs $p^k_{i,ij}(i,j=1,2,...,N$ and $k=0,1,...,n-1)$ of $\alpha_i\times m_{ij}$ are generated by M transformation in parallel. Next, partial sums $ps_{(i,ij)}{}^s_r$ $(i,j=1,2,...,N,\ s=1,2,...\log_2 n$ and

$r=0,1,\ldots,n/2$) are generated, in succession, by a binary-tree algorithm until the products $p_{i,ij}$ $(i,j=1,2,\ldots,N)$ are obtained. Finally, β_j $(j=1,2,\ldots,N)$ are obtained by applying the binary-tree algorithm to $p_{i,ij}$.

Assuming there are 2 elements (α_1, α_2) in the vector and 2×2 elements $(m_{11}, m_{12}, m_{21}, m_{22})$ in the matrix. Their digits are all four. Fig. 3 illustrates the process of vector-matrix multiplication. There are 16 PPs $p^k_{i,ij}$, 8 partial-sums $ps_{(i,ij)^s r}$, and 4 products $p_{i,ij}$ of $\alpha_i \times m_{ij}$ $(i,j=1,2;s=1,2;k=0,1,2,3$ and $r=0,1)$ in the first, second, and third column, respectively. The final results β_j $(j=1, 2)$ are shown in the right. $ps_{(i,ij)^s r}$, $p_{i,ij}$ and β_j $(i,j=1,2,\ s=1,2,\ and\ r=0,1)$ are all obtained by a binary-tree algorithm. The top and bottom parts show the process of the computation of β_j $(j=1, 2)$, respectively.

4 Experiment of OVMM and Results

An experiment is to demonstrate the process of OVMM on TOC. We employ the pixel redundancy technique, that is to say, the adjacent 4×4 pixels are viewed as a basic operating unit (BOU). Thus there is a 16×8-BOU array in every part. For example,

$$(3 \quad 1)_{10} \times \begin{pmatrix} -1 & 2 \\ -2 & -3 \end{pmatrix}_{10} = (11 \quad 1\bar{1})_{MSD} \times \begin{pmatrix} \bar{1}1 & 10 \\ 10 & \bar{1}\bar{1} \end{pmatrix}_{MSD}$$

The steps taken to obtain the optical vector-matrix multiplication are as follows:

◆   Step 1, generate the PPs by M transformation in parallel. The output of the M transformation is illustrated in Fig. 4(a). In order to facilitate the experiment observation, the BOUs used by the first digit in every part have been marked in real-line box. At the same time, the BOUs through which light can pass have been also marked in broken-line box. After being decoded, the results are 0011, 0-1-10, 0000, 0-110 and 0000, 0110, 00-11, 0-110.

◆   Step 2, carry out simultaneously T and W transformations on the results of step 1. Their outputs are illustrated in Fig. 4(b). The results are 0-101,0-110,0110,0-101 and 010-1, 01-10, 0-1-10, 010-1. For the next step, the results of T transformation are shifted left in a circular into -1010, -1100, 1100, -1010.

◆   Step 3, carry out simultaneously T' and W' transformation on the results of step 2. Their outputs are shown in Fig. 4(c). The results are 0000, 0100, 0000, 0000 and -111-1, -10-10, 10-10, -111-1. The results of the T' transformation are adjusted into 0000, 1000, 0000, 0000.

◆   Step 4, carry out the T transformation on the results of step 3. The outputs are shown in Fig. 4(d). The results are -111-1, 00-10, 10-10, -111-1. Now the products of corresponding elements in vector and matrix are obtained in parallel. They are -3, -2, 6, and -3 in decimal numbers, respectively.

◆   Step 5 is to repeat steps 2 to 4 on the products to obtain the VIPs, that is, to accomplish the OVMM. Their outputs are shown in Fig. 4(e-g). The final results in Fig. 4(g) are 00-1-11 and 01-1-11, viz. -5 and 3 in decimal number. Now the vector-matrix multiplication is obtained optically in parallel.

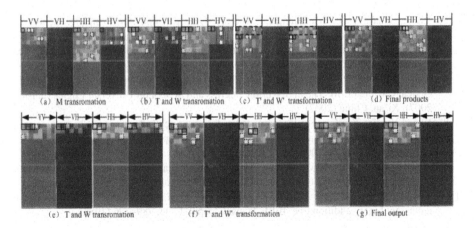

(a) M transromation   (b) T and W transromation   (c) T' and W' transformation   (d) Final products

(e) T and W transromation   (f) T' and W' transformation   (g) Final output

Fig. 4. Output of computing a vector-matrix multiplication

The experiment verifies the feasibility and correctness of OVMM on TOC. From the whole process, we can see that it is the M transformation that uses the most BOUs in OVMM. If no pixel redundancy is employed, we can in 5 steps implement the OVMM of a 1×32 vector with a 32×32 matrix whose elements are all single-digit.

5 Conclusion

This study has implemented OVMM on TOC, a novel optical architecture, by using five transformations in the MSD number system and obtaining PPs in completely in parallel and using VIPs in a binary-tree algorithm. The OVMM has many advantages:

- It obtains both the PPs and VIPs in parallel;
- It has scalability, that is, it is easily expanded to thousands of digits;
- It combines light intensity and polarization to represent information, thus that the operating accuracy and speed are improved significantly.

The operating speed is not discussed in detail because of the limitation of experimental conditions. At the same time, the utilization of hardware is also not considered here.

References

[1] Heinz, R.A., Artman, J.O., Lee, S.H.: Matrix Multiplication by Optical Methods. Applied Optics 9(9), 2161–2168 (1970)

[2] Avizienis, A.: Signed-digit number representations for fast parallel arithmetic. IRE Trans. Electron. Comp. EC-10, 389–400 (1961)

[3] Goodman, J.W., Dias, A.R., Woody, L.M.: Fully parallel, high-speed incoherent optical method for performing discrete Fourier transforms. Optics Letters 2(1), 1–3 (1978)

[4] Draker, B.L., Bocker, R.P., Lasher, M.E., et al.: Photonic Computing Using the Modified Signed-Digit Number Representation. Optical Engineering 25(1), 38–43 (1986)

[5] Yi, J., Huacan, H., Yangtian, L.: Ternary Optical Computer Principle. Scince in China(Series F) 46(2), 145–150 (2003)

[6] Yi, J., Hua-can, H., Yang-tian, L.: Ternary Optical Computer Architecture. Physica Scripta, 98–101 (2005)

[7] Yi, J., Junyong, Y., Kaizhong, Z.: Hardware Design of Reconstructed Ternary Logic Optical Calculator. In: The 2nd World Congress and School on Universal Logics (uni-log 2007), Xi'an, China (2007)

[8] Yan, J.Y., Jin, Y., Zuo, K.: Decrease-radix design principle for carrying/borrowing free multi-valued and application in ternary optical computer. Scince in China (Series F) 51(10), 1415–1426 (2008)

[9] Li, M., Jin, Y., He, H.-c.: A New Method for Optical Vector-Matrix Multiplier. In: International Conference on Electronic Computer Technology (ICECT 2009) (accepted)

[10] Takagi, N., Yasuura, H., Yajima, S.: High speed VLSI multiplication algorithm with a redundant binary addition tree. IEEE Trans. Comput. C-34, 789–796 (1985)

Ultra High Throughput Implementations for MD5 Hash Algorithm on FPGA

Yuliang Wang, Qiuxia Zhao, Liehui Jiang, and Yi Shao

China National Digital Switching System Engineering and Technological R&D Center,
450002, Zhengzhou, China
wyl5257@163.com

Abstract. This paper first presents a new architecture of MD5, which achieved the theoretical upper bound on throughput in the iterative architecture. And then based on the general proposed architecture, this paper implemented other two different kinds of pipelined architectures which are based on the iterative technique and the loop unrolling technique respectively. The latter with 32-stage pipelining reached a throughput up to 32.035Gbps on an Altera Stratix II GX EP2SGX90FF FPGA, and the speedup achieved 194x over the Intel Pentium 4 3.0 processor. At least to the authors' knowledge, this is the fastest published FPGA-based design at the time of writing. At last the proposed designs are compared with other published MD5 designs, the designs in this paper have obvious advantages both in speed and logic requirements.

Keywords: Secure hash algorithm; MD5; Filed Programmable Gate Array (FPGA); Pipelining; Loop unrolling; Speedup.

1 Introduction

With the development of information technology and Internet communication, the security and credibility of information become more and more important. Message authentication is an essential technique to verify that received messages come from the alleged source and have not been altered. Data integrity assurance and data origin authentication are essential security services in financial transactions, electronic commerce, electronic mail, software distribution, data storage and so on. And the best way to implement these security services is to use the cryptographic hash algorithms such as MD5 and SHA-1.

Implementing a hash function on hardware presents numerous advantages. Hardware implementations present higher throughput than software, thus being more adaptable for high speed applications. Moreover, they operate uninterruptible, contrary to software implementations in a multitask environment. Furthermore, hardware provides higher level of security than software in cases of hacking attempts.

Only few publications have been published concerning FPGA acceleration of the MD5 algorithm. Deepakumara achieved throughputs of 165Mbps and 354Mbps on a Virtex 1000 FPGA in his iterative and full loop unrolling designs [1]. Implementation by Diez et al. achieved a throughput of 467Mbps on a Xilinx Virtex-II XC2V3000 FPGA [2]. A throughput of 756Mbps on Virtex-II 2V400 were achieved by Ioannis

W. Zhang et al. (Eds.): HPCA 2009, LNCS 5938, pp. 433–441, 2010.

Yiakoumis [3]. And Kimmo Jarvinen achieved a throughput of 5.8Gbps in his 10 parallel MD5 blocks implementation [4]. Based on the analysis of the MD5 algorithm and the previous publications, this paper optimized the critical path of MD5 first, whose delay was equal to the iteration round of MD5 proposed in [5]. And then based on the general proposed architecture, this paper presented other two different kinds of pipelined architectures which were based on the iterative technique and the loop unrolling technique. Compared with other published designs even commercial MD5 IP Cores, the presented implementations in this paper have obvious advantages both in speed and logic requirements.

The paper is organized as follows: A description of the MD5 algorithm is presented in Section 2. The optimized architecture of the MD5 algorithm is introduced and analyzed in section 3. The loop unrolling and pipelining techniques are analyzed in section 4. Two different kinds of pipelined architectures are implemented on FPGA in section 5 and the results of the proposed implementations are presented and compared to other published implementations in Section 6.

2   The MD5 Algorithm

MD5 is a hash algorithm introduced in 1992 by professor Ronald Rivest, it consists of five steps (Please refer to [6] for more details, here we only introduce the main step).

The heart of MD5 is an algorithm which is used for the processing of the message. The message M is divided into 512-bit blocks which are processed separately. The algorithm consists of four rounds, each of which comprises 16 steps. The algorithm is performed as follows: first, values of A, B, C and D are stored into temporary variables. Then, every step operations are performed for $i = 0$ to 63 as follows:

$$B_{i+1} \leftarrow B_i + ((R(B_i,C_i,D_i) + A_i + T_{i+1} + M_j[i+1]) \lll S_{i+1})$$
$$A_{i+1} \leftarrow D_i, C_{i+1} \leftarrow B_i, D_{i+1} \leftarrow C_i \tag{1}$$

Finally, the values of the temporary variables are added to the values obtained from the algorithm, and the results are stored in the registers A, B, C and D. When all the message blocks have been processed, the message digest of M is in A, B, C, and D.

3   Analysis and Optimization for MD5

The heart of MD5 is the algorithm which is used for calculating the values of A, B, C, and D in every step operations. From Eq.1, we can see that the values of A, C, D can be got directly, while the calculation of B is quite complicated, which consists of four mod 2^{32} additions, a logical function and a circular shift left operation, forming the critical path of the MD5 algorithm. And the delay of the critical path is: $T=4 \times Delay(+) + Delay(R) + Delay(\lll S)$, which is much larger than the iteration bound $T\infty = 2 \times Delay(+) + Delay(R) + Delay(\lll S)$ proposed in [5]. Therefore, to achieve a throughput optimal design, we must optimize the iterative architecture to shorten the critical path.

As can be seen from equation $B_{i+1}=B_i+((R(B_i,C_i,D_i)+A_i+T_{i+1}+M_j[i+1]))<<S_{i+1}$, T_{i+1} and S_{i+1} are constants in every clock cycle, $M_j[i+1]$ is a 32-bit message in a 512-bit message block, which also can be seen as a fixed constant after the 512-bit message block inputted, and the value of A_i equals to D_{i-1}, so if we introduce a temporary variable $Temp_i$ in the ith clock cycle, and let $Temp_i$ be $D_{i-1}+M_j[i+1]+T_{i+1}$, then in the $i+1th$ clock cycle, B_{i+1} can be simplified as:$B_{i+1}=B_i+((R(B_i,C_i,D_i)+Temp_i))<<S_{i+1}$, some pre-computation is performed. After the optimization, every step operations are:

$$B_{i+1} \leftarrow B_i + ((R(B_i,C_i,D_i) + Temp_i) <<< S_{i+1})$$
$$A_{i+1} \leftarrow D_i, C_{i+1} \leftarrow B_i, D_{i+1} \leftarrow C_i \tag{2}$$
$$Temp_{i+1} \leftarrow D_i + T_{i+2} + M_j[i+2]$$

Since register A of Eq.2 is not used in the following calculations, the value of $Temp_i$ can be stored in register A_i, i.e. $A_{i+1}=D_i+T_{i+2}+M_j[i+2]$. Moreover, a Carry Save Adder (CSA) can also be used in $D_i+T_{i+2}+M_j[i+2]$, which can save some area and reduce some delay.

After the optimization, the critical path of the algorithm is shortened, there are only two additions instead of four, which improves the speed significantly. And the delay of the critical path is $T=2\times Delay(+)+Delay(R)+Delay(<<S)$, which is equal to the iteration round of MD5 proposed in [5], according to [5], the optimized architecture achieves the theoretical upper bound on throughput in the iterative architecture. Moreover, the logic area of the optimized structure is not increased almost compared to the original structure.

4   Analysis of Pipelining and Loop Unrolling Techniques

After the optimization in section 3, the speed of the algorithm increases obviously, while it is still an iterative architecture, the sequential nature of the MD5 algorithm is not changed, and there is only one message block can be processed simultaneously. In order to increase the throughput, it must introduce the loop unrolling and pipelining techniques.

The purpose of pipelining is to increase the total amount of data being processed simultaneously, and make the algorithm be able to process multiple message blocks at the same time, thereby enhancing the throughput of the algorithm. In the pipelined mode, how many pipelined stages will process how many message blocks simultaneously.

According to the structure of the MD5 algorithm, the reasonable number of pipelined stages are $p = 1$ (an iterative design), $p=2$, $p=4$, $p=32$ and $p=64$ (a fully pipelined design). If some other number of pipelined stages, e.g. $p = 8$ or $p = 16$ is used, major enhancement in either area requirements or in delay, while only little faster performance is achieved with considerably larger area requirements [4].

The loop unrolling technique means here that several of the MD5 steps are unrolled and then processed in one clock cycle. Because the loop unrolling technique can reduce parts of the clock delay and registers delay, the total delay of the implementation is reduced, which can increase the throughput of the algorithm significantly.

Based on the analysis above, this paper implemented one stage pipelining (an iterative architecture), four-stage pipelining (each round acts as a stage pipelining), and
two different kinds of 32-stage pipelining architectures. The two 32-stage pipelining
architectures are based on the iterative technique and the loop unrolling technique
respectively.

5   The Hardware Implementations of the MD5 Algorithm

As can be seen from [6], the steps 1-2 of MD5 can be easy and fast performed with
the software, and all the designs in this paper only implemented steps 3-5. The two
different kinds of pipelined architectures are described in section 5.1 and 5.2 respectively. For convenience, we take the 4-stage pipelining architectures for introduction.

5.1   The Pipelined Architecture Based on Iterative Technique

The General Architecture. The 4-stage pipelined architecture based on iterative
technique is presented in Fig.1, which adds registers between every round calculation,
and each round acts as a stage pipelining. In each round, the 16 steps of iterative operations use the same functional unit and register, and every step is performed in one
clock cycle, so one round calculation will be performed in 16 clock cycles. Since this
structure is based on 4-stage pipelining, it can calculate four different 512-bit message
blocks simultaneously, except the first 512-bit message block will be performed in 64
clock cycles, the later ones will be performed in only 16 clock cycles.

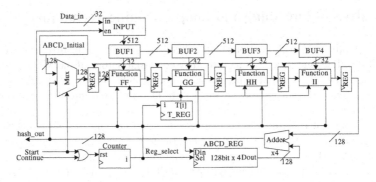

Fig. 1. The pipelined architecture based on iterative technique

The system consists of four blocks, the input block, the memory block, the count-
ing block and the encrypting block.

The input block is used for controlling the input of the data and control signals.
The message is given for the design with Data_in signal, and the width of Data_in can
be chosen freely, 32 bits were used for implementations in this paper. ABCD_Initial
signal is used to keep the initial value of A, B, C and D. Processing of the algorithm is
started with the Start or Continue signals. Start signal is used when a derivation of a

new message digest is started, for example, when M_0 is processed, and Continue signal is used for the later ones, such as M_j, where $j \geq 1$.

The counter in the architecture counts from 0 to 64 and it is reset to zero when Start or Continue signal is high. Other blocks, such as the input block, the memory block and the encrypting block are all controlled by the counter.

The memory block comprises four 512-bit BUF register blocks, four 128-bit ABCD_REG register blocks and a T_REG register block. And the four BUF blocks are used to keep four different groups of 512-bit message blocks, which are used for the four encrypting blocks respectively. The ABCD_REG blocks are used to keep four different groups of middle results of the A, B, C and D. T_REG is used to keep the constant T.

The four encrypting blocks are the main functional units of the algorithm, which are used for the four rounds of calculations respectively. Each encrypting block is connected to the corresponding BUF block, and which can just only process the data in the connected BUF block. After processing the corresponding data, the result will be transferred to the next encrypting block, and the data of the connected BUF block are also transferred to the next BUF block. This pattern has the advantages as follows: first, it avoids the bus competition, and each encrypting block can own the whole bandwidth of the connected BUF block, which reduce the delay of the design. Second, this pattern simplifies the logic control, and it also reduces the logic requirements demanding. In addition, this structure has well expansibility, when it needs to increase or decrease the pipelined stages, we can add or delete the corresponding encrypting blocks and the connected BUF blocks simply. Take the one stage pipelining in this paper for example, which is only needed to delete three encrypting blocks and the three connected BUF blocks from the structure in Fig.1. And for the 32-stage pipelining, we just only need to add the encrypting blocks and the corresponding BUF blocks to 32.

The Inner Structure of the Encrypting Block. The encrypting block is the main functional unit of the MD5 algorithm which calculates Eq.2 presented in Fig.2.

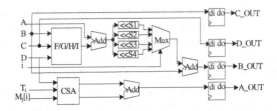

Fig. 2. The inner structure of the encrypting block

Each round calculation uses the same non-liner logic function, so in the pipelined architecture, only one function needs to be implemented instead of all four. In addition, the shifter can also be reduced from the design, because there are only four values of s per round, which can be hardwired into the design. Shifting by a constant can be performed trivially by rearrange the bit vector, which reduces both delay and area requirements. In hardware design, shifting is quite a logic resources demanding and long delay operation, while the speed of hardwired design is quite high, so through this way it can reduce the delay and the area requirements significantly, and the whole system can improve fast performance greatly.

5.2 The Pipelined Architecture Based on the Loop Unrolling Technique

The 4-stage pipelined architecture based on the loop unrolling technique is presented in Fig.3, which introduces the loop unrolling technique based on Fig.1. It unrolls all the 16 steps in each round, and performed in one clock cycle, so in this architecture, each round calculation will be processed in only one clock cycle. In the 4-stage pipelining, except the first 512-bit message block will be performed in 4 clock cycles, the later ones will be performed in only one clock cycle.

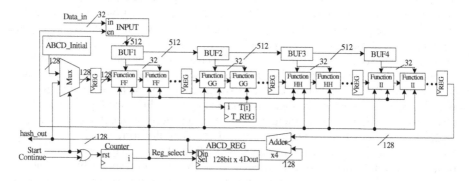

Fig. 3. The pipelined architecture based on the loop unrolling technique

Compared the two different kinds of pipelined architectures above, each has its own advantages. In the aspects of clock frequency and the reuse of the resources, the former acts better, all the 16 steps in each round reuse the same functional unit, each step will be performed in one clock cycle, the critical path is relatively simple, and which has a higher clock frequency. While the every step of the latter uses its own functional unit with large resources, moreover, several steps combined together as a larger combinational logic circuit performed in one clock cycle, and its critical path is much longer than the former, which require a relatively long clock cycle, so the latter has a lower clock frequency. In the aspect of storage space, the former needs 512·$p$bit and 32·$p$bit storage space respectively to store M_j and T, while each step of the latter has its own combinational logic circuit, so the constant T_i can be hardwired into the design instead of T_REG. In addition, the value of the s in every step of the latter is a constant, the multiplexer in fig.2 can also be reduced. In the aspect of throughput, the latter reduces parts of the clock delay and registers delay, the total delay of the implementation is reduced, which increases the throughput of the algorithm. Take the single step into consideration, the latter reduces both time delay and area requirements, while each step requires a combinational logic circuit, the overall area requirements of the latter are much larger than the former.

6 Results of the Implementations and Conclusions

6.1 The Results of the Implementations

This paper presented the optimization of the MD5 algorithm, the design method of the pipelined architecture, as well as several FPGA-based implementations of the algorithm. All the implementations were designed in Verilog HDL and implemented on an Altera Stratix II GX EP2SGX90FF1508C3 FPGA, Quartus 7.2 was used in design entry, synthesis, placement & routing, programming and configuration. Simulation was performed with Modelsim 6.1g, and the results running on the board were entirely correct.

For convenience, the iterative, 4-stage pipelining, 32-stage pipelining based on iterative technique and the 32-stage pipelining based on loop unrolling technique designs are renamed to MD5_iterative, MD5_4_i_pipe, MD5_32_i_pipe and MD5_32_u_pipe respectively. All the results were presented in Table 1. And the throughput and speedup, respectively, defined with the following formula:

$$throughput = (block\ size \times clock\ frequency \times p)\ /\ latency$$
$$speedup = software\ run\text{-}time\ /\ hardware\ run\text{-}time \tag{3}$$

where block size is 512 bits, p is the stages of pipelining, clock frequency and latency are given by the implementations.

The software running environment of the MD5 algorithm is: Intel Pentium 4 3.0G processor, 1G memory, Windows Xp operating system. Encrypting the same length of message (here we selected 512bits, 1024bits and 50kbits), the speedup of the four hardware implementations of the MD5 algorithm achieve 4.90, 18.40, 130.00 and 193.90, respectively, as shown in Table 1.

Table 1. Results of the Hardware Implementations

Design	Pipe_line	Clock (Mhz)	logic utilization	ALUTs	Total registers	latency	Throughput (Mbps)	Speedup
MD5_iterative	1	102.7	2%	1352	462	65	810	4.90
MD5_4_i_pipe	4	97.95	9%	5929	3484	66	3039	18.40
MD5_32_i_pipe	32	86.32	53%	36296	25767	66	21428	130.00
MD5_32_u_pipe	32	66.48	57%	36790	26758	34	32035	193.90

7 Conclusion

The results of the four implementations in this paper compared with other publications are presented in Table 2. Other open-literature designs in the comparison are [1], [2], [3] and [4]. Three commercial designs by [8], [9] and [10] have been also included into the comparison although only limited information of these designs is available. All the designs in this paper were implemented on an Altera board, while other published designs were implemented on Xilinx boards. Generally, a Xilinx's Slice comprises two LUTs and two registers [11], hence, the equivalent numbers of LUTs and registers of Xilinx devices were showed as the figures with * in table 2. In other published designs, MD5-FP [4] is a fully pipelined design, MD5-HT4P [4] is a

Table 2. Comparison of other Published FPGA-based Implementations

Design	Device	Clock (Mhz)	ALUTs (Altera)	registers (Altera)	Slices (Xilinx)	BRAMs	latency	Throughput (Mbps)	Throughput /ALUT
MD5_iterative	Stratix II GX	102.7	1352	462	0	0	65	810	0.60
MD5_4_i_pipe	Stratix II GX	97.95	5929	3484	0	0	66	3039	0.51
MD5_32_i_pipe	Stratix II GX	86.32	36296	25767	0	0	66	21428	0.59
MD5_32_u_pipe	Stratix II GX	66.48	36790	26758	0	0	34	32035	0.87
Iterative [1]	Virtex V1000-6	21.00	1760*	1760*	880	0	65	165	0.09
Full loop unrol[1]	Virtex V1000-6	71.40	9526*	9526*	4763	0	n.a.	354	0.04
Diez et al. [2]	Virtex-II 2V3000	60.20	2738*	2738*	1369	n.a.	66	467	0.17
Ioannis [3]	Virtex-II -6	96.00	1594*	1594*	797	n.a.	n.a.	756	0.47
MD5-I[4]	Virtex-II 2V4000	75.50	1294*	1294*	647	2	66	586	0.45
MD5-I[4]	Virtex-II 2V4000	78.30	2650*	2650*	1325	0	66	607	0.23
MD5-FP[4]	Virtex-II 2V4000	93.40	15994*	15994*	7997	0	66	725	0.05
MD5-HT4p[4]	Virtex-II 2V4000	80.70	11464*	11464*	5732	0	66	2395	0.21
MD5-HT10i[4]	Virtex-II 2V4000	75.50	22996*	22996*	11498	0	66	5857	0.25
Amphion [8]	Virtex-II	60.00	1688*	1688*	844	n.a.	n.a.	472	0.28
Helion [9]	Virtex-II -6	96.00	1226*	1226*	613	1	n.a.	744	0.61
Ocean Logic[10]	Virtex-II -6	62.00	1218*	1218*	614	n.a.	n.a.	488	0.38

4-stage pipelining, MD5-HT10i [4] uses 10 parallel iterative MD5 blocks, Full loop unrol [1] unrolls all the steps, Ioannis [3] is a inner pipelined design, and the others are the iterative architectures. It can be seen that the MD5_iterative structure has the highest clock frequency and throughput in all the iterative structures, and the value of Throughput/ALUT is slightly lower than Helion [9]. The MD5_4_i_pipe and the MD5-HT4P [4] are both 4-stage pipelining, but the former is much better than the latter both in logic requirements and speed, which owe to that the former optimized the critical path. The MD5_32_u_pipe design in this paper achieves a throughput of 32035Mbps, and the value of Throughput/ALUT reached 0.87, at least to the authors' knowledge, this is the fastest published FPGA-based architecture at the time of writing.

The compared results above show that the designs in this paper perform very well both in required area and performance, although an exact comparison to certain implementations is difficult, because different FPGA device families are used. The main reason for the good performance of the designs in this paper is most probably efficient use of the reasonable architectures, especially, the optimized critical path, the loop unrolling technique and the reasonable pipelined stages.

The proposed design methodology in this paper can also be used by other hash algorithms such as SHA-1, RIPEMD-160, etc.

References

1. Deepakumara, J., Heys, H.M., Venkatesan, R.: FPGA Implementation of MD5 Hash Algorithm. In: Proceedings of the Canadian Conference on Electrical and Computer Engineering, CCECE 2001, Toronto, Canada, May 13-16, vol. 2, pp. 919–924 (2001)

2. Diez, J.M., Bojanić, S., Stanimirovicć, L., Carreras, C., Nieto-Taladriz, O.: Hash Algorithms for Cryptographic Protocols:FPGA Implementations. In: Proceedings of the 10th Telecommunications Forum, TELFOR 2002, Belgrade, Yugoslavia, November 26-28 (2002)

3. Yiakoumis, I., Papadonikolakis, M., Michail, H.: Efficient Small-Sized Implementation of the Keyed-Hash Message Authentication Code. In: EUROCON 2005, Serbia & Montenegro, Belgrade, November 22-24 (2005)
4. Jarvinen, K., Matti, T.: Hardware Implementation Analysis of the MD5 Hash Algorithm. In: Proceedings of the 38th Hawaii International Conference on System Sciences (2005)
5. Lee, Y.K., Chan, H., Verbauwhede, I.: Design Methodology for Throughput Optimum Architectures of Hash Algorithms of the MD4-class. Journal of Signal Processing Systems 53(1-2), 89–102 (2008)
6. Rivest, R.L.: The MD5 Message-Digest Algorithm. RFC 1321, MIT Laboratory for Computer Science and RSA Data Security, Inc. (April 1992)
7. Sklavos, N., Dimitroulakos, G., Koufopavlou, O.: An Ultra High Speed Architecture for VLSI Implementation of Hash Functions. In: Proceedings of ICECS, pp. 990–993 (2003)
8. Amphion. CS5315, High Performance Message Digest 5 Algorithm (MD5) Core. Datasheet (2004), http://www.amphion.com/acrobat/DS5315.pdf
9. Helion Technology. Datasheet, High Performance MD5 Hash Core for Xilinx FPGA (2004), http://www.heliontech.com/downloads/md5_xilinx_helioncore.pdf
10. Ocean Logic Ltd., http://www.ocean-logic.com
11. Jihua, W., Cheng, W.: Altera FPGA/CPLD design. Posts & Telecom Press, Beijing (2005)

Stability Analysis and Numerical Simulation for a Class of Multi-variable Networked Control Systems

Lisheng Wei[1], Ming Jiang[1], and Minrui Fei[2]

[1] Anhui University of Technology and Science, Wuhu 241000, China
Lshwei_11@163.com, my_kjjm@163.com
[2] School of Mechatronics and Automation, Shanghai University, Shanghai 200072, China
mrfei888@x263.net

Abstract. The issue of asymptotical stability for continuous-time multi-variable networked control systems is researched, where its network transmission is connected with network-induced delay. The complete mathematical model of the system is derived. The sufficient condition for asymptotical stability is analyzed and the maximum allowable delay conditions for systems are derived by using the 2nd Lyapunov stability theory. And the criteria of delay-dependent asymptotical stability for systems are derived. The merit of the proposed design methods lies in their less conservativeness, which is achieved by using free-weighting matrices techniques. The efficacy and feasibility of the proposed methods is shown by presenting simulation results from multi-variable networked control example.

1 Introduction

The concept of Networked Control Systems (NCSs) was proposed in 1980s, which was called Integrated Communication and Control Systems (ICCS) at that moment [1]. NCSs are the feedback control loops closed through a real time network. That is, in NCSs, communication networks are employed to exchange the information and control signals between control system components [2]. The aim of such systems is to ensure data transmission and coordinating manipulation among spatially distributed components. Compared with conventional point-to-point control systems, Advantages of NCSs include low cost, high reliability, ease of diagnosis and maintenance, small volume of wiring and so on. It is well known that NCSs have been widely applied to many complicated control systems, such as, manufacturing plants, vehicles, aircraft, and spacecraft [3].

Despite of the great advantages and wide applications, the insertion of the communication network will lead to time delay and data packet dropout inevitably, which might be potential sources to instability and poor performance of NCSs [4-5]. Recently, many researchers have studied stability/ stabilization of NCSs in the presence of network-induced delay [2-3, 6-8]. There are some preliminary results studying the problems of time delay and packet dropout compensation. Among these problems, network-induced delays are of prior importance, and are usually the major causes of

W. Zhang et al. (Eds.): HPCA 2009, LNCS 5938, pp. 442–449, 2010.
© Springer-Verlag Berlin Heidelberg 2010

the deterioration of the dynamic performance of the system and potential instability of the system. Wei et al. propose the novel real-time optimization grey prediction method for modeling the network- induced delay, based on the research of grey theory and optimization theory. By using AGO to smooth the original data sequence, the random characteristic of the network-induced delay can be reduced [7]. Luo et al. establish the continuous time model of NCSs, and consider the delay-independent stability of linear differential delay NCSs Based on the 2nd Lyapunov method [8]. Huang et al. analyze the integrity design of NCSs with actuator failure by using delay-dependent approach and integral-inequality method. And they get the sufficient stabilizability condition of system with memory-less networked state feedback controller based on linear matrix inequalities [9].

As we can see, the stability analysis methods presented above are usually based on Lyapunov theory. However, the relationships of states with random delays are not involved in Lyapunov-Krasovskii functional candidate. In order to reduce the conservativeness, free-weighting matrix approach is used to derive the delay-dependent asymptotical stability of multi-variable continuous-time NCSs.

The remainder of this paper is organized as follows. In Section 2, the sufficient condition for convergence of the proposed method is derived. And the maximum allowable transfer interval is used in its place to ensure absolute stability of NCSs. In Section 3, numerical simulation results with the proposed control scheme are obtained. Finally conclusion remarks are presented in Section 4.

2 Stability Analysis of Multi-variable NCSs

2.1 System Modeling

Consider the block diagram of a class of Multi-variable NCSs as shown in Fig.1 [8, 10]. There are n_p states x_p, M inputs u_p, and R outputs y_p in the plant model, and n_c states x_c, R inputs u_c, and M outputs y_c in the controller dynamics model. Using τ_{sc} and τ_{ca} to represent the sensor-to-controller and controller-to-actuator delays, respectively.

The continuous-time state-space model of the plant can be described by

$$\begin{cases} \dot{x}_p(t) = A_p x_p(t) + B_p u_p(t) \\ y_p(t) = C_p x_p(t) \end{cases} \tag{1}$$

And the continuous-time state-space model of the controller by

$$\begin{cases} \dot{x}_c(t) = A_c x_c(t) + B_c u_c(t) \\ y_c(t) = C_c x_c(t - \tau_c) + D_c u_c(t - \tau_c) \end{cases} \tag{2}$$

where A_p, A_c, B_p, B_c, C_p, C_c, D_c are known constant real matrices with proper dimensions, τ_c is the calculation delay of controller.

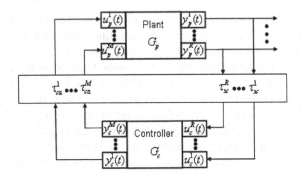

Fig. 1. The block diagram of a class of Multi-variable NCSs

For the convenience of investigation, without loss of generality we make the following assumptions [11-14]:

1) All the sensors are time-driven, the sample period is T, and the time gas among the sensors' nodes can be neglected, the controllers and the actuators are event-driven.

2) The data is transmitted with multi-data packet through the communication network at every sampling period.

Since u_p and u_c are delayed version of y_c and y_p respectively, then we have

$$u_p^j(t) = y_c^j(t - \tau_{ca}^j)$$
$$u_c^j(t) = y_p^j(t - \tau_{sc}^j)$$

(3)

According to Equation (3), multi-variable NCSs can be written as the following equivalent form

$$\dot{x}(t) = \begin{bmatrix} \dot{x}_p(t) \\ \dot{x}_c(t) \end{bmatrix} = Ax(t) + \sum_{j=1}^{r} A_j x(t - \tau_1^j) + \sum_{i=1}^{m} B_i x(t - \tau_2^i) + \sum_{i=1}^{m}\sum_{j=1}^{r} C_{ij} x(t - \tau_3^{i,j})$$

(4)

where

$$A = \begin{bmatrix} A_p & 0 \\ 0 & A_c \end{bmatrix}, \quad A_j = \begin{bmatrix} 0 & 0 \\ B_c E_j & 0 \end{bmatrix}, \quad B_i = \begin{bmatrix} 0 & B_p F_i \\ 0 & 0 \end{bmatrix}, \quad C_{ij} = \begin{bmatrix} B_p G_{ij} & 0 \\ 0 & 0 \end{bmatrix}$$

$$\tau_1^j = \tau_{sc}^j, \quad \tau_2^i = \tau_{ca}^i + \tau_c, \quad \tau_3^{i,j} = \tau_{ca}^i + \tau_{sc}^j + \tau_c$$

For brevity of our discussion, rearranging Equation (4), we have

$$\dot{x}(t) = Ax(t) + \sum_{i=1}^{N} A_i x(t - \tau_i) = \left[A + \sum_{i=1}^{N} A_i \right] x(t) - \sum_{i=1}^{N} A_i \left[x(t) - x(t - \tau_i) \right]$$

(5)

This model takes network-induced delay of multi-variable NCSs into consideration.

For the same reason, when the data is transmitted with one data packet through the communication network. That is, a single packet is enough to transmit the plant output at every sampling period. And the real memory-less state feedback control input $u(t)$ realized through zeroth-order hold in Equation (2) is a piecewise constant function.

$$u(t) = Kx(t)$$

If we consider the effect of the network-induced delay on the NCSs, then the real control system (5) can be rewritten as

$$\dot{x}(t) = Ax(t) + A_1 x(t - \tau_1) \tag{6}$$

where τ_1 is the time delay, which denotes the time from the instant when the sensor nodes sample sensor data from a plant to the instant when actuators transfer data to the plant. Then we assume that $u(t) = 0$ before the first control signal reaches the plant and a constant $\tau > 0$ exists such that $0 \leq \tau_1 \leq \tau < \infty$.

With these models, the stability sufficient condition is proposed in the next section.

2.2 Asymptotical Stability of Multi-variable NCSs

In the actual industrial applications, we often use single packet transmission method in order to facilitate the design and reliability.

Before the development of the main result, the following lemmas will be used.

Lemma 1 (Schur complement theorem) [15]: Given any symmetric matrix $S = S^T$

$$S = \begin{bmatrix} S_{11} & S_{12} \\ S_{21} & S_{22} \end{bmatrix} \tag{7}$$

where $S_{11} \in R^{r \times r}$, S_{12}, S_{21}, S_{22} are known real matrices with proper dimensions. The following three conditions are equivalent

(1) $S < 0$

(2) $S_{11} - S_{12} S_{22}^{-1} S_{12}^T < 0$ and $S_{22} < 0$

(3) $S_{22} - S_{12}^T S_{11}^{-1} S_{12} < 0$ and $S_{11} < 0$

Theorem 1: considering the closed-loop system (6), given positive constant $0 \leq \tau$, if there exist positive matrix P, Q, Z and X, matrix N_1, N_2 with proper dimensions such that the LMI (8) holds.

$$\Phi = \begin{bmatrix} \Phi_{11} & \Phi_{12} & \tau A^T Z \\ * & \Phi_{22} & \tau A_1^T Z \\ * & * & -\tau Z \end{bmatrix} < 0 \quad ; \quad \Pi = \begin{bmatrix} X_{11} & X_{12} & N_1 \\ * & X_{22} & N_2 \\ * & * & Z \end{bmatrix} \geq 0 \tag{8}$$

Then system (6) is asymptotically stable when all network-induced delay satisfies $0 \leq \tau_1 \leq \tau$. Where $*$ denotes the symmetric terms in a symmetric matrix, and

$$\Phi_{11} = PA + A^T P + N_1 + N_1^T + Q + \tau X_{11}; \quad \Phi_{12} = \Phi_{21}^T = PA_1 - N_1 + N_2^T + \tau X_{12}$$

$$\Phi_{22} = -N_2 - N_2^T - Q + \tau X_{22}; \quad X = \begin{bmatrix} X_{11} & X_{12} \\ X_{21} & X_{22} \end{bmatrix} \geq 0$$

Proof: Construct a Lyapunov-Krasovskii function is presented as follows [15]:

$$V(t, x) = V_1(t, x) + V_2(t, x) + V_3(t, x) \tag{9}$$

where P、Q and R are symmetric positive matrices, and

$$V_1(t,x)=x^T(t)Px(t);\ V_2(t,x)=\int_{-\tau_1}^{0}\int_{t+\beta}^{t}\dot{x}^T(\alpha)Z\dot{x}(\alpha)d\alpha d\beta;\ V_3(t,x)=\int_{t-\tau_1}^{t}x^T(\alpha)Qx(\alpha)d\alpha$$

On the one hand, from the Leibniz-Newton formula, we have

$$x(t)-x(t-\tau_1)=\int_{t-\tau_1}^{t}\dot{x}(\alpha)d\alpha \tag{10}$$

Then the following equation is true for any free-weighting matrices N_1 and N_2 with appropriate dimensions.

$$2\left[x^T(t)N_1+x^T(t-\tau_1)N_2\right]\times\left[x(t)-x(t-\tau_1)-\int_{t-\tau_1}^{t}\dot{x}(\alpha)d\alpha\right]=0 \tag{11}$$

On the other hand, give the symmetric positive matrices X as

$$X=\begin{bmatrix}X_{11}&X_{12}\\ *&X_{22}\end{bmatrix}\geq 0 \tag{12}$$

Then we have

$$\tau\bar{x}^T(t)X\bar{x}(t)-\int_{t-\tau_1}^{t}\bar{x}^T(t)X\bar{x}(t)d\alpha\geq 0 \tag{13}$$

where $\bar{x}(t)=\left[x^T(t)\quad x^T(t-\tau_1)\right]^T$.

Calculating the derivative of $V(t)$ along the solutions of system (6) and adding the left side of equation (11) and inequality (13) into it, we have

$$\dot{V}(t,x)=\dot{V}_1(t,x)+\dot{V}_2(t,x)+\dot{V}_3(t,x)$$

$$\leq x^T(t)\left(PA+A^TP\right)x(t)+2x^T(t)PA_1x(t-\tau_1)+x^T(t)Qx(t)$$

$$+x^T(t-\tau_1)Qx(t-\tau_1)+\tau\dot{x}^T(t)Z\dot{x}(t)-\int_{t-\tau_1}^{t}\dot{x}^T(\alpha)Z\dot{x}(\alpha)d\alpha$$

$$+2\left[x^T(t)N_1+x^T(t-\tau_1)N_2\right]\times\left[x(t)-x(t-\tau_1)-\int_{t-\tau_1}^{t}\dot{x}(\alpha)d\alpha\right] \tag{14}$$

$$+\tau\bar{x}^T(t)X\bar{x}(t)-\int_{t-\tau_1}^{t}\bar{x}^T(t)X\bar{x}(t)d\alpha$$

$$=\bar{x}^T(t)\Omega\bar{x}(t)-\int_{t-\tau_1}^{t}\tilde{x}^T(t)\Pi\tilde{x}(t)d\alpha$$

where

$$\tilde{x}^T(t)=\left[x^T(t)\quad x^T(t-\tau_1)\quad\dot{x}^T(t)\right]^T$$

$$\Omega = \begin{bmatrix} \Phi_{11} + \tau A^T ZA & \Phi_{12} + \tau A^T ZA_1 \\ * & \Phi_{22} + \tau A_1^T ZA_1 \end{bmatrix}; \Pi = \begin{bmatrix} X_{11} & X_{12} & N_1 \\ * & X_{22} & N_2 \\ * & * & Z \end{bmatrix} \geq 0$$

$$\Phi_{11} = PA + A^T P + N_1 + N_1^T + Q + \tau X_{11}; \Phi_{12} = \Phi_{21}^T = PA_1 - N_1 + N_2^T + \tau X_{12}; \Phi_{22} = -N_2 - N_2^T - Q + \tau X_{22}$$

It can be proved that if the following matrix inequality (15) holds, then the closed-loop NCSs (6) is asymptotically stable by the Lyapunov-Krasovskii functional theorem.

$$\Omega < 0 \qquad \Pi \geq 0 \qquad\qquad (15)$$

By the Schur complement theorem, and according to inequality (17), we have

$$\Omega = \begin{bmatrix} \Phi_{11} + \tau A^T ZA & \Phi_{12} + \tau A^T ZA_1 \\ * & \Phi_{22} + \tau A_1^T ZA_1 \end{bmatrix} \qquad ; \quad \Pi \geq 0$$

$$= \begin{bmatrix} \Phi_{11} & \Phi_{12} \\ * & \Phi_{22} \end{bmatrix} - \begin{bmatrix} \tau A^T Z \\ \tau A_1^T Z \end{bmatrix} (-\tau Z)^{-1} \begin{bmatrix} \tau A^T Z \\ \tau A_1^T Z \end{bmatrix}^T = \begin{bmatrix} \Phi_{11} & \Phi_{12} & \tau A^T Z \\ * & \Phi_{22} & \tau A_1^T Z \\ * & * & -\tau Z \end{bmatrix} = \Phi < 0 \qquad (16)$$

So we can see inequality (16) is the same as inequality (8) in Theorem 1.

The proof of Theorem 1 is completed.   ∎

3 Numerical Simulations

In this section, the effectiveness of the proposed delay-dependent asymptotical stability of multi-variable NCSs is demonstrated by numerical simulations.

Consider the following multi-variable system

$$A = \begin{bmatrix} -10.38 & -0.2077 & 6.715 & -5.676 \\ -0.5814 & -4.29 & -10 & 0.675 \\ 1.067 & 4.273 & -6.653 & 5.893 \\ 0.048 & 4.273 & 1.343 & -2.104 \end{bmatrix}; B = \begin{bmatrix} 0 & 0 \\ 5.679 & 0 \\ 1.136 & -3.146 \\ 1.136 & 0 \end{bmatrix}; C = \begin{bmatrix} 1 & 0 & 1 & -1 \\ 0 & 1 & 0 & 0 \end{bmatrix}$$

$$k = \begin{bmatrix} -0.0907 & 0.4222 & -1.7898 & 0.5445 \\ -0.2190 & -0.9225 & -0.1876 & -1.8060 \end{bmatrix}$$

So we have A_1 in system (6).

$$A_1 = \begin{bmatrix} 0 & 0 & 0 & 0 \\ 0.5152 & -2.3976 & 10.1641 & -3.0922 \\ -0.5860 & -3.3817 & 1.4431 & -6.3003 \\ 0.1031 & -0.4796 & 2.0332 & -0.6185 \end{bmatrix}$$

By Theorem 1 in the paper, the maximum allowable transfer interval (MATI) that guarantees the stability of system is $\tau_{max} = 165.1ms$. However, using Theorem 1 in reference [10], the maximum value of $\tau_{max} \approx 2.4ms$. Therefore, the free-weighting matrix introduced in Theorem 1 improves the result of reference [10] and has less conservation. The simulation results are shown in the flowing figures.

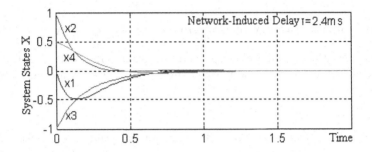

Fig. 2. Simulation results (network-induced delay=2.4ms)

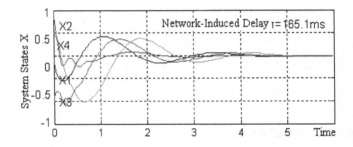

Fig. 3. Simulation results (network-induced delay=165.1ms)

As can be seen from the simulation results, two experiments are conducted to test the asymptotical stability of multi-variable NCSs when network-induced delay is 2.4ms and 165.1ms respectively. By simulating a multi-variable plant, we successfully improve the system control performances and reduce the conservation. The results are better than the ones that the theorem 1 in reference [10] can provide.

4   Conclusions

In this paper, a method of analysis the asymptotical stability sufficient condition for an continuous-time multi-variable NCSs with random communication network-induced delays has been proposed. Based on Lyapunov stability theory combined with LMIs techniques, a sufficient convergence condition is derived by introducing a new Lyapunov-Krasovskii functional candidate. When the single packet transmission method is used, the criteria of delay-dependent asymptotical stability for systems are achieved by using free-weighting matrices techniques which can be selected properly to lead to much less conservative results. Numerical simulation results indicate the effectiveness and robustness of the proposed methods.

Acknowledgments. This work was supported by National Natural Science Foundation of China under grant 60774059, 10902064 and 60843003, the Priming Scientific Research Foundation for the Introduction Talent in Anhui University of Technology and Science under grant 2009YQQ003, Anhui Provincial Natural Science Foundation under grant 090412071, sunlight Plan Following Project of Shanghai Municipal Education Commission, Shanghai Leading Academic Disciplines under grant T0103.

References

1. Halevi, Y., Ray, A.: Integrated communication and control Systems: part I-analysis. ASME J. Dyn. Syst., Meas., and Control 110(4), 367–373 (1988)
2. Zhang, W., Branicky, M.S., Phillips, S.M.: Stability of networked control system. IEEE Control Systems Magazine 21(2), 84–99 (2001)
3. Walsh, G.C., Ye, H., Bushnell, L.G.: Stability analysis of networked control systems. IEEE Transactions on Control Systems Technology 10(3), 438–446 (2002)
4. Hespanha, J.P., Naghshtabrizi, P., Xu, Y.: A Survey of Recent Results in Networked Control Systems. Proceedings of IEEE 95(1), 138–162 (2007)
5. Yang, T.C.: Networked control system: a brief survey. IEE Proceedings of Control Theory Applications 153(4), 403–412 (2006)
6. Gao, H., Meng, X., Chen, T.: Stabilization of Networked Control Systems with a New Delay Characterization. IEEE Transactions on Automatic Control 53(9), 2142–2148 (2008)
7. Wei, L.S., Fei, M.R.: A Real-time Optimization Grey Prediction Method for Delay Estimation in NCS. In: The 6th IEEE International Conference on Control and Automation, Guangzhou, China, May 30-June 1, pp. 514–517 (2007)
8. Dongsong, L., Zhiwen, W., Ge, G.: Modeling and Stability Analysis of MIMO Networked Control Systems. In: Proceedings of the 27th Chinese Control Conference, Kunming, Yunnan, China, July 16-18, pp. 240–242 (2008)
9. Huang, H., Han, X., Ji, X., Wang, Z.: Fault-tolerant Control of Networked Control System with Packet Dropout and Transmission delays. In: IEEE International Conference on Networking, Sensing and Control, Sanya, China, April 6-8, vol. 8, pp. 325–329 (2008)
10. Wei, L., Fei, M.: Modeling and Stability Analysis of Multi-variable Networked Control Systems. Journal of System Simulation 20(14), 3759–3762 (2008) (in Chinese)
11. Wei, L., Fei, M., Hu, H.: Modeling and stability analysis of grey–fuzzy predictive control. Neurocomputing 72(1-3), 197–202 (2008)
12. Liu, G.P., Chai, S.C., Rees, D.: Networked Predictive Control of Internet/Intranet Based Systems. In: Proceedings of the 25th Chinese Control Conference, Harbin, Heilongjiang, August 7-11, pp. 2024–2029 (2006)
13. Schenato, L.: Optimal Estimation in Networked Control Systems Subject to Random Delay and Packet Drop. IEEE Transactions on Automatic Control 53(5), 1311–1317 (2008)
14. Yue, D., Han, Q.-L., Peng, C.: State feedback controller design of networked control systems. IEEE Trans. on Circuits and Systems-II 51(11), 640–644 (2004)
15. li, Y.: Robust Control- Linear Matrix Inequalities. Press of Qinghua University, Beijing (2002) (in Chinese)

The Oblique Water Entry Impact of a Torpedo and Its Ballistic Trajectory Simulation

Zhaoyu Wei[1], Xiuhua Shi[1], Yonghu Wang[2], and Yuanbo Xin[1]

[1] School of Marine, Northwestern Polytechnical University, Xi'an 710072, P.R. China
[2] Flight Technology college, civil aviation flight university of China, 618307, P.R. China
weimuru@163.com

Abstract. The torpedo water entry impact has a great effect on its underwater ballistic trajectory. In the paper, by wind tunnel experiments we get the torpedo water entry drag coefficient, amending it with supercavitation continuous factor and local cavity effect factor, and then the torpedo motion equation is established. Finally, the large scale nonlinear finite element software MSC.dytran is used to simulate the initial water entry impact of a Disk-Ogive-Head [1] torpedo. Then the motion parameters in the end of this stage are input into the motion equation as initial input values; finally, two parts of data are combined to get the whole parameters. The model uses cavitation number to determine torpedo's cavity, supercavitation, partial cavity or full wet navigation stage.

1 Introduction

In modern naval warfare, the concealment of torpedoes is a key issue to be researched, for high-speed is very important to concealment. However, high-speed naked torpedo will face enormous fluid force, the load may cause damage to its structure and even internal components. It is necessary to accurately compute the fluid-solid interaction and its effect. As computer-aided technology rapidly develops, finite element analysis has been widely used in transient dynamics analysis [2], especially high speed torpedo water entry impact, which can greatly improve efficiency and save spending [3]. MSC.dytran can effectively deal with multi-material fluid-solid coupling problems, and simulate the impact when torpedo hits the water.

2 Dytran Numerical Model

All parameters use the IS Units. The finite element model is shown in figure 1. Euler region is divided into two parts, the air and water domain, filled respectively with ideal compressible gas and non-viscous fluid material. The rigid structure of torpedo is divided into lagrange shell elements. The weight is 150kg. The initial attack angle is 0 degree, pitch angle is 10,20,30,50 degrees, and initial velocity is 150m/s.

The entire torpedo surface is defined as coupling face, using general coupling algorithm. All fluid free surfaces are defined as flow in and out boundary by FLOW [4]

W. Zhang et al. (Eds.): HPCA 2009, LNCS 5938, pp. 450–455, 2010.

card. Card MATRIG [4] defines the mass center, shell's polar inertia moment and equatorial inertiain moment in local coordinate system. The parameters of torpedo outputs mass center movement in horizontal and vertical component, velocity, acceleration and impact force time history. The fluid only outputs deformation. Global and local coordinate systems are, respectively, shown in figure 2 and 3.

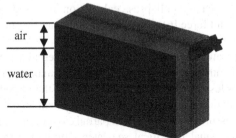

Fig. 1. Water entry three-dimensional FE model

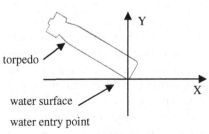

Fig. 2. Global coordinate system

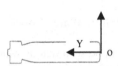

Fig. 3. Local coordinate system

Fig. 4. Model installation in wind tunnel

3   Theoretical Modeling

3.1   Experiment and Drag Coefficient Testing

The experiment was performed in NF3 wind tunnel in NWPU, mechanics parameters of a similar model are tested, the main parameters is the relationship of attack angle and fluid drag coefficient. The model is fixed as figure 4, and the drag coefficient of corresponding attack angle is shown in figure 5. The drag coefficient is amended according to torpedo's surface area and the largest cross-sectional area.

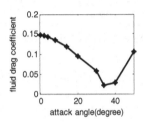

Fig. 5. Attack angle and drag characteristic curve

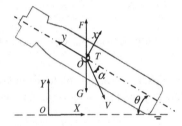

Fig. 6. Diagram of pitch

3.2 Theoretical Modeling

The model describes the phase from impact end to stable navigation. This article has adopted a method to amend the drag coefficient by supercavitation continuous factor and partial cavitation effect factor changing with the cavity number. Establishment of a six freedom degrees space motion equations only considers the water force, which is based on some assumptions [5]. Before cavity collapses, calculation is based on semi-empirical formula. The important fluid force [6] weight in horizontal and vertical direction is calculated as the reference.

Then, quotient of critical sea water saturation vapor pressure to supercavitation continuance factor is calculated and contrasted to cavitation number, making the judgments:(1) If the cavitation number is less than or equal to the quotient, the torpedo is in supercavitation stage; (2)If the cavitation number is bigger than quotient and less than critical seawater saturation vapor pressure, the torpedo is in partial cavitation;(3) If the cavitation number is greater than or equal to critical seawater saturation vapor pressure, the torpedo moves in totally wet stage.

4   Result of Simulation and Analysis

4.1   Analysis of Impact Load and Impact Coefficient of Oblique Water Entry

The over load and load curve is shown in figure 7 and 8. It can be seen that as water entry angle increases, over load and load peak value correspondingly increases. It is concluded that the vertical situation has the biggest peak value. In addition, it is shown that after impact peak value the curves nearly level off. In general, the water entry impact has a very short duration, with the level of a millisecond.

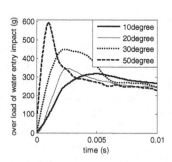
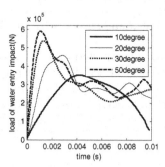

Fig. 7. Water entry impact over load   **Fig. 8.** Water entry impact load

The impact coefficient of four angles water entry impact is compared, which is calculated by the following formulation [1].

$$C_D = F_{imp} / (\frac{1}{2}\rho_w \pi V_0^2 R_0^2) \tag{1}$$

Where, F_{imp} is impact load; ρ_w is fluid density; V_0 is torpedo's initial velocity; R_0 is cylinder diameter. The time history of impact coefficient has been shown in Figure 9, it can be seen from the figures that the law of impact coefficient appears the same trend with over load and load curves.

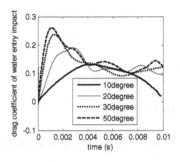
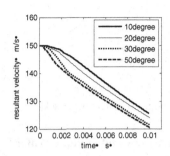

Fig. 9. Drag coefficient time history   **Fig. 10.** Water entry velocity time history

4.2 Water Entry Velocity

The four water entry velocity curves are shown in figure (10). The resultant velocity drops greatly for huge over load. As water entry load and over load increase with water entry angle, the velocity change quantity increases. The 10 degree angle water entry has a velocity drop of 24.42m/s, for that of 50 degree it is 29.57 m/s.

Table 1. Parameters of water entry impact comparison

parameter	corresponding data			
Trajectory angle(degree)	10	20	30	50
Velocity Change （m/s）	24.42	25.99	28.405	29.57
Attitude angle Change (degree)	1.19	0.82	0.76	0.49
overload peak value （g）	309.2	345.9	449.0	591.8
load peak value （N）	351837	459350	536982	591275

4.3 Whip and Attitude Angle Analysis

During impact, bend torque causes angular velocity mutation around horizontal axis. When it become serious whip happens. The tracks curves and pitch angles are shown in figure 11 and 12. For its Disk-Ogive-Head, four curves in figure 11 are almost straight, the whip could be avoided.

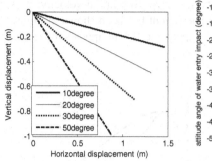

Fig. 11. Water entry tracks   **Fig. 12.** Time history of attitude angles

4.4   Water Flow and Oblique Water Entry Supercavitation Status Analysis

(a) 10 degree   (b) 20 degree   (c) 30 degree   (d) 50 degree

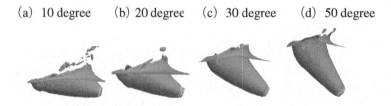

Fig. 13. Torpedo oblique water entry supercavitation

The high-speed water entry causes strong fluid-solid coupling interaction, so water medium could get a high velocity and forms splashing, which is shown in figure 13. As shown in the chart, supercavitation size decreases as the angle increase. The cavity status table 2 shows that as attitude angle become smaller, the cavity navigation lasts longer. In addition, the bigger angle water entry condition also has a bigger stable velocity, for smaller angle water entry gets a bigger drag in navigation.

Table 2. Cavitation status of torpedo in different water entry angle (second, s, velocity, v)

Angle	Supercavitation	Local cavity	Full wet	Steady V
50degree	0-0.24s	0.24-0.72s	0.72-3s	10.55m/s
30degree	0-0.29s	0.29-0.81s	0.81-3s	10.23m/s
20degree	0-0.38s	0.38-0.93s	0.93-3s	9.94m/s
10degree	0-0.43s	0.43-1.1s	1.1-3s	9.65m/s

5   Conclusion

In this paper, some parameters of torpedo are studied; the trajectory is divided into two parts, impact and navigation with cavity to stability. Water entry impact has a great influence on its head and trajectory behavior. The movement equation is gotten by introducing supercavitation continuous factor and local cavitation impact factor to amend the drag coefficient. Then two parts data combines to get the whole trajectory. After analysis, the initial velocity and angle have a great influence on ballistic behavior, but for its Disk-Ogive-Head whip couldn't happen.

References

1. Yonghu, W.: Dynamic Response Analysis of Airborne Torpedo and Deep-mine during Water-Entry Impact and Research of the Relative Technology. Ph.D, NWPU (2008)
2. Seddon, C.M., Moatamedi, M.: Review of water entry with applications to aerospace structures. International Journal of Impact Engineering 32, 1045–1067 (2006)
3. Zhonghua, L.: Theoretical Analysis and Numerical Simulation of Ogive-Nose Projectiles Penetrating into Water and Sand Medium. Master, Institute of Structural Mechanics China Academy of Engineering Physics, Mianyang, Sichuan (2002)
4. Dytran 2008 r1 Reference Manual (2008)
5. Yuwen, Z.: Torpedo Profile design. NWPU Press, Xi'an (1998)
6. Yuwen, Z.: Trajectory and ballistic design of torpedo. NWPU Press, Xi'an (1999)

Intelligent Traffic Simulation Grid Based on the HLA and JADE

Junwei Wu[1] and Xiaojun Cao[2]

[1] Shanghai Development Center of Computer Software Technology
wjw@stcsm.gov.cn
[2] Shanghai Jiao Tong University

Abstract. The application of Intelligent Traffic Simulation generally is composed of massive microscopic entities. These entities to reach certain scale are needed in order to achieve the accuracy and credibility of the simulation results, and each entity has its own patterns of behavior. The Intelligent Traffic Simulation must implement the simulation of microscopic traffic entities and the scalability of traffic solution. This paper introduces an ongoing research, which combines HLA and JADE to support microscopic traffic simulation framework, implements a prototype system to prove the feasibility of framework, and improves the prototype system based on the performance analysis. Some considerations about key technical issues of simulation framework are also discussed.

1 Introduction

As the construction of basic infrastructure, such as Car GPS, induction coil of crossroads and e-policeman as the basic facilities of the city, which generates massive amounts the transportation information data(TID) from different systems. It is fundamental to analyze and forecast traffic status. The amounts of TID in each system are huge. In order to simulate the detail traffic information of a scenario, further reduce the traffic congestion, provide real-time traffic information to decision makers and transportation planning managers, the government must develop the intelligent transportation simulation systems (ITSS) based on sophisticated information technology, which aims to build up a information share platform to integrate various transportation systems as a whole.

According to the degree of the simulation model described in detail on the transport system, we divide the simulation model into the following three categories:

- *Macro-simulation model.* It is great rough to describe the behavior of each interactive object in the traffic network.
- *Micro-simulation model.* It can describe more details the system entities and the individual the behavior of each interactive entity.
- *Meso-Simulation Models.* It can also describe the most of the system entities with accurate detail.

W. Zhang et al. (Eds.): HPCA 2009, LNCS 5938, pp. 456–464, 2010.
© Springer-Verlag Berlin Heidelberg 2010

So the Micro-simulation model is especially suitable for precision emersion network of actual transportation condition in the computer. This characteristic enables microscopic simulation to be really come evaluating the most objective tool in intelligent transportation system (ITS) influence. And it wants to process of data quantity is also biggest in threes. Fortunately, the grid technology provides us with conditions to implement micro-simulation of the traffic information[1,2].

Using the grid technology to implement micro-simulation of the large-scale traffic data need to solve two key issues: firstly, how achieve the scalable distributed applications to make use of grid compute resources; secondly, how simulate the microcosmic traffic entities to meet the demand for simulation. The distributed open framework is the more advanced technology to solve the scale problems currently for the first question, the High Level Architecture is the most representative among them [3,4]; On the other hand, we must consider theirs requirements to the independence and intelligence for the construction of the entity model. Multi-Agent Decision System is a relatively mature technology [5]. JADE (Java Agent Development Kit) [6] is a more popular Agent Kit. This paper mainly surrounds the HLA and the JADE technique to develop a discussion, research and achieve a method of the intelligent traffic micro-simulation.

The paper is organized as follows. Section 2 gives a belief introduction to related technique the background of the HLA and Agent. Section 3 discusses how integrate the HLA with JADE and use their respective advantages to achieve Intelligent Traffic Simulation. Section 4 describes the method we developed based on a prototype system and its performance analysis. Finally, the paper concludes the research and points out some future works in Section 5.

2   Technology Background

HLA (High Level Architecture) is that the U.S. Department of DefenseDoD rules formally standard technology framework for simulation projects. It is released as IEEE1516 in September 2000, becoming international general use standard, and is a relatively mature currently of open general simulation platform. To solve traditional simulation models often lack two desirable properties: reusability and interoperability, and high development and maintenance costs, As shown in Fig. 1, HLA defines a distributed simulation, it is called a federation, and each individual simulator is referred as a federate, one point of attachment to the Runtime Infrastructure (RTI).Meanwhile, HLA provides a series of HLA Interface API to achieve simulation management functions, including the Federal Management, Declaration Management, Object Management, Ownership Management, Time Management and Data Distribution Management.

A more intuitive way is that a series of related micro-entities are regarded as an object managed by a federate. There must be defined interaction object model achieves communication between federates. We can consider a complex simulation program as a hierarchy of components of increasing levels of aggregation by designing and developing hierarchy interaction function between federations and federates in accordance with the HLA interface specification.

The federations or federates can arbitrarily join or leave from RTI under certain conditions during the runtime. They can distribute in the different physical nodes. For a use scale as a target to simulate application, if granularity of federation and federates are defined correctly, it can attain requirements of the quantity and performance theoretically. Users can create simulation object based on HLA in order to implement micro-simulation applications. These objects can be regarded as federates or object model in HLA.

Agent itself has not been clearly defined. In the field of computer, it is widely recognized Wooldridge and Jennings' definition [7] that: "An agent is a computer system capable of autonomous flexible action in some environment in order to meet its design objectives." Agent is said to be the software or hardware which has some intelligent characteristics, such as autonomy, sociability, responsiveness, pro-activity. The intelligent characteristic of Agent system is reflected in behavior decision. One technology of achieving the intelligent decision-making power is BDI reasoning [8]. BDI is mainly to build up a decision tree Brief, the Decision and Intention are a main behavior decision system of a simulation entity in Brief, direct behavior performance from the Intention , indirect decision from the Decision , but the target or mission owned by that entity is decide by the Brief.

Java Agent Development KitJADEprovides a platform to create agent model. It defines general framework of abstract entities through inheritance patterns to add the behavior of specific type in order to define different patterns of different kinds entities objects. JADE also provides a series of interactive mechanisms, such as Agent Communication LanguageACL Messagewhich is the main communication way that followed FIPA protocol between Agents.

In other words, the main interactive mode among Agents is message passing mechanism. O2AMessage as the communication interface between Agent and external application can send application message to the specific agent. However, this application cannot necessarily run in the JADE platform. O2AMessage provides a method that can control the life cycle. It is also an interactive way from HLA to JADE platform. JADE platform also supports multi-node agent's migration and mobility based on FLPA protocol and can achieve dynamic load balancing function by combining with the middleware of resource management.

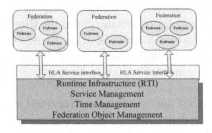

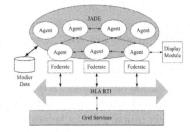

Fig. 1. HLA structure and function diagram

Fig. 2. System framework

3   Integration of HLA and JADE

The integration of HLA and JADE is the key to solve the scale problem in the large-scale micro-simulation and the technical difficulties on complex behavior of the simulation model. As shown in Fig. 2, HLA provides component hierarchy for the management of simulation system, and the JADE defines the multi-agent system prototype and model to create simulation object. HLA implements multi-agent simulation functions. They includes object management, time management and builds up the scalable distributed simulation framework, which Simulates the various objects in the real world through the behavioral model of agent in order to achieve fine-grained simulation of micro-objects. Considering the performance requirements of the distributed micro-simulation application, we divide the Agent, and achieve the indirect control through the direct management for some part in HLA. The main aspects of management include entity management model, simulation time strategy and interactive way.

3.1   The Abstract Definition of Simulation Entities

The entities of quantify and the interaction between entities in Micro-simulation applications are the bottleneck of performance decision. Suppose that there are n entities to communicate with each other in the simulation pool and every communication is composed of "request" and "response". Then the amount of data sent by an entity in a beat is $n-1$ and it has a total of $n(n-1)$ information to send. If the entities of quantity is very huge, even if broadcasting is used(only one copy in the entity message queue), there is great pressure to the network load and response time. We can add some entities and define different functions to achieve an abstract hierarchical structure to solve the problem of traffic.

A possible definition is to set Control, Coordinator, as well as Entity. Control is regarded as the only one of the integrated control entities, and Coordinator is responsible for process communications and management between the entities. The communication of all entities are transmitted through the Coordinator in accordance with this mode, then the traffic achieving an exchange of information is reduced to: n + n=2n. Suppose that there is n entities to communication with the Coordinator, then the total of message that Coordinator receive and send is 2n. According to this model, simulation objects are defined as:

- *Entity.* Simulation entity that corresponds to the simulated reality object;
- *Coordinator.* Management coordinator as a special Agent entity is responsible for the management of Entity's communications and the provision of environmental information, equal to a Federate in the HLA level;
- *Control.* Agent as the central is responsible for processing massive amounts of micro-information generated by macro-information, as well as managers of the whole object model; it is the only one in the system.

Under general cases, entity objects communicate with their corresponding Coordinator, and all of the Coordinators communicate with Control. In such a

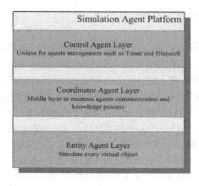

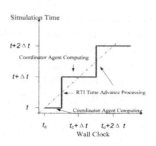

Fig. 3. The level division of multi-agent

Fig. 4. Time Management

division level, the same type of communication must be control of transmitting by the upper, and added a transmitting process reduces the quantity of message. The division structure as shown in Fig. 3.

The significance of the Agent role level division is as follows:

- Different Agents have different responsibilities, which facilitates simulation management.
- Division can reconstruct effectively the relation of entities, and further impact on performance links, such as communications, information processing.
- An abstract sense of the hierarchical structure can be extended as a generic hierarchical micro-entities model for the different requirements of micro-simulation application.

The formulary of abstract level division can achieve modeling of the complex simulation objects by recursion method. For example, in some special cases, coordinator collaborating with agent can be regarded as some Coordinators' entity objects.

3.2   Strategy of Simulation Time

The HLA provides some time management strategies, such as conservative time advance, event-based triggered advance, and timestamp-based management and so on. Time management means that the HLA runs RTI to coordinate and control Coordinator and Entity in the use of micro-simulation system constructed by JADE and HLA. All event management strategies mentioned above can be applied. That more easily to comprehend and in brief among them is uniformity time advance method, as shown in Fig. 4. Each time advance made by the federate is of a fixed duration of simulation time. In fact, the CPU time for processing data may not exactly equal, so every step length may not be completely equal. In the uniform step length, the simulation interval time is t, the time to perform T and CPU processing time Tc meet the equation: $T = \sum_{t=1}^{n} Tc + t$. Suppose that the simulation interval time is 1s, and the average CPU processing time of each simulation entity Tc is 0.0001s. If there are 100 simulation entities in the system, the time to perform each simulation step length is $0.0001 \times 100 + 1s = 1.01$ seconds, With the increasing number of entities, Tc value becomes more and more big, and peer-to-peer communication way will produce square magnitude growth. The processing time can be better to reduce to linear growth through abstract layer model.

3.3   Interaction Management

The interaction process among Coordinator, HLA/RTI and Entity is as shown in Figure 5:

1) Coordinator Agent requests RTI time advance by calling TimeAdvance Request() function at the beginning of each step length;
2) RTI responds to the request and advance simulation time through callback TimeAdvanceGrant() function. And it notifies all of the Coordinator that time is advanced. Advance callback response may be different based on different time advance algorithm. Only can unrestricted Federation actively send response advance request. Others restricted federation must wait and can not receive a unified response from RIT until the unrestricted Federations send request;
3) It interacts with all its management of Entity on this time step length after Coordinator receives the message from Callback TimeAdvanceGranted() function;
4) It requests RTI time advance after completion of all of the information exchange, then go into the next simulation step length. The CPU process time is used for passing message and processing information of each Agent in this time management mode.

HLA /RTI communicate directly with Coordinator of JADE in order to achieve the time management. All of the agent entities don't request directly the time synchronization, but can achieve this through their respective Coordinators. This division of granularity can support a simulation system with huge quantity of entities. The Communication Control between Coordinator Agent and Entity Agent can use approach of loosely coupled message-based request - response, tightly coupled sharing data, and middleware transmitting.

4   Experiment

According to the framework principle proposed the author achieves a simple distributed micro-simulation prototype system which simulate vehicles and pedestrians at a crossroad in the real world. The bottom layer of simulation framework adopts HLA RTI, uses the Agent simulation abstract system as the simulation model, and achieves the integration of HLA and JADE by Coordinator Agent,

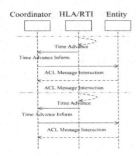

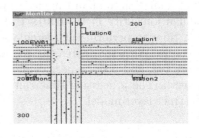

Fig. 5. Interactive Management

Fig. 6. The operation interface of the prototype system

moreover, this prototype system uses time-slice-based uniform advance strategies as well as message-based interactive way to implement. The soft hardware environment and test data of the prototype are as follows. Fig. 6 illustrates the operation interface of the prototype system.

Fig. 11 reflects on the initial performance of the prototype system. The performance testing shows that the CPU time of the system each period would increase along with growth of the quantity of simulation entities. This phenomenon reflects on the existence of the system performance bottleneck that has a directly link with simulation entities. According to this idea, the author analyzes performance of the whole system framework and makes the appropriate improvements.

1. *Reduce the information content.* It converts the original object serialization into the binary string format through the definition of ontology and format of the message. As shown in Table 1:
2. *Improve the ability of distributed parallel processing.* It set up node level singleton to achieve knowledge management function. All the messages in the prototype simulation system must be processed by Coordinator Agent and written into its local knowledge domain. The data is received, updated and sent in a simulation step length. The basic attributes of Agent is thread, so it can reduce the cost that caused by receiving and sending message through sharing memory, increase the handling capacity through parallel processing maximally, and reduce the load that caused by Coordinator as the processing hub.

Table 1. Information conversion

Object Serialization	Ontology	Binary String Format
Class PosMessage implements Serializable { int posX = 11; int posy = 120; }	PosMessage: (int)posX;(int)posY	PosMessage:11;120*

Machine	CPU	RAM	Virtual Memory
Dell Optiplex 120L*2	P4 3.06GHz	0.99GB	1524MB

Fig. 7. Hardware Testing Environment

	The number of road	Start simulation road segment
CASE A	2	SimulationW001, Simulation1
CASE B	3	SimulationW001, 1, 1008

Fig. 8. CASE A and CASE B

IDE	JDK	HLA version	JADE version
Eclipse 3.2.1	1.5.0_06	1.3NG-V6	1.4.2

Fig. 9. Software Testing Environment

Entity Number	20	40	80	160
CPU Time(ms)	204	1344	2281	2328
	703	1297	625	734
	1781	953	703	766
	1984	1328	516	3000
	578	1000	828	859
	1672	1625	1015	2157
	1750	969	906	1718
	1078	953	4125	1500
	1250	766	766	1125
	797	609	2203	4281
	984	1953	3579	2250
	1313	953	703	766
	1781	1188	2609	4980
	719	1032	1000	5968
	1625	875	4047	5516
	1547	796	2047	4328
	766	1156	859	3685
Average(ms)	1171.94	1115.25	1756.81	2824.69
Exception(ms)	N/A	4484	6265	N/A
	N/A	3125	8141	N/A
	N/A	3359	13219	N/A
	N/A	3703	6437	N/A

Fig. 10. Response Time

3. *Improve the time management.* The timestamp is added to the agent platform for exchanging information. It also adds a global clock behavior and advance RTI time at intervals of fixed CPU time. The HLA time management used by the system simulation is time-slice-based uniform advance strategies. It can request the RTI Time Advance at intervals and send the response to Agent platform. If it spent more time in processing in the Agent platform, it will affect the call of RTI advance, which will cause each step length of CPU time to grow linearly along with the increase of Entity Agent. The Agent platform uses the timestamp-based management in accordance with the new model. However, the HLA/RTI still uses the uniform Time Advance, which can ensure that system advance a step at every fixed interval (such as 1 second). With the increasing quantity of entities, all the information may not be dealt with in a step length, but the global clock advances accordance to set the starting time step. The information that originally belonged to the beat but not have the time to deal with will be retained to the next beat to deal with in accordance with its timestamp. Because of the Agent state's update, processing and adding mechanism, there is very little data on the no synchronous situation. The performance analysis of improved system is as shown in Fig. 12.

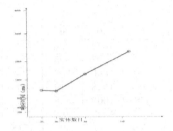

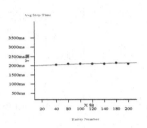

Fig. 11. The diagram of prototype system initial performance data

Fig. 12. The diagram of improved performance testing

5   Conclusions and Future Work

This paper combined HLA simulation system with Multi-Agent technology and solved the distributed systems' scalability and complexity in the application of Intelligent Traffic Micro-Simulation grid. Specific entity management, timing and interaction strategies are proposed and discussed in detail. A usable prototype system is implemented. The author also analyzes its performance and improves the system. However, what we simulate the scenarios are not enough complicated, we will take more complex factors into account to verify the method and technology proposed in this paper in the future.

References

1. Li, Y., Li, M., Cao, J., et al.: Towards Building Intelligent Transportation Information Service System on Grid. In: Shen, H.T., Li, J., Li, M., Ni, J., Wang, W. (eds.) APWeb Workshops 2006. LNCS, vol. 3842, pp. 632–642. Springer, Heidelberg (2006)
2. Cao, J., Li, M., Huang, L., et al.: Towards Building an Intelligent Traffic Simulation Platform. In: The 6th IEEE International Symposium on Cluster Computing and the Grid Workshops(CCGRIDW 2006) (2006)
3. Adnersson, J., et al.: HLA as Conceptual Basis for a Multi-Agent Environment. Technical Report 8TH-CGF-033, Pitch Kunskapsutveckling AB (1999)
4. IEEE Standard 1516 (HLA Rules), 1516.1 (Interface Specification) and 1516.2 (OMT) (September 2000), http://www.dmso.mil/public/transition/hla/
5. Eugénio, O., Klaus, F., Olga, S.: Multi-agent systems: which research for which applications. Robotics and Autonomous Systems 27(1-2), 91–106 (1999)
6. JADE - Java Agent DEvelopment Framework (March 2006), http://jade.tilab.com/
7. Wooldridge, M.J., Jennings, N.R.: Intelligent Agents: Theory and Practice. Journal of Knowledge Engineering Review 10(2), 115–152 (1995)
8. Rao, A.S., Georgeff, M.P.: BDI Agents: From Theory to Practice. In: Proceedings of the 1st International Conference on Multi-Agent System (ICMAS 1995), San Francisco, USA, June 1995, pp. 312–319 (1995)

The Research and Emulation on PIM-SM Protocol[*]

Libing Wu[1], Shengchao Ding[2], Chanle Wu[1], Dan Wu[3], and Bo Chen[1]

[1] School of Computer, Wuhan University, Wuhan, 430072, China
{wu,chanlewu,chenbo99}@whu.edu.cn
[2] Institute of Computing Technology, Chinese Academy of Sciences,
Beijing, 100190, China
dingshengchao@ict.ac.cn
[3] School of Computer Science, University of Windsor, Windsor,
Ontario, N9B3P4, Canada
danwu@windsor.edu.ca

Abstract. This paper summarizes the concept of multicast and the routing protocols, analyzes the principles of PIM-SM, and simulates PIM-SM in three scenarios on OPNET. As the simulation results show, in contrast to unicast, PIM-SM consumes less bandwidth, resulting in lower link occupancy rate. However, the higher end-to-end delay makes the switching from RPT to SPT long. Besides, when the recipient router locates between the sending router and RP, PIM-SM forwards redundant packets, and it is possible that the end-to-end delay of group members can be reduced. Furthermore, this paper explores the disadvantages of the standard PIM-SM and gives some improvements.

1 PIM-SM Routing Protocol

PIM-SM routes multicast packets and sets up distribution tree via WAN, because this protocol can use any unicast routing information, such as the information of RIP or OSPF. This protocol does not depend on any specific unicast routing information, so it is called "protocol-independent" [1-3].

In PIM-SM, if a host wants to add into a multicast group, it must join the shared tree which is also known as the RP tree (RPT, Rendezvous Point Tree). This tree relies on a central router called RP (Rendezvous Point), which receives all communications from sources and then forwards to receivers. The members around RP must send "add" info to RP. Designated Router is responsible for sending the "add / delete" information to RP. Generally the highest IP address in sub-network is chosen as DR. When a receiver joins a multicast group, it informs the Designated Router through Internet Group Management Protocol (IGMP). DR calculates the RP of this group by a Hash function, sends a unicast PIM message, and creates a forwarding table for the multicast group if necessary [4]. The designated router sends delete info to RP when group members leave the group, and then the corresponding part of the tree was deleted [5-7].

---

[*] Support by the National Science Foundation for Post-doctoral Scientists of China and the Natural Science Foundation of Hubei Province.

W. Zhang et al. (Eds.): HPCA 2009, LNCS 5938, pp. 465–472, 2010.

2 Simulation of PIM-SM Routing Protocol

This paper focuses on the working process and some disadvantages of PIM-SM protocol. So we design a series of scenarios to simulate the protocol in OPNET.

2.1 Simulation of Multicast

Using the multicast technology, the sender needs to set up only a session process for all receivers. Thus, the sender only need send out a copy of data to make all receivers to get the data, that is, the number of packets sent out is a constant in contrast with the number of the receivers.

As shown in figure 1, the first simulation is conducted in a school, which includes three departments and one administration. From the figure, it is clear that every department has the same deployment of LAN, that is, one HUB links to two workstations, among which one is the receiver of a video conference. In the administration's LAN, one HUB links to two workstations, among which one is the sender of the video conference. These four LANs are linked by two routers—Backbone Router1 and Backbone Router2, which are linked by the backbone.

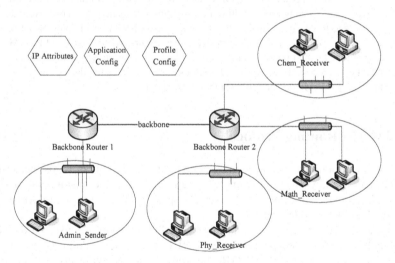

Fig. 1. Network topology of the multicast test

For the convenience of comparing unicast with multicast, we simulate unicast based on this scenario at the step one. In OPNET, Profile Config is used to define the applications which the tests support. OPNET has defined 14 standard applications, such as Email, Database Access, File Transfer, Web Browsing, and so on. In view of the testing target, we configure three identical applications, which correspond to three video unicast to three receivers. The deviation of starting time of each application conforms to the Uniform Distribution, which is configured as uniform(5,10). Their operation mode is set to simultaneous mode, and the applications run until the end of the test.

Then we set up three applications in the Application Definitions of Application Config, and set the sending frame rate of each video conference to 10 frame/s and the size of each frame of the receiving flow, as well as the sending flow, to 5000 Bytes (in the configuration window of Frame Size Information). The destination addresses are set respectively to the receivers of the three departments, that is, Chem_Receiver, Math_Receiver and Phy_Receiver. The other configurations use the default values.

IP Attributes are used to determine whether the scenario supports the multicast technology. Because we test the unicast at first, we do not change them, just using the default values. Then we configure the simulation time and the statistics. We set the link utilization as the statistic and set the simulation time to 1 hour, then start the simulation.

At the step two, we carried out the multicast test based on that scenario. For simplicity, this paper uses the RP-specified method. We set the IP Multicast RP Information of the IP Attributes and add an item, in which the multicast address is 224.0.6.1 and the RP address is 192.0.1.1, that is, we set the Backbone Router2 as the RP of that multicast application. Then we set the destination name as "Multicast Receiver" in the Application Config. Because of the use of multicast technology, the configuration of the Profile config needs only one application, which is set to video conference and configured as above.

Apart from setting "Application: Destination Preferences" to "Multicast Receiver", the configurations of the sender are configured as the above scenario. As to the configurations of the three receivers, we change "Application: Multicasting Specification" to "Video", and set the moment of joining the application to the 10th min. The receivers leave the multicast group until the end of the simulation.

As to the routers of the two backbones, we set the IP multicast to support PIM-SM, and set "PIM-SM Interval" and "PIM-SM Source Threshold" to infinity, which indicates that we do not take account of the case of PIM-SM switching from RPT to SPT. For convenience of comparison, the statistics and simulation time are the same as the step one.

2.2 Simulation of Switching from RPT to SPT

The second simulation scenario adds a new LAN (English Department) based on the first one. As shown in figure 2, the new LAN's configurations are the same as the other three LANs. We set the Backbone Router2 as RP, and set "PIM-SM Interval" of Backbone Router3 to 600 seconds, "PIM-SM Source Threshold" to 0.5 packets/sec (to ensure switching from RPT to SPT). That is, let the Backbone Router3 calculate the transport rate of packets every 600 seconds. If the rate is more than 0.5 packets/sec, then switch from RPT to SPT.

At the same time, mark the paths of RPT and SPT in the figure. The path to Eng_Receiver(RPT) is Router1 – Backbone Router2 – Backbone Router3, which is indicated by solid arrows. The corresponding path of SPT is Backbone Router1 – Backbone Router3, which is indicated by dashed arrows.

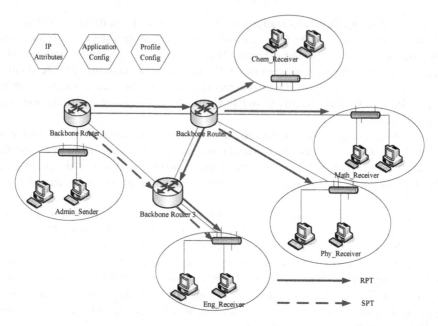

Fig. 2. Test of switching from RPT to SPT

The third simulation scenario is designed to focus on a particular network topology as shown in figure 3. SPT of the sender to RP and RPT of the receivers are all of coincidence, that is, the receivers are between RP and the sender. Router Center set its "PIM-SM Interval" to 600 seconds and "PIM-SM Source Threshold" to 0.5 packets/sec.

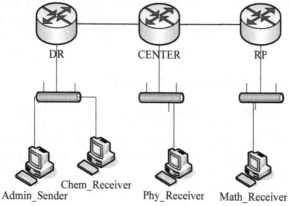

Fig. 3. Network topology of the receivers locating between RP and the sender

2.3 Simulation Results and Analysis

In the first scenario, through analysis of experimental results as follows we get following conclusions:

(1) The traffic of PIM-SM multicast is less than that of unicast, and the link occupancy rate is also lower. Because that simulation is taken in the absence of background application and noise interference, the data traffic of unicast is about 3 times of that of multicast (traffic of unicast is 30 packets/sec, and that of multicast is 10 packets/sec). It illuminates that the need of the bandwidth to realize the video conference by unicast is in direct proportion to the number of the group members. It is because that the data source must send a copy of data packets to every group member, while the source only needs to send the same data packets once in the multicast case.

(2) The end-to-end delay of multicast using PIM-SM is more than that of unicast. In our simulation, the end-to-end delay of not using RPT-SPT-switch technology is two times of that of unicast. It is because that the data source host needs to send the packets to RP, and then RP forwards them to every receiver in the group.

In the second scenario, it is clear that PIM-SM has a particular delay when switching from RPT to SPT. Hereinto, the link occupancy of Backbone Router2 to Backbone Router3 is based on RPT, while the link occupancy of Backbone Router1 to Backbone Router3 is based on SPT. Because the routers calculate the data transmit rate every 600 seconds and the first result is over the threshold value 0.5 packets/sec, there is a switchover at the 10th minute. Apparently, the crossing point of the two curves represents the moment when switching from RPT to SPT. Before and after the switchover, the sum occupancy of the two backbones is a constant value, as the same as our expectation. Switching from RPT to SPT is not direct but a course.

In the third scenario, we get the results of the end-to-end delay from the three receivers in the different locations. We found that the end-to-end delay of Chem_Receiver is the smallest, because Chem_Receiver which is in the same LAN of the sender can receive the data packets directly rather than receive them through routers. The turning points emergence at the moment of CENTER switching from RPT to SPT. The end-to-end delay of Phy_Receiver reduces after switching from RPT to SPT, because the multicast packets of Phy_Receiver received are forwarded along DR->CENTER->RP->CENTER before the switchover, and forwarded along DR->CENTER after the switchover. The end-to-end delay of Math_Receiver increases after switching to SPT, because the multicast packets of Math_Receiver received are both forwarded along DR->CENTER->RP before and after the switchovers, and DR needs to forward multicast packets to CENTER in the SPT besides forwarding packets to RP. As shown in figure 4(a) and 4(b), the number of packets of DR sending to CENTER has doubled after switching to SPT. Thus, forwarding dual packets increases the processing time of routers, so the end-to-end delay of Math_Receiver increases as a result.

Figure 4(c) and 4(d) show the traffic between RP and CENTER. As expected, the number of packets of RP sending to CENTER reduces to half of the former number when CENTER is switched to SPT. Apparently the forwarding policy of PIM-SM is not optimal when the receivers locate between the sender and RP. PIM-SM still forwards some redundant multicast packets, and it is possible to reduce the end-to-end delay.

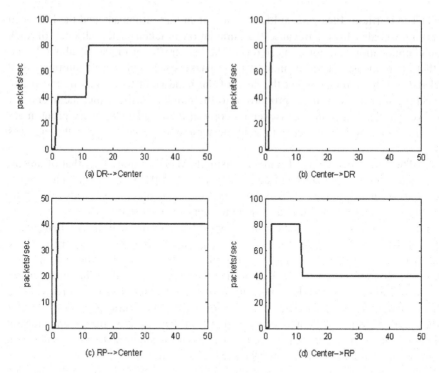

Fig. 4. Traffic of inter-routers

3 Improvements of the PIM-SM Protocol

From the test results and analysis of the above scenarios, it is clear that there are some disadvantages in the standard PIM-SM as follows: the routers or hosts cannot get packets from their upriver router which already has group members when the packets pass by the router in the course of the sender sending packets to RP, and they can only receive from RP; in the case of the router switching from RPT to SPT and their paths being some or all of coincidence, the router conforming to PIM-SM will still send some superfluous multicast packets, and the forwarding policy is not optimal. For the purpose of reducing the number of packets and the end-to-end delay of group members, we present some improvements on PIM-SM as follows.

(1) Improvement of the format of the routing item
The routers supporting PIM-SM include two types of routing items about PIM-SM. One is (*,G) and the other is (S,G). In fact, those two types of items can be represented by the same data structure, and distinguished only by a flag. At the same time, we optimize the routing item of PIM-SIM, which saves the storage and improves the router processing speed.

Besides saving the storage space of PIM-SM routing entities(items) in the routers, another more important advantage of this design is that it merges the item (*,G) and

(S,G), and makes them to use the same export list, and considers the item (S,G) in priority. So it can solve the problem of the PIM-SM router forwarding dual packets when SPT and RPT are some or all of coincidence.

(2) Registering routing items of the source host

The source host S sends packets to RP through its DR according to the shortest unicast path. The standard PIM-SM carries out the course in the direction of RP in the form of unicast. Different from the standard one, the ameliorated PIM-SM will check if there is the item (S,G) or (*,G) besides forwarding packets along the shortest unicast path, in order to decide whether there is a need to forward packets to the interfaces besides RP. The improvement solves the problem of the packets not being forwarded immediately by the routers which have multicast members when the packets pass by these routers in the course of the source sending packets to RP. After the routers along the path receive the registration info of the source host, PIM-SM will run as follows:

  a) Check if there is the routing item (S,G); if not, then create the item (S,G);

  b) Set the import list of (S,G) include the interfaces which have received packets;

  c) Check if there is the routing item (*,G); if there is, then copy the export list of the routing item (*,G) into that of the routing item (S,G), and grid rid of the interfaces which is included in the import list of (S,G) from the export list;

  d) If there is not an item (*,G), and if this router self is the RP of a designated group, then set the export list of (S, G) as (null), otherwise set it as the exit to RP;

  e) If the export list of (S, G) is not null, then forward packets to the interfaces included in the list.

4 Conclusion

Presently, PIM-SM is the standard Multicast Routing Protocol. Its design makes it effective to run on the WAN where the multicast groups are distributed sparsely. PIM-SM retains the traditional IP multicast service model in which the receivers initialize the group membership, and supports the shared tree and the shortest path tree.

This paper makes an analysis of PIM-SM, and carries out the corresponding simulations by OPNET. The simulations realize the basic functions of this protocol and design three scenarios. As the simulation results show, in contrast to unicast, PIM-SM consumes less bandwidth, resulting in lower link occupancy rate. However, the higher end-to-end delay makes the switching from RPT to SPT long. We have also found that PIM-SM will forward redundant packets when the recipient router locates between the sender router and RP. It is possible that the end-to-end delay of group members can be further reduced. At the end, the paper analyzes the disadvantages of the standard PIM-SM and presents some improvements. Research on the management of multicast in complex networks is our major work in future.

References

1. Bae, K.-J., Kwon, D.-H., Kim, W.-J., Suh, Y.-J.: An Efficient Multicast Routing Protocol in Multi-rate Wireless Ad Hoc Networks. In: Zhou, X., Sokolsky, O., Yan, L., Jung, E.-S., Shao, Z., Mu, Y., Lee, D.C., Kim, D.Y., Jeong, Y.-S., Xu, C.-Z. (eds.) EUC Workshops 2006. LNCS, vol. 4097, pp. 93–102. Springer, Heidelberg (2006)
2. Chen, S.-C., Dow, C.-R., Wang, R.-D., et al.: A Reliable Multicast Routing Protocol Based on Recovery Points and FEC in Mobile Ad-hoc Networks. Wireless Personal Communications 19(5), 76–82 (2008)
3. Xia, D., Li-min, S., Jian-xin, W., et al.: On-demand multicast routing protocol based on node classification in MANET. Journal of Central South University of Technology 13(2), 190–195 (2006)
4. Wen, C.-C., Wu, C.-S., Chen, K.-J.: Centralized Control and Management Architecture Design for PIM-SM Based IP/MPLS Multicast Networks. In: Proceedings of Global Telecommunications Conference, GLOBECOM 2007, November 26-30, pp. 443–447. IEEE Computer Society, Los Alamitos (2007)
5. Li, D., Wu, J., Xu, K., et al.: Performance analysis of multicast routing protocol PIM-SM. In: Proceedings of Advanced Industrial Conference on Telecommunications/Service Assurance with Partial and Intermittent Resources Conference, pp. 157–162. IEEE Computer Society, Los Alamitos (2005)
6. Lin, Y.-D., Hsu, N.-B., Pan, C.-J.: Extension of RP relocation to PIM-SM multicast routing. In: Proceedings of IEEE International Conference on Communications, 2001. ICC 2001, June 2001, vol. 1, pp. 234–238. IEEE Computer Society, Los Alamitos (2001)
7. SungHei, K., SoYoung, P., ShinGak, K.: PIM Multicast Spam Countering Method Using Blacklist in Rendezvous Point. In: Proceedings of 10th International Conference on Advanced Communication Technology, 2008, ICACT 2008, February 2008, vol. 1, pp. 539–543. IEEE Press, Los Alamitos (2008)

A Method for Querying Conserved Subnetwork in a Large-Scale Biomolecular Network

Jiang Xie[1,2], Weibing Feng[1], Shihua Zhang[3], Songbei Li[1], Guoyong Mao[4], Luwen Zhang[1], Tieqiao Wen[2], and Wu Zhang[1,2]

[1] School of Computer Engineering and Science,
Shanghai University, Shanghai 200072,
`jiangx@shu.edu.cn`
[2] Institute of Systems Biology, Shanghai University, Shanghai 200444
[3] Academy of Mathematics and Systems Science, CAS, Beijing 100080
[4] Department of Electronic Information and Electric Engineering,
Changzhou Institute of Technology, Changzhou 213002

Abstract. To uncover conserved pathways using systems biology methods, comparing various kinds of networks among different species or within a species becomes an increasingly important problem. With more and more molecular data being available, most of the current methods cannot deal with the large-scale networks owing to the computational scale limitation on a single PC or workstation. In this paper, we adopted an Immediate Neighbors-in-first Method for the biomolecular network querying problem. In contrast to other methods, we developed the parallel computing algorithm to treat large-scale networks. The efficient parallel performance of the present method is shown by Parkinson's Disease related protein interaction network.

1 Introduction

Since the birth of molecular biology, a great deal of knowledge on biological molecules has been accumulated. With further in-depth research and biotechnology development, investigators pay more and more attention to interactions between molecules and networks constructed by them rather than single molecule. Studies on those molecular networks provide new opportunities for understanding life science at a system-wide level [1,2].

Network alignment and network querying are typical network comparison methods [3]. In recent years, many investigators have contributed themselves to this field and made great progress [4,5,6,7,8]. A few querying tools have been developed, but searching a sub-network from a large network is a problem of local network comparison, involving large scale computation and belongs to NP hard cluster. The existing network querying tools are still at an early stage and far from perfect [3]. The bottleneck is that biomolecular networks are complex networks and querying a sub-network is computationally demanding.

To meet the demand of computational complexity and deal with large-scale biomolecular networks, an effective way is to adopt parallel computation. In this

W. Zhang et al. (Eds.): HPCA 2009, LNCS 5938, pp. 473–478, 2010.

paper we adopt the Immediate Neighbors-in-first Method (INM) for biomolecular network and propose its parallel computing algorithm, and the performance of parallel computing is demonstrated by Parkinson's Disease related protein interaction network (PIN).

2   Biomolecular Network Querying

A biomolecular network can be represented as a undirected or directed graph. Each node in the graph represents a molecule, and each edge represents the relationship between two molecules.

The biomolecular network querying problem that we will study in this paper, aims to discovery sub-networks that are identical or most similar to the target within or cross species in the biological sense. The characteristics of the proposed method is that it bases on attributes (such as sequences or function) of molecules themselves and increases the chance that two molecules will be matched if their neighbors have been matched. We call the algorithm Immediate Neighbors-in-first Method(INM). The INM for querying sub-networks from graph G_0 is divided in four phases here.

2.1   Initialize the Similarity Scores of Molecules

Let $G_0 = (V_1, E_1)$ (undirected graph) or $G_0 = (V_1, E_1, \lambda)$ (directed graph), where $|V_1| = n_1$, and $G_t = (V_2, E_2)$ (undirected graph) or $G_t = (V_2, E_2, \lambda)$ (directed graph), where $|V_2| = n_2$. Here G_t is the target sub-network. G_0 and G_t are represented by their adjacency matrix $A_1(n_1 \times n_1)$ and $A_2(n_2 \times n_2)$. $A_{n_1 \times n_2}$ is the similarity matrix S, where the entry $S(a, b)$ indicates the similarity coefficient between the node $a \in G_0$ and node $b \in G_t$. The initial value of $S(a, b)$ is $Sim(a, b)$.

In the case of the metabolic graphs, the similarity between enzymes can be defined as Tohsato [9] or Pawlowski [10] did. If it is the PIN or gene regulatory network, we compute the initial similarity by E-value, which is computed by BLAST [11], converted into number between 0 and 1, and treated as initial value. Regardless of the manner in which the initial value of $S(a, b)$ is obtained, $Sim(a, b)$ expresses relationship of the function or sequence of molecule a and b.

2.2   Computation of Similar Scores between Molecules

Biomolecular networks are different from each other not only because of differences in their components, but also in their network architectures. To take into account both of the two aspects, the topological information of network and the initial values should be put together.

Similarity of network topological structure can be described as $A1$-$A4$ and $D1$-$D4$ proposed by [12] [13] for general network querying. Considering incorrectness and incompleteness of experiment data [14,15,16], the INM computes the similar coefficient in matrix S as follows, in which mathematical definition of $A1$-$A4$ can be found in [13].

Initialization

$$S^0(a,b) = Sim(a,b) \qquad (1)$$

Iteration

$$S^{(k+1)}(a,b) = \frac{A_1^k(a,b) + A_2^k(a,b) + A_3^k(a,b) + A_4^k(a,b)}{2} \times Sim(a,b) \qquad (2)$$

Normalization

$$S \leftarrow \frac{S}{\| S \|_2} \qquad (3)$$

So the similarity information of network topology is added upon initial value, and the similar coefficient that involves both function and topology information of molecules is obtained by iteration.

2.3   Querying by Immediate Neighbors-In-First

After building the similarity matrix S, we are ready to start implementation of network querying. Molecules in same functional module often have similar function, take part in one molecular process, or form one signaling pathway etc., so based on NBM [17], the INM is immediate neighbors-in-first, which creases similarity of their neighbors while two nodes have been matched. Then according to the similarity matrix S of G_0 and G_t, the matched nodes and the edges between them in G_0 construct the result sub-network G_s [18].

2.4   Computing Graph Similarity Score

As mentioned above, similarity of two biomolecular networks is not only the similarity of their molecules, but also that of the relationship between the molecules. So the similarity score of G_s and G_t is computed as [18].

3   Parallel Computing

The INM aims at studying the similarity between biomolecular networks. So far for some species such as Fly, Yeast and Human, magnitude of proteins that their interactions exist in databases is about 10^3, the interactions is 10^4, and these data is rising continuously [20]. Challenge is emerging with dramatically growth of data resource. In order to meet requirements of computing large scale biomolecular network, we designed the parallel strategy of the INM.

3.1   Method

The parallel computing environment is the cluster of workstations (COW): 14 IBM HS21 blade servers and 2 x3650 servers are the computing and management nodes, each node is equipped two dual-cores CPU and 4GB memory, and connected to each other by 1KM Ethernet and 2.5G infiniBand. The storage is distributed and memory shared. The operation system for this COW is Linux, programming environment is Message Passing Interface (MPI), and the language is C/C++.

As described above, the INM is mainly composed of two parts: one is initialization of the similarity matrix S of G_t and G_0, the other is network querying. The former is $n_0 \times n_t$ iteration of matrix (where number of nodes is n_0 and n_t in G_0 and G_t respectively), and the computational complexity is $O((n_0 \times n_t)^2)$. The latter is querying the similar nodes and increasing the similarity coefficient of their neighbors, and the computational complexity is $O(n_1 \times n_2)$. So most computational time is cost for the former part, namely the initialization of similarity matrix.

Therefore, partition of parallel tasks for the INM is to decompose the initialization process of the similarity matrix S. Let entry $s_{ij} = S(a, b)$ in S indicates the similarity score between node $a \in G_0$ and $b \in G_t$, where $i = 0...n_0 - 1, j = 0...n_t - 1$, we decompose S by row to partition parallel tasks. The initialization process of S in parallel algorithm is as follows.

1. Send S_x (initial value is S_0) to each processor.

2. According to the number of itself, each processor judges which row in S_x will be computed in the local, the rule is: entry s_{ij}^x $(j = 0...n_t - 1)$ in row i is computed by node which number is $(i \bmod k)$, where k is the total number of processors.

3. Each processor computes similarity between s_{ij}^x $(j = 0...n_t - 1)$ that need to process in the local and each entries in S_x, obtains s_{ij}^{x+1} $(j = 0...n_t - 1)$, and sends the result to NO.0 processor.

4. No. 0 processor adjudges whether S_{x+1} has converged. If not, then S_x is replaced by S_{x+1}, and repeat steps 1-4. Otherwise stop computing.

3.2 Performance Evaluation

To study Parkinson's Disease (PD), our biological research group obtained some differentially expressed proteins in the Fly model. Based on the PIN dataset in [16], which includes 7038 proteins and 20720 interactions, we construct the target sub-network G_t, which includes 60 proteins and 100 interactions of Fly. The G_0 is PIN of human that is obtained from HPRD [19] and involves 6340 proteins and 23591 interactions.

The computing time as a function of the number of processors used for querying sub-network G_t in G_0 is shown in Table 1. As we know, performance of parallel computing is often evaluated by two indicators, one is the speedup, and the other is the scalability. The two indicators of this parallel algorithm are shown in Fig. 1. It indicates that the algorithm has good performance.

Table 1. Computing time for different processors

processors	1	2	4	6	8	10	12
time (s)	244.26	169.2	129.98	77.08	66.41	54.21	46.73

(A)   (B)

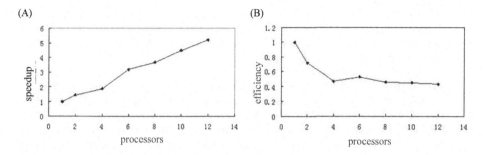

Fig. 1. (A). Speedup of parallel computing. (B). Efficiency of parallel computing.

4 Conclusions and Future Work

Similarity between biomolecular networks is of great significance in species evolution and diseases investigation. With expansion of biomolecular networks, the computing scale of conventional sequential algorithms gradually cannot meet the requirements of bioinformatics. The INM is developed to achieve biomolecular network querying, hence sub-networks that are identical or similar to the target network within or cross species in a biological sense can be discovered. The parallel algorithm of the INM is developed to treat with large-scale networks. Experimental results demonstrate that its speedup and scalability are promising.

To keep pace with the development of bioinformatics, some challenging problems should be considered in the future studies. Heuristic algorithm should be taken into account to reduce correlation between molecules during iteration, and new parallel strategies should be adopted to further improve parallel efficiency. Moreover, computational results should be labored to mine more information in biomolecular networks.

Acknowledgement

This work is part supported by the National Basic Research Program of China under Grant No.2006CB500702, Shanghai Leading Academic Discipline Project under Grant No.J50103 and Shanghai University Systems Biology Research Fund.

References

1. Zhang, S.H., Zhang, X.S., Chen, L.: Biomolecular network querying: a promising approach in systems biology. BMC Systems Biology 2, 5 (2008)
2. Zhao, X.M., Wang, R.S., Chen, L.N., Aihara, K.: Uncovering signal transduction networks from high-throughput data by integer linear programming. Nucl. Acids Res. 36(9), e48 (2008)

3. Sharan, R., Ideker, T.: Modeling cellular machinery through biological network comparison. Nature Biotechnology 24(4), 427–433 (2006)
4. Kelley, B.P., Yuan, B., Lewitter, F., Sharan, R., Stockwell, B.R., Ideker, T.: Path-BLAST: a tool for alignment of protein interaction networks. Nucleic Acids Research, w83–w88 (2004)
5. Sharan, R., Suthram, S., Kelley, R.M., Kuhn, T., McCuine, S., Uetz, P., Sittler, T., Karp, R.M., Ideker, T.: Conserved patterns of protein interaction in multiple species. PNAS 102(6), 1974–1979 (2005)
6. Kelley, B.P., Sharan, R., Karp, R.M., Sittler, T., Root, D.E., Stockwell, B.R., Ideker, T.: Conserved pathways within bacteria and yeast as revealed by global protein network alignment. PNAS 100(20), 11394–11399 (2003)
7. Pinter, R.Y., Rokhlenko, O., Yeger-Lotem, E., Ziv-Ukelson, M.: Alignment of metabolic pathways. Bioinformatics 21(16), 3401–3408 (2005)
8. Shlomi, T., Segal, D., Ruppin, E., Sharan, R.: QPath: a method for querying pathways in a protein-protein interaction network. BMC Bioinformatics 7, 199 (2006)
9. Tohsato, Y., Matsuda, H., Hashimoto, A.: A Multiple Alignment Algorithm for Metabolic Pathway Analysis Using Enzyme Hierarchy. In: Proceedings of the Eighth International Conference on Intelligent Systems for Molecular Biology, pp. 376–383. AAAI Press, Menlo Park (2000)
10. Pawlowski, K., Jaroszewski, L., Rychlewski, L., Godzik, A.: Sensitive sequence comparison as protein function predictor. In: Pac. Symp. Biocomput., pp. 42–53 (2000)
11. Altschul, S.F., Gish, W., Miller, W., Myers, E.W., Lipman, D.J.: Basic Local Alignment Search Tool. Journal of Molecular Biology 215, 403–410 (1990)
12. Heymans, M., Singh, A.K.: Deriving phylogenetic trees from the similarity analysis of metabolic pathways. Bioinformatics 19, i138–i146 (2003)
13. Heymans, M., Singh, A.K.: Building phylogenetic trees from the similarity analysis of metabolic pathways. Department of Computer Science, University of California, Santa, Barbara, 2002-33 (2002)
14. Maslov, S., Sneppen, K.: Specificity and stability in topology of protein networks. Science 296, 910–913 (2002)
15. Deane, C.M., Salwinski, L., Xenarios, I., Eisenberg, D.: Protein interactions: two methods for assessment of the reliability of high throughput observations. Molecular Cell Proteomics 1(5), 349–356 (2002)
16. Bandyopadhyay, S., Sharan, R., Ideker, T.: Systematic identification of functional orthologs based on protein network comparison. Genome Research 16, 428–435 (2006)
17. He, H., Singh, A.K.: Closure-Tree: An Index Structure for Graph Queries. In: ICDE 2006: Proceedings of the 22nd International Conference on Data Engineering, p. 38. IEEE Computer Society, Washington (2006)
18. Xie, J.: Numerical simulation of protein interaction network. Doctoral thesis of Shanghai University (2008)
19. Mishra, G., Suresh, M., Kumaran, K., Kannabiran, N.: Human Protein Reference Database - 2006 update. Nucleic Acids Research 34, D411–D414 (2006)
20. Xie, J., Zhang, X., Zhang, W.: PSE-Bio: a grid enabled problem solving environment for bioinformatics. In: Proceedings of the Third IEEE International Conference on e-science and Grid Computing, pp. 529–535 (2007)

Conflict Analysis of Multi-source SST Distribution

Lingyu Xu[1], Pingen Zhang[1], Jun Xu[1], Shaochun Wu[1],
Guijun Han[2], and Dongfeng Xu[3]

[1] Department of Computer Engineer and Science,
Shanghai University Shanghai, 200072 Shanghai, China
xly@shu.edu.cn
[2] National marine Data and Information Service
[3] The Second Institute of Oceanography, SOA

Abstract. This article focuses on evaluating the quality of sea surface temperature (SST) observed by satellite remote sensing. Due to the Grubbs test's limitations [1] when analyzing multi-source satellites SST, an improved algorithm is proposed, which is found to be more effective than the traditional variance method when quantifying the differences and conflicts of SST. And the improved method is applied in SST product in East China Sea waters for the year 2006: confirming a set of highly consistent points, finding and eliminating outlying data, digging out abnormal waters, and providing references for the subsequent researchers to evaluate the quality of marine information.

1 Introduction

As the development of satellite remote sensing technique, it can do repeated measurement in the same temporal and spatial in most of global areas, the series satellites which could provide high-quality and large-scale SST data, mainly including HY-1, FY-2 (china), NOAA, SeaWiFS, EOS/MODIS (US) and MTSAT(Japan) [2]. SST, being one of the most important geophysical parameters in the ocean, plays an important role in global climate change. The technique to obtain SST has the problems of coverage overlapping, information redundancy and so on. Therefore, how to discover the conflict relationship and inconsistency has become an important subject as to investigate the marine information. Hosoda [3] used standard deviation to conduct cross-validation on GLI SST and AMSR SST, and drew a conclusion that the general value was about $\leq 1°C$. Iwasaki [4] made mutual contrast validation on the following four kinds of data: (CAOS) SST, (MWOI) SST, (MGD) SST and (RTG) SST, and he also analyzed the difference and defect of each data. Barton [5] conducted inter-comparison on the data (NOAA-16/AVHRR SST, ENVISAT/AATSR SST, Terra & Aqua/MODISSST) for the year 2003, then obtained the conclusion that the temperature error is $\leq 0.61°C$ near the waters of Australia.

The methods available for judging the outliers among the data of remote sensor satellites, including comparing with the field measured data [6,7], variance criterion and so on. The variance criterion is widely used to describe the confliction among the satellites data. However, these methods all have limitation in different degree. Refer-

W. Zhang et al. (Eds.): HPCA 2009, LNCS 5938, pp. 479–484, 2010.

ences [6,7] both adopted comparison modes to measure abnormality in satellites data, and argued that the best manner to check the accuracy of remote sensor satellites SST is to conduct field measurement while satellites pass the area. Taking field measured data as true value. Whether satellite data contains outlier, is identified by comparing it with the field measurement.

2 Grubbs Test and Analysis

Grubbs test is a prevailing method to detect the outlying data in dataset, and had been collected by the Chinese criterion (G1B4883-85) and US criterion test method (ASTM E178-68).

2.1 Grubbs Test[1]

Assuming to conduct equally precise and independent multi-measurement on a certain variable, then we have $x_1, x_2, \cdots, x_n$.

Where, x_i obeys normal distribution, $\bar{x} = \dfrac{1}{n}\displaystyle\sum_{i=1}^{n} x_i$ is the mean, and $v_i = x_i - \bar{x}$ is the residual variance.

According to Bessel formula, we have standard deviation: $\sigma \approx \sqrt{\dfrac{\displaystyle\sum_{i=1}^{n} v_i^2}{(n-1)}}$ order to test whether there exists any gross error within x_i ($i = 1, 2, 3, \cdots, n$), arranging x_i into statistics $x_{(i)}$ ranked in the order of $x_{(1)} \leq x_{(2)} \leq \cdots \leq x_{(n)}$.

Two equations are obtained: $g_{(n)} = \dfrac{x_{(n)} - \bar{x}}{\sigma}$ and $g_{(1)} = \dfrac{\bar{x} - x_{(1)}}{\sigma}$

where, $x_{(n)}$ =largest observation and $x_{(1)}$ = smallest observation. Setting the value of significance level α (normally is 0.05 or 0.01), and we can query the critical value $g_0(n, \alpha)$ [1]. Then two equations are obtained as following:

$$P\left(\frac{\bar{x} - x_{(1)}}{\sigma} \geq g_0(n, \alpha) \right) = \alpha \quad \text{and} \quad P\left(\frac{x_{(n)} - \bar{x}}{\sigma} \geq g_0(n, \alpha) \right) = \alpha$$

If $x_{(1)}$ and $x_{(n)}$ are questionable observations, let $g_{(1)} = \dfrac{\bar{x} - x_{(1)}}{\sigma}$ and $g_{(n)} = \dfrac{x_{(n)} - \bar{x}}{\sigma}$.

If $g_{(i)} \geq g_0(n, \alpha)$, the ith measurement is supposed to be a possible outlier. The largest value exceeding the threshold is regarded to be an outlier and the measurement is removed from the dataset. Then the Grubbs test is performed again to see if there is any more outlier.

On mathematics, it had been proved that if there is only one outlier in dataset, Grubbs test is the best method compared to other test methods. The most significant problem, however, lies in the situation that the standard deviation and mean are affected by two or multiple outlying values so that no outliers are detected. The limitation of Grubbs test tends to cause the phenomenon of false alarm or missing alarm. Missing alarm means taking abnormal value as normal value, while false alarm means taking normal value as abnormal value.

3 Improved Grubbs Test

Grubbs test has obviously limitation, and no outlier will be detected when the test is applied to the dataset with multiple outliers, for the outliers may be masked by large standard deviation. When the standard deviation of dataset is too large or too small, it is tend to cause the phenomenon of false alarm or missing alarm. Therefore, in order to avoid missing alarm and false alarm caused by Grubbs test, Grubbs test should be improved. According to the character of SST data and the experience of experts, this paper sets threshold values for the group of satellites observation, which can effectively compensate the limitation of Grubbs test. The improved method is presented by the following Table 1:

Table 1. Explanation of improved algorithm

interval / Improved method \ Original method	confliction	non-confliction
(0~0.3)	False alarm	non-confliction
(0.3~0.5)	confliction	non-confliction
>0.5	confliction	Missing alarm

As seen from Table 1, the improved method mainly through setting the threshold value for standard deviations, it conducts judgment basing on the result of Grubbs test. When the standard deviation of a group observation is (0~0.3), but Grubbs test proved it has confliction; then we think dataset has false alarm according to the improved method. When the value of standard deviation is (>0.5), and Grubbs test verdict it has no confliction; then it exists missing alarm according to the improved method.

4 Experiment

This paper chose East China Sea waters as trial area to conduct the analysis of conflict relationship, area coverage $(16.125°N \sim 33.125°N, 122.125°E \sim 139.875°E)$, date Jan 1,2006, spatial resolution 4.7km. Eleven products of remote sensing satellites were adopted in this study. The location, with 7 observations at least, was chosen within the observation area coverage, and 905 data samples were totally gained.

To address the validity of the improved method, a comparison with respect to original method and improved method was done, based on the experiment result of the two methods. The comparing result is shown in Fig. 1.

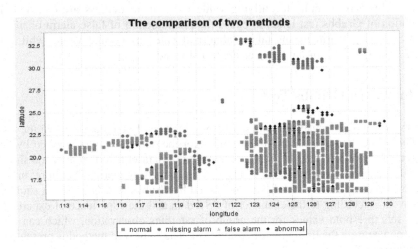

Fig. 1. The comparison between two methods. As seen from Fig.1, red diamond, black lozenge, blue circle and green triangle were respectively used to represent non-confliction area, confliction area, error alarm area and missing alarm area in this paper.

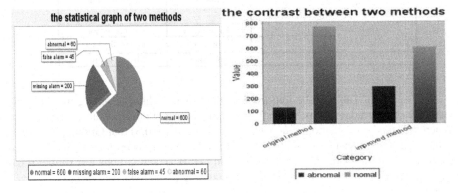

Fig. 2. The statistical graph of the result. The numbers of non-confliction area, confliction area, false alarm area and missing alarm area are respectively 600, 200, 45 and 60. The improved method can identify 295 confliction areas, however, the original method is only 129.

5   Argo Float Data Prove the Correctness of Improved Method

50 argo float data were gained in this study, the area coverage is $(16.125°N \sim 33.125°N, 122.125°E \sim 139.875°E)$, and the date is July.1 2006. Firstly, original method and improved method were respectively used to identify the conflicting relationship of these 50 satellites remote data in responding place; then argo float data were used to validate the results of these two methods. As seen from Fig.3.

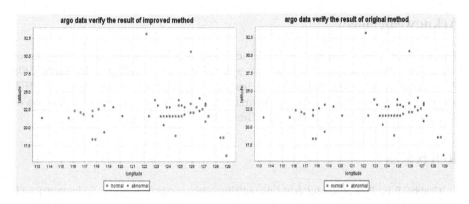

Fig. 3. Using argo float data to validate the original method. As to the data under test, 19 outlying data and 31 normal data were identified by original method; while 30 outlying data and 20 normal data were identified by improved method. Through analyzing, it is discovered that there are 13 right results and 37 wrong results found by original method compared to 42 right results and 8 wrong results found by improved method.

6   Application of Improved Method

In the following, this paper will apply the improved method to analyze area confliction relationship of satellite field data in East China Sea waters, the area arrange is $(16.125°N \sim 33.125°N, 122.125°E \sim 128.875°E)$. The analyzing results as seen in Fig.4.

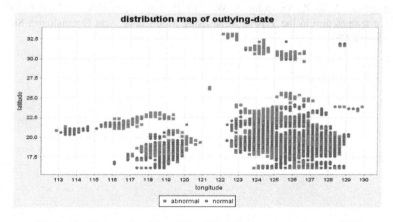

Fig. 4. Conflict relationship of East China Sea waters in the year 2006

Through the analyses of Fig.4, it was discovered that the conflicting relationship of the satellites data is quite serious in the East China Sea waters, where the area coverage is about $(19.125°N \sim 21.125°N, 123.875°E \sim 125.875°E)$; the phenomenon is likely caused by the warm current or cold snap in this area. However, in the area where the coverage range is about $(21.300°N \sim 25.125°N, 123.125°E \sim 126.875°E)$, the SST data among satellites is reliable.

Acknowledgements

This research were supported by the Hi-tech Research and Development Program of China (863 Program 2006A-A09Z138), and the project of Advance Research (908 Program 908-03-01-05), and Shanghai leading Academic Discipline Project J50103, and the fifth season key subject of Shanghai, and the Natural Science Foundation of Shanghai Municipality of China under Grant No. 08ZR1408400.

References

1. Grubbs, F.E.: Procedures for detecting outlying observations in samples. Technometrics 11, 1–10 (1969)
2. Shi, S.: Study on Soft Fusion Strategy of Multi-Channel Incertitude Information in Digital Ocean, pp. 16–74. Northeastern University, Shenyang (2005)
3. Hosoda, H., Murakami, H., et al.: Difference Characteristics of Sea Surface Temperature Observed by GLI and AMSR Aboard ADEOS-II. Journal of Oceanography 62, 339–350 (2006)
4. Iwasaki, S., Kubota, M., Tomita, H.: Inter-comparison and evaluation of global sea surface temperature products. International Journal of Remote Sensing 29, 500–512 (2008)
5. Barton, I., Pearce, A.: Validation of GLI and other satellite-derived sea surface temperatures using data from the Rottnest Island ferry. Western Australia Journal of Climate 16, 73–87 (2006)
6. Gao, G.-p., Qian, C.g.-c., Bao, X.-w., Shi, M.-c.: Difference between the PFSST and the in-situdata in East China Sea. Acta Oceanalogica Sinica 23, 122–124 (2001)
7. Chun-gui, Z., Xing, Z., Yin-dong, Z., Wei-hua, P., Jing, L.: Retrieval and validation of sea surface temperature in the Taiwan Strait using Modis data. Acta Oceanalogica Sinica 30, 153–160 (2008)

Scientific Application Based Performance on Magic Cube*

Ying Xu, D.D. Zhang, and Lei Xu

Shanghai Supercomputing Center, Shanghai, China, 201203
{yxu,ddzhang,lxy}@ssc.net.cn
http://www.ssc.net.cn

Abstract. Magic Cube at Shanghai Supercomputing Center is the fastest supercomputer in east Asia. It is configured with 1920 16-Way SMP compute nodes, which gives 233 TFLOPS theoretical peak performance. The compute nodes are connected using Infiniband switches. In this study, we use STREAM micro-benchmark, random access in HPCC benchmark suite to understand the memory performance of Magic Cube's SMP compute node. The multi-zone version of NAS Parallel Benchmark suite (NPB-MZ) servers as the application performance evaluation tools.

1 Introduction

Developing scientific and engineering simulations for large-scale high performance system is a challenge task, especially with petascale supercomputer merging on TOP 500 list [7]. The high performance computing technology for these simulations will rely on a balance among the speed of processors, memory, memory bandwidth, network and etc.. The balance among these factors becomes more difficult with technologies such as multicore widely used in the supercomputers. Most systems in high-performance computing (HPC) feature a hybrid hardware design: shared memory nodes with several multi-core CPUs connected via high speed network.

The dominant programming models on hierarchically structured hardware are: pure MPI (Message Passing Interface), pure OpenMP and hybrid MPI+OpenMP. Most of the high-end supercomputers now virtually all consist of multi-core nodes connected by a high speed network. The idea of using OpenMP threads to exploit the multiple cores on computer nodes while using MPI to communicate among the nodes appears natural. It is always feasible to use pure MPI and treat each CPU cores as a separate MPI processor with its own memory space. However, with the hybrid programming model, the message passing inside the SMP node can be avoided and OpenMP threads provides the light-weighted parallel programming model. Several researchers recently conducted the performance study on some

* Sponsored by NSFC under Grant No. 90612017, National high-tech research development plan of China under Grant No. 2006AA01A112, Grand No. 2006AA01A117. and Grant No. 2006AA01A125.

W. Zhang et al. (Eds.): HPCA 2009, LNCS 5938, pp. 485–490, 2010.

large-scale supercomputers, such as SGI Altix 4700, Cray XT4, IBM Power5+ and etc.[6,5,1].

Magic Cube with peak floating point operation as 233.5Tflops is one of the top supercomputer in Asia and ranked No. 10 on November 2008 TOP 500 list. This Linux Cluster is configured with 1920 16-way blades connected via several Infiniband full crossbar switches. Each node is composed of 4 quad-core AMD Barcelona CPU with 2.0 GHz giving a theoretical peak performance of 128 Gflops/node per node. While the system offers nearly 2000 nodes and each node consists of 16-way multi-core configuration, Magic Cube enables a massive parallel computation and provides the researchers with various possible ways of multi-level, hybrid parallel computing options. The trend of increasing core per socket and per compute node will continue as the major chip manufactures improve the performance by increasing the core density. Hence the multi-level parallel computing is inevitable and this requires a strategic approach for better and more efficient computational performance.

In this study, we use the High Performance Computing Challenge (HPCC) [2] and STREAM micro-benchmarks [3] to develop a controlled understanding of Magic Cube, and then use this information to analyze and interpret the performance of the NAS Parallel Benchmark Multi-Zone version (NPB-MZ) [8]. In the following section, the benchmark suites used for this study are described in Section 2, followed by performance results and analysis in Section 3. The summary of the analysis will be presented in Section 4.

2   Benchmarks

In this study, the STREAM [3] and the random access benchmark in HPCC [2] are selected for the memory benchmark tests. NPB-MZ [8] is chosen as the scientific application performance tests. Although these benchmarks do not cover wide spectrum of various HPC applications, they provide an essential performance measure for a new supercomputer system.

The Multi-Zone version of the NAS Parallel Benchmark (NPB-MZ) is a hybrid parallel version of the three application benchmarks in NPB. The original NPBs exploit fine-grain parallelism in a single zone, while the multi-zone version enables in-depth analysis of hybrid and multi-level parallelization with its coarse-grain parallelism between zones with MPI and loop-level parallelism within each zone using OpenMP [8]. NPB-MZ contains three application benchmarks: BT-MZ, SP-MZ and LU-MZ. BT-MZ (uneven-sized zones) and SP-MZ (even-sized zones) test both coarse-grain and find-grain parallelism and load balance. LU-MZ is similar to SP-MZ but use a fixed number of zones (4×4). Load balancing for SP-MZ benchmark cases are relatively easy since the zone size is the same. On the other hand, mesh partition of BT-MZ generates different size zones due to the problem characteristics, which is closer to real application problems. Hence, with the imbalance load in BT-MZ benchmarks, to identify the best performance with hybrid parallel mode for BT-MZ could be critical in this study.

NPB-MZ suite has two hybrid versions. One is MPI+OpenMP, and the other option is SMP+OpenMP. The MPI+OpenMP mode is used for this study because it is suitable for the system architecture of Magic Cube, where MPI is used for communication between nodes and OpenMP is used for parallelization within one node. Selected problem size of NPB-MZ for the benchmark is Class C. The number of zones for BT-MZ and SP-MZ is 16×16 and the aggregate mesh sizes is $480 \times 320 \times 34$. The memory requirement is approximately 0.8 GB.

3   Benchmark Results and Results Analysis

In this section, the results from STREAM and random access benchmarks are discussed. We can understand the memory bandwidth of the compute node on Magic Cube from these two benchmarks' results. The NPB-MZ benchmark with problem size class C is discussed later this section.

3.1   STREAM and Random Access Benchmarks

With the multi-core architecture on the Magic Cube compute node, the OpenMP version STREAM benchmark is used, where the parallel for OpenMP directive is used in the benchmark. Since there are totally 16 physical cores on one compute node, the maximum number of OpenMP threads used here is 16. We use the environment variable provided by PGI compiler [4,9] to bind the OpenMP threads with the physical core ID. The following test cases are used to compare the effects of core binding with the random core binding scheduled by the operating system (seen in Table 1). In Table 1, CPU0, CPU1, CPU2 and CPU3

Table 1. Core binding test case for STREAM benchmark

Test Case ID	Description
8a	CPU0(0,1,2,3), CPU1(0,1,2,3)
8b	CPU0(0,1,2,3), CPU3(0,1,2,3)
8c	CPU0(0,1), CPU1(0,1), CPU2(0,1), CPU3(0,1)
12a	CPU0(0,1,2,3), CPU1(0,1,2,3), CPU2(0,1,2,3)
12b	CPU0(0,1,2), CPU1(0,1,2), CPU2(0,1,2), CPU3(0,1,2)

represent the CPU ID, and the numbers in the brackets are the core ID on one CPU. The test case with 16 OpenMP threads is also tested and the results are shown in Figure 1.

The results show that except Np=16, the memory bandwidth measured with core-binding is higher than that measured with OpenMP threads scheduled by the operation system, where the largest performance gain is almost 20% for test case 8a and 8b. The results for case 8c, 12b and Np=16 are very uniform across the compute nodes of Magic Cube exhibiting a performance of approximately 16GB/s for one compute node. The memory bandwidth of the test case 8c, 12b and Np=16 is around $5.34\% - 28.22\%$ higher compared with the memory bandwidth from the case where OpenMP threads are scheduled to physical CPU cores (no core binding case) by OS. Hence, with OpenMP threads evenly distributed to physical cores, the memory bandwidth is significantly improved compared with OpenMP threads bound to one or two CPUs and leaving other CPUs on the same node idle.

The random access benchmark is one of the seven benchmarks in HPC Challenge benchmark, which measures the rate of integer random updates of memory. A small percentage of random memory accesses (cache misses) in an application can significantly affect the overall performance of that application [2]. In the random access benchmark, MPI (message passing interface) is used to manage the multi-core processors on one compute node. In this study, the following three scenarios are tested: 4 cores on one CPU (4a), one core on each CPUs (4b) and all 16 cores used. The benchmark results are shown in Figure 2.

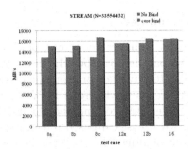

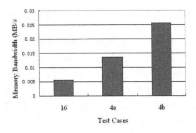

Fig. 1. The STREAM results   **Fig. 2.** Random Access results

It is noted that with MPI processors assigned to 16 cores on one compute node, the random access memory bandwidth is lowest among all three cases. The highest random access is obtained with 4 MPI processors assigned to 4 CPUs individually. Since random access benchmark does not update data along the cache line, with one MPI processor per CPU, the random access can utilize the shared L3 cache on one CPU and obtain best performance for this particular benchmark.

3.2   NPB-MZ Results Analysis

In this study, the application benchmarks using NPB-MZ are performed with BT-MZ and SP-MZ cases. There are six different size class in NPB-MZ, Class C is chosen to understand the scalability of Magic Cube. The problem size with Class D and E will be tested in the near future. The class C size requires running on a minimum of 8 processors and a maximum of 256 MPI processors. The number of OpenMP thread is chosen to be 2, 4, 8 here because compute nodes have a total of 16 CPU cores.

For the case SP-MZ, the overall mesh is partitioned such that the zones are identical in size, which makes it relatively easy to balance the load of the parallel application. However, BT-MZ (Block Tri-diagonal) case has unevenly partitioned zone size, where the size of zones spans significantly. The ratio of the largest zone over the smallest zone size is approximately 20, which makes it more difficult to balance the load than the load balance of SP-MZ.

For SP-MZ, the speedup in logarithmic scale is illustrated in Figure 3(a), where the speedup is calculated using the Mflops from serial performance as reference point. For the pure MPI runs, speedup (solid line with square symbols) is slightly higher than the ideal linear speed-up line, where the speedup for 256 MPI processes is more than 300. The speedups for hybrid runs with two and four OMP threads is slightly less than the linear speedup. With 8 OpenMP threads used, the speedup for 256 MPI processors (a total of 2048 cores) is 697, which is far less than the ideal linear speedup. These show that the fork/join of OpenMP threads consumes extra resource, and the overhead due to OpenMP threads increases with the number of OpenMP threads used.

For BT-MZ hybrid, the speedup of pure MPI illustrated in Figure 3(b) turns downward after running with 64 MPI processors, which clearly shows the scalability limitation of the pure MPI application. For BT-MZ hybrid runs with 2 and 4 OpenMP threads, the speedup is close to the linear speedup with 128, 256 and 512 cores used. For 8 OpenMP threads per MPI task, the speedup slightly decreases with a total of 1024 cores used. This result indicates that running in a hybrid mode using MPI processors with multiple OpenMP threads produces better scalability when the application has performance bottleneck owing to the communication overhead. With 8 OpenMP threads per MPI task, the overhead of OpenMP threads should still be taken into account.

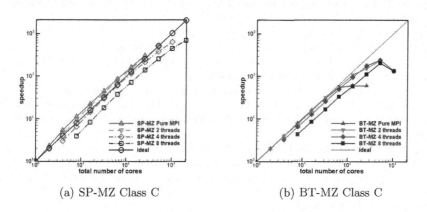

(a) SP-MZ Class C   (b) BT-MZ Class C

Fig. 3. Speedup for Class C: (a) SP-MZ; (b) BT-MZ

4   Conclusion

A series of benchmarks are performed using STREAM, Random access and NPB-MZ on Magic Cube in order to investigate the memory bandwidth and scalability of the system. STREAM benchmark shows a rather uniform performance of 16

GB/s memory bandwidth across the whole nodes. We also conduct a series of tests to investigate the STREAM performance with OpenMP threads bound to physical CPU core ID. With OpenMP threads evenly bound with physical CPUs, the memory bandwidth will be significantly improved compared to OpenMP threads bound to one or two CPUs and with CPU cores left idle.

The application-based benchmark test using NPB-MZ in hybrid mode were also performed. The study shows that running applications in hybrid mode using multiple OpenMP threads per MPI processor increase the scalability of the application. The pure MPI scientific applications usually hit performance bottleneck at a certain number of MPI processors. As the MPI processors number increases, the computational load partitioned on each MPI processors decreases while the communication overhead becomes greater. Increasing number of CPUs cores for MPI processors will deteriorate the scalability of the parallel applications. Using hybrid parallel programming mode offers additional opportunity for better scalability. With the MPI processors number kept the same, using more CPU cores per MPI tasks will increase the computational performance, while the communication time is still around the same level. Hence, the scalability can be improved substantially. In the future, NPB-MZ with the problem size class D and E will be investigated.

References

1. Kim, B.D., Cazes, J.E.: Performance and scalability study of SUN constellation cluster Ranger using application-based benchmarks. In: TeraGrid 2008 Conference (2008)
2. Koester, D., Lucas, B.: Hpc challenge benchmark: Randomaccess, http://icl.cs.utk.edu/projectsfiles/hpcc/RandomAccess/
3. McCalpin, J.D.: Stream: Sustainable memory bandwidth in high performance computers, http://www.cs.virginia.edu/stream/
4. PGI Group, PGI User's Guide, http://www.pgroup.com/doc/pgiug.pdf
5. Rabenseifner, R., Hager, G., Jost, G.: Hybrid MPI/OpenMP parallel programming on clusters of multi-core SMP nodes. Parallel, Distributed and Network-based Processing (427) (2009)
6. Saini, S., Talcott, D., Jespersen, D., Djomehri, J., Jin, H., Biswas, R.: Scientific application-based performance comparison of SGI Altix 4700, IBM Power5+, and SGI ICE 8200 Supercomputers. In: Supercomputing Conference. ACM, New York (2008)
7. http://www.top500.org/
8. Van der Wijingaart, R.F., Jin, H.: NAS parallel benchmarks, multi-zone versions. Technical report, NAS Technical Report NAS-03-010 (2003)
9. Xu, L., Zhang, D.D., Xu, Y.: A study of OpenMP multithread application execution performance on multicore architecure. Submitted to HPC China (October 2009)

Computation of Bounds for Exact Quantities of Interest in Elasticity Based on FEM and SFEM

Zhaocheng Xuan, Yaohui Li, and Hongjie Wang

Department of Computer Science, Tianjin University of Technology and Education,
Tianjin 300222, China
xuanzc@tute.edu.cn
Tel.: +86 22 2819 6397; Fax: +86 22 2819 6397

Abstract. We compute lower and upper bounds for the quantities of interest that are the functions of displacements in elasticity by finite element method (FEM) and smoothed finite element method (SFEM). An important feature of FEM based on the minimum potential energy principle is that it bounds the true strain energy of the structure from below, whereas SFEM, which has been found recently, generally provides bounds from above. We use the two methods to compute outputs–local displacements, local reaction and stress intensity factor in the elastic problems, and find that they do give the lower and upper bounds for the true outputs.

Keywords: Bounds, Quantities of interest, FEM, SFEM.

1 Introduction

A key ingredient for computing the output interval is the computation of global upper and lower bounds to the total strain energy [1–3]. We know that an approximation based on the potential energy principle (displacement method) which uses displacements as variables will give a lower bound to the global strain energy. Conversely, the complementary energy principle (equilibrium method) that uses stresses as variables will give an upper bound to the global strain energy [4, 5]. The difficulties arising with equilibrium methods are the processing of boundary conditions. The right hand side of the resulting discrete algebraic equation is zero if the displacement is zero on the Dirichlet boundary, and the applied loads cannot be implemented by merely striking out rows and columns of the flexibility equations, which is the usual way in which displacement boundary conditions are normally implemented in the displacement/stiffness method [6]. Recently a modified FEM with strain smoothing, SFEM, has been used to solve mechanics problems, and it has been found that in some situations the strain energy computed by SFEM bounds the exact strain energy from above [7, 8].

In this paper we study SFEM and give some inequalities for comparing the strain energies computed with FEM and SFEM. We then extend SFEM to compute lower and upper bounds to general linear output of linear elasticity.

W. Zhang et al. (Eds.): HPCA 2009, LNCS 5938, pp. 491–496, 2010.
© Springer-Verlag Berlin Heidelberg 2010

2   The Smoothed Finite Element Method

The problem domain Ω is divided into smooth subdomains $\Omega = \Omega_1 \cup \Omega_2 \cup ... \cup \Omega_N$ and $\Omega_i \cap \Omega_j = \emptyset$, $i \neq j$, where N is the number of total field nodes located in the entire problem domain. The smoot domain Ω_k for node k is created by connecting sequentially the mid-edge point to the centroid of the surrounding triangles of the node as shown in Fig. 1. Using the nodal based smoothing operation, the strain to be used in the smoothed method is assumed to be the smoothed strain on the smooth domain Ω_k. $\hat{\varepsilon}_k = \int_{\Omega_k} \omega(x - x_k)\varepsilon d\Omega$, where $\omega(x)$ is a diagonal matrix of the smoothing function $\omega(x)$. The smoothed strain $\hat{\varepsilon}_k$ is a constant over the smooth domain Ω_k. For two dimensional elasticity problems, the diagonal matrix $\omega(x) = \mathrm{diag}\{\omega(x), \omega(x), \omega(x)\}$. For simplicity, the smooth function $\omega(x)$ is taken as

$$\omega(x - x_k) = \begin{cases} 1/A_k, & \text{if } x \in \Omega_k \\ 0, & \text{if } x \notin \Omega_k \end{cases}$$

where $A_k = \int_{\Omega_k} d\Omega$ is the area of smoothing domain for node k. Therefore the smoothed strain in the smooth domain k will be $\hat{\varepsilon}_k = \frac{1}{A_k} \int_{\Omega_k} \varepsilon d\Omega$. Let us

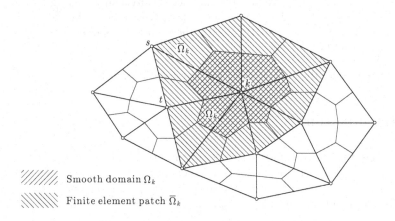

/////// Smooth domain Ω_k

\\\\\\\ Finite element patch $\overline{\Omega}_k$

Fig. 1. The finite element mesh and smooth domain

define the smoothed finite element solution to be $\hat{u}_h$ as the approximation of the solution, u, to the partial differential equation of elasticity, and Φ_i is the shape function matrix for node i, for example, for two dimensional problems the shape function matrix $\Phi_i(x) = \mathrm{diag}\{\phi_i(x), \phi_i(x)\}$, where $\phi_i(x)$ is the shape function for node i, the smoothed finite element solution is then expressed as $\hat{u}_h = \sum_{i=1}^{N} \Phi_i(x)\hat{u}_h^i$, where $\hat{u}_h^i = \{\hat{u}_{hx}^i, \hat{u}_{hy}^i\}^T$ is the vector of displacement at node i. Strain is given by the derivative of displacement, then we define the approximate strain obtained from the approximate displacements and not being smoothed as $\varepsilon(\hat{u}_h)$, that is $\varepsilon(\hat{u}_h) = \sum_{i=1}^{N} D\Phi_i(x)\hat{u}_h^i$, where D is the derivative matrix. By replacing ε with $\varepsilon(\hat{u}_h)$, we obtain the smoothed strain

$\hat{\varepsilon}_k$, $\hat{\varepsilon}_k(\hat{\boldsymbol{u}}_h) = \frac{1}{A_k} \int_{\Omega_k} \varepsilon(\hat{\boldsymbol{u}}_h) d\Omega$, and more specifically, $\hat{\varepsilon}_k(\hat{\boldsymbol{u}}_h) = \frac{1}{A_k} \sum_{i \in \mathcal{N}_k} \hat{\mathcal{B}}_k^i \hat{\boldsymbol{u}}_h^i$, where $\mathcal{N}_k$ includes all nodes in patch $\bar{\Omega}_k$ that is formed by the elements containing node k, and $\hat{\mathcal{B}}_k^i = \int_{\Omega_k} \mathcal{D}\Phi_i(\boldsymbol{x}) d\Omega$. In the next step we will derive the stiffness matrix. The strain energy in the smooth domain Ω_k is

$$\int_{\Omega_k} \hat{\varepsilon}_k^T(\hat{\boldsymbol{u}}_h) \boldsymbol{E} \hat{\varepsilon}_k(\hat{\boldsymbol{u}}_h) d\Omega = \frac{1}{A_k} \sum_{i \in \mathcal{N}_k} \sum_{j \in \mathcal{N}_k} \hat{\boldsymbol{u}}_h^{iT} \hat{\mathcal{B}}_k^{iT} \boldsymbol{E} \hat{\mathcal{B}}_k^j \hat{\boldsymbol{u}}_h^j.$$

Therefore the stiffness matrix associated with node k is obtained as $\hat{\boldsymbol{K}}_{ij(k)} = \frac{1}{A_k} \hat{\mathcal{B}}_k^{iT} \boldsymbol{E} \hat{\mathcal{B}}_k^j$, and the global stiffness matrix for smoothed method will be $\hat{\boldsymbol{K}}_{ij} = \sum_{k=1}^N \hat{\boldsymbol{K}}_{ij(k)}$. The entries (in sub-vectors of nodal forces) of the force vector $\hat{\boldsymbol{f}}$ in the right hand side of the algebraic system can be simply expressed as $\hat{\boldsymbol{f}}_i = \sum_{k \in \mathcal{N}_k} \hat{\boldsymbol{f}}_{i(k)}$. The above integration is also performed by a summation of integrals over smoothing domains; hence, $\hat{\boldsymbol{f}}_i$ is an assembly of nodal force vectors at the surrounding nodes of node k, $\hat{\boldsymbol{f}}_{i(k)} = \int_{\Omega_{(k)}} \Phi_i(\boldsymbol{x}) \boldsymbol{b} d\Omega + \int_{\Gamma_{t(k)}} \Phi_i(\boldsymbol{x}) \boldsymbol{t} d\Gamma$. Note that the force vector obtained in the smoothed method is the same as the one gotten in FEM, if the same order of shape functions is used. This simplifies the implementation of the smoothed method.

For any approximate strain computed by direct differentiation of the approximate displacement solutions, obtained on finite element mesh $\mathcal{T}_h$, and the smoothed strain, obtained on the same mesh, we have the so called orthogonal property for the smoothed method, that is

$$\int_{\Omega} \varepsilon^T(\hat{\boldsymbol{u}}_h) \boldsymbol{E} \hat{\varepsilon}(\hat{\boldsymbol{u}}_h) d\Omega = \int_{\Omega} \hat{\varepsilon}^T(\hat{\boldsymbol{u}}_h) \boldsymbol{E} \hat{\varepsilon}(\hat{\boldsymbol{u}}_h) d\Omega, \tag{1}$$

we should notice that $\hat{\varepsilon}(\hat{\boldsymbol{u}}_h)$ is a piecewise constant function over the whole domain.

With the above orthogonality we can obtain the property of the smoothed method assuring that the strain energy computed with the smoothed strain in $\mathscr{X}_h$ always bounds the strain energy obtained with the non-smoothed strain in $\mathscr{X}_h$ from below,

$$\int_{\Omega} \hat{\varepsilon}^T(\hat{\boldsymbol{u}}_h) \boldsymbol{E} \hat{\varepsilon}(\hat{\boldsymbol{u}}_h) d\Omega \leq \int_{\Omega} \varepsilon^T(\hat{\boldsymbol{u}}_h) \boldsymbol{E} \varepsilon(\hat{\boldsymbol{u}}_h) d\Omega. \tag{2}$$

Since the above inequality holds for any displacement in mesh $\mathcal{T}_h$, we can certainly replace $\hat{\boldsymbol{u}}_h$ with $\boldsymbol{u}_h$, i.e. the finite element solution expressed as $\boldsymbol{u}_h = \sum_{i=1}^N \Phi_i(\boldsymbol{x}) \boldsymbol{u}_h^i$, and obtain the lower bounds to the strain energy computed with FEM,

$$\int_{\Omega} \hat{\varepsilon}^T(\boldsymbol{u}_h) \boldsymbol{E} \hat{\varepsilon}(\boldsymbol{u}_h) d\Omega \leq \int_{\Omega} \varepsilon^T(\boldsymbol{u}_h) \boldsymbol{E} \varepsilon(\boldsymbol{u}_h) d\Omega. \tag{3}$$

The weak form for FEM is $\int_{\Omega} \varepsilon^T(\boldsymbol{u}_h) \boldsymbol{E} \varepsilon(\boldsymbol{v}) d\Omega = \int_{\Omega} \boldsymbol{b}^T \boldsymbol{v} d\Omega + \int_{\Gamma_N} \boldsymbol{t}^T \boldsymbol{v} d\Gamma$, for all $\boldsymbol{v} \in \mathscr{X}_h$, after imposing $\boldsymbol{v} = \boldsymbol{u}_h$ into the above equation, we have $\int_{\Omega} \varepsilon^T(u_h) E\varepsilon(u_h)d\Omega = \int_{\Omega} b^T u_h d\Omega + \int_{\Gamma_N} t^T u_h d\Gamma$. Both FEM and smoothed method have the same right hand side in the discrete form when the same shape function is used in mesh $\mathcal{T}_h$, then with the finite element solution u_h as the test function to the smoothed method we get $\int_{\Omega} \hat{\varepsilon}^T(\hat{u}_h) E\hat{\varepsilon}(u_h)d\Omega = \int_{\Omega} b^T u_h d\Omega + \int_{\Gamma_N} t^T u_h d\Gamma$, by comparing the above two equations, we have $\int_{\Omega} \varepsilon^T(u_h) E\varepsilon(u_h)d\Omega = \int_{\Omega} \hat{\varepsilon}^T(\hat{u}_h) E\hat{\varepsilon}(u_h)d\Omega$. We can omit the hat of $\hat{\varepsilon}(u_h)$ on the right hand side of the above equation, and obtain $\int_{\Omega} \hat{\varepsilon}^T(\hat{u}_h) E\hat{\varepsilon}(u_h)d\Omega = \int_{\Omega} \hat{\varepsilon}^T(\hat{u}_h) E\varepsilon(u_h)d\Omega$, then we have $\int_{\Omega} \varepsilon^T(u_h) E\varepsilon(u_h)d\Omega = \int_{\Omega} \hat{\varepsilon}^T(\hat{u}_h) E\varepsilon(u_h)d\Omega$. Therefore the followin inequality holds

$$\int_{\Omega} \varepsilon^T(u_h) E\varepsilon(u_h)d\Omega \leq \int_{\Omega} \hat{\varepsilon}^T(\hat{u}_h) E\hat{\varepsilon}(\hat{u}_h)d\Omega. \qquad (4)$$

With equations (2), (3) and (4), we obtain a sequence of inequalities for the strain energies computed with the strains obtained with both FEM and SFEM. More detailed derivation of these inequalities can be found in [9]. [7] gave the same inequality (4), and tried to prove that the strain energy computed with the smoothed method is also an upper bound to the exact strain energy under the hypothesis that shape functions exist for exact solutions. Many numerical examples show that the smoothed method really gives the upper bounds to the true strain energy, except for some cases with too coarse meshes.

3   An Example

In the example, linear triangle finite element approximations are used for both primal and dual problems, and uniform mesh refinement is used to illustrate the bounding property with respect to the mesh size. The example is a square elastic body with two rectangular holes, under the assumption to be in plane

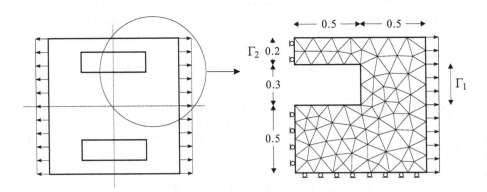

Fig. 2. An elasticity problem with symmetric geometry and load condition, a quarter of the structure is used for the finite element modeling. The finite element mesh shown in the right figure is the initial mesh with 132 elements.

stress state as shown in Fig. 2. A uniformly distributed force, $p = 1$, is applied on the left and right sides of the body. The non-dimensionalized Young modulus is 1.0 and Poisson ratio is 0.3. Since the geometry and load conditions in this problem are symmetric with respect to both the x- and y-axes, we only use a quarter of the body for the finite element model.

One output is considered in this example, it is the average normal displacement over the boundary Γ_1, $\ell_1^O(u) = \int_{\Gamma_1} u^T n \mathrm{d}\Gamma$, in which n is the unit outward normal to the boundary. The initial (coarse) mesh with respect to mesh size H is plotted in Fig. 2. The uniformly refined meshes are based on mesh sizes $H/2$, $H/4$, $H/8$, and $H/16$ respectively. The results for $\ell_1^O(u)$ and $\ell_2^O(u)$ including the outputs calculated with the finite element solutions, the upper and lower bounds, and the average of the upper and lower bounds are plotted in Fig. 3.

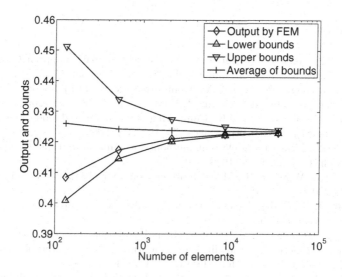

Fig. 3. The upper and lower bounds of the displacement output $\ell_1^O(u)$ (left) and the reaction output $\ell_2^O(u)$ (right)

4   Conclusions and Discussion

We have examined the smoothed method with linear triangle elements and extended it to compute upper and lower bounds to general linear outputs of displacements in elasticity. In the examples we have introduced the smoothed method behaves like an equilibrium method and the strain energy converges to the true strain energy from above. We also find that in some cases the energy norm of the solution by the smoothed method does not reach the exact strain energy, but it stays as an upper bound indication. But in most cases, the smoothed method really gives an upper bound for the strain energy and, consequently, also gives upper and lower bounds to general linear outputs. One of the most important advantages of bounds computation by the smoothed method is that they are very easy to implement. We do not need to revise many lines of our finite element code to implement the smoothed method. This is an advantage over the equilibrium method to obtain upper bounds. We also note that many a posteriori error estimates proposed in literature are an order of magnitude more expensive to be computed than the finite element solution. In contrast, the computation of upper bounds using the smoothed method is only about as expensive as solving the regular finite element problem.

Acknowledgement

This work is supported by the National Natural Science Foundation of China under the grant no. 10872146.

References

1. Xuan, Z.C., Peng, J.W.: A goal oriented numerical simulation approach for computing stress intensity factors in bimaterials. Mater. Sci. Forum 575, 249–254 (2008)
2. Xuan, Z.C., Feng, Z.S., Gao, D.Y.: Computing lower and upper bounds on stress intensity factors in bimaterials. Int. J. Nonl. Mech. 42, 336–341 (2007)
3. Xuan, Z.C., Khoo, B.C., Li, Z.R.: Computing bounds to mixed mode stress intensity factors in elasticity. Arch. App. Mech. 75, 193–205 (2006)
4. Arnold, D.N.: Mixed finite element methods for elliptic problems. Comput. Meth. Appl. Mech. Eng. 82, 1–88 (1990)
5. Arnold, D.N., Winther, R.: Mixed finite elements for elasticity. Numer. Math. 92, 401–419 (2002)
6. Gallagher, R.H.: Finite element structural analysis and complementary energy. Finite Elem. Anal. Des. 13, 115–126 (1993)
7. Liu, G.R., Zhang, G.Y.: Upper bound solution to elasticity problems: A unique property of the linearly conforming point interpolation method (LC-PIM). Int. J. Numer. Meth. Engng 74, 1128–1161 (2008)
8. Chen, J.S., Wu, C.T., Yoon, S., You, Y.: A stabilized conforming nodal integration for Galerkin mesh-free methods 50, 435–466 (2001)
9. Xuan, Z.C., Lassila, T., Rozza, G., Quarteroni, A.: Computing upper and lower bounds for linear outputs of elasticity by the smoothed finite element method. Submitted to Int. J. Numer. Meth. Engng.

Development of a Scalable Solver for the Earth's Core Convection*

Chao Yang[1], Ligang Li[2], and Yunquan Zhang[1,3]

[1] Institute of Software, Chinese Academy of Sciences, Beijing 100190, P.R. China
yang@mail.rdcps.ac.cn, zyq@mail.rdcps.ac.cn
http://www.rdcps.ac.cn/~yang
http://www.rdcps.ac.cn/~zyq
[2] Shanghai Astronomical Observatory, Chinese Academy of Sciences,
Shanghai 200030, P.R. China
[3] State Key Lab. of Computer Science, Chinese Academy of Sciences,
Beijing 100190, P.R. China

Abstract. A scalable parallel solver is developed to simulate the Earth's core convection. With the help from the "multiphysics" data structure and the restricted additive Schwarz preconditioning in PETSc the iterative solution of the linear solver converges rapidly at every time-step. The solver gains nearly 20 times speedup compared to a previous solver using least-squares polynomial preconditioning in Aztec. We show the efficiency and effectiveness of our new solver by giving numerical results obtained on a BlueGene/L supercomputer with thousands of processor cores.

1 Introduction

There has been an increasing interest in simulating the fluid motion in the Earth's outer core, which is commonly believed to be essentially related to the geomagnetic field around the Earth. One stepstone for the numerical dynamo simulations is the non-magnetic model in a rotating spherical shell (test case 0 in [5]), which can be written in the following non-dimensional form

$$
\begin{cases}
\frac{\partial \mathbf{u}}{\partial t} - L_1(\mathbf{u}) - R_1(\Theta) + G(P) = -\mathbf{u} \cdot \nabla \mathbf{u}, \\
\frac{\partial \Theta}{\partial t} - L_2(\Theta) - R_2(\mathbf{u}) = -\mathbf{u} \cdot \nabla \Theta, \\
D(\mathbf{u}) = 0,
\end{cases}
\tag{1}
$$

where

$$
\begin{aligned}
&L_1(\mathbf{u}) = \nabla^2 \mathbf{u} - \tfrac{2}{E}(\hat{\mathbf{z}} \times \mathbf{u}), \quad R_1(\Theta) = \tfrac{Ra}{Er_o}(\Theta\,\mathbf{r}), \quad G(P) = \tfrac{1}{E}\nabla P, \\
&L_2(\Theta) = \tfrac{1}{Pr}\nabla^2\Theta, \quad\quad\quad\;\; R_2(\mathbf{u}) = \tfrac{r_i r_o}{r^3}\mathbf{u}\cdot\mathbf{r}, \quad D(\mathbf{u}) = \nabla \cdot \mathbf{u}.
\end{aligned}
$$

* Project supported by the National High Technology Research and Development Program of China (No. 2006AA01A125 and No. 2006AA01A102), the National Natural Science Foundation of China (No. 10801125 and No. 60533020) and the National Basic Research Program of China (No. 2005CB321702).

W. Zhang et al. (Eds.): HPCA 2009, LNCS 5938, pp. 497–502, 2010.

Here $\hat{z}$ is the unit vector pointing in the direction of the rotating axis and $Ra = 100$, $E = 1.0 \times 10^{-3}$, $Pr = 1$ are non-dimensional parameters. The spherical coordinates are (ϕ, θ, r) with $\phi \in [\phi_0, \phi_0 + 2\pi)$, $\theta \in [0, \pi]$, $r \in [r_i, r_o]$, where $\phi_0 = -\frac{\pi}{4}$, $r_i = \frac{7}{13}$ and $r_o = \frac{20}{13}$, are used throughout this paper. The boundary conditions for (1) are $\mathbf{u} = 0$, $\Theta = 0$ at $r = r_i, r_o$. Zero initial velocity and the nonzero initial temperature suggested in [4,5] can be used to start the calculation. The final quasi stationary state of the problem is a steadily traveling wave $(\mathbf{u}, \Theta) = g(r, \theta, \phi - \omega t)$ with drift frequency ω.

We use a second order MAC scheme [8] to discretize the main system (1) on a staggered Arakawa-C mesh [1]. The mesh is uniform in both θ and ϕ directions but nonuniform in the radius direction to better resolve the Ekman boundary layers, details can be found in [4]. A fixed time-step size is used during the whole calculation and the time-stepping method is based on the second order approximate factorization method [6] together with Crank-Nicolson (C-N) scheme. The nonlinear terms $\mathbf{f}_1 = \mathbf{u} \cdot \nabla \mathbf{u}$, $f_2 = \mathbf{u} \cdot \nabla \Theta$ at half time-step are approximated using second-order Adams-Bashford formula $f^{n+\frac{1}{2}} = \frac{3}{2}f^n - \frac{1}{2}f^{n-1} + \mathcal{O}(\Delta t^2)$ and $f^{\frac{1}{2}} = f^0$. The whole time-stepping procedure is as follows.

Step-1. Compute the matrices

$$A = I - \frac{\Delta t}{2}\begin{pmatrix} \mathcal{L}_1 & \mathcal{R}_1 \\ \mathcal{R}_2 & \mathcal{L}_2 \end{pmatrix}, \quad B = \frac{\Delta t}{2}\mathcal{D}\mathcal{G},$$

where $\mathcal{L}_1, \mathcal{R}_1, \mathcal{L}_2, \mathcal{R}_2, \mathcal{D}, \mathcal{G}$ are the second-order finite difference operators of L_1, R_1, L_2, R_2, D, G respectively, see [4] for details.

Step-2. Begin time integration with $n = 0$.

Step-2.1. Calculate the nonlinear terms and let $\tilde{\mathbf{u}}^n = \mathbf{u}^n - \frac{\Delta t}{2}\mathcal{G}p^n$. Solve

$$A\begin{pmatrix} \tilde{\mathbf{u}}^{n+\frac{1}{2}} \\ \Theta^{n+1} \end{pmatrix} = (2I - A)\begin{pmatrix} \tilde{\mathbf{u}}^n \\ \Theta^n \end{pmatrix} - \Delta t \begin{pmatrix} \mathbf{f}_1^{n+\frac{1}{2}} \\ f_2^{n+\frac{1}{2}} \end{pmatrix}. \tag{2}$$

Step-2.2. Solve a discrete Poisson equation for pressure

$$Bp^{n+1} = \mathcal{D}\tilde{\mathbf{u}}^{n+\frac{1}{2}}, \tag{3}$$

and correct velocity $\mathbf{u}^{n+1} = \tilde{\mathbf{u}}^{n+\frac{1}{2}} - \frac{\Delta t}{2}\mathcal{G}p^{n+1}$.

Step-2.3. If final convection state is not attained, increase $n \leftarrow n + 1$ and go to Step-2.1.

There are two linear systems to be solved at each time-step, i.e., the velocity-temperature equation (2) and the pressure equation (3). In practice, these two systems are the most time-consuming parts of the whole calculation.

2   Linear Solvers and Preconditioners

Both the linear systems (2), (3) are solved iteratively using Krylov subspace methods with certain preconditioning techniques. Instead of solving the original linear system, say, $Ax = b$, we seek an approximate inverse M^{-1} of A and solve an equivalent system $M^{-1}Ax = M^{-1}b$. The performance of the linear solver depends greatly on the efficiency and effectiveness of the preconditioner M^{-1}.

For parallel computation, the matrix distribution on each processor core is generally determined from the global ordering of the unknowns. The "field-splitting" ordering of the unknowns is a popular choice for staggered mesh, as was done in our previous solver using Aztec. With the field-splitting ordering the velocity-temperature matrix takes the following form

$$A = \begin{pmatrix} A_{uu} & A_{uv} & A_{uw} & 0 \\ A_{vu} & A_{vv} & A_{vw} & 0 \\ A_{wu} & A_{wv} & A_{ww} & A_{w\Theta} \\ 0 & 0 & A_{\Theta w} & A_{\Theta\Theta} \end{pmatrix}, \tag{4}$$

where each block entry is the discretization to the field-coupling between physical variables on the staggered mesh. The matrix distribution on each processor core is then done based on (4), i.e., the first several rows of A in (4) is locally owned by the first processor core, then the second several rows go to the second processor core, and so on. One main disadvantage of the field-splitting ordering is that different processor cores could own different physical coupling matrices. This could lead to severely unbalanced local working loads and global communications. Besides, with the field-splitting ordering, domain decomposition preconditioner M^{-1} can only be done in a purely algebraic manner and has no geometry explanations and thus no theoretical support.

To better utilize the mesh information and access higher parallel efficiency, we decompose the whole computational domain Ω, into $np = p_1 \times p_2 \times p_3$ non-overlapping rectangular subdomains, Ω_j, $j = 1, \ldots, np$. Here np is also the number of processor cores and p_i is the number of subdomains for a one-dimensional decomposition in the i-th direction. An illustration for the domain decomposition to a two-dimensional staggered mesh is given in Fig. 1. To obtain an overlapping decomposition of the domain, we extend each subdomain Ω_j to a larger subdomain $(\Omega_j)'$ with δ layers of mesh points in each direction.

For every overlapping subdomain we define A_j as the restriction of A to the overlapping subdomain Ω_j'. Here each submatrix A_j takes an analogous form as A in (4). Then the left restricted additive Schwarz (RAS) preconditioner [3] is defined as

$$M^{-1} = \sum_{j=1}^{np}(R_j^0)^T A_j^{-1} R_j^\delta, \tag{5}$$

Let m be the total number of mesh points in Ω and m_j' the total number of mesh points in Ω_j'. Then R_j^δ serves as a restriction matrix because its multiplication by a $m \times 1$ vector results in a smaller $m_j' \times 1$ vector by dropping the components corresponding to elements outside Ω_j'. In particular R_j^0 is a restriction to the non-overlapping subdomain.

We implement our algorithm using the PETSc [2] library. The Arakawa-C staggered mesh is implemented with the help from the "multi-physics" data

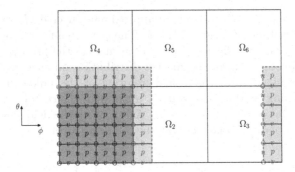

Fig. 1. A two-dimensional illustration of the domain decomposition to the Arakawa-C mesh: six subdomains, periodic boundary conditions in ϕ direction, overlapping factor $\delta = 1$. The non-overlapping subdomain for the first processor core, Ω_1, is marked in darker shaded color. The discretized variables owned by Ω_1 are indicated in blue. The extended area from Ω_1 to the overlapping subdomain Ω_1' is marked in lighter shaded color. The discretized variables owned by the extended area are indicated in green.

structure. The velocity-temperature system is solved by using TFQMR [7] with a relative tolerance of 1.0×10^{-14} and the pressure system is solved by using Bi-CGSTAB [10] with a relative tolerance of 1.0×10^{-12}. A constant null space is attached to the pressure solver to make the solution unique. The preconditioners for both linear solvers are constructed using RAS with zero overlap and with ILU(0) subdomain solvers.

The two matrices A and B for the velocity-temperature equation (2) and the pressure equation (3) are generated before time loop. An "aij" matrix format in PETSc is used for both the matrices and necessary matrix pre-allocations are performed to get better cache performance. The ILU factorizations of all submatrices are obtained and stored at the first time-step and used repeatedly thereafter. To further reduce the iteration number, the initial guesses of the two linear systems are chosen to be the solutions at previous time-step.

3   Performance Tests

The Blue Gene/L (BG/L) supercomputer, a 1024 node system with a peak performance of 5.7 TFLOPS located at NCAR, is used for performance tests. Each BG/L node has a dual-core PowerPC-440 processor running at 700 MHz and 512 MB local memory.

In practice use the following mesh

$$(G1): \quad N_\phi = 128, \quad N_\theta = 128, \quad N_r = 96, \quad \Delta t = 1 \times 10^{-4}$$

for the calculation. The simulation reaches to the final quasi stationary state within about $t = 0.8$. The convergence history of the mean kinetic energy $E_{\text{kin}} = \frac{1}{2V} \int_V |\mathbf{u}|^2 dV$ and the temperature distribution on the mid-depth sphere at convergence are provided in Fig. 2.

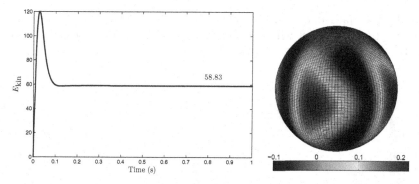

Fig. 2. The convergence history of the mean kinetic energy E_{kin} (left) and the temperature distribution on the mid-depth sphere at convergence

Next we compare our solver with a previous solver [4] developed by utilizing the parallel library Aztec. Except for using a different parallel strategy and the least-squares polynomial preconditioning, the iterative methods and the relative tolerances used in the old solver are the same to those in the new one. We run both the old and the new solvers for 10 time-steps with gradually increased the number of processor cores to do the performance tests. The averaged number of iterations per time-step and the total solution time for both the velocity-temperature system and the pressure system are provided and compared in Table. 1. Although no improvement on the number of iterations is observed, the solution time for the two linear systems benefits dramatically from the new domain-decomposition preconditioners. Besides, the extra costs at each time-step, including the cost for the velocity correction and the cost for the generations of the right-hand-side vectors, are negligible compared to those in the old solver. In total, the averaged computing time at each time-step is saved from 93.3% upto 96.4%, i.e., nearly 20 times speedup is gained, when the new solver is used.

Table 1. Performance comparisons using mesh (G1), results averaged on 10 time steps

	Velocity-Temperature						Pressure						Extra		Total		
	Iterations		Time (s)				Iterations		Time (s)				Time (s)		Time (s)		
np	old	new	old	new	%		old	new	old	new	%		old	new	old	new	%
64	-	51.8	-	12.89	-		-	272.6	-	9.65	-		29.7	0.02	-	22.6	-
128	55.8	45.3	71.3	5.61	7.9		228.6	285.8	55.8	4.92	8.8		29.7	0.01	156.9	10.5	6.7
256	50.9	47.3	40.5	2.87	7.1		244.1	318.1	43.8	2.66	6.1		29.7	0.01	114.1	5.5	4.9
512	56.0	45.9	29.3	1.39	4.7		227.2	320.4	20.6	1.44	7.0		29.7	0.00	79.6	2.8	3.6
1024	58.1	82.4	16.0	1.18	7.4		257.1	358.4	8.6	0.92	10.7		29.8	0.00	54.4	2.1	3.9
2048	62.5	81.2	12.6	0.77	6.2		236.4	412.7	4.1	0.88	21.3		29.8	0.00	46.5	1.7	3.6

It can be seen from Table. 1 that the mesh (G1) is not fine enough to show the scalability of the new solver since the averaged solution time for a linear system at each time-step is only about one second when $np = 1024$. However, when we use a finer mesh

$$(G2): \quad N_\phi = 192, \quad N_\theta = 192, \quad N_r = 128, \quad \Delta t = 5 \times 10^{-5}$$

the old solver fails due to insufficient memory for allocation. The new solver scales up to $np = 2048$ with an almost optimal scalability curve, as seen in Fig. 3.

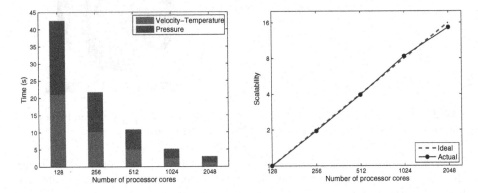

Fig. 3. The solution time for the two linear systems (left) and the overall strong scalability (right). Results are obtained using mesh (G2), averaged on 10 time-steps.

References

1. Arakawa, A., Lamb, V.: Computational design of the basic dynamical processes of the UCLA general circulation model. Methods in Computational Physics 17, 174–267 (1977)
2. Balay, S., Buschelman, K., Gropp, W., Kaushik, D., Knepley, M., McInnes, L., Smith, B., Zhang, H.: PETSc Users Manual, Argonne National Laboratory (2008)
3. Cai, X.-C., Sarkis, M.: A restricted additive Schwarz preconditioner for general sparse linear systems. SIAM J. Sci. Comput. 21, 792–797 (1999)
4. Chan, K., Li, L., Liao, X.: Modelling the core convection using finite element and finite difference methods. Phys. Earth Planet. Interiors 157, 124–138 (2006)
5. Christensen, U., Aubert, J., et al.: A numerical dynamo benchmark. Phys. Earth Planet. Interiors 128, 25–34 (2001)
6. Dukowicz, J., Dvinsky, A.: Approximate factorization as a high order splitting for the implicit incompressible flow equations. J. Comput. Phys. 102, 336–347 (1992)
7. Freund, R.W.: A Transpose-Free Quasi-Minimal Residual algorithm for non-Hermitian linear systems. SIAM J. Sci. Comput. 14, 470–482 (1993)
8. Harlow, F., Welch, J.: Numerical calculatin of time-dependent viscous incompressible flow of fluid with free surface. Phys. Fluids 8, 2182–2189 (1965)
9. Tuminaro, R., Heroux, M., Hutchinson, S., Shadid, J.: Official AZTEC Users Guide: Version 2.1 (1999)
10. van der Vorst, H.A.: A fast and smoothly converging variant of Bi-CG for the solution of nonsymmetric linear systems. SIAM J. Sci. Stat. Comput. 13, 631–644 (1992)

A Virtualized HPC Cluster Computing Environment on Xen with Web-Based User Interface[*]

Chao-Tung Yang[1,**], Chien-Hsiang Tseng[1,2], Keng-Yi Chou[1], and Shyh-Chang Tsaur[3]

[1] High-Performance Computing Laboratory
Department of Computer Science, Tunghai University, Taichung, 40704, Taiwan, ROC
{ctyang,g97357006,g97350007}@thu.edu.tw
[2] ARAVision Incorporated, Sindian City, Taipei Count, 23141, Taiwan, ROC
warp@aracity.com
[3] Department of Electronics
National Chin-yi University of Technology, Taichung County 411 Taiwan, ROC
sctsaur@gmail.com

Abstract. Nowadays, large-scale computing solutions are common issues. A PC cluster computing system is the solution to problems faced by end users. And problems associated with System Virtualization are evenly popular issues in recently years. This technology is necessarily needed for enterprises and end users in the future applications, indeed. This paper introduces how to implement and integrate virtualization with cluster computing system on Xen and how it works, and, also explains and contrasts the differences between non-virtualization and virtualization. The virtual cluster computing system is more efficient in operations and economic in power than the traditional cluster computing system; the virtualized cluster computing system is a trend of cluster system. This virtual cluster computing system is used to deal with large-scale problems instead of using the transitional cluster computing system.

Keywords: Cluster Virtualization, Cluster Computing System, Virtualization computing.

1 Introduction

Over the past 50 years, human beings have changed ecosystems more rapidly and extensively than any comparable period of time in human history, largely due to meet rapidly growing demands for food, fresh water, timber, fiber and fuel. The rapid loss of earth resources is a significant issue in recently years.

Taiwan, one of members in the earth village, demands immediate attention to deal with the global warming and climate change. A traditional cluster system, consisting of many real computers consumes a great deal of powers and the heat energy generated

---

[*] This work is supported in part by National Science Council, Taiwan R.O.C., under grants no. NSC 96-2221-E-029-019-MY3 and NSC 98-2220-E-029-004.
[**] Corresponding author.

W. Zhang et al. (Eds.): HPCA 2009, LNCS 5938, pp. 503–508, 2010.
© Springer-Verlag Berlin Heidelberg 2010

by this system, causes the global warming. Therefore, the virtual cluster computing system is a trend to save energy and protect environment in the future development.

This paper introduces how to implement and integrate virtualization with cluster computing system on Xen and how it works, and, also explains and contrasts the differences between non-virtualization and virtualization [1-7]. The virtual cluster computing system is more efficient in operations and economic in power than the traditional cluster computing system; the virtualized cluster computing system is a trend in the cluster system. This virtual cluster computing system is used to deal with large-scale problems instead of using the transitional cluster computing system.

The rest of this paper is stated as follows. In section 2, we will discuss the virtual cluster computing system in details. In section 3, we will mention our system architecture, web interface, resource broker, and experiments by using efficient virtualization. Finally, conclusions and the future work are stated in section 4.

2 Background Review

A virtual Cluster Computing System is a system consisting of cluster computers connected and virtualization of computing.

2.1 Cluster Systems

A cluster system is a group of linked computers, working together so closely to complete jobs that in many respects they form a single computer. The components of a cluster are commonly, but not always, connected to each other through a fast LAN, and each of them is called a "node". A cluster skeleton is divided into homogeneous and heterogeneous types. Frame clusters, based on function, can be categorized as three types: High Availability Clusters, Load Balancing Clusters and High Performance Computing Clusters.

2.2 Virtualization

Virtualization is simply the logical separation of the request for some service from the physical resources that actually provide that service. There are five or more virtualization technologies, but we just discuss two of them, which are known by most people.

In order to evaluate the viability of the difference between virtualization and non-virtualization, the virtualization software we used in this paper is XEN. XEN is chosen to be our system's virtual machine monitor because it provides better efficiency, supports different operating systems simultaneously, and gives each operating system an independent system environment.

3 System Implementation

In our entire framework, a cluster computing system with XEN is a major architecture to achieve the economization of power.

3.1 System Architecture

A Beowulf cluster uses a multi-computer architecture. It features a parallel computing system that consists of one or more head nodes and available tail nodes, compute nodes, or cluster nodes, which are interconnected via widely available network interconnects. All of the nodes in a typical Beowulf cluster are commodity systems consisting of PCs, workstations, or servers-running commodity software.

Based on a traditional cluster framework mentioned before, we introduce an ideas of virtualization in the cluster system to economize power; therefore, there are some differences on framework of cluster; all physical compute hosts use message passing interface to perform communication, but in the virtualization computing cluster, fully paravirtualized machines are used instead of physical machines.

Our cluster system was built up with four homogeneous computers; the system of these computers is equipped with Intel Xeon CPU E5410 2.33GHz, eight gigabytes memory, 500 gigabytes disk, fedora 8 operating system, and the network connected to a gigabit switch.

Referring to the next chapter of experiment, besides the master node can be NFS, NIS server, etc., it can also be a compute node during job computing. We will compare virtualization with non-virtualization on the effect of computing efficiency and power economization, including two software stack diagrams, with XEN and without XEN. The software stack diagrams (with XEN) are shown on Fig. 1.

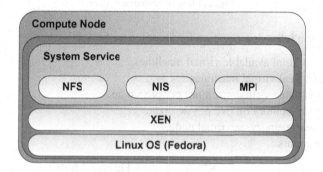

Fig. 1. Software stack of node with Xen

3.2 Resource Broker

It's a good idea to use resource broker, end users can easily provide their jobs. In this portal, we can support VM environment and non-VM environment. In VM environment, we can provide heterogeneous platforms, which also support to upload, and compile their job files automatically.

The resource broker is the soul of this system; it controls the total computing resources, assigns available resources to end users, and manages licenses for this system. The flow between end users and computing resources is shown on Fig. 2. The working flow is listed in the following:

1. Upload source code by UI
2. Request available resources

3. Request management and booting resources
4. Start computing
5. Get results
6. Use UI to download results

Working Flow

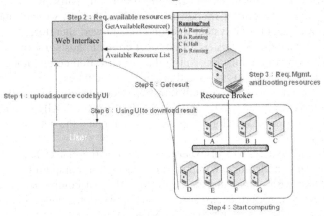

Fig. 2. Flow of resource broker

We define the following equation for the resource broker.

- $Node_{Totalvnum}$: Total available virtual machines.
- $Node_{Realvnum}$: Real virtual machines.
- C_n: Total available virtual machines per physic node.
- Mem_p: Physic memory on one physic node.
- Mem_v: Virtual memory on virtual node.
- L: License counts.

$$Node_{Totalvnum} = \sum_{n=1}^{n=L} C_n \qquad C_n = (Mem_p / Mem_v)$$
$$Node_{Totalvnum} > Node_{Realvnum}$$

Using this equation, we can

1. Count virtual machine's numbers.
2. Avoid using physics swap. Performance is achieved because total virtual machine's memory can be no larger than physics machine's memory.
3. Control license counts.

3.3 Experimental Results

We focus on economization of power and compare efficiency between a traditional cluster and a virtual cluster. Therefore, by using matrix multiplication, LINPACK and LU test sets are used to verify that a virtual cluster will economize more power and operate more efficiently than a traditional cluster.

Matrix Multiplication in mathematics is the operation of multiplying a matrix with either a scalar or another matrix. Besides this matrix multiplication, the matrix size could be varied into a different value.

We focus on economizing power, and then the matrix multiplication is the test set to verify that virtualization can save more power than non-virtualization. Here we compare a physical cluster, which consists of four real computers, that each has eight cores, with four virtual machines, each with eight cores on one real computer.

Therefore, we can calculate the power consumption of virtualization and non-virtualization by mathematic equations shown below:

Equation 1
$$(Watt\ of\ CPU\ used) \times (CPU\ number) = Machine\ Watt$$

Equation 2
$$(Machine\ watt) \times (Machine\ number) = Cluster\ watt$$

Equation 3
$$\frac{(Cluster\ watt) \times (Job\ Execute\ Time)}{3600} = Thermal\ power\ of\ Cluster$$

The CPU, Intel Xeon E5410, needs 80 watts to operate, so our computer needs 160 watts by equation 1. And through equation 2, the cluster watt is 640 watts for non-virtualization and 160 watts for virtualization. By equation 3, we get a set of values about thermal power for non-virtualization and virtualization. All data sets are shown in table 1.

Because our real cluster is eight cores for each computer, and then there are 32 cores. Therefore, the matrix size has to begin from 32 or more. By using experiment data, we draw a linear illustration to make a description of thermal power between non-virtualization and virtualization as shown in Fig.3.

4   Conclusions and Future Work

It is a trend to integrate virtualization with a cluster computing system. Virtualization is simply the logical separation of the request for some service from the physical resources that actually provide that service. Regardless of efficiency or economization of power, the experiment shows that a virtualization cluster is more efficient and economical on power than a non-virtualization cluster. But virtualization is not all good for every application, it's just better than non-virtualization on some applications, such as email server, ftp server and http server, etc... that can use virtualization to build up and manage. Since a cluster also can be virtualized to be the compute node, so it not only saves power but also let other physical computers execute other works.

And the next stage of our system, we will build more functions in user interface for end users, who do not major in the computer science domain and need to use cluster computing to solve a large scale problem. The resource broker proposed is used to handle all physical and virtualization resources, and dispatch resource that end users have authority to use. Adding more logic functions in resource broker will enhance better management.

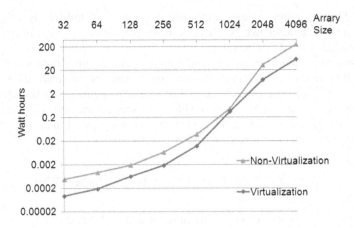

Fig. 3. Thermal power matrix multiplication with watt hour

References

1. Dong, Y., Li, S., Mallick, A., Nakajima, J., Tian, K., Xu, X., Yang, F., Yu, W.: Extending Xen with Intel Virtualization Technology. Intel® Technology Journal 10(03), 1–14 (2006)
2. Sharifi, M., Hassani, M., Mousavi, S.L.M., Mirtaheri, S.L.: VCE: A New Personated Virtual Cluster Engine for Cluster Computing. In: 3rd International Conference on Information and Communication Technologies: From Theory to Applications, 2008. ICTTA 2008, April 7-11, pp. 1–6 (2008)
3. Liu, J., Huang, W., Abali, B., Panda, D.K.: High Performance VMM-Bypass I/O in Virtual Machines. In: Proceedings of USENIX 2006 (2006)
4. Huang, W., Liu, J., Abali, B., Panda, D.K.: A Case for High Performance Computing with Virtual Machines. In: ICS 2006: Proceedings of the 20th annual international conference on Supercomputing, pp. 125–134. ACM Press, New York (2006)
5. Menon, A., Santos, J.R., Turner, Y., Janakiraman, G., Zwaenepoel, W.: Diagnosing Performance Overheads in the Xen Virtual Machine Environment. In: VEE 2005: Proceedings of the 1st ACM/USENIX international conference on Virtual execution environments, pp. 13–23. ACM Press, New York (2005)
6. Cherkasova, L., Gardner, R.: Measuring CPU Overhead for I/O Processing in the Xen Virtual Machine Monitor. In: USENIX 2005 Annual Technical Conference, pp. 387–390 (2005), http://www.usenix.org/events/usenix05/tech/general/cherkasova.html
7. Smith, J.E., Nair, R.: The Architecture of Virtual Machines. Computer 38(5), 32–38 (2005)

Performance-Based Parallel Loop Self-scheduling on Heterogeneous Multicore PC Clusters*

Chao-Tung Yang[1,**], Jen-Hsiang Chang[1], and Chao-Chin Wu[2]

[1] High-Performance Computing Laboratory
Department of Computer Science, Tunghai University Taichung, 40704, Taiwan ROC
{ctyang,g95290009}@thu.edu.tw
[2] Department of Computer Science and Information Engineering
National Changhua University of Education, Changhua, 50074, Taiwan
ccwu@cc.ncue.edu.tw

Abstract. In recent years, Multicore computers have been widely included in cluster systems. They adopt shared memory architectures. However, previous researches on parallel loop self-scheduling did not consider the feature of multicore computers. It is more suitable for shared-memory multiprocessors to adopt OpenMP for parallel programming. In this paper, we propose a performance-based approach that partitions loop iterations according to the performance weighting of cluster nodes. Because the iterations assigned to one MPI process will be processed in parallel by OpenMP threads running by the processor cores in the same computational node, the number of loop iterations to be allocated to one computational node at each scheduling step also depends on the number of processor cores in that node. Experimental results show that the proposed approach performs better than previous schemes.

Keywords: Self-scheduling, Parallel loop scheduling, Multicore, Cluster, OpenMP, MPI.

1 Introduction

Recently, more and more cluster systems include multicore computers because almost all the commodity personal computers are multicore architectures. The primary feature of multicore architectures is that multiple processors on the same chip can communicate with each other by directly accessing the data in the shared memory.

In this paper, we revise popular loop self-scheduling schemes to fit cluster computing environments. The HPCC Performance Analyzer [1] is used to estimate performance of all nodes rather accurately. The MPI library is usually used for parallel programming in the cluster system because it is a message-passing programming language. However, MPI is not the best programming language for multicore computers. Instead, OpenMP is very suitable for multicore computers because it is a

---

* This work is supported in part by National Science Council, Taiwan R.O.C., under grants no. NSC 96-2221-E-029-019-MY3 and NSC 98-2220-E-029-004.
** Corresponding author.

W. Zhang et al. (Eds.): HPCA 2009, LNCS 5938, pp. 509–514, 2010.

shared-memory programming language. Therefore, in this paper we propose to use hybrid MPI and OpenMP programming mode to design the loop self-scheduling scheme for the cluster system with multicore computers.

2 Background Review

2.1 Multicore and Cluster Systems

In a multicore processor, two or more independent cores are combined in a single integrated circuit. A system with n cores is most effective when presented with n or more concurrent threads. The degree of performance gain, resulting from use of a multicore processor, depends on the problem being solved and the algorithms used, as well as on their implementation in software. The main features allow dividing large-scale programs into several smaller programs for parallel execution by more than one computer in order to reduce processing times, and include modern cluster systems that communicate mainly through Local Area Networks (LANs), and can be broadly divided into homogeneous and heterogeneous systems.

2.2 Loop Self-scheduling Schemes

Self-scheduling schemes are mainly used to deal with load balancing [8] and they can be divided into two types: static and dynamic [6, 7]. Static scheduling schemes decide how many loop iterations are assigned for each processor at compile time. The number of processors available for distribution and the calculated dynamics of each machine are taken into consideration when implementing programs with static scheduling. The advantage of static scheduling schemes is no scheduling overhead at runtime.

In contrast, dynamic scheduling is more suitable for load balancing because it makes scheduling decisions at runtime. No estimations and predictions are required. Self-scheduling is a large class of adaptive and dynamic centralized loop scheduling schemes. Initially, a portion of the loop iterations is scheduled to all processors. As soon as a slave processor becomes idle after it has finished the assigned workload, it requests the scheduling of unscheduled iterations.

3 Proposed Approach

Fig.1 explains our approach. All the loop iterations are kept in the global scheduler. No slave cores are allowed to request iterations directly from the global scheduler. Instead, they have to request from the local scheduler in the same computing node. To utilize the feature of shared-memory architectures, every MPI process of the local scheduler will create OpenMP threads for each processor core on its resident computing node. The messages between the global scheduler and the local scheduler are inter-node communications. They are MPI messages. In contrast, the messages between the local scheduler and the processor core are intra-node communications.

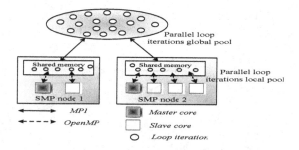

Fig. 1. Multicore computing node communications with MPI processes and OpenMP threads

In this context, we propose to allocate $\alpha\%$ of workload according to the performance weighted by CPU clock speed and the HPCC [1] measurement of all nodes, and the remaining workload is dispatched by some well-known self-scheduling scheme such as GSS [5]. By using this approach, we need to know the real computer performance with HPCC benchmarks. Then, we can distribute appropriate workloads to each node, and load balancing can be achieved. The more accurate the estimation is, the better the load balance well be.

$$PW_j = \beta \frac{CS_j}{\sum_{\forall node_i \in S} CS_i} + (1 - \beta) \frac{HPL_j}{\sum_{\forall node_i \in S} HPL_i}, 0 \leq \beta \leq 1 \tag{1}$$

where S is the set of all cluster nodes, CS_i is the CPU clock speed of node i, and it is a constant attribute. HPL_i is the HPL measurement of HPCC, and this value is analyzed above; β is the ratio between the two values.

This algorithm is based on a message-passing paradigm, and consists of two modules: a master module and a slave module. The master module makes the scheduling decision and dispatches workloads to slaves. Then, the slave module processes the assigned work. This algorithm is just a skeleton, and the detailed implementation, such as data preparation, parameter passing, etc., might be different according to requirements of various applications.

4 Experimental Environment and Results

The performance of our scheme is then compared with that of other static and dynamic schemes on the heterogeneous cluster. In this work, we implemented three classes of applications in C language, with MPI and OpenMP directives to parallelize code segments for execution on our testbed: Matrix Multiplication, Mandelbrot Set Computation and Circuit Satisfiability.

4.1 Hardware Configuration and Specifications

We have built a testbed consisting of fourteen nodes. The hardware and software configuration is specified in Table 1. The network route is stated in Fig.2.

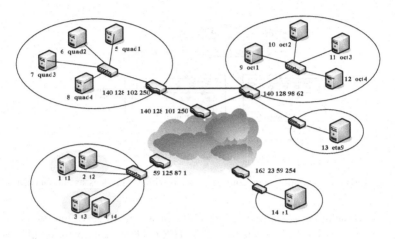

Fig. 2. Network route state

Table 1. Our cluster system configuration

Host	Processor Model	#of CPU	# of Core	RAM	NIC	OS version
quad1	Intel™ Core™2 Quad CPU Q6600 @ 2.40GHz	1	4	2GB	1G	2.6.23.1-42.fc8
quad2	Intel™ Core™2 Quad CPU Q6600 @ 2.40GHz	1	4	2GB	1G	2.6.23.1-42.fc8
quad3	Intel™ Core™2 Quad CPU Q6600 @ 2.40GHz	1	4	2GB	1G	2.6.23.1-42.fc8
quad4	Intel™ Core™2 Quad CPU Q6600 @ 2.40GHz	1	4	2GB	1G	2.6.23.1-42.fc8
oct1	Intel(R) Xeon(R) CPU E5410 @ 2.33GHz	2	8	8G	1G	2.6.21-xen_Xen
oct2	Intel(R) Xeon(R) CPU E5410 @ 2.33GHz	2	8	8G	1G	2.6.21-xen_Xen
oct3	Intel(R) Xeon(R) CPU E5410 @ 2.33GHz	2	8	8G	1G	2.6.21-xen_Xen
oct4	Intel(R) Xeon(R) CPU E5410 @ 2.33GHz	2	8	8G	1G	2.6.21-xen_Xen
t1	Intel(R) Xeon(R) CPU E5310 @ 1.60GHz	2	8	8GB	1G	2.6.25.4-10.fc8
t2	Intel(R) Xeon(R) CPU E5310 @ 1.60GHz	2	8	8GB	1G	2.6.25.4-10.fc8
t3	Intel(R) Xeon(R) CPU E5410 @ 2.33GHz	2	8	8GB	1G	2.6.25.4-10.fc8
t4	Intel(R) Xeon(R) CPU E5410 @ 2.33GHz	2	8	8GB	1G	2.6.25.4-10.fc8
eta9	Intel(R) Xeon(R) CPU E5420 @ 2.50GHz	2	8	4G	1G	2.6.25-14.fc9
s1	Intel(R) Xeon(R) CPU E5310 @ 1.60GHz	2	8	4GB	1G	2.6.18-128.1.6.el5

4.2 Experimental Results

In our experiments, first, the HPL measurements and CPU speed of all nodes were collected. Next, the impact of the parameters α, β, on performance was investigated. With this approach, a faster node will get more workloads than a slower one proportionally.

In the matrix multiplicatoin experiment, we find that the proposed schemes get better performance when α is 40 and β is 0.4. Fig. 3 illustrates execution time of traditional scheme, dynamic hybrid (matn*ss3) and the proposed scheme (matn*ss3_omp).

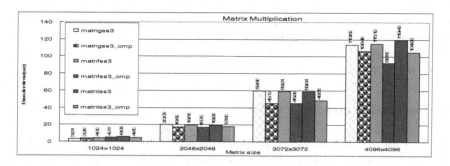

Fig. 3. Performance improvement comparison for (matn*ss) and (matn*ss_omp) different applications

In Mandelbrot set computation example, we found that the proposed schemes got better performance when α was 40 and β was about 0.4. Fig. 4 shows execution times for the proposed scheme (mann*ss3), and for the proposed scheme of OpenMP (mann*ss3_omp) on the GSS, FSS, and TSS group approaches.

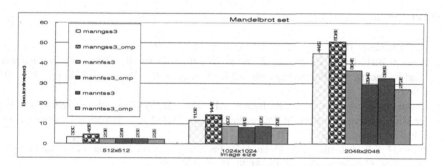

Fig. 4. Performance improvement comparison for (mann*ss) and (mann*ss_omp) different applications

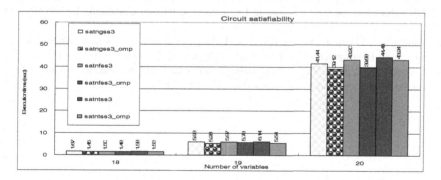

Fig. 5. Performance improvement comparison for (satn*ss) and (satn*ss_omp) different applications

In Circuit Satisfiability example, we found that the proposed schemes got better performance when α was 30 and β was about 0.5. Fig. 5 shows execution times for the proposed scheme (satn*ss3) and the proposed scheme of OpenMP (satn*ss3_omp).

5   Conclusion and Future Work

In this paper, we use the hybrid programming model MPI with OpenMP to design parallel loop self-scheduling schemes for heterogeneous cluster systems with multi-core computers. We propose a heuristic scheme, which combines the advantages of static and dynamic loop scheduling schemes, and compare it with previous algorithms by experiments in this environment. In each case, our approach can obtain performance improvement on previous schemes. Furthermore, we hope to find better ways to model the performance functions, such as incorporating amount of memory available, memory access costs, network information, CPU loading, etc. Also, a theoretical analysis of the proposed method will be addressed.

References

1. HPC Challenge Benchmark, http://icl.cs.utk.edu/hpcc/
2. Bennett, B.H., Davis, E., Kunau, T., Wren, W.: Beowulf Parallel Processing for Dynamic Load-balancing. In: Proceedings on IEEE Aerospace Conference, vol. 4, pp. 389–395 (2000)
3. Chronopoulos, A.T., Andonie, R., Benche, M., Grosu, D.: A Class of Loop Self-Scheduling for Heterogeneous Clusters. In: Proceedings of the 2001 IEEE International Conference on Cluster Computing, pp. 282–291 (2001)
4. Hummel, S.F., Schonberg, E., Flynn, L.E.: Factoring: a method scheme for scheduling parallel loops. Communications of the ACM 35, 90–101 (1992)
5. Polychronopoulos, C.D., Kuck, D.: Guided Self-Scheduling: a Practical Scheduling Scheme for Parallel Supercomputers. IEEE Trans. on Computers 36(12), 1425–1439 (1987)
6. Yang, C.-T., Cheng, K.-W., Shih, W.-C.: On Development of an Efficient Parallel Loop Self-Scheduling for Grid Computing Environments. Parallel Computing 33(7-8), 467–487 (2007)
7. Yang, C.-T., Cheng, K.-W., Li, K.-C.: An Enhanced Parallel Loop Self-Scheduling Scheme for Cluster Environments. The Journal of Supercomputing 34(3), 315–335 (2005)
8. Yagoubi, B., Slimani, Y.: Load Balancing Strategy in Grid Environment. Journal of Information Technology and Applications 1(4), 285–296 (2007)

Sharing University Resources
Based on Grid Portlet

Shuhua Yu, Jianlin Zhang, and Chunjuan Fu

Information Engineering College, Capital Normal University, Beijing, China
yushuhua456@126.com, jlzhang66@263.net,
fuchunjuan1986@163.com

Abstract. Accessing and using the grid service portal is the most important and the most basic function. This paper is to use this feature to address such a problem that a legitimate user who leaves the campus LAN environment cannot use information resources of the university. By using the grid-portlet-based grid service portal, students on any computer connected to the internet can access the university resources, such as storage resources, computing resources, and valuable information resources.

Keywords: grid technology, grid portal, portlet, information resources.

1 Introduction

The grid portal technology based on portlet has been used in many fields, such as the research in high-energy physics of a new generation, the experiments of particle astrophysics, the grid platform and portal of the cosmic ray observation experiment in Yangbajing [1], biological data processing and bio-computing [2], and the implementation of enterprise portal. In addition, the portlet-based portal technology has also been used for campus digitization [3-5]. But research on the application of the grid-portlet based technology used in the university resources planning is exiguous. So far, the research of grid technology in campus digitization is only about the resources inside the university. The study on how to use campus resources when we are outside the LAN is rare. This problem is very meaningful. Normally, students are the main applications of university resources. 12 months of the year, students have more than nine months on campus. During the period of off-campus students cannot take full use of campus resources, such as the valuable resources of university academic resources, which results in the waste of resources. In order to make the best use of university resources, this paper studies and uses the portlet-based grid service portal technology to solve the problem, and enables the university resources available beyond the campus as well.

2 The Problem

There is always a problem for the legal users of the university intranet, that is, either you are a teacher or a student, when you are beyond the intranet of university, you

W. Zhang et al. (Eds.): HPCA 2009, LNCS 5938, pp. 515–521, 2010.
© Springer-Verlag Berlin Heidelberg 2010

can't make use of the information resources of the university. For example, a student when he was outside university, he can not query the bibliographic of library, can not submit homework on-line and so on. In order to resolve the problem, this paper put forward a general model using the technology of grid portlet.

3   The Significance of Problem-Solving

The service gird portal which based on portlet technology can make fully use of university resources. No matter where teachers and students are, as long as you can access the internet, you can make use of the information resources of the university as conveniently as you are inside the intranet of the college. You can submit your homework on-line, query the bibliographic of library, and you also can read the electronic journals that have been purchased by your school.

4   The Main Technology that the Service Grid Portal Used

Ian Foster and Carl Kesselman make the initial definition of grid in their book in 1998. The name of the book is the Grid: Blueprint for a New Computing Infrastructure. The definition is computational grid is a reliable, consistent, ubiquitous, inexpensive hardware and software infrastructure, used for high-end computing as in [6].

Grid wants to make the Local Area Network, Metropolitan Area Network and even Internet into a huge supercomputer, achieve the overall share of knowledge resources, storage resources, computing resources, information resources and expert resources. As the same as internet, the concept of grid computing comes from the needs to achieve sharing resources among universities. The main feature of the grid is the share sharing of resources as in [7].

4.1   Grid Portlet

The introduction of the portlet is in order to overcome the limitations of the first generation of the grid portal. It is used to constitute the second generation of the grid portal. From a user's point of view, portlet is a window in the portal, is able to provide specific services, such as calendar and information flows. From the point of view of an application development, portlet is a software component using Java language, managed by the portlet container. It deals with the request of users and generates dynamic content. As a pluggable interface component for users, portlet can send information to the presentation layer of the portal system. The portlet of the grid portal is not just a conventional portlet that can insert into portal, but also associated with a background service of grid. We call the portlet that associated with grid services grid portlet.

4.1.1   Portlet Criterion
In order to achieve the aim that shares the information resources of universities, it is necessary to develop portlet of different providers. So we need to use a standard portlet API to develop portlet. At present, there are two groups committed to the

development of portlet standards. One is OASIS (Organization for the Advancement of Structures Information Standards), the other is JCP (Java Community Process).

4.1.2 The Portal Framework that Portlet Supported

Currently, Jetspeed, WebSphere and GridSphere are the more popular and representative portal framework .The three portal frameworks have been widely used in the constituting of Web portal by portlet technology. They integrate grid services and use grid portlet to constitute grid portal.

4.2 The Solutions with Grid Portlet Technology

Grid service portal is an entry point of accessing the grid system, and provides interface which starts up the application program for users. The application program will use the resources and services provided by the grid, these resources include computing resources, software resources, storage resources and information resources. Accessing and using grid services are the most fundamental and important functions of service grid portal. In this paper, in order to resolve the problem of sharing university resources, the author uses the portlet based grid technology constituting a service grid portal.

The figure 1 describes how you can access the resources of grid services of university by grid portlet. When the users issue a request for their own operations, servlet will change the user request into portlet request through grid portal and passes it to the Grid portlet. The grid portlet mainly adopts MVC framework, grid portlet through open grid services and grid middleware system called the campus grid resources. Finally, the grid portal presents the obtained resources to users in web pages. In this way, Internet users can easily use the resources of university, provided that the user is a legitimate user, after authentication. Grid service portal provides different users with different user interfaces. There are two major categories of users, administrators and ordinary users. Administrators have the purview of operating management, user management, resource management, system management and system auditing authority, and ordinary users can only modify their own registration and related information, submit work, query operating state, the use of portal resources, there is no system administration authority. Grid portlet for different targets, their deployment is different, which is respectively described as follows.

4.2.1 The Implementation and Deployment of Grid Service Oriented Portlet

The basic class structure inherits the abstract base class of AbstractGridServcie from the ServiceInterface. All class of grid service is inherited from ServiceInterface. Take CounterGridService as an example to specify the implementation of Grid Service. It implements the calling of two main methods for the user interface. One is the method named GetValue, it is used for obtaining the current value of the counter, the other is the Add method, and it is used for adding value to specific counter. First of all, send the request that creates an instance of service to the grid service provider which is appointed by user and call the setGRS method to obtain the handle of grid service instance. Then call the corresponding operation to complete the user's request, acquire the value of the current counter and increase it.

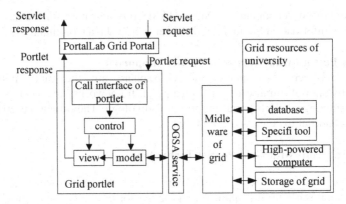

Fig. 1. The model of access the resources of university grid portal by portlet

Firstly, users select the providers of grid services, send the URL request of the services updating and the portlet verify the validity of URL, and send the request creating an instance for gird services to the providers of grid services. After the initialization, Client sends request to the back-end server named OGSA by specific communication protocol as SOAP. The OGSA server creates the service instances for users and response to users with the URL of service instance. Finally, the user can obtain URL of calling the specific service instances and WSDL description of corresponding services. Portlet-based grid service portal provides different interfaces for different users. The functions for different types of users are as in figure 2.

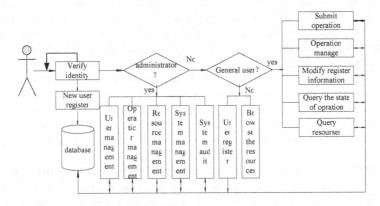

Fig. 2. Framework of user functions

4.2.2 The Implementation and Deployment of Computing Service Oriented Portlet

In Grid Portal, we provide a submission interface for users to calculate. Users can select a specific document and submit it to specific server to calculate. There are two solutions for achieving the specific calculation, (1) using the management services of the operations of OGSA ,submit operation request to the service node that deployed the cluster of Globus Toolkit3 and use the standard MPI to achieve computing. (2)P2P-based computing model and implementation of using Web Service methods, when the server side acquires the operating documents which users submit, it starts to distribution operations to the peer client as in [9].

4.3 Part Experimental Data of Grid Service Portlet and Analyses

The author of this article has developed an initial resource sharing grid portal, it bases on java language, run with tomcat 5.5 or tomcat 6.0. In order to test the function of the grid portal, we use two clusters of computers to constitute the network environment. Specific cluster configuration is shown in the table 1.

Table 1. Configuration of the cluster

Host name	Node number	CPU	Core storage
Wo.grid.cnu.edu.cn	4+1	Intel(R)Core(TM)2Duo2.00Ghz	1014MB
Hao.grid.cnu.edu.cn	8+1	Server (2×PIII2.2Ghz) Node(2×PIII2.00Ghz)	1014MB

Experimental conditions: We will carry out a reasonable arrangement of cluster Wo, so that any computer of the cluster can connect the Internet, Hao will be arranged as a cluster LAN, we constitute grid with the resources of the cluster in this Local Area Network. If you want to know how to make the information resources to be grid, you should refer [10], we don't talk about it in this paper.

1) Cluster Wo direct access resources of cluster Hao
The results showed that any computer of Wo cluster can use part resources of the cluster Hao. When users submit a work, we measured the different times of two different clusters by calculating as in the table 2.

Table 2. The calculate time of the cluster

Compute quantity	1000	2000	4000	8000	10000
Time of Wo(s)	104	216	401	720	930
Time of Hao(s)	80	162	320	610	801

This experiment has the same effect as outside the intranet of campus, non-grid services portal, directly accessed university resources. We can test in person, outside the campus network, any computer even if it can link to the internet, even legitimate users of the school network, for example, students can not use all the resources of the Intranet in schools, particularly valuable papers.

2) Cluster Wo through Grid service portal access grid resources of cluster Hao
The results showed that the any computer of the cluster Wo can used all resources of the cluster Hao, including computing resources, storage resources, and information resources and so on. This experiment has the same effect as on a random computer

connected to the internet outside the intranet of campus accessing the campus grid resources through grid services. Figure 1 is the realization of the model.

When users submit a work, we measured the different computation time as shown in table 3.

Table 3. The calculate time of the cluster

Compute quantity	1000	2000	4000	8000	10000
Time of Wo(s)	88	164	315	614	803
Time of Hao(s)	60	102	200	480	670

Compare tables 2 and 3, we can see that through the Service Grid portal accessed the Grid resources of university can reduce the computing time, which is proved from another point of view, Wo Cluster through Grid service portal uses Hao Grid resources can make a higher resource utilization, which makes the best use of the resources of Hao cluster.

5 Epilogue

The design and achievement of the service grid portal of university, not only make the best use of the university information resources, enlarge the number of users for some expensive and no copy resources, but also avoid resource and information waste, provide a safe, reliable and extensible Web environment for users. Any one who verifies the identity can access the application of the service gird portal by browsingon any computer that can access the Internet. You can send your operation and examine the state of execution. Accordingly, if grid portlet of different providers can access each other, then each university can accesses the other's information resources, so we can achieve the idea of One University. Otherwise, grid portal is individual, users can customize specific gird portal if he needs. By the use of grid portal, wherever you are, whoever you are, if you can access the internet and verify your identity, you can make use of the resources of university as conveniently as you are inside the intranet of university.

References

1. Chen, Z., Chen, G.: Introduction and Application of Portlet-based Grid Portal. Sciences Journal of graduate school of Chinese Academy 23, 442–446 (2006)
2. Zhang, G.: Study on the Application of Service of Grid Computing Environment. Southeast University, Nanjing (2004)
3. Liuand, Y., Yang, G.: Design and Implementation of Portlet-based Framework for Teaching Grid Portal. J. Beijing Institute of Machinery Industry 23, 42–46 (2008)
4. Tian, C., Zhang, S.: Achieve the Resources of Digital Campus Intergration Using Portlet Technology. Science of computer 34(8), 293–295 (2007)
5. Wang, Z.: Design and Impementation of Portlet-based Campus Information Portal. J. Computer Simulation 22, 103–110 (2004)

6. Foster, I., Kesselman, C. (eds.): The grid: Blueprint for a New Computing Infrastructure, 1st edn. Morgan Kaufmann, San Francisco (1998)
7. Zhang, Y.: The Technical Guidelines for System Analyst. TsinghuaUniversity Press, Beijing (2007)
8. Maozhenli, Baker, M.: Core Technology of Grid Computing. TsinghuaUniversity Press, Beijing (2006)
9. Feng, Z.: Portlet-based Framwork for Service-oriented GRID Portal Implementation. J. Computer Engineering 30, 91–115 (2007)
10. Liu, F.: Research of Campus Computing Grid of GT4 Based. Middle and Southern University, Hunan (2007)

A Hybrid Particle Swarm Optimization Algorithm Based on Space Transformation Search and a Modified Velocity Model

Song Yu[1], Zhijian Wu[1], Hui Wang[1], and Zhangxing Chen[2]

[1] State Key Lab of Software Engineering, Wuhan University,
Wuhan 430072, P.R. China
[2] Department of Chemical and Petroleum Engineering, Schulich School of
Engineering, University of Calgary, Calgary 2500, Canada

Abstract. Particle Swarm Optimization (PSO) has shown its fast search speed in many complicated optimization and search problems. However, PSO often easily falls into local optima because the particles would quickly get closer to the best particle. Under these circumstances, the best particle could hardly be improved. This paper proposes a new hybrid PSO (HPSO) to solve this problem by combining space transformation search (STS) with a new modified velocity model. Experimental studies on 8 benchmark functions demonstrate that the HPSO holds good performance in solving both unimodal and multimodal functions optimization problems.

Keywords: Space Transformation Search (STS), evolutionary algorithm, Particle Swarm Optimization (PSO), optimization.

1 Introduction

Particle swarm optimizer (PSO), which was firstly introduced by Kenedy and Eberhart in 1995[1,2], emulates the flocking behavior of birds to solve optimization problems. In PSO, each potential solution is considered as a particle. All particles have their own fitness values and velocities. These particles fly through the D-dimensional problem space by learning from the historical information of all the particles. A potential solution is represented by a particle that adjusts its position and velocity according to equation (1) and (2):

$$v_{id}^{(t+1)} = \omega v_{id}^{(t)} + c_1 r_1 (p_{id}^t - x_{id}^t) + c_2 r_2 (p_{gd}^t - x_{id}^t), \tag{1}$$

$$x_{id}^{(t+1)} = x_{id}^{(t)} + v_{id}^{(t+1)}, \tag{2}$$

where t is the time index, i is the particle index, and d is the dimension index. p_i is the individual best position. p_g is the known global best position. ω is the inertia weight described in [3]. c_1 and c_2 are the acceleration rates of the cognitive and social parts, respectively. r_1 and r_2 are random values different for each particle i as well as for each dimension d. The position of each particle

W. Zhang et al. (Eds.): HPCA 2009, LNCS 5938, pp. 522–527, 2010.

is also updated in each iteration by adding the velocity vector to the position vector.

One problem found in the standard PSO is that it could easily fall into local optima in many optimization problems. One reason for PSO to converge to local optima is that particles in PSO can quickly converge to the best position once the best position has no change. When all particles become similar, there is a little hope to find a better position to replace the best position found so far. In this paper, a new hybrid PSO algorithm called HPSO is proposed. It avoids premature convergences and allows STS-PSO [4] to continue searching for the global optima by applying space transformation-based learning and to break away from local optimal with a new disturbing factor and a convergence monitor. Our HPSO has been tested on both unimodal and multi-modal function optimization problems. Comparison has been conducted among HPSO, standard PSO and STS-PSO. The rest of this paper is organized as follows: Section 2 presents the new HPSO algorithm. Section 3 describs the benchmark continuous optimization problems used in the experiments, and gives the experimental settings. Section 4 presents and discusses the experimental results. Finally, Section 5 concludes with a summary.

2   HPSO Algorithm

2.1   Space Transformation Search (STS)

Many evolutionary optimization methods start with some initial solutions, called individuals, in an initial population, and try to improve them toward some optima solution(s). The process of searching terminates when some predefined conditions are satisfied. In some cases, the searching easily stagnates, when the population falls into local optima. If the stagnation takes places too early, the premature convergence of search is caused. Under these circumstances, the current search space hardly contains the global optimum. So it is difficult for the current population to achieve better solutions. However, Space transformation search, based on opposition learning method[5], originally introduced by Hui Wang [4], has proven to be an effective method to cope with lots of optimization problems. When evaluating a solution x to a given problem, we can guess the transformed solution of x to get a better solution x'. By doing this, the distance of x from optima solution can be reduced. For instance, if x is -10 and the optimum solution is 30, then the transformed solution is 40. But the distance of x' from the optimum solution is only 20. So the transformed solution x' is closer to the optimum solution. The new transformed solution X^* in the transformed space S can be calculated as follows:

$$x^* = k(a + b) - x, \tag{3}$$

where $x \in R$ within an interval of $[a, b]$ and k can be set as 0,0.5,1 or a random number within $[0, 1]$.

To be more specific, we put it in an optimization problem, let $X = (x_1, x_2, x_n)$ be a solution in an n-dimensional space. Assume $f(X)$ is a fitness function which is used to evaluate the solution's fitness. According to the definition of the STS, $X^* = (x_1^*, x_2^*, x_n^*)$is the corresponding solution of X in the transformed search space. If $f(X^*)$ is better than $f(X)$, then update X with X^*; otherwise keep the current solution X. Hence, the current solution and its transformed solution are evaluated simultaneously in order to continue with the fitter one. The interval boundaries $[a_j(t), b_j(t)]$ is dynamically updated according to the size of current search space. The new dynamic STS model is defined by

$$X_{ij}^* = k[a_j(t) + b_j(t)] - X_{ij}, \tag{4}$$

$$a_j(t) = min(X_{ij}(t)), b_j(t) = max(X_{ij}(t)) \tag{5}$$

$$i = 1, 2, ..., PopSize, j = 1, 2, ..., n$$

2.2   Modified Velocity Model

In the PSO, particles are attracted to their corresponding previous best particles $pbest_i$ and the global best particle $gbest$. With the movement of particles, particles are close to $pbest_i$ and $gbest$, and then $pbest_i - X_i$ and $gbest - X_i$ becomes small. According to the updating equation of velocity, the velocity of each particle become small. Once the $pbest_i$ or $gbest$ fall into local minima, all the particles will quickly converge to the positions of them. The cognitive part and social part of each particle will be near to 0 because of $X_i = pbest_i = gbest$. As a result, the velocity of each particle tends to 0, and the updating equation of position is invalid. Finally, all the particles will be stagnate and hardly escape from local optima.

In order to avoid this situation, this paper proposes a new modified velocity model to perturb the position of particles by monitoring each $pbest_i$ and $gbest$. If the $pbest_i$ or $gbest$ has no changes in a predefined number of generations, it is considered to be trapped into local optima. To help it escape from local optima, we conduct a disturbance to the particle to help the trapped particle jump to another position accordingly, if the $Monitor\_pbest_i > T_1$, the cognitive part of PSO turns to be:

$$c_1 r_1 (p_{id}^t - d_1 x_{id}^t), \tag{6}$$

where $Monitor\_pbest_i$ records the number of times the $pbest$ did not change, and the T_1 is the predefined threshold, and d_1 is a random number within [0,1]. If the $Monitor\_gbest > T_2$, the social part of PSO turns to be:

$$c_2 r_2 (p_{gd}^t - d_2 x_{id}^t), \tag{7}$$

where $Monitor\_gbest$ records the number of times the $gbest$ did not change, and the T_2 is a predefined threshold, and d_2 is a random number within [0,1]; Accordingly the equation (1) can be modified to be:

$$v_{id}^{(t+1)} = \omega v_{id}^{(t)} + c_1 r_1 (p_{id}^t - d_1 x_{id}^t) + c_2 r_2 (p_{gd}^t - d_2 x_{id}^t) \tag{8}$$

Table 1. The main steps of HPSO

Begin
 n = dimensional size;
 P = current population;
 TP = the transformed population of P;
 t = the generation index;
 $[a_j(t), b_j(t)]$ = the interval boundaries of the j_{th} dimension in current population;
 ps = the probability of STS;
 $best\_fitness$ = the fitness value of the best particle found by all particles so far;
 accuracy = fixed accuracy level;
 MAX_{NE}=the maximum number of evaluation;
 while($best_f itness > accuracy$&&$NEMAX_{NE}$);
  if $(rand(0, 1) < ps)$;
   update the dynamic interval boundaries $[a_j(t), b_j(t)]$incurrent population according to equation 5;
   for $i = 1$ **to** $PopSize$
    Calculate the transformed particle TP_i of P_i according to equation 4;
    The velocity of TP_i keeps the same with P_i;
    Calculate the fitness value of particle TP_i;
   for end
   select $PopSize$ fittest particles in P and TP as a new population;
   Update $pbest, gbest$ in the new population if needed;
  else
   for $i = 1$ **to** $PopSize$
    if $(Monitor\_pbest_i >= T_1)$
     $d_1 = random[0, 1]$;
    else $d_1 = 1$;
    if $(Monitor\_gbest >= T_2)$, $d_2 = random[0, 1]$;   **else** $d_2 = 1$;
    Calculate the velocity of particle $P(i)$ according to equation 8;
    Update the position of particles $P(i)$ according to equation 2;
    Calculate the fitness value of particle $P(i)$;
    update $pbest$ if needed
    if ($pbest$ changed), $Monitor\_pbest_i = 0$;
     else $Monitor\_pbest_i + +$;
   for end
   Update $gbest$ if needed;
   if ($gbest$ changed), $Monitor\_gbest$=0;
    else $Monitor\_gbest + +$;
  while end
End

Table 2. Minimum values of the function, and X Rn is these search space

Test Function	Dim	X	f_{min}
$f_1(x) = \sum_{i=1}^{n} x_i^2$	30	[-100,100]	0
$f_2(x) = \sum_{i=1}^{n} |x_i| + \prod_{i=1}^{n} x_i$	30	[-10, 10]	0
$f_3(x) = \sum_{i=1}^{n} (\sum_{j=1}^{i})$	30	[-100,100]	0
$f_4(x) = max|x_i|$	30	[-100, 100]	0
$f_5(x) = \sum_{i=1}^{n} (x_i + 0.5)$	30	[-100, 100]	0
$f_6(x) = \sum_{i=1}^{n} (x_i^2 - 10 \cos(2\pi\ x_i) + 10)$	30	[-5.12,5.12]	0
$f_7(x) = -20 \exp(-0.2\sqrt{\frac{1}{n} \sum_{i=1}^{n} x_i^2}) - \exp(\frac{1}{n} \sum_{i=1}^{n} \cos(2\pi x_i)) + 20 + e$	30	[-32, 32]	0
$f_8(x) = \frac{1}{4000} \sum_{i=1}^{n} x_i^2 - \prod_{i=1}^{n} cos\frac{x_i}{\sqrt{i}} + 1$	30	[-600, 600]	0

3   Numerical Experiments

3.1   Test Functions

A comprehensive set of benchmark functions [6], including 8 different global optimization problems, have been chosen in our experimental studies. According

Table 3. The comparison results among PSO, STS-PSO and HPSO

Function	PSO		STS-PSO		HPSO	
	Mean	NFC	Mean	NFC	Mean	NFC
f_1	9.23e-16	39644	8.81e-16	57069.3	3.52e-16	22600
f_2	8.48e-16	105972	9.16e-16	90714.7	8.44e-16	39708
f_3	9.05e-16	44100	8.99e-16	57853.3	6.57e-16	23800
f_4	3.23e-06	200000	1.45e-04	200000	7.97e-16	48694
f_5	1.15	123560	0	15228	0	5210
f_6	46.3153	200000	56.746	200000	0	22200
f_7	1.41334	200000	9.59e-13	200000	9.56e-13	200000
f_8	2.3e-2	200000	9.34e-16	46400	7.66e-16	24200

to the properties, they are divided into two classes: unimodal functions ($f_1 - f_4$), multimodal functions ($f_5 - f_8$). All the functions used in this paper are to be minimized. The description of the benchmark functions and their global optimum(s) are listed in Table 2.

3.2 Experiment Setup

There are three variant PSO algorithms including the proposed HPSO used in the following experiments. The algorithms and parameters settings are listed below: The standard PSO (PSO);A space transformation search PSO (STS-PSO); Our Hybrid PSO (HPSO);

For PSO, STS-PSO and HPSO, $w = 0.72984$, $c_1 = c_2 = 1.49618$, and the maximum velocity V_{max} is set to the half range of the search space on each dimension. For all algorithms, the population size is set to 40 and the maximum number of evaluations is set to 200,000. The accuracy of functions $f_1 - f_4, f_7, f_8$ is set to 1e-15 and that of functions f_5, f_6 is set to 0. If the fitness value of the best fitness found by all particles so far (best fitness) reaches to the fixed accuracy, the current population is considered to obtain the global optimum, and then the algorithm is terminated. The probability of STS ps is set to 0.25. All the experiments are conducted 50 times with different random seeds, and the average results throughout the optimization runs are recorded.

3.3 Experimental Results

Table 3 shows the comparison among PSO,STS-PSO, HPSO for function f_1 to f_8, where "Mean" indicates the mean best function values found in the last generation, and "NFC" stands for the average number of function calls over 50 trials.From the result, it is obvious that HPSO performs better than standard PSO and STS-PSO. The significant improvement achieved by HPSO can be contributed to the space transformation search and the disturbing factor. The space transformation search method adds the changing probability of particles, and the modified velocity model proposed in this paper improves the accuracy of convergence. Therefore, HPSO gets better solutions than the standard PSO and STS-PSO.

4 Conclusion

The idea of HPSO is to improve PSO based on space transformation search method and a new velocity model with convergence monitor to help avoid local optima and accelerate the convergence of PSO. The new proposed velocity model is to monitor the changes of fitness values of each $pbest_i$ and $gbest$. If a $pbest_i$ or $gbest$ has no improvements in a predefined generations, it is considered to fall into local minima and at the same time we present some disturbances to these particles to break away the local optima. By combining these methods , HPSO is able to find better solutions than other improved PSO. HPSO has been compared with the standard PSO, STS-PSO on both 4 unimodal functions and multimodal functions. The results have shown that HPSO has faster convergence rate on those simple unimodal functions and superior global search ability on those multimodal functions compared to other PSO.

However, according to no free lunch theory[7], in some cases, this hybrid PSO can still not avoid premature convergence, in some more complex problems. This will be an important work to continue. Besides the 8 multimodal functions, more test functions will be selected in further work.

Acknowledgment

This work was supported by the National Basic Research Program of China(973 program, No.: 2007CB310801).

References

1. Kennedy, J., Eberhart, R.C.: Particle swarm optimization. In: Proceedings of IEEE International Conference on Neural Networks, pp. 1942–1948 (1995)
2. Eberhart, R.C., Shi, Y.: Comparison between genetic algorithms and particle swarm optimization. In: Proceedings of the 7th Annual Conference on Evolutionary Programming, pp. 69–73 (1998)
3. Shi, Y., Eberhart, R.C.: A modified particle swarm optimization. In: Proceedings of IEEE Congress Evolutionary Computation, pp. 69–73 (1998)
4. Wang, H., Wu, Z.J., Liu, Y.: Space Transformation Search: A New Evolutionary Technique. Genetic and Evolutionary Computation (2009) (in press)
5. Rahnamayan, S., Tizhoosh, H.R., Salama, M.M.A.: Opposition-Based differential evolution. In: Proceedings of IEEE Congress Evolutionary Computation, vol. 12, pp. 64–79 (2008)
6. Yao, X., Liu, Y., Lin, G.: Evolutionary programming made faster. IEEE Transaction on Evolutionary Computation 3, 82–102 (1999)
7. Wolpert, D.H., Macready, W.G.: No free lunch theorems for optimization. IEEE Transaction on Evolutionary Computation 1, 67–82 (1997)

Adaptive Control in Grid Computing Resource Scheduling

Jia-bin Yuan, Jiao-min Luo, and Bo-jia Duan

Nanjing University of Aeronautics and Astronautics, Postfach 21 00 16
30 yudao street nanjing jiangsu province, China
jbyuan@nuaa.edu.cn

Abstract. In this article, we present a method of improving the genetic algo-rithms in the task scheduling of grid environment due to the dynamic variability characteristic of grid. First, we review the crossover probability P_c and mutation probability P_m, the key parameters affecting the performance of genetic algo-rithm. Next, using the adaptive thinking and population fitness which represents the performance of grid resource scheduling, we present an adaptive genetic algorithm, giving a reasonable way to select crossover probability and mutation probability. It helps P_c and P_m can be adjusted automatically with the change of the population fitness; therefore we can get a good resource scheduling. Finally, we describe the results of the test, showing that the improved adaptive genetic algorithms can make the grid resource scheduling have good population fitness.

1 Introduction

With the rapid development of the grid, the task scheduling problem in grid computing has become increasingly important. Task scheduling, also known as task mapping, aims at assigning different tasks to the corresponding grid nodes to complete in the most reasonable way, taking into consideration of the parameters such as calculation performance of the grid node and communication between nodes in the grid environ-ment of numerous computers[1]. As the dynamic change of speed and host load and time of network communications of the processor in the grid environment, task scheduling problem has also become difficult [2]. At present, lots of research work has been made at home and abroad around the task scheduling algorithms of grid com-puting [3-6]. The task scheduling algorithm is mainly divided into static and dynamic scheduling algorithms. Static scheduling algorithm refers to that all the tasks and task mapping strategies have been identified before the implementation of the task sched-uling. Dynamic scheduling algorithm refers to that the tasks and task mapping strate-gies are determined in accordance with the actual situation during the period of the implementation of the task scheduling.

In this paper, we present a method of improving the genetic algorithms in the task scheduling of grid environment due to the dynamic variability characteristic [7-8]. First, we analyze the characteristics and architectures of Grid technology, as well as the basic idea of adaptive. Next, self-adaptive genetic algorithms are proposed to solve the

W. Zhang et al. (Eds.): HPCA 2009, LNCS 5938, pp. 528–533, 2010.

task scheduling problem in grid environment. We also adjust the key parameters which affect the behavior and performance of genetic algorithm to obtain a good resource scheduling.

2 Genetic Algorithms

GA (genetic algorithms) is a technology used to search a large solution space, applied to specific problem areas (heterogeneous environment). We use GA to a given meta-task scheduling under the environment of the grid heterogeneous. Set up a population has r chromosomes, each chromosome is one-dimensional vector, the position i in one-dimensional vector represents the task t_i, which records the machine allocated to the task t_i.

There are two methods for the initial population selection: (a) r chromosomes are assigned with the same random way; (b) one chromosome comes from the matching program of the Min-min scheduling algorithm, while others are randomly generated. The second method is known as population method with Min-min chromosome. After the population is initialized, all chromosomes would be to calculate the corresponding fitness values.

First of all, we come into the "Choice" steps of the algorithm cycle: a roulette-based selection strategy is used to select chromosome evolution. This strategy may make a number of chromosomes be copied, also may delete some other chromosomes (the chromosome to be better matched has the higher probability of being copied), in order to ensure good matching program retain in the population. Next, we operate "hybrid": select chromosomes in population randomly and operate the "single point of hybridization" on the pairs of chromosomes, setting up the "hybrid" probability of each pair of chromosomes is P_1. Then we operate the "mutation": select a chromosome and a task of the chromosome randomly, and redistribute the tasks to a new machine randomly, setting up the probability of "variation" of each chromosome is P_2. Finally, each chromosome of the future population is reassessed their fitness value.

A cycle of the above algorithm has been completed. The cycle of algorithm ends when one of the following occurs: a) the stated number of the evolution has been completed; b) in the limited cycle, the major chromosomes of the population have not changed; c) all the chromosomes are gathered into the same map.

3 Improved Adaptive Genetic Algorithm

Since the integrity of the structure and the theory of genetic algorithms were introduced, research and applications of the genetic algorithm never stopped [9]. In this paper, we review the crossover probability and mutation probability, the key parameters affecting the performance of genetic algorithm. Then we present two adaptive genetic algorithms, giving a reasonable way to select crossover probability and mutation probability, using the adaptive thinking and population fitness which represents the performance of grid resource scheduling.

3.1 Improved GA1

The parameters crossover probability P_c and mutation probability P_m of genetic algorithm are the key parameters impacting the behavior and the performance of genetic algorithm. It is a direct impact on the convergence and performance of the algorithms. The greater the P_c is, the faster the new individual arises. If P_c is too large, the damage possibility of the genetic model is greater, which make a high fitness individual structure will soon be destroyed. If P_c is too small, the search process will be slow down and stagnate. For mutation probability P_m, if P_m is too small, it is not easy to generate new individual structure; if the value P_m is too large, the genetic algorithm will be turned into a purely random search algorithm. Therefore, the choice of P_c and P_m is an important work in genetic algorithm. However, the choices of P_c and P_m should be determined according to different optimization problems by repeated experiments and it is very difficult to find the best value for each question.

This paper presents an improved adaptive genetic algorithm based on adaptive thinking, it helps P_c and P_m can be adjusted automatically with the change of the population fitness. The specific approach is: when the population fitness of the individual is close to or become the best at the local, P_c and P_m increase; when the group fitness dispersed, P_c and P_m reduced; at the same time, the individuals whose fitness is higher than the average fitness groups, correspond to lower P_c and P_m so that the solution can be protected to access to the next generation; and the individuals whose fitness is lower than the average fitness groups, correspond to a higher P_c and P_m so that the solution can be eliminated. Thus, the design of adaptive laws of parameters in genetic algorithm is shown as the formula (1-2). Demand that P_c and P_m can provide the best value of a relative solution algorithm and can ensure its convergence when it maintains the population diversity.

$$P_c = \begin{cases} \dfrac{k_1(f_{\max} - f')}{f_{\max} - f_{avg}}, & f' \geq f_{avg} \\ k_2 & f' < f_{avg} \end{cases} \tag{1}$$

$$P_m = \begin{cases} \dfrac{k_3(f_{\max} - f)}{f_{\max} - f_{avg}}, & f \geq f_{avg} \\ k_4 & f < f_{avg} \end{cases} \tag{2}$$

f_{max} represents the maximum fitness value of the population, f_{avg} represents the average fitness value of each generation, f' represents the larger fitness value of two crossover individual, f represents the fitness value of variance individual. k_1, k_2, k_3, k_4 are parameters, each value is in $(0,1)$.

3.2 Improved GA2

In 3.1 we give an improved adaptive genetic algorithm. When the fitness value is lower than the average fitness value, it shows that the performance of the individual is not good, then we set cross-rate and variability rate larger; if the fitness value is higher than the average fitness value, it shows that the performance of the individual is adaptable, then we set the cross-rate and mutation rate in accordance with its corresponding value. As it can be seen, when the fitness value is closer to the largest fitness value, the crossover rate and mutation rate is smaller; when it is equal to the maximum fitness value, the crossover rate and mutation rate is zero.

At the early evolution of the population, the better individual is almost in a stable state and the good individual may not be the most optimal global solution, so it is easier for the evolution to turn to the local optimal solution. Therefore the improved algorithm 1 is positive for the groups in the latter evolution, but negative for the early evolution. Thus, the adaptive genetic algorithm can be further improved to make the individuals' cross-rate and mutation rate with the largest fitness value is non-zero, and make them increase to P_{c2} and P_{m2}. This situation increases the cross-rate and mutation rate of the individuals with good performance in the group, making them away the state of stagnation. In order to ensure the individual with good quality of each generation will not be damaged, elite selection strategy is used to make them copy to the next generation directly. The improved design of expression is as follows (3-4):

$$P_c = \begin{cases} \dfrac{(P_{c1} - P_{c2})(f' - f_{avg})}{f_{max} - f_{avg}}, & f' \geq f_{avg} \\ P_{c1} & f' < f_{avg} \end{cases} \quad (3)$$

$$P_m = \begin{cases} \dfrac{(P_{m1} - P_{m2})(f_{max} - f)}{f_{max} - f_{avg}}, & f \geq f_{avg} \\ P_{m1} & f < f_{avg} \end{cases} \quad (4)$$

for each parameter, $P_{c1} = 0.9$, $P_{c2} = 0.6$, $P_{m1} = 0.1$, $P_{m2} = 0.001$.

4 Test Analysis

Java language was used to compile the task scheduling based on both improved adaptive genetic algorithm and general genetic algorithm. The improved adaptive genetic algorithm and general genetic algorithm were compared. Set the number of resources at 6, the number of task at 20, record the average fitness value and the individual maximum fitness value during the evolution of 10 generations of population respectively. The results are shown in Table 1-2.

From the data in the table, it can be seen that some individuals evolve while others degenerate in the process of generating offspring using the genetic algorithms to allocate the tasks. This indicates that when the number of individual of the population is small, the genetic algorithm can not show its own advantages. Moreover, in the evolution of populations it may occur that some new populations degenerate.

Table 1. The fitness value of GA

Generation of population	Average fitness value f_{avg}	Maximum fitness value f_{max}
Initial population	0.034863554	0.055555556
The 1th generation	0.03474636	0.055555556
The 2nd generation	0.03351257	0.05
The 3th generation	0.034116037	0.045454547
The 4th generation	0.033231862	0.05
The 5th generation	0.031385913	0.05
The 6th generation	0.035160933	0.05
The 7th generation	0.037903365	0.055555556
The 8th generation	0.03631475	0.05
The 9th generation	0.035923343	0.05
The 10th generation	0.034972034	0.05

Table 2. The fitness value of Improved adaptive GA

Generation of population	Average fitness value f_{avg}	Maximum fitness value f_{max}
Initial population	0.040378146	0.0625
The 1th generation	0.04164709	0.06666667
The 2nd generation	0.03731074	0.0625
The 3th generation	0.03907328	0.0625
The 4th generation	0.035878647	0.05882353
The 5th generation	0.036360785	0.05263158
The 6th generation	0.037200257	0.05
The 7th generation	0.038251955	0.05
The 8th generation	0.039156914	0.05
The 9th generation	0.039733935	0.05
The 10th generation	0.04042905	0.06666667

5 Conclusion

In this paper, we study the task scheduling problem in the grid environment, giving a method of improving the genetic algorithms in the task scheduling of grid environment due to the dynamic variability characteristic. The following test results show that the improved adaptive genetic algorithms can make the grid resource scheduling have a good population fitness, which presents the availability of the genetic algorithm.

References

1. Foster, I., Kesselman, C., Tuechke, S.: The Anatomy of the Grid (2001)
2. Zhi-hui, D., Yu, C., Peng, L.: Grid Computing, vol. 21, 28, pp. 65–72. Tsinghua University Press, Beijing (2002)
3. Hai-bo, C., Yi, Z.: Scheduling Resources Based on Improved Genetic Algorithm. Computer Simulation (June 2008)
4. Mei-yun, G., Bo, Y., Zhi-gang, C.: Trustworthy Task Scheduling Based on Grid Resource Hypergraph Model. Computer Engineering (13) (2008)
5. Ling, S.H., Lam, H.K., Leung, F.H.F.: A variable-parameter neuralnetwork trained by improved genetic algorithm and its application. In: Proc of International Joint Conference on Neural Networks, Montreal, pp. 1343–1348 (2005)
6. Song, S., Kwok, Y.K., Hwang, K.: Trusted Job Scheduling in Open Computational Grids:Security-driven Heuristics and a Fast Genetic Algorithm. In: Proceedings of the19th IEEE International Parallel&Distributed Processing Symposium, pp. 33–40. IEEE Press, Denver (2005)
7. Jun, C.: Improved genetic algorithm applying to automatic generation of function. Computer Engineering and Design (09) (2008)
8. Da-bin, Z., Jing, W., Gui-qin, L., Hou, Z.: Fuzzy adaptive genetic algorithm. Computer Engineering and Design (18) (2008)
9. Jia-bin, Y., Hai-chen, P.: E-mail Information Classifier of Neural Network Based on Genetic Algorithm Optimization. Journal of Nanjing University of Science and Technology (Natural Science) (01) (2008)

Study on Synchronously Driving Control System of Linear Move Irrigator[*]

Yanwei Yuan, Xiaochao Zhang, Wenhua Mao, and Huaping Zhao

Institute of Mechatronics Technology and Application,
Chinese Academy of Agricultural Mechanization Sciences,
Box25, No.1, Beishatan, Dewai St., Beijing, 100083, P.R. China
yyw215@163.com

Abstract. Spray Irrigation is more efficient in water-saving and yield-increasing than other irrigation methods. Large scale linear move spray irrigation system is widely used in China. But the traditional go-stop-go driving method makes the linear move irrigator hard to control and gets bad irrigation performance. New control way with high efficiency in operation and low consumption of water, electricity, other materials and human resource is needed. Because of the difficulty of examination, virtual reality technology is used to simulate the controlling and driving system in this thesis. Three-dimension models of the irrigation system departments are built according to their scale, and three-dimensional scenes of farmland, as well as mechanical models of the irrigation system are established according to the principles of ground vehicle dynamics. Through simulation a better control method is obtained, which is used in field test, and controlling the large scale irrigator movement almost in a line, with an angle error less than 0.06°.

1 Introduction

Compared with traditional irrigation way, spray irrigation has the following two advantages: avoid excavation of the ridge and furrow irrigation so that conserved arable land area, and use water pipes to avoid leakage losses from irrigation channels and leakage in deep layer of the field [5,12], thus spray irrigation is widely used in China [6,7,16].

Large-scale irrigation system has the character of high degree of automation and low consumption of electricity, water and human resource. Linear move irrigation is the most extensive used large-scale irrigator, which is composed of motors, joist, towers, rear suspension, driving parts and walking components and so on. It has higher coverage rate but more complex structure, and need a higher precision synchronization of the tower. So electrical driving control system is needed to keep all towers go ahead in a horizontal line.

Research projects have been done on precision irrigation systems by different groups [4,14]. These precision irrigation systems were developed for continuous

---

[*] This work was mainly funded by the Chinese National High Technology Program ("863" program) (No. 2006AA10A305), and the "11th five year" program (No. 2006BAD11A01) of China.

W. Zhang et al. (Eds.): HPCA 2009, LNCS 5938, pp. 534–541, 2010.

linear move irrigation systems with a design for variable rate water application control either by Programmable Logic Controller or by addressable devices on a bus system connected to solenoid valves [2]. Traditional experiment methods need long time and more recourses waste. While virtual experiment method has the following character: Without experiment of spray irrigation, analysis the linear move irrigation on process, performance, controlling effect and so on. So the repeating running, detecting, perfecting and so on can be done on virtual environment, which makes the experiment periods short and reduces water and human resource cost [9,16].

In the thesis, we built 3-D models of the irrigation system according to their scale with Pro/ENGINEER, and 3-D scenes of farmland with Multigen Creator software, as well as mechanical models of the irrigation system according to the principles of ground vehicle dynamics. Visual C++ and Multigen Vega were used to program an application, which load the three-dimension models of the irrigation system into the scenes of farmland. Then simulated the control system and drive system to monitor in real-time.

2   Methodology

2.1   Build 3D Models

Disassemble the linear move irrigator and measure every part, build three dimension models of each part with the software of Pro/ENGINEER according to the measured size, and then save the models as .obj formats. Import the .obj file to Multigen Creator, and assemble those models to a whole machine model for each tower (Fig. 1).

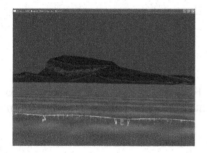
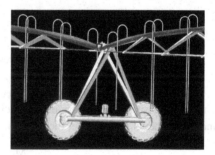

Fig. 1. Interface of the linear move irrigation control system

Fig. 2. Motor driving control interface of linear move irrigator

Get Digital Elevation Model (DEM) of the field to be experimented, and translate the DEM data to Digital Elevation Data (DED) style that can be imported to Multigen Creator. Set parameters to DED and generate three dimension terrain models, add textures to the model and then get the virtual scenes (Fig. 1).

2.2   Driving of 3D Models

The large scale irrigator we studied is composed of six joists, which were sustained by eight towers. Each tower was driven by a variant frequency motor through gear change mechanism fixed on it. On the connections of each two connected sections, there was one linear displacement sensor to detect the angle between the two connected sections (Fig. 2).

2.2.1 Force Analysis of the Irrigator Tower

The linear move irrigation system is composed of towers, joists, sprinklers, cantilevers, motors, driving system and navigation system and so on (Fig. 1). Each joist is fixed to tow towers, and there are many cantilevers with low pressure sprinklers fixed to a joint. Every two joists are connected by a flexible joining. On each tower there is a motor, which was controlled by the controlling system to keep the all the towers move ahead in give direction and keep in a horizontal line [13].

As the speed of the linear move irrigator is very low, which is 0.03m/s~0.035m/s, when force anglicizing on the tower, we take it for granted that each tower is a three dimension rigid body move, and will never jump. The two wheels have the same radius, when driving on sloping field, the force in portrait plane is shown as Fig. 3.

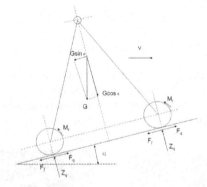

Fig. 3. Schematic diagram of forces on tower walking along a field slope

In Fig. 4, G is gravity the tower accept, F_q is driving force of former and back wheels, F_f is resistance of former and back wheels, M_f is resistance moment of former and back wheels, then we get the equation :

$$M_f = F_f * r_q \tag{1}$$

r_q is the radius of the wheel. Suppose Z_q is the counterforce of the ground, α is grade of the field, then the drive balance equation of the ground is:

$$F_q = f\,G\,\cos\alpha + G\,\sin\alpha \tag{2}$$

Where f is roll resistance coefficient of the tower.

When it works in the field, the driving power of one motor is:

$$N_q = F_q\,v\,/\,60 \tag{3}$$

Where: v is the speed of the tower.

The torque M_q is generated by motor, through transmission system that composed of reducers, gimbals, transmission shafts and wheel reducers and so on, transmitted to driving wheels. Suppose i_g is transmission rate of the motor reducer, i_c is transmission rate of the wheel reducer, η_r is the mechanical efficiency of transmission system, then we get:

$$M_q = M_{qt}\, i_g\; i_0\, \eta_r \qquad (4)$$

And the driving force of tower is:

$$F_q = M_{qt}\, i_g\; i_0\, \eta_r / r_q \qquad (5)$$

2.2.2 Collaborative Simulation of Machine and Motors

Change each motor's output power by computer keyboard, calculate the forces of each tower according to the terrain condition and the corresponding motor driving force, calculate each tower's acceleration, and then speed by integral [1]. Detect the speed of each tower and the angles between every two conterminous joists, calculate the errors between speeds detected and given one, feed the errors back to the controlling motor [11], and change the output power of each motor to keep the angles between every two conterminous joists small enough. Data flow of virtual simulation is as Fig. 4.

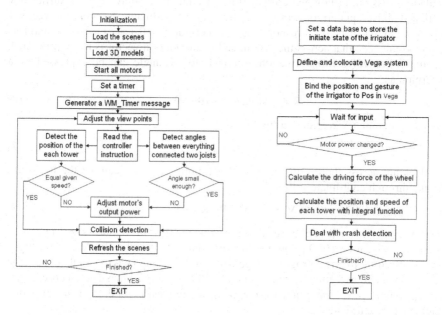

Fig. 4. Data flow of virtual simulation   **Fig. 5.** Rocess of linear move irrigation driving

As Fig. 4, we initialize the program first, give initial positions to each tower of the irrigation system, start all motors fixed on each tower, according to terrain character, forces between other joists, weight of towers and joists, all kinds of resistances and so on, calculate the position and gesture of every tower, and refresh the scenes.

Detect the angles between every two connected joists, and keep the angles little enough so that all joists are moving forward in a horizontal line through change the motors' output power. Fig. 5 shows the driving process of linear move irrigation.

2.2.3 Collaborative Simulation Programming

As the force, speed, position and gesture of the irrigator are all parameters of three dimension co-ordinations, we must express those parameters with vector. When calculate the gesture and position in virtual scene, API function of Vega must be used. There are four kinds of coordinates in Vega: absolute coordinate, observer coordinate, rule object coordinate and user-defined coordinate. The position should be calculated in absolute coordinate system, the gesture should be calculated in rule object coordinate and absolute coordinate, while forces should be calculated in rule object coordinate system, then, coordinates transform is necessary.

The gesture of the 3D model is usually described with Euler angle (x, y, z, θ, ψ, φ), where θ, ψ and φ are pitch, yaw, and roll angles that the model revolving around x, y and z axis. As the gimbals lock character of Euler function, when the revolving angle is near $90°$, the infinite number will occur in the commutation matrix, which will terminate the simulation.

Poisson kinematics function can avoid the singularity of Euler function, but as the simulation goes on, orthogonal error will be accumulated. To avoid the insufficiency mentioned above, quaternion was used to transform coordinates. Suppose the vector v = (x, y, z) in 3D space is corresponding to quaternion V = 0 + x i + y j + z k, and L is a circumrotate axis that across the origin, and its orientation vector is n = (n_1, n_2 , n_3), then the circumvolve transformation around L for θ angle can be expressed by a quaternion as:

$$R = \cos(\theta/2) + \sin(\theta/2)\, n \qquad (6)$$

The quaternion that V rotates θ around L is:

$$V_1 = R\, V\, R^{-1} \qquad (7)$$

If L does not across the origin, suppose P is a point of L, we can get the transform formula through coordinate shift as:

$$V_1 = R\, (\, V - P\,)\, R^{-1} + P \qquad (8)$$

The software system described in this thesis is running in Windows XP operation system and Visual C++ 6.0 programming environment. Besides, the API of Multigen Vega is also used to write programs together with C++ language to simulate the large scale linear move irrigation system cooperation between machines and electrical controlling system. In the program, we import three dimension models of the irrigation system and virtual field scenes.

Console application cannot satisfy the request of virtual reality simulation, and the API of Windows is perplexing and low efficiency to use, so we use an efficient and simple way to program, that is, with LynX of Vega and MFC configurations to build the program.

Build a single document interface, write code to load the .flt file of the 3D model. The function runVega() of myMFCVegaView is used to check whether the ADF file has necessary Vega class. To control the movement, we use input Devices class of

Vega and user-defined movement model, with CALLBACK function and vgMotRegister() to realize the control of the model.

The structure vgMotionCallbackStruct is used as a parameter to transmit the motion model. Then message responding function OnKeyDown and OnKeyUp is used to receive key-press messages.

3 Results and Discussion

When linear move irrigator works in the field, because of the difference of field gradient, ground messiness and moisture and glutinosity of the field, the resistance is very complicated. At different position, we give resistance as random values.

When experiment in virtual scenes, the eight motors start with the same frequency of 7.5 Hz, drive the wheels move through derailleur, and the towers which were fixed on tow wheels respectively move ahead, because of the difference of resistance, the

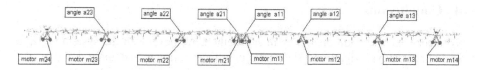

Fig. 6. Angles and motors serial numbers of linear move irrigator

Table 1. Data of irrigator system in field test

No.	Angle of the sensors (°)						Frequency of motors (Hz)								Position
---	a11	a12	a13	a23	a22	a21	m11	m12	m13	m14	m24	m23	m22	m21	(meter)
1	0	0	-.02	0	0	-.02	8.99	8.29	7.73	7.63	7.12	7.35	7.13	7.29	632
2	-.02	0	-.04	0	.02	0	7.84	7.9	7.48	7.01	7.31	7.57	6.51	5.81	638
3	.04	-.02	-.02	.02	0	.04	8.41	8.05	6.99	6.2	6.81	7.36	5.85	5.09	645
4	-.02	-.02	-.02	0	-.04	-.04	6.55	7.01	7.31	6.66	9.18	8.5	9.6	11.9	650
5	0	0	0	.06	0	-.02	7.22	7.64	7.2	5.23	11.59	6.95	6.59	6.71	657
6	0	.02	0	.04	-.02	0	8.14	8.21	7.29	7.36	6.8	7.52	7.4	7.24	661
7	.02	-.02	-.02	.04	.02	0	8.46	7.42	7.52	7.39	6.76	7.6	6.12	5.28	667
8	-.02	-.02	-.02	.02	0	0	7.16	7.26	7.58	7.43	7.08	7.42	6.78	6.04	673
9	-.02	0	-.02	.04	0	-.02	6.56	7.44	7.44	7.31	6.7	7.56	7.5	7.66	682
10	0	0	-.02	.04	.02	0	7.87	7.89	7.39	7.25	6.87	7.61	6.31	5.93	686
11	0	-.02	-.04	.02	.02	0	7.31	6.97	7.59	7.2	7.02	7.41	6.43	6.21	691
12	-.02	-.02	-.02	.02	0	-.02	7.26	7.48	7.52	7.34	6.86	7.48	7.14	7.16	692
13	0	0	0	.04	0	-.02	7.79	7.69	7.45	7.5	6.68	7.55	6.99	7.17	694
14	0	-.02	0	.02	.02	0	7.49	6.89	7.47	7.39	6.82	7.53	6.43	6.19	699
15	0	0	-.02	0	0	0	7.67	7.51	7.49	7.34	7.25	7.51	6.73	6.65	704

speed of each tower is different, which caused the distortion of the whole irrigation system. Detect the values of each linear displacement sensor, calculate the angles between every two connected joists, then aggrandize the motor frequency whose position is behind others, and decrease the motor frequency whose position is ahead, so as to keep all the towers in a line. Simulation show that when adjust the angles from the middle to two sides, like shown in Fig. 6, when adjust angle a11 and angle a21, followed by angle a12 and a22, and then a13 and a23, we can get best results.

Then used this control method to field test, we get good result too. Table 1 is the angles, motor frequencies and positions of linear move irrigation system driving.

The frequencies of each motor changed according to the corresponding angle, to increase or decrease the speed of each tower, so as to keep all joists and towers in a horizontal line. Data in table 1 show us the linear move irrigator move from the position of 632 meters to 704 meters, and during the whole 72 meters' process, the largest angle error is 0.06°.

4 Conclusions

To ameliorate the traditional experiment method, we developed the system of large scale linear move irrigation system. Through the experiment and analysis we get the conclusion: (1), this system can do experiment expediently; (2), simulation shows that when adjust the angles from middle to two sides can get best results; (3), when use the control method obtained from virtual simulation into field test, the large scale irrigation we used can move almost in a line with an angle error of no more than 0.06°.

References

1. Dukes, M., Perry, C.: Uniformity testing of variable-rate center pivot irrigation control systems. Precision Agriculture 7(3), 205–218 (2006)
2. Sadler, E.T., Evan, R.G.: Site-Specific, Variable - Rate Precision Irrigation: More Overhead Boom Improvement. Irrigation Journal 51(6) (2001)
3. Evans, G.W., Harting, G.B.: Precision irrigation with center pivot systems on potatoes. In: Proc. ASCE 1999 International Water Resources Engineering Conference, August 8-11 (1999)
4. Evans, R.G., Buchleiter, G.W., Sadler, E.J., King, B.A., Harting, G.B.: Control for precision irrigation with self-propelled systems. In: Evans, R.G., Benham, B.L., Trooien, T.P. (eds.) Proc. 4th Decennial National Irrigation Symposium, pp. 322–331. ASAE, St. Joseph, Mich. (2000)
5. Hongzhi, J.: Indraught and experience of large scale irrigation. Country mechanization (3), 38–39 (1999)
6. Hongzhi, J.: The application and development of large scale irrigation in China. Water saving irrigation 24-26(4), 155–158 (1998)
7. Lin, M.C., Gottschalk, S.: Collision Detection between Geometric Models: A Survey. In: Proceedings of IMA Conference on Mathematics of Surfaces. Bath Information Geometers 1998, pp. 1–20 (1998)

8. James, M.H., Klosowski, T., Joseph, S.B., et al.: Evaluation of Collision Detection Methods for Virtual Reality Fly-Through. In: Conf. Computational Geometry C. Gold, Canada, pp. 205–210 (1995)
9. Klocke, N.L., Hunter, C., Alam, M.: Application of a linear move sprinkler system for limited irrigation research. In: 2003 ASAE Annual Meeting (2003)
10. Oksanen, T., Visala, A.: Optimal control of tractor-trailer system in headlands. In: ASAE International Conference on Automation Technology for off-road Equipment, Kyoto, Japan, pp. 255–263 (2004)
11. Perry, C., Pocknee, S., Hansen, O.: Variable-rate irrigation. Resource 10(1), 11–12 (2003b)
12. Robinson, E.: GPS-guided center pivot eliminates need for buried wire. Southwest Farm Press (April 17, 2003)
13. Sadler, E.J., Camp, C.R., Evans, D.E., Millen, J.A.: Corn canopy temperatures measured with a moving infrared thermometer array. Trans. ASAE. 45(3), 531–591 (2002)
14. Seattle, Wa, Y., Chung-Kee, Liao, Y.-T.: Development of a GPS - operated sprayer - Spraying at a destined field and by a fixed flow rate. In: Proceedings of International Symposium on Automation and Mechatronics of Agricultural and Bioproduction Systems, November 2002, vol. 1, pp. 344–349 (2002)
15. Haijun, Y.: Study on variable rate technology based water distribution uniformity of center point and linear move irrigation system. Chinese agricultural University, Beijing (2004)
16. Szalavári, Z., Eckstein, E., Gervautz, M.: Collaborative Gaming in Augmented Reality. In: Proceedings of VRST 1998, Taipei, Taiwan, November 2-5, pp. 195–204 (1998)

A Fast Morphological Reconstruction Algorithm for MRI Brain Image Simplification

Bofeng Zhang, Hui Zhu, Anping Song, and Wu Zhang

School of Computer Engineering and Science, Shanghai University
200072 Shanghai, China
bfzhang@shu.edu.cn

Abstract. The MRI (Magnetic Resonance Imaging) brain image simplification has become one of important pre-processing steps for medical researches and clinical applications. Usually, the fast hybrid reconstruction algorithm, one of the common algorithms of image simplification, requires multiple iterations of reconstruction, so the time complexity is high. In 2004, Robinson gave a downhill filter to overcome this shortage, but it usually remains brighter regions because this algorithm targets MRCP (Magnetic Resonance Cholangiopancreatography) data. In response to the characteristics of MRI brain image simplification, this paper proposes a fast morphological reconstruction algorithm. Firstly, regional maxima concept is introduced to modify the initialization condition, then improved downhill filter algorithm is applied to reconstruct image. Experimental results show that the mean reduction of the execution time is about 73.68% compared to the fast hybrid reconstruction algorithm, and it can achieve good result when it is used to the contour extraction from the MRI brain image.

Keywords: MRI brain image simplification, Morphological reconstruction, Downhill filter.

1 Introduction

The research on the segmentation of interest regions of medical image is the most important basis of the medical image analysis, and the most extensive and in-depth study of the field. Watershed transform is a common technique for image segmentation which has been widely used in many fields of image processing, including medical image segmentation. However, if the watershed transform is applied directly to image segmentation, the problem of over-segmentation caused by insignificant structures or noise will be very serious. So image segmentation is typically done by preprocessing, and then using the watershed transform [1]. The purpose of pre-processing is to remove the image details, which are not necessary to the segment and to produce flat zones. This process is usually called image simplification.

In recent years, several morphological reconstruction filters have been developed as tools for image simplification. These filters indeed produce flat zones while preserving

W. Zhang et al. (Eds.): HPCA 2009, LNCS 5938, pp. 542–549, 2010.

the contour information. The classical filter is morphological reconstruction by dilation which is first proposed by Serra [2]. Then there are many varied instances of this kind filter, but there is a problem: the inefficiency of the 'iterate until convergence' approach. So a number of optimizations and algorithmic efficiencies have been detailed for this and similar procedures in both binary and grayscale morphology including structuring element decomposition [3] and manipulation[4, 5], flat zones [6], interval coding [7], and the use of ordered pixel queues [8]. These algorithms have a common drawback that is the procedure still remains computationally expensive and highly data dependant.

In order to enhance the computing speed, Robinson proposed an efficient morphological reconstruction method which is called the downhill filter [9]. This is an improved algorithm based on the alternative reconstruction by dilation procedures. It can achieve the same filtering effect in a single pass through the data and as such is both fast and linear time in its execution. But the downhill filter usually remains brighter regions because this algorithm targets MRCP (Magnetic Resonance Cholangiopancreatography) data. Thus, in this paper, downhill filter algorithm will be improved to be better for the MRI brain image simplification.

2   Morphological Reconstruction

The reconstruction transformation[10] is relatively well-known in the binary case, where it simply extracts the connected components of an image which are "marked" by another image. However, reconstruction can be defined for grayscale images, where it turns out to be extremely useful for several image analysis tasks. It can be thought of conceptually as repeated dilations of an image, called the marker image, until the contour of the marker image fits under a second image, called the mask image. In morphological reconstruction, the peaks in the marker image "spread out," or dilate. Each successive dilation operation is forced to lie underneath the mask. When further dilations do not change the marker image any more, the processing is finished. The final dilation creates the reconstructed image. The most commonly used algorithm is alternative definition of grayscale reconstruction which is defined as follows:

Let J and I be two grayscale images defined on the same domain, taking their values in the discrete set $\{0,1,\cdots,N-1\}$ and such that $J \leq I$ (i.e., for each pixel $p \in D_I, J(p) \leq I(p)$). The elementary geodesic erosion $\delta_I^{(1)}$ of grayscale image $J \leq I$ above I is given by

$$\delta_I^{(1)}(J) = (J \oplus B) \wedge I. \tag{1}$$

In this equation, $\wedge$ stands for the pointwise minimum and $J \oplus B$ is the dilation of J by flat structuring element B. These two notions are the direct extension to the grayscale case of respectively intersection and binary dilation by B. The grayscale geodesic dilation of size $n \geq 0$ is then given by

$$\delta_I^{(n)}(J) = \underbrace{\delta_I^{(1)} \circ \delta_I^{(1)} \circ \cdots \circ \delta_I^{(1)}}_{n \text{ times}} (J) \qquad (2)$$

The grayscale reconstruction $\rho_I(J)$ of I from J is given by

$$\rho_I(J) = \bigvee_{n \geq 1} \delta_I^{(n)}(J) \qquad (3)$$

There are four algorithms described in [10] for the two dimensional eight connected and three dimensional six connected cases:

A Standard Technique: this algorithm works by iterating elementary dilation followed by pointwise minimum until stability. It is not suited to conventional computers, because the image pixels can be scanned in an arbitrary order. It requires the iteration of numerous complete image scanning, sometimes several hundreds. Its execution time is often minutes.

B Sequential Reconstruction Algorithm: this algorithm first propagate the information in a raster scanning and then upwards in an anti-raster scanning, so it usually requires only a few image scanning (typically a dozen) until stability is reached, but it does not deal well with "rolled-up structures" like several other sequential algorithms.

C Reconstruction Using a Queue of Pixels: in this algorithm the boundary pixels of the marker image are loaded into a FIFO (first-in-first-out) queue at the initialization. Then pixels are removed, their neighbors examined, changed, and added to the queue as required. Processing continues repeating until the queue is empty. However, this algorithm may be slowed down by the initial determination of the boundary pixels.

D Fast Hybrid Reconstruction Algorithm: this algorithm takes advantage of the strong points of the previous two algorithms described in the last two sections without retaining their drawbacks.

3   Downhill Filter Algorithm and Improvement

3.1   Downhill Filter

The downhill filter algorithm is an optimal implementation of the reconstruction by dilation procedure. As with the third and fourth algorithms above, the downhill filter operates on a pixel queue. Folded or rolled up structures in the input image for instance seriously compromise the execution speeds achieved by all four approaches so that no guarantees can be given as to the processing time required in the general case. This algorithm exhibits no such level of variability in its execution speed.

The downhill filter can be presented in two stages. In the first algorithm restrict the marker image in order to make computing easier. Initialization methods state as follows: each pixel in the marker is either equal to the corresponding pixel in the mask or it is equal to zero.Eq.4.

$$\forall p: D \cdot ((J[p] = I[p]) \vee (J[p] = 0)) \tag{4}$$

Then the reconstruction will be determined directly in the marker image J. Let m be the maximum value of the pixels in J and maintain m lists which from $L[1]$ to $L[m]$. So each pixel is set to its final value will be placed in the list corresponding to that value. While the current list is not empty the next element is removed and its neighborhood is examined. For each neighbor pixel which has not already been finalized, J is set equal to the lesser of the current list number and the value in I at this location and the neighbor is added to the corresponding list. If it was already in a list it is also removed from that location.

The process above ensures the scanning from a high gray value to a low gray value pixel by pixel after initialization, and then gets the final reconstruction image. Because a random access queue is implemented instead of a *FIFO* queue in order to allow the processing of pixels in an optimal order, every pixel is addressed only once in the course of the algorithms execution. Specific operations can be referenced in [9].

3.2   Improvement of Downhill Filter Algorithm

The downhill filter algorithm is much faster than the four techniques mentioned above. But it is not suitable for all kind of medical images, because it is improved just for data like MRCP and usually remains the brighter regions. The purpose of the simplification of MRI brain image is to produce flat zones to separate the skull, brain and other structures. So when it is used for the MRI brain image simplification, much important boundary information will be lost except cerebrospinal fluid (CSF). Thus, this paper improves the downhill filter algorithm for the MRI brain image simplification. The drawback occurs in the initialization cause the progress starting from the maximum pixel, so this paper introduces a concept of regional maxima to solve this problem.

A regional maximum M of a grayscale image I is a connected components of pixels with a given value h (plateau at altitude h), such that every pixel in the neighborhood of M has a strictly lower value. It can be defined as follows: A regional maximum at altitude h of grayscale image I is a connected component C of $T_h(I)$ such that $C \cap T_{h+1}(I) = \emptyset$ ($T_h(I)$ is threshold of I at level h.). $R(I)$ is used to denote the regional maxima:

$$R(I)(p) = \begin{cases} I(p), & \text{if } p \text{ belongs to a maximum} \\ 0, & \text{otherwise} \end{cases} \quad \forall p \in D_I \tag{5}$$

In practice, the process of initialization after introducing regional maxima method is described as follows: First, let the marker image value equals the mask image value, or equals zero. Then, find the regional maxima at the region of non-zero pixels, and modify pixels values in accordance with the Eq.5. The final image J will include more important pixels related to different part of image. Each of the regional pixels is added to the corresponding list, then use the part of the downhill filter algorithm to reconstruct image.

Algorithm: Improved reconstruction algorithm by downhill filtering:

```
I :grayscale mask image
J :grayscale marker image, defined on domain D_I , J ≤ I
Reconstruction is determined directly in J
    Compute regional maxima of J:J ← R(J),
    Initialization of the queue with pixels of maxima:
     For every pixel p ∈ D_I:
      If J(p) ≠ 0 and p ∉ R(J),J(p) = 0
    Find m,the maximum pixel value in image J
    Place each non-zero pixel in J into its appropriate list
     For every pixel p ∈ R(J):
      If J(p) ≠ 0 , L[J[p]] ← L[J[p]]^p
    Process the m lists from high to low:
      For n = m ⋯ 1
       While L[n]_emptey( ) = false
        p ← L[n]_first( )
         For every pixel q ∈ N_G(p)
          If J(q) < min (n, I[q])
           If J(q) ≠ 0
            L[J[q]] ← squash(L[J[q]] ▷ {q})
           J(q) ← min (n, I[q])
           L[J[q]]_add() ← L[J[q]]^p
```

Symbol definitions.

$N_G(p)$	–	The neighbours of pixel p on the grid G
$I[p]$	–	The pth pixel in image I
←	–	Assignment (to differentiate from = for equality)
▷	–	Range subtraction: removes a specified element from a list
squash	–	Closes up holes in a list (e.g. left by range subtraction)

4   Experiments

In order to demonstrate the efficiency of the proposed method, it has been implemented and tested on the MRI brain image data from the Shanghai Renji hospital. The scanning apparatus is Philips MR scanner and slice thickness is 1.5mm. In all cases the image size is 512×512 pixels, and the data is eight bit (256 grey value levels). Two experiments have been carried out on the images with different characteristics.

The first experiment is to perform a series of the validation test to confirm the improved algorithm could be correctly implemented. So this paper designed an experiment about the MRI brain image contour extraction. First, this paper use multi-scale alternating sequential filtering reconstruction to simplify the input image, here using the improved reconstruction algorithm, then use the marking extraction technology to get the gradient image, at last the watershed transform algorithm is applied to the marked gradient images to get the contour of brain.

The results are shown in Fig. 1. Fig. 1(a) is the original image. For the purpose of comparison, the simplified images obtained by multi-scale alternating sequential filtering reconstruction are showed in Fig. 1(b)~(e) respectively. The results show that simplification process can transform homogenous regions into flat zones and preserve the contours of skull and brain well according the images. In Fig. 1(b) the structure element (SE) size is 5×5. In Fig. 1(c) the SE size is 20×20. In Fig. 1(d) the SE size is 25×25. In Fig. 1(e) the SE size is 30×30. Fig. 1 (f) is the final result of contour extraction after using mark extraction watershed transformation. Obviously, the experiment could obtain good segmentation results, thus confirmed that the algorithms performed correctly.

The second experiment is the comparisons about execution times for two reconstruction algorithms tests. These methods are: (1) Fast hybrid reconstruction algorithm; (2) The proposed algorithm of this paper. All tests were performed on a 2.8GHz Duo CPU with 2GB of RAM. Table 1 indicates the computing result with a same structure

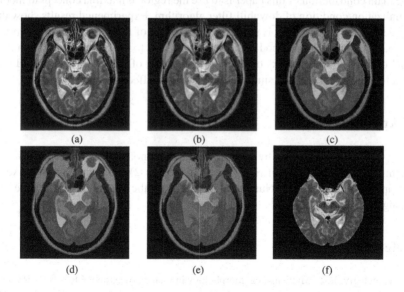

(a)   (b)   (c)

(d)   (e)   (f)

Fig. 1. MRI brain image simplification

element (disk-shaped, size 3×3). In Table 1 the execution times are presented in milliseconds for each of the algorithm as applied to each of four test slices. The rate of reduction is 77.64% based on 4 slices. After tested on almost 60 slices, the mean reduction of the execution time is about 73.68% compared to the fast hybrid reconstruction algorithm. It means that the execution times are reduced significantly.

Table 1. Comparison of execution times for two reconstruction algorithms (milliseconds)

Methods	Slice1	Slice2	Slice3	Slice4	Average
Fast hybrid reconstruction	97.65	101.72	89.22	95.31	95.975
This paper method	21.35	26.86	17.49	20.56	21.565
Rate of reduction	78.14%	73.59%	80.40%	78.43%	77.64%

5   Conclusions

The MRI brain image simplification has become an important pre-processing step for many medical researches and clinical applications. Usually, the process of image simplification requires multiple iterations of reconstruction. Therefore, the efficiency of the reconstruction algorithm is a key problem. This paper has proposed a fast reconstruction algorithm for MRI brain image simplification based on downhill filter. The main contribution of this paper is to use the regional maxima concept to modify the initialization condition of downhill filter algorithm. Experimental results show that the efficiency of this algorithm is much better than that of fast hybrid reconstruction algorithm, and it can achieve good result when it is used to the contour extraction from the MRI of brain. Further works on automatic selection of structure element and times of iteration aim at achieve the simplified image more effectively.

Acknowledgment

This work was supported by Scientific and Technological Project of Science and Technology Commission of Shanghai (08511501702), Shanghai Leading Academic Discipline Project, Project Number (J501030), and the Postgraduate Creative Fund of Shanghai University (284).

References

1. Dougherty, E.R.: Mathematical morphology in image processing. CRC, Boca Raton (1992)
2. Serra, J.: Image analysis and mathematical morphology. Academic Press, Inc., Orlando (1983)
3. Park, H., Yoo, J.: Structuring element decomposition for efficient implementation of morphological filters. IEE Proceedings-Vision, Image and Signal Processing 148, 31–35 (2001)

4. Sivakumar, K., Patel, M.J., Kehtarnavaz, N., Balagurunathan, Y., Dougherty, E.R.: A constant-time algorithm for erosions/dilations with applications to morphological texture feature computation. Real-Time Imaging 6, 223–239 (2000)
5. Van Droogenbroeck, M., Talbot, H.: Fast computation of morphological operations with arbitrary structuring elements. Pattern Recognition Letters 17, 1451–1460 (1996)
6. Salembier, P., Serra, J.: Flat zones filtering, connected operators, and filters by reconstruction. IEEE Transactions on image processing 4, 1153–1160 (1995)
7. Ji, L., Piper, J., Tang, J.Y.: Erosion and dilation of binary images by arbitrary structuring elements using interval coding. Pattern Recognition Letters 9, 201–209 (1989)
8. van Vliet, L.J., Verwer, B.J.H.: A contour processing method for fast binary neighbourhood operations. Pattern Recognition Letters 7, 27–36 (1988)
9. Robinson, K., Whelan, P.F.: Efficient morphological reconstruction: A downhill filter. Pattern Recognition Letters 25, 1759–1767 (2004)
10. Vincent, L.: Morphological grayscale reconstruction in image analysis: Applications and efficient algorithms. IEEE Transactions on Image Processing 2, 176–201 (1993)

On Chip Cache Quantitative Optimization Approach: Study in Chip Multi-processor Design

Chi Zhang and Xiang Wang

School of Electronic and Information Engineering, Beihang University,
100191, Beijing, China
zhangchi8620@gmail.com, wxiang@buaa.edu.cn

Abstract. The nanoelectroincs era promotes multi-core processor (or chip multiprocessor, CMP) improvements with a good deal of both opportunities and challenges. In CMP systems based on SMP organization, cache is much more important than before because performance promoted by multiprocessor is easily degraded by memory latency in shared symmetric multiprocessors. A quantitative optimization cache design is presented in SMP based CMP systems. Cache design strategies in uniprocessor systems are implemented in multiprocessor simulator by executing parallel programs for different number of processors. Evaluation result shows that designing principles in uniprocessor are partly applicable to multiprocessor systems while some traditional designs deteriorate system performance. Increasing cache sizes results in hit rates augment from 15.01% to 43.83% in various simulation conditions, while hit rates is an extremal function for block size. For large caches (128KB), Random algorithm overrides LRU for 6.041% hit rate at most.

1 Introduction

Development of Integrated Circuits techniques promotes high increase of transistors capacity in chip. More than a billion transistors are integrated on a single chip which enables multiprocessor chip (CMP) to be the next generation's dominant architecture [1]. SMP (Symmetric Multi-Processor) designs have long been implemented using discrete processors since SMP has been the most popular architecture in multiprocessor systems [2]. In the case of chip multi-processor (CMP), the SMP involves symmetric processors architecture-- where two or more identical processors shared main memory and are connected by one or many buses or switches. As the clock frequencies increase and the feature sizes decrease, wire delays have been more critical than gate delays in performance degradation, so the system composed of small scale basic units gains better locality. CMP architecture is divided into a number of processors; each one is relatively simple and is conducive to optimizing the system. Reproduction of simple and similar processors is the way SMP architecture uses to lower costs. Chip Multiprocessor takes use of the realizable implementation architecture SMP system. CMP employing SMP architecture is promising in the future CMP designs.

Gap between processors and off-chip main memory, which is called memory wall, is increasing and especially serious in SMP based CMP machines [3]. Performance improvement gained by the reproductions of multiprocessors is most likely to be

W. Zhang et al. (Eds.): HPCA 2009, LNCS 5938, pp. 550–556, 2010.

counteracted by the bus utilization since data access behavior has a strong influence on it, inducing degrading efficiency of communication among multiprocessors. Therefore, it is necessary to make good use of caches in SMP systems [4]. In uniprocessor system, cache size, block size, set associative and replacement policy have been carefully investigated and are implemented in real systems [1] [5]. Nowadays, cache related discussions mostly focus on coherence problem [6] [7].

According to the restricted area and transistors in a single chip multiprocessor, a refined cache design in SMP based CMP systems is introduced, then we evaluate the performance with different number of multiprocessors by configuring various cache size, block size and replacement policy.

2 Characterization of Cache Design Principles

Miss rate is selected as the criterion to estimate memory systems performance due to two reasons. Miss rate is independent from hardware speed. Besides, it is difficult to obtain exact access time in distinct CMP systems. Therefore memory performance is evaluated by miss rates instead of average memory access time. As a kind of UMA (Uniform Memory Access) architectures, SMP system has the same latency for every processor to access the memory.

2.1 Cache Architecture Designs in CMP

Cache in CMP is organized by tag arrays and data arrays in n-ways set-associative organization. Characters of primary factors in cache designs such as cache size, block size, mapping, and replacement policies.

In cache design, tradeoff between size and access time should be comprehensively considered. Small size results in low cost, less access time but worse hits rate while considerable large size raises the prize, increases the access time and hits rate. Both hits rate and access time affect the overall performance of a system.

2.2 Performance Evaluation Methods

CPU time is a critical performance criterion in evaluating the whole systems. Equation 1 shows that Memory Stall Clock Cycles can affect CPU time. Larger Memory Stall Clock Cycles means longer CPU time. Consequently, reducing Memory Stall Clock Cycles will decrease CPU time significantly. In equation 2, miss rate composes part in the Memory Stall Cycles. From Eq 1 and 2, it can be determined that miss rate is involved in improving CPU time.

Combing Eq 3 with discussion in section 2.1, access time (hit time) and penalty time (miss penalty) also affect system performance. However, miss penalty time is much longer than access time in CMP system.

$$CPU\ time = IC \times (CPI_{execution} + \frac{Memory\ Stall\ Clock\ Cycles}{Instruction}) \times Clock\ Cycle\ Time \qquad (1)$$

$$\text{Memory Stall Cycles} = \text{Number of Misses} \times \text{Miss Penalty}$$

$$= IC \times \frac{\text{Misses}}{\text{Instruction}} \times \text{Miss Penalty} \qquad (2)$$

$$= IC \times \frac{\text{Memory Accesses}}{\text{Instruction}} \times \text{Miss Rate}$$

$$\text{AMAT} = \text{Hit Time} + \text{Miss Rate} \times \text{Miss Penalty} \qquad (3)$$

Therefore, in this paper access time is ignored in evaluation the performance. With the necessary theory analysis, it can be concluded that miss rate is an important factor in SMP based CMP system design.

2.3 Simulation and Benchmarks

SMPcache [8] is chosen as the simulator. Parameters that can be designed in the simulator are: cache coherence protocols, policies of bus arbitration, mapping, replacement policies, cache size (blocks in cache), number of cache sets, number of words by block (memory block size) and word wide. Taking good use of the simulator, we can observe program locality, influence of the number of processors and so on.

Being a MIMD (Multiple Instruction stream, Multiple Data stream) system, CMP requires parallel programs executed in multiprocessors to take full advance of SMP architecture's computation capacity. Table 1 shows four parallel programs for two, four and eight processors respectively, which represent several typical programs in real application. We keep the problem size constant in every simulation configuration. To be specific, all the parallel programs executed with various scale of SMP have the same memory traces.

Table 1. Details of parallel benchmarks

Name	References	Language	Description
FFT	7,451,717	Fortran	Parallel application that simulates the fluid dynamics with FFT
Simple	27,030,092	Fortran	Parallel version of the SIMPLE application
Weather	31,764,036	Fortran	Parallel version of the WEATHER application, which is used for weather forecasting.

3 Simulation Results

There is no cache design that can adapt to all working loads because of the diversity of programs and cache sensitiveness to different loads. Nevertheless, optimized cache organization is possible to exhibit satisfying performance for most programs according to locality merits most working loads have. Taking real uniprocessor system for example, level 1 cache size is usually 16KB and 32KB, which are suitable for most serial programs executed in the uniprocessor machine. For SMP based CMP systems, It takes parallel programs for two, four and eight processors respectively to simulate working conditions of level 1 cache.

3.1 Cache Size and Performance Evaluation

The hit rate (H) is constructed owing to the cache size(c), block size (b) and number of blocks' (n) contribution. Since c can be represented by n and b, as showed in set of Eq 4, the corresponding hit rate can be obtained.

Figure 1 illustrates the change in hit rate as cache size is increased for three different multiprocessor configurations. Simulation results show that despite of processors amount the system has, the cache size increasing always has a beneficial impact on performance, since it reduces the frequency of costly cache misses. $H'(c) > 0$ in Eq 5 denotes that H is a monotonic increasing function while $H''(c) < 0$ represents that curve H is convex, which means the increase of H is slower when increasing cache size consistently.

$$\begin{cases} H = f(b,n,c......) \\ c = b \times n \end{cases} \Rightarrow H = F(b,c......) \tag{4}$$

$$\begin{cases} H'(c) > 0 \\ H''(c) < 0 \end{cases} \tag{5}$$

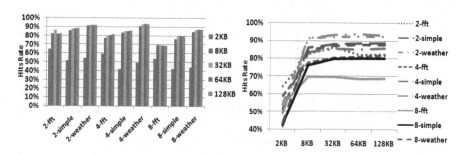

Fig. 1. Hit rate for benchmarks with 2, 4, 8 processors respectively

As the number of processors is increased, total miss rates rise for that communication among processors increase, which leads to more coherence misses. When magnitude of coherence misses overweighs capacity misses, overall miss rates of CMP systems are higher than uniprocessor systems.

Cache sizes and hit rates in FFT, simple, weather benchmarks with two, four, and eight processors SMP systems are simulated and the results are displayed in Figure 1. Configuration is MESI coherence protocol, LRU bus arbitration, 16 bits words wide, 4-way set-associative with LRU replacement policy and fixed 64 bytes block size. There have been distinct decreases for different parallel programs according to diverse localities they have.

3.2 Block Size and Performance Evaluation

Simulation configuration is the same as in section 3.1 except the parameters block size and cache size. FFT is selected as benchmark program. Figure 2 shows tradeoffs between miss rates and block size with various cache sizes in multiprocessors. From the simulation results, conclusion can be drawn that increasing block size is another approach to decrease miss rates although this approach is not always effective. This principle is true for both uniprocessor and multiprocessor systems.

There exists a positive number ζ such that for every H such that $b - \zeta < H < b$ we have $H'(b) > 0$, and for every H such that $b < H < b + \zeta$ $H'(b) < 0$ can be deduced, then it has a local maximum at $b = b_{opt}$.

Quantitative analysis and simulation results illustrate that in multiprocessors block size also has the optimal value for fixed cache size. Figure 3 represents that in all multiprocessor configurations, differences between 64bytes block size and 16bytes block size are high in small cache size. Differences in 8 bytes-16 bytes, 16bytes-32bytes and 32 bytes-64bytes are significant in 32 KB, 64 KB, and 128KB caches respectively. Data flow is transferred frequently in SMP systems so that spatial locality of working loads is hammed through communication among multiprocessors. Large blocks in small caches are especially suffered from this discipline. Fragmentized data increasing bus transactions, causing higher miss rate. Decrease is sharp in such conditions.

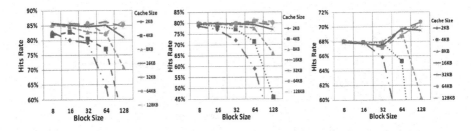

Fig. 2. Hits rate for different block size in 2, 4, 8 processors

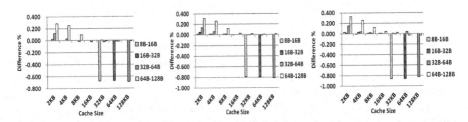

Fig. 3. Hit rates differences for neighboring block sizes in 2, 4, 8 processors

3.3 Replacement Policy and Performance

A variety of replacement policies have their own advantages. Via the evaluation on SPECfp2000 and SPECint 2000 [2] in uniprocessor systems, it can be summed that, for large cache size configuration, LRU and random have little difference in affecting performance, while for small cache LRU is the most efficient policy and FIFO has a better performance than random policy. In real machines, random policy is widely used for it can be implemented on hardware easily. LRU is much more complicated with better adaption to locality optimization. Simulation configuration is the same and results are exhibited below in Figure 4. Bold statistics are the highest hit rates in corresponding cache size.

Comparing with three replacement policies in two, four and eight multiprocessor systems, it comes to the conclusion that in a small cache (eg, 8KB), LRU algorithm has the best performance. In the middle scale cache (64KB), FIFO leads to highest hit rate and in large cache capacity (eg, 128KB), random policy is evaluated as the best one. Therefore, replacement policy has little connection with number of processors but quite close relation with cache size. In large cache design which tends to be popular, Random policy is a good choice not only for the easily implementation in hardware but also for the low miss rates.

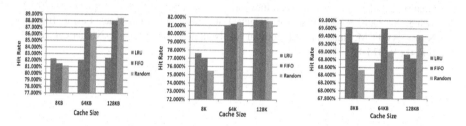

Fig. 4. Replacement Policy simulation in 2, 4, 8 processors

4 Conclusion

Several cache design strategies in SMP based CMP systems are introduced, benefits brought by which are also quantitatively analyzed. By simulation cache organization in multi-processors configurations, this work contributes some general design disciplines: a) Larger caches brought by increasing processor numbers lead to lower hit rates for its poor overall locality, while in various fixed processor numbers, increasing cache sizes results in hit rates augment from 15.01% to 43.83% generally; b) block size always has a optimal value with fixed cache size; c) LRU-FIFO-Random replacement policy are most efficient for small, middle and large scale respectively. For large caches (128KB), Random algorithm overrides LRU for 6.041% hit rate at most. These principles are fully examined and concluded in SMP based multiprocessor simulation with parallel benchmarks.

Considering merits of parallel programs in SMP based CMP systems, designer cannot completely imitate designing experiences in uniprocessor systems. So designs suggested would provide some useful strategies in multiprocessor systems manufactures.

References

1. Chen, M., et al.: The Stanford Hydra CMP. In: Hot Chips 1999. Talk slides (August 1999)
2. David, A., Patterson, J.L.: Computer architecture: a quantitative approach, 4th edn. China Machine Press, Beijing (2007)

3. Shi, X., Su, F., et al.: CMP cache performance projection: Accessibility vs. capacity. In: Workshop on Design, Architecture and Simulation of Chip Multi-Processors (2006)
4. Yung, R., Rusu, S., et al.: Future Trend of Microprocessor Design. M. Schlett, Trends in Embedded-Microprocessor Design, Computer 31(8), 44–49 (1998)
5. Patterson, D.A., Hennessy, J.L.: Computer Organization and Design: The Hardware Software Interface, 3rd edn. Morgan Kaufmann, San Francisco (2004)
6. Loghi, M., Poncino, M., Benini, L.: Cache Coherence Tradeoffs in Shared Memory MPSoCs. ACM Transactions on Embedded Computing Systems 4(3) (2005)
7. Loghi, M., Letis, M., et al.: Exploring the Energy Efficiency of Cache Coherence Protocols in Single-Chip Multi-Processors. In: Proceedings of the ACM Great Lakes Symposium on VLSI (GLSVLSI), pp. 276–281 (2005)
8. Vega Rodrguez, M.A., et al.: Simulation of Cache Memory Systems on Symmetric Multiprocessors with Educational Purposes. In: Proceedings of the First International Congress in Quality and in Technical Education Innovation, September 2000, vol. 3, pp. 47–59 (2000)
9. Wang, X., Guo, R.: Multi-sensor Targets Data Association and Track Fusion Based on Novel AWFCM. International Journal of Nonlinear Science and Numerical Simulation 10(3), 875–885 (2009)

A Novel CT Image Dynamic Fuzzy Retrieval Method Using Curvelet Transform

Guangming Zhang[1], Zhiming Cui[1,2], and Shengrong Gong[1]

[1] The Institute of Intelligent Information Processing and Application Soochow University, Suzhou 215006, China
[2] JiangSu Province Support Software Engineering R&D Center for Modern Information Technology Application in Enterprise, Suzhou 215104, China
gmwell@126.com, {szzmcui,shrgong}@suda.edu.cn

Abstract. Curvelet transform as time-frequency and multiresolution analysis tool is often used in the domain of image processing, especially for image characteristic extraction. This paper proposes a novel CT image retrieval method which is combining curvelet transform and dynamic fuzzy theory. Firstly, the image was decomposed by curvelet transform to obtain the different subbands coefficients. Then the entropy from certain subband was calculated, and a membership function based on dynamic fuzzy theory was constructed to adjust the weight of coefficients similarity. At last a model was constructed to obtain the similarity degree for CT image retrieval. The precision of our model could be applied to CT image retrieval practically.

Keywords: fuzzy retrieval, curvelet transform, similarity degree, CT image.

1 Introduction

In recent years, the curvelet transform has received more and more attention due to its particular characters. Many Classical multiresolution ideas only address a portion of the whole range of possible multiscale phenomena, like the classical wavelet viewpoint, there are objects, e.g. images that do not exhibit isotropic scaling and, thus, call for other types of multiscale representation. Candes and Donoho [1] developed a new theory of multiresolution analysis called the curvelet transform. This mathematical transform differs from wavelet and related other mathematical transform. Curvelets take the form of basis elements, which exhibit a very high directional sensitivity and are highly anisotropic. In two dimensions, for instance, curvelets are localized along curves and in three dimensions along sheets. Because this new mathematic transform is based on the wavelet transform and radon transform. It has overcome some limitations of wavelet transform in CT image retrieval.

CT imaging [2] is even used for the diagnosis and treatment of certain vascular diseases that undetected and untreated. By analyzing the characters of CT medical images, we find that each images are taken by the same instrument at different time. And most of the medical images are gray pictures. Due to this character, when we retrieve the medical image we should analysis the similarity in a certain scope. And the change trend of similarity could be used in retrieval process. This technique is based on dynamic fuzzy logic.

W. Zhang et al. (Eds.): HPCA 2009, LNCS 5938, pp. 557–562, 2010.

There are a great number of developments in the domain of fuzzy mathematics' theory to solve those static problems, since L. A. Zadeh proposed fuzzy sets in 1965 [3]. Dynamic fuzzy logic as an effective theory to solve dynamic fuzzy problems is very useful. Due to the fuzzy character of the image retrieval, we combined DFL with curvelet transform for CT medical image retrieval.

The rest of this paper is organized as follows. The curvelet transform analysis is given in Sections 2. Dynamic Fuzzy Curvelet Transform Retrieval Model is given in Sections 3. Section 4 proposes the experiment and discusses the results. Conclusions are presented in last section.

2 Curvelet Transform Analysis

Curvelet transform [1] as a newly developed mathematical transform is often used as time-frequency and multiresolution analysis tool in the signal and image processing domain. It was developed by Cand'es and Donoho which combined the anisotropic of ridgelet with the multiscale characteristic of wavelet. The prominent characteristic of curvelet is multiscale and high anisotropic. Like the wavelet transform, curvelet transform[4] is a multiscale transform, with frame elements indexed by scale and location parameters. Unlike the wavelet transform, it has directional parameters, and the curvelet pyramid contains elements with a very high degree of directional specificity. In addition, the curvelet transform is based on a certain anisotropic scaling principle which is quite different from the isotropic scaling of wavelets. Generally speaking, curvelet transform extends the ridgelet transform to multiple scale analysis. This means that ridgelet can be tuned to different orientations and different scales to create the curvelets. Curvelets have a complete cover of the spectrum in frequency domain [5-6]. That means, there is no loss of information in curvelet transform in terms of fusing the frequency information from images[7].

The image could be decomposed into a set of wavelet bands, and each band could be analyze by a ridgelet transform. The block size can be changed at each scale level. These formal properties are very similar to those one expects from an orthonormal basis, and reflect an underlying stability of representation. The Curvelet Transform includes four stages:

(1) Sub-band decomposition:

$$f \mapsto \left(P_0 f, \Delta_1 f, \Delta_2 f, \ldots\right) \tag{1}$$

(2) Smooth partitioning:

$$h_Q = w_Q \cdot \Delta_s f \tag{2}$$

A grid of dyadic squares is defined as follows:

$$Q_{(s,k_1,k_2)} = \left[\frac{k_1}{2^s}, \frac{k_1+1}{2^s}\right] \times \left[\frac{k_2}{2^s}, \frac{k_2+1}{2^s}\right] \in \mathbf{Q}_s \tag{3}$$

$\mathbf{Q}s$ – all the dyadic squares of the grid.

(3) Renormalization:

$$\left(T_Q f\right)\!\left(x_1, x_2\right) = 2^s f\!\left(2^s x_1 - k_1, 2^s x_2 - k_2\right) \tag{4}$$

$$g_Q = T_Q^{-1} h_Q \tag{5}$$

(4) Ridgelet analysis:

$$\alpha_{(Q,\lambda)} = \left\langle g_Q, \rho_\lambda \right\rangle \tag{6}$$

There is also procedural definition of the reconstruction algorithm. The Inverse of the Curvelet Transform:

(1) Ridgelet Synthesis:

$$g_Q = \sum_\lambda \alpha_{(Q,\lambda)} \cdot \rho_\lambda \tag{7}$$

(2) Renormalization:

$$h_Q = T_Q g_Q \tag{8}$$

(3) Smooth Integration:

$$\Delta_s f = \sum_{Q \in \mathbf{Q}_s} w_Q \cdot h_Q \tag{9}$$

(4) Sub-band Recomposition:

$$f = P_0\!\left(P_0 f\right) + \sum_s \Delta_s\!\left(\Delta_s f\right) \tag{10}$$

Curvelet transform is defined via above concepts.

3 CT Image Retrieval by Curvelet Transform and DFL

In order to apply dynamic fuzzy logic theory [8] in the domain of image retrieval, we introduce the dynamic fuzzy logic concepts firstly.

3.1 Dynamic Fuzzy Logic (DFL)

Definition 1. A statement having character of dynamic fuzzy is called dynamic fuzzy proposition that is usually symbolized by capital letter A, B, C···

Definition 2. A dynamic fuzzy number $(\overleftarrow{a}, \overrightarrow{a}) \in [0,1]$ which is used to measure a dynamic fuzzy proposition's true or false degree is called dynamic fuzzy proposition's true or false. It is usually symbolized by $(\overleftarrow{a}, \overrightarrow{a})$, $(\overleftarrow{b}, \overrightarrow{b})$, $(\overleftarrow{c}, \overrightarrow{c})$, Here $(\overleftarrow{a}, \overrightarrow{a}) = \overleftarrow{a}$ or $\overrightarrow{a}$, $\min(\overleftarrow{a}, \overrightarrow{a}) \triangleq \overleftarrow{a}$, $\max(\overleftarrow{a}, \overrightarrow{a}) \triangleq \overrightarrow{a}$, the same are as follows.

Definition 3. A dynamic fuzzy propositions can be regarded as a variable whose value is in the interval [0,1]. The variable is called dynamic fuzzy proposition variable that is usually symbolized by small letter.

Dynamic fuzzy calculus formation can be defined as follows:

(1) A simple dynamic fuzzy variable itself is a well formed formula.

(2) If $(\bar{x},\vec{x})$p is a well formed formula, then $\overline{(\bar{x},\vec{x})P}$ is a well formed formula, too.

(3) If $(\bar{x},\vec{x})$P and $(\bar{y},\vec{y})$Q are well formed fomulas, then $(\bar{x},\vec{x})$P$\vee$$(\bar{y},\vec{y})$Q, $(\bar{x},\vec{x})$P$\wedge$$(\bar{y},\vec{y})$Q, $(\bar{x},\vec{x})$P$\rightarrow$$(\bar{y},\vec{y})$Q, $(\bar{x},\vec{x})$P $\leftrightarrow$ $(\bar{y},\vec{y})$Q are also well formed formulas.

(4) A sting of symbols including proposition variable connective and brackets is well formed formula if and only if the strings can be obtained in a finite number of steps, each of which only applies the earlier rules(1), (2) and (3).

3.2 Dynamic Fuzzy Curvelet Transform Retrieval Model

The medical image is contributed to only a few coefficients with some block size after curvelet transform. Therefore, since the image information is concentrated in these coefficients, it is possible to calculate weight of each image's coefficients with some block size to construct retrieval model.

In this paper, a new model which assesses the similarity for CT image by DFL is proposed to retrieval process.

$$S = \begin{cases} E \times W & \text{if } 0 \leq W \leq 0.5 \\ E \times (1-W) & \text{if } 0.5 \leq W \leq 1 \end{cases} \tag{11}$$

Where E is the entropy of the certain levels of image after curvelet transformation; W is the weight of each each scale level; S is similarity scores of all the CT images. The final retrieval result is decided by the order of S.

The model has some attributes as follows:

• The number of levels of curvelet transform could be chosen by the precision of retrieval, the large number means high precision but cost more time to computer.

• The entropy of the certain subband of image after curvelet transformation is a objective parameter of this similarity compution via weight adjustment.

• The W was adjusted for the purpose of computer the similarity degree of entropy after curvelet transform. Because the value of W is in the interval [0,1], so DFL was applied to construct a membership function to adjust the weight of coefficients similarity. The membership function was constructed as follows:

$$\bar{A}(\bar{u}) = \begin{cases} 0 & \text{if } 0 \leq \bar{u} \leq \overleftarrow{0.15} \\ (1+(\frac{\bar{u}-0.15}{0.05})^{-2})^{-1} & \text{if } \overleftarrow{0.15} \leq \bar{u} \leq \bar{1} \end{cases} \quad \vec{A}(\vec{u}) = \begin{cases} 0 & \text{if } 0 \leq \vec{u} \leq \overrightarrow{0.15} \\ (1+(\frac{\vec{u}-0.15}{0.05})^{-2})^{-1} & \text{if } \overrightarrow{0.15} \leq \vec{u} \leq \vec{1} \end{cases}$$

$$\bar{B}(\bar{u}) = \begin{cases} 0 & \text{if } 0 \leq \bar{u} \leq \overleftarrow{0.85} \\ (1+(\frac{\bar{u}-0.85}{0.05})^{-2})^{-1} & \text{if } \overleftarrow{0.85} \leq \bar{u} \leq \bar{1} \end{cases} \quad \vec{B}(\vec{u}) = \begin{cases} 0 & \text{if } 0 \leq \vec{u} \leq \overrightarrow{0.85} \\ (1+(\frac{\vec{u}-0.85}{0.05})^{-2})^{-1} & \text{if } \overrightarrow{0.85} \leq \vec{u} \leq \vec{1} \end{cases} \tag{12}$$

By using the constructed membership function of DFL, we could find the trend of weight adjustment, so the order of similarity degree could be calculated by it.

4   Experimental Results and Discussion

Before the experiment, we get a lot of CT images from the First Affiliated Hospital of Soochow University, including different parts of human body CT images.In order to retrieve the CT medical image, we proposed a new model combine curvelet transform and DFL. The steps of this processing method as follows:

- All CT images are decomposed into low-frequency subband and high-frequency subband based curvelet transform.
- Calculate the entropy from different subbands of CT medical image.
- Construct a model based on DFL to obtain the similarity degree in order.

In order to lookup certain image quickly and accurately and make best use of these data, the CT medical images retrieval technology are applied to adjuvant therapy and surgical planning purposes. In the experiment, the CT image retrieval result is shown in Fig. 1. Use this paper's arithmetic, the result similarity with the descending order is shows in the Table 1. The high precision of our model could be applied practically.

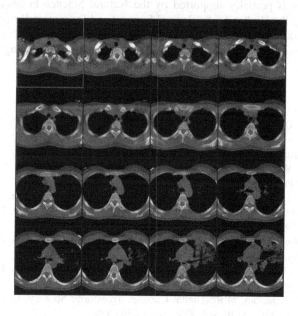

Fig. 1. CT image retrieval result

Table 1. Data analysis

Order	Entropy	Weight	Similarity	Precision
1	3.728	0.95	100.00%	88.56%
2	3.856	0.83	87.37%	87.78%
3	3.922	0.77	81.05%	86.37%
4	3.975	0.68	71.58%	85.39%
5	3.996	0.62	65.26%	85.25%

5   Conclusions

A novel model using curvelet transform and dynamic fuzzy theory was proposed in this paper to retrieve CT image. Firstly, the image was decomposed by curvelet transform to obtain the different subbands information. Then the entropy from the different subbands was calculated, and a membership function based on dynamic fuzzy theory was constructed to adjust the weight of coefficients. At last a novel model was construct to obtain the similarity degree in order for CT image retrieval. This model is very adaptive to gray medical image retrieval.

Acknowledgement

This research was partially supported by the Natural Science Foundation of China (No.60673092), the Higher Technological Support and Innovation Program of Jiangsu Province (BE2008044), the Natural Science Foundation of Jiangsu Province, and the Project of Jiangsu Key Laboratory of Computer Information Processing Technology.

References

1. Candes, E.J., Donoho, D.L.: Curvelets,
   http://www-stat.stanford.edu/~donoho/Reports/1999/
   curveletsurprise.pdf
2. Madison, N.: What is ct imaging, http://www.wisegeek.com
3. Zadeh, L.A.: Fuzzy sets. J. Information and Control. 8, 338–353 (1965)
4. Cohen, A., Rabut, C., et al.: Curvelets A surprisingly effective nonadaptive representation for objects with edges. In: Curve and Surface Fitting: Saint-Malo 1999. Vanderbilt Univ. Press, TN (1999)
5. Do, M.N., Vetterli, M.: Orthonormal finite ridgelet transform for image compression. In: Proc. IEEE Int. Conf. Image Processing, ICIP (2000)
6. Starck, J., Candès, E.J., Donoho, D.L.: The Curvelet Transform for Image Denoising. IEEE Transactions on Image Processing 11(6), 670–684 (2002)
7. Donoho, D.L., Duncan, M.R.: Digital Curvelet Transform: Strategy, Implementation and Experiments. In: Proc. SPIE, vol. 4056, pp. 12–29 (2000)
8. Fanzhang, L.: Dynamic Fuzzy Logic and Its Applications. Nova Science Pub. Inc., New York (2008)

An Implementation Method of Parallel Finite Element Computation Based on Overlapping Domain Decomposition*

Jianfei Zhang[1], Lei Zhang[2], and Hongdao Jiang[1]

[1] School of Civil Engineering, Hohai University, Nanjing 210098, China
{jianfei,hdjiang}@hhu.edu.cn
[2] China Institute of Water Resources and Hydropower Research, Beijing 100044, China
zhangl@iwhr.com

Abstract. An implementation method of parallel finite element computation based on overlapping domain decomposition was presented to improve the parallel computing efficiency of finite element and lower the cost and difficulty of parallel programming. By secondary processing the nodal partition obtained by using Metis, the overlapping domain decomposition of finite element mesh was gotten. Through the redundancy computation of overlapping element, finite element governing equations could be parallel formed independently. And the uniform distributed block storage could be achieved conveniently. The interface to the DMSR data format was developed to meet the need of Aztec parallel solution. And the solver called the iterative solving subroutine of Aztec directly. This implementation method reduced the change of the existed serial program to a great extent. So the main frame of finite element computation was kept. Tests show that this method can achieve high parallel computing efficiency.

1 Introduction

The finite element method is one of the most effective ways for structural analysis currently. With the increasing size and increasing complexity of engineering structures, using the traditional finite element method in the serial computer to solve these problems will inevitably face problems of insufficient computing resources. Parallel finite element computation is undoubtedly an important way to solve these large problems [1].

At present, the mainstream of parallel finite element methods are the methods based on the domain decomposition method. These methods not only need not explicitly form the global stiffness matrix, but also can adapt to the current most popular distributed memory architecture in the field of high-performance computing. So these methods can get a higher degree of parallelism. Based on the overlap or not, the domain decomposition method is classified into overlapping domain decomposition and non-overlapping domain decomposition. Because of the simple and direct formula, the parallel finite element method based on non-overlapping domain decomposition

---

* This work was supported by Natural Science Foundation of Hohai University.

W. Zhang et al. (Eds.): HPCA 2009, LNCS 5938, pp. 563–570, 2010.

has a wide range of applications. The parallel substructure method [2, 3], FETI [4] method are all developed based on non-overlapping domain decomposition. However, parallel finite element method based on non-overlapping domain decomposition needs data communication between sub-domains during formation of governing equations of finite element. And the non-overlap method also does not facilitate the parallel sub-block formation and distribution of the governing equations. So the main framework of finite element method will be destroyed, and the original serial program needs to be changed to a greater extent. So the method can not be acceptable to general users.

This paper presents an implementation method based on overlapping domain decomposition. This method can facilitate the sub-block formation and uniform distribution of the finite element equation. The open source software is used in parallel programming. The method maintains the main framework to a great extent, and reduces the destruction and revision of the original serial procedures, so the difficulty and cost of development is reduced and the development cycle is shortened. This method is helpful to the further popularization of parallel applications of finite element computation.

2 Parallelism Analyses

In finite element computing, element analysis usually accounts for around 20% of the total volume of the whole analysis and the solution of equations accounts for more than 70% [5].

According to the theory of finite element method, element stiffness matrix, element equivalent nodal load and element strain and stress calculation only need the information of the element without relating to other elements. So they can be completely parallelized without data communications.

The global stiffness matrix and equivalent nodal load are assembled with all element stiffness matrix and equivalent nodal load according to the relationship between the local nodal number and the global number. The assemble uses equation (1)and(2)below, where selective matrix $\mathbf{C_e}$ element plays a transforming role between the local number and the global number. If the use of non-overlapping domain decomposition, the parts of the global stiffness matrix and equivalent nodal load relating to the interface nodes need to use the element stiffness matrix and equivalent nodal load of adjacent sub-domains. So the data communications are inevitable. If using overlapping domain decomposition, the data communication can be avoided and the global stiffness matrix and equivalent nodal load of each sub-region can be computed in parallel independently.

$$\mathbf{K} = \sum_e \mathbf{C_e^T k C_e} \tag{1}$$

$$\mathbf{R} = \sum_e \mathbf{C_e^T R^e} \tag{2}$$

The coefficient matrix of finite element governing equation is usually a large sparse symmetric positive definite matrix. The solution of these equations mainly includes direct and iterative method. In spite of the stability of the direct method, but factoring sparse matrix will bring the inevitable non-zero filling. So the amount of storage capacity and computation will increase. The parallel algorithms and programming of direct solver are more complex than iterative solvers and the degree of parallelism of direct method is relative low. Iterative methods have not the problem of non-zero fill, so the storage capacity should be less than the direct method. The computation mainly includes matrix and vector computation which are more suitable for parallel processing. So the iterative method can get better parallelism. The parallel algorithms and programming is also relatively simple. However, iterative methods often can not guarantee the convergence and can not predict computing time. There are many precondition technologies used to improve the convergence rate of iterative methods now. Preconditioned iterative methods have been successfully applied in the finite element analysis of large and complex structure.

3 Implementation of Over-lapping Domain Partition

3.1 Graph Partition and Metis

Before parallel finite element computing based on domain decomposition, the finite element mesh needs to be partitioned firstly. There are two main principles of partition: the nodes of each sub-domain are uniform and the number of nodes on interface between sub-domains is minimal. The role of these two principles is load-balancing and minimizing data communication [6]. At present, the main method used to partition finite element mesh is the methods of graph partition. In the graph, each node is regarded as vertex and side between nodes is regarded as edge. They are called nodal graph. It also can regard each element as vertex and edge exists when two elements have shared points, edges or faces. They are called dual graph. Corresponding to the two partition methods, there are nodal partition and element partition. There are many software packages to be used to partition graph now. The most representative is the Metis [7]. Metis provides a number of procedures, including procedures transforming finite element to nodal graph and dual graph to be partitioned. By using Metis, we can get the partition based on nodes or elements easily. These partitions are both non-overlapping.

3.2 Domain Partition Based on Nodes

Node-based overlapping mesh partition with Metis transforms mesh to nodal graph firstly. Then partition the graph and generate non-overlapping partition as shown in Figure 1. Cycling all the elements, as long as one of the nodes of an element belongs to the current partition, it belongs to the current sub-domain, too. The Metis formed a non-overlapping domain partition. Nodes and elements all belong to a unique sub-domain. When the cycle ends, a one-element over-lapping partition is gotten, as shown in Figure 2. Then the global stiffness matrix and nodal equivalent load of each sub-region can be computed in parallel independently and the data communication can be avoided.

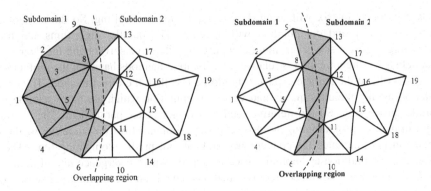

Fig. 1. Non-overlapping domain decomposition   **Fig. 2.** Overlapping domain decomposition

For example, sub-domain stiffness matrix is assembled according to equation (3). Where $\sum_{e}$ denotes sum of all matrix element with the same subscript. In figure 1, if r and s are internal nodes, corresponding matrix element can be computed in independently. If r and s are boundary nodes, corresponding matrix element are computed needing data communication between sub-domains.

$$\mathbf{K}_{rs} = \sum_{e} \mathbf{k}_{rs} \tag{3}$$

Because the finite element nodes relate rows and columns of equations, node-based domain partition can partition coefficient matrix by the row assigned to each processor. For each sub-region, element analysis and the formation of the global stiffness matrix are completely parallel. The boundary conditions can be dealt with fully parallel too. In this way, the finite element governing equations can be distributed evenly in each processor.

4   Implementation of Parallel Solver

4.1   Aztec

Aztec [8] is a parallel linear solver to solve the system of linear equations such as the equation $Ax=b$, where A is n × n sparse matrix, b is a n-dimension vector, x is a solution of n-dimensional vector.

Aztec provides many Krylov Iterative Methods, such as the conjugate gradient method (CG), generalized minimum residual method (GMRES), stabilized bi-conjugate gradient method (BiCGSTAB). These Krylov methods are preconditioned with a number of preconditioners, such as polynomial pre-conditioner, LU or incomplete LU decomposition preconditioner.

Aztec offers two special sparse matrix storage formats: modified sparse row (MSR) and variable block row (VBR). The corresponding distributed data formats are DMSR and DVBR. Aztec generates data suitable for Aztec with a transform function.

4.2 Formation and Storage of Equations

The DMSR format is a generalization of the MSR format [9]. The data structure consists of an integer vector *bindx* and a double precision vector *val* each of length *N_nonzeros* +1 where *N_nonzeros* is the number of nonzeros in the local submatrix. For a submatrix with *m* rows the DMSR arrays are as follows:

bindx: *bindx[0]* $=m+1$

      bindx[k+1]-bindx[k] =number of nonzero off-diagonal elements in *k'*th row, *k<m*

      bindx[ks...ke]   =column indices of the off-diagonal nonzeros in row *k* where *ks=bindx[k]* and *ke=bindx[k+1]-1*.

val: *val[k]* $= A_{kk}, k<m$

      val[ki]   =*the (k,bindx[ki])'*th matrix element where *ks≤ki≤ke* with *ks* and *ke* as defined above.

Global equations are stored by the use of sparse storage format according to the data format required by Aztec. This storage must be translated to the DMSR format required by the solving function of Aztec. Node-based domain partition is equivalent to distribute the global stiffness matrix by rows. The right hand load vector is naturally distributed according to the global stiffness matrix.

Element analysis consists of element stiffness matrix and equivalent node load vector. The elements and nodes participating in the calculation are all the elements and nodes in a sub-domain (including the overlapping zone and boundary nodes). After the element stiffness matrix and equivalent node load vector is completed, according to equation (1) and (2), the global stiffness matrix and load vector assemble. The global stiffness matrix stores with DMSR format. The algorithm to form DMSR storage of the global stiffness matrix is as follows:

(1) Determine non-zero structure of the stiffness matrix and form *bindx* array. According to finite element theory, the corresponding elements of the stiffness matrix are non-zero when the nodes in the same element. So two nested loops can be used to determine the related nodes of each node, of which the outer loop is all the nodes in a sub-domain, the inner loop is all the element in a sub-domain. The non-zero structure is stored in the array *bindx*.

(2) Store the non-zero elements of global stiffness matrix and form the array *val*. After *bindx* array is formed, the calculation of element stiffness matrix and index matrix of element stiffness matrix can be performed by loop over all elements. The distributed global stiffness is assembled by adding of element stiffness matrix element to the global matrix according to index matrix *bindx*. The process of this assemble is according to equation (4) ~ (5) below where *i* is the global row number and *il* is the local row number.

$$K_{ii} = val(il) \tag{4}$$

$$K_{ij} = val(bindx(k_s, \cdots, k_e)), i \neq j \tag{5}$$

$$k_s = bindx(il), k_e = bindx(il+1) - 1 \tag{6}$$

5 Parallel Tests

5.1 Test of Domain Partition

The quality of domain partition is important to efficiency of parallel computing. Domain partition not only needs load balancing, but also minimizing communication between processors. That is, the number of elements in sub-domain is uniform and the nodes in interface are minimal. As an example of 810,000 hexahedral elements and 836,381 nodes, the domain partition method presented above is used to divide it into 4 sub-regions. The number of elements in each sub-domain and overlapping elements of both cases is shown in table 1 and the running time for domain partition is given in table 2.

Table 1. Number of elements in each sub-domain

Sub-domain 1	Sub-domain 2	Sub-domain 3	Sub-domain 4	Number of Common Elements
202327	205522	200336	201815	20696

Table 2. Running time of mesh partition (unit: s)

Number of sub-domains	4	16	64	256
I/O	2.350	2.350	2.400	2.370
Partition	3.730	3.750	4.130	4.700
Total running time	6.080	6.100	6.530	7.070

Tests show that uniformity of elements is good and non-uniform deviation is less than 2.5%. There are 20,696 elements in overlapping region and the increased computing volume in each region is around 5000 elements accounting for about 2.5%. So the increase of computation due to overlapping is small. But the small increase can avoid more communication during assembling the global stiffness matrix. And the communication can be reduced and the programming complexity decreases.

From table 2, we can see that the partition of more than 80 million elements only takes a few minutes. Compared with the overall finite element computing time, it is negligible and can be run in serial.

5.2 Goble Test

Based on the presented parallel finite element implementing method, a parallel solving module and a domain partition module of parallel finite element computing for three-dimensional elastic problem are developed. They are used to solving initial stress field of an arch dam. The computing environment is a cluster of 5 IBM Blade-Center HS20 servers which has two Xeon 3.2G CPUs, 2G memory. The interconnection network uses Gig-Ethernet and the operating system is Redhat 4.0 Enterprise

Edition. The parallel environment is GCC and MPICH. The preconditioned conjugate gradient method (PCG) solver is selected and preconditioner is incomplete LU based on domain decomposition.

The arch dam has been meshed with 310,122 e tetrahedral elements and 57,936 nodes. The mesh is divided into 4 sub-domains by using node-based partition strategy with Metis. The partitioned mesh of the arch dam is shown in Figure 3.

The finite element computing results are shown in figure 4. The computing time with variable processors is listed in table 3. From table 3, we can see that the speedup of solving equations is good. The efficiency with 4 processors a little decreased because the number of processors increase and the problem remain the same size. The parallel overhead increases when the number of processors is increase.

Fig. 3. Finite element mesh partition of the arch dam   **Fig. 4.** Vertical stress of the arch dam

Table 3. Parallel computing time and speedup

Number of processors	1	2	4
Solving Equation(s)/speedup	20.6/—	10.5/1.96	7.5/2.75
Total running time(s)/speedup	69/—	37/1.86	25/2.76

6 Conclusions

Parallel finite element computation is an important way to enlarge the size of problem, improve solving accuracy and speed up the analysis. An implementation method of parallel finite element computation based on overlapping domain decomposition is presented in his paper from the angles of efficiency and utility. Through the node-based overlapping domain decomposition, the communication is avoided during forming the governing equations of finite element method and the uniform distribution of the equations can be gotten easily. The DMSR data format interface is developed to meet the parallel solver of Aztec for solving equations directly. This method parallelizes all the key steps of finite element method. The communication between processors is reduced so the parallel computing efficiency and parallel scalability are improved.

This method can maintain the frame of the existing serial program to a great extent and raise the computing efficiency. The cost and difficulty of parallel finite element computing can significantly reduce so the method is suitable to be popularized.

References

1. Chao-jiang, F., Wu, Z.: Progress in parallel processing in finite element structural analysis. Advances in Mechanics 36(3), 354–362 (2006)
2. Ju-ching, C.: Parallel computational algorithm of substructure method of large-scale structure analysis. Applied Mathematics and Mechanics 12(1), 93–100 (1991)
3. Thomas, H.R., Yang, H.T., He, Y.: A sub-structure based parallel solution of coupled thermo-hydro -mechanical modelling of unsaturated soil. Engineering Computations 16(4), 428–443 (1999)
4. Farhat, C., Roux, F.X.: A method of finite element tearing and interconnecting and its parallel solution algorithm. International Journal for Numerical Methods in Engineering 32(6), 1205–1227 (1991)
5. Ding, K.Z., Qin, Q.H., Cardew-Haw, M., Kalyanasundaram, S.: Efficient parallel algorithms for elasto-plastic finite element analysis. Computational Mechanics 41(4), 563–578 (2008)
6. Jianfei, Z., Hongdao, J.: Performance analysis in FEM substructure parallel algorithm. Mechanics in Engineering 24(5), 35–37 (2002)
7. Karypis, G., Kumar, V.: METIS A Software Package for Partitioning Unstructured Graphs, Partitioning Meshes, and Computing Fill-Reducing Orderings of Sparse Matrices Version 4.0. (September 1998),
   http://glaros.dtc.umn.edu/gkhome/metis/metis/download
8. Ray, S., Heroux, T.M., Hutchinson, S.A., et al.: Official Aztec User's Guide (November 1999), http://www.cs.sandia.gov/CRF/Aztec_pubs.html
9. Jian-ping, W., Zheng-hua, W., Xiao-mei, L.: Efficient solving and parallel computing of sparse linear equations, pp. 52–53. Hunan science and technology Press, Changsha (2004)

Numerical Simulation of Unsteady Flow in Centrifugal Pump Impeller at Off-Design Condition by Hybrid RANS/LES Approaches

Wei Zhang, Yunchao Yu, and Hongxun Chen

Shanghai Institute of Applied Mathematics and Mechanics, Guang Yan road 123.
20072 Shanghai, China
{waynezw0618,yuyunchao,chenhx}@shu.edu.cn

Abstract. A new kind of hybrid RANS/LES turbulence modeling method - SST based SAS model is first time used for studying the stall phenomena in a centrifugal pump impeller at off-design condition in present paper. The previous reported "two channel" non-uniform flow structure has been gotten with this model. The numerical result is compared with LES and unsteady SST model, also the PIV result in reference paper. The time average result of flow show good agreements in general. The difference in turbulence quantities will affect the time average field in high turbulence intensity area to make SAS having close to LES. To achieve this effect, more computation consumption has been taken.

Keywords: Flow visualization, centrifugal impeller, hybrid RANS/LES, off-design condition.

1 Introduction

For most application centrifugal pump works at a wide flow range especially at the partial load condition. This will result more complex unsteady flow in pumps.

By using PIDV, N.Paone[1] has detected the complex and unsteadiness flow field in centrifugal pump in 1989.In Manish Sinha[2]-[3] has also done the PIV study for centrifugal impller. After that a LES simulation has also taken by him.

There are lots of studies of unsteady flow especially in off-design condition. G.Wuibaut[4] has done the PIV measurements in the impeller and vaneless diffuser of radial flow pump at off design condition. In 2003, Hong Wang [5] has studied the unsteady pressure fluctuations comparing with experiment result and numerical one.

Lots of the numerical works have been done with RANS method or unsteady RANS method, like in reference papers [6]-[8]. According C.Kato[9], RANS has inherent limitations in predicting unsteady nature of flow field, so he used the LES to simulate the internal flow of pump. But LES method cost greatly for industry application. The most recently work of Feng.J[10] in 2009 has used DES, which is a hybrid RANS/LES method, to study the part-load condition of radial diffuser pump. In present paper a new kind of hybrid RANS/LES, SST based SAS method has been employed to study the unsteady flow in a centrifugal impeller.

W. Zhang et al. (Eds.): HPCA 2009, LNCS 5938, pp. 571–578, 2010.

2 Numerical Modeling

Pump Impeller in this study is a shrouded, low-specific-speed pump impeller (shown in Fig 1). It is scaled from impeller of an industrial multistage pump. The performance curve (shown in Fig 2) of studying impeller is calculated by similar transformation from original pump impeller. The numerical study is taken with a partial load condition (Q=25% Q_d) in this paper, Pederson [11]has studied the flow by PIV and LDV measurements, and R.K.Byskov [12]has performed the numerical studying by LES method with only two passages and total 385,000 mesh element.

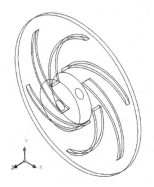
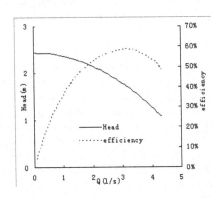

Fig. 1. 3D wireframe view of the impeller   **Fig. 2.** Performance curve of the impeller[11]

The simulation has been done with ANSYS CFX 11.0, unsteady governing equation under Single Rotating Frame (SRF) can be written as following:

$$\begin{cases} div\vec{W} = 0 \\ \rho\dfrac{d\vec{W}}{dt} = -gradp + \mu divgrad\vec{W} + \rho\omega^2 r\vec{i}_r - 2\rho(\vec{\omega}\times\vec{W}) \end{cases} \tag{1}$$

The $\vec{W}$ is relative speed in the rotating frame. The absolute velocity $\vec{C}$ is computed by vectorial-addition of local circumferential impeller speed to the relative velocity. The centrifugal force term $\rho\omega^2 r\vec{i}_r$, and the coriolis force term $-2\rho(\vec{\omega}\times\vec{W})$ are added to the Navier-Stokes equation, as compensation.

To resolve the unsteady turbulence flow in the centrifugal impeller, A type of Scale Adaptive Simulation (SAS) based on the shear stress transport (SST) model has been chosen. It is a new approach of hybrid RANS/LES (F.R.Mentors[13]). It allows the simulation of unsteady flow with both RANS and LES content in a single model environmental. Simulations with and unsteady SST model and LES (sub-grid scale stress is modeled by smagorinsky model) are also taken to make comparison. To modeling the flow near wall, "Automatic near wall treatment" has been used in SST based SAS model and unsteady SST model. In LES simulation, the Van Driest wall damping function is used to modeling the flow near wall. Details of the models can be found in [14].

The transient term is discretized by second order backward Euler method. The advection term is discretized by high resolution scheme in ANSYS CFX 11.0.It is Blended between Central differencing and Upwind differencing locally.

To discrete the entire impeller, full hexahedron mesh element is used in ICEM-CFD 11.0 with blocking method. That is totally 2,088,474 mesh elements(see Fig.3). According to the result, all near wall element could satisfy the requirement of Y+ smaller then 1 for near wall treatment methods of all turbulence modeling methods used in this paper. The sensitive test of mesh independence has not been done with the unsteady simulation, but for Standard $k - \varepsilon$ model. The grid independency result showed that the flow pattern is not sensitive to the mesh at such mesh level. For Discretization of temporal, the time step size for unsteady flow has been set to 1.15e-5 second, which is equivalent to time for impeller rotating 1/20 degree. The total time of simulation is for impeller rotating 3 revolutions, flow field has revealed statically stable after that.

3 Result and Discussion

3.1 Computation Cost

The computation was taken on Ziqiang 3000 in Shanghai University High Performance Computation Centre with 8 nodes, with 2 HP X3.0/800-2M cpus per nodes. The comparison of computation consumption has shown in Fig.4.comsumption of SAS is between LES and unsteady SST.

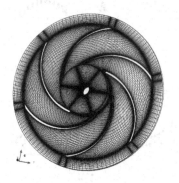

Fig. 3. 3D view of surface mesh   **Fig. 4.** Comparison of computation consumption

3.2 Time Average Field

Like the PIV result of Pederson and LES result of R.K.Byskov for two passages, the flow in the impeller at Q=25% Q_d is not uniform for passages, "two channel"

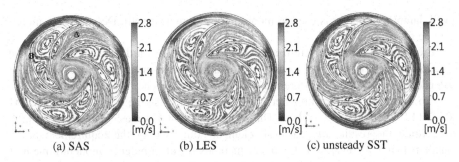

(a) SAS   (b) LES   (c) unsteady SST

Fig. 5. streamline plot colored by velocity magnitude at the impeller mid-height, $z/b_2=0.5$

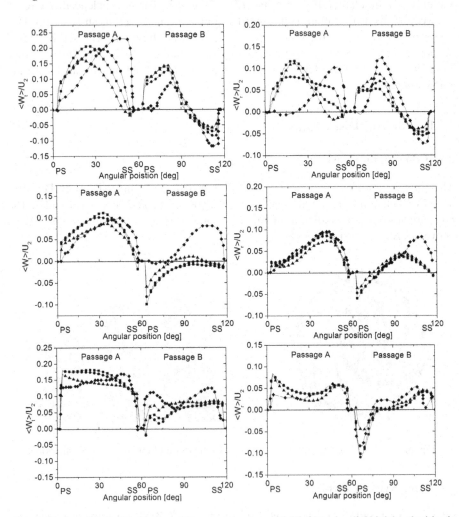

Fig. 6. Blade to Blade distribution of time average tangential(left) and radial(right) velocities in the impeller mid-height $z/b_2=0.5$, at radial position a)$r/R_2=0.5$,(b)$r/R_2=0.75$ and (b)$r/R_2=0.90$. -■-SAS,-▲-LES,-●-unsteady SST,-◆-PIV of *Pederson*

phenomenon consisting of alternate stalled and unstalled passages has been captured with full impeller simulation for SST based SAS,LES and unsteady SST as shown in Fig.5. There is almost no difference for three kinds of method to modeling the time averaged velocity field in impeller from the view at the impeller mid-height.

See Fig.6,the comparisons of blade to blade distribution of time average velocity profile are also taken between three CFD results and PIV measurements of Pederson for this partial load condition.

For passage A, all three turbulence modeling methods used in this work do well in calculating velocity profile compared with PIV result, except for radial position $r/R_2=0.5$. At such position, SAS model has predicted a contrast profile which is close to the LES result. The reason of this difference is consider being of pre-rotation in reference paper [11]. Unsteady SST model has predicted a relative flat for tangential velocity profile and so does the radial velocity profile here. For other positions the time average velocity profile predicted by SAS is quiet close to the SST model.

In the passage B, close to the unsteady SST, all profiles predicted by SAS model could capture the steady separation bubble. The different in the velocity profile to LES is of the different in prediction of separation point and scale of separation bubble near passage outlet for models. It seems that for velocity profile prediction, SAS model behave close to LES model in upstream, and to unsteady SST in downstream.

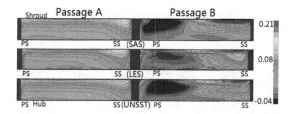

Fig. 7. Contour plot of Time-averaged radial velocity at position of constant radius equivalent to trailing edge

It could be find that, in the partial load condition,steady separation bubble, resulting from positive incidence angle at impeller suction side near leading edge, generate the obstructions in passage B, so the net flux of mass flow in passage B is relative small. To make the balance of mass flow of inlet and outlet of impeller, there is more mass flow goes into the passage A with large momentum. This also decreases the positive incidence angle for the blade between passage A and passage B. From the view of turbo surface at position of constant radius equivalent to trailing edge (see Fig.7) of passage B, this bubble is tridimensional, for large area negative radial velocity near pressure side and shroud, also a positive one near suction side and shroud.

3.3 Turbulence Behavior

A sample instantaneous iso-surface of the invariant of velocity gradient tensor in Fig.8 has given a general view of turbulence flow in this impeller running at Q=25% Qd captured by different methods. Unlike time average velocity field, the turbulence structure prediction is quiet different for each. It is clear that LES could get lots of small scale vortex structure in turbulence fluctuation. But for unsteady SST, only some large scale structure can be calculated, lots of information of turbulence fluctuation will be smoothed, and result some large viscosity ratio area near inlet and outlet part of passages. SAS model captured something between LES and SAS. At passage inlet part, especially in the unstalled passages, SAS model seems switch to behave like LES, and gets lots of small scale structure. That would be the reason for SAS predict a time average velocities profiles close to LES at radial position r/R₂=0.5 in passage A(discussed before), and for other position, it is close to unsteady SST.

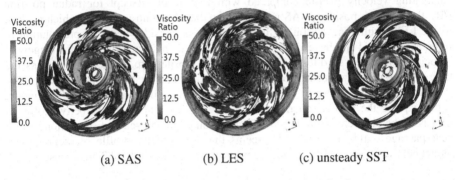

(a) SAS   (b) LES   (c) unsteady SST

Fig. 8. Sample instantaneous iso-surface of the invariant (Ω^2-S^2 =10^5 [s^{-2}]) colored by viscosity ratio (=eddy viscosity/ dynamic viscosity)

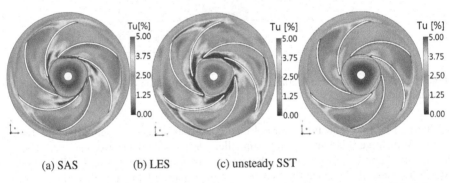

(a) SAS   (b) LES   (c) unsteady SST

Fig. 9. Contour plots of Turbulence Intensity (Tu) in the impeller mid-height,z/b2=0.5

From Fig.9, It is clearly that the largest turbulence intensity (Tu) is in the inlet part of passages and outlet of stalled passages. The flow there is quiet unstable. Near the inlet part of passage, the high turbulence intensity flow is blocked outside of stalled passages, but it goes into unstalled passages, and then decays rapidly from 5% to smaller than 1%. In the stall passages, Turbulence intensity is around 1%, smaller then in the unstalled passages. A high turbulence intensity flow could be found starting from trailing edge of stalled passage suction side, and stopping at the pressure side of this passage. This is not found in unstalled passages. It is the result from flow bypassing the blades.

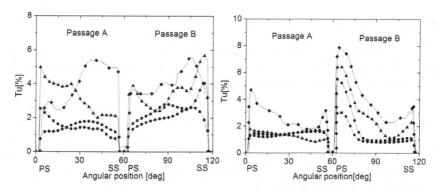

Fig. 10. Blade to blade distribution of turbulence intensity (Tu) in the impeller mid-height, $z/b_2=0.5$, at radial position $r/R_2=0.65$ (left) and $r/R_2=0.90$ (right). -■-SAS, -▲-LES,-●-unsteady SST,-◆-PIV of *Pederson*

Compared with unsteady SST model, SST based SAS model could get higher turbulence intensity close to the LES method, especially in the inlet part of unstalled passage. Considering the velocity profile there, when turbulence intensity is large enough, SST based SAS model could develop LES-like solutions in unsteady regions.

The comparisons of blade to blade distribution of turbulence intensity are given in Fig.10 for radial position $r/R2=0.65$ and $r/R2=0.90$. At $r/R2=0.65$, the turbulence intensity predicted by SAS decline from pressure side to suction side in passage A like LES, but is about 50% of LES`s. This is different for PIV result. And unsteady SST get a relative flat profile here. In passage B, SAS also get the same trend as LES and PIV, that Tu profile is increase from pressure side to suction side. The value predicted by SAS is about 2% smaller than LES.

At $r/R2=0.90$, the PIV has got a "V" type profile for turbulence intensity with higher turbulence intensity in pressure side than suction side for both passages, the peak value is at pressure of passage B.

4 Conclusion

SST based SAS model is a new kind of hybrid RANS/LES method to modeling the turbulence especially in centrifugal impeller. It is first time used for numerical study of centrifugal impeller especially for partial load condition calculation to study stall in the impeller passages.

From above discussing, the time average parameters of unsteady turbulence flow in the centrifugal impeller can be calculated close for both unsteady RANS method, hybrid RANS/LES and LES method. The previous reported "two channel" structure, captured by PIV can be gotten for both. And the time average velocity has compared for all numerical work and PIV result of reference paper. As SST based SAS model consume more computation of resource than unsteady SST turbulence model, but less than LES, It get unsteady structure close to LES, which cannot be captured in unsteady RANS model by unsteady SST model, this difference will cause SAS model to get more close time average value to LES in high turbulence intensity area.

Acknowledgments

This work has been supported by Shanghai University innovation fund of graduated student (A.16-0401-08-006). Author also wants to thanks High Performance Computation Center of Shanghai University and Wang X.W.

References

1. Paone, N., Riethmuller, M.L., et al.: Experimental investigation of the flow in the vaneless diffuser of a centrifugal pump by practical image displacement velocimetry. Experimental in Fluid 7, 371–378 (1989)
2. Sinha, M., Katz, J.: Quantitative visualization of the flow in a centrifugal pump with diffuser vanes-I: on Flow structure and turbulence. ASME J. Fluid Eng. 122, 97–107 (2000)
3. Sinha, M., Katz, J.: Quantitative visualization of the flow in a centrifugal pump with diffuser vanes-II: Addressing passage-average and Large Eddy simulation modeling issures in turbomahchinery flows. ASME J. Fluid Eng. 122, 108–116 (2000)
4. Wuibaut, G., Gbois, P., Dupont, et al.: PIV measurements in the impeller and vaneless diffuser of radial flow pump in design and off-design Operation condition. ASME J. Fluid Eng. 124, 791–797 (2002)
5. Wang, H., Tsukamoto, H.: Experimental and Numerical study of unsteady flow in a diffuser Pump at off-design conditions. ASME J. Fluid Eng. 125, 767–777 (2003)
6. Gonzales, J., Santolaria, C.: Unsteady flow Structure and Global Variables in a centrifugal pump. ASME J. Fluid Eng. 128, 937–945 (2006)
7. Gonzalez, J.F., Blanco, E., Santolaria, C.: Numericalsimulation of the dynamic effects due to impellervoluteinteraction in a centrifugal pump. ASME J. Fluid Eng. 124, 348–355 (2002)
8. Cheah, K.W., Lee, T.S., Winoto, S.H., Zhao, Z.M.: Numerical Flow Simulation in a Centrifugal Pump at Design and off-Design Conditions. Inter. J. Rotating mach., 1–8 (2007)
9. Kato, C.: Applications of LES in Mechanical Engineering, ADP013624
10. Feng, J., Benra, F.K., Dohmen, H.J.: Unsteady flow visualization at part load conditions of radial diffuser pump:by PIV and CFD. J. of visualization 12, 65–72 (2009)
11. Pedersen, N., Larson, P.S., et al.: Flow in a centrifugal pump impeller at design and off-design conditions-Part I: Particle Image Velocimetry (PIV) and Laser Doppler Velocimetry(LDV) measurements. ASME J. Fluid Eng. 125, 61–72 (2003)
12. Byskov, R.K., Jacbsen, C.B., Pedersen, N.: Flow in a centrifugal pump impeller at design and off-design conditions-Part I: Large Eddy Simulations. ASME J. Fluid Eng. 125, 73–83 (2003)
13. Menter, F.R., Kuntz, M., Bender, R.: A scale Adaptive Simulation Model for turbulent flow predictions. In: AIAA 2003-0767 (2003)
14. ANSYS CFX-Solver Theory Guide (November 2006)

A Two-Level Stabilized Nonconforming Finite Element Method for the Stationary Navier-Stokes Equations

Liping Zhu[1] and Zhangxin Chen[2]

[1] Faculty of Science, Xi'an Jiaotong University, Xi'an 710049, and Faculty of Science, Xi'an University of Architecture and Technology, Xi'an 710054, P.R. China
[2] Department of Chemical and Petroleum Engineering, Schulich School of Engineering, University of Calgary, Calgary, AB T2N 1N4, Canada

Abstract. In this paper, we combine a stabilized nonconforming finite element method with a two-level method to solve the stationary Navier-Stokes equations. Numerical results are presented to show the convergence performance of this combined algorithm.

Keywords: Navier-Stokes equations, two-level algorithm, nonconforming finite element method, numerical results.

1 Introduction

When the finite element methods are used to solve the Navier-Stokes equations, the approximations for velocity and pressure must satisfy the inf-sup condition to have a stable solution. Although the low order mixed finite element pairs $P_1 - P_1$, $P_1 - P_0$, $Q_1 - Q_1$, and $Q_1 - P_0$ do not satisfy this condition, they have the practical importance in scientific computation for their computational simplicity and convenience. Moreover, compared with the conforming finite element method, the nonconforming finite element method [1] is more attractive for discretizing the Stokes problem since it has more favorable stability properties. Much work has recently been devoted to the low order nonconforming finite element method [2–6].

In practice, the numerical solution of a nonlinear system of equations arising in the discretization of nonlinear partial differential equations can be time consuming. A two-level method aims to compute a discrete approximation of the solution of the nonlinear system with less computational work and with the same order of convergence as the solution (e.g., see [7, 8] for stationary semi-linear elliptic equations, [9–13] for the stationary Navier-Stokes equations, and [12, 14–17] for the nonstationary Navier-Stokes equations). Recently, some multi-level strategies have also been studied for the nonstationary Navier-Stokes equations [18, 19].

In this paper we combine the stabilized low order nonconforming finite element method with the two-level method to solve the two-dimensional stationary Navier-Stokes problem, and present a numerical convergence study for this combined algorithm. Optimal convergence rates are obtained.

W. Zhang et al. (Eds.): HPCA 2009, LNCS 5938, pp. 579–585, 2010.

2 Functional Setting of the Navier-Stokes Equations Problem

Let Ω be a bounded domain in $\Re^2$, with a Lipschitz continuous boundary $\partial\Omega$. We consider the Navier-Stokes problem: Find velocity $u = (u_1, u_2)$ and pressure p defined on Ω such that

$$\begin{cases} -\nu\Delta u + (u \cdot \nabla)u + \nabla p = f & \text{in} \quad \Omega, \\ \operatorname{div} u = 0 & \text{in} \quad \Omega, \\ u = 0 & \text{on} \quad \partial\Omega, \end{cases} \tag{2.1}$$

where f is the body forces per unit mass and $\nu > 0$ is the dynamic viscosity.

For the mathematical setting of this problem, we introduce the Hilbert spaces

$$X = \left(H_0^1(\Omega)\right)^2, \quad Y = \left(L^2(\Omega)\right)^2, \quad M = \left\{q \in L^2(\Omega) : \int_\Omega q dx = 0\right\}.$$

The spaces $\left(L^2(\Omega)\right)^m$, $m = 1, 2, 4$, are endowed with the L^2-scalar product $(\cdot, \cdot)$ and the L^2-norm $\|\cdot\|_0$. The spaces $H_0^1(\Omega)$ and X are equipped with their usual scalar product $(\nabla u, \nabla v)$ and norm $\|\nabla u\|_0$.

We define the continuous bilinear forms $a(\cdot, \cdot)$ and $d(\cdot, \cdot)$ on $X \times X$ and $X \times M$ respectively, by

$$a(u, v) = \nu(\nabla u, \nabla v) \quad \forall u, v \in X, \quad d(v, p) = (\operatorname{div} v, p) \quad \forall v \in X, p \in M,$$

a generalized bilinear form on $(X, M) \times (X, M)$ by

$$\mathcal{B}((u, p), (v, q)) = a(u, v) - d(u, q) - d(v, p) \quad \forall (u, p), (v, q) \in X \times M,$$

and a trilinear form on $X \times X \times X$ by

$$b(u; v, w) = = ((u \cdot \nabla)v, w) + \frac{1}{2}((\operatorname{div} u)v, w)$$
$$= \frac{1}{2}((u \cdot \nabla)v, w) - \frac{1}{2}((u \cdot \nabla)w, v) \quad \forall u, v, w \in X.$$

It is well known that $b(\cdot; \cdot, \cdot)$ satisfies the following properties [10]:

$$b(u; v, w) = -b(u; w, v) \quad \forall u, v, w \in X, \tag{2.2}$$

$$|b(u; v, w)| \leq N\|u\|_1\|v\|_1\|w\|_1 \quad \forall u, v, w \in X, \tag{2.3}$$

where N is a positive constant depending on the domain Ω. Then the variational formulation is to find $(u, p) \in X \times M$ such that

$$\mathcal{B}((u, p), (v, q)) + b(u; u, v) = (f, v) \quad \forall (v, q) \in X \times M. \tag{2.4}$$

Let $h > 0$ be a real positive constant, and $\tau_h(\Omega)$ be a regular triangulation of Ω into elements $\{K_j\}$: $\overline{\Omega} = \cup \overline{K}_j$. Denote the boundary edge of K_j by $\Gamma_j = \partial\Omega \cap \partial K_j$, the interface between elements K_j and K_k by

$$\Gamma_{jk} = \Gamma_{kj} = \partial K_j \cap \partial K_k,$$

and the centers of Γ_j and Γ_{jk} by ξ_j and ξ_{jk}, respectively. Then the nonconforming finite element spaces for the velocity is

$$NCP_1 = \{v \in Y : v|_K \in (P_1(K))^2 \; \forall \, K \in \tau_h(\Omega), v(\xi_{jk}) = v(\xi_{kj}), v(\xi_j) = 0, \forall j, k\},$$

and the conforming finite element spaces for the pressure is

$$P_1 = \{p \in H^1(\Omega) \cap M : p|_K \in P_1(K) \quad \forall \, K \in \tau_h(\Omega)\}.$$

The space NCP_1 is not a subspace of X. For any $v \in NCP_1$, the following compatibility conditions hold for all j and k:

$$\int_{\Gamma_{jk}} [v] \, ds = 0 \quad \text{and} \quad \int_{\Gamma_j} v \, ds = 0,$$

where $[v] = v|_{\Gamma_{jk}} - v|_{\Gamma_{kj}}$ denotes the jump of the function v across Γ_{jk}. We define the (broken) energy semi-norm

$$\|v\|_{1,h} = \Big(\sum_j |v|^2_{1,K_j}\Big)^{1/2}, \quad v \in NCP_1.$$

Let $(\cdot, \cdot)_j = (\cdot, \cdot)_{K_j}$ and $\langle \cdot, \cdot \rangle_j = \langle \cdot, \cdot \rangle_{\partial K_j}$. Then the discrete bilinear and trilinear forms are given as follows:

$$a_h(u, v) = \nu \sum_j (\nabla u, \nabla v)_j, \quad d_h(v, q) = \sum_j (\mathrm{div}\, v, q)_j, \quad b_{1h}(u; v, w) = \sum_j \Big(\sum_{i=1}^{2} u_i \partial_i v, w\Big),$$

and

$$b_h(u; v, w) = \frac{1}{2}[b_{1h}(u; v, w) - b_{1h}(u; w, v)].$$

For any $u, v, w \in (H^1(K_j))^2$ for each j, integration by parts on each element gives

$$b_{1h}(u; v, w) = b_h(u; v, w) - \frac{1}{2}\sum_j ((\mathrm{div}\, u)v, w)_j + \frac{1}{2}\sum_j \langle (u \cdot n_j)v, w \rangle,$$

where n_j is the unit outward normal to ∂K_j. Also, the trilinear term $b_h(\cdot; \cdot, \cdot)$ satisfies

$$b_h(u_h; v_h, w_h) \le N\|u_h\|_{1,h}\|v_h\|_{1,h}\|w_h\|_{1,h} \quad \forall u_h, v_h, w_h \in NCP1.$$

The $NCP_1 - P_1$ does not satisfy the inf-sup condition. To remedy this, we add a simple, local, and effective stabilization form $G(\cdot, \cdot)$:

$$G(p, q) = \sum_{K_j \in \tau_h(\Omega)} \Big\{\int_{K_{j,2}} pq \, dx - \int_{K_{j,1}} pq \, dx\Big\}, \quad p, q \in L^2(\Omega),$$

where $\int_{K_{j,i}} pq \, dx$ indicates an appropriate Gauss integration over K_j that is exact for polynomials of degree i, $i = 1, 2$, and pq is a polynomial of degree not greater than two. Consequently, we define the L^2-projection operator $\pi_h : L^2(\Omega) \to W_h$ by

$$(p, q_h) = (\pi_h p, q_h) \quad \forall p \in L^2(\Omega), q_h \in W_h, \tag{2.5}$$

where $W_h \subset L^2(\Omega)$ denotes the piecewise constant space associated with $\tau_h(\Omega)$. Now, using (2.5), we can define the bilinear form $G(\cdot, \cdot)$ as follows:

$$G(p, q) = (p - \pi_h p, q) = (p - \pi_h p, q - \pi_h q).$$

Then the nonconforming finite element approximation of (2.4) is to find a pair $(u_h, p_h) \in (NCP_1, P_1)$ such that

$$\mathcal{B}_h((u_h, p_h), (v_h, q_h)) + b_h(u_h; u_h, v_h) = (f, v_h) \quad \forall (v_h, q_h) \in (NCP_1, P_1),$$

where

$$\mathcal{B}_h((u_h, p_h), (v_h, q_h)) = a_h(u_h, v_h) - d_h(v_h, p_h) - d_h(u_h, q_h) - G(p_h, q_h)$$

is the bilinear form on $(NCP_1, P_1) \times (NCP_1, P_1)$.

3   The Two-Level Stabilized Nonconforming Finite Element Method

In this section the constant $H > 0$ is associated with a coarse grid, and $h > 0$ is associated with a fine grid, where $H >> h > 0$. We construct the associated nonconforming finite element spaces X_H, X_h for velocity and the conforming finite element spaces M_H, M_h for pressure as in the previous section. Then we will consider two two-level stabilized nonconforming finite element methods.

3.1   Simple Two-Level Nonconforming Finite Element Method

Step I: Solve the Navier-Stokes problem on a coarse mesh; i.e., find $(u_H, p_H) \in (X_H, M_H)$ such that

$$a_h(u_H, v) - d_h(v, p_H) - d_h(u_H, q) - G(p_H, q) + b(u_H, u_H, v) = (f, v) \quad \forall (v, q) \in (X_H, M_H), \tag{3.1}$$

Step II: Solve the Stokes problem on a fine mesh; i.e., find $(u^h, p^h) \in (X_h, M_h)$ such that

$$a_h(u^h, v) - d_h(v, p^h) - d_h(u^h, q) - G(p^h, q) + b(u_H, u_H, v) = (f, v) \quad \forall (v, q) \in (X_h, M_h). \tag{3.2}$$

It can be shown that the solution (u^h, p^h) of (3.1) and (3.2) satisfies

$$\|u - u^h\|_{1,h} + \|p - p^h\|_0 \leq c(h + H^2).$$

Hence, if we choose H such that $h = O(H^2)$, then the two-level stabilized nonconforming finite element method is of the same order of convergence as that of the usual stabilized nonconforming finite element method. However, our method is simpler to implement.

3.2   Newton Two-Level Stabilized Nonconforming Finite Element Method

Step I: Solve the Navier-Stokes problem on a coarse mesh; i.e., find $(u_H, p_H) \in (X_H, M_H)$ such that

$$a_h(u_H, v) - d_h(v, p_H) - d_h(u_H, q) - G(p_H, q) + b(u_H, u_H, v) = (f, v),$$

for all $(v, q) \in (X_H, M_H)$.

Step II: Solve the general Stokes problem on a fine mesh; i.e., find $(u^h, p^h) \in (X_h, M_h)$ such that

$$a_h(u^h, v) - d_h(v, p^h) - d_h(u^h, q) - G(p_h, q) + b(u_h, u_H, v) + b(u_H, u_h, v) = (f, v) +$$

$$b(u_H, u_H, v),$$

for all $(v, q) \in (X_h, M_h)$. It can be proven that

$$\|(u - u^h)\|_{1,h} + \|p - p^h\|_0 \le c(h + |\ln h|^{1/2} H^3),$$

and

$$\|u - u^h\|_0 \le c(h^2 + H^3).$$

4   Numerical Examples

In this section we evaluate the performance of the two-level stabilized noncon-forming finite element method described. We consider a unit-square domain with a driven-cavity flow solution, which is a very popular problem in testing various numerical methods, with $\nu = 0.1$:

$$u(x_1, x_2) = (u_1(x_1, x_2), u_2(x_1, x_2)), \quad p(x_1, x_2) = \cos(\pi x_1)\cos(\pi x_2),$$
$$u_1(x_1, x_2) = 2\pi \sin^2(\pi x_1)\sin(\pi x_2)\cos(\pi x_2),$$
$$u_2(x_1, x_2) = -2\pi \sin(\pi x_1)\sin^2(\pi x_2)\cos(\pi x_1).$$

where f is determined by (2.1). The numerical results are presented in Tables 1 and 2 in terms of the $H^1(\Omega)$ and $L^2(\Omega)$-convergence rates. These rates are consistent with the theoretical results obtained.

Table 1. Numerical results of the simple two-level method

H	h	$\frac{\|u-u^h\|_0}{\|u\|_0}$	$\frac{\|u-u^h\|_{1,h}}{\|u\|_1}$	$\frac{\|p-p^h\|_0}{\|p\|_0}$	u_{H^1}rate	p_{L^2}rate
1/5	1/25	0.0328743	0.131147	0.0519094		
1/6	1/36	0.0154519	0.0860781	0.0355032	1.15	1.04
1/7	1/49	0.011722	0.0619583	0.026597	1.07	0.94
1/8	1/64	0.0095464	0.0468163	0.0206697	1.05	0.94
1/9	1/81	0.00780026	0.0366353	0.0164926	1.04	0.96
1/10	1/100	0.00648638	0.0294869	0.0134903	1.03	0.95

Table 2. Numerical results of the Newton two-level method

H	h	$\frac{\|u-u^h\|_0}{\|u\|_0}$	$\frac{\|u-u^h\|_{1,h}}{\|u\|_1}$	$\frac{\|p-p^h\|_0}{\|p\|_0}$	u_{L^2}rate	u_{H^1}rate	p_{L^2}rate
1/5	1/25	0.0096909	0.0916197	0.0559245			
1/6	1/36	0.0054821	0.0634003	0.0305551	3.125	1.009	1.658
1/7	1/49	0.00320268	0.0464736	0.0186414	3.487	1.007	1.603
1/8	1/64	0.00201017	0.035535	0.0122728	3.488	1.004	1.565
1/9	1/81	0.00130388	0.028052	0.00818116	3.675	1.003	1.722
1/10	1/100	0.000874452	0.0227089	0.00559618	3.791	1.002	1.802

References

1. Chen, Z.: Finite Element Methods and Their Applications. Springer, Heidelberg (2005)
2. Douglas Jr., J., Santos, J.E., Sheen, D., Ye, X.: Nonconforming Galenkin methods based on quadrilateral elements for second order elliptic problems. Math. Modelling and Numerical Analysis 33, 747–770 (1999)
3. Cai, Z., Douglas Jr., J., Ye, X.: A stable nonconforming quadrilateral finite element method for the stationary Stokes and Navier-Stokes equations. Calcolo (36), 215–232 (1999)
4. Kim, Y., Lee, S.: Stable nonconforming quadrilateral finite elements for the Stokes problem. Applied Mathematics and Computation 115, 101–112 (2000)
5. Li, J., Chen, Z.: A new local stabilized nonconforming finite element method for the Stokes equations. Computing (82), 157–170 (2008)
6. Zhu, L., Li, J., Chen, Z.: A new local stabilized nonconforming fintite element method for the stationary Navier-Stokes equations (submitted for publication)
7. Xu, J.: A novel two-grid method for semilinear elliptic equatios. SIAM J. Sci. Comput. 15, 231–237 (1994)
8. Xu, J.: Two-grid finite element discritizations for nonlinear PDEs. SIAM J. Numer. Anal. 33, 1759–1777 (1996)
9. Layton, W.: A two-level discretization method for the Navier-Stokes equations. Comput. Math. Appl. 26, 33–38 (1993)
10. Layton, W., Lenferink, W.: Two-level Picard and modified Picard methods for the Navier-Stokes equatios. Appl. Math. Comput. 69, 263–274 (1995)
11. Layton, W., Tobiska, L.: A two-level method with backtracking for the Navier-Stokes equations. SIAM J. Numer. Anal. 35, 2035–2054 (1998)
12. Girault, V., Lions, J.L.: Two-grid finite element scheme for the transient Navier-Stokes problem. Math. Model. and Numer. Anal. 35, 945–980 (2001)
13. He, Y., Li, J., Yang, X.: Two-level penalized finite element methods for the stationary Navier-Stokes equations. Intern. J. Inform. System Sciences 2, 1–16 (2006)
14. Olshanskii, M.A.: Two-level method and some a priori estimates in unsteady Navier-Stokes calculations. J. Comp. Appl. Math. 104, 173–191 (1999)
15. He, Y.: Two-level method based on finite element and Crank-Nicolson extrapolation for the time-dependent Navier-Stokes equations. SIAM J. Numer. Anal. 41, 1263–1285 (2003)

16. He, Y.: A two-level finite Element Galerkin method for the nonstationary Navier-Stokes Equations, I: Spatial discretization. J. Comput. Math. 22, 21–32 (2004)

17. He, Y., Miao, H., Ren, C.: A two-level finite Element Galerkin method for the nonstationary Navier-Stokes equations, II: Time discretization. J. Comput. Math. 22, 33–54 (2004)

18. He, Y., Liu, K.M.: Multi-level spectral Galerkin method for the Navier-Stokes equations I: time discretization. Adv in Comp. Math. 25, 403–433 (2006)

19. He, Y., Liu, K.M., Sun, W.W.: Multi-level spectral Galerkin method for the Navier-Stokes equations I: Spatial discretization. Numer. Math. 101, 501–522 (2005)

Author Index

Allen, Gabrielle   272
Analoui, Morteza   337

Ben, Sheng-lan   404

Cao, Xiaojun   456
Chang, Jen-Hsiang   509
Che, Jianhua   96
Chen, Bo   465
Chen, Hongxun   571
Chen, Qingfa   183
Chen, Shaojun   218
Chen, Shengbo   102
Chen, Zhangxin   58, 88, 579
Chen, Zhangxing   139, 522
Cheng, Bin   108
Cheng, Haiying   114
Chou, Keng-Yi   503
Chunman, Huang   206
Cortés, Ana   1
Cui, Deqi   119
Cui, Ming   127
Cui, Yanbao   410
Cui, Zhiming   557

Deng, Li   8
Deng, Yazhu   127
Ding, Haiyan   169
Ding, Shengchao   465
Do, Hiep-Thuan   133
Dong, Bin   242
Dong, Xiaojian   139
Douglas, Craig C.   8, 38
Du, Chuanbin   69
Du, Siqi   350
Duan, Bo-jia   528

Efendiev, Yalchin   8

Fan, Jiang   206
Fei, Minrui   442
Feng, Jianzhou   146
Feng, Weibing   17, 473
Fu, Chunjuan   515

Ge, Baoshan   58
Ge, Ning   390
Gong, Bin   236, 325
Gong, Shengrong   557
Gong, Zhigang   390
Guan, Qinghua   280
Guo, Zhaolu   58
Gu, Wei   27

Haase, Gundolf   8, 38
Hamzei, Mohammad   305
Han, Guijun   479
Han, Jungang   264
He, Bing   17
He, Guo-qiang   295
He, Liqiang   153
He, Ning   161
He, Qinming   96
Hong, Jiangshou   398
Hou, Lei   169
Hu, Changjun   177
Hu, Jianhua   183
Hu, Jungao   191
Hu, Yue   410
Huang, Dawei   96
Huang, Linpeng   350
Huang, Ping   317
Huang, Tingzhu   230
Huang, Xiaofang   198
Huang, Yingmen   183
Huang, Yunqing   48
Hussain, Khalid   212

Irshad, Azeem   384
Irshad, Ehtsham   384

Jiang, Hongdao   563
Jiang, Liehui   433
Jiang, Ming   442
Jin, Shengye   102
Jin, Yi   377, 426

Khanum, Surraya   212, 384
Kolditz, Olaf   418
Kong, Lingfu   146
Kong, Qingyue   344
Kucher, Andreas   8

Lao, Dezheng   183
Lei, Yongmei   218
Li, Cuijin   264
Li, Dan   224
Li, Guanglei   390
Li, Hanling   169
Li, Hao   369
Li, Jianjiang   177
Li, Jianlei   230
Li, Jichun   48
Li, Kangshun   58
Li, Lei   236
Li, Ligang   497
Li, Lingxiong   398
Li, Mei   377, 426
Li, Songbei   473
Li, Xiuqiao   242
Li, Yaohui   491
Li, Ying   108
Liang, Dong   69
Liao, Ningfang   119
Liebmann, Manfred   38
Limet, Sébastien   133
Lin, Yu   119
Liu, Chaoqun   78
Liu, Fuheng   257
Liu, Hui   325
Liu, Jingfa   250
Liu, Xuhong   257
Liu, Yali   177
Liu, Youyao   264
Lodder, Robert   8
Löffler, Frank   272
Long, Dongyang   398
Lu, Yaohui   280
Luo, Jiao-min   528

Ma, Yan   236
Ma, Yingying   344
Mao, Guoyong   288, 473
Mao, Wenhua   534
Melin, Emmanuel   133
Meng, Ze-hong   295

Noshairwan, Wajahat   384

Oliveira, Maria   78
Ouyang, Shan   426

Pan, Jinji   250
Parsa, Saeed   305, 311

Peng, Hongbo   390
Peng, Hui   317
Peng, Junjie   377, 426
Peng, Ying   325
Plank, Gernot   38

Qin, Bin   161
Qin, Guan   8
Qiu, Lin   169

Rao, Wenbi   331
Rezvani, Mohammad Hossein   337
Ruan, Li   242

Schnetter, Erik   272
Shao, Huagang   114
Shao, Yi   433
Shao, Yonghong   344
Shariati, Saeed   311
Shen, Fei   350
Shen, Lihua   356
Shen, Zhangyi   426
Sher, Muhammad   212
Shi, Dinghua   362
Shi, Weixia   331
Shi, Xiuhua   450
Shi, Yunmei   257
Soltani, Neda Reza   311
Song, Anping   17, 542
Su, Guang-da   404

Tan, Boneng   119
Tang, Guo   369
Tao, Jian   272
Teng, Liang   377
Tian, Yingai   257
Tong, Weiqin   108, 410
Tsaur, Shyh-Chang   503
Tseng, Chien-Hsiang   503

Usman, Muhammad   212, 384

Wang, Bailing   390
Wang, Banghai   398
Wang, Hongjie   491
Wang, Hongwei   114
Wang, Hualin   114
Wang, Hui   522
Wang, Jue   177
Wang, Licheng   198
Wang, Mei   404

Wang, Ting   410
Wang, Wenqing   418
Wang, Xianchao   426
Wang, Xiang   550
Wang, Xiaohuan   146
Wang, Xin   27
Wang, Xingang   108
Wang, Yali   250
Wang, Yang   17
Wang, Yonghu   450
Wang, Yuliang   433
Wei, Lisheng   442
Wei, Qiong   390
Wei, Zhaoyu   450
Wen, Tieqiao   473
Wu, Chanle   465
Wu, Chao-Chin   509
Wu, Dan   465
Wu, Junwei   456
Wu, Libing   465
Wu, Pingbo   280
Wu, Shaochun   479
Wu, Wenmin   119
Wu, Zhijian   139, 522

Xiang, Cong   161
Xiao, Limin   242
Xiaoli, Zhi   191
Xie, Jiang   288, 473
Xin, Yuanbo   450
Xu, Dongfeng   479
Xu, Jun   479
Xu, Lei   485
Xu, Lingyu   479
Xu, X. Frank   356
Xu, Yabin   257
Xu, Ying   485
Xuan, Zhaocheng   491

Yanbao, Cui   191
Yang, Chao   497
Yang, Chao-Tung   503, 509
Yang, Fei   280

Yan, Yu   218
Yao, Shaowen   369
Yao, Wei   317
Ye, Kejiang   96
Yijun, Wang   206
Yu, Shuhua   515
Yu, Song   139, 522
Yu, Yunchao   571
Yuan, Jia-bin   528
Yuan, Yanwei   534
Yue, Hu   191

Zafar, Rehab   212
Zeng, Jing   280
Zhang, Bofeng   542
Zhang, Chi   550
Zhang, D.D.   485
Zhang, Guangming   557
Zhang, Guangyong   153
Zhang, Hongbo   362
Zhang, Jianfei   563
Zhang, Jianlin   515
Zhang, Lei   563
Zhang, Luwen   473
Zhang, Miao   17
Zhang, Pingen   479
Zhang, Qi   161
Zhang, Shihua   473
Zhang, Wei   571
Zhang, Wu   17, 473, 542
Zhang, Xiaochao   534
Zhang, Xuqing   102
Zhang, Yanxin   325
Zhang, Yunquan   497
Zhao, Huaping   534
Zhao, Qiuxia   433
Zhao, Zhen-yu   295
Zhi, Xiaoli   410
Zhong, He   88
Zhongwei, Liang   206
Zhou, Keping   183
Zhu, Hui   542
Zhu, Liping   579